Feelings and Emotions

Emotions are central to human behavior and experience. Yet scientific theory and research during most of the twentieth century largely ignored the emotions until a quite dramatic change that took place during its last thirty years, which witnessed an upsurge of interest in emotions in a number of disciplines. Just after the turn of the century therefore seemed to be an appropriate time to take stock of current scientific reflection on emotions. This book arose from the twenty-four keynote papers presented at a symposium held in June 2001 that bore the same title. The aim of that meeting was to review the current state of the art of research on emotions from a multidisciplinary perspective. Each chapter here is authored by an acknowledged authority in the respective field. Together they provide an overview of what is currently being studied and thought about the emotions in disciplines ranging from neurophysiology and experimental psychology to sociology and philosophy.

Antony S. R. Manstead is Professor of Psychology at Cardiff University.

Nico Frijda is Extraordinary Professor in the Study of Emotion at the University of Amsterdam.

Agneta Fischer is Professor in the Department of Psychology at the University of Amsterdam.

STUDIES IN EMOTION AND SOCIAL INTERACTION
Second Series

Series Editors

Keith Oatley
University of Toronto

Antony S. R. Manstead
Cardiff University

This series is jointly published by Cambridge University Press and the Éditions de la Maison des Sciences de l'Homme, as part of the joint publishing agreement established in 1977 between the Fondation de la Maison des Sciences de l'Homme and the Syndics of Cambridge University Press.

Cette publication est publiée en co-édition par Cambridge University Press et les Éditions de la Maison des Sciences de l'Homme. Elle s'intègre dans le programme de co-édition établi en 1977 par la Fondation de la Maison des Sciences de l'Homme et les Syndics de Cambridge University Press.

Feelings and Emotions

The Amsterdam Symposium

Edited by

ANTONY S. R. MANSTEAD
Cardiff University and University of Amsterdam

NICO FRIJDA
University of Amsterdam

AGNETA FISCHER
University of Amsterdam

CAMBRIDGE
UNIVERSITY PRESS

PUBLISHED BY THE PRESS SYNDICATE OF THE UNIVERSITY OF CAMBRIDGE
The Pitt Building, Trumpington Street, Cambridge, United Kingdom

CAMBRIDGE UNIVERSITY PRESS
The Edinburgh Building, Cambridge CB2 2RU, UK
40 West 20th Street, New York, NY 10011-4211, USA
477 Williamstown Road, Port Melbourne, VIC 3207, Australia
Ruiz de Alarcón 13, 28014 Madrid, Spain
Dock House, The Waterfront, Cape Town 8001, South Africa

http://www.cambridge.org

First published 2004

Printed in the United States of America

Typeface Palatino 10/12 pt.   *System* LATEX 2$_\varepsilon$ [TB]

A catalog record for this book is available from the British Library.

Library of Congress Cataloging in Publication Data
Feelings and emotions : the Amsterdam symposium / edited by Antony S.R. Manstead,
Nico Frijda, Agneta Fischer.
   p.   cm. – (Studies in emotion and social interaction)
Symposium held in June 2001 in Amsterdam, Netherlands.
ISBN 0–521–81652–1 – ISBN 0–521–52101–7 (pb.)
1. Emotions – Congresses.   2. Emotions – Social aspects – Congresses.
I. Manstead, A. S. R.   II. Frijda, Nico H.   III. Fischer, Agneta, 1958–   IV. Series.
BF531.F445   2003
152.4 – dc21   2003043960

ISBN 0 521 81652 1 hardback
ISBN 0 521 52101 7 paperback

Contents

Contributors

Gary G. Berntson
Ohio State University
Department of Psychology
1885 Neil Avenue
Columbus, OH 43210, U.S.A.
berntson.2@osu.edu

Kent C. Berridge
University of Michigan
Department of Psychology
East Hall, 525 East University
Ann Arbor, MI 48109-1109, U.S.A.
berridge@umich.edu

John T. Cacioppo
University of Chicago
Department of Psychology
5848 South University Avenue
Chicago, IL 60637, U.S.A.
Cacioppo@uchicago.edu

Candace Clark
Montclair State University
Department of Sociology
Upper Montclair, NJ 07043, U.S.A.
clarkc@mail.montclair.edu

Antonio R. Damasio
University of Iowa
Interdisciplinary Graduate Program of Neuroscience
The University of Iowa Hospitals and Clinics
200 Hawkins Drive
Iowa City, IA 52242, U.S.A.
damasio@mail.medicine.uiowa.edu

Frans B. M. de Waal
Emory University
Living Links Center, Yerkes Regional Primate Research Center
954 N. Gatewood Road
Atlanta, GA 30322, U.S.A.
dewaal@rmy.emory.edu.

Raymond J. Dolan
University College London
Wellcome Department of Imaging Neuroscience
12 Queen Square
London WC1N 3BG, U.K.
m.bennett@fil.ion.ucl.ac.uk

Judy Dunn
University of London
Institute of Psychiatry
Social, Genetic, and Developmental Psychiatry Research Centre
De Crespigny Park, Denmark Hill
London SE5 8AF, U.K.
judy.dunn@iop.kcl.ac.uk

Paul Ekman
University of California at San Francisco
Human Interaction Laboratory
401 Parnassus Avenue
San Francisco, CA 94143, U.S.A.
ekman@compuserve.com

Jon Elster
Columbia University
Political Science Department
International Affairs Building, Floor 7
420 West 118th Street
New York, NY 10027, U.S.A.
je70@columbia.edu

Agneta H. Fischer
University of Amsterdam
Faculty of Social and Behavioral Sciences
Roetersstraat 15
1018 WB Amsterdam, Netherlands
A.H.Fischer@uva.nl

Robert H. Frank
Cornell University
Johnson Graduate School of Management
327 Sage Hall
Ithaca, NY 14853-2801, U.S.A.
rhf3@cornell.edu

Nico H. Frijda
University of Amsterdam
Faculty of Social and Behavioral Sciences
Roetersstraat 15
1018 WB Amsterdam, Netherlands
N.H.Frijda@uva.nl

Alice M. Isen
Cornell University
Johnson Graduate School of Management
359 Sage Hall
Ithaca, NY 14853-2801, U.S.A.
ami4@cornell.edu

Marja Kokkonen
University of Jyväskylä
Department of Psychology
Agora/Psykocenter, Mattilanniemi PL 35
40351 Jyväskylä, Finland
Marja.Kokkonen@psyka.jyu.fi

Jeff T. Larsen
Texas Tech University
Department of Psychology
Lubbock, TX 79409, U.S.A.
jeff.larsen@ttu.edu

Paulo N. Lopes
Yale University
Department of Psychology
P.O. Box 208205
New Haven, CT 06520, U.S.A.
paulo.lopes@yale.edu

Antony S. R. Manstead
Cardiff University
School of Psychology
P. O. Box 901
Cardiff CF10 3YG, U.K.
MansteadA@cardiff.ac.uk

Hazel Rose Markus
Department of Psychology
Stanford University
Stanford, CA 94305-2130, U.S.A.
markus@psych.stanford.edu

John D. Mayer
University of New Hampshire
Department of Psychology
Conant Hall
Durham, NH 03824, U.S.A.
jack.mayer@unh.edu

Barbara A. Mellers
University of California, Berkeley
Haas School of Business
Berkeley, CA 94720, U.S.A.
mellers@haas.berkeley.edu

Batja Mesquita
Wake Forest University
P.O. Box 7778 Reynolds Station
Winston Salem, NC 27109, U.S.A.
mesquita@wfu.edu

Keith Oatley
University of Toronto
Ontario Institute for the Study of Education
Toronto, Ont. M5S 1V6, Canada
keith_oatley@tednet.oise.utoronto.ca

Arne Öhman
Karolinska Institute Z6
Department of Clinical Neuroscience
Section of Psychology
171 76 Stockholm, Sweden
arne.ohman@cns.ki.se

Jaak Panksepp
Bowling Green State University
Department of Psychology
Bowling Green OH 43403-0228, U.S.A.
and Northwestern University
Falk Center for Molecular Therapeutics
Department of Biomedical Engineering
Evanston, IL 60201 U.S.A.
jpankse@bgnet.bgsu.edu

Peter Salovey
Yale University
Department of Psychology
2 Hillhouse Avenue, P.O. Box 208205
New Haven, CT 06520-8205, U.S.A.
Peter.Salovey@yale.edu

Klaus R. Scherer
University of Geneva
Department of Psychology
40, Boulevard du Pont d'Arve
CH-1205 Geneva, Switzerland
Klaus.Scherer@pse.unige.ch

Nancy Sherman
Georgetown University
Department of Philosophy
224 New North NW
Washington, DC 20057, U.S.A.
shermann@georgetown.edu

Richard A. Shweder
University of Chicago
Committee on Human Development
5730 S. Woodlawn Avenue
Chicago, IL 60637, U.S.A.
rshd@dura.spc.uchicago.edu

N. Kyle Smith
Ohio Wesleyan University
Department of Psychology
Phillips Hall
Delaware, OH 43015, U.S.A.
nksmith@cc.owu.edu

Robert C. Solomon
University of Texas
Department of Philosophy
Austin, TX 78712, U.S.A.
rsolomon@mail.utexas.edu

Peggy A.Thoits
Vanderbilt University
Department of Sociology
Box 1811, Station B
Nashville, TN 37235, U.S.A.
THOITSPA@ctrvax.Vanderbilt.Edu

Stefan Wiens
Karolinska Institute Z6
Department of Clinical Neuroscience
Section of Psychology
171 76 Stockholm, Sweden
stefan.wiens@cns.ki.se

Joel S. Winston
University of London
Functional Imaging Laboratory
Wellcome Department of Imaging Neuroscience
12 Queen Square
London WC1N 3BG, U.K.
j.winston@fil.ion.ucl.ac.uk

Robert B. Zajonc
Stanford University
Department of Psychology
Stanford, CA 94305, U.S.A.
zajonc@psych.stanford.edu

1

Introduction

Antony S. R. Manstead, Nico H. Frijda, and Agneta H. Fischer

THE AMSTERDAM SYMPOSIUM

This book arose from the twenty-four keynote papers presented at a meeting that had the same title as this volume: "Feelings and Emotions: The Amsterdam Symposium." It was held in June 2001, in Amsterdam, and was hosted by the Department of Psychology at the University of Amsterdam.

Our purpose in organizing this symposium was to review the current state of the art of research on emotions from a multidisciplinary perspective. Stock-taking of this kind has been undertaken before. In 1927 a meeting was held under the title *Feelings and Emotions: The Wittenberg Symposium* (Reymert, 1928). In 1948 *Feelings and Emotions: The Mooseheart Symposium* was held in Chicago (Reymert, 1950); and in 1969 *Feelings and Emotions: The Loyola Symposium* took place at Loyola University, again in Chicago (Arnold, 1970). Those interested in knowing more about these earlier *Feelings and Emotions* symposia can find the title pages of all three of these books reproduced in the present volume, following p. 4.

The Amsterdam Symposium was inspired by these previous efforts and borrowed its title from them. The turn of the century seemed to be an appropriate moment to take stock of current scientific reflection on emotions. Emotions are central to human behavior and experience. This central role notwithstanding, theory and research had largely ignored emotions during most of the twentieth century. This situation changed rather dramatically during the last thirty years of that century, however. An upsurge of interest was apparent in a number of disciplines, including psychology, biology, sociology, anthropology, philosophy, neuroscience, economics, psychiatry, and cognitive science. Important research was performed in all of these fields, and major new insights were obtained. It seemed worthwhile to us, the organizers of the symposium, to reflect on where we now stand.

1

FIGURE 1.1. Pictured above are eighteen of the twenty-four speakers at the Amsterdam Symposium. From left to right: Batja Mesquita, Nancy Sherman, Candace Clark, Frans de Waal, Robert Frank (in rear), Bob Solomon (in front), Keith Oatley, John Cacioppo, Arne Ohman, Rick Shweder, Klaus Scherer, Jaak Panksepp, Bob Zajonc, Peter Salovey, Kent Berridge, Peggy Thoits, Jon Elster, and Nico Frijda.

With the assistance of an advisory board of eminent figures in the field of emotion, twenty-four keynote speakers were invited to summarize their views of the domain. They represented most of the disciplines mentioned above. Each speaker made a forty-five-minute presentation; and following each half-day group of three lectures there was a forty-five-minute general discussion. The number of keynote speakers was limited by our expectation that four days would be the maximum that most participants (speakers and audience alike) could devote to the symposium, and by our determination to avoid parallel sessions. The speakers invited therefore emerged from a severe selection process. We began with a much longer list of speakers, each of whom would have merited an invitation. Although we were of course disappointed and frustrated by not being able to include some prominent and productive researchers, we were (and remain) convinced that the final selection of speakers struck a good balance between the importance of the speaker's own theoretical contribution to emotion research and the need to have a range of academic disciplines.

In addition to the keynote presentations and general discussions, two poster sessions were held. About 150 posters were accepted by the program committee. These sessions enabled the presenters (many of whom were Ph.D. students or postdoctoral researchers) to present their own work and interests to others, including, of course, the keynote speakers and other established researchers who attended the meeting.

As well as thanking the keynote speakers, all of whom are repre-sented in this volume, and the audience, who helped to create lively and interesting discussions, we would like to acknowledge the financial support that made the symposium (and therefore this book) possible. Generous support was received from the Royal Netherlands Academy of Science (KNAW); the Netherlands Organization for Scientific Research (NWO); the Netherlands Convention Bureau; the European Commission; the European Association of Experimental Social Psychology; the board of the University of Amsterdam; the Department of Psychology at the University of Amsterdam, and the experimental and social psychology programs within that department.

We also thank the members of the advisory committee who helped in suggesting potential keynote speakers from the various disciplines and to evaluate proposals made by the organizers: Roy D'Andrade, Paul Ekman, Jan van Hooff, Richard Lazarus, George Mandler, Martha Nussbaum, Keith Oatley, Jaak Panksepp, W. Gerrod Parrott, Bernard Rimé, Herbert Simon, and Robert Zajonc.

Last but not least, we express heartfelt gratitude to Reyna Veldhuis, who was a superb conference manager, and our sincere thanks to Albina Shayevich, who provided invaluable help with the indexing of this book.

THE PRESENT VOLUME

The rest of the chapters in this book provide what we believe to be a representative coverage of the major research domains in the study of emotions. These include the nature of basic emotional mechanisms, from a psychological and from a neuroscientific point of view (Berridge, Cacioppo et al., Isen, Öhman & Wiens, Panksepp, Zajonc); the neural correlates of emotional processes (Damasio, Winston & Dolan, Panksepp); the nature of emotional feelings (Cacioppo, Damasio, Winston & Dolan, Frijda, Panksepp); the relationships of emotions to action, rationality, and decisions (Elster, Frijda, Isen, Mellers); the nature of the processes leading to, as well as constituting, emotions (Dunn, Ekman, Scherer); and critical issues surrounding the very concept of emotions, such as those of its presumed passivity, or its distinction from rationality (Elster, Oatley, Shweder, Solomon). In several chapters the authors investigate the fundamental role of emotions in social interaction and in moral issues (Clark, de Waal, Frank, Salovey et al., Sherman), and the complex ways in which emotional experience and behavior relate to the social and cultural context (Clark, Mesquita & Markus, Shweder).

The chapters also clearly reflect the diversity of current methodological approaches to the study of emotions: neuroscientific investigations (Berridge, Damasio, Winston & Dolan, Panksepp); experimental psychological approaches (Cacioppo et al., Isen, Öhman, Mellers, Scherer, Zajonc); questionnaire research in experimental or interview contexts (Mesquita, Salovey); ethologically inspired observations of humans (Dunn) and infrahumans (de Waal); sociological and/or anthropological analyses (Clark,

Shweder, Thoits); the analysis of fiction (Oatley); and theoretical reflection (Ekman, Elster, Frank, Frijda, Sherman, Solomon).

We feel that the keynote presentations are representative of current research efforts and orientations with respect to emotions. Together they provide an overview of what is currently being studied and thought about emotions in the variety of disciplines concerned. We could have structured the chapters in a number of ways, each of which would have had a certain logic and coherence. The way they are organized is in terms of five themes: (1) the nature of feelings and emotions; (2) basic psychological processes in feelings and emotions; (3) the impact of affect; (4) feelings and emotions in their sociocultural context; and (5) feelings, emotions, and morality. The papers that formed the basis of these chapters generated a great deal of interest and discussion during the symposium. We believe that readers will also find them informative and provocative.

References

Arnold, M. B. (Ed.) (1970). *Feelings and emotions: The Loyola symposium*. New York: Academic Press.
Reymert, M. L. (Ed.) (1928). *Feelings and emotions: The Wittenberg symposium*. Worcester, MA: Clark University Press.
Reymert, M. L. (Ed.) (1950). *Feelings and emotions: The Mooseheart symposium*. New York: McGraw-Hill.

THE INTERNATIONAL UNIVERSITY SERIES IN PSYCHOLOGY

FEELINGS AND EMOTIONS

THE WITTENBERG SYMPOSIUM

by

Alfred Adler
F. Aveling
Vladimir M. Bekhterev
Madison Bentley
G. S. Brett
Karl Bühler
Walter B. Cannon
Harvey A. Carr
Ed. Claparède
Knight Dunlap
Robert H. Gault
D. Werner Gruehn
L. B. Hoisington
D. T. Howard
Erich Jaensch
Pierre Janet
Joseph Jastrow

Carl Jörgensen
David Katz
F. Kiesow
F. Krueger
Herbert S. Langfeld
William McDougall
Henri Piéron
W. B. Pillsbury
Morton Prince
Carl E. Seashore
Charles E. Spearman
Wilhelm Stern
George M. Stratton
John S. Terry
Margaret F. Washburn
Albert P. Weiss
Robert S. Woodworth

Edited by
Martin L. Reymert

WORCESTER, MASSACHUSETTS
CLARK UNIVERSITY PRESS
1928

Feelings and Emotions

the MOOSEHEART SYMPOSIUM
in cooperation with THE UNIVERSITY OF CHICAGO

ANTON J. CARLSON, *President-of-Honor*
MARTIN L. REYMERT, *General Chairman*
JAMES G. MILLER, *Cochairman*

Edited by MARTIN L. REYMERT, Ph.D.

New York   Toronto   London
McGRAW-HILL BOOK COMPANY, INC.
1950

Feelings

and

Emotions

The Loyola Symposium

Edited by
Magda B. Arnold

1970

ACADEMIC PRESS　New York　San Francisco　London
A Subsidiary of Harcourt Brace Jovanovich, Publishers

PART I

THE NATURE OF FEELINGS AND EMOTIONS

2

On the Passivity of the Passions

Robert C. Solomon

ABSTRACT

How much control do we have over our emotions? Does it make any sense to say that we *choose* our emotions? Psychologists talk about "emotion regulation," leaving it open to what extent and in what ways the languages of control or of choice might apply. Philosophers have long taken the position, in part because of their celebration of reason, that we can control (but not choose) our emotions only by constraining them, or by controlling their expression. But are questions of regulation, control, and constraint perhaps misleading? In this chapter, I suggest that the *active* and even *willful* dimension of emotion has been too often dismissed, ignored, or what is the same, caricatured so that it makes no sense at all. I defend a model in which such voluntaristic talk captures some important insights about our emotions and consider several objections to this thesis.

> The existentialist does not believe in the power of passion. He will never regard a grand passion as a destructive torrent upon which a man is swept into uncertain actions as by fate, and which, therefore is an excuse for them.
> Sartre, "Existentialism Is a Humanism," p. 33

How much control do we have over our emotions? Does it make any sense to say that we *choose* our emotions? Psychologists talk about "emotion regulation," leaving it open to what extent and in what ways the languages of control or of choice might apply. Philosophers have long taken the position, in part because of their celebration of reason, that we can control (but not choose) our emotions only by constraining them, or by controlling their expression. But is the question of control and constraint perhaps the wrong question? Or a much too limited question? Is controlling an emotion something like controlling a wild animal within? (Horace: "Anger is like riding a wild horse"). Is it like controlling one's blood pressure, or one's cholesterol level, something that (certain Yogis excepted) we can do only indirectly? Or is it rather like a boss controlling his or her employees by way of various threats and incentives, the "boss" being reason? (Plato's model in *The Republic*). Or is controlling an emotion like controlling one's thoughts, one's speech, one's arguments, putting them into shape, choosing one's mode of expression as well as one's timing? (The difference between spontaneously "blurting" out a comment and giving a considered response may be applicable here.) Or is it like coordinating one's actions through practice, like riding a bike, which may be "mindless" (that is, wholly unreflective and unselfconscious) but is nevertheless wholly voluntary and both very much within one's control and a continuous matter of choice?

The question of responsibility (for one's emotions) has been largely neglected in both philosophy and the social sciences. I have tried to move such matters to center stage. In my first (and I admit very polemical) book on emotions, *The Passions*, I argued outright that emotions should be construed as "actions," as "doings," as matters of "choice." There, and in subsequent books and essays, I have suggested that such emotions as love and anger might sometimes be better understood in terms of the choices we make rather than in terms of visceral reactions, metaphorical or neurological "chemistry," or passively undergone feelings. Critics and commentators have correctly noted that I was (and still am) influenced by the philosophical psychology of the French "existentialist," Jean-Paul Sartre. They also noted that Roy Schafer was pursuing much the same line of argument for the disciplines of psychiatry and psychoanalysis. My own aim, following Sartre, was to reinforce the role of responsibility with regard to our emotions. As my work developed, this became part of a larger Aristotelian conception of ethics centering on the cultivation of good character, including the "right" emotions.

There are two immediate obstacles to the argument that emotions are akin to actions, and even a matter of choice. The first is the obvious fact that emotions *seem* to happen to us, quite apart from our preferences or intentions. There are occasions in which we are "overwhelmed" by emotion (and the action impulses that immediately follow). And our emotions are often manifested in thoughts that "haunt" us and of which (try as we might) we cannot rid ourselves. The phenomenological point is reinforced by a semantic-syntactic observation, that the language of the passions (starting with the word "passion") is riddled with passivity, "being struck by" and so on. (This set of observations should be balanced with another, that we sometimes feel guilty or even proud about feeling what we feel and that we often assess our emotions as warranted or not, wise or foolish, appropriate or inappropriate.) The second obstacle is the enormous range of emotions and emotional experiences – from being startled to carefully plotting one's revenge, from inexplicable panic upon seeing a small spider to a well-warranted fear of being audited by the Internal Revenue Service, from falling "desperately" in love to conscientiously cultivating a life-long loving relationship, from "finding oneself" in a rage to righteous and well-considered indignation and a hatred of injustice. And it is not merely the difference between various emotions that is at stake here, but (as several of the listed examples indicate) a difference in kinds of emotional experiences in the same sort of emotion (fear, anger, love).

The enormous range of emotions suggests that no single claim or analysis will suit all emotions, or *emotion as such*. But each and every emotion also has different *aspects* (although I do not endorse the popular "components" analysis). I take it that every emotion has five such aspects: (1) behavioral (including everything from facial expressions and verbal expressions ("Damn!") and reports ("I love you") to elaborate plans for action; (2) physiological (hormonal, neurological, neuromuscular); (3) phenomenological (everything from "physical" sensations to ways of seeing and describing the "objects" of one's emotions and "meta-emotions"); (4) cognitive (including appraisals, perceptions, thoughts, and reflections *about* one's emotions); and (5) the social context (from the immediacy of interpersonal interactions to pervasive cultural considerations). These aspects are often interwoven (e.g., behavioral and physiological, phenomenological, cognitive, and cultural), and they should not be construed as competing conceptions of emotion. As a philosopher, I have always paid the most attention to the phenomenological and cognitive (belatedly cultural) aspects of emotion, but I now think it was a (heuristically fruitful) mistake to insist that "emotions are judgments" insofar as that was intended to elevate the cognitive aspects of emotion at the expense of the others. But the different aspects of emotion require very different sorts of arguments regarding the voluntary-involuntary, active-passive status of emotions.

Moreover, there is a broad range of claims regarding such status that might be made regarding emotions, from the relatively innocent view that one can always do something not only to control but to "set up" (or prevent) particular emotions (see Ekman, this volume), to the mild (but still controversial) insistence that we are responsible for our emotions (whether or not we can control or choose them), to the view that emotions are active and do not just "happen" to us, to the very strong claim that an emotion is a matter of choice, something voluntary and even willful. And since different aspects (and different aspects of those aspects) invite very different conclusions, the discussion of the passivity of emotions is no simple matter and yields no single conclusion. We sometimes hold people responsible for what they think. We usually hold them responsible for what they do. Some expressions of emotion are voluntary, but not all are. But in what sense are we responsible for what we believe, judge, appraise? And does it make any sense at all to say that we are responsible for what happens in our brains (leaving aside the willful intake of mind-altering substances) or that we are responsible for what we feel? What does happen when we choose or force ourselves to have an emotion (like Arlie Hochschild's stewardesses), and is the resultant emotion therefore "inauthentic"? Or is it rather only

the "setup" of an emotion for which we can (sometimes) be held responsible, knowingly getting ourselves into a situation (e.g., taking a job that
requires congeniality or entering into a confrontation with one's ex-wife's
new boyfriend) in which we will almost certainly be "moved" by one or
another emotion?

I now see that my early emphasis on action and choice was misleading,
but not because I so flagrantly flew in the face of what seems obvious to
us, the passivity of the passions. Rather, I ignored or gerrymandered the
many differences and distinctions alluded to above and tried to defend
a thesis about emotions *simpliciter*. But it will not do simply to separate
the different emotions (that is, different kinds of emotions) into groups –
for instance, "basic emotions" or "affect programs," on the one hand, and
"higher cognitive emotions," on the other, and make separate arguments
for each. Fear and anger, two "basic" emotions on almost every researcher's
list, have many different manifestations. Contrast sophisticated fear (say,
of being audited by the tax authorities) with sheer panic. Or, righteous and
well-thought-out anger and indignation, on the one hand, with "blind"
rage on the other. I have no qualms about saying that there is something
involuntary, something that "overwhelms us," in the cases of panic and
rage (which is not to say that there is *no* sense in which we are responsible
for them). On the other hand, sophisticated fear and righteous and well-
thought-out anger are shot through with judgments, choices, and plans for
behavior that are clearly matters of choice and responsibility (as evidenced
by the fact that, in righteous anger, for instance, we happily *take* responsibility for our emotion). And in the so-called realm of higher cognitive
emotions, it is not necessarily the case that cognition implies responsibility. Those emotions, too, have to be examined case by case. (For instance,
in what sense is a person responsible for his or her own embarrassment,
or shame, or guilt? Surely it depends on the case and the context.)

Nevertheless, as a general strategy, I would like to push the idea that
we choose and are responsible for our emotions as hard as I can, if only
because the opposite idea, that our passions render us passive, has such a
grip on both our ordinary thinking and the rich literature on the emotions.
In general, I think that questions of agency and responsibility regarding
the physiological aspects of most emotions are out of order (aside from
questions about medication and, much more subtly, the ways in which our
cultivation of emotional habits have measurable effects on our physiology).
But where behavior is concerned, even such "programmed" movements
as facial expressions are at least subject to question. Our facial expressions
may sometimes "betray" our emotions, but we also quite conscientiously
"express" our emotions with our faces. A wince or a frown may be beyond
our control, but a hearty handshake or a caress is surely within the realm
of appropriate and inappropriate behavior. And when our focus turns to
the phenomenological and cognitive, at least when we are talking about

such matters as ways of seeing the world and thoughts and judgments, the questions of choice and responsibility are always looming.

CLEARING THE GROUND

The idea that our passions render us passive, often taken to be a defining characteristic of emotions, tends to assume that emotions are all more or less the same and treats them as an undifferentiated block phenomenon. Thus Peters and Mace, years ago, and Robert Gordon (1987), more recently, have argued that emotions are of a single kind, a kind that can be summed up in terms of "the category of passivity."[1] Even Paul Griffiths (1999), who most vehemently denies that emotions form a "natural kind," nevertheless does not flinch from describing all emotions as "irruptive." So, too, Jon Elster in a recent book (Elster, 1999, p. 306), asks "Actions or Passions?" and comes down solidly on the side of "the traditional view," "that emotions are involuntary, suffered in a passive mode." This treatment of emotions as essentially passive has led to a number of overblown and mistaken interpretations of my claim that emotions are voluntary and involve choices.

First of all, I certainly did not mean that emotions were *deliberate* actions, the results of overt plans or strategies. We do not think our way into most emotions. Nor do emotions fit the philosophical paradigm of intentional action, that is, actions that are preceded by intentions – combinations of explicit beliefs and desires and "knowing what one is going to do." Insofar as the emotions can be defended in terms of a kind of activity or action, it is not fully conscious intentional action that should be our paradigm. But the realm of semiconscious, inattentive, quasi-intentional, habitual, spontaneous, and even "automatic" activity and action has received little attention in philosophy, despite the efforts of such seminal figures as William James and Maurice Merleau-Ponty. Between intentional and full-blown deliberate action and straightforward passivity – getting hit with a brick, suffering a heart attack or a seizure – there is an enormous range of behaviors and "undergoings" that might nevertheless be considered within the realm of activity and action and (more generally) as matters of responsibility.

Second, I was not claiming that having an emotion is or can be what Arthur Danto once called a "basic action" (namely, an action one performs *without performing any other action*, such as wiggling one's little finger). One cannot "simply" decide to have an emotion. One can, however, decide to do any number of things – enter into a situation, not take one's medication, think about a situation in a different way, "set oneself up" for a fall – that

---

[1] R. S. Peters, "Emotions and the Category of Passivity": "judg[e]ments being disturbed, clouded or warped by emotion, of people not being in control of their emotions" (Peters & Mace, 1961–1962, p. 119); Gordon, 1987, pp. 110–127.

will bring about the emotion. Or one might *act as if* one has an emotion, act angrily, for instance, from which genuine anger may follow. There is William James's always helpful advice: "Smooth the brow, brighten the eye, contract the dorsal rather than the ventral aspect of the frame, and speak in a major key, pass the genial compliment, and your heart must be frigid indeed if it does not gradually thaw." But this does not mean that we simply "manipulate" or "engineer" our emotions, as if *we* perform actions which affect or bring about *them*. Following Danto, one might say that virtually all human actions – writing a letter, shooting a rifle, signaling a left-hand turn, working one's way through law school – involve doing something by doing something else, and this does not mean that the latter action *causes* the former. The one act (or course of action) *constitutes* the other. Thus (as Paul Ekman has argued, in pursuit of a very different kind of theory), one's intentional smoothing of the brow is already constitutive of the ensuing kindly emotion.

Third, although it is certainly true that most of our emotions are not premeditated or deliberate, it is not as if *all* emotions are devoid of premeditation and deliberation. As I shall argue in what follows, we often pursue love – the having of the emotion and not just the beloved – and we "work ourselves into a rage," at least sometimes with obvious objectives in mind (e.g., intimidating the other person). It is simply not true that intending (even announcing) that one is going to have a certain emotion (when realized) is insincere or in any sense not "genuine." Nor in so intending (or announcing) does one merely *predict* one's emotional state. The intention (and perhaps the announcement) rather help bring the emotion about, and whether or not that emotion is genuine or sincere is a complex and subtle matter that is by no means reducible to the simple formula "if it is by choice, then it cannot be genuine." (This argument is often conflated with an argument about the expression of emotion, namely, that insofar as the expression [for instance, a smile] is "faked," then not only does it not express the emotion but it is also not a genuine smile.)

Even where an emotion is premeditated and deliberate, however, we may not experience the emotion as a choice among options. We may not think to ourselves, "I could get angry now, I could just resign myself to the fact that I'm a loser, *or* I could just forget about it." Given the situation, I simply get angry. Nevertheless, I think that the notion "choice," like the notion of "action," is instructive in such contexts. It suggests a very different kind of framework for the study of emotion, one in which choice, intention, purpose, and responsibility play important if not central roles at least some of the time. And when we look for moments in the process of having an emotion where choice, intention, purpose, and responsibility might be playing relevant roles we may very well be surprised by how much we can find.

THE "PASSIVITY" PARADIGM OF EMOTION:
EMOTIONS AS EMERGENCIES

It is often supposed that our emotions are to be construed primarily in terms of "ways of being acted upon" (Robert Gordon, 1987, 1999, p. 223). They are, after all, called "passions" for just that reason. But though our emotions are often reactions to events or things that happen to us it does not follow that the emotion itself is something that happens to us. We talk of anger "overwhelming us" and of love "sweeping us away," but as colorful and common as this Sturm und Drang language of emotion may be, it remains on the level of picturesque speech. It should be viewed suspiciously. Are we really the victims of an internal emotional tempest? Or are we instead not only the subject but in some sense the *agent* of our emotions as well? This is not to say, again, that we usually deliberate and choose our immediate emotional responses. But the question of agency here is a subtle matter, and it is by no means resolved by way of the simple-minded disjunction: *either* an emotion is a full-blown deliberate intentional action *or* it is something that happens to us or victimizes us "from the inside," so to speak. Agency involves many different kinds of responses that are something less than "willful."

There is a vital if obvious distinction to be made from the outset here between the situation that evokes emotion and the emotion itself. I acknowledge that we do not (usually) deliberate and choose our immediate emotional responses, and it does (usually) seem as if our emotions arise unbidden, "spontaneously," in the face of some unexpected or (in James's phrase) "disturbing" situation. *But it is the situation and the circumstances that suddenly confront us, not the emotion.* I am driving along a mountain pass and I suddenly see a rock slide in front of me.[2] The rock slide is unexpected and does indeed "happen to me," but my emotional response is quite a different matter. Depending on my driving skills, my self-confidence, and my previous experience (not to mention my temperament, tendency to panic, etc.) both my emotional response and my actions (which cannot be easily separated) are just that, *my responses*. They may be spontaneous, un-thinking, and if I am practiced in the art of dangerous driving, habitual. My response need not be fully conscious. It certainly need not be articulated or explicitly "thought" at the time. There is no room for deliberation. What I do and feel no doubt depends on my history of habits and kindred experiences, but it is the situation, not my emotion, that suddenly confronts me. My response, whatever else it may be, is a *response*, an action of

---

[2] As the genealogy of examples has become a certain concern in emotions research, let me note that this particular example I borrow from Jerome Schafer, from his article "Emotions" in Irani and Myers, *Emotions* (Haven, 1983) which I first used myself in my "Beyond Reason: The Place of Emotions in Philosophy," in J. Ogilvy, ed., *Revisioning Philosophy* (SUNY, 1992).

sorts, not a reflex. I am not its recipient or its victim. I am the *agent* of my emotion, and as Aristotle argued in his *Ethics*, twenty-five hundred years ago, we are responsible for *even those actions which are involuntary* if we can be held responsible for the *cultivation* of the relevant habits, perhaps from childhood.

But the example I have chosen – the most plausible kind of example for those who wish to view emotions as "happening to us," is by no means the only or the best kind of paradigm of emotion. Many of our emotions are not suddenly provoked, nor are they provoked by sudden circumstances.[3] Our emotions do not always depend on the immediate situation. Often the evoking situation or incident is emblematic or symbolic of a much more general, perhaps repetitive, set of events, as when a colleague's ongoing sarcastic comments finally provide "the last straw" and I get furious. Thus Gordon reminds us that emotions and actions share "an ontogenesis in propositional attitudes" ("by way of beliefs and attitudes") rather than in "brute causes exclusively" (Gordon, 1986, p. 372; 1987). Sometimes *no* situation or incident confronts us. Thinking back to my colleague's behavior over the past few months, I "work myself into" a rage. Or thinking back to my junior high school sweetheart, I find myself "falling in love all over again" – or, at any rate, enjoying an interesting combination of nostalgia and arousal, mixed, perhaps with a tinge of regret.

Starting from nothing, or perhaps from the most fleeting association or fantasy, we "work ourselves into" a passion. Anger and jealousy are most familiar in this regard. We quite intentionally seek out evidence, review the situation, build a case, even provoke the very behavior that concerns us (perhaps as a kind of "test"). One might still hesitate to call such a carefully cultivated emotional response "deliberate." One might insist that what we cultivate is the "setup" and not the emotion (which predictably follows), but this says something about the subtlety and complexity of our emotional lives. It certainly does not suggest that our emotional lives are "out of our hands." Falling in love is not (as the metaphor suggests) a sudden "fall" but a slow campaign – looking for, finding, and to some extent creating ever new charms and virtues in the beloved (what Stendhal famously calls "crystallization"). It is not a matter of "falling" but of making incremental decisions and commitments and occasional major ones (for example, saying "I love you" for the first time), nurturing both the beloved's good feelings and (more to the point) one's own. Even grief, which of all emotions would seem to be the most obvious candidate for an emotion that simply befalls us, turns out to be a (more or less) cultivated response to tragedy. As the grief goes on, we get to make many choices which

---

[3] Thus I disagree with those who insist that emotion is bound up with change, except, perhaps, in the trivial sense in which it is the emotion itself that changes things (as when one falls in love or gets angry with a friend).

will – directly or indirectly – affect the trajectory of both the grief and our lives.

The rock-slide example would suggest that our emotions are by their very nature "short-lived." I sense the rock slide; I have a quick emotional reaction and make the (more or less) skilled move necessary to come to a safe and non-skid stop. Or (with more phenomenological accuracy), I stop and *then* (in safety) experience (that is, *notice*) my emotional reaction. My heart is beating furiously, sweat pours down my brow, morbid thoughts race through my mind, and this continues for several minutes until I "compose" myself and I can drive on.[4] But, again, the example is by no means typical or paradigmatic of emotion. Nico Frijda and I have both argued for years that restricting emotions to short-term responses is arbitrary and limiting (not to mention a grotesque violation of common usage). A stipulative definition of emotions as momentary and short-lived may be highly convenient to theorists who wish to utilize episodic measures or techniques (changes caused by the autonomic nervous system, MRI scans, spontaneous facial expressions, immediate retrospective reports). But I see no justification for shutting the door on all of the other emotions that do not fit this artificial paradigm. An emotion is *not* what happens in the first 120 milliseconds of arousal. In the current climate, I cannot emphasize this point enough. An emotion is not the initial neurological reaction, which is involuntary to be sure. An emotion is a process that continues via the cerebral hemispheres and thus by way of thought and self-recognition, for minutes, hours, weeks, or years. Moreover, not all emotions involve such arousal. Long-term love, "simmering" resentment, and "cold" vengeful anger seem to me to be cases in which the presumption that all emotions involve momentary arousal is extremely doubtful.

Thus I distinguish what has often been conflated, the sometimes sudden and urgent circumstances under which we have many emotions, on the one hand, and the nature of the emotion response itself. To be sure, in cases where the circumstances constitute a sudden emergency our emotional response may also be sudden and urgent. (Indeed, it would be hard to explain the evolutionary development of emotions without some such notion of a capacity for immediate response.) But suddenness and urgency are compatible with skill and spontaneity, and the fact that we find ourselves in an emergency situation does not mean that our emotional response is similarly imposed upon us. One might make some exception for the extremes of emotional response, for instance, panic and rage, where the response is indeed more "hard-wired" and more a matter of neurology than psychology, but it is certainly not the case that all emotions should be so understood (indeed, not even such "basic" emotions as fear and anger).

[4] In his classic *Get Shorty*, Elmore Leonard's character Chilli Palmer turns to his girlfriend after nearly getting shot and says, "I *was* afraid, but how long do you want me to be scared?"

The emergency paradigm suggests that the emotions necessarily happen first and experience and reflection only afterward, a thesis that has been reinforced by some powerful but misleading perceptual and neurological arguments.[5] But we often *produce* an emotional state in ourselves through deliberation and reflection, starting from nothing (or nothing emotional). In this sense, in particular, we can be said to "choose" our emotions. We "work ourselves into" an emotional state, building a case for getting angry at someone who, we come to realize, has offended us. We nurture grief (even if we begin by not feeling any) by forcing ourselves to remember the person who has just died and the many ways in which he or she affected one over the years. (This is a particularly important technique at funerals, and it is helped along, of course, by participating in the funeral "service" as well.) In any case, it is simply false that we should generally construe our emotions in terms of "ways of being acted upon." Our emotions do not render us passive but are sometimes the engines of our behavior and the motivators of meaningful action.

EMOTIONS AS THOUGHTS AND THE QUESTION OF AGENCY

On almost any account of freedom and responsibility, I am the undisputed agent of my coolly calculated, long-planned, and clearly intended actions, for which I have ready any number of more or less convincing reasons. But when the action in question is not a matter of planning, not deliberate, not even voluntary or clearly intentional, then the question of agency, responsibility, and choice becomes much more subtle and discerning. Take, for example, matters of habit, actions that are carried out unthinkingly, as a matter of "second nature" (such as Aristotle described the proper expression of the virtues). I shake the outstretched hand that greets me without thinking about it, more or less automatically, because this is what I do, what I have always done, what I have always been taught to do. In fact, my mind may be entirely elsewhere, noting (with fascination) the dancing elephant motif on my acquaintance's tie or worrying (with alarm) whether or not I remember his name. Nevertheless, even in the absence of all deliberation there is little doubt that the act of "mindlessly" shaking his hand is *mine*

---

[5] Robert Zajonc has long argued against the analysis of emotion as appraisal or cognition on the grounds that (subliminal) perception precedes the cognitions involved in emotion by several seconds. But reflection (noticing) our emotional responses is not the same thing as having them. Joseph Le Doux, in particular, has made much of the argument that the emotion response, indicated and measured in neurological terms, happens much more quickly than cognition, by which he means the reflective recognition *of* the emotion. But as I have already argued, having an emotion and (reflectively) experiencing an emotion are quite different, if not always distinct, and even the most primitive neurological emotional response involves some kind of *recognition* (a form, obviously, of cognition) as an initial stimulus. (We are not just talking about poking and prodding neurons here.)

(and not just in the minimal sense that it is *my* hand that does the shaking).[6] So, too, I thoughtlessly scratch the fresh, itchy scab, utterly mindless of the nurse's explicit warnings, making it bleed again profusely. Doing so is my responsibility (or irresponsibility), no question about it. But at least the itch provides a clear-cut reason for scratching, and thus the action was intentional even if thoughtless. The issue becomes much more complicated with *unintended* actions, such as mistakes and forgetting and Freudian slips. Nevertheless, we no longer refuse to attribute agency to such acts. Indeed, that was the whole point of Freud's radical and enduring insight.

Do such considerations apply to strictly "mental" acts, that is, thoughts, desires, and emotions that may have only minimal expression in overt behavior? Consider thoughts. Our emotions are a lot like thoughts, and not only in the sense that emotions typically involve thoughts. Jerome Neu, following Spinoza, suggests that emotions simply *are* thoughts (Neu, 1977 and 2000). Some thoughts are carefully and conscientiously cultivated, as when we "think our way through" a problem. On some occasions, it may make sense to say that the thoughts are "invited," for instance, when we have been mulling over a philosophical puzzle, given up on it for the day, and find that the answer "comes to us" in the middle of dinner or the middle of the night. But thoughts also come to us unbidden, even unwanted, and such cases support Nietzsche's famous observation that "a thought comes when *it* will, not when I will." Nevertheless, I have always thought that Nietzsche's observation served mainly to throw the whole idea of agency open for closer examination, not (as it is often interpreted), as a rejection of the notion of agency as such. The fact is that most of us take full responsibility for our thoughts, no matter how unbidden, so long as they fit into our personal agendas, particularly if it is an original or particularly brilliant thought. But also, more generally, we accept responsibility and take a thought as "our own" if it fits a problem we are working on or an issue in which we are engaged. This might suggest to some (as Nietzsche is taken to argue) that there is no need for such concepts of "agency" at all, but I think it rather relocates the question. It suggests that our sense of agency is far more expansive than the limited realm of "the will," that is, what we conscientiously *try* to do, and so, too, is our sense of responsibility.

Thoughts, whatever else they are, are telltale symptoms of emotion. When we find ourselves having certain thoughts – for instance, momentary homicidal or sexual fantasies – even in the absence of any other evident signs of emotion, that is some reason to accept the attribution of the relevant

---

[6] Indeed, having my hand grabbed and shaken without my participation is a very different and very upsetting experience. What is at stake here is what Wittgenstein famously queried as "the difference between my raising my arm and my arm going up." But for our purposes here, it is sufficiently evident that we are discussing the former and not the latter, shaking the other person's hand and not simply having one's own hand shaken.

emotions (fury and eros, respectively). If the thought is sufficiently horrifying, we may well dismiss it as nothing but fleeting and insignificant; but if it comes back, again and again, mere dismissal is no longer plausible. Freud may have been wrong when he early on insisted that all such thoughts are manifestations of a wish, but he was surely right that they are manifestations of *some* desire or emotion. But are thoughts a kind of action? Are we responsible for them? Thoughts as products of thinking, certainly. Invited thoughts, perhaps. Thoughts uninvited, no. But it is not always easy to tell the difference between a thought that appears in the process of thinking and an invited or even an uninvited thought.

These complex observations apply to emotions insofar as emotions involve thoughts. I do not deny that thoughts can be obsessive, that as manifestations of powerful (and perhaps repressed) emotions they "haunt" us without mercy. But when working on a problem I may be "haunted" by thoughts as well, and this does not compromise my responsibility both for having those particular thoughts or for thinking about the problem in the first place. Depending on the intensity as well as the circumstances and acceptability of the emotion, we tend to "own" the emotion or not, embrace it as an aspect of the ego, or confront it as the unwanted product of the unscrupulous id. In many cases, I would argue that the matter of acknowledging agency with regard to our emotions rests with how we think of the emotion in question, whether we (and others) consider it part of ourselves or not, whether it fits into our emotional narratives. This is not to suggest that all emotions that "fit" are flattering or acceptable, of course. A person who recognizes his or her envious or resentful nature will grudgingly accept envy or resentment as his or her own and acknowledge the larger narrative in which these unflattering emotions play a part.

A further source of our responsibility for our emotions is our ability to think *about* our emotion. Thus one might suggest that we exemplify agency and responsibility in how we think about our emotions (and consequently what we intend to do about them). Here again we come back to the intimate relation between having an emotion and experiencing the emotion, or between emotion and reflection (and, looking to a larger set of questions, between emotion and reason). But insofar as emotions are cognitive, cognitions *in* and cognitions *about* one's emotion tend to be logically connected. One's thoughts of being wronged that are constitutive of anger and one's thoughts about one's anger (for example, that it is justified, and it is justified because one has been wronged) tend to be very much of a piece. Thus, what one thinks about one's emotion and what one feels and thinks in virtue of having the emotion are not necessarily different thoughts, and what one thinks about his or her emotion may well be instrumental in changing or reinforcing the thoughts and thinking that are constitutive of the emotion.

EMOTIONS AS ACTS OF JUDGMENT

I will not here repeat my now familiar arguments for a "cognitive" theory of emotions in which emotions are primarily constituted by judgments. Suffice it to say that judgment (and more generally "cognition") remains one of the essential aspects of emotion. But we *make* judgments. Judgments are acts for which we can be held responsible. But this is not to say (as in many traditional philosophical analyses) that the judgments in question are necessarily conscious or deliberative or even articulate. Indeed, one might even doubt they are intentional (in the strong sense of following an intention).[7] But they are intentional in a weaker sense (which is all that we need here), in that they are based on one's beliefs and desires. They are purposive in that they serve (not consciously anticipate) a purpose. For instance, kinesthetic and aesthetic judgments (to which many emotional judgments are kindred) are usually or at least often inarticulate and not deliberative. We judge that the size of the next step on the stairway will be identical to the several we have already descended and move our bodies accordingly, our minds entirely on the conversation we are having with our companion. Walking down a set of uneven or crumbling steps, or descending the stairway after an accident, we become acutely aware of the nature of these judgments. Having once tripped and hurt ourselves, we make such judgments quite consciously, even reminding ourselves articulately ("now lower your left foot slowly") as we go.[8] But usually, such judgments are and remain quite unconscious.

So, too, we "find ourselves" liking an abstract painting, or a piece of music, or a view, without being able to say much of anything about why we like it. We need not even acknowledge that we like it, and yet our behavior (pausing before the painting and smiling, swaying to the music, gravitating to the landscape) indicates that we do.

But, of course, a great deal of this remains unconscious and unanalyzed. An art critic might be trained to identify and skillfully articulate those aspects of the painting which so move her, but for most of us, most of the time, the closest to articulation and consciousness we come is to think, "I like that." So, too, with emotions: we get annoyed without thinking "I am annoyed" and often without being aware of what annoys us. We find our

---

[7] Nico Frijda suggests that I borrow John Searle's distinction between intentions *in* action and actions that follow intentions here. In Frijda (1986) he suggests that intentional action is guided by the prospect of a future state. Impulsive action is guided by a desired change from a current state. I think the distinction here is subtle, at best (as many philosophers have pointed out that the present is "specious"), but the point is well taken. Nevertheless, impulsive action, insofar as it is based on one's beliefs and desires (unlike a "hard-wired" reaction or a reflex) is intentional in the sense specified.

[8] Cf. Michael Stocker's poignant account of how he felt walking on ice having once slipped and seriously hurt himself (*Valuing Emotions* [Cambridge, 1999]).

beloved charming and lovable without thinking, "She is so charming" or reflecting on the fact that we love her or being able to say, even if queried, what it is about her that we find so charming or lovable. But, of course, we can also become exquisitely articulate about such matters, and thus it would be as much of a mistake to insist that emotions in general are unconscious as it would be to insist that they are always conscious. And this is even before we enter that dangerous territory mapped out by Doctor Freud.

Using kinesthetic and aesthetic judgments as test cases, let me again ask the question whether it makes sense to say that we are active, perhaps even that we choose and are responsible for making our judgments. That we do "make" them may, of course, be an accident of grammar (just as the passivity patterns in the vernacular may be accidents of grammar), but it certainly gives the voluntariness of judgment a prima facie plausibility. But it is also true that, often, we do so unconsciously, without thinking or reflection, and this, it could be argued, suggests that we do not make our judgments voluntarily. We rather "find ourselves" making (or having made) them.

But the fact that a judgment is "unconscious" (in a non-Freudian sense) is no argument against its being voluntary or an aspect of our activity. Our many habitual actions are similarly unconscious, not because we habitually behave in ways that are devoid of intention, but rather because we do not pay attention. Some habits – for instance, strumming on the table with one's fingers – are devoid of any intention other than the minimal or "basic" one, namely, to strum one's fingers. Sometimes they have a minimally ulterior motive – for instance, to release some tension by strumming on the table with one's fingers. Sometimes they involve the intention to annoy. Other habitual actions are rich with intention and purpose – for instance, one's skillful typing on the keyboard, trying to express one's thoughts. But the typing itself is (and better be) unconscious in the relevant (non-Freudian) sense. Unconscious actions are still actions, and unconscious intentional actions are still intentional actions.

Speaking of intentional actions is different from speaking of "choice," which is clearly appropriate when an action (or judgment) is deliberate. But where an action (or a judgment) is not deliberate, is "choice" still appropriate? It is often said that "choice" remains appropriate where it is evident that one could choose or have chosen otherwise, even if one did not think of and in any sense weigh alternative options. On these grounds, a great many more of our judgments as well as our actions and habits count as chosen, whether or not there is any process of deliberation or conscious awareness of choice and options. We blame a man, for example, for making racist judgments (and not only pronouncements) whether or not it ever occurred to him that he might not make them. (This matter of "prereflective" consciousness and choice is critical to Sartre, who rejects the idea that we are responsible only for what we think of. This would let too much bad behavior "off the hook.") One is responsible not just for his or her immediate choices but for at least some of the history in which they are cultivated.

It is not unimportant that we usually *find ourselves* making such judgments (and performing such habitual actions). But it does not follow from this that we do not *do* them, or do them voluntarily. One might say that they are "spontaneous," which is not to say that they just happen but rather that we do them without preliminary thought or intention. (It is important to follow Frijda and distinguish between an intention that precedes action and an action that is intentional, which means that it is performed for some purpose. I would add only that the sorts of judgments and actions we are talking about here might sometimes *both* lack a prior intention and not be intentional.) Even spontaneously, making judgments is something we do. On reflection, we may come to discover, sometimes to our horror, that we have *already made* this or that judgment and, accordingly, are already in an emotional state. But to find oneself already doing something or in a "state" is not to deny that it is our doing. Spontaneity does not mean passivity.

Most of our kinesthetic judgments are sufficiently "automatic" that they might seem to be more bodily mechanism than an activity bound to perception. And, in a sense, this may be true. There is what W. B. Cannon famously described as "the wisdom of the body," which current research has only rendered more impressive. It is truly remarkable how the body responds to stress and circumstances, much of it never reaching the level of consciousness, much less full reflection. Some of this, I will argue, is a matter of confusing autonomic bodily responses, bodily expressions of emotion, and action. But much of it reveals an important point, often neglected by philosophers in particular. And that is (as I have argued elsewhere) that judgments should not be construed as "mental acts" alone. One can and sometimes must speak of "bodily judgments" (although, to be sure, a creature must have a mind if it is to make sense to speak of "judgment" at all). But it does not follow that if a judgment is bodily and utterly unreflective that it is therefore not done, not voluntary, and not intentional. To think so is to put much too much emphasis on the paradigm of reflective judgment, and more often than not to confuse cultivated (but still unreflective) judgments with mere autonomic bodily responses.

PASSIVITY AND THE EXPRESSION OF EMOTION

The question of the activity versus passivity of the passions is often conflated with the question of the voluntariness of expressions of emotion. This is quite understandable, since many philosophers and psychologists (and by no means all of them "behaviorists") have argued that an essential aspect or component of emotion is behavioral expression, and it is primarily through the expression of emotion that other people can recognize that one has any emotion at all. But we should distinguish among various sorts of expressions of emotion, such as bodily expressions, verbal expressions, facial expressions, various sorts of postures and gestures, full-blown actions and courses of action, and actions performed because of or "out of" emotion. There are many psychologists, seizing on one or another of these sorts of expression, who would more or less identify the emotion with its expression, and I think this is a healthy suggestion. The distinction between emotion and expression has so often been overdrawn, and so many philosophers (myself once included) have insisted on the "purely mental" status of emotions, emotions as experience, that the obvious connections between emotion and emotional behavior either get lost altogether or are rendered quite mysterious. It is illustrative, for example, that until very recently few philosophers who discussed emotion (even going back to Aristotle) said much of anything about the face and facial expression. They rather referred (as in James) to "the urge to vigorous action." Against this background of neglect Paul Ekman's strong equating of emotion and facial expression makes a lot of sense, so long, of course, as we do not thereby deny the experiential aspects and other expressions of emotion.

If we restrict our attention for the moment to full-blown action (as opposed to facial expressions, gestures, and more "basic" bodily responses), there is some question which actions count as expression of emotion and which are related to the emotion in some other way. Thus Peter Goldie distinguishes "acting out of emotion" from true emotional expression, although his criterion for distinguishing such action from expression of emotion is not the mere fact of delay but rather the "ends-means" nature of the action.[9] If an action is subsequent to and distinct from the emotion, we might well hesitate to call it an expression of emotion, but I think the distinction here founders. I say, "I love you." I blurt it out in the midst of a passion. And then I say it again the next morning in calm repose because I want to be sure that you know that I do love you. Does it make sense to say that the first is an expression of love but the second is not? Need we say that it is an "act of love" as opposed to an expression of love? or a *report* of one's love?[10] Doesn't it make more sense to understand the whole history

---

[9] In short, expressions of emotion have no better explanation than the fact that they just are expressions of that emotion. Actions, by contrast, have a belief-desire or ends-means structure that puts them firmly in the field of intentional action. I find this distinction illusory; first, because it presumes to recognize when an action has or does not have "ulterior" motives, and second, because habitual and practiced actions may be purposive even if they themselves have no purpose "in mind" – e.g., scowling as an expression of anger and intimidating those around you, or saying "I love you."

[10] This, I take it, is what Wittgenstein's much-muddled insistence about first-person mental reports is about. His concern is to deny that first-person reports are *reports* and to insist

of my loving behavior as an ongoing expression of my love and, if you like, focus on some acts that are more direct expressions of my emotion, others that are motivated in part by more divers concerns? Thus my saying "I love you" may sometimes be nothing other than an expression of love; at other times it may also serve as reassurance; and at others it may even serve as a threat, a warning, or a plea.[11] My making breakfast for you on a Sunday morning is almost certainly an expression of love, but that surely does not preclude its also being my way of assuring that you get your proper nutrition for the day, my way of hurrying up your morning so we can leave on our road trip on time, my chalking up "points" in our domestic arrangement to more or less evenly distribute the household duties, and so on. Indeed. It makes sense to say that my just *being* with you, quite apart from the particulars of my behavior, is an expression of my love.[12]

All of these examples of expression are more or less voluntary actions. Insofar as the expression is an action and is part of (and not only subsequent to) the emotion, the emotion itself is, *to that extent*, clearly in the realm of action and responsibility. But if we are to argue this position, we should also be prepared to confront those less obviously voluntary aspects of expression that might therefore be argued to drag the emotion down into the category of passivity.

Facial expressions, as Ekman and others have shown, are often unconscious and involuntary (which is not to deny that facial expressions might also be straightforwardly voluntary, e.g., "making a face"). Various postures and gestures would seem to fall into the same category. Autonomic expressions – sweating, blushing, the various immediate effects of an "adrenalin rush" – are clearly involuntary but therefore might not count as "expressions" (rather as "symptoms" or "manifestations"). It is important not to follow James in overemphasizing autonomic responses or in conflating these various sorts of expression, all of which do not lead to the same conclusions about either the relationship between emotion and expression or the voluntariness of emotion. What links these sorts of expressions together is the fact that they need not be conscious or in any way

that, rather, they are *expressions* of emotion in order to get around the Cartesian claim that a person has "privileged access" to his or her own mental states. But whatever the merits of the Cartesian case, it is certainly no good argument that denies the obvious, that sometimes people recognize and acknowledge their emotion and that acknowledgment becomes part of the emotion.

[11] I have discussed the complexity of such verbal expressions in my chapter on "I love you" in Solomon, 2001.

[12] One could throw in here a general set of qualifications, beginning with the assumption that I actually love you and depending on my general demeanor – just "being" is surely not enough if the particulars of my behavior are for the most part contemptuous or resentful. And one might add: in the absence of any overwhelming need – say, to hold onto my rights to the apartment in a tight real-estate market – such that my continuing to be with you can be wholly explained by motives that have nothing to do with love.

attended to, and they are most often not attended to and in that sense are "unconscious."

People are typically unaware of their facial expressions and equally oblivious to their posture as expressive of emotions. So, too, such expressions as "nervous" fidgeting are only rarely the object of one's self-consciousness. But it is important to note that such behavior is not strictly speaking involuntary, as it is the "voluntary" musculature that makes it possible. One can learn to act out various facial expressions of emotion without feeling the emotion (Ekman has famously mastered the art of doing so), and of course actors have long mastered the arts of semblance. Yet there is a difference between "spontaneous" emotional expression and voluntary expressions, and the seeming involuntariness of "spontaneous" expression is often used as an argument that the emotions themselves are involuntary. But here again I think the paradigm of immediate emotional response, as opposed to longer-term emotional process, misleads us. Even in those emotions we choose – for instance, going to a meeting where we know we will be outraged – the immediate emotional response will be involuntary. There is no reason to deny full "expression" status to such unintentional and unconscious behavior, but neither does the involuntariness of the expression render the emotion involuntary.

All in all, to the extent that an emotion *is* its expression there are very good arguments for denying what has long been called the passivity of the passions. And insofar as we want to distinguish an emotion (as experience) from its expression, it is essential that we not think of the experience in its stripped-down and utterly minimal form, as just a sensation produced by visceral disturbances. Nor should we think of the expression in its stripped-down and utterly minimal form as mere bodily movement, which does not even distinguish it from muscle spasms and reflex arcs. But once we have fleshed out the intimate relation between emotion and expression, it seems that the weight of the argument falls heavily on the side of activity. It is not that we are responsible *both* for the emotion and its expression. It is rather that we are (often) responsible for the emotion *as* its expression, for ultimately the two cannot be separated.

CONCLUSION

One can look at emotions from several different perspectives, but how we *think* about our emotions – as something we suffer or as something we "do" – will deeply affect both our behavior and our understanding of our behavior. In other words, theses about emotions tend to be self-confirming. If one thinks of oneself as the victim of irrational forces, there is no need to examine the reasons and motives for behaving as one does. On the other hand, if one thinks of oneself as the author of his or her emotions (perhaps not "the captain of one's fate," but in any case the oarsman who makes a significant contribution), one does reflect in such a way as to affect and possibly alter one's emotions. That is enough, I believe, to insist that we often and to a significant extent choose our emotions and are responsible for them.

References

Elmore, L. (1988). *Get Shorty*. New York: William Morrow.

Elster, J. (1999). *Alchemies of the mind*. Cambridge: Cambridge University Press.

Frijda, N. H. (1986). *The emotions*. Cambridge: Cambridge University Press.

Gordon, R. (1987). The passivity of emotions. In *The Structure of Emotions*. Cambridge: Cambridge University Press, pp. 110–127.

Griffiths, P. (1997). *What emotions really are*. Chicago: University of Chicago Press.

Neu, J. (1977). *Emotion, thought, and therapy*. London: Routledge and Kegan Paul.

Neu, J. (2000). *A tear is an intellectual thing*. New York: Oxford University Press.

Peters, R. S. (1963). *The concept of motivation*. London: Routledge and Kegan Paul.

Peters, R. S., & Mace, C. A. (1961–1962). Emotions and the category of passivity. *Proceedings of the Aristotelian Society, 6*, 117–142.

Plato. *The Republic* (Trans. G. M. A. Grube). Indianapolis: Hackett, 1993.

Robert, G. (1987). *The structure of emotions*. Cambridge: Cambridge University Press.

Sartre, J. P. (1948). *Existentialism is a humanism* (Trans. P. Mairet). New York: Philosophical Library, 1948.

Schafer, J. (1984). Emotions. In Irani and Myers (Eds.), *Emotions*. New York: Haven.

Schafer, R. (1976). *A new language for psychoanalysis*. New Haven, CT: Yale University Press, 1976.

Solomon, R. C. (1993). *The passions*. Indianapolis: Hackett.

Solomon, R. C. (1997). Beyond reason: The place of emotions in philosophy. In J. Ogilvy (Ed.), *Revisioning philosophy*. New York: SUNY Press.

Solomon, R. C. (2001). *About love*. Lanham, MD: Rowman and Littlefield.

Stocker, M. (1999). *Valuing emotions*. New York: Cambridge University Press.

Zajonc, R. C. (1980). Feeling and thinking: Preferences need no inferences. *American Psychologist, 35*, 151–175.

3

Emotions and Rationality

Jon Elster

ABSTRACT

The issue of emotion versus rationality is intertwined with the more traditional issue of passion versus reason. This chapter discusses the impact of emotion on impartial reasoning and then considers how instrumental rationality can be affected by emotion, drawing on ancient and modern moralists as well as on recent work on emotion and decision making.

REASON AND RATIONALITY

The relation between emotion and rationality is a tangled one. To untangle it, we first need to distinguish between *reason* and *rationality*. From antiquity onward, philosophers and moralists have opposed reason and passion. By "passion," they mean more or less what modern writers mean by "emotion." What they mean by "reason" varies across writers and periods. The ancient moralists, of whom I shall take Seneca as my example, had a more restricted idea of reason than what we find, for instance, in James Madison. Both conceptions of reason differ, however, from the modern conception of rationality. The relation between emotion and reason or rationality naturally varies with the way we understand the latter.

Given his vast influence on later writers, we may take Seneca as an exponent of the classical opposition between reason and passion. His treatise *On Anger*, in particular, has a number of instructive observations.[1] He was well aware, for instance, of the distinction between occurrent emotions and emotional dispositions: "The difference between [anger] and irascibility is evident; it is like the difference between a drunken man and a drunkard,

---

[1] See Harris (2001) for the broader context of this treatise.

I am grateful to Kent Berridge and Olav Gjelsvik for their comments on an earlier draft of this chapter.

30

between a frightened man and a coward. An angry man may not be an irascible man; an irascible man may, at times, not be an angry man" (I.iv). He also insisted on the involuntary and often all-consuming nature of the emotions: "they await no man's gesture and are not possessed, but possess" (I.xvi).

Seneca further observed that "Reason wishes the decision that it gives to be just; anger wishes to have the decision which it has given seem the just decision" (I.xviii). Here, Seneca is not only making a distinction between reason and passion as motivations; he is also claiming that, even from the point of view of the passionate agent, reason is the superior motivation. When la Rochefoucauld said that "Hypocrisy is a tribute vice pays to virtue" (Maxim 218), he did not go that far. He implied only that the vicious man must present himself to *others* as being motivated by reason. Seneca is claiming that he must also present himself to *himself* as being swayed by this motivation. There is a normative hierarchy of motivations that does not merely regulate our behavior in public but our self-image as well.

Seneca actually *defined* passion in terms of its capacity to overcome reason: "A man thinks himself injured, wishes to take vengeance, but dissuaded by some consideration immediately calms down. This I do not call anger, this prompting of the mind [*motum animi*] which is submissive to reason; anger is that which overleaps reason and sweeps it away" (II.iii). The spontaneous urge of the angry man to take revenge, or of the envious man to destroy the object of his envy, is a brute fact of human nature – neither rational nor irrational.[2] These urges are not passions. They become passions only when they override reason rather than submitting to it. Yet even when overriding reason, passion wants, as we have seen, to justify itself by reason.

Seneca also made one of the first theoretical comments on precommitment or self-binding:

While we are sane, while we are ourselves, let us ask help against an evil that is powerful and oft indulged by us. Those who cannot carry their wine discreetly and fear that they will be rash and insolent in their cups, instruct their friends to remove them from the feast; those who have learned that they are unreasonable when they are sick, give orders that in times of illness they are not to be obeyed. (III.xiii)

Reason, in other words, can take precautions against passion. The converse cannot happen, for two reasons. First, as noted, passion stands in a relation of deference to reason. Second, anger is typically too shortsighted or

---

[2] Observations to this effect by Aquinas, Dr. Johnson, and Kant are cited in Elster, 1999a, p. 168.

myopic to engage in strategic interaction with reason.[3] Reason, by contrast, is farsighted, at least in the modern conception.

As Seneca did not propose an explicit definition of reason, let me try to reconstruct one. In the reconstruction, the ancient idea of reason is defined by four features: orientation toward the future, lack of urgency, accurate belief formation, and justice or impartiality. (In the modern idea of reason, the first feature is modified.) The reasonable person is swayed by the future rather than by the past. Referring to someone who is free from anger, Seneca writes that

in every case of punishment he will keep before him the knowledge that one form is designed to make the wicked better, the other to remove them; in either case he will look to the future, not to the past. For as Plato says, "A sensible person does not punish a man because he has sinned, but in order to keep him from sin; for while the past cannot be recalled, the future may be forestalled." (I.xix)

Before I define urgency, let me define a more general category of *prudence*, which I shall understand as the absence of both *impatience* and *urgency*. I define impatience as a preference for early reward over delayed reward; hence the prudent person is not only oriented toward the future, but toward the distant future, in the sense of being able to be swayed by long-term consequences of present behavior. I define urgency as a preference for earlier action over delayed action. Thus understood, impatience and urgency are independent phenomena: each can occur without the other. Seneca denounces urgency in many places, but there is no unambiguous denunciation of impatience.[4] I do not know the corpus of classical writers well enough to assert whether this imbalance is characteristic. In modern writers we certainly find the opposite imbalance: impatience is routinely denounced, urgency more rarely. Although proverbial wisdom recognizes the fact of "Marry in haste, repent at leisure," modern political philosophers and social scientists have paid less attention to the phenomenon.

A paradigmatic case of prudence as absence of urgency is the Roman general Fabius, the "hesitater," about whom Seneca asks:

How else did Fabius restore the broken forces of the state but by knowing how to loiter, to put off, and to wait – things of which angry men know nothing? The state, which was standing then in the utmost extremity, had surely perished if Fabius had ventured to do all that anger prompted. But he took into consideration the

---

[3] I consider some exceptions to this statement in Elster, 2000, pp. 23–24.

[4] In an ambiguous denunciation, Seneca writes about Gaius Caesar that "so impatient was he of postponing his pleasure – a pleasure so great that his cruelty demanded it without delay – that he decapitated some of his victims by lamplight, as he was strolling with some ladies and senators on the terrace of his mother's gardens, which runs between the colonnade and the bank of the river. But what was the pressing need?" (I.xviii).

well-being of the state, and, estimating its strength, of which nothing now could be lost without the loss of all, he buried all thought of resentment and revenge and was concerned only with expediency and the fitting opportunity; he conquered anger before he conquered Hannibal. (I.xi)

One reason why urgency is harmful is that it impedes rational belief formation. (I shall later discuss other reasons.) "Reason grants a hearing to both sides, then seeks to postpone action, even its own, in order that it may gain time to sift out the truth; but anger is precipitate" (I.xvii). Here, anger causes suboptimal investment in information. In addition, anger prevents us from drawing correct inferences from the information that we do possess. Although the relevant passages are mostly too rhetorical to permit accurate analysis, it seems that Seneca had in mind that anger tends both to cloud the mind (without biasing it) and to bias it (e.g., through self-deception or wishful thinking).

Finally, reason is closely related to justice and fairness. As Seneca says, reason wishes the decision that it gives to be just. The kind of justice he has in mind is clearly consequentialist: the reasonable person "will openly kill those whom he wishes to have serve as examples of the wickedness that is slow to yield, not so much that they themselves may be destroyed as that they may deter others from destruction" (I.xix). To my knowledge, the idea that individual rights and duties might constrain or preempt consequentialist reasoning was unknown to him. For Seneca, the public interest was the dominant concern.

The next step in the development of the idea of rationality was taken, I believe, by the seventeenth-century French moralists. A particularly striking formulation can be taken from La Bruyère: "Nothing is easier for passion than to overcome reason; its greatest triumph is to conquer interest" (*Characters*, 4:77). In this maxim, La Bruyère distinguishes among three motivations: reason, passion, and interest. Although he does not tell us what he means by reason, we can perhaps reconstruct his meaning. When he says that reason is a weaker motivation than interest, in the sense of being more easily overridden by passion, it seems plausible to conclude that reason must be a disinterested or impartial motivation. We might ask a further question about the relative strength of these motivational forces. If passion can override both reason and interest, and with less resistance from reason than from interest, is interest also able to override reason? It does not follow, and La Bruyère does not tell us.

Writing a hundred years later, James Madison answered this question in the following terms:

To those who do not view the question through the medium of passion or of interest, the desire of the commercial States to collect, in any form, an indirect revenue from their uncommercial neighbors, must appear not less impolitic than it is unfair; since it would stimulate the injured party, by resentment as well as interest, to resort to less convenient channels for their foreign trade. But the mild voice of reason, pleading the cause of an enlarged and permanent interest, is but too often drowned, before public bodies as well as individuals, by the clamors of an impatient avidity for immediate and immoderate gain.[5]

Although the text is not as crystal clear as one would wish, Madison seems to be saying that passion and interest *when impatient* are both able to override reason. If asked whether patient or long-term interest is capable of overriding reason, he would probably have answered that the two are unlikely to conflict. From Montaigne onward there was a long-standing idea in moral philosophy that long-term self-interest and morality tend to generate the same behavior. "Even if I did not follow the right road for its rightness, I would still follow it because I have found from experience that, at the end of the day, it is usually the happiest one and the most useful."[6] To some extent, therefore, the reference to an "enlarged and permanent interest" is redundant. If interest is permanent, it is also enlarged.

The language of interest is not yet the language of instrumental rationality. We have to add two elements and subtract one. The two elements to be added are (1) the idea of deliberate choice of means and (2) the extension of rationality to cover beliefs as well as actions. The element to be subtracted is the idea of self-interest.

The idea of interest does not by itself include the idea of a choice among several possible means to realize a given end. The pursuit of interest is sometimes described in words that would also apply to the activity of pursuing of a hare simply by running after it. It is a mechanical and mindless activity. In reality, the intelligent pursuit of one's interest may require considerable sophistication. In fact, even the pursuit of a hare may require a great deal of thought. Rather than just running in the direction where the hare is at any given moment, one may do better by running in the direction where it will be at some later point in time. In doing so, one may initially have to run away from the hare rather than toward it: "reculer pour mieux sauter." Similarly, the pursuit of economic welfare may require a sacrifice of welfare now for the sake of greater welfare later. More generally, the efficient pursuit of economic interest requires the agent to choose among alternative means. The profit-maximizing entrepreneur, for instance, has to choose among input combinations according to the relative prices of the factors of production. Ricardo or Marx never understood this principle. In the history of Western thought, the idea of the rational economic agent

---

[5] *Federalist*, no. 42.

[6] Montaigne, 1991, p. 709. At the Federal Convention in Philadelphia, George Mason, Gouverneur Morris, and Roger Sherman all appealed to arguments of this general kind (Farrand, 1966, vol. 1, pp. 49, 531: vol. 2, p. 3. (See also n. 29 below.) A modern game-theoretic form of this argument is that, although a rational egoist would never cooperate in a one-shot Prisoner's Dilemma, he or she might do so in an indefinitely repeated interaction.

first emerged in the writings of the marginalists in the 1870s, and received a formal codification in the writings of Max Weber.

The pursuit of interest can hardly be called rational if it is based on irrational beliefs. For a belief to be rational, we should not require it to be true, only to be *well-grounded* in the evidence available to the agent. Actually, as Seneca noted, we should require a bit more: the agent should invest an optimal amount of resources (time, money, energy, etc.) in acquiring evidence or information. If these two conditions are satisfied, we might say that the agent pursues "enlightened self-interest." In contemporary as well as in earlier usage, however, that phrase is ambiguous. We may take it to mean that the agent acts on *rational beliefs*, but we could also use it to express the idea of acting according to *long-term interest*. Earlier, I noted that, as far as we can judge from Seneca, the ability to be motivated by long-term reward was no part of the ancient idea of reason. As I shall explain more fully, it is not part of the modern conception of rationality either. It is, however, part of the modern conception of reason.

At the same time, there is no need to limit instrumental rationality to the sphere of self-interest. Although both defenders and critics of rational-choice theory sometimes assume that rational agents must be self-interested, that assumption cannot be justified. Instrumental efficiency is obviously valuable in the pursuit of *any* end, whether self-interested or not. Altruism as well as hatred can fall within the domain of instrumental rationality. An individual who wants to alleviate poverty will naturally want to choose the charity that will use his donation most efficiently. He will avoid charitable organizations with high overhead costs and those whose funds end up lining the pocket of dictators rather than helping the poor. Unlike anger, which typically clouds or biases the mind, hatred is consistent with clear-headed instrumental rationality. The Holocaust – the greatest act of hatred in history – was carried out with notorious efficiency.

The spheres of reason and rationality overlap, in the sense that neither is a subset of the other. Instrumental rationality can be harnessed to the pursuit of private as well as public interest. Conversely, the modern concept of reason includes noninstrumental components. At the Federal Convention, Madison denounced "the immediate interest which one party may find in disregarding the rights of another or the good of the whole." What Madison calls "the good of the whole" is what I have referred to as the public interest. The notion of individual rights cannot, however, be directly assimilated to the public interest. Generally speaking, the idea of the rational pursuit of interest – private or public – is *consequentialist*. The rational agent chooses the means that will have the best consequences with regard to the interest he or she is pursuing or promoting. Rights, by contrast, are valued on nonconsequentialist grounds. The rights to life, liberty, security, and property are intrinsically valuable, over and above whatever value they might have on consequentialist grounds.

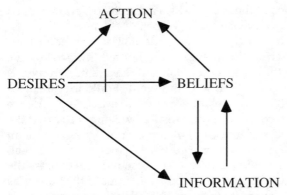

FIGURE 3.1. Rational-choice explanation of behavior

Rights and duties are correlative. The right to property, for instance, implies that other agents have a duty to abstain from taking it and that the state has a duty to prevent them from doing so. The right to work, if taken literally, implies that the state has a duty to provide employment for those who cannot find it in the labor market. Yet from Kant onward many have argued for duties that are not mere correlatives of rights, but independently justifiable. To the extent that these duties are prescribed universally and impartially, they, too, fall within the modern conception of reason. This conception, then, is richer than the ancient conception in two ways. It includes nonconsequentialist elements and it requires a long-term perspective. What has dropped out, it seems, is the idea that reason and urgency are incompatible.[7]

THE MODERN CONCEPTION OF RATIONALITY

We now are in a position to state more explicitly the modern theory of rational choice. The theory has two main aspects: it is explanatory and subjective. It aims at explaining behavior by assuming that agents do as well as they can by their own lights. The theory is summarized in Figure 3.1.

I have depicted a blocked arrow from desires to beliefs to indicate that processes such as wishful thinking and self-deception are inconsistent with rationality. Note, however, that the diagram leaves room for an indirect influence of desires on beliefs. How much evidence we collect depends on our prior beliefs about the expected costs and benefits of gathering new information. As indicated in the diagram, it also depends on our desires. To take a simple example, a person whose desires are very present-oriented,

---

[7] The idea, to be sure, is ignored, rather than denied.

in the sense that he does not take much account of future consequences of present behavior, would not rationally invest many resources in finding out what those consequences might be.

This remark brings out the fact that rational-choice theory is radically subjective. One might want to say that someone who pays little attention to future consequences of present behavior is unwise, or downright stupid. His or her life is likely to be nasty, brutish, and short. Surely, we might want to say, drug addicts are not rational. Well, they can be. They are far from always rational, but the idea is not absurd. Imagine someone who for genetic or cultural reasons pays little attention to long-term reward and focuses almost totally on the short term. Under some circumstances, taking drugs might well be optimal. The person might even anticipate that drug taking will induce a deficit of rationality in the future, but decide that this effect is just a cost on a par with the financial and medical consequences of drug taking. All the conditions for rationality might well be fulfilled. The choice to become an addict could be a rational one. I do not believe this is true of most addicts, but it could be true of some.[8]

In light of what I have said, what kinds of things can be assessed as more or less rational? Actions, beliefs, and investment in information can be rational or not, optimal or suboptimal. But desires cannot be assessed as more or less rational. In the diagram, there are arrows going from desires, but no arrows going to desires; in the machinery of action, desires are the unmoved mover. This is not strictly true. To some extent we can choose our desires. Suppose I do not get any pleasure from classical music but observe that my friends do. I might then decide to expose myself to a great deal of classical music on the assumption that I will come to like it as much as they do. Although we should not say that the desire to listen to classical music is rational, the decision to develop that desire might well be. These cases are not common, but they exist.

There is a severe constraint, however, on the choice of desires. The consequences of having a new desire must be judged desirable in terms of the present desires, otherwise we would not want to develop the new desire. The classical music case satisfies that constraint. But here is a case that does not. Suppose I suffer from an inability to defer gratification, that is, from being unable to take account of future consequences of present behavior. And suppose scientists came up with a discounting pill, which would increase the weight of future rewards in present decisions. If I took the pill, my life would go better. In retrospect, I would be grateful I took the pill. But if I had a choice to take the pill or not, I would refuse. Any behavior that the pill would induce is already within my reach. I could stop smoking, start exercising, or start saving money right now, but I don't. Since I do not

---

[8] For a fuller discussion, see Elster, 1999b, chap. 5.

want to do it, I would not want to take a pill that made me do it. Or, to put it differently, to want to be motivated by long-term consequences of present behavior *is* to be motivated by long-term consequences of present behavior.[9]

The person with a short time horizon is trapped. As the saying goes, "The eye cannot see beyond its horizon." A very myopic person may not be able to locate the optician who could provide him with the glasses he needs: he is trapped. In a similar way, a person can be caught in a belief trap. Gerry Mackie argues that

women who practice infibulation [a form of female genital mutilation] are caught in a belief trap. The Bambara of Mali believe that the clitoris will kill a man if it comes in contact with the penis during intercourse. In Nigeria, some groups believe that if a baby's head touches the clitoris during delivery, the baby will die. I call these self-enforcing beliefs: a belief that cannot be revised, because *the believed costs of testing the belief are too high.*[10]

THE MODERN CONCEPTION OF EMOTION

I shall define occurrent emotions in terms of six features, which I shall first enumerate and then discuss at greater length.[11] They are:

- physiological arousal
- physiological expressions
- valence
- cognitive antecedent
- intentional object
- action tendency

When I discuss specific features, I draw attention to some of the ways in which they are relevant for the comparison with rationality. It is important to keep *all* the features in mind. Reducing emotions to "affect," that is, to arousal, can be misleading. Reducing them to their positive or negative "valence" can be equally misleading. The explanatory force of the emotions often lies in their fine grain. People behave quite differently under the influence of anger, indignation, resentment, hatred, or envy, although all these emotions are instances of negative affect.

By "arousal" I mean any departure from the physiological baseline – for instance, a decrease in the heart rate as well as an increase. This criterion is

---

[9] For a fuller development of this argument, see Elster, 2000, pp. 26–29, and Skog 2001.

[10] Mackie, 1996, p. 1009; italics added.

[11] This definition relies heavily on Nico Frijda's work, notably Frijda, 1986. In Elster 1999a, ch.II.2, I argue that Aristotle also imputed these six features to occurrent emotions. In ch.IV.2 of the same work, I elaborate on each of the six features and comment on various exceptions.

important to distinguish emotions proper from other phenomena referred to by the same words. The term "fear," for instance, may denote visceral fear or fear proper, but it can also denote a simple belief-desire complex, as when I say I'm afraid it's going to rain.[12] Whereas visceral fear may short-circuit rationality, fear as a desire-belief complex will typically induce rational action, such as taking an umbrella. Similarly, the term "regret" may refer to a wrenching experience or to a mere wish that one had acted differently.

The fact that emotions have physiological expressions makes it possible for the emotion felt by one person to shape the behavior of other agents. When an expression is perceived as the forerunner of action directed toward another, the latter may take steps to defuse or encourage such action. If my antagonist can see from my face and posture that I am angry, he may back down. If a woman can infer from my facial expression that I may be about to make an advance to her, she may modify her behavior to encourage or discourage me. To the extent that these expressions are under the control of the conscious will, or can be approximated by deliberate simulation, they invite instrumentally rational exploitation.

The valence of the emotions – the pain and pleasure that accompany them – offers an obvious bridge to rational-choice theory. One might indeed think that the pain and pleasure of emotions are simply negative and positive utilities that may contribute to the overall expected utility of a given choice. For reasons I have spelled out elsewhere, I believe the picture is more complicated.[13] Here, let me simply note that the level of pain and pleasure derived from emotions are inversely related to the probability of the events that generate these emotions. As Barbara Mellers and her colleagues have shown, surprise is an important magnifier of affect.[14] In the choice between an action that is unlikely to generate high pleasure and one that is quite likely to do so, one might rationally choose the former.

The emotions I shall consider are indeed triggered by beliefs. The triggering beliefs may, like any other belief, be rational or irrational. Moreover, if the triggering belief is irrational, it may be because it is distorted by a prior emotion. When I compare your success with my failure, I experience a pang of envy. To rid myself of the feeling of inferiority, I tell myself a story according to which your success was due to immoral or illegal behavior. On the basis of this emotionally motivated belief I now feel indignation rather than envy. In such processes, emotions enter both as causes and as effects of beliefs.

---

[12] Gordon, 1987; see also Harris, 2001, p. 108.

[13] Elster, 1999a, pp. 154–156, 179–181, 301–306.

[14] Mellers, Schwartz, and Ritov, 1999. Paradoxically, perhaps, anticipation is also a magnifier of affect, as it enables us to savor the emotional experience before it actually occurs (Loewenstein, 1987).

TABLE 3.1. *Action Tendencies of Emotions*

Emotion	Action Tendency
Anger	Cause the object of anger to suffer (revenge)
Hatred	Cause the object of hatred to cease to exist
Contempt	Ostracism
Shame	"Sink through the floor"; suicide
Guilt	Confess; make repairs; hurt oneself
Envy	Destroy the envied object or its possessor
Fear	Flight; fight
Love	To approach and touch the other

Moreover, emotions have intentional objects: they are about something, or directed toward something. In the important case of emotions that target individuals, the object may be an action committed by a person or it may be that person's character. Anger, guilt, admiration, and pride are directed toward actions; hatred, contempt, shame, liking, and pridefulness are directed toward the person's character. The object of envy is not the envied person but the fact that he has something I want, in both senses of that word. But if what he has and I lack is moral goodness, or beauty, this distinction becomes tenuous.

Emotions, finally, have action tendencies. Some examples are given in Table 3.1.

Some emotions may be associated with wishes rather than with desires. One may wish that a certain state obtain, or one may desire to bring it about. In hatred, what matters is that the hated person or group disappear from the face of the earth. In envy, what matters is that the envied person lose his or her possessions. In neither case is there an additional emotional satisfaction derived by the state of affairs being realized through my agency. In hatred, I may take action if I am well placed to do so, but I might be just as happy, or even happier, if someone else did it for me. In envy, I may even have a positive preference for the other's ruin not coming about through my agency.[15] Some people who would abstain from calling the fire brigade if their neighbor's house were on fire would not themselves set fire to it (and not merely because of the risk of detection). By contrast, anger, contempt, love, guilt, and shame activate desires where it matters that they are realized through *my* agency. My desire for revenge is not slaked if the object is injured in a car accident. My desire for atonement is not alleviated if the person I have harmed wins the jackpot in a lottery. My feeling of contempt requires *me* to isolate myself from the object, not merely that the person be ostracized by others.

---

[15] Seneca, *On Anger* III.v.

RATIONALITY AND EMOTION

Rationality, as summarized in Figure 3.1, requires three optimizing operations. First, the action must be the optimal means of realizing the agent's desire, given the beliefs. Second, the beliefs must be rational or well-grounded, given the evidence. Exactly what this means is controversial, but in many cases the general idea is unproblematic. Third, the agent must have invested optimally in acquiring the evidence that is needed to form a belief before acting. Violations of rationality may occur in any of these three optimizing operations. Such violations can have many causes. Here I only consider those which can be traced back to the interference of emotion with rationality. I have already mentioned many emotion-induced violations of reason that are also violations of rationality. These are emotionally induced cognitive flaws that arise through urgency, clouded thinking, or biased thinking.[16]

I now want to consider violations that are not due to flawed cognitive processes. To do so, I need to be more explicit about the objects of the "desires" or preferences that generate behavior. In the standard case, agents have primitive preferences over outcomes of action and outcome-induced preferences over actions. Who desires the end (and the side effects) desires the means. In other cases, agents have non-outcome-induced preferences over actions. In still other cases, agents have preferences over outcomes that are shaped by (their beliefs about) the actions that brought them about or, more accurately, that caused the set of outcomes to be restricted in a particular way.

In the standard case, assuming correct cognitive processing, the ensuing action will be rational. In making this assertion I ignore some famous literary cases of weakness of the will. Medea, when killing her children, says: "I know indeed what evil I intend to do. But stronger than all my afterthoughts is my fury."[17] Racine's Phèdre asks her confidante to "serve my fury, and not my reason." I do not know whether such states, characterized by the coexistence of lucidity and extreme passion, occur outside of literature.[18] I have more faith in Seneca's claim that "anger wishes to have the decision which it has given seem the just decision." Be this as it may, I shall focus on the two nonstandard cases.

Consider first non-outcome-induced preferences over actions. These are closely related to the action tendencies associated with emotion. Also, they

---

[16] Although we tend to think of emotional bias as taking the form of wishful thinking, the opposite bias is also possible. A French proverb says, "We believe easily what we hope *and what we fear.*" Othello illustrates the latter, underexplored mechanism.

[17] See Harris, 2001, p. 169, n. 52, for some of the complications that arise in interpreting this text.

[18] Racine's *Andromaque* is unique among his plays in that it recognizes that passion tends to undermine the lucidity of the agent (see Elster, 1999a, pp. 111–117).

are closely related to the idea of urgency. In my earlier discussion, I have assumed that the impact of urgency is mediated by cognition, and in particular by the suboptimal investment in information gathering. Urgency can also have a direct impact, however. This is the case when the agent takes early action even when he or she knows (1) that the outcome of action would be better if the action were delayed; and (2) that the outcome itself will not be not delayed by delaying the action. By assumption (1), it is not a matter of faulty cognitive processing. By assumption (2), it is not a matter of impatience.

A more complicated and probably more common case is the following. The agent can act at time 1 or time 2. If action is taken at time 1, the outcome occurs at time 3. If action is taken at time 2, it occurs at time 4. (The times succeed each other in the numbered order.) The interval between time 1 and 2 is relatively long. The interval between time 3 and time 4 is relatively short. The outcome at time 4 is substantially better than the outcome at time 3. These vague phrases are intended to convey the idea that in a nonemotional state the agent would be able to defer gratification from time 3 to time 4. If the emotional state induces the agent to choose the earlier action and the smaller reward, the mechanism could be either urgency (a preference for an earlier action) or a temporary increase in the rate of time discounting (a stronger preference for an earlier reward).[19] If the choice of the earlier action is due to urgency, it violates the canons of rationality.[20] If it is due to increased impatience, it does not.[21] In practice, it might be hard to identify the culprit.

Social norms provide an important special case of non-outcome-induced preferences over actions. Consider two injunctions: "Always wear black in strong sunshine" and "Always wear black at a funeral." The former is instrumentally rational advice, as air circulates more quickly under dark

---

[19] In the related case of addiction, several writers have discussed the idea of endogenous changes in discounting rates (Becker, 1996, p. 120; Orphanides & Zervos, 1998; O'Donoghue & Rabin, 1999). The idea that emotions, too, can shorten the time horizon of the agents is more or less clearly stated by various writers. Yet the (crucial) question is rarely asked whether emotion undermines the agent's awareness of remote consequences or causes him to attach less weight to them in his utility function.

[20] A counterargument might be that someone who has an urgent desire to act will get rid of the urge by acting. Since having an unsatisfied urge is painful, and acting can relieve the pain, early action is rational if the gains from relieving the pain earlier rather than later offset the loss of receiving the smaller rather than the larger reward. The objection, in my view, is misguided. Although acting on the urge will relieve the urge, it is not typically instrumental action for the *purpose* of relieving the urge, in the way one can take Methadone to relieve oneself from a painful craving for heroin.

[21] Some might object to this statement. If a person who is normally able to defer gratification loses that ability in an emotional state, is that not the very paradigm of irrationality? There is indeed a temptation to assess desires and preferences as more or less rational on the basis of the way in which they have come about, but it is one we should resist. I am grateful to Kent Berridge and Olav Gjelsvik for pressing this point on me.

clothes. The latter has no instrumental aspect at all. It is a social norm that is maintained by internalized emotions (shame) and sanctioning behavior by others in the community. Here are some other salient examples of social norms:

Norms regulating the use of money. (1) Suppose someone walks up to the person at the head of a bus queue and asks to buy that person's place. If the offer is accepted, two persons gain and nobody loses. If it is rejected, nobody loses. Yet there is a norm against making such offers. (2) In a small suburban community, Mr. H. mows his own lawn. His neighbor's son would mow it for $12. He wouldn't mow his neighbor's same-sized lawn for $20. This suggests that the value to him of the time it takes him to mow the lawn is both less than $12 and more than $20. The puzzle is resolved by noting the existence of a norm in such communities against monetary transactions of this kind among adults.[22]

Medical norms.[23] (1) Medical ethics tell doctors to treat the more severe cases first. Yet these are often (as in liver transplants) the patients who are too ill to benefit from treatment. (2) Doctors follow a norm of thoroughness, which tells them that once a patient has been admitted, he or she should get "the full treatment." Yet other patients might benefit much more from the time he spends on the later tests, since with respect to any given patient the doctor's time has decreasing marginal productivity. Both norms violate instrumental rationality with regard to the objective of saving lives or improving overall health.

The paradox of voting. Why do people bother to vote in national elections? Since no such election has ever been won by a single vote, an individual vote makes no difference to the outcome, and may entail considerable trouble for the voter. Yet people do vote in large numbers, to fulfill their "civic duty."

Norms of revenge.[24] People often seek revenge for an insult, even when (1) doing so is costly or risky, (2) they know that they will not be able to undo the harm that was done to them, and (3) they know the revenge will not dissuade others from harming them in the future. In other words, people seek revenge even when there are no tangible benefits and some tangible costs. Although many forms of revenge behavior occur spontaneously (this was Seneca's main concern), some societies have powerful social norms that reinforce the spontaneous tendency.

Norms of cooperation.[25] (1) The norm of fairness tells individuals to cooperate if and only if others do. The norm makes cooperation contingent on other people's behavior and not on the outcome of the agent's behavior. (2) The norm of "everyday Kantianism" tells individuals to cooperate if, and only if, it would be better for all if all cooperated than if nobody did. This norm makes cooperation contingent on hypothetical outcomes of behavior rather than on the actual outcome of the agent's behavior.

---

[22] Thaler (1980), from whom this example is taken, explains it in terms of loss-aversion. Yet as Amos Tversky pointed out to me a long time ago, the norm explanation is also plausible.

[23] For a fuller exposition, see Elster, 1992, pp. 91–94, 147–149.

[24] For a fuller exposition see Elster, 1999a, chap. 3, p. 4.

[25] For a fuller exposition, see Elster, 1989, chap. 3.

I am making two claims about such norm-guided behavior. First, these norms violate instrumental rationality by subverting the goals of the agents who subscribe to them. Second, the norm following is induced or sustained by emotions. Both claims might be met by the objection that if people are sanctioned by others for violating the norm, norm following *is* instrumentally rational because it enables the agent to avoid punishment. I have two responses. First, we still have to explain why others sanction norm violators. The response that they do so because nonsanctioners will also be sanctioned (and so on at higher degrees) becomes implausible at more than two or three removes away from the original violation. Second, and more fundamentally, the objection rests on a misunderstanding of the impact of sanctioning. When I refuse to deal with a person who has violated a social norm, that person may suffer a financial loss. Far more important, however, the other will see the sanction as a vehicle for my emotions of contempt or disgust and suffer shame as a result. The material aspect of the sanction that matters is *how much it costs the sanctioner to penalize the target*, not how much it costs the target to be penalized. The more it costs me to refuse to deal with you, the stronger you will feel the contempt behind my refusal and the more acute will be your shame. The emotional meaning of sanctions was recognized by Aristotle, who wrote that "Shame is the imagination of disgrace, in which we shrink from the disgrace itself and *not from its consequences*" (*Rhetoric* 1384a; italics added).

In the second nonstandard case, agents have preferences over outcomes that depend on how they are brought about. I shall develop this idea by referring to the Ultimatum Game (Fig. 3.2).[26]

In this game, the first player proposes a division of ten dollars between himself and the second player. Proposals can be made only in whole dollars. The second player can reject the proposal, in which case neither player gets anything, or accept it, in which case the proposed division is implemented. In experiments, participants interact anonymously, through computer terminals. Also, in the experiments I shall consider there is only one-shot interaction, with no room for reputation building. Given these conditions, there is no reason to think that the players care about each other or that they might be concerned with building a reputation for the future. We would expect them to be concerned only with the payoffs in the experiment. If they are rational, and know each other to be rational, Player I will propose nine dollars for himself and one dollar for Player II, who will accept the proposal. What happens in experiments is quite different. Player I typically offers something like seven dollars for himself and three for Player II. Player II typically rejects any proposal that gives her less than three dollars.

Consider three interpretations of these findings, in terms of (a sense of) fairness, envy, and resentment. First, we could imagine that those in the

[26] For a survey of Ultimatum Game experiments, see Roth, 1995.

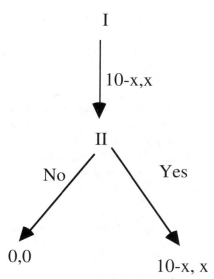

FIGURE 3.2. The Ultimatum Game

position of Player I are moved (although not only) by a sense of fairness when they abstain from making the most self-interested proposal, and that those in the position of II are moved (although not only) by fairness when they reject the most unfavorable proposals. Yet in experiments with the "Dictator Game," in which Player II simply has to accept the proposal without the option of rejecting it, Player I typically makes a more selfish proposal. This finding suggests that even in the Ultimatum Game Player I is motivated mainly by the anticipated rejection by Player II of an unfavorable proposal, rather than by a sense of fairness. Moreover, it is not really plausible to explain the rejection in terms of a sense of fairness. If an agent were genuinely moved by considerations of fairness, these would move him or her in the position of Player I as well as in that of Player II. Since participants are randomly assigned to the positions of Players I and II, there should not be any systematic difference in the sense of fairness displayed in their behavior. As those in the position of Player I are not (or not strongly) moved by fairness, it seems plausible to explain the behavior of those in the position of Player II in terms of envy or resentment rather than by a (genuine) sense of unfairness, and the behavior of those in the position of Player I by their anticipation of such envy or resentment.

Let us now consider the two emotion-based explanations in terms of envy and resentment. Whereas envy is an outcome-based emotion, resentment is action-based.[27] One can imagine that Player II, if facing an 8,2 proposal, might reject it out of envy. If that is the case, she should also

[27] Hirshleifer, 1987.

reject the same proposal if Player I were constrained to choose, say, between (10,0) and (8,2). Intuition suggests and experiments confirm that Player II will be much more likely to reject in this constrained case than in the unconstrained case.[28] The explanation of the behavior in the Ultimatum Game must be resentment rather than envy.

To show the relevance of this issue, let me cite from a comment made by George Mason at the Federal Convention in Philadelphia. The discussion concerned whether the Western lands that would accede to the Union in the future should be admitted with the same rights as those of the original thirteen states. When Gouverneur Morris argued that they should be admitted as second-rate states, so that they would never be able to outvote the original states, Mason argued strongly for the opposite view:

If the Western States are to be admitted into the Union, as they arise, they must be treated as equals, and subjected to no degrading discriminations. They will have the same pride & other passions which we have, and will either not unite with or will speedily revolt from the Union, if they are not in all respects placed on an equal footing with their brethren.[29]

Mason appeals to the "pride and passions" of the new states, not to their self-interest. Even if it would in fact be in their interest to accede to the Union on unequal terms rather than remain outside, they might still, out of resentment, prefer to stay outside. Implicitly, he appeals to the self-interest of the old states, not to their sense of justice.[30]

Is the resentful player in the Ultimatum Game who rejects the (8,2) proposal *irrational?* I cannot see any way in which the behavior can be said to serve his or her ends. An envious rejection might maximize a utility function in which the consumption of others enters on a par with the agent's own consumption, but I submit that there is no noncontrived utility function that would rationalize rejection out of resentment.

CONCLUSION

I have defended the traditional view that emotions interfere with and subvert instrumental rationality. This is not to say that we would be better off

---

[28] Camerer, 2003, chap. 3. 7. 5.

[29] Farrand, 1966, vol. 1, pp. 578–579. Sherman's veil-of-ignorance argument (n. 6 above) was made in the same context: "We are providing for our posterity, for our children & our grand Children, who would be as likely to be citizens of New Western States, as of the old States. On this consideration alone, we ought to make no such discrimination as was proposed by the motion."

[30] Actually, he used both arguments. By admitting the Western states on equal terms, the Framers would do "what we know to be right in itself" (Farrand, 1966, vol. 1, p. 578). To those who might not accept that argument, he added that the new states would in any case be unlikely to accept a degrading proposal.

if we had no emotions. Emotions provide us with a sense of goal and direction in life, but also prevent us from going steadily in that direction. Except in unacceptably loose language, the first part of the previous sentence does not imply that "emotions are rational."

Could emotions *enhance* instrumental rationality? Although several writers have proposed arguments to this effect, I have not found any of them convincing.[31] The fact that efficient decision making and normal affect are impaired by the same brain lesions does not show that the latter is a condition for the former. The fact that an emotional action tendency can provide a more efficient response to danger than an exhaustive assessment of all options and their consequences shows only that the latter procedure is irrational, not that the former is superior to a rational response.

Might not emotions themselves fall under the scope of rational choice? I believe that occurrent emotions are largely unchosen. Although emotional dispositions are (at least partly) the result of action, I do not think we know enough about the causal mechanisms involved to be able to act efficiently on our dispositions. Even if we could, the costs might be prohibitive – five years of psychoanalysis can add up to twice the annual income of a middle-class professional.

More generally, there is in the social sciences, partly because of the dominating influence of economics, a pervasive tendency to "rationalize" all aspects of human behavior. This tendency is shown by the large number of "just-so" or "as-if" stories that, in my opinion, discredit their authors. We cannot deal rationally with irrationality if we refuse to accept its existence.

References

Becker, G. (1996). *Accounting for tastes*. Cambridge, MA: Harvard University Press.

Camerer, C. (2003). *Behavioral game theory*. Princeton, NJ: Princeton University Press.

Elster, J. (1989). *The cement of society*. New York: Cambridge University Press.

Elster, J. (1992). *Local justice*. New York: Russell Sage.

Elster, J. (1999a). *Alchemies of the mind*. New York: Cambridge University Press.

Elster, J. (1999b). *Strong feelings*. Cambridge, MA: MIT Press.

Elster, J. (2000). *Ulysses unbound*. New York: Cambridge University Press.

Farrand M. (Ed.) (1966). *Records of the Federal Convention*, vols. 1–3. New Haven, CT: Yale University Press.

Frijda, N. (1986). *The emotions*. Cambridge: Cambridge University Press.

Gordon, R. M. (1987). *The structure of emotions*. Cambridge: Cambridge University Press.

Harris, W. (2001). *Restraining rage: The ideology of anger control in classical antiquity*. Cambridge, MA: Harvard University Press.

Hirshleifer, H. (1987). The emotions as guarantors of threats and promises. In J. Dupré (Ed.), *The latest on the best* (pp. 307–326). Cambridge, MA: MIT Press.

---

[31] See comments on Damasio and de Sousa in Elster, 1999a, pp. 287–298.

Loewenstein, G. (1987). Anticipation and the valuation of delayed consumption. *Economic Journal, 97*, 667–684.

Mackie, G. (1996). Ending footbinding and infibulation: A convention account. *American Sociological Review, 61*, 999–1017.

Mellers, B. A.; Schwartz, A.; & Ritov, I. (1999). Emotion-based choice. *Journal of Experimental Psychology: General, 128*, 1–14.

Montaigne, M. de. (1991). *The complete essays* (Trans. M. A. Screech). Harmondsworth: Penguin.

O'Donoghue, T., & Rabin, M. (1999b). Addiction and self-control. In J. Elster (Ed.), *Addiction: Entries and exits* (pp. 169–206). New York: Russell Sage.

Orphanides, A., & Zervos, D. (1998). Myopia and addictive behavior. *Economic Journal, 108*, 75–91.

Roth, A. (1995). Bargaining experiments. In J. H. Kagel and A. E. Roth (Eds.), *Handbook of experimental economics* (pp. 253–348). Princeton, NJ: Princeton University Press.

Skog, O.-J. (2001). Theorizing about patience formation. *Economics and Philosophy, 17*, 207–219.

Thaler, R. (1980). Towards a positive theory of consumer choice. *Journal of Economic Behavior and Organization, 1*, 39–60.

4

Emotions and Feelings

A Neurobiological Perspective

Antonio R. Damasio

ABSTRACT

After receiving remarkable attention from scientists during the nineteenth century, emotion was relatively neglected throughout the 20th century, especially within the field of neuroscience. Recently, however, neuroscientists have begun again to advance the understanding of the neural mechanisms behind emotion.

Emotion is as much amenable to scientific study as any other aspect of behavior. Moreover, emotion is not a luxury: it is an expression of basic mechanisms of life regulation developed in evolution, and is indispensable for survival. It plays a critical role in virtually all aspects of learning, reasoning, and creativity. Somewhat surprisingly, it may play a role in the construction of consciousness.

In this chapter I review a theoretical framework which places emotion and the phenomenon that follows emotion, feeling, in an evolutionary perspective and discuss their biological roles in homeostasis. I shall also review some current evidence on neural systems involved in emotion and feeling based on the lesion method and functional neuroimaging studies.

What are emotions and feelings from the neurobiology perspective? How do organisms produce these phenomena and, in particular, how does the brain implement them? What are emotions and feelings for? Recent advances in biology, cognitive science, and neuroscience are beginning to help us answer these questions – not completely, by any means, but in ways that suggest progress is being made. In this chapter I give a sketch of some possible answers.

Let me begin with the matter of what emotions and feelings are. The statement of the problem suggests that a research distinction can be drawn with advantage between the two, that emotions and feelings are not the same thing as objects of study, notwithstanding the fact that, in real time and real life, emotion and feeling seemingly occur as if they were merely two sides of the same coin, affect pure and simple. Many are skeptical about the need for such a distinction. Some argue that the current usage of these terms has made them synonymous and that it is difficult if not impossible to expunge the conflation. Others contend that the term "emotion" is perfectly adequate to describe both emotions and feelings. Still others will say that "feeling" is a hopeless concept: too vague, too slippery, too bad. By now, however, we know enough about the nature of affective processes to state that there are distinctive, albeit interrelated, physiological and mental events that benefit from separate designations. We also know that different names allow for a clearer communication regarding the profile of these events and the related theories and hypotheses. The fact that the words chosen to designate the two sets of phenomena are, respectively, emotion and feeling, is neither divinely ordained nor arbitrary. The two words effectively interconnect a historical tradition with our current understanding of the phenomena they are supposed to denote. They are rather good words for the purpose.

WHAT EMOTIONS AND FEELINGS ARE

The following are definitions of these phenomena, as I see them today. Note that these definitions are provisional, that they are neither the definitions of the problems with which I remember starting my work on this subject nor the definitions we are likely to come to, in the years ahead, as new findings change the ways in which we conceive these problems and carve out revised descriptions. Working hypotheses in the form of definitions is perhaps the best way to designate the statements that follow.

In the simplest and most general wording possible, emotions are *bioregulatory reactions* that aim at promoting, directly or indirectly, the sort of physiological states that secure not just survival but survival regulated into the range that we, conscious and thinking creatures, identify with *well-being*.

What are these reactions made of? They are constituted by a *patterned collection of chemical and neural responses* that the brain produces when it detects the presence of an *emotionally competent stimulus*. The processing of the stimulus may be conscious or nonconscious, but in either case the responses are produced automatically.

And what is an emotionally competent stimulus? It is an object or a situation actually perceived or recalled from memory. Some stimuli achieve competent status in the course of evolution. As a result of the brain's design, stimuli that belong to certain classes of objects and events predictably cause the repertoires of action, internal and external, which we call emotions. Eventually, the brain associates other objects and events that occur in individual experience with those which are innately set to cause emotions, and as a consequence an additional set of emotionally competent stimuli arises. By the ripe age at which one gets invited to write scientific essays, most if not all objects and situations in the world evoke *some* emotion, strong or weak. The world comes in shades of "good" or "bad"; and precious little in it is neutral. Moreover, in relation both to the evolutionarily set stimuli and to those stimuli which are acquired, a lifetime of experience is continually remodeling their "competence," revising their power to trigger emotions. In other words, neither innate nor acquired stimuli are fixedly competent. They can be more or less competent over time, which really means that their ability to cause emotions is in part a function of how our lives have been lived. They change as a function of the individual's autobiography.

Does the notion that emotions can be triggered nonconsciously and automatically deny the classical notion of an "appraisal" phase preceding emotions? Not at all. The process by which, at a given moment, an object or situation *becomes* an emotionally competent stimulus often includes a conscious, cognitive appraising of the circumstances. Besides, even when the process is nonconscious, the current context may play a role and enhance or reduce the competence of the stimulus. In the end, the emotional competence of a given stimulus depends on several major factors: evolutionary history; personal history; and current context. In some instances, the same stimulus may cause virtually the same emotion for a lifetime; in other instances, the emotional competence varies over time. In other words, it is not true that emotions, conceived in the manner outlined here, are necessarily stereotyped and genetically set reactions. The machinery that produces the responses is genetically set, for certain, but past individual experience and current context can modulate the evolutionary wisdom to a greater or smaller degree.

The emotionally competent stimulus produces its action by activating certain brain regions that in my framework I designate as *triggering* or *induction* regions. The activity of those regions leads to the *execution* of the emotion. Once the emotion cascade is triggered and its execution begins, the emotional responses target both the body and other regions of the brain that are not part of the triggering set of regions. The responses alter the state of the internal milieu (using, for example, hormonal messages disseminated in the bloodstream); the state of the viscera; the state of the musculoskeletal system; and they lead a body now prepared by all these functional changes into carrying out varied actions or complex behaviors. The latter actions and behaviors range from facial and postural expressions to the acts that define, say, fight and flight behavior, or parenting, or sympathy; from *approach* to *withdrawal* behaviors; from behaviors we associate with the notion of *pleasure* and *reward* to behaviors we associate with the notion of *pain* and *punishment* or *aversion*. In the social context in which emotions often occur, the emotional state also alters the state of other individuals who perceive and react to that emotional state.

While the core of an emotion is the set of homeostasis-related bodily changes I just described, emotions involve changes in the brain itself. Along with the overt body changes there are subtle changes in the way the brain operates within those systems which support cognition, especially those which govern attention and mental image production. For example, sadness is often accompanied by a reduced rate of new image formation and by increased allotment of attention to those images. Happiness is often accompanied by the opposite circumstances: high rates of new image production and shorter attention spans. Moreover, as emotional states get established, a number of thoughts congruent with the emotion are also evoked. For example, the emotion of sadness provokes the recall of thoughts on the theme of loss and worthlessness, thoughts that are often referred to as "sad thoughts." They are sad thoughts by virtue of their association with the state of the body that defines sadness. In brief, even in this oversimplified description, an emotion is a complicated matter: a collection of preparatory body changes and ensuing behaviors that is accompanied by a particular style of mental operation.

Using the same perspective, how can we define feelings, specifically, feelings of emotion? My working definition of feelings indicates that *feelings are the mental representation of the physiologic changes that occur during an emotion*. The essence of feelings of emotion is the mapping of the emotional state in the appropriate body-sensing regions of the brain. But *feeling an emotion also includes the mapping of changes that occur in the cognitive processing style, as well as the evocation of thoughts that are congruent with the feeling state*.

In the broadest possible definition a feeling is the perception of an emotional state, as enacted in the body, an essential content of which is the perception of some variation of the sense of pleasure or pain (establishing a connection to the subset of reward and aversion mechanisms that are an integral part of emotive behavior). Along with the perception of body changes there is also a perception of a certain mode of thinking, and of thoughts with certain themes. Thus feeling depends on the perception of a changed body state alongside the perception of a certain style of mental processing and the production of thoughts with themes consonant with the emotion.

VARIETIES OF EMOTION

The definition of feelings offered above is quite specific and yet broad enough to encompass feelings from three classes of emotion: background emotions, primary emotions, and social emotions (so-called secondary emotions). The application of the definition to all three classes of emotion/feeling, however, raises intriguing issues, some of which deserve comment.

First, it is apparent that the emotions that are currently part of the rosters of the above categories are extremely varied in terms of their emotionally competent stimulus, their physiological profile, and the homeostatic benefits they bring to an organism, directly or indirectly. Second, there is no general agreement about what to include or leave out from such lists of emotions, although it is fair to say that there is a consensus regarding most of what is or is not currently judged to be an emotion. Third, not everyone would agree with the suggestion that those emotions whose status gathers a broad consensus fit the definition I offered above. The objections would revolve around the regulatory, homeostatic role of emotions. For example, while fear or disgust produce indisputable advantages for the emoting subject, the benefits of sadness or happiness are often doubted.

Fourth, applying the above definition in the case of social emotions – for example, applying it to pride or despair – raises understandable questions. Is it indeed the case that such emotions engage the body in a distinctive way? Are pride and despair significantly deployed in the body at all? Is it not the case that what counts when we feel proud or desperate are the thoughts that lead to pride and despair, as well as the thoughts that follow? What has the body got to do with such processes?

My answer to these questions is that the definitions of emotion and feeling that I provided earlier *do* apply, as stated, to pride and despair. The bodily mise-en-scène of pride and despair is indeed powerful and distinctive. Can one imagine mistaking the behavior of a person in a fit of pride from that of a person in the throes of despair? Not really. Not even bad actors manage to confuse the two. The facial mask and the bodily countenance are specific to each of these emotions, and that goes only for what we can see with the naked eye, and not for what the viscera and the internal milieu manage to contribute away from sight.

Do I have any doubt that thoughts about the circumstances surrounding episodes of pride and despair are an important aspect of the comprehensive experience of pride and despair? I do not. But I believe that thoughts about the circumstances surrounding episodes of fear or sadness cannot be dismissed either, or regarded as of lesser importance. The differences in these emotions, and there are differences, have to do with the subtlety of the emotional expression – fear and sadness, perhaps, are more obvious, more variegated than pride and despair – and with the setting, which is perhaps more importantly sociocultural in the case of pride and despair. The body-relatedness is not different, however, and the universality of these emotions/feelings comes from bodily expressions that cut across cultures and species – just consider, for example, the proud demeanor of the leading male in a troop of monkeys. I suspect the objection arises mostly when the "bodily basis" of feelings is conceived too narrowly, along the visceral dimension only. The inclusion of the extensive signaling from musculoskeletal and internal milieu processes addresses the objection.

Although it would not be possible for me to agree to a definition of, say, pride or despair that would not factor body-specific components, I would be sympathetic to the argument if it were cast in the following

manner: that although there is considerable evidence for a body component
to social emotions, there is not enough empirical data showing that, say,
pride and despair have entirely distinct profiles across a wide number of
physiological parameters; I would agree that the strong view implied by
my provisional definitions should not be regarded as definitely proven
but rather as plausible and supported by preliminary evidence. In the end,
however, when someone says that he or she feels proud but that someone
believes the process of that feeling consists exclusively of thoughts about
the circumstances surrounding the episode of pride, I suggest that the
person does not "feel" pride at all, but rather "thinks" pride. If feeling sad or
desperate or happy is a mere matter of thoughts about circumstances, then
the appropriate description is "thinking" sadly or desperately or happily.
Why use the term "feeling" at all? Depriving an emotion or a feeling of
their body-related components empties out their respective concepts.

   That emotions and feelings are enmeshed with nonemotional mental
events is quite apparent. That the human importance of emotions and
feelings comes in great part from those other mental events with which they
become associated is just as obvious. But the specifics of our understanding
of the neurophysiology of emotion reside in elucidating the mechanisms
that permit the realization of an emotional state and of the ensuing feeling,
rather than with the mental events that bracket those mechanisms as either
competent causes or consequences.

THE NEURAL BASIS FOR EMOTION AND FEELING

The composition of the neural systems involved in the production of emotion is being identified as a result of studies in humans and animals. The
identification of these systems and of their key components has barely begun. For example, an emotionally competent stimulus, actual or recalled,
consciously or nonconsciously appraised, is processed in sensory regions
and results in the availability of neural signals at a variety of sites from
which emotions can be triggered. Such sites include the amygdala and the
ventromedial frontal cortices, which thus operate as interfaces between the
appraisal process – the "gathering" of an emotionally competent stimulus –
and the actual execution of an emotion. Sites such as the amygdala are part
of multi-region systems that trigger emotions. On the other hand, sites in
the hypothalamus, the basal forebrain (e.g., the nucleus accumbens), and
in the brainstem (e.g., the nuclei in the periaqueductal gray), are the principal executors of an emotion. These are the structures that directly signal,
chemically and neurally, to the body and brain targets whose changes will
come to constitute an emotional state.

   It is possible that some regions that operate as triggering sites also contribute to the execution of emotions (some nuclei in the amygdala), while
other regions probably operate exclusively as effectors (the ventromedial

prefrontal cortices). Only further empirical work will tell. However, none of the triggering/effector regions is likely to participate in the process that follows on the heels of an emotion, namely, feeling.

What can we currently say about the neural basis for the experiencing of emotions? Recent functional imaging studies show that body-sensing areas such as the somatosensory cortices of the insula and of the second somatosensory region (S2), the cingulate cortex, and some nuclei in the brainstem tegmentum, show a significant pattern of activation or deactivation when normal individuals experience the emotions of sadness, happiness, fear, and anger, and that, moreover, the patterns vary among the emotions. Of all regions receiving body signals the insula now appears to be the key cortical component in the process of feeling. Intriguingly, the insula receives signals from the bulk of the viscera and internal milieu conveyed by dedicated peripheral nerve systems, spinal cord and brainstem pathways, and even a specific thalamic nucleus. In brief, the recent findings indicate that the mapping of body states is significantly modified during the process of feeling an emotion and that those patterns of activation and deactivation are correlates of the mental states we call feelings.

The important notion to emphasize here is that the neural patterns exhibited in these regions are the substrate for the mental patterns we call feelings. This fact leads to an important question that must be raised at this point: how do the neural patterns in body-sensing regions arise in the first place? In my answer I propose three possible mechanisms.

The basic mechanism is the result of a straightforward mapping of body changes. The areas these studies identify are the recipients of signals hailing from the body, as changed by the emotional state. Just as emotion is produced by chemical and neural signals, so feelings too are based on chemical and neural signaling. In this first mechanism the chemical signals arrive at regions such as the area postrema, in the brainstem, and from there neural signals carry on the message inside the brain; the neural signals arrive at every segment of the spinal cord and also at the level of the brainstem via cranial nerves.

The second mechanism is a variant of the first. As a result of interference with signal processing, the information conveyed from the body is modulated at sites such as the spinal cord and brainstem, resulting in a particular map of the body state that takes into account the context of the organism and that varies to a smaller or larger degree from the map of the actual body state.

The third mechanism, which I have termed the "as-if-body-loop," produces, in its pure form, a neural map of the body state "as-if" it were occurring in the body, without the body being fully involved or involved at all in its actual execution. It is in effect a "simulation" and is probably akin to "mirror-neuron mechanisms" described more recently. Whether based fully or partly on the body, however, the body-relatedness of the maps that underlie feelings is the key issue.

The notion that the neural basis of feelings would be out of scientific reach is no longer tenable. The mental events we call feelings are associated with changes in the neural mapping of the body state. The finding of such correlations is the beginning of the unraveling of the neurophysiological mysteries behind one of the most critical aspects of human experience. We now know where to look further for the sort of changes – cellular and molecular – that provide the deeper underpinning of feelings. I note, however, that the success of this new stage of understanding of the physiology of affective phenomena depends on the research distinction between emotion and feeling I outlined above. The majority of emotional responses are directly observable either with the naked eye or with the appropriate scientific probes, for example, endocrine assays, psychophysiological and neurophysiological measurements. Emotional responses are perfectly objective, and emotions can be investigated in the numerous laboratory species that exhibit them, namely Drosophila, Aplysia, and rodents. The idea that they are subjective is an artifact of the improper conceptualization of the phenomena, in fact, a result of confusing objective emotions with subjective feelings. Emotions are *not* subjective, *not* private, *not* elusive, *not* intangible, *not* indefinable. Their neurobiology can be investigated objectively, and understanding their neurobiology opens the way to elucidating the neurobiology of feelings.

WHAT ARE EMOTIONS AND FEELINGS FOR?

The general role of emotions has been apparent for some time. For obvious reasons the role of feelings has been less clear or in dispute. Emotions allow organisms to cope successfully with a variety of objects and situations that are potentially dangerous or potentially advantageous. This is true of fear and disgust, of sadness and happiness, of sympathy and love, of shame and pride. The directness of the effect does vary immensely – the results of fear or disgust are immediate and pertain to the subject having the emotion; the results of sympathy or shame are often delayed and also involve others; the same is true of happiness, in many instances. Emotions are just the most visible and complex part of a tall edifice of biological regulation that includes basic homeostatic reactions, (e.g., those which maintain one's metabolism); basic reflexes; pain and pleasure behaviors; and appetitive drives and motivations.

Whereas emotions provide an immediate reaction to certain challenges and opportunities faced by an organism, feeling the emotions provides the organism with a mental alert for the significance of the object that caused the emotion and for the thoughts consequent to responding emotionally. The adaptive value of feelings comes from amplifying the mental impact of a given situation and increasing the probabilities that comparable situations can be anticipated and planned for in the future so as to avert risks and take advantage of opportunities.

References

Damasio, A. R. (1994). *Descartes' error: Emotion, reason, and the human brain.* New York: Putnam.

Damasio, A. R. (1999). *The feeling of what happens: Body and emotion in the making of consciousness.* New York: Harcourt.

Damasio, A. R. (2003). *Looking for Spinoza: Joy, sorrow and the feeling brain.* New York: Harcourt.

Damasio, A. R.; Grabowski, T. J.; Bechara, A.; Damasio, H.; Ponto, L. L. B.; Parvizi, J.; & Hichwa, R. D. (2000). Subcortical and cortical brain activity during the feeling of self-generated emotions. *Nature Neuroscience, 3,* 1049–1056.

Davidson, R. J.; Goldsmith, H. H.; & Scherer, K. (Eds.) (2001). *Handbook of affective science.* New York: Oxford University Press.

Frijda, N. H. (1986). *The emotions.* New York: Cambridge University Press.

Lane, R. D., & Nadel, L. (Eds.). (2000). *The interface of emotion and cognitive neuroscience.* New York: Oxford University Press.

LeDoux, J. (1996). *The emotional brain: The mysterious underpinnings of emotional life.* New York: Simon and Schuster.

Rolls, E. T. (2000). Précis of the brain and emotion. *Behavioral and Brain Sciences, 23,* 177–191.

5

The Concept of an Evolved Fear Module and Cognitive Theories of Anxiety

Arne Öhman and Stefan Wiens

ABSTRACT

Consistent with theories that postulate appraisal as a key mechanism of emotion, the theoretical rationale behind the currently prominent cognitive therapy for disorders of anxiety and depression stresses the role of conscious processing in the generation of fear and anxiety. This emphasis, however, runs counter to recent developments in physiological, cognitive, and social psychology that document the importance of automatic processes in many psychological contexts. The point of departure for this chapter can be summarized in terms of the concept of an evolved fear module: a relatively independent behavioral, mental, and neural system that has evolved as a response to recurrent survival threats in mammalian evolution. The module is postulated to be selective, automatic, encapsulated, and realized in specific neural circuitry centered on the amygdala.

Research using masked stimuli show that the fear module is independent of conscious cognition. From this perspective, consciously accessible cognition has little role in the activation of fear and anxiety but may be important in maintaining the emotion over time.

When we think of emotions, fear is the one that most readily comes to mind. As an experience shared among humans, it is, perhaps more than we like, an integral part of human existence. In the science of emotion, furthermore, all theorists that accept the notion of basic or fundamental emotions agree that fear is one of them. Fear is also central to the adjacent field of stress research, because many of the experimental manipulations used to induce and study stress have been imported from research on fear and its close ally, anxiety. Fear is an activated, aversive emotion that serves

The research reported in this chapter was supported by grants to the first author from the Bank of Sweden Tercentennial Foundation and by the Swedish Council for Research in the Humanities and Social Sciences.

Address correspondence to Arne Öhman. Psychology Section, Department of Clinical Neuroscience, Karolinska Institutet at Karolinska Hospital, Z6, S-171 76 Stockholm, Sweden.

to motivate escape and avoidance of threatening circumstances (Öhman, 2000b). Thus, it is essentially a coping emotion that is associated with attempts to handle threats to physical or psychological integrity (Epstein, 1972). If the coping attempts fail and the situation becomes uncontrollable, fear turns into anxiety (Öhman, 2000a).

A novel understanding of the basic neurophysiological mechanisms of fear has emerged in the last decades (see reviews by, e.g., Davis & Lee, 1998; Lang, Davis, & Öhman, 2000; LeDoux, 1996; Öhman, 2000b; Rosen & Schulkin, 1998). The purpose of this chapter is to present a contemporary, evolutionarily inspired perspective on fear (Öhman & Mineka, 2001) and to discuss its implications for the current understanding of clinical anxiety. According to this perspective, fear originates in an evolutionarily derived predatory defense system whose basic characteristics are shared among mammals. The function of this system is to handle survival threats in the surroundings by facilitating information uptake concerning the threat, and rapid escape or avoidance if the threat is imminent (Fanselow, 1994). If the threat is distant, the typical effect is behavioral inactivity and scanning of the environment to assess the risk involved and the chance of avoiding the threat (Blanchard & Blanchard, 1988). As the imminence of the threat increases (e.g., a predator gets closer) there is gradual activation of autonomic nervous system activity (e.g., skin conductance increases, heart rate decreases, blood pressure increases) and potentiation of defensive reflexes (e.g., the startle reflex; see Lang, Bradley & Cuthberg, 1997).

Öhman and Mineka (2001) introduced the concept of an evolved fear module to provide a general description of this fear system. Briefly, the fear module reflects an evolutionarily shaped neural circuit centered on the amygdala in the anterior medial temporal lobe, which represents a common mammalian heritage. It is the characteristics of this circuit that determine the behavioral characteristics of the module. These characteristics include selectivity with regard to effective stimuli for activating the module, automaticity of activation, and encapsulation with regard to cognitive input.

Several aspects of the fear module provide challenges to the appraisal-oriented cognitive theories of anxiety that dominate contemporary clinical management of anxiety disorder. In this chapter we will present the fear module construct and its database before we conclude by discussing the similarities and differences between the two approaches to clinical anxiety.

THE SPECIFIC NEURAL CIRCUITRY OF THE FEAR MODULE

The fear module is controlled by a specific neural circuit that has been evolutionarily shaped to mediate functional relationships between ecological threats and defensive behavior. Because the module reflects a common mammalian heritage, it is primarily located in subcortical and brainstem areas of the brain. Thus, it served animals with primitive brains long before more recent biological families with more developed cortices emerged. In particular, this circuit was firmly established at the base of the brain that eventually, during relatively recent hominid evolution, became the site of cortical neural networks serving language and advanced cognition. The circuit is organized around the amygdala, a limbic structure in the medial temporal lobe, immediately anterior to the hippocampus (see reviews by Davis & Lee, 1998; Davis & Whalen, 2001; Emery & Amaral, 2000; Fendt & Fanselow, 1999; Lang, Davis, & Öhman, 2000; LeDoux, 1996). The amygdala, and primarily its lateral nucleus, receives input from thalamic and cortical sites, which constitute "low-" and "high-routes" mediating only preliminarily or fully processed sensory information, respectively (LeDoux, 1996). Thus, the amygdala may be accessed by a direct, monosynaptic link from the thalamus that activates the fear response even before the fear-evoking stimulus is identified through full processing in the multiple synapses of the sensory regions of the cortex (e.g., Öhman, 2000b). In this way, fear may be rapidly activated after minimal stimulus processing, giving the organism a potentially crucial temporal advantage in escaping, for example, an attacking predator (LeDoux, 1996). The central nucleus of the amygdala complex projects to hypothalamic and brainstem nuclei that control various aspects of overt fear behavior, such as fight/flight, sympathetic activation, facial expression, and defensive reflexes (see reviews by Davis & Whalen, 2001; Fendt & Fanselow, 1999; LeDoux, 1996). Note that the amygdala has extensive projections to the cortex via the generalized cholinergic arousal system originating in the basal nucleus of the forebrain (e.g., LeDoux, 1992) and via direct projections to several levels of sensory-processing areas (Emery & Amaral, 2000). Thus, the ancient origin and the anatomical connections of the amygdala suggest that it is relatively independent of higher conditions, rather controlling than being controlled from the cortex (LeDoux, 1996).

THE SELECTIVITY OF THE FEAR MODULE

Evolutionarily shaped behavioral systems are likely to be selective with regard to input. Accordingly, the fear module is assumed to be particularly likely to respond to stimuli that have been correlated with threatening encounters in the evolutionary past. By limiting the set of effective stimuli, ready-made neural mechanisms could be devised for identifying critical events after only minimal neural processing, to capture attention, and to promote rapid defense activation. Further, the range of stimuli that activates the fear module can be vastly expanded through Pavlovian conditioning. Thus, stimuli that signal activation of the fear module can, after co-occurrence of the signal and the threat it signals, produce such activation themselves.

Classification of Fear Stimuli

Fear in animals can be elicited by heterogeneous sets of stimuli (e.g., Russell, 1979). However, in spite of the variability there are a number of common themes that suggest evolutionary influences in determining which stimuli are effective in engaging the fear module (e.g., Marks, 1987). Mayr (1974) distinguished between social and nonsocial (i.e., physical) ecological contexts for behavioral acts in terms of whether they elicited active responses from the environment, that is, whether they were directed toward living creatures or not. Mayr (1974) argued that behavior eliciting active responses had to be tightly genetically controlled to assure stable social signaling between members of the same species, for instance, in aggressive or sexual encounters (intraspecific communicative behavior), or to deal with the time constraints of predatory encounters (interspecific communicative behavior). Behavior directed at the physical environment (noncommunicative behavior), on the other hand, was assumed to be more open to environmental influences (e.g., learning where to forage for food and other resources). Öhman, Dimberg, and Öst (1985) noted that, if applied to fear, this classification system would result in three broad domains of fear stimuli: social fears, animal fears, and nature fears. Not only do these categories figure prominently in factor analytical work on human fear stimuli (e.g., Arrindell, Pickersgill, Merckelbach, Ardon, & Cornet, 1992) but they also conform to three important classes of phobias in the *Diagnostic and Statistical Manual of Mental Disorders* (4th ed., DSM-IV; American Psychiatric Association, 1994): social phobias, animal phobias, and nature phobias. Thus, one would expect that the fear module would be easily activated by threatening social stimuli (e.g., threatening faces); animal stimuli associated with predatory threat in evolution (e.g., snakes); or natural events persistently related to threat to safety (e.g., thunder). Because of the importance of mobilizing defense in threatening circumstances, such stimuli also would be effective in capturing attention.

Evolutionary Fear Stimuli Capturing Attention

Öhman, Flykt, and Esteves (2001) tested if attention is preferentially captured by evolutionary fear stimuli such as spiders and snakes. In a visual search task, participants were shown matrices of pictures (snakes, spiders, flowers, and mushrooms) that either were all showing objects from the same category (e.g., flowers) or included a discrepant target stimulus from another category (e.g., a snake among flowers). Results showed that participants were faster in detecting discrepant snakes and spiders among flowers and mushrooms than vice versa. This effect was independent of the number of distracters (3 or 8) in the display and was enhanced in snake and spider fearful participants, suggesting that the effect was automatic and potentiated by fear. Similarly, Öhman, Lundqvist, and Esteves (2001) used carefully controlled schematic facial stimuli (see Lundqvist, Esteves, & Öhman, 1999) to test the hypothesis that social-threat faces would be preferentially detected in crowds of faces (cf. Hansen & Hansen, 1988; Purcell, Stewart, & Skov, 1996). Again, across five experiments, threatening faces were detected faster and more accurately than nonthreatening faces, and this was true across different crowd sizes.

The Preparedness Hypothesis

Another aspect of the fear module's selectivity with regard to input is the assumption that fear learning (Pavlovian conditioning) is more effective to evolutionary fear-relevant than fear-irrelevant stimuli (Öhman et al., 1985; Öhman & Mineka, 2001; Seligman, 1971). Öhman and Mineka (2001) reviewed the literature and concluded that there is strong converging evidence that evolutionary fear-relevant stimuli such as snakes, spiders, and angry faces show a special affinity for becoming associated with aversive events. The strongest evidence comes from experiments in lab-reared rhesus monkeys that had never been exposed to snakes, and that showed no initial signs of fear in response to snake-related stimuli. However, after the monkeys were shown a video in which a conspecific model acted fearfully to such stimuli, they quickly developed strong fear (Cook & Mineka, 1989; 1990). Similar effects were not observed when the model monkey acted fearfully to a flower or a toy rabbit, even though these stimuli supported learning as well as snakes in the context of appetitive learning (Cook & Mineka, 1990). Likewise, in an extensive series of studies using psychophysiological dependent variables, Öhman and coworkers (see reviews by Öhman, 1979; Öhman, 1993) demonstrated that human participants showed enhanced resistance to extinction (i.e., responding decreased less quickly) after conditioning to fear-relevant stimuli (snake, spiders, angry faces) compared to when the conditioned stimuli (CSs) were fear-irrelevant (flowers, mushrooms, happy faces). Such effects were not obtained with nonaversive unconditioned stimuli (Öhman, Fredrikson, & Hugdahl, 1978) or for culturally determined threat stimuli such as electrical equipment (Hugdahl & Kärker, 1981) or guns (Cook, Hodes, & Lang, 1986). Finally, when an aversive stimulus such as a shock was as likely to follow fear-relevant (e.g., snakes) as fear-irrelevant (e.g., mushrooms) stimuli, participants consistently overestimated the relation between fear-relevant stimuli and shock, particularly if they had been selected to fear the fear-relevant stimulus (e.g., Tomarken, Cook, & Mineka, 1989; see review by Öhman & Mineka, 2001). Interestingly, even though participants' ratings of immediate likelihood of shock did not differ between pictures of snakes and broken electrical equipment, they showed the retrospective illusory correlation with aversive events only for the biologically fear-relevant stimulus (Amin & Lovibond, 1997; Tomarken, Sutton, & Mineka, 1995; Kennedy, Rapee, & Mazursky, 1997).

THE AUTOMATICITY OF THE FEAR MODULE

The fear module was originally assembled in animals with primitive brains that had midbrain structures such as the superior colliculi as the most advanced area in the visual system (Allman, 1999). In humans, this subcortical input may access the fear module independent from conscious cognition (LeDoux, 1996; Morris et al., 1999; 2001). However, this input to the fear module is rather crude in terms of visual details; nonetheless, it has to be specific enough to identify crucial life-threatening stimuli, probably on the basis of specific features. Accordingly, data on the selectivity of input imply that evolutionary fear stimuli contain features that can activate the fear module from relatively early structures in the visual pathways that operate prior to object recognition.

To examine automatic activation of the fear module, Öhman and colleagues (see reviews in Öhman, 1996; 2000b) have used backward masking to rule out conscious recognition as a mediating factor in the activation of fear.

Backward Masking

In backward masking, a brief target stimulus is immediately followed by a masking stimulus. If the interval between the onsets of these two stimuli (the stimulus-onset asynchrony, SOA) is relatively long (on a neural time scale) (e.g., >100 ms), both stimuli may be consciously perceived. However, if the SOA is sufficiently short, the target stimulus cannot be recognized (i.e., is backward masked) and only the masking stimulus can be consciously recognized.

Öhman and Soares (1993, 1994) used masking stimuli constructed from randomly cut, reorganized, and rephotographed pictures of the target stimuli to examine effects of the SOA on participants' ability to recognize masked images of snakes, spiders, flowers, and mushrooms. Participants were instructed that on each trial two brief images would be presented consecutively, and that their task was to identify whether the first image (the target stimulus) of each pair was a snake, a spider, a flower, or a mushroom. Participants also rated their confidence in the answers. At relatively long

SOAs (80, 120, and 180 ms), participants recognized correctly almost all of the images and were sure of their answers. At a 30-ms SOA, on the other hand, participants performed at chance level and indicated that they were guessing. Similar results have been reported for emotional facial stimuli (Esteves & Öhman, 1993).

Autonomic Responses to Masked Stimuli

Based on the well-established finding that phobics show elevated psychophysiological responses to phobic stimuli (e.g., Fredrikson, 1981; Globisch, Hamm, Esteves, & Öhman, 1999; Hamm, Cuthbert, Globisch, & Vaitl, 1997), Öhman and Soares (1994) tested the automaticity of the fear module by examining responses to masked presentations of feared stimuli. A questionnaire measure was used to select participants who were afraid of snakes but not of spiders (snake-fearful), afraid of spiders but not of snakes (spider-fearful), or unafraid of both spiders and snakes (control). The results showed elevated skin conductance responses (SCRs) only in fearful participants to stimuli that were relevant to their specific fear, even if conscious recognition was prevented by backward masking. Thus snake-fearful participants showed larger responses to masked snakes than to masked spiders, whereas the opposite was true for spider-fearful participants.

However, because SCR has also been used as a measure of attention (orienting response), it is unclear if the enhanced SCR to masked fear stimuli in the Öhman and Soares (1994) study represents a general attentional process or a process specific to fear.

Facial Responses to Masked Stimuli

Dimberg (1982) reported that participants tended to mimic the emotional expression of stimulus faces in their facial muscle responses as assessed by electromyography (EMG). Thus, when exposed to an angry face they showed increases in activity of the *corrugator supercilii* muscle mediating the frown of anger, and little change in the *zygomatic major* muscle mediating a smile. With a happy face, however, the opposite pattern was found, with increases in the zygomatic and no change or a decrease in the corrugator muscle. To examine whether this patterned EMG response was automatically elicited, Dimberg, Thunberg, and Elmehed (2000) examined facial responses to masked facial stimuli. They presented angry, neutral, and happy faces very briefly (30 msec) and immediately masked by a 5 sec presentation of a neutral face to three different groups of normal unselected participants. Even though participants in the three groups consciously could perceive only the neutral masking face, they nevertheless showed differential facial EMG responses depending on the preceding target face. The masked happy face elicited a larger zygomatic response than the neutral or angry face, whereas the masked angry face elicited a larger corrugator response than the neutral or happy faces. These differences, furthermore, emerged relatively quickly, within the first 500 msec after stimulus onset. Thus, it appears that not only a nonspecific response such as the SCR but also a more specific emotional response could be elicited by masked fear stimuli.

Automatic Fear Responses in the Human Amygdala

Morris, Öhman, and Dolan (1998) used positron-emission tomography (PET) to measure regional cerebral blood flow responses to conditioned angry faces. Before PET scanning, participants were conditioned to one angry face (the CS+) by having it paired with an aversive noise, whereas a different angry face (CS−) was not paired with the noise. During PET scanning, the CS+ and the CS− were presented either nonmasked or masked with neutral faces. SCR data confirmed reliable differential conditioning to both masked and nonmasked presentations; that is, responses to CS+ exceeded those to CS− in both conditions. Confirming the hypothesis that nonconscious responding in human fear conditioning involves the amygdala, contrasts between PET images obtained during presentations of the masked CS+ and CS− showed enhanced activation to the CS+, specifically in the right amygdala region.

Whalen et al. (1998) used functional magnetic resonance imaging (fMRI) to directly measure responses of the human amygdala to masked presentations of facial stimuli. Contrasting regional blood flow in the amygdala during periods of repeated presentation of a masked fearful face with periods of repeated presentation of a masked happy face, they reported specific increases in amygdala activation to the fearful faces. Thus, even though conscious recognition of the stimuli was prevented by backward masking, these two studies showed reliable activation of the central structure of the fear circuit, the amygdala (e.g., Fendt & Fanselow, 1999; Lang et al., 2000; LeDoux, 1996), to emotionally relevant faces.

In further support for the automaticity of the amygdala response to threatening faces, Vuilleumier, Armony, Driver, and Dolan (2001) showed that amygdala activation was unaffected by whether the spatial location of a fearful face was attended or not. Right fusiform cortex, on the other hand, showed additive effects of attention and facial emotion.

Subcortical Mediation of the Automatic Fear Response

Morris et al. (1999) analyzed the neural connectivity between the amygdala and other brain regions during masked stimulation to examine whether the activation of the amygdala reported by Morris et al. (1998) occurred through a subcortical route involving the thalamus, as predicted from LeDoux's (1996) model. In support of this hypothesis, they reported that masked activation of the (right) amygdala could be reliably predicted from activation in the superior colliculus and the right pulvinar of the thalamus, but not from any cortical regions. Similar results were obtained from a patient with blindsight when emotional faces were presented in his blind field (Morris et al., 2001), suggesting that the amygdala can be accessed from the same pathways that mediate blindsight. The research by Morris et al. (1998; 1999; 2001) is important in demonstrating that a similar system to that previously delineated in the rodent brain for fear conditioning (see review by, e.g., LeDoux, 1996; Fendt & Fanselow, 1999) appears also to be operating in the brains of humans. Consistent with the automaticity assumption of the fear module, therefore, these data suggest that fear can be activated from a coarse perceptual analysis of biologically fear-relevant stimuli that is based on perceptual features rather than on a full-meaning analysis based on the recognition of objects.

THE ENCAPSULATION OF THE FEAR MODULE

A second aspect of the fear module's independence of cognition is encapsulation, that is, it is relatively impenetrable to other modules with which it lacks direct connections (Fodor, 1983). Thus, once activated, the fear module may run its course with few possibilities for other processes to interfere with or stop it. However, even though the fear module is relatively impenetrable to conscious influences, influences may be possible in the other direction, in which its influence is likely to be distorting – promoting, for example, exaggerated expectancies of bad outcomes (e.g., Davey, 1995). In this section, we review differential conditioning studies with masked and nonmasked stimuli that support the notion of encapsulation of the fear module.

Effects of Masking on Conditioned Skin Conductance Responses

Research suggests that whereas masking has strong effects on participants' ability to recognize masked pictures, masking has small, if any, effects on conditioned SCRs. For example, in a study by Parra, Esteves, Flykt, and Öhman (1997), participants rated after each picture how certain they were whether or not they had seen the picture before. Results showed that although participants rated nonmasked pictures as very familiar and masked pictures as very unfamiliar, the conditioned SCRs in extinction were similar for masked and nonmasked pictures. This finding suggests that, although masking had strong effects on familiarity ratings, it had negligible effects on conditioned SCRs (see Figure 5.1, left panels). In another study by Parra et al., participants were instructed to rate their expectancy of shock immediately after each picture. Although participants differentiated

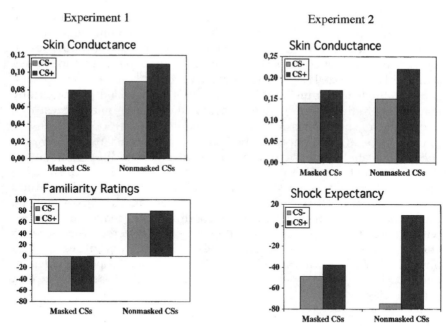

FIGURE 5.1. Skin Conductance Responses (SCRs) and Familiarity Ratings (*left panel*), and SCRs and Shock Expectancy Ratings (*right panel*) to masked and nonmasked presentations of angry (CS+, *dark bars*) and happy (CS−, *light bars*) faces that had been paired with (CS+) or without shock (CS−). Note that SCRs primarily reflect the conditioning contingency (larger response to the CS+ than the CS−), whereas the ratings primarily reflect whether stimuli were masked.

in their ratings between CS+ and CS− trials, this effect showed a strong interaction with masking. As shown in the right panel of Figure 5.1, participants who were shown nonmasked pictures showed much larger rating differences between CS+ and CS− trials than participants who were shown masked pictures. In contrast, masking had no effect on conditioned SCRs. These findings of the relatively small effects of masking on the conditioned SCRs were replicated in several other studies that also used pictures of human faces (Esteves, Dimberg, & Öhman, 1994; Morris, Öhman, & Dolan, 1998) and were obtained also for spider and snake pictures (Öhman & Soares, 1993; Soares & Öhman, 1993). In sum, these findings suggest that emotional response, as indexed by SCRs, is relatively unaffected by whether or not participants are aware of the emotional stimuli.

Effects of Instructions on Conditioned Skin Conductance Responses

Studies using differential conditioning paradigms have further found that even when participants are instructed that no more shocks will be administered, they continue to show conditioned SCRs provided that the stimuli are evolutionary fear-relevant. Thus, instruction immediately took away differential responding in participants conditioned to neutral stimuli, whereas it had no effect in participants conditioned to snakes and spiders (Hugdahl & Öhman, 1977). Assuming that the conditioning procedure had accessed the fear module only in participants conditioned to biologically fear-relevant stimuli (Öhman & Mineka, 2001), these data suggest that knowledge of shock omission had no effect on the fear module, thus supporting its postulated encapsulation from cognition. Soares and Öhman (1993) replicated this basic finding and showed, in addition, that conditioned differential SCRs to snakes and spiders survived both instruction of shock omission and masking, whereas differential SCRs to flowers and mushrooms did neither. Further, Schell, Dawson, and Marinkovic (1991) found that participants who had been conditioned to snakes and spiders with a short CS–US interval continued to show differential SCRs even after a six-month delay and when differential shock expectancies were extinguished. These results show that the fear module can operate independently from cognition, in that it produced SCRs in the absence of explicit expectancies.

Acquisition of Emotional Responses to Masked Stimuli

The encapsulation of the fear module is further supported by findings that participants could acquire emotional responses to masked stimuli that they were unable to recognize. In two experiments, Esteves, Parra, Dimberg, and Öhman (1994) showed that participants could acquire differential conditioned SCRs to masked angry faces. Because findings of conditioned SCRs were not obtained for happy faces, results suggest that conditioning of SCRs depends on the fear-relevance of the conditioned stimuli. Consistent with these findings, Öhman and Soares (1998) found that participants could acquire conditioned SCRs to masked spiders and snakes but not to masked flowers and mushrooms. The finding of conditioned SCRs to masked snakes and spiders was replicated in a follow-up study in the same lab (Öhman & Soares, 1998) and also in a different lab (Katkin, Wiens, & Öhman, 2001).

Because these data demonstrate that participants acquired conditioned SCRs to masked fear-relevant stimuli despite their inability to recognize the conditioned stimuli, the findings provide evidence that fear learning can occur outside of awareness and, thus, support the notion that the fear module is encapsulated (see Lovibond & Shanks, 2002, and Wiens & Öhman, 2002, for a discussion of awareness and conditioning in masking studies). Further, because findings of conditioned SCRs to masked pictures were obtained for angry faces (but not happy faces) and for spiders and snakes (but not flowers and mushrooms), the findings further support the notion of the selectivity of the fear module to fear-relevant stimuli.

Effects of Conditioning to Masked Stimuli on Shock Expectancy: Evidence for Gut Feelings?

Studies that used dependent variables other than SCRs provide evidence that self-report may also be a sensitive measure of conditioning to masked fear-relevant stimuli. In a study by Öhman and Soares (1998), participants were conditioned to masked spiders and snakes. When a picture was followed by a shock (i.e., on CS+ trials), the shock was administered four seconds after the picture was shown. During the four seconds after each picture, participants rated their expectancy of shock or no shock. Results from a forced-choice recognition task showed that participants were unable to discriminate between the masked spiders and snakes. Nonetheless, they showed differential shock expectancies on shock trials (CS+) and no-shock trials (CS−); that is, participants were more expectant of shocks on CS+ trials than on CS− trials. Thus, shock expectancy, in contrast to recognition, was sensitive to the conditioning contingency. Based on the finding that participants also acquired a conditioned fear response, as indexed by SCRs, Öhman and Soares (1998) suggested that they might have been able to predict shocks based on autonomic cues associated with the conditioned fear response. However, inconsistent with this suggestion, conditioned SCRs were found to be uncorrelated with shock expectancy ratings.

Katkin, Wiens, and Öhman (2001) postulated that it may not be the mere occurrence of autonomic responses, but their *sensation*, that allows shock prediction. To test this hypothesis, Katkin et al. administered the same conditioning task as was used by Öhman and Soares (1998), but assessed also participants' general sensitivity to visceral cues in a separate part of the experiment. Participants' general sensitivity to visceral cues was indexed by their ability to detect their own heartbeats (Katkin, 1985). Results showed that, even though good and poor heartbeat detectors did not differ in their conditional SCRs, only the good detectors showed differential shock expectancy ratings on CS+ and CS− trials (see Figure 5.2). These results are consistent with the idea that participants may have used the sensation of visceral cues associated with the conditioned fear response in their prediction of shock. Thus, the findings suggest that "gut feelings" may actually involve the sensation of visceral cues. Furthermore, they suggest that the fear module, even though it is encapsulated from cognition, can affect conscious cognition indirectly, through feedback from autonomic responses in a way that is consistent with an important line of thought in research on emotion (e.g., James, 1884; Mandler, 1975; Damasio, 1994).

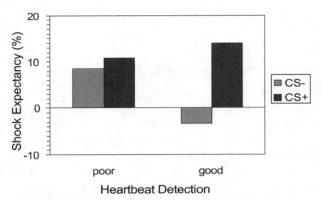

FIGURE 5.2. Shock expectancy ratings to masked shock-associated stimuli (CS+) and non-shock-associated stimuli (CS−) for participants sensitive or insensitive to their autonomic nervous system activity (good or poor heartbeat detectors). Note that only good heartbeat detectors showed differential shock expectancy ratings on CS+ and CS− trials.

DISCUSSION: THE FEAR MODULE VERSUS COGNITIVE THEORIES OF ANXIETY

In the preceding sections, we have reviewed extensive data that document the characteristics of the fear module proposed by Öhman and Mineka (2001), that is, specialized neural circuitry, selectivity, automaticity, and encapsulation. In this section of the chapter we shall examine more directly the implications of the fear module for the understanding of anxiety and anxiety disorder, particularly in relation to the currently dominating cognitive perspective as it has emerged and developed from the work of Beck, Emery, and Greenberg (1985).

Characteristics of Cognitive Theory

In many respects, the concept of the fear module is strikingly different from the view of fear and anxiety that is dominating the current scene, which stresses the role of cognitive mechanisms in the generation and clinical management of anxiety (e.g., Barlow, 1988; Beck, Emery, & Greenberg, 1985; Clark, 1999; Rapee, 1996). Premised on the ancient doctrine that we are not disturbed by the things themselves but by what we make of them, these approaches have a close affinity to appraisal theories of emotion (see Roseman & Smith, 2001; Scherer, 1999). Thus, they emphasize the person's interpretation of the situation in the generation of emotions such as anxiety (e.g., Beck et al., 1985). An important implication of this statement is that anxiety is determined by mental activity, or put more bluntly, by thoughts. When questioned thoroughly, even patients suffering from panic attacks appearing to come "right out of the blue" report that the attack was preceded by worries or thoughts about threat (Hibbert, 1984). These thoughts, however, need not be activated at center stage in consciousness, but may remain relatively inaccessible automatic thoughts (Beck et al., 1985).

For a situation to be interpreted as anxiety-provoking, cognitive theory posits that the perceptual information it conveys is processed in relation to the belief systems of the individual – information called up from long-term memory to define threatening circumstances. The belief systems of anxiety-prone individuals are particularly elaborated when it comes to threat and danger, typically by exaggerating risks and deflating coping potential. For example, misattributing an innocuous (perhaps emotionally induced) perceived change in heart rate to an impending heart failure may set the stage for a vicious cycle in which rising anxiety promotes more heart rate changes confirming the catastrophic interpretation, and so on, eventually culminating in a full-blown panic attack (Clark, 1986). Belief systems are shaped by the history of individuals in their social context, and even though individuals may not be consciously aware of all aspects of their beliefs, it is commonly assumed that these can be assessed by self-reports (e.g., McNally, 2001).

Cognitive models of anxiety typically assume a linear series of appraisal stages from input to output, and that several of these stages are accessible in conscious awareness. Thus, input from the environment is elaborated by appraisal processes to converge in consciousness, where options for action are evaluated and decisions to act are taken. This is in accordance with the intuitive psychology that sees consciousness as the focal point where all determinants of psychological events converge, and where actions are initiated. Again, because causal factors typically are consciously accessible, they can be assessed by self-reports.

An interesting feature of cognitive theories is that they are "notably rationalistic" (McNally, 2001, p. 514), that is, rather than showing the "irrationality" expected for neurotic anxiety, anxiety responses are seen as following logically from faulty beliefs and appraisals. It is not the anxiety, but the preceding cognitive activity, the appraisal of threat, that is irrational. For example, consistent with the cognitive theory, phobic patients report in effect innocuous phobic situations or objects as more dangerous than do non-phobic controls (Menzies & Clark, 1995; Thorpe & Salkovskis, 1995) and as more likely to be encountered (Öst & Csatlos, 2000). It is this malign misattribution of danger that is assumed to pave the way for anxiety disorder. Consequently, curing anxiety disorder requires modification of the cognitive schemas that govern threat appraisal. The goal of treatment is rationalistic – to make the beliefs more veridical by improving their fit with the actual circumstances.

The Fear Module Perspective

In striking contrast to the tenets of cognitive theory, the fear module concept claims that fear can be automatically activated by subcortical pathways before the eliciting stimulus is consciously represented (e.g., Öhman & Soares, 1994; LeDoux, 1996). Thus, the fear response may be activated before the eliciting stimulus is fully perceived. These pathways represent evolutionarily shaped perceptual systems that efficiently locate threatening information prior to object recognition (Morris et al., 1999; Morris et al., 2001) and that are not available to self-report. Rather, the characteristics of these systems must be inferred from experimental data (e.g., Öhman, Flykt, & Esteves, 2001; Öhman, Lundqvist, & Esteves, 2001; Öhman & Mineka, 2001).

The fear module perspective suggests that the primary problem in anxiety disorder is not that fear activation is rigidly determined by unrealistic cognitions but that it is disconnected from cognition (even though, of course, it might interact with it, see, e.g., LeDoux, 1989). Fear is a strong, stimulus-driven aversive response that may be evoked by incompletely processed stimuli, and particularly by features of threat stimuli that derive their potency from evolutionary sources. Individuals may differ in their vulnerability to anxiety disorder because their fear modules (for genetic or developmental reasons) may be differentially sensitive to threat. Furthermore, individuals may be differentially prepared for associating activation of the module with new stimuli through Pavlovian conditioning. Because of the automaticity and encapsulation of the fear module, sufferers from anxiety disorders repeatedly find themselves in situations in which they experience anxiety for reasons to which they have little conscious access, and/or which they have little means of influencing by their cognitions. It is the independence of cognition that may make fear and anxiety appear strange ("pathological") and irrational given the prevailing circumstances. However, what may appear strikingly irrational given these circumstances may make eminent sense in terms of evolutionary logic. That is, the fear module is biased by evolution to go for false positives rather than false negatives (i.e., respond to what turns out to be innocuous rather than miss a real danger; LeDoux, 1990; Mineka, 1992). For example, to experience a full-blown panic attack when watching an attacking snake on a TV movie no doubt is irrational, but having this emotional response triggered by the same stimulus pattern at some other time might save one's life if it promotes rapid flight.

What anxious individuals may do when they find themselves responding with fear without knowing why is what humans often do in such circumstances: use their elaborate cognitive systems to justify and explain the fear (Öhman & Mineka, 2001). Humans have a deep need to make sense of their experience, to interpret and incorporate experiences into a coherent narrative of themselves (Gazzaniga, 1998). Such interpretations no doubt may aggravate and maintain anxiety. From this perspective, exaggerated beliefs in the danger and likelihood of encountering phobic objects and situations (e.g., Thorpe & Salkovskis, 1995; Öst & Csatlos, 2000) should be understood as effects (justifications for) rather than causes of fear.

The fear module concept appeals to a different type of reason than cognitive theory – that reflected in biological evolution rather than what appears to be rational from the perspective of the belief system of an individual. No doubt evolution is rational in the sense that it results in adjustments of the frequency of gene alleles in the gene pool of species to achieve better fit with ecological demands. But what is rational on the aggregate level of the gene pool may be quite irrational in the specific ecological niche occupied by an individual, particularly if the environmental contingencies have changed. For example, for the small mammals that had to survive in a world ruled by reptiles, it was rational indeed to fear and avoid reptiles. For their distant descendants, humans living in an urban environment, however, reptiles do not provide any real threat, and therefore their excessive avoidance qualifies as psychopathology.

The Zajonc Debate

Taken at face value, the data reviewed in this chapter suggest that fear activation is independent of, and often precedes, conscious cognition. They suggest that fear is rapidly activated, before there is time for a complete perceptual analysis of the situation and for representing the end product of the analysis in consciousness. Our conclusion, therefore, appears to correspond closely to Zajonc's (1980) influential thesis that "preferences need no inferences." This thesis directly contradicts the basic tenet of the cognitive theory, that anxiety is always triggered by preceding thoughts or images (Beck et al., 1985).

Zajonc's (1980) claim that affect precedes cognition, however, has been controversial. A primary line of defense for those wanting to retain the basic assumption of appraisal theory, that emotion always depends on cognition, has been to argue that an affective stimulus in itself cannot trigger emotion but has to be at least minimally processed before it can do so, and even minimal processing of a stimulus qualifies as cognition (e.g., Lazarus, 1984). What we are left with, then, is a semantic controversy over how to define "cognitive" (Leventhal & Scherer, 1987), and which comes first, emotion or cognition, becomes a rather arbitrary issue. Specifically, Leventhal and Scherer (1987) suggested that arguing about definition is seldom productive, and that efforts should be directed toward uncovering the mechanisms behind the activation of emotion rather than quarreling about what is cognitive and what is not.

We think that the research that we have reviewed in this chapter goes some way toward specifying these mechanisms at a neurophysiological level (see LeDoux, 1989; 1996). As a result, we are inclined to side with Zajonc (1980; 1984) rather than with the appraisal theorists (Lazarus, 1984; Leventhal & Scherer, 1987) in this debate. Thus, we concur with Zajonc's (1984) argument that the term "cognitive" should be reserved for postperceptual processes, and that it is important to distinguish such processes from the sensory and perceptual processes preceding object recognition. This argument, in fact, can be boosted by the emerging knowledge about the neurophysiology of visual processing. For example, backward masking has been shown to interfere with processing stages earlier than those involved in object recognition (e.g., identifying objects as specific faces; Rolls & Tovée, 1994; Rolls, Tovée, & Panzeri, 1999). Therefore, because masking interrupts perceptual processing at the level in which the conscious percept is constructed (Marcel, 1983), it provides a methodological means for segregating "noncognitive" pre- and "cognitive" postperceptual information processing. Hence, it is reasonable to claim that emotional responses to masked visual stimuli (e.g., Öhman & Soares, 1994) do not depend on prior cognitive activity. In fact, because emotional responses to masked stimuli appear to be mediated by way stations early in the visual system that operate on features rather than objects (Morris et al., 1999; 2001), it should be considered pre-perceptual, and thus as definitely "noncognitive." From this argument, we think that a strong claim can be made to the effect that, at least for fear (and thus for anxiety), emotional activation precedes cognitive appraisal of the stimulus. Therefore, Beck's (Beck et al., 1985) insistence that anxiety is crucially dependent on thought lacks support from the data reviewed in this chapter. Rather than preceding and determining anxiety, cognition follows and is shaped by anxiety.

Our argument is summarized in Figure 5.3, the upper panel of which shows our interpretation of the traditional cognitive theory, which puts relatively advanced appraisal processes at center stage in the construction of an emotion. The lower panel shows our perspective (Öhman & Mineka, 2001), according to which the fear module is inserted between the stimulus and the appraisal processes. As shown in the figure, it is important to remember that the fear module is more than a stimulus-processing system, in that its primary purpose is rapidly to call on attention, to recruit defensive reflexes, and to mobilize resources for action. This interpretation of the processes governing fear activation is predicated on our conclusion that the evidence argues quite strongly against the basic postulate in the cognitive approach to anxiety. However, although they are relatively unimportant for initial activation of fear and anxiety, cognitive factors as manifested in appraisal are more important for the further development and interpretation of the emotional response, and when it comes to the maintenance of anxiety over time (Clark, 1999).

(a) Cognitive Theory

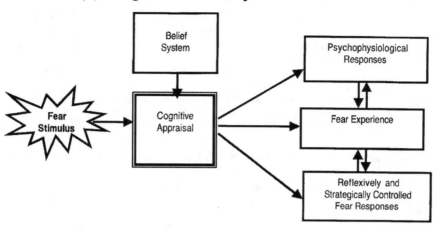

(b) The Fear Module

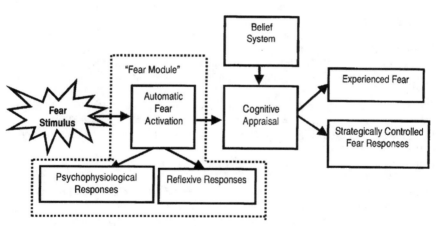

FIGURE 5.3. The contrast between the cognitive view (*upper panel*) and the fear module perspective (*lower panel*) in the activation of fear and anxiety.

References

Allman, J. M. (1999). *Evolving brains*. New York: Scientific American Library.

American Psychiatric Association. (1994). *Diagnostic and statistical manual of mental disorders*. 4th ed. Washington, DC: Author.

Amin, J. M., & Lovibond, P. F. (1997). Dissociation between covariation bias and expectancy bias for fear-relevant stimuli. *Cognition and Emotion, 11,* 273–289.

Arrindell, W. A.; Pickersgill, M. J.; Merckelbach, H.; Ardon, M. A.; & Cornet, F. C. (1991). Phobic dimensions: III. Factor analytic approaches to the study of common phobic fears: An updated review of findings obtained with adult subjects. *Advances in Behaviour Research and Therapy, 13*, 73–130.

Barlow, D. H. (1988). *Anxiety and its disorders: The nature and treatment of anxiety and panic.* New York: Guilford.

Beck, A. T.; Emery, G.; & Greenberg, R. L. (1985). *Anxiety disorders and phobias: A cognitive perspective.* New York: Basic Books.

Blanchard, D. C., & Blanchard, R. J. (1988). Ethoexperimental approaches to the biology of emotion. *Annual Review of Psychology, 39*, 43–68.

Clark, D. M. (1986). A cognitive approach to panic. *Behaviour Research and Therapy, 24*, 461–470.

Clark, D. M. (1999). Anxiety disorders: Why they persist and how to treat them. *Behaviour Research and Therapy, 37*, S5–S27.

Cook, E. W.; Hodes, R. L.; & Lang, P. J. (1986). Preparedness and phobia: Effects of stimulus content on human visceral conditioning. *Journal of Abnormal Psychology, 95*, 195–207.

Cook, M., & Mineka, S. (1989). Observational conditioning of fear to fear-relevant versus fear-irrelevant stimuli in rhesus monkeys. *Journal of Abnormal Psychology, 98*, 448–459.

Cook, M., & Mineka, S. (1990). Selective associations in the observational conditioning of fear in rhesus monkeys. *Journal of Experimental Psychology: Animal Behavior Processes, 16*, 372–389.

Damasio, A. R. (1994). *Descartes' error: Emotion, reason, and the human brain.* New York: G. P. Putnam's Sons.

Davey, G. C. L. (1995). Preparedness and phobias: Specific evolved associations or a generalized expectancy bias? *Behavioral and Brain Sciences, 18*, 289–325.

Davis, M., & Lee, Y. (1998). Fear and anxiety: Possible roles of the amygdala and bed nucleus of the stria terminalis. *Cognition and Emotion, 12*, 277–305.

Davis, M., & Whalen, P. J. (2001). The amygdala: Vigilance and emotion. *Molecular Psychiatry, 6*, 13–34.

Dimberg, U. (1982). Facial reactions to facial expresssions. *Psychophysiology, 19*, 643–647.

Dimberg, U.; Thunberg, M.; & Elmehed, K. (2000). Unconscious facial reactions to emotional facial expressions. *Psychological Science, 11*, 86–89.

Emery, N. J., & Amaral, D. G. (2000). The role of the amygdala in primate social cognition. In R. Lane and L. Nadel (Eds.), *The cognitive neuroscience of emotion* (pp. 156–191). New York: Oxford University Press.

Epstein, S. (1972). The nature of anxiety with emphasis upon its relationship to expectancy. In C. D. Spielberger (Ed.), *Anxiety: Current trends in theory and research* (Vol. 2, pp. 292–338). New York: Academic Press.

Esteves, F.; Dimberg, U.; & Öhman, A. (1994). Automatically elicited fear: Conditioned skin conductance responses to masked facial expressions. *Cognition and Emotion, 8*, 393–413.

Esteves, F., & Öhman, A. (1993). Masking the face: Recognition of emotional facial expressions as a function of the parameters of backward masking. *Scandinavian Journal of Psychology, 34*, 1–18.

Esteves, F.; Parra, C.; Dimberg, U.; & Öhman, A. (1994). Nonconscious associative learning: Pavlovian conditioning of skin conductance responses to masked fear-relevant facial stimuli. *Psychophysiology, 31,* 375–385.

Fanselow, M. S. (1994). Neural organization of the defensive behavior system responsible for fear. *Psychonomic Bulletin and Review, 1,* 429–438.

Fendt, M., & Fanselow, M. S. (1999). The neuroanatomical and neurochemical basis of conditioned fear. *Neuroscience and Biobehavioral Reviews, 23,* 743–760.

Fodor, J. (1983). *The modularity of mind.* Cambridge, MA: MIT Press.

Fredrikson, M. (1981). Orienting and defensive reactions to phobic and conditioned fear stimuli in phobics and normals. *Psychophysiology, 18,* 456–465.

Gazzaniga, M. S. (1998). *The mind's past.* Berkeley: University of California Press.

Globisch, J.; Hamm, A. O.; Esteves, F.; & Öhman, A. (1999). Fear appears fast: Temporal course of startle reflex potentiation in animal fearful subjects. *Psychophysiology, 36,* 66–75.

Hamm, A. O.; Cuthbert, B. N.; Globisch, J.; & Vaitl, D. (1997). Fear and the startle reflex: Blink modulation and autonomic response patterns in animal and mutilation fearful subjects. *Psychophysiology, 34,* 97–107.

Hansen, C., & Hansen, R. (1988). Finding the face in the crowd: An anger superiority effect. *Journal of Personality and Social Psychology, 54,* 917–924.

Hibbert, G. A. (1984). Ideational components of anxiety: Their origin and content. *British Journal of Psychiatry, 144,* 618–624.

Hugdahl, K., & Kärker, A. C. (1981). Biological vs experiential factors in phobic conditioning. *Behavioural Research and Therapy, 19,* 109–115.

Hugdahl, K., & Öhman, A. (1977). Effects of instruction on acquisition and extinction of electrodermal responses to fear-relevant stimuli. *Journal of Experimental Psychology: Human Learning and Memory, 3,* 608–618.

James, W. (1884). What is an emotion? *Mind, 9,* 188–205.

Katkin, E. S. (1985). Blood, sweat, and tears: Individual differences in autonomic self-perception. *Psychophysiology, 22,* 125–137.

Katkin, E. S.; Wiens, S.; & Öhman, A. (2001). Nonconscious fear conditioning, visceral perception, and the development of gut feelings. *Psychological Science, 12,* 366–370.

Kennedy, S. J.; Rapee, R. M.; & Mazursky, E. J. (1997). Covariation bias for phylogenetic versus ontogenetic fear-relevant stimuli. *Behaviour Research and Therapy, 35,* 415–422.

Lang, P. J.; Bradley, M. M.; & Cuthbert, B. N. (1997). Motivated attention: Affect, activation, and action. In P. J. Lang, R. F. Simons, and M. T. Balaban (Eds.), *Attention and orienting: Sensory and motivational processes* (pp. 97–136). Hillsdale, NJ: Erlbaum.

Lang, P. J.; Davis, M.; & Öhman, A. (2000). Fear and anxiety: Animal models and human cognitive psychophysiology. *Journal of Affective Disorders, 61,* 137–159.

Lazarus, R. S. (1984). Thoughts on the relation between emotion and cognition. *American Psychologist, 37,* 1019–1024.

LeDoux, J. E. (1989). Cognitive-emotional interactions in the brain. *Cognition and Emotion, 3,* 267–289.

LeDoux, J. E. (1990). Fear pathways in the brain: Implications for a theory of the emotional brain. In P. F. Brain, S. Parmigiani, R. J. Blanchard, and D. Mainardi (Eds.), *Fear and defence* (pp. 163–178). London: Harwood.

LeDoux, J. E. (1992). Brain mechanisms of emotion and emotional learning. *Current Opinions in Neurobiology, 2,* 191–197.

LeDoux, J. E. (1996). *The emotional brain.* New York: Simon & Schuster.

Leventhal, H., & Scherer, K. R. (1987). The relationship of emotion to cognition: A functional approach to a semantic controversy. *Cognition and Emotion, 1,* 3–28.

Lovibond, P. F., & Shanks, D. R. (2002). The role of awareness in Pavlovian conditioning: Empirical evidence and theoretical implications. *Journal of Experimental Psychology: Animal Behavior Processes, 28,* 3–26.

Lundqvist, D.; Esteves, F.; & Öhman, A. (1999). The face of wrath: Critical features for conveying facial threat. *Cognition and Emotion, 13,* 691–711.

Mandler, G. (1975). *Mind and emotion.* New York: John Wiley.

Marcel, A. J. (1983). Conscious and unconscious perception: An approach to the relations between phenomenological experience and perceptual processes. *Cognitive Psychology, 15,* 238–300.

Marks, I. M. (1987). Fears, phobias, and rituals. *Panic, anxiety, and their disorders.* Oxford: Oxford University Press.

Mayr, E. (1974). Behavior programs and evolutionary strategies. *American Scientist, 62,* 650–659.

McNally, R. J. (2001). On the scientific status of cognitive appraisal models of anxiety disorder. *Behaviour Research and Therapy, 39,* 513–521.

Menzies, R. G., & Clarke, J. C. (1995a). Danger expectancies and insight in acrophobia. *Behaviour Research and Therapy, 33,* 215–221.

Mineka, S. (1992). Evolutionary memories, emotional processing, and the emotional disorders. *The Psychology of Learning and Motivation, 28,* 161–206.

Morris, J. S.; DeGelder, B.; Weiskrantz, L.; & Dolan, R. J. (2001). Differential extrageniculostriate and amygdala responses to presentation of emotional faces in a cortically blind field. *Brain, 124,* 1241–1252.

Morris, J.; Öhman, A.; & Dolan, R. J. (1998). Modulation of human amygdala activity by emotional learning and conscious awareness. *Nature, 393,* 467–470.

Morris, J. S.; Öhman, A.; & Dolan, R. J. (1999). A subcortical pathway to the right amygdala mediating "unseen" fear. *Proceedings of the National Academy of Sciences, 96,* 1680–1685.

Öhman, A. (1979a). Fear relevance, autonomic conditioning, and phobias: A Laboratory model. In P.-O. Sjödén, S. Bates, & W. S. Dickens III (Eds.), *Trends in behavior therapy* (pp. 107–134). New York: Academic Press.

Öhman, A. (1993). Stimulus prepotency and fear learning: Data and theory. In N. Birbaumer and A. Öhman (Eds.), *The structure of emotion: Psychophysiological, cognitive, and clinical aspects* (pp. 218–239). Seattle: Hogrefe & Huber.

Öhman, A. (1996). Preferential preattentive processing of threat in anxiety: Preparedness and attentional biases. In R. M. Rapee (Ed.), *Current controversies in the anxiety disorders* (pp. 253–290). New York: Guilford.

Öhman, A. (2000a). Anxiety. In G. Fink (Ed.), *Encyclopedia of stress* (Vol. 1, pp. 226–231). San Diego: Academic Press.

Öhman, A. (2000b). Fear and anxiety: Evolutionary, cognitive, and clinical perspectives. In M. Lewis and J. M. Haviland (Eds.), *Handbook of emotions* (2d ed.; pp. 573–593). New York: Guilford.

Öhman, A.; Dimberg, U.; & Öst, L.-G. (1985). Animal and social phobias: Biological constraints on learned fear responses. In S. Reiss and R. R. Bootzin

(Eds.), *Theoretical issues in behavior therapy* (pp. 123–178). New York: Academic Press.

Öhman, A.; Flykt, A.; & Esteves, F. (2001). Emotion drives attention: Detecting the snake in the grass. *Journal of Experimental Psychology: General, 130*, 466–478.

Öhman, A.; Fredrikson, M.; & Hugdahl, K. (1978). Orienting and defensive responding in the electrodermal system: Palmar-dorsal differences and recovery rate during conditioning to potentially phobic stimuli. *Psychophysty, 15*, 93–101.

Öhman, A.; Lundqvist, D.; & Esteves, F. (2001). The face in the crowd revisited: An anger superiority effect with schematic stimuli. *Journal of Personality and Social Psychology, 80*, 381–396.

Öhman, A., & Mineka, S. (2001). Fears, phobias, and preparedness: Toward an evolved module of fear and fear learning. *Psychological Review, 108*, 483–522.

Öhman, A., & Soares, J. J. F. (1993). On the automatic nature of phobic fear: Conditioned electrodermal responses to masked fear-relevant stimuli. *Journal of Abnormal Psychology, 102*, 1221–1232.

Öhman, A., & Soares, J. J. F. (1994). "Unconscious anxiety": Phobic responses to masked stimuli. *Journal of Abnormal Psychology, 103*, 231–240.

Öhman, A., & Soares, J. J. F. (1998). Emotional conditioning to masked stimuli: Expectancies for aversive outcomes following nonrecognized fear-relevant stimuli. *Journal of Experimental Psychology: General, 127*, 69–82.

Öst, L. G., & Csatlos, P. (2000). Probability ratings in claustrophobic patients and normal controls. *Behavior Research and Therapy, 38*, 1107–1116.

Parra, C.; Esteves, F.; Flykt, A.; & Öhman, A. (1997). Pavlovian conditioning to social stimuli: Backward masking and the dissociation of implicit and explicit cognitive processes. *European Psychologist, 2*, 106–117.

Purcell, D. G.; Stewart, A. L.; & Skov, R. B. (1996). It takes a confounded face to pop out of a crowd. *Perception, 25*, 1091–1108.

Rapee, R. M. (Ed.). (1996). *Current controversies in the anxiety disorders.* New York: Plenum.

Rolls, E. T., & Tovée, M. J. (1994). Processing speed in the cerebral cortex and the neurophysiology of visual masking. *Proceedings of the Royal Society, London, Series B, 257*, 9–15.

Rolls, E. T.; Tovée, M. J.; & Panzeri, S. (1999). The neurophysiology of backward masking: Information analysis. *Journal of Cognitive Neuroscience, 11*, 300–311.

Roseman, I. J., & Smith, C. A. (2001). Appraisal theory: Overview, assumptions, varieties, controversies. In K. R. Scherer, A. Schorr, and T. Johnstone (Eds.), *Appraisal processes in emotion* (pp. 3–19). New York: Oxford University Press.

Rosen, J. B., & Schulkin, J. (1998). From normal fear to pathological anxiety. *Psychological Review, 105*, 325–350.

Russell, P. A. (1979). Fear-evoking stimuli. In W. Sluckin (Ed.), *Fear in animals and man* (pp. 85–124). New York: Van Nostrand Reinhold.

Schell, A. M.; Dawson, M. E.; & Marinkovic, K. (1991). Effects of the use of potentially phobic CSs on retention, reinstatement, and extinction of the conditioned skin conductance response. *Psychophysiology, 28*, 140–153.

Scherer, K. R. (1999). Appraisal theory. In T. Dalgleish and M. Power (Eds.), *Handbook of cognition and emotion* (pp. 637–663). London: Wiley.

Seligman, M. E. P. (1971). Phobias and preparedness. *Behavior Therapy, 2*, 307–320.

Soares, J. J. F., & Öhman, A. (1993). Preattentive processing, preparedness, and phobias: Effects of instruction on conditioned electrodermal responses to masked and non-masked fear-relevant stimuli. *Behaviour Research and Therapy, 31,* 87–95.

Thorpe, S. J., & Salkovskis, P. M. (1995). Phobic beliefs: Do cognitive factors play a role in specific phobias? *Behaviour Research and Therapy, 33,* 805–816.

Tomarken, A. J.; Cook, M.; & Mineka, S. (1989). Fear-relevant selective associations and covariation bias. *Journal of Abnormal Psychology, 98,* 381–394.

Tomarken, A. J.; Sutton, S. K.; & Mineka, S. (1995). Fear-relevant illusory correlations: What types of associations promote judgmental bias? *Journal of Abnormal Psychology, 104,* 312–326.

Vuilleumier, P.; Armony, J. L.; Driver, J.; & Dolan, R. J. (2001). Effects of attention and emotion on face processing in the human brain: An event-related fMRI study. *Neuron, 30,* 829–841.

Whalen, P. J.; Rauch, S. L.; Etcoff, N. L.; McInerney, S. C.; Lee, M. B.; & Jenike, M. A. (1998). Masked presentations of emotional facial expression modulate amygdala activity without explicit knowledge. *Journal of Neuroscience, 18,* 411–418.

Wiens, S., & Öhman, A. (2002). Unconsciousness is more than a chance event. Comment on Lovibond and Shanks (2002). *Journal of Experimental Psychology: Animal Behavior Processes, 28,* 27–31.

Zajonc, R. B. (1980). Feeling and thinking: Preferences need no inferences. *American Psychologist, 35,* 151–175.

Zajonc, R. B. (1984). On the primacy of affect. *American Psychologist, 39,* 117–123.

6

Deconstructing the Emotions for the Sake of Comparative Research

Richard A. Shweder

ABSTRACT

One of the central aims of the discipline of cultural psychology is to develop a theoretical language for the comparative study of mental states that makes it possible to understand and appreciate the mental life of members of other cultures. In this chapter the author suggests that the language of the emotions is not an ideal theoretical language for making progress on the study of mental states across human populations. It is argued that the idea of an emotion is a complex synthetic notion, composed of wants, beliefs, feelings and values; and that human mentalities may vary in how they give shape, and lend meaning, to the more fundamental and direct experience of wanting certain things, valuing certain things, knowing certain things and having particular somatic and affective feelings. The chapter considers the advantages of temporarily privileging the study of "feeling" over the study of the "emotions."

What types of cross-cultural variations in "feelings and emotions" are we able to imagine, given our understanding of what it means to be a person (that is, a mentally endowed human being)? And what types of evidence on mental functioning in other cultures would we want to collect to convince us that those imaginable (and hence logically conceivable) variations in feelings and emotions are actually real? What predictions, if any, follow from the idea of having an "emotional" life? And what predictions, if any,

I wish to thank Agneta Fischer and Anna Wierzbicka for their timely and useful comments on the original draft of this essay. Thanks as well to my fellow participants in the "Cultural Psychology" reading group at the University of Chicago Committee on Human Development, where the issue of the cross-cultural diagnosis of mental states was critically examined and debated during the 2000–2001 academic year. Without in any way holding them responsible for my own views, I have gained much from my discussions of this topic with Bertram Cohler, Jennifer Cole, Raymond Fogelson, Joe Gone, Rebecca Lester, John Lucy, Tanya Luhrmann, McKim Marriott, Tanya Menon, and Debjani Mukerjee.

follow from the idea of having a mental life organized by some particular emotion, such as sadness, envy, guilt, or love?

I suspect those questions are unavoidable in a scholarly discipline such as cultural psychology, which aims to develop a credible account of psychological differences across cultural groups (see, e.g., Briggs, 1970; Cole, 1988, 1990, 1996; Bruner, 1990; Nisbett & Cohen, 1995; D'Andrade, 1984, 1987; Geertz, 1973; Goddard, 1997; Good & Kleinman, 1984; Haidt, Koller, & Dias, 1993; LeVine, 1990; Levy, 1984; Lutz, 1985; Lutz & White, 1986; Markus & Kitayama, 1991; Markus, Kitayama, & Heiman, 1998; Miller, 1997; Rosaldo, 1984; Shweder, 1988, 1991, 2003; Shweder et al., 1998; Shweder & LeVine, 1984; Shweder & Sullivan, 1992; Wierzbicka, 1993, 1999). Nevertheless, my main reason for raising these questions on this occasion is to explore a particular argument made by the comparative descriptive linguists Anna Wierzbicka and Cliff Goddard (Wierzbicka, 1999; also see Wierzbicka, 1986, 1990, 1993; Goddard, 2001; Goddard & Wierzbicka, 1994). Wierzbicka and Goddard have argued that the complex mental states referred to with English words for emotions (words such as "sadness," "envy," "guilt," or "love") should be theoretically decomposed into more elementary mental processes such as wanting, knowing, feeling, and evaluating things as good or not good. They have suggested that the ideas of thinking, feeling, wanting, knowing, and evaluating things as good (or not good) are semantically simple, intuitively obvious, readily available universal folk concepts, which is why those ideas have been found by linguists to be natural language "primes." (A natural language prime is any idea that has been lexically encoded – there is a single wordlike element for it – in every known human language.) Wierzbicka and Goddard have suggested that this is not true of the idea of emotions, which at the very least is semantically complex, not universally acknowledged as a folk concept, and not a linguistic prime. Their main point is that, for the sake of the development of a universal theoretical language for comparative research on the meaning and translation of mental states across cultural groups, the idea of "feeling" ought to take theoretical precedence over the idea of an "emotion." Alternatively stated, the language of the emotions per se (the language of sadness, envy, guilt, love) is not an ideal "etic" language (Pike, 1967) for making progress on the cross-cultural study of human mental functioning.

Of course, emotions are not words. But what they are is something we must form an idea of, conceptualize and define, or at least elucidate, if we are to know what we are talking about when we use words to theorize about the emotions and record them. My interest in Anna Wierzbicka and Cliff Goddard's proposal, which they derive from work in comparative linguistics, is undoubtedly related to the fact that a cognate argument can be found in some of my own writings in cultural psychology (e.g., Shweder, 1994; Shweder & Haidt, 2000). In those formulations it has been suggested that certain empirical questions about emotions (for example, are there universal or "basic" emotions?) are best answered by analyzing or semantically "deconstructing" the concept of an emotion into a series of component meanings. It has been proposed that those components of meaning – for example, the semantic components of "anger" involving a "desire" (for revenge) plus (e.g.) an "affective feeling" (of arousal, agitation, or tension) should be empirically sampled for their co-occurrence and distribution properties across mental events or mental episodes. One can then ask whether those components of meaning actually combine in identical ways in the mental life of members of all cultural communities.

Paralleling Wierzbicka and Goddard's proposal, I have suggested that the idea of an emotion is a complex synthetic notion; and particular emotions (e.g., sadness, envy, guilt, and love) are derivatives of various combinations of wants, beliefs, feelings, and values.[1] From that theoretical perspective in cultural psychology, "emotions" are but one of several possible ways to give shape and lend meaning to the more fundamental and direct experience of wanting certain things, valuing certain things, knowing certain things, and having certain somatic and affective "feelings." Consequently, here I consider the advantages of privileging the study of somatic and affective feelings (the feelings of the body – e.g., dizziness or pain – and the feelings of the "self" or "soul" – e.g., emptiness or frustration) over the study of the emotions. In some small measure I seek to elaborate on the Wierzbicka and Goddard claim that the language of emotions per se is not an ideal theoretical language for making progress on the study of mental states across human populations.

A caution to the reader, however. Although I theoretically privilege feelings over emotions, I certainly do not rule out the possibility that some particular combinations of wants, feelings, beliefs, and values (e.g., those combinations labeled with the English words "anger" or "fear" or "sadness") are readily synthesized and occur everywhere in the world. If and when they occur, those universal combinations of wants, feelings, beliefs, and values may, of course, occur whether or not such "emotions" are symbolically available as a single word in some natural language. I do maintain, however, that the theoretical deconstruction of the emotions into their components of meaning is a necessary step for research in cultural psychology. Unless that step is taken, cultural psychology will have little hope of ever empirically engaging or credibly critiquing the claim that human emotional functioning is pretty much the same wherever you go. Unless that

---

[1] The ideas of "true" and "false" (not "true") are also semantically simple, intuitively obvious, readily available universal folk concepts. I use the term "beliefs" throughout this chapter to refer to the universal condition of thinking that one knows that something is true. I also assume, for the sake of the argument, that the "something" can be represented in the form of a proposition about "the world." Beliefs, at least by my account, should thus be part of any theoretical language for comparative research on mental states.

step is taken, cultural psychology will also have little hope of ever establishing that particular combinations of wants, feelings, beliefs, and values are distinctive of particular cultural mentalities and are unequally distributed across the mental lives of members of different cultural groups.

CULTURAL VARIATIONS IN FEELINGS AND EMOTIONS: WHICH ARE IMAGINABLE?

Before undertaking an empirical investigation aimed at documenting differences in psychological functioning across human populations, it is a useful exercise to identify types of mental differences that one might conceivably or plausibly discover. When trying to imagine possible cross-cultural differences in feelings and emotions, in particular, there is a continuum of hypothetical possibilities that runs from those which are easy to bring to mind to those which seem impossible even to conceptualize.

On the easy-to-imagine side of things, one can readily understand and accept that the particular "environmental determinants" or "eliciting events" for particular emotions may be different in other cultures; for example, that there are places in the world where receiving a compliment on one's pregnancy may not elicit pride or gratitude but rather anxiety or fear (e.g., of the "evil eye" or of the effects of other people's wicked intentions). Thus, we readily acknowledge and can easily see that the things experienced as "threatening" or the events experienced as a "loss" or as an "insult" or as the "blockage of one's goals" may not be the same from place to place. No particular conceptual difficulties arise in this type of case, because we are confident that we can relate the differential "emotional" impact of the eliciting event to some variation in culturally endorsed beliefs or in the real or perceived consequence of the event in that local cultural context.

We also find it rather easy to imagine other types of differences in the psychological functioning of members of different cultural groups. We can quickly assent to the idea that in some other culture some particular emotion (say, anger or envy or sadness) may not be displayed, expressed, or communicated to others (or even to oneself). This might be so, we readily and coherently consider, even when the emotion is mentally active and consciously or unconsciously experienced by members of that society. Again, no particular conceptual difficulties arise in this type of case, because we imagine that we can relate the absence of any outward signs of the emotion to some anticipated advantage that follows from keeping the emotion hidden.

There are, of course, certain presuppositions upon which we rely when making this interpretation, viz., that people around the world anticipate the future consequences of their own expressive behavior and also want to have more of the things they desire or think of as "good." Nevertheless, those presuppositions fit squarely within our picture of what it means to be a "person." Hence, no interpretive problems arise if some anthropologist interested in cultural psychology reports the following: that many Balinese Hindus believe it makes things really difficult for the soul of the deceased (and also brings bad luck) if anyone cries or expresses grief at cremation ceremonies. Hence, on such occasions there is no public display of negative emotions; indeed, the event appears to be a celebration.

There are other cross-cultural differences in feelings and emotions that are easy to imagine. I would include the possibility that changes in biological state are not experienced or "felt" in the same way across cultural groups. Biologically "normal" human beings in all cultures have an autonomic arousal system, which has the capacity to increase the rate of heart contractions and redirect the flow of blood from the gut and skin to the muscles. As a result of autonomic arousal the skin blanches and cools. During a state of autonomic arousal it is widely reported that the gut "feels empty." Nevertheless, some cross-cultural researchers (most recently, Hinton & Hinton, 2002) have raised the possibility that not all peoples respond in the same way to changes in biological state. The Hintons draw our attention to the phenomenon of "autonomic response specificity."

The idea of autonomic response specificity invites us to entertain the possibility that some peoples characteristically experience autonomic arousal with distinctive somatic and affective feelings. For example, among Cambodians, autonomic arousal is often associated with such "feelings" and experiences as dizziness, tinnitus (ringing in the ears), blurred vision, neck tension, joint pains, muscle aches, and perhaps even a sense of panic linked to an anticipation of death. Reading Hinton and Hinton (2002; also Hinton, Um, & Ba, 2001), one realizes that one can and must admit for consideration the logical possibility that autonomic arousal (an objective state of the body) does not produce the same sensations, feelings, or subjective experiences everywhere you go. This type of evidence challenges us to come up with an account of either local Cambodian biology or local Cambodian beliefs about illness and the body that might explain the existence of culturally distinctive subjective experiences under conditions of autonomic arousal. One aspect of the Hintons' own explanation is discussed later.

We also find it rather easy to entertain the possibility that the "same emotion," take guilt, for example, may be coped with or managed differently in different cultures. Again, no particular conceptual difficulty arises if it should turn out that in some corner of India people do not confess their sins and transgressions but rather unload them in some other kind of way. This coping process might unfold by passing along or transferring one's own spiritual debts to beggars via alms, thereby increasing the relative amount of one's own religious merit. Indeed, for some residents in the temple town of Bhubaneswar in Orissa, India, where I have done some research, the mental experience of giving alms (or "charitable dona-tions") to a beggar amounts to the feeling of a transfer of "sins" from the giver of the "gift" to the receiver. In this system for shaping and structur-ing one's feelings and emotions, the beggar plays the part of scapegoat, who by accepting material gifts (rice or money) from those who are better off, also takes on the burden (including the karmic consequences) of their sins. The giver, by means of the gift, feels relieved of his or her spiritual debts, and also somewhat cleansed because unburdened of some measure of accumulated transgressions against the moral order of things.

Of course at this point I find myself wondering, am I really merely talking here of some universal emotion (named "guilt" in English), which is just coped with in different ways in different cultural communities? Or do all these special aspects – the idea of spiritual debts and the practice of transferring one's sins to others – suggest a different type of mental state? The first way of talking – guilt plus local coping strategy – surely is intellectually coherent; and the possibility that guilt might be unloaded in ways other than confession does seem, at the very least, imaginable.

The idea of gifts as transfers of guilt is coherent and intelligible, es-pecially if one is prepared to assume three things. First, that the idea of "guilt" refers to an emotion caused or conditioned upon personal viola-tions of the moral order or deviations from what one knows to be right, good, or dutiful. Second, that wherever there are personal transgressions of the moral order there is also going to be the mental experience of guilt, at least among "normal" human beings. Third, that people may differ in their metaphysical beliefs.

For example, some peoples may classify the experience of guilt as a purely subjective mental event existing "only in the head"; while other peoples may have a different metaphysical view of the "same" experience. They may classify the experience of guilt as the concomitant of a special type of event called the occurrence of a sin. Such an event (a sin) may be un-derstood to have an objective or "thing-like" nature with causal properties of its own, which can weigh on your mind and influence your fate, until it is transferred to someone else. With regard to this example, of course, we may not subscribe to that particular metaphysical picture of the world, but that does not block us from understanding it. In fact, in this case we seem to have no difficulty making all three of the assumptions mentioned above, leading us to conclude that it is conceivable that guilt is coped with or managed in different ways in different parts of the world.

The application or use of the idea of guilt may not be the only way, or even the best way, to understand the mental life of Oriya Hindus in this instance. One might be tempted to argue in favor of an alternative approach in which differences between peoples in their metaphysical be-liefs (e.g., the idea that "faults" are objective, not subjective) are used as one of several ways to identify differences in mental states. Nevertheless, the interpretation of universal guilt plus culture-specific coping strategy is certainly imaginable.

Not all claims about cultural variations in feelings and emotions are so readily imaginable. For example, I find it impossible to make much sense of the statement "X particular emotion [for example, sadness] does not have the same meaning in the culture in which I work as it does in your culture." Imagine an anthropologist who returns from years of field research and reports, "Among the people I studied in the highlands of New Guinea 'sadness' is the good feeling people have when they manage to acquire the things they most want." I find that statement incoherent because the idea of any particular emotion (for example, the idea of sadness) is what it is, and means what it means, and neither feeling good nor managing to acquire the things you most want is what "sadness" is about. In other words, the idea of (e.g.) "sadness" (that is, its meaning or definition) remains the same, regardless of where on the globe you happen to be when you find yourself thinking about it: it remains the same regardless of whose mental life (a New Guinea Highlander's or a Scotsman's) one is trying to understand when one decides to put the idea of sadness to interpretive use. Whether and when one should be inclined to put an emotion concept (such as "sadness") to use is quite another matter, to which I now turn.

THE USE OF EMOTION CONCEPTS IN COMPARATIVE RESEARCH: A MISGIVING

The idea of sadness can be used to illustrate some of the problems that arise if one uncritically adopts the theoretical language of emotion concepts as an analytic scheme for the comparative study of mental states (see Shweder, 1993). The idea of sadness, at least as I understand it, can be roughly defined as follows (concerning the definition of "sadness" see Smedslund, 1991, who discusses it as an example of "psychologic"; also Lazarus, 1991, who individuates emotions such as sadness by their "core relational themes"). "Sadness" refers to the particular way that a normal person will feel when the things he or she wants or likes are believed to be permanently unattainable or lost, and the distinctive way that a normal person acts when he or she has those beliefs and feelings.

Of course, to actually arrive at an adequate specification of the idea of sadness those particulars and also some of the presuppositions of the definition would need to be filled in. At a minimum they would include all of the following. Among the particulars we would want to know something about the quality of the feelings that are experienced by "normal" people when the things they want or like are thought to be permanently unattainable (or lost). This might include a description of both their somatic feelings (e.g., feeling tired, "chilled") and their affective feelings (e.g., feeling deflated, empty, passive, contracted). We would also want to know something about the quality of the actions toward which normal people incline (e.g., withdrawal from social interactions, ruminating about the futility of life) when they believe that the things they want or like have been lost forever. Among the various presuppositions of the definition is a utilitarian moral theory. Thus, it is presupposed by the very idea of sadness that human beings have wants and likes and that it is good for them to have the things they want and like.

Even this brief and superficial attempt at a definition of sadness suggests the richness and complexity of the meaning of a typical emotion concept. I have not even addressed the issue of whether the idea, concept, or definition of sadness includes (or ought to include) a reference to nonmental (physiological, neurological, hormonal) states. Should our attempt at a *definition* of the idea of sadness also say, "Sadness is the way a 'normal person' feels, thinks, and acts when their biological systems are in the following material states," followed by a list of brain states, hormone levels, and so forth?

An even deeper analysis might try to show the way the idea of an emotion contains within itself the notion that human beings will be motivated by their feelings and desires to maintain the social order as a moral order. Fear, for example, is an idea associated with issues of safety and harm, and the mental state it identifies is meant to motivate us to eliminate the conditions that produce that mental state by making our world safer. Anger, especially in the form of indignation, is associated with issues of fairness, equity, and just desert and is meant to motivate us to eliminate injustice from the world. Love and compassion are associated with protection of the vulnerable and are meant to motivate us to take care of others. Thus the semantic analysis of the idea of any particular emotion will reveal a good deal about the social, moral, and mental world of any normal human being whose wants, feelings, beliefs, and values are in fact packaged in that particular way.

But is it true that wherever you go in the world human mental life (decomposable into wants, feelings, beliefs, and values) is in fact packaged that way (as "emotions")? Which are the "emotionalized" packages of wants, feelings, beliefs, and values that actually play a part in the mental life of this or that people? And how can we find out? This is where I start to get nervous about the privileging of our received emotion concepts in research on cultural psychology. I get nervous because I think it is very hard to answer those questions if one begins one's comparative research by applying emotions as universally relevant theoretical categories. The prior adoption of such an analytic scheme makes it very difficult ever to conclude that the analytic scheme itself is either inappropriate or insufficiently revealing of the mental states of others.

Consider, for example, the observation made by several anthropologists about the ways people in some cultures respond to apparent loss (such as the death of a child). They do not respond with visible or direct signs of "sadness" – no tears, no subjective reports of deflation, no predicted facial expressions, no mournful retreat from life, and no use of a word for a negative emotion. Rather, they respond with "fatigue, sickness, or other kinds of bodily distress" (such as backaches and headaches). In the light of such anthropological observations (for the sake of argument let us assume that they are reliable) what should we say about the mental life of such a people? What should we say about the cultural relevance of the particular package of wants, beliefs, feelings, and values known as "sadness"?

Typically what happens in this case is that the theoretical idea of sadness is put to use, creatively generating various interpretive possibilities for making sense of what has been observed. The problem with this is that all the interpretations simply presuppose the relevance of the "idea of sadness," leaving us with no empirical basis for examining the validity of that presupposition.

For example, one possible interpretation is the following. Something the "native" very much wanted has become permanently unattainable (a child has died); therefore, he or she must be mentally experiencing sadness. According to this interpretation there is no visible and direct manifestation of mental sadness because the native either denies being sad, psychologically defends against it (for example, by "somatizing" the mental state), or does not have a language or vocabulary for describing, communicating, or expressing sadness; or any or all of the above. For those who elect to interpret things in this way, the somatization option is viewed as an unconscious psychological strategy or defense that makes it possible to retreat from daily life in a socially acceptable way (as "sick") without having to acknowledge feelings of demoralization.

A second possible interpretation is that the native shows no visible or direct manifestation of sadness because the significance of the eliciting event is other than it seems. According to this interpretation, the death of the child was not really appraised as a loss (for reasons yet to be discovered); hence there was no manifestation of "sadness," because there actually was no mental sadness in the first place. In other words, the set of things that might sadden the anthropologist are not necessarily coincidental with the set of things that might sadden the people whose behavior is being observed, whose mental states we are trying to infer, whose minds we are seeking to read.

A third possible interpretation is that something must be wrong with these "natives." Normal human beings, we suppose, here relying on our received theory of the emotions, are saddened to discover that the things they want and like have become permanently unobtainable. Various types of psychopathology might be suspected. A pathology of knowing (that something of great significance has been lost), a pathology of wanting (to have the things you like), a pathology of feeling (appropriate feelings), a pathology of valuing (the right sorts of things), and so forth.

From the point of view of making progress in the field of cultural psychology, I think there is something a little troubling when interpretation proceeds in this way, although it is hard to say precisely what it is or to give the problem a name. Roughly stated, I think the difficulty is this. Under the theoretical influence of the idea of sadness far too many "top-down" interpretations of the mental states of the "other" can be generated. And all of these interpretations seem to presuppose the relevance of the idea of sadness without ever reconsidering that presupposition.

Moreover, the connection of actual evidence to any of these interpretations seems loose at best. The most manifest evidence, based on anthropological observation, suggests that apparent loss is not typically associated with sadness in some cultures, but rather with headaches or backaches or other forms of bodily distress. Nevertheless, the relevance of the emotion concept to the case at hand is never doubted. And, given the range and types of possible interpretations generated under the influence of the idea of sadness, it is not even apparent what would count as evidence that sadness is not the mental state of relevance in this case.

Imagine interviewing some apparently unsaddened native suffering from bodily aches and pains who, when asked, explicitly denies that the death of his or her child is a loss. Well, given that "denial" remains an interpretative option, we might certainly discount his or her testimony. On the other hand, imagine the opposite. A native explicitly confirms appraising the death as a permanent loss of something that was wanted and highly valued, yet he or she gives no signs of the mental experience of sadness. Given the way emotion concepts work as analytic tools, we are still free to assume that he or she really is sad, or else suspect some form of pathology. Notice that once we have presupposed the relevance of the idea of sadness, actual self-reports about wants, feelings, beliefs, and values appear to be neither necessary nor sufficient as evidence for or against our interpretations. But what conceivable evidence would convince us that it is possible for a normal person in another culture to lose something he or she truly wants and values without automatically activating the mental state we identify with the idea of sad? As far as I can tell, this entire exercise in "mind reading" the mental state of others in the circumstance described is constrained primarily by one's prior commitment to the idea of "sadness" as a basic theoretical category for making sense of the mental life of all human beings. That seems to me a problem, because we seem to be blocked from ever even imagining that there might be other ways for "normal" human beings to package their wants, feelings, beliefs, and values.

PUTTING THE "EMOTIONS" TO THE SIDE
IN CULTURAL PSYCHOLOGY

One of the several aims of cultural psychology as a discipline is to develop a language for the comparative study of mental states that makes it possible to understand and appreciate the mental life of others. "Others" refers to members of some different cultural community who by virtue of lifelong membership in that group ascribe meaning to their lives in the light of wants, feelings, values, and beliefs that are not necessarily the same as one's own. Following Wierzbicka's (1999) proposal, one might suggest that wants, feelings, values (evaluating things as good or bad), and beliefs be taken as fundamental or basic to the mental life of peoples in all cultures, indeed as constituent elements of what it means to have a mental life. Wanting, feeling, knowing, and valuing (as good or bad) would thus circumscribe cultural psychology's "theory of mind." But what about the emotions?

Setting aside the emotions in cultural psychology really amounts to decomposing them into more elementary or constituent meanings, for example, of the type proposed by Wierzbicka and Goddard. In earlier work of my own (Shweder, 1994; Shweder & Haidt, 1999; also see Menon & Shweder, 1994) it has been proposed that the idea of an emotion (e.g., sadness, fear, anger, envy, disgust, or love) is a complex. It is not something separable from the conditions that justify it, from the somatic and affective experiences that are ways of being touched by it, from the actions it demands, and so on. The emotion is the whole story. It is a kind of somatic event (fatigue, chest pain) and affective event (panic, emptiness, expansiveness). It is caused by the perception of some antecedent condition (e.g., the death of a friend) and by the recognition of the personal implications of the event for the self (e.g., loss, gain, threat, goal blockage, degradation, or elevation of status). This motivates a plan for action (e.g., attack, withdraw, hide, confess, celebrate) to preserve or enhance one's sense of identity and purpose in life. The idea of an "emotion" is about the entire mental, moral, and social episode. It is about the unitary experience of the whole package deal or the simultaneous experience of all the components of meaning.

For analytic purposes and for the sake of cross-cultural research on the universality versus culture-specificity of human mental states, I have thus suggested that it might be helpful to decompose the idea of an emotion into various components of meaning. Many other theorists have done so as well (Ekman, 1980, 1984; Ellsworth, 1991; Frijda, 1986; Lazarus, 1991; Russell, 1991; Scherer, Walbott, & Summerfield, 1986). Paul Ekman, for example, talks of antecedent events, appraisal, behavioral response, physiology, and expression. I like to ask whether different members of different cultural groups are alike or different in mental functioning in this broad domain by dividing that question into several more specific ones, focusing on the following seven components of the meaning of an "emotion."

1. Environmental determinants: Are members of different cultural groups alike or different in the antecedent conditions of the world (e.g., job loss, violating a rule) that elicit somatic and affective feelings? This is about what people know.
2. Self-Appraisal: Are members of different cultural groups alike or different in the perceived implications of those antecedent conditions for their personal identity and projects in life (e.g., status loss, fame, goal blockage)? This is about what people want, know, and value.
3. Somatic phenomenology: Are members of different cultural groups alike or different in their somatic reactions (e.g., muscle tension, headaches) to 1 and 2 above? This is about what people feel.
4. Affective phenomenology: Are members of different cultural groups alike or different in their affective reactions (e.g., feelings of emptiness, calm, expansiveness) to 1 and 2 above? This is also about what people feel.
5. Social appraisal: Are members of different cultural groups alike or different in the extent to which displaying those somatic and affective reactions has been socially baptized a vice or virtue or a sign of sickness or health? This is about what people value.
6. Self-management: Are members of different cultural groups alike or different in the plans for self-management (e.g., attack, withdraw, hide, confess, transfer sins) that are activated as part of an action routine? This is about what people want, know, and value.
7. Communication: Are members of different cultural groups alike or different in the iconic or symbolic vehicles (e.g., facial expressions, voice quality, posture) for expressing the whole package of interconnected components (1–6 above)?

If we proceed in this way, deconstructing the emotions and temporarily setting them aside as analytic or theoretical categories, it certainly seems possible that certain wants, feelings, beliefs, and values might be universal and similarly packaged together in all cultures. Many researchers will be betting on anger, fear, and sadness as mental states (each consisting of a complex but unique way of packaging wants, feelings, beliefs, and values) that are readily synthesized and available to all "normal" human beings. It also seems possible, however, indeed likely, that not all wants, feelings, beliefs, and values are shared across cultures or packaged together in the same way everywhere. There may well be many culture-specific emotions, that is to say, coactivations of particular wants, feelings, values, and beliefs that play a part and are significant in the mental lives of members of some cultures but not others. It is precisely because these are things to be discovered rather than presupposed that I am sympathetic to the view that emotion concepts should not, at least for the moment, be part of the basic theoretical language of cultural psychology.

Work in medical anthropology focused primarily on what I would call feelings (what they call "sensations and symptoms") rather than on emotions per se has uncovered several culture-specific coactivations of the sort I have in mind. For example, Hinton and Hinton (2002; also Hinton, Um, & Ba, 2001) have examined what they refer to as the "sore-neck syndrome" (*rooy go*) among Khmer Cambodian populations. Their research is in the broad territory of anxiety experiences, feelings of panic and autonomic arousal. For Khmer Cambodians that experience is associated with a cluster of feelings and sensations including dizziness, ringing in the ears, blurred vision, joint pains, muscle aches, shoulder and neck soreness as well as anxieties about death. None of those feelings, sensations, or symptoms is a universal feature of autonomic arousal or panic attacks. During such mental episodes Khmer Cambodians also experience palpitations, shortness of breath, and profuse perspiration. As Hinton and Hinton point out, not all populations of peoples in the world are prone to "motion sickness" (for example, on a boat or in a car) or dizziness (for example, when quickly standing up) to the same degree. Human physiology is not uniform around the world, and there is probably no reason to assume a priori that all populations of peoples have identical feelings under equivalent circumstances. Among Khmer Cambodians, however, there is also a well-developed cultural conceptualization of human physiology (which appears to have its origins in South Asian medical theories about the "humors" of the body). And it may play a part in how they feel, think, and react when they "panic."

Here I recapitulate Hinton and Hinton (2002, pp. 163–164) on how "each symptom of autonomic arousal will be appraised and apperceived given the local ethnophysiology." "Wind" is one of the humors of the body, and the prototypical symptom of wind is "dizziness." As the Hintons note, "the complaint of dizziness, immediately indicating wind illness, implies a complex physiology." Khmer Cambodians believe, the Hintons note, that excessive "wind" can be caused by poor diet, little sleep, or wind penetrating the pores of the body. "If there is too much wind in the body, often the vessels carrying wind and blood become acutely blocked, especially at the knees and elbows, preventing outward flow along the limbs. The obstruction is said to cause hand and foot coldness, numbness, weakness, and muscle aches as well. . . . The Khmer believe that permanent limb paralysis may result from this tubal obstruction. Furthermore, according to the Khmer ethnophysiology, if wind is blocked at the limb joints, it tends to reverse its flow and surge toward the neck and head, possibly rupturing the neck vessels as well as causing a pressure increase at the head. Wind is said to shoot out the ears causing them to ring. Some patients describe dizziness as resulting from an actual spinning of brain matter."

One could go on – wind impeding breathing, compressing the heart, and then rushing to the head, "coining" as one of several measures to reduce the pressure of wind and alleviate the feeling of dizziness – but I hope the point has been made. Research of this type points us in the direction of a cultural psychology of mental states that is "bottom-up" (starts by identifying wants, feelings, beliefs, and values) rather than "top-down" (starts with the idea of "emotions"). It begins with the documentation of how particular wants, feelings, beliefs, and values get linked or co-occur during actual mental events or mental episodes in particular populations.

That is not to say that there are no universal emotions. It is to say that particular emotion concepts should be introduced into the theoretical language for comparative research on human mental states only after they have been induced and convincingly shown to be empirical universals. It won't do simply to presume the universal usefulness of particular emotion concepts, or to design research projects that offer no way to displace that assumption. It won't do to rely on judgments of bilingual informants or on dictionaries for evidence about the mental life of people in other cultures. One way to get from here to there might be to follow Anna Wierzbicka and Cliff Goddard's analytic proposal, adding to it an inductive step in which we actually document the distribution of particular wants, feelings, beliefs, and values across mental events or mental episodes in different cultural groups. Even to contemplate that step is fairly mind-boggling and reveals how far we have to go. It will require the development of an approach to the sampling of actual mental events or episodes across a chosen set of cultural groups that is representative of the major cultural regions of the world. It will require the interdisciplinary coordination of techniques and methods (from linguistics, ethology, ethnography, psychology, and biology) for assessing wants, feelings, beliefs, and values, including their content, and to do so "on-line" or in ecologically valid ways. Fortunately, this is a great moment for the coordination of interdisciplinary research in the area of feelings and emotions, and many of us are eager to take the step.

References

Briggs, J. L. (1970). *Never in anger: Portrait of an Eskimo family.* Cambridge, MA: Harvard University Press.

Bruner, J. S. (1990). *Acts of meaning.* Cambridge, MA: Harvard University Press.

Cole, M. (1988). Cross-cultural research in the socio-historical tradition. *Human Development, 31*, 137–157.

Cole, M. (1990). Cultural psychology: A once and future discipline? In J. J. Berman (Ed.), *Cross-cultural perspectives.* Nebraska symposium on motivation, 1989. Lincoln: University of Nebraska Press.

Cole, M. (1996). *Cultural psychology: A once and future discipline.* Cambridge, MA: Harvard University Press.

D'Andrade, R. G. (1984). Cultural meaning systems. In R. A. Shweder and R. A. LeVine (Eds.), *Culture theory: Essays on mind, self, and emotion* (pp. 88–119). Cambridge: Cambridge University Press.

D'Andrade, R. G. (1987). A folk model of the mind. In N. Quinn and D. Holland (Eds.), *Cultural models in language and thought.* Cambridge: Cambridge University Press.

Ekman, P. (1980). Biological and cultural contributions to body and facial movement in the expression of emotions. In A. Rorty (Ed.), *Explaining emotions* (pp. 73–101). Berkeley: University of California Press.

Ekman, P. (1984). Expression and the nature of emotion. In K. Scherer and P. Ekman (Eds.), *Approaches to emotion* (pp. 319–343). Hillsdale, NJ: Erlbaum.

Ellsworth, P. (1991). Some implications of cognitive appraisal theories of emotion. *International Review of Studies of Emotion, 1,* 143–161.

Frijda, N. (1986). *The emotions.* Cambridge: Cambridge University Press.

Geertz, C. (1973). *The interpretation of culture.* New York: Basic Books.

Goddard, C. (1997). Contrastive semantics and cultural psychology: "Surprise" in Malay and English. *Culture and Psychology, 2,* 153–181.

Goddard, C. (2001). Lexico-semantic universals: A critical overview. *Linguistic Typology, 5,* 1–66.

Goddard, C., & Wierzbicka, A. (1994). *Semantic and lexical universals – theory and empirical findings.* Amsterdam: John Benjamins.

Good, B. J., & Kleinman, A. M. (1984). Culture and anxiety: Cross-cultural evidence for the patterning of anxiety disorders. In A. H. Tuma and J. D. Maser (Eds.), *Anxiety and the anxiety disorders.* Hillsdale, NJ: Erlbaum.

Haidt, J.; Koller, S.; & Dias, M. (1993). Affect, culture, and morality, or is it wrong to eat your dog? *Journal of Personality and Social Psychology, 65,* 613–628.

Hinton, D.; & Hinton, S. (2002). Panic disorder, somatization, and the new cross-cultural psychiatry; or the seven bodies of a medical anthropology of panic. *Culture, Medicine and Psychiatry, 26,* 155–178.

Hinton, D.; Um, K.; & Ba, P. (2001). A unique panic-disorder presentation among Khmer refugees: The sore-neck syndrome. *Culture, Medicine and Psychiatry, 25,* 297–316.

Lazarus, R. S. (1991). *Emotion and adaptation.* New York: Oxford University Press.

LeVine, R. A. (1990). Infant environments in psychoanalysis: A cross-cultural view. In J. Stigler, R. Shweder, and G. Herdt (Eds.), *Cultural psychology: Essays on comparative human development.* New York: Cambridge University Press.

Levy, R. I. (1984). Emotion, knowing and culture. In R. A. Shweder and R. A. LeVine (Eds.), *Culture theory: Essays on mind, self, and emotion* (pp. 214–237). Cambridge: Cambridge University Press.

Lutz, C. (1985). Depression and the translation of emotional worlds. In A. Kleinman and B. Good (Eds.), *Culture and depression: Studies in the anthropology and cross-cultural psychiatry of affect and disorder* (pp. 63–100). Berkeley: University of California Press.

Lutz, C., & White, G. (1986). The anthropology of emotions. *Annual Review of Anthropology, 15,* 405–436.

Markus, H. R., & Kitayama, S. (1991). Culture and the self: Implications for cognition, emotion and motivation. *Psychological Review, 98,* 224–253.

Markus, H. R.; Kitayama, S.; & Heiman, R. (1998). Culture and "basic" psychological principles. In E. T. Higgins and A. W. Kruglanski (Eds.), *Social psychology:
Handbook of basic principles*. New York: Guilford.

Menon, U., & Shweder, R. A. (1994). Kali's tongue: Cultural psychology and the
power of "shame" in Orissa, India. In H. Markus and S. Kitayama (Eds.), *Culture
and the emotions*. Washington, DC: APA Publications.

Miller, J. G. (1997). Theoretical issues in cultural psychology. In H. Triandis (Ed.),
Handbook of cross-cultural psychology (Vol. 1, pp. 85–128). Boston: Allyn and Bacon.

Nisbett, R. E., & Cohen, D. (1995). *The culture of honor: The psychology of violence in
the South*. Boulder, CO: Westview Press.

Pike, K. (1967). *Language in relation to a unified theory of the structure of human behavior*.
The Hague: Mouton and Company.

Rosaldo, M. Z. (1984). Toward an anthropology of self and feeling. In R. A. Shweder
and R. A. LeVine (Eds.), *Culture theory: Essays on mind, self, and emotion* (pp. 137–
157). Cambridge: Cambridge University Press.

Russell, J. A. (1991). Culture and the categorization of emotions. *Psychological Bulletin, 110*, 426–450.

Scherer, K. R.; Walbott, H. G.; & Summerfield, A. B. (1986). *Experiencing emotion: A
cross-cultural study*. Cambridge: Cambridge University Press.

Shweder, R. A. (1988). Suffering in style. (Review of the *Social origins of disease and
distress* by Arthur Kleinman). *Culture, Medicine and Psychiatry, 12*, 479–497.

Shweder, R. A. (1990). Cultural psychology: What is it? In J. Stigler, R. Shweder,
and G. Herdt (Eds.), *Cultural psychology: Essays on comparative human development*
(pp. 1–43). New York: Cambridge University Press.

Shweder, R. A. (1991). *Thinking through cultures: Expeditions in cultural psychology*.
Cambridge, MA: Harvard University Press.

Shweder, R. A. (1993). Everything you ever wanted to know about cognitive appraisal theory without being conscious of it. *Psychological Inquiry, 4*, 322–326.

Shweder, R. A. (1994). You're not sick, you're just in love: Emotion as an interpretive
system. In P. Ekman and R. Davidson (Eds.), *Questions about emotion*. New York:
Oxford University Press.

Shweder, R. A. (2003). *Why do men barbecue? Recipes for cultural psychology*.
Cambridge, MA: Harvard University Press.

Shweder, R. A.; Goodnow, J.; Hatano, G.; LeVine, R. A.; Markus, H. R.; & Miller, P.
(1998). The cultural psychology of development: One mind, many mentalities.
In W. Damon (Ed.), *Handbook of child psychology*, Vol. 1, 5th ed. New York: Wiley.

Shweder, R. A., & Haidt, J. (1999). Cultural psychology of the emotions: Ancient
and new. In M. Lewis and J. Haviland (Eds.), *The handbook of emotions*. New York:
Guilford.

Shweder, R. A., & LeVine, R. A. (1984). *Culture theory: Essays on mind, self and emotion*.
Cambridge: Cambridge University Press.

Shweder, R. A., & Sullivan, M. A. (1993). Cultural psychology: Who needs it? *Annual
Review of Psychology, 44*, 497–523.

Smedslund, J. (1991). The pseudoempirical in psychology and the case for psychologic. *Psychological Inquiry, 2*, 325–328.

Wierzbicka, A. (1986). Human emotions: Universal or culture-specific? *American
Anthropologist, 88*, 584–594.

Wierzbicka, A. (1990). Special issue on the semantics of the emotions. *Australian Journal of Linguistics, 10 (2)*.

Wierzbicka, A. (1993). A conceptual basis for cultural psychology. *Ethos, 21*, 205–231.

Wierzbicka, A. (1999). *Emotions across languages and cultures: Diversity and universals.* New York: Cambridge University Press.

7

From the Emotions of Conversation to the Passions of Fiction

Keith Oatley

ABSTRACT

In this chapter I argue that narratives provide contexts to make sense of emotions, by linking emotions to the principal aspect of their meaning – namely goals. In literature a character is a person who has goals and who enacts plans to pursue those goals. Narrative plays an integrative role by relating emotions to a narrative line and attributing them to characters. Fiction contributes to the building of characters by means of emotions. Four aspects of story structure are discussed, and it is shown how they elicit emotions in the reader, but also how they enable us to understand emotions.

INTRODUCTION: EMOTION, NARRATIVE, CHARACTER

Grief over the death of a parent, suicidal despair, contempt for women, disgust at sexuality, delight upon seeing a friend, curiosity and dread toward the unexplained – how can we make sense of such emotions? Incidents of this kind are recognizable to emotion researchers. They are what we study. Yet, in this form – raw emotions caused by certain events and directed at certain objects – neither the person who experiences them nor we who read about them could understand their meanings. Something else is necessary.

One necessary aspect is a narrative line. Let me add one and run the sequence again. Hamlet, dressed in black, is asked by his mother why he continues to grieve for his dead father. When she departs, accompanied by her new husband, Hamlet feels suicidal: "Oh that this too too sullied flesh would melt," he thinks. He reflects on his mother's too-hasty marriage to her husband's brother. He is filled with contempt: "frailty thy name is woman." He is disgusted at the thought of his mother and his uncle

I thank Angela Biason, Laurette Larocque, Seema Nundy, and Mitra Gholamain for their contribution to these ideas and data, and the SSHRC of Canada for grant support.

in bed together. In the next scene, he is delighted to see his close friend Horatio, and is both eager and afraid at the news that the ghost of his father has been seen on the castle's battlements (Shakespeare, 1600). The narrative line starts to makes sense of emotions. There is another necessary aspect: character. Hamlet is one of the most famous characters in world literature.

A narrative line provides a context for understanding how emotions depend on goals and plans, and how one emotion may transform into another, as anger may arise from fear, or distrust from disappointment. Character supplies a yet more personal context. Hamlet is profoundly affected by his emotions. In the play he is driven strongly by one of them: angry vengeance. Hamlet is such a distinctive character that he becomes acutely conscious of the implications of this banal urge. Merely to enact it would put him on the same level as his uncle Claudius, who killed out of lust for Hamlet's mother and for the crown. It would make him indistinguishable from anyone enacting a crass scheme of revenge.

In those works of world literature that we value most, narrative line and character combine. It is by means of the one that we understand the other. In such works, we see a cast of emotions, each of which throws a different light upon the others so that characters come alive. A narrative line, therefore, is what first links emotions to the principal aspect of their meaning, namely goals. The meaning is not complete without the idea of who the agent is who possesses the goals. Character, then, in literary theory, is an idea of a person who has goals, and who enacts plans that derive from them. In a literary character, emotions potentiate the goals. Thus Hamlet at the beginning of the play is grieving; his goals are as yet inchoate. They are made actual by the command of his father's ghost: "if thou didst ever thy dear father love ... Revenge his foul and most unnatural murder" (1. 5. 23–25). Then there is a reflexive aspect: planful actions that flow from a character's goals give rise to incidents that produce further emotions, which then elaborate the idea we have of the character. Thus, Hamlet the avenger of a crime himself becomes a criminal when, by mistake, he kills Polonius, the father of another son, Laertes. The light of Hamlet's guilt (and man's dual nature as both wronged and wrongdoer) shines upon his goal of angry vengeance; Hamlet says of Laertes: "For by the image of my cause, I see / The portraiture of his" (5. 2. 76–77).

My argument is that narrative has an integrative role (Oatley, 1992). Without assimilating emotions to a narrative line and attributing them to characters (our own or other people's) they remain almost meaningless: gusts of neural activity causing little tempests of experience. Brewin, Dalgleish, and Joseph (1996) have argued that the experiences of people who have suffered traumata are processed in two ways. One is nonverbal and largely involuntary. It is characterized by flashbacks of emotional scenes that are triggered by situational cues. The other is verbal; in it, people explain what happened to them – such explanation being in narrative form – and the emotional experiences become part of their identity. Once an experience has been articulated in this way, it can be recounted voluntarily, and integrated.

These conclusions link to the research of Pennebaker and Seagal (1999), who found that when people write narratives of a personal kind about events that have been emotionally stressful in their lives, they experience substantial health benefits. Experience that is not narrated is not integrated; that which can be integrated conduces to health. Antonovsky (1979) found that people who had survived concentration camps or the experience of being refugees who had some degree of psychological health were those who could assimilate emotionally painful experiences to meaningful understandings of their life. Without the ability to make narrative accounts – explicitly in language or implicitly in a language of mind – traumatic emotional experiences would be isolated islands of experience.

THE LINKING NARRATIVE OF PLANS, OUTCOMES, AND EMOTIONS

Bruner (1986) has proposed that narrative is a distinctive mode of thought. It is, indeed, that mode of thought within which we conceptualize human beings as having goals and plans, which meet vicissitudes. Narrative, then, is folk theory articulated, as the philosophers have said, in terms of beliefs and desires. Emotion researchers should add the element emotion – because vicissitudes almost invariably cause emotions – so one may call this the folk theory of beliefs, desires, and emotions. One can therefore see narratives as made up of episodes that have the following form:

Character with goals → Plans in the → Vicissitudes → Outcomes of an
of an emotional kind   social world   (problems)   emotional kind

Over the last thirty years or so, many researchers have thrown doubt on whether psychology should have any truck with folk theory. In physics, goes one argument, folk theory has been shown to be wrong, not just in detail but completely and utterly. Folk theory in psychology has the same vices of being unresponsive to evidence, so why should we pay attention to it (Churchland, 1986)?

Within cognitively based emotion research, however, the argument has been different. It is that folk theory of desires (goals), beliefs, and emotions, expressed in something like the narrative format given above, runs parallel to scientific theory. Thus, Tomkins (1979) has proposed that emotions are embedded in scripts; and Frijda (1987) that emotions are processes which have a structure not unlike the narrative schema proposed, in which a principal property of emotions is motivational: emotions are tendencies toward action. With Frijda's formulation we may see the first term in this series (goals of an emotional kind) as motivating the plan and hence the episode. By the last term in the series (outcomes of an emotional kind) the goals may have been accomplished (a happy outcome) or lost (a sad outcome), or transformed so that the emotional outcome becomes the start of a new episode.

Evidence that the folk theory on which narrative stands does have a scientific basis comes from the construction of joint plans, in which people coordinate their actions. Oatley and Larocque (1995) have shown that people make many joint plans each day. They arrange to meet, they arrange formal and informal contracts, they arrange to complete different parts of joint tasks, and so forth. We have found that, although errors certainly happen, they happen only in about one in twenty of the joint plans. If there were no mapping between folk theory (in which these plans are arranged) and behavior, if beliefs and desires were constructs of a theory that was deluded, no joint plan would be successful. There would be no "you do this, and I'll do that, then together we can accomplish so and so." There would be no Amsterdam Symposium. There would be no Amsterdam. In other words, the folk theory based on beliefs, desires, and emotions is the successful means by which humans coordinate actions among each other. It allows talk about emotions of satisfaction when actions are accomplished, and of anger and sadness when they are not. The language of beliefs, desires, and emotions is the human interface between minds.

Perhaps human thinking within the folk theory of beliefs, desires, and emotions can never be correct more than 70 percent (or some other percentage) of the time. This theory, however, is the means by which we humans form complex models of each other and of ourselves, in ways that enable us to carry out joint intentions and to think about the emotions that occur when these intentions do not go as expected. Conversation and fiction are, respectively, the spontaneous and the elaborated ways of explaining human action and emotions in folk theoretical terms.

The Topics of Conversation

What do human beings converse about? The answer given by Dunbar (1996) is that some 70 percent of human conversations are about character: people we know, ourselves, and the interactions in our social group. In most cases some element of emotion is present both for the person who is the object of discussion and for the conversants. In addition, Rimé et al. (1998) have shown that people almost invariably do share emotional experiences with others. In such human narrating – with family, friends, loved ones – we strive to make sense of emotional experience.

Typically, human beings who are not emotion researchers are uninterested in an emotion as such. In conversation we offer, as it were, little character references. We are interested in an emotion as it contributes to a mental model of another person. In spontaneous conversation, we observe some of the elements of the literary idea of character being built, and see that this idea is essential to understanding emotions in relation to models of others, often by comparison – who we are like and who unlike – to models of ourselves.

The Evolution of Conversation and Development of Mental Models

Dunbar (1996) has argued that the large size of the primate brain, and the especially large size of the human brain (about 1,300 cc in modern humans, as compared with about 180 cc for a typical non-primate mammal of our body weight), has been selected for because of social life. More specifically, one might say that this large size is needed to house our characterological models of each other. Dunbar (1993) argues that increasing brain size among primate species is associated with living in interactive social groups of progressively larger numbers of individuals as primate evolution progressed.

What people talk about in conversations, as mentioned above, is largely the emotion-prompting doings of members of their social group, on which people base their characterological models. In this way, each of us has the emotional capacity, and the brain capacity, to maintain a set of friendly relationships, as well as a set of less friendly relationships, in a social nexus of up to 150 individually known people. The characterological models we construct of ourselves and others in the narratives of conversation enable us to be human.

CHARACTER IN EMOTION-BASED NARRATIVE

Human emotions in mental models of other people allow us to know how we shall treat these others, whether we shall like them or feel shy in their presence or feel aggressive toward them. As we get to know people better, we tend to like them more, or less. We come to trust or not to trust them. A progressively elaborated characterological model contains more or less explicit character sketches: this person is invariably cheerful despite misfortune; that one is cold even though sociable; another is full of barely suppressed anger. Emotions in models of the self are also important. They yield such functions as optimism and self-esteem. Such models are not of self-in-isolation, but of self-with-other, and they act as guides to how we act toward others.

Here are three hypotheses about mental models of character.

1. Mental models of another person or of ourselves have, at their core, emotional dispositions that are largely interpersonal.

2. Incidents that are caused by the vicissitudes of plans in interactions with others give rise to emotions, which prompt the formation of mental models of the others involved in the interactions; in some cases, they also prompt changes in our models of ourselves.
3. Our abilities in forming such models are elaborated in conversation, in play, and in fiction.

As to the first of these hypotheses, Jenkins and Greenbaum (1999) have found that children between the ages of eight and ten have a ready ability to describe the socioemotional goals and emotions of others in their social group. Children in the same school class were interviewed with such questions as: "How important is it to [child's name] to get other people to take up his/her ideas?" (dominance goal) and "How important is it for [child's name] to get to know others really well and get close to them?" (affiliation goal). As to dominance goals, there was high agreement among their peers about the children in the group, and high agreement, also, between peers' and teachers' ratings of these same children. Peers and teachers also agreed about which children were frequently angry. Agreement about children's affiliation goals was also generally significant, but the associations were less strong than for the dominance goals.

As to the second hypothesis: the effects of friendly turning-things-over in conversation are augmented by the formation of shared beliefs and commitment to shared plans (Oatley & Larocque, 1995). When such plans go well, they contribute to the affection in which the other person in the plan is held. When they go badly, they affect the relationship adversely; in such cases repairs or readjustments are needed. Oatley and Larocque, and Grazzani-Gavazzi and Oatley (1999) asked participants in Canada and Italy to keep diaries of incidents in which a joint plan had been formed and something had gone wrong with it. We found that errors in joint plans almost invariably caused emotions, anger being the most frequent. The anger typically included blaming the other person for not having done what had been agreed. Other emotions such as sadness and anxiety also occurred.

Participants in these studies were asked to record in their diaries their thoughts about the other person. These thoughts provide an important window into mental models that people form of others in the press of emotion. In one study, 50 of 157 participants ascribed negative personality traits to the other after an error: "unreliable," "disrespectful," "dishonest," "irresponsible," "careless," "self-involved," "stupid," "a bitch," and so forth. Participants who were angry, as compared to not angry, were far more likely to form negative trait ascriptions of the other, and this difference was highly significant. Such derogatory ascriptions were mostly made when participants did not know the other person well.

In the cauldron of anger following an error, a mental model of that person can be formed with the core emotional component of the person depicted as untrustworthy. In one error in our corpus, a participant waited for a new colleague in one restaurant while he sat for over an hour in a different location of the same chain of restaurants, waiting for her. The participant stated that the fact that he had "stood her up" would remain at the back of her mind the next time she had dealings with him. She said this although her explanation indicated that he had been no more at fault than she, and indeed that he had been the one to telephone to find out what had gone wrong and had attempted repairs. In other words, the emotional core of her mental model of him in relation to her – that he had not valued her – would dominate the next phase of any relationship they might have.

As to the third of these hypotheses, Dunn and Brown (1991) have shown the emergence of shared meaning from protolanguage in infant conversation, as in this example from a twenty-one-month-old child and his mother.

CHILD: Eat my Weetabix [breakfast cereal]. Eat my Weetabix. Crying.
MOTHER: Crying weren't you? We had quite a battle. "One more mouthful, Michael." And what did you do? You spat it out.
CHILD: (*Pretends to cry.*)

Mother and child are here discussing breakfast time, with the child naming the emotion: "crying." Maybe the child is apologizing; maybe he is wondering what breakfast will be like tomorrow. What is clear is that he and his mother are constructing a joint meaning of the emotional event, in narrative and interpersonal terms.

Part of the argument of this chapter is that fiction also contributes to the building of mental models of others. It allows readers and audience members to build models of the individuality of people other than themselves, who can be understood with a degree of inwardness.

POETICS: HOW FICTION WORKS

Aristotle's *Poetics* remains in the West the textbook of how to make stories with emotionally absorbing qualities. Indeed, the terms "poetics" and "fiction" both derive from verbs meaning "to make." In the Indian literary tradition, which is of comparable antiquity, the word for poet, *kavi*, is different. It has the root of one who perceives, who is wise (Lehmann, 1996). In this tradition the poet's art has a moral quality, in which social life is intended to imitate this art. In this tradition, also, the listener or reader is the maker of meaning, so in this sense the East has anticipated the recent Western movement of reader-response theory.

The more deeply one looks into fiction, the more highly structured it appears. One piece of structure that has been widely acknowledged, and seems to apply to all fiction, was pointed out by the Russian formalists nearly a hundred years ago. They distinguished *fabula*, usually translated

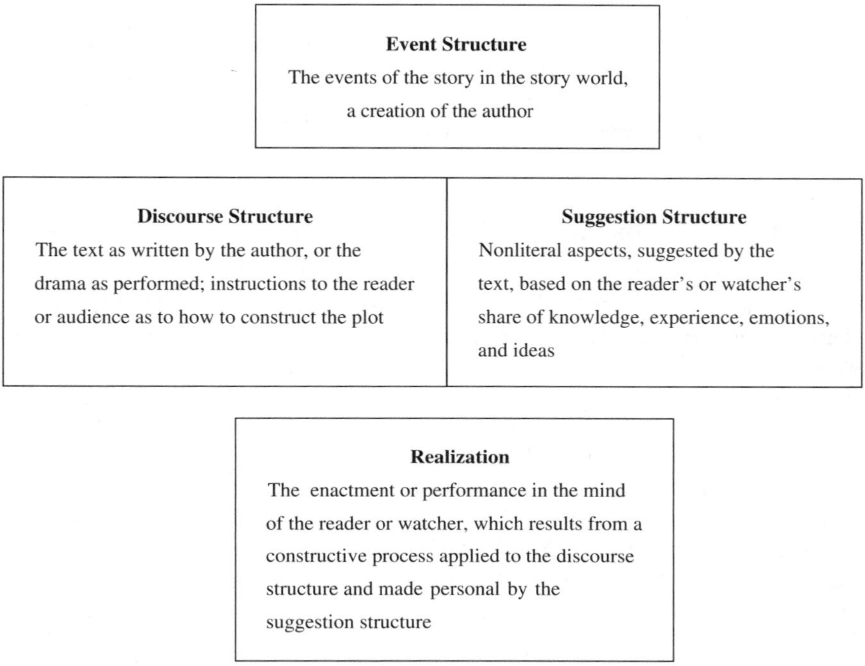

Event Structure

The events of the story in the story world,
a creation of the author

Discourse Structure

The text as written by the author, or the
drama as performed; instructions to the reader
or audience as to how to construct the plot

Suggestion Structure

Nonliteral aspects, suggested by the
text, based on the reader's or watcher's
share of knowledge, experience, emotions,
and ideas

Realization

The enactment or performance in the mind
of the reader or watcher, which results from a
constructive process applied to the discourse
structure and made personal by the
suggestion structure

FIGURE 7.1. Four Aspects of Story Structure (after Oatley, 2001)

as "story" but better termed "event structure," as illustrated in Figure 7.1, from *siuzhet,* which used to be translated as "plot," but in Figure 7.1 is called the "discourse structure" (Brewer & Lichtenstein, 1981).

Event Structure and Discourse Structure

Event structure in a story is a set of events of a story world: this happened and then that. For any story it is important that there are such events, but their recitation as such would sustain no interest. Discourse structure is the discourse of the author to the reader or audience, the equivalent of speech acts in conversational discourse; it is the story as written, told, or enacted.

The discourse structure is a construction of sequenced language by the author intended to prompt the absorbing qualities that will bring the story alive. In a previous section, I remarked that conversation is a means for building mental models of others. Conversation has a quality of emotional absorption, and so, as Harris (1998) has remarked, has pretend play. Also, as Goffman (1961) has pointed out: "there seems to be no agent more effective than another person in bringing a world for oneself alive . . . it is only here that a definition of a situation has a favored chance of taking on the vivid character of sensed reality" (p. 41).

One of the striking features of the story, the drama, and the novel – forms in which elements of conversation and of pretend play have joined – is that these, too, can be emotionally absorbing even when the usual face-to-face elements are absent. Part of the task of the discourse structure, then, is to provide the basis of absorption, even when another person is not present.

Suggestion Structure

I have proposed (Oatley, 1999, 2001) that some further analysis is necessary, beyond the event structure and discourse structure, in order for the nature of fiction and its structure to be understood. (I concentrate on fiction, but some of what I say applies equally to some genres of nonfiction such as biography, history, and social anthropology.) One further aspect, beyond that of the event and discourse structures, is the suggestion structure (see Figure 7.1), the means by which emotions, memories, and thoughts that are not paraphrases of the text are prompted in the reader.

The suggestion structure is the means by which emotions and other personal reactions are evoked in a reader. It was described by Abhinavagupta, a literary theorist who lived in the area that is now Kashmir about a thousand years ago (Ingalls, Masson, & Patwardhan, 1990). He and others in the same tradition argued that the heart of literary stories lies in their suggestive qualities (*dhvani*), which can prompt literary emotions (*rasas*). Hogan (2000) has argued that these suggestions are carried primarily by processes that are recognized in modern cognitive psychology as priming. One of Abhinavagupta's examples is this verse spoken by a young woman to a male traveler who comes to her house to stay while her husband is away.

> Mother-in-law sleeps here, I there:
> Look, traveler, while it is light.
> For at night when you cannot see
> You must not fall into my bed.
> (Ingalls et al., 1990, p. 98)

"Sleep" suggests (or primes) the sexual connotation of "to sleep with." This is a metonymic figure, but the suggestive quality of *dhvani* does not depend closely on figures of speech. Abhinavagupta explains: "The sprout of love has suddenly arisen in a traveler as he looks at a young woman whose husband is away from home. By means of this prohibition she gives him permission" (pp. 98–99). Abhinavagupta continues for three paragraphs about the suggestions of this verse. He includes the idea of the traveler being made blind by something other than mere darkness, and of the lovers having to be quiet in their lovemaking. The *rasa* that is suggested here is love, or the amorous. We all know that once an amorous atmosphere has been established, a large number of things one might say can have a suggestive quality.

The oldest extant Indian writing on the *rasas*, thought to be based on contributions by multiple authors from the fifth century B.C.E. to the third century C.E., is a fifth-century C.E. text called the Natyasastra, attributed to Bharata. *Rasa* literally means something like "essence" or "taste." It is sometimes translated as "sentiment" and is a stable mental state. There were thought to be eight fundamental emotions of everyday life. Here they are, with (in parentheses) their corresponding literary *rasas* (Gnoli, 1968; Gerow, 1977; Jussawalla, 1994): delight (the amorous), laughter (the comic), sorrow (the pitiable or tragic), anger (the furious), heroism (the heroic), fear (the terrible), disgust (the odious), and wonder (the marvelous). A ninth was added later: serenity (the peaceful). Indian fundamental emotions map onto basic emotions (e.g., Oatley & Johnson-Laird, 1996), but *rasa* is a notion absent from Western literary theory. There is something of its sense in Vygotsky's aesthetic theory (Kozulin, 1990) according to which, alongside the causal structure of the plot, there is said to be a much more indirect aesthetic sense, something like the emotion-arousing music that accompanies movies. For Vygotsky, in the dialectical relationship between them, the aesthetic sense of the story was thought capable of overcoming the plot line.

In Indian literary theory, it was argued that a good literary work should concentrate on just one of the *rasas*, though often by way of others, and usually via what the Indian theorists called transient mental states, such as discouragement, weakness, and apprehension. This theory had strong spiritual aspects and postulated *rasa* as being a perception of the infinite, which both was and was not dependent on ordinary mental processes. I believe that concepts of the suggestive (*dhvani*) and sentiments (*rasas*) are of central importance for understanding the emotions of literature. The argument is that literature can allow us to see deeply into the nature of things in a way that transcends the egotism of everyday emotions.

Empirically, among the best ways of demonstrating the emotions of reading is a development from the work of Larsen and Seilman (1988). They asked readers of a short story to mark passages in which a memory came to mind during reading. In my research group, we ask readers of short stories to mark the margin with an M when a memory occurs, with an E when they experience an emotion, and a T if a thought occurs that is not a direct paraphrase of the text. Almost all readers can do this easily. We take these as measures of the effects of the suggestion structure, of the reader's absorption in the story. At the end of a reading we can count the Ms, Es, and Ts, and ask the reader to relate the content of any or all of them. Biason and Oatley (see Oatley, 1996) asked high school students to read one of two short stories about adolescent identity, either one by Alice Munro that had a female protagonist or one by Carson McCullers that had a male protagonist. Whereas the female students had plentiful Ms and Es while reading the stories with either the male or the female protagonist, boys had many fewer Es and Ms with the story of the female protagonist. In other words, the girls were able to identify with a protagonist of either sex, whereas the boys were much less able (or willing) to identify with the female protagonist.

Using a second type of method, we have given readers a short story and measured their emotions before and after reading. In this way Nundy and Oatley (Oatley, 1996) studied readers' responses to Russell Banks's (2001) short story "Sarah Cole."

In the opening paragraph of this story, a first-person narrator says that, at the time of the story's events, "I was extremely handsome," and that Sarah was "the homeliest woman I have ever known." He says he is telling the story ten years after its events occurred, and that he will tell the story objectively so as not to be biased. He then continues in the third person, calling himself "the man." The man starts an affair with Sarah. After the affair has continued for some months, he ends it cruelly, saying to her, "Leave me now, you disgusting, ugly bitch."

The story ends in an ambiguous way. After our readers had finished the story, we asked them three questions about its ambiguities, as follows:

Question 1: From the narrator's point of view, why do you think the story says, "She's transformed into the most beautiful woman he had ever seen?"

Question 2: From the narrator's point of view, why do you think the story says, "It's not as if she has died; it's as if he has killed her?"

Question 3: What do you think the meaning of the story is from the narrator's point of view?

We categorized the kinds of reasoning in response to these questions and found 91 percent agreement between two raters. One category was of what is known in studies of reasoning as backward chaining: stating a conclusion and then giving reasons to support it. Here is an example, part of one participant's response to Question 1.

He no longer sees Sarah as belonging to him. She breaks away from him probably more strongly than he tries to separate from her. He is also not truly capable of a true respectful love . . . and maybe feels guilty and envious that she was giving in the relationship he was never honestly in.

Now here is an example of forward chaining, stating a set of reasons and then a conclusion; another participant's response to Question 2 was:

He knew she knew and everyone else that she was "homely." Perhaps it was perverse or pity that he engaged in a relationship with her. But despite her physical appearance which she struggled with, she had feelings. . . . So out of guilt he might as well have killed emotionally – cut deep into the soul at any rate.

"Sarah Cole" is an unusual story in that it elicits widely differing emotions from different readers. Though not all the participants used reasoning in response to interpretive questions, in those who did, we found that those who became sad engaged predominantly in backward chaining. Participants who grew angry engaged predominantly in forward chaining. This difference was highly significant for each of the three interpretive questions.

Readers became emotionally absorbed in the story, and their mode of thinking was different depending on what emotion was predominant. Sadness is a mode in which one starts from the current state and reasons backward to try to understand its causes. In anger, one reasons forward from the current state about what to do next. This result is just from a single study, but it is consistent with the idea that a story is suggestive for readers in ways that prompt emotions which are idiosyncratic to them.

Not only does the suggestive in literature evoke emotions, but, as the medieval Indian literary theorists argued and as the study with the story "Sarah Cole" suggests, once a mood has been created, the interpretation of a story is affected by it. This is not all: emotions not only change thought (as in the story of Sarah Cole), they are themselves the principal agents in changing emotions. As Greenberg (2002) has argued, change in psychotherapy occurs when one emotion comes to replace another, for instance, when anger at some other person is replaced by sadness as one realizes one's own part in a rift that has occurred. In a comparable way, Miall and Kuiken (2001) have argued that what occurs in literary and dramatic works is that one emotion, for instance pity, comes to replace and reinterpret another. If this idea is applied to *Hamlet,* what occurs at the beginning is that, first, his awe in response to the ghost changes into vengeful emotions. By the end of the play, these vengeful feelings are transformed, and the whole play can be understood in terms of empathetic sorrow for Hamlet's plight, and for the predicament of mankind generally.

Realization

The fourth aspect of fiction shown in Figure 7.1 is what I have called the realization. It contains elements of interpretation that, as Dante (1304–1308) pointed out, can take various forms, including the literal and the allegorical. But realization is not just interpretation. It is the listener's own enactment or performance of the piece. The critical conceptualization here, as Mithen (2001) has argued, is imagination, or as some writers of the nineteenth century (e.g., Stevenson, 1888) described it, fiction as a kind of dream. In modern cognitive-psychological terms, one may argue that the realization is a kind of simulation – a simulation that runs not on computers but on minds (Oatley 1992, 1999).

The distinction between *fabula* and *siuzhet* is exactly equivalent to the distinction between the parts of a computer program that represent, respectively, the elements of the ordinary world that are being simulated and the commands to the computer about how to compute over these elements. In the simulation of a story, the listener or reader allows his or her own self, and the projection of that self into the future by means of plans, to be guided by the discourse structure. At the same time, the reader is affected by the associations of the suggestion structure to produce his or her own enactment.

Among the emergent properties of a literary simulation are the social emotions prompted by the suggestion structure. Emotions are based on goals, so social emotions are based on social goals. Jenkins and I have argued (Oatley, 2000; Oatley & Jenkins, in preparation) that there are three fundamental kinds of social goal: attachment, assertion, and affiliation. From these flow most of our social emotions. There are in addition the emotions of the physical world, such as curiosity and fear of physical danger, and also what one might call the antisocial emotions, those of contempt and disgust.

The emotions and the roles they afford – physical, social, and antisocial – are capable of intermixture. Friends enjoy joining in competition against a common opponent. As well as being affectionately warm, lovers also act as attachment partners, and so on. Perhaps most disastrously for us, we humans are easily capable of uniting the emotions of angry assertion with the antisocial emotions of contempt. This alloy produces perhaps the most blatant emotional stains on human character: our capacities for war against those we take to be outsiders and for disdain toward the powerless.

Human narratives, then, become means by which we seek to understand the problematics of our emotional legacy. Each of the social emotional-motivational systems has inner contradictions, and with their easy entry into emotional alloys, the contradictions grow more stark. These become the stuff of the imaginative world of narrative fiction, a principal means by which we try to make sense of our own socioemotional makeup, just as in pretend play children seek to make sense of social roles.

Mithen (2001) has argued that what we call imagination is a distinct phase of mental life that, in evolutionary terms, emerged in Homo sapiens after our divergence from the line that led to the Neanderthals. Before that, Mithen argues, thinking was domain-specific and skill-specific, with different skills and domains of knowledge being encapsulated and limited in scope. He bases this conclusion on the restricted range of stone tools that have been found before this time and the lack of artifacts of decoration or art. His argument is that metaphor is quintessentially a domain-crossing mental operation. When Hamlet says, "Denmark's a prison"

(*Hamlet*, 2. 2. 239), domains are crossed. Artistic activities, moreover, depend on externalizations, such as those of a story or ritual, or of a painting, memento, or ornament.

Fictions are simulations of social interaction by which we may explore the paradoxes of our social-motivational systems and discover cultural forms that resonate with the identities we construct. Among the operations of computer simulations are the setting of variables into ordered list structures and the assigning of arguments to functions. Among the operations of the simulations of fiction are the linking of emotions to segments of narrative line, their attribution to characters, and the transition from one emotion to another.

HUMAN EMOTION: THE PASSIONATE HEART OF FICTION

Nonfictional writing tends to be about explanation of the world. An essential question is whether the world really is or was, empirically speaking, as the author describes. Fiction, by contrast, has a different center: the emotions, which are the means by which we become absorbed in stories. They derive principally from the suggestion structure, and they are enacted in the realization. It is not that emotions are all that fiction is concerned with – the empirically valid and the emotionally engaging need not be at odds with each other – but the emotions are fiction's joints and muscles.

I have proposed five modes in which readers experience emotions in fiction (Oatley, 1994). Two occur in common with other forms of art: the pleasure of assimilation to existing schemas, and the more ambiguous pleasure of having one's schemas accommodate. Three modes are specific to the world of literature where we enter an imagined world as through a magic door in a garden wall.

Identification

The psychological mode of identification is a principal means by which a reader or audience member enters a story. First one comes to like a main character, or narrator; then, by taking on his or her goals and running the simulation, one becomes like the character, even becomes the character. I propose that this literary process is paralleled in ordinary life by empathy: entering rather fully by means of imagination into someone else's life, and perhaps losing aspects of oneself by doing so.

Sympathy

A second means by which we feel emotions within a story is on behalf of characters, because we perceive the appraisal patterns – which T. S. Eliot

(1919) called objective correlatives – with which they are confronted. Here the reader does not give up him- or herself to a story character, but feels emotions on behalf of that character. The best treatment of these effects has been given by Tan (1996) and, as he has argued, the best means we have for inducing them is film, which he has called an emotion machine. The effects also occur readily in novels and short stories. The sympathetic reader/watcher is like a fly on the wall. But why should he or she take an interest? One evolutionary psychological answer is that this sympathy is not as disinterested as it seems: three scenarios that easily produce sympathetic emotions correspond to the three motivational/emotional systems discussed earlier. People like watching sex and its anticipations (based on a specific aspect of the affiliation motive). Is this because in our genes, as in the genes of our closest primate cousins the bonobos, watching sex is closely associated with having sex? People like watching infants: is this because our attachment and care-giving schemas are pleasurably activated by doing so? More alarmingly, people like watching fights. Is this because a fight we watch easily turns into a fight that we join?

Memory

The third important means by which emotions are elicited specifically from within the story world is memory, best treated by Scheff (1979). A story can elicit autobiographical memories of emotionally significant episodes that, because of the constructive nature of the enactment of the story, allow us to reexperience and rework those aspects of the memory which are important to our emotional identity.

CONCLUSION

In the understanding of visual perception, much of the argument is conducted by demonstrations that make underlying processes salient in the experience of the perceiver: cues to three-dimensional depth, color contrast, successive stimulation that gives rise to perception of movement, and so forth. Similarly, fiction provides a set of constructed demonstrations, based on underlying emotional processes – identification, sympathy, memory, and so forth – which show the commonality between the constructed (fictional) and real (everyday) experience of the social world. Each of the modes of emotional absorption described in the previous section offers a means of resonance with a reader and can make a story personal. By showing the links from emotions to goals and character, narrative lets us see into the heart of the social world.

References

Antonovsky, A. (1979). *Health, stress, and coping.* San Francisco: Jossey-Bass.

Aristotle, (c. 330 B.C.). (1970). *Poetics* (Trans. G. E. Else). Ann Arbor: University of Michigan Press.

Banks, R. (2001). *The angel on the roof.* Toronto: Random House.

Brewer, W. F., & E. H. Lichtenstein (1981). Event schemas, story schemas and story grammars. In J. Long & A. Baddeley (Eds.), *Attention and performance* (9: 363–379). Hillsdale, NJ: Erlbaum.

Brewin, C. R.; Dalgleish, T.; & Joseph, S. (1996). A dual representation theory of post-traumatic stress disorder. *Psychological Review, 103,* 670–686.

Bruner, J. (1986). *Actual minds, possible worlds.* Cambridge, MA: Harvard University Press.

Churchland, P. S. (1986). *Neurophilosophy.* Cambridge, MA: MIT Press.

Dante Alighieri. (1304–1308; 1989). *Il Convivio (The Banquet).* Saratoga, CA: Anma Libri.

Dunbar, R. I. M. (1993). Coevolution of neocortical size, group size, and language in humans. *Behavioral and Brain Sciences, 16,* 681–735.

Dunbar, R. I. M. (1996). *Grooming, gossip and the evolution of language.* London: Faber & Faber.

Dunn, J., & Brown, J. (1991). Relationships, talk about feelings, and the development of affect regulation in early childhood. In J. Garber and K. Dodge (Eds.), *The development of emotion regulation and dysregulation* (pp. 89–108). Cambridge: Cambridge University Press.

Eliot, T. S. (1919). *Hamlet.* In J. Hayward (Ed.), *T. S. Eliot: Selected prose* (pp. 104–109). Harmondsworth: Penguin.

Frijda, N. H. (1987). Emotion, cognitive structure and action tendency. *Cognition and Emotion, 1,* 115–143.

Gerow, E. (1977). *Indian poetics.* Wiesbaden: Harrassowitz.

Gnoli, R. (1968). *The aesthetic experience according to Abhinavagupta.* Varanasi: Chowkhamba Sanscrit Series Office.

Goffman, E. (1961). *Encounters: Two studies in the sociology of interaction.* Indianapolis: Bobbs-Merrill.

Grazzani-Gavazzi, I., & Oatley, K. (1999). The experience of emotions of interdependence and independence following interpersonal errors in Italy and Anglophone Canada. *Cognition and Emotion, 13,* 49–63.

Greenberg, L. (2002). *Emotion-focused therapy.* Washington, DC: American Psychological Association.

Harris, P. (1998). Fictional absorption: Emotional responses to make-believe. In S. Braten (Ed.), *Intersubjective communication and emotion in early ontogeny* (pp. 336–353). New York: Cambridge University Press.

Hogan, P. C. (2000). *Philosophical approaches to the study of literature.* Gainesville: University Press of Florida.

Ingalls, D. H. H.; Masson, J. M.; & Patwardhan, M. V. (1990). *The Dhvanyaloka of Anandavardana with the Locana of Abhinavagupta.* Cambridge, MA.: Harvard University Press.

Jenkins, J. M., & Greenbaum, R. (1999). Intention and emotion in child psychopathology: Building cooperative plans. In P. D. Zelazo, J. W. Astington, and D. R. Olson (Eds.), *Developing theories of intention: Social understanding and self-control* (pp. 269–291). Mahwah, NJ: Erlbaum.

Jussawalla, F. (1994). Indian theory and criticism. In M. Groden and M. Kreisworth (Eds.), *The Johns Hopkins guide to literary theory and criticism* (pp. 399–404). Baltimore: Johns Hopkins University Press.

Kozulin, A. (1990). *Vygotsky's psychology: A biography of ideas.* Cambridge, MA: Harvard University Press.

Larsen, S. F., & Seilman, U. (1988). Personal meanings while reading literature. *Text, 8,* 411–429.

Lehmann, W. P. (1996). Poetic principles in the South Asian literary tradition: Interrelatedness of grammar, prosody, and other elements of language. *College Literature (Special issue on Comparative Poetics: Non-Western traditions of literary theory), 23 (1),* 111–123.

Miall, D. S., & Kuiken, D. (2001). A feeling for fiction: Becoming what we behold. *The Work of Fiction: Cognitive Perspectives.* Conference, Bar-Ilan University, Ramat-Gan, Israel, 4–7 June 2001.

Mithen, S. (2001). The evolution of imagination: An archeological perspective. *SubStance* (nos. 94/95), 28–54.

Oatley, K. (1992). Integrative action of narrative. In D. J. Stein and J. E. Young (Eds.), *Cognitive science and clinical disorders* (pp. 151–170). San Diego, CA: Academic Press.

Oatley, K. (1994). A taxonomy of the emotions of literary response and a theory of identification in fictional narrative. *Poetics, 23,* 53–74.

Oatley, K. (1996). Inference and emotions in narrative and science. In D. R. Olson and N. Torrance (Eds.), *Modes of thought.* New York: Cambridge University Press.

Oatley, K. (1999). Why fiction may be twice as true as fact: Fiction as cognitive and emotional simulation. *Review of General Psychology, 3,* 101–117.

Oatley, K. (2000a). The sentiments and beliefs of distributed cognition. In N. Frijda, A. S. R. Manstead, and S. Bem (Eds.), *Emotions and beliefs: How feelings influence thoughts* (pp. 78–107). Cambridge: Cambridge University Press.

Oatley, K. (2000b). Social goals and emotion. Report of invited talk at the 2000 British Psychological Society Annual Conference, *The Psychologist, 13,* 290–291.

Oatley, K. (2002). Emotions and the story worlds of fiction. In T. C. Brock, J. J. Strange, and M. C. Green (Eds.), *Narrative impact: Social and cognitive foundations.* Mahwah, NJ: Erlbaum.

Oatley, K., & Johnson-Laird, P. N. (1996). The communicative theory of emotions: Empirical tests, mental models, and implications for social interaction. In L. L. Martin and A. Tesser (Eds.), *Striving and feeling: Interactions among goals, affect, and self-regulation* (pp. 363–393). Mahwah, NJ: Erlbaum.

Oatley, K., & Larocque, L. (1995). Everyday concepts of emotions following every-other-day errors in joint plans. In J. Russell, J.-M. Fernandez-Dols, A. S. R. Manstead, and J. Wellenkamp (Eds.), *Everyday conceptions of emotions: An introduction to the psychology, anthropology, and lingusitics of emotion. NATO ASI Series D 81* (pp. 145–165). Dordrecht: Kluwer.

Pennebaker, J. W., & Seagal, J. D. (1999). Forming a story: The health benefits of narrative. *Journal of Clinical Psychology, 55,* 1243–1254.

Rimé, B.; Finkenauer, C.; Luminet, O.; Zech, E.; & Philippot, P. (1998). Social sharing of emotion: New evidence and new questions. *European Review of Social Psychology, 9,* 145–189.

Scheff, T. J. (1979). *Catharsis in healing, ritual, and drama.* Berkeley: University of California Press.

Shakespeare, W. (1600; 1981). *Hamlet* (Ed. J. Jenkins). London: Methuen.

Stevenson, R. L. (1888). A chapter on dreams. *Scribner's Magazine,* January. Reprinted in *R. L. Stevenson Essays and Poems* (Ed. C. Harman). (1992). London: Dent Everyman's Library (pp. 1189–1199).

Tan, E. S. (1996). *Emotion and the structure of film: Film as an emotion machine.* Mahwah, NJ: Erlbaum.

Tomkins, S. S. (1979). Script theory: Differential magnification of affects. *Nebraska Symposium on Motivation, 1978* (Ed. H. E. Howe & R. A. Dienstbier), *26,* 201–236. Lincoln: University of Nebraska Press.

PART II

BASIC PSYCHOLOGICAL PROCESSES IN FEELINGS AND EMOTIONS

8

What We Become Emotional About

Paul Ekman

ABSTRACT

The different ways in which emotions are triggered are analyzed. Working from the premise that emotions evolved to prepare us to deal with important events, the most common of these is an automated appraisal system, referred to here as "autoappraisers." Eight further ways in which emotions are generated are also identified.

We can all remember times when our emotional reaction was inappropriate. It is not that our emotional reaction was too intense, or that our way of expressing it was incorrect; it is that we were feeling the wrong emotion. The problem is not that we got too angry, or that we showed it in the wrong way; we realized afterward that we should not have become angry at all. The issue here is why an inappropriate emotion was being triggered.

The question would not arise if we all reacted the same way when something happened, if every event triggered the same emotion in everyone. Clearly that is not the case; some people are afraid of heights, others are not; some people mourned the death of Princess Diana as if she had been their close relative, while others could not have cared less. Yet there are some triggers that do generate the same emotion in everyone; near-miss car accidents invariably spark a moment of fear. How does this happen? How do we each acquire our own unique set of emotional triggers and at the same time have the same emotional reaction that everyone else has to other triggers? How do we acquire the emotion triggers that we wish we did not have?

This chapter is taken from chapter 2 of my book *Emotions Revealed* (London: Weidenfeld & Nicolson, and New York: Times Books, 2003). My research was supported in part by an NIMH Senior Research Scientist Award, KO5-MH06092.

We do not become emotional about everything; we are not in the grip of emotion all the time. Emotions come and go. We feel an emotion one moment, and may not feel any emotion at another moment. The most common way in which emotions occur is when we sense, rightly or wrongly, that something is happening or is about to happen that seriously affects our welfare, for better or worse. (Later, I describe eight other paths for generating emotion that do not directly involve our own welfare.) It is a simple idea – emotions evolved to prepare us to deal quickly with those events in our lives that are most vital to us.

Recall a time when you were driving your car and suddenly another car appeared, going very fast, seeming as if it were about to hit you. Let us suppose that your conscious mind was focused on something else, perhaps an interesting conversation with a friend sitting in the passenger's seat, or a program on the radio. In an instant, before you had time to think, before the conscious, self-aware part of your mind could consider the matter, danger was sensed and fear began.

As an emotion begins, it takes us over in those first milliseconds, directing what we do and say and think. Without consciously choosing to do it, you automatically turned the steering wheel to avoid the other motorist, hitting the brake with your foot. At the same time an expression of fear flashed across your face – brows raised and drawn together, eyes opened very wide, and lips stretched back toward your ears. Your heart began to pump more rapidly, you began to sweat, and the blood rushed to the large muscles of your legs.

Emotions prepare us to deal with the most important events in our lives, without our having to think about what to do. You would not have survived that near-miss car accident if part of you had not been continually monitoring the world for signs of danger. Nor would you have survived if you had had to think consciously about what you should do to cope with the danger once it was apparent. Emotions do this without your knowing it is happening, and much of the time that is good for you, as it would be in a near-miss car accident.

When the emotion is strong and it starts abruptly, as in the car example, our memory of the emotion episode after it is over will not be very accurate. You cannot know what your brain did, what processes were involved in recognizing the danger posed by the other car. You would know that you turned the wheel and hit the brake, but you probably would not be aware of the expression that flashed across your face. You would have felt some of the sensations in your body, but it would be hard for you to find words to describe those sensations. If we wanted to know how it was that you were even able to sense the danger when you had been focused on your conversation or the music on the car radio, you would not be able to tell us. You were not a witness to the processes within you that saved your life.

If the process were slower, we might be aware of what is happening inside our brains, but we would not survive near-miss car accidents; we would not be able to act quickly enough. In that first instant, the decision or evaluation that brings forth the emotion is extraordinarily fast and outside of awareness. We must have *automatic* appraising mechanisms that are continually scanning the world around us, detecting when something important to our welfare, to our survival, is happening. When we get to the point where we can actually observe the operation of automatic appraising in the brain, I expect we will find many mechanisms, not one; so from now on I will use the plural form when referring to automatic appraising mechanisms, which I will abbreviate as "autoappraisers."

Nearly everyone who does research on emotion today agrees with what I have described so far: First, that emotions are reactions to matters that seem to be very important to our welfare; and second, that emotions often begin so quickly that we are not aware of the processes in our mind that triggered them (although a few emotion theorists still cling to the notion that we consciously decide when we will become emotional). Research on the brain is consistent with what I have so far suggested. We can make very complex evaluations very quickly, in milliseconds, without being aware of the evaluative process.

We can now rephrase the first set of questions about how there can be both universal and individual specific emotion triggers. What are the autoappraisers sensitive to, and how did they become sensitive to those triggers? How do the emotion triggers become established? The answers could tell us why we have an emotion when we do. Why do we sometimes have emotions that do not seem to us to be at all appropriate? Why at other moments are our emotions perfectly tuned to what is happening, and may even save our lives?

We can infer something about what events our autoappraisers are sensitive to by examining when emotions happen. Most of what we know has not come from actually observing when people experience one or another emotion. Instead it comes from their answers to questionnaires about when they remember feeling one or another emotion. In his insightful book, philosopher Peter Goldie (2000) calls this kind of information post-rationalizing. This is not to dismiss such information. The answers people give on such questionnaires, like the explanations we give to ourselves after an emotional episode to account for why we did what we did, may be incomplete and perhaps stereotyped because they go through the filters of what people are aware of and remember. On questionnaires there is the additional issue of what people are willing to tell others. But the answers can still teach us quite a bit.

Similar research on students was conducted by Boucher and Brandt (1981) in Malaysia and in the United States and, some years later, by Klaus Scherer and his collaborators (Scherer, Walbott, & Summerfield,

1986) in eight Western cultures. Both sets of researchers found evidence of universals – the same kinds of triggers were reported to evoke the same emotions across very different cultures. Both sets of investigators also found evidence of cultural differences in the specific events that call forth an emotion. So, here again is the problem: How did the autoappraisers become sensitive both to emotional triggers that are found in everyone, the universals, and to triggers that call forth different emotions across individuals even within a culture?

The autoappraisers must be scanning for events that everyone encounters, events that are important to the welfare or survival of all human beings. For each emotion there might be a few such events that are stored in the brains of every human being. It might be a schema, an abstract outline, or the bare bones of a scene, such as the threat of harm for fear and some important loss for sadness. Another equally likely possibility is that what is stored is not at all abstract but is a specific event, such as the loss of support or something coming at us so quickly that it is likely to hit us, for fear. For sadness, the universal trigger might be the loss of a loved one, a person to whom one is strongly attached. There is no scientific basis yet for choosing between these two possibilities, but it does not make a difference for how we lead our emotional lives.

Many psychologists have focused on a related but different set of issues, which is how the automatic appraisers evaluate a new event to determine, in my terms, whether it fits an item already in the emotional appraisal data base. I have some doubts about whether the findings of Scherer, Roseman, or Ellsworth (cf. Scherer, Schorr, & Johnstone, 2001) tell us what actually happens, as it is based on what people tell them, and none of us is aware of what our mind is doing at the moment it is doing it in the automatic appraisal process. What this research has provided is good models to account for how people explain what makes them emotional (see Parkinson & Manstead, 1992, 1993). For an excellent compilation of the different approaches to this issue, see a new book on appraisal theory (Scherer et al., 2001) and Roseman and Smith's (2001) review of the different approaches in that book. In any case, their suggestions are not directly relevant to the theory I suggest in the rest of this chapter about what we become emotional about, when we become emotional, and whether we can change these things.

Over the course of our lives we encounter many specific events that we learn to interpret in such a way as to frighten, anger, disgust, sadden, surprise, or please us, and these are added to the universal antecedent events, expanding on what the autoappraisers are alert to. These learned events may closely or distantly resemble the originally stored events. They are elaborations of or additions to the universal antecedent events. They are not the same for all people, but vary with what we each experience. When I studied members of a Stone Age culture in New Guinea in the late

1960s, I found they were afraid of being attacked by a wild pig. In urban America, people are more afraid of being attacked by a mugger, but both cases represent a threat of harm.

In an earlier book (Ekman & Friesen, 1975) I and my coresearcher Wally Friesen described the scenes we thought were universal for seven emotions. Richard Lazarus (1991) later made a similar proposal. He used the phrase "core relational themes" to reflect his view that emotions are primarily about how we deal with other people, a point I very much agree with (although impersonal events such as a sunset or an earthquake can also trigger emotions). The word "theme" is a good one, because we can then talk about the universal themes and the *variations* on those themes that develop in each person's experiences.

When we encounter a theme, such as the sensations we experience when a chair unexpectedly collapses under us, it triggers an emotion with very little evaluation. It may take a bit longer for the autoappraisers to evaluate any of the variations on each theme, the ones we learn in the course of growing up. The further removed the variation is from the theme, the longer it may take; until we get to the point where what I call *extended appraising* occurs. In extended appraising, we are consciously aware of our evaluative processes; we are thinking and considering what is happening. Suppose someone heard that there was going to be a cutback in the work force at her place of employment. She would think about whether she is likely to be hit, and as she thinks about this potential threat, she might become afraid. She can't afford to lose that job, she needs the money it provides to support her. The event is related to the theme of loss of support – if indeed that is one of the themes for fear – but it is far enough removed that the appraising would not be automatic but extended. Her conscious mind is in on the process.

It is obvious how the idiosyncratic variations, each person's own emotional triggers, are acquired. They are learned, reflecting what each of us experiences (mugger or wild pig). But how are the universal themes acquired, how do they get stored in our brain so that the autoappraisers are sensitive to them? Are they, too, learned, or are they inherited, the product of our evolution? It is worth taking the time to consider this carefully, because the answer to this question – how the universal themes are acquired – has implications for how readily they can be modified or erased. Regrettably, there is no evidence about how the universal themes are acquired. Elsewhere (Ekman, 2003) I have spelled out two alternatives – species constant learning and natural selection.

It seems to me very unlikely that natural selection would not operate on something as important and central to our lives as what triggers our emotions. I propose that the themes for which the autoappraisers are constantly scanning our environment, typically without our knowing it, were selected over the course of our evolution. We are born prepared, sensitive to some events, and these are the events that were relevant to the survival of our species in their ancestral environment as hunters and gatherers. We are also sensitive to the variations on those themes, the variations being events that have been relevant to our own personal survival, not the survival of our ancestors.

Evidence consistent with this view comes from a brilliant series of studies by Arne Öhman (2000). He reasoned that, over most of our evolutionary history, snakes and spiders had been dangerous. Those of our ancestors who learned quickly that they were dangerous and avoided them would have been more likely to survive, to have children and to be able to care for them, than those who were slow to learn to be afraid of snakes and spiders. If indeed we are prepared by our evolution to become afraid of what has been dangerous in our past environment, then people today, he predicted, would learn more quickly to be afraid of snakes and spiders than of flowers, mushrooms, or geometric objects. That is exactly what he found.

I am convinced that one of the most distinctive features of emotion is that the events that trigger emotions are influenced, not just by our individual past experience, but also by our ancestral past. I am grateful to Tooby and Cosmides' (1990) writings about emotion for emphasizing this point. Emotions, in the felicitous phrase of Richard Lazarus, reflect the "wisdom of the ages," in both the emotion themes and the emotion responses. The autoappraisers are scanning for what has been important to survival, not just in our own individual lives, but also in the lives of our hunter-gatherer ancestors.

What we respond to may not always be appropriate to our current environment. If we visit a country where they drive on the other side of the road, our automatic processing can kill us, for we can easily do the wrong thing when we come to a traffic circle (roundabout) or make a turn. We cannot have a conversation or listen to the radio: we must consciously guard against the automatic decisions that we would otherwise make. Sometimes we may find that emotionally we are living in another "country," another environment than the one to which our automatic appraising mechanisms are sensitive. Then our emotional reactions may be inappropriate to what is happening.

That would not be much of a problem if it were not for another built-in benefit of our emotional appraising mechanisms – that they operate so incredibly quickly. If they were slower they would not be as useful, but there would be time for us to become conscious of what was making us become emotional. Our conscious evaluations could allow us to interrupt the process when we thought it inappropriate or not useful to us, before an emotion began. Nature did not give us that choice. If on odds it had been more often useful to have slow rather than fast appraising mechanisms, more useful over the history of our species on this planet, then we would not have such rapid, out-of-awareness, automatic appraising mechanisms.

Sometimes we respond emotionally to matters that were important in our earlier lives but are no longer relevant to our current lives. The variations on each theme that add and provide detail to what is identified through automatic appraising begin to be learned very early in life, some in infancy, others in childhood. We may find ourselves responding inappropriately because we are responding to things that angered, frightened, or disgusted us earlier, reactions that we now deem inappropriate to our adult life. There is a greater likelihood that we will make mistakes in our early learning of emotional triggers simply because our learning mechanisms are less well developed. Yet what we learn early in life may have greater potency, greater resistance to unlearning, than what we learn later in life.

The autoappraisers are powerful, scanning continuously, out of our conscious awareness, watching out for the themes and variations of the events that have been relevant to our survival. To use a computer metaphor, the automatic appraising mechanisms are operating on an *emotional alert database* that is written in part by our biology, through natural selection, and in part by our individual experience. (Remember that what is written by natural selection may not be triggers themselves, but preparation that allows some triggers to quickly become established in the database.)

This database is open, not closed; information gets added to it all the time (Myer, 1974). Throughout life we encounter new events that may be interpreted by automatic appraising as similar to a theme or variation stored in the database, and when that happens an emotion is triggered. Nico Frijda (1986) importantly emphasized that what I am calling the variations are not just the result of prior direct experience, but often are new stimuli we encounter that seem relevant to one of our *concerns*. Frijda emphasizes that we do not respond just to stimuli, but to stimuli that we appraise as relevant to our welfare. Remember my definition of emotion at the start of this chapter – emotions occur when we sense, rightly or wrongly, that something is happening or is about to happen that seriously affects our welfare, for better or worse. The something that is happening or about to happen may resemble a theme, it may be a variation we have learned through conditioning, or it may be something that we have not encountered before that fits one of our emotional concerns, resembling things we have learned that could affect our welfare. Consider for a moment the theme of loss of an object to which we are attached. What objects we are attached to – a hope, a desired position, a residence – is the result of our individual experience that forms our sadness set of concerns. When the autoappaisers detect a stimulus in the environment relevant to those concerns, an emotion occurs. Appraisal theorists such as Scherer propose how we determine that a new event is relevant to our concerns.

We are more likely to make a mistake, to misconstrue what is happening, when the autoappraisers are responding to a variation on one of the themes, matching something that is happening in the environment with one of our concerns. Automatic appraising does not always correctly evaluate the meaning of what is happening in our environment at any given moment. Remember, automatic appraisal is accomplished very quickly, in milliseconds, prior to our conscious awareness of what is happening. A few moments later, when we become aware of what we are feeling and how we are reacting, we could then correctly interpret the scene and realize that we are responding in an inappropriate way, but that awareness does not always change our emotional reaction.

Peter Goldie (2000) gives an example in which fear endures despite knowledge that there is no basis for being afraid. "You are on a cliff walk, and you turn towards the sea view. You believe that you are at a perfectly safe distance from the edge of the cliff (ten meters, say), and that there is no wind or slippery slope to drive you towards it. So, according to your beliefs, there is absolutely no reason to feel fear, as there is no possibility of falling. Yet you feel fear.... Even though you may be able to control your actions, managing simply to turn away from the view and proceed on your cliff walk, nevertheless you tremble, feel a damp sweat, and . . . you cannot help but feel fear: waves of fear overcome you, and these feelings are not *cognitively penetrable* as they are not affected by our persistent beliefs about the cliff – that you could not slip that far, that no one is going to push you, and so forth – in sum, that you are in no danger" (p. 76; italics added).

This example shows that knowledge or beliefs may not override the autoappraisers that generate our emotional response. Even after our emotional responses have begun and we consciously access knowledge which shows that we need not be emotional, the emotion persists. I suspect that this happens when the trigger is an evolved emotional theme or a learned trigger that is close to the theme. When the learned trigger is more distantly related to the theme, our conscious knowledge may be better able to interrupt the emotional experience. Put in other terms, if our concerns are only distantly related to a theme, we may be able to override them by choice.

There is another, more serious way in which emotions override what we know and believe. In the example of being afraid on a cliff walk, we are consciously aware that we need not be emotional, but that knowledge does no good. What I want to consider next is that emotions initially can prevent us from having access to what we know. We can be, for a time, gripped by an inappropriate emotion, directed by that emotion to interpret what is happening in a way that will fit, for a time, with the emotion we are feeling.

Once they begin, emotions change how we see the world and how we evaluate the actions of others (see Frijda et al., 2000, and Lazarus, 1991). We do not seek to challenge but to confirm why we are feeling a particular emotion. We evaluate what is happening in a way that is consistent with the emotion we are feeling, thus justifying and maintaining the emotion. This may be of great service to us, focusing our attention on what is relevant to what is at stake, guiding our thinking to what will be most useful in dealing with the problem at hand. But it can also be a problem, for when we are gripped by an emotion we discount or ignore knowledge we have that could disconfirm the emotion we are feeling, just as we ignore or discount new information coming to us from our environment that does not fit our emotion. In other words, the same mechanism that guides and focuses our attention can distort our ability to deal with new information and stored knowledge.

Jerry Fodor (1983) describes a process in which information is encapsulated, by which he means that information that might not fit with a way of interpreting the world, information the person has stored and knows, becomes inaccessible for a time. Suppose a person is furious about having been insulted in public. In that fury the insulted person will not easily be able to reconsider whether the person who made the insult actually meant it seriously, or really meant what he said as an insult. Past knowledge about that person and about the nature of insults will be only selectively available; only that part of the knowledge that supports the fury will be remembered, not that which would contradict it. If the insulting person explains or apologizes, the furious person may not immediately incorporate this information.

When we feel a strong emotion our thinking is organized to serve that emotion, to abet the actions, ideas, and plans that have been useful to us in the past. This may be useful to us, preventing us from being distracted; or it may be destructive, by not allowing us to use information that would disconfirm how we are feeling. Our attention is focused and narrowed in a way that serves the emotion we are feeling. It may help to think that for a time we are in a *refractory* state, during which our thinking does not incorporate information that does not fit, maintain, or justify the emotion we are feeling. This refractory state may be of more benefit than harm if it is brief, lasting only for a second or two. Then it focuses our attention on the problem at hand, using the most relevant knowledge that can guide our initial actions, and on preparations for further actions. However, difficulties can arise, or inappropriate emotional behavior may occur when the refractory period lasts much longer – for minutes or perhaps even hours. By keeping the emotion alive, it can bias the way we see the world and ourselves.[1]

---

[1] My thinking on this issue was sharpened by the discussion of these ideas at a meeting with the Dalai Lama about destructive emotions (Mind and Life, 2000: The Destructive Emotions, 20–24 March 2000, Dharmsala, India); see the recent book about this meeting (Goleman, 2003). I am especially grateful to Alan Wallace for the problems he raised about my earlier formulation.

With the near-miss car accident, we do not remain in a state of fear once we have avoided the other car. We realize very quickly that the danger has passed and wait for our breathing and heart rate to return to normal, which happens in five to fifteen seconds. But suppose the fear is about something that cannot be so instantly or dramatically disproven. Suppose a person is afraid that the ache he is feeling in his lower back is a symptom of liver cancer. During the refractory period he will reject contradictory information, forgetting that yesterday he helped move his friend's furniture, and that this is why his back hurts.

Our nervous system does not make it easy to change what makes us emotional, to unlearn either the connection between what Donald Hebb (1949) and Joe LeDoux (1996) called an *emotional cell assembly* and a response, or between a trigger and an emotional cell assembly. The emotional alert database is an open system, in that new variations continually get added to it, but it is not a system that allows anything to be easily removed once entered. Our emotion system was built to keep triggers in, not get them out, to mobilize our emotional responses without thought, not to allow us to interrupt them readily.

Every driver has had the experience, when sitting in the passenger seat, of having his foot involuntarily shoot out toward a nonexistent brake pedal when it seems that another car is veering toward him. Note that hitting the brake pedal is a learned response to the fear of being hit by another car. Not only is the response learned, but so also is the trigger. Cars were not part of the environment of our ancestors; a car veering toward us is not a built-in theme but a learned variation. We learn it quickly because it is very close to one of the likely fear themes – anything that moves quickly into our sight, moving toward us as if it is about to hit us.

While most of us will, when sitting in the passenger seat, involuntarily press down on a nonexistent brake pedal when we sense danger, driving instructors learn not to do so. They may learn to interrupt the response only, in which case they will still feel afraid, but they will not make the response. Or, they may learn to break the connection between the trigger – that car lurching toward them – and the cell assembly in the brain that was established for this fear trigger. (We could find out which one they do by measuring their physiology when this happens, but it doesn't really matter for my point here.) Perhaps what they do is more finely tune the connection between the trigger and the cell assembly, so that fear is aroused and the protective brake-pedal response activated only when the danger is very likely to occur. But if they have had a bad night's sleep, or are still mulling over an unfinished argument with their spouse that morning, that foot will shoot out once again, just as it would for any of us who are not driving instructors, who have not learned to interrupt this trigger. That reaction shows that the links between trigger, cellular connections, and response have not been erased, only weakened to the point where nothing happens except under unusual circumstances. It is not gone, not deleted, just weakened.

Not everything that makes us emotional is a result of conditioning, however. Frijda (1986) points out that emotions "result . . . , to a large extent, from inferred consequences or causes . . . A majority of emotional stimuli have . . . little to do with having experienced aversive or pleasurable consequences accompanying a particular stimulus. Losing one's job, receiving criticism, perceiving signs of being neglected or slighted, being praised, and seeing norm violations are all quite indirectly or remotely connected to the actual aversive or pleasurable conditions that they somehow signal and that give them emotional life" (p. 310). I will soon suggest that the more indirect and remote the connection, the easier it is to interrupt emotional behavior and weaken the connection between stimulus and cell assembly.

While emotions are most often triggered by automatic appraising mechanisms, that is not the only way in which they can begin. Let us turn now to consider eight other pathways that generate emotion. Some of them provide more opportunity to control whether or not we are going to become emotional.

Sometimes emotions begin following more *extended appraising*, in which we consider consciously what is occurring because we are not sure what it means. As we think about it we are aware of our evaluations. Then, as the situation unfolds or our understanding of it proceeds, something clicks; it fits something in our emotional alert database and the automatic appraising mechanisms take over. This more extended appraising deals with ambiguous situations, situations to which the automatic appraising mechanisms are not already tuned. Suppose you meet someone who begins to tell you about her life, and it is not clear why she is telling you, or what point she is trying to make. You think about what she is saying, trying to figure out what, if anything, it means to you. At some point you may figure it does not mean much, and your attention may wander, whereas after analyzing what she is saying, or after she says more, it may click into place that she is threatening your job, at which point the automatic appraisal mechanism takes over.

We are aware of what is going on during extended appraisal; our conscious mind runs the show. But there is a price we pay for extended appraisal – time. It is precisely those moments or minutes that the automatic appraising mechanisms save us. Often, literally by not taking extended time, our automatic appraisals can and do save us from disaster. Think of how many accidents would occur if we had to consciously think and evaluate what that car that is lurching toward us is really doing before we hit the brake and twist the steering wheel.

When emotions begin as a result of extended appraisal there is an opportunity for us to influence what transpires.[2] To do so we need to be well acquainted with our own emotional hot triggers – the specific variations on the universal themes that are most prominent in our lives for each emotion. If we know our hot triggers, then we can make a deliberate effort not to allow them to bias our interpretation of what is transpiring.

Suppose a trigger for your sadness/anguish reaction is the subtlest hint that a woman is going to abandon you because she has discovered your closely guarded secret, your learned feelings of fundamental worthlessness. Knowing this, in an extended appraisal you can guard against allowing yourself to make the judgment that you are being abandoned. It will not come easily, but with practice it may be possible to decrease the chance that you will snap into sadness/anguish when you were not really being abandoned. Extended appraisal offers your conscious mind more of a role. You have the opportunity to learn how to deliberately guard against the likelihood of misinterpreting what is happening.

We can also become emotional when remembering a past emotional scene. We may choose to remember a past emotional scene, reworking it in our mind, going over it to figure out what happened, or why it happened, or how we might have acted differently. Or the memory may not be a choice; it may be unbidden, popping into our mind. Regardless of how the memory begins, whether by choice or unbidden, the memory may include from the start not just the scene and the script of what transpired emotionally, but an emotional reaction. It may replay the emotions we felt in the original scene, or we may now feel a different emotion. For example, a person might now be disgusted with herself for having been so afraid in the original scene, feeling only the disgust and not the fear that was originally felt. It can also happen that initially we have the memory about the emotional events but do not again experience those or other emotions. Or the emotions may begin only as the scenes unfold in our mind.

We have used a memory task to produce emotions in the laboratory so we could study the expressions and physiological reactions that mark each emotion. The "we" refers to one of my longtime research collaborators, Robert Levenson, who studies the Autonomic Nervous System (ANS). We thought it would be hard for people to reexperience past emotional scenes when they knew they were being videotaped and wires had been attached

---

[2] After speaking with the Dalai Lama about what he terms "destructive emotions" and the attempts made through Buddhist practices to become free of them, I had the impression that what he and others have achieved is substituting extended for automatic appraising. He and others who have engaged in many years of practice seem to have the choice, most of the time, not to become emotional, or if emotional not to act and speak in a way that will be harmful to others. See more about this in my book *Emotions Revealed* (2003).

to different parts of their body to measure their heart rate, respiration, blood pressure, sweating, and skin temperature. It was just the opposite. Most people seem eager for an opportunity to replay and reexperience a past emotional scene. Just give them the chance to do so, and it happens almost immediately, maybe not for all emotions, but for some of them.

We asked people to remember their own personal version of one of the events that has been found to be universal for each emotion. So, for example, to call forth sadness we asked people to remember a time in their lives when someone they were attached to had died. Who had died varied from person to person; it might have been a friend, grandparent, lover, or pet. We asked them to visualize a moment when they had felt the most intense sadness and then try to experience again the emotion they had felt when the death first happened.

Almost before these short instructions were over, their ANS was changing as they reexperienced the remembered emotion. We found that the memory route did succeed in generating the physiological changes, the subjective feelings, and, in some people, even the facial expressions that characterize emotions. This should be no surprise, as everyone has had the experience of remembering an important event and feeling an emotion as a result. What was not known before our research was whether those changes that occur when emotions are remembered actually resemble the changes that occur when emotions begin by other means, and indeed they do. Memories about emotional events, those which we choose to call to mind without immediately reexperiencing the originally felt emotions, provide an opportunity to learn how to reconstrue what is happening in our lives so that we have a chance to change what is making us emotional.

Imagination is still another way in which we can bring about an emotional reaction. If we use our imaginations to create scenes that we know make us emotional, we may be able to cool off the trigger. We can, in our own minds, rehearse and try out other ways of interpreting what is occurring so that it does not fit our usual hot triggers.

So far I have described four ways in which emotions can begin: automatic appraisal, extended appraisal, memory of a past emotional event, and imagination. A fifth way is by talking about past emotional experiences. We might be telling the very person with whom we had an emotional reaction about how we felt and why we think we felt that way. Or, we may tell someone who was not there, such as a friend or a psychotherapist. Sometimes the simple act of talking about an emotion episode will cause us to reexperience the emotion all over again, just as it happens in our experiments when we ask people to try to do so (Scheff, 1979).

Reexperiencing the feelings we had in a past emotional episode can have benefits. It may give us a chance to bring matters to a different end; it may elicit support or understanding from the person with whom we are talking.

Of course, sometimes reexperiencing the emotions gets us into trouble. You might have thought you could talk dispassionately with your spouse about a misunderstanding that happened a few days earlier, only to find that you became angry again, just as angry or even angrier than you were originally. That can happen even if you had hoped it would not, for we do not have control, most of the time, over when we will become emotional.

Let us suppose you are talking to a friend about how terrible you felt when the vet told you that your dearly loved dog would not survive his illness. Telling the story causes you to reexperience and show grief, and as your friend listens, she also begins to look very sad. That is not uncommon, even though it is not your friend's dog, not your friend's loss. All of us can feel the emotions that others feel, when we feel emotions empathetically. This is a sixth way in which emotions can begin, by witnessing someone else's emotional reaction.

It need not be our friend whose misfortune sets off our empathic emotional reaction. It can be a perfect stranger, and that stranger may not even be in our presence. We see that person on the television screen, or in a movie, or read about the person in the newspaper or a book. Although there is no doubt that we can become emotional by reading about a stranger, it is amazing that something that came so late in the history of our species – written language – can generate emotions. I assume that written language is converted into sensations, pictures, sounds, smells, or even tastes, in our mind, and once this happens, these images are treated like any other event by the automatic appraisal mechanisms to arouse emotions. If we could block the production of those images, I do not think emotions would be felt, but there is no research on that.

In the vicarious pathway to emotion we witness by some means the emotional reactions of others and feel their emotions (Bandura, 1977). Our automatic appraisal system responds as if it were happening to us. It does not always happen; it will not happen if we do not care about the person, if we do not in some way identify with the stranger. And sometimes we witness someone's emotions and feel an entirely different emotion. We may be contemptuous of them for being so angry or afraid, or afraid of the anger they show, and so forth.

The symbolic pathway is when we are told directly what to be afraid of, to get angry about, to enjoy, and so forth. Most likely this instruction will have been given by a caregiver in our early life, and its impact will be strengthened when it is emotionally charged. We may also learn what to feel emotions about by observing what people who are significant in our lives become emotional about, and unwittingly adopt their emotion variations as our own.

Most of those who have written about emotions have discussed norm violations, the emotions we feel when we ourselves or someone else has violated an important social norm. We may be angry, disgusted, contemptuous, ashamed, guilty, surprised, perhaps even amused and pleased. It depends on who violated the norm and what the norm was about. Norms are, of course, not universal; they may not even be shared entirely within a national group or culture. We learn norms about what people should do early in life and throughout our life.

Here is the last way in which emotions can begin – a novel, unexpected way. Voluntarily making the facial expressions that have been found to be universal generates emotion-specific changes in the autonomic and central nervous system (Levenson, & Friesen, 1983; Levenson, Carstensen, Friesen, & Ekman, 1991; Levenson, Ekman, & Friesen, 1990; Levenson, Ekman, Heider, & Friesen, 1992). While our findings have recently been criticized by Boiten (1996), a reanalysis of our and his data has strengthened our results (Levenson & Ekman, 2002). Generating emotional experience, changing your physiology by deliberately assuming the appearance of an emotion, is probably not the most common way in which people experience emotion. But it may occur more often than we think.

I have described nine paths for accessing or turning on our emotions. The most common one is through the operation of the autoappraisers, the automatic appraising mechanisms. A second path begins in extended appraisal, which then clicks on the autoappraisers. Memory of a past emotional experience is a third path, and imagination is a fourth. Talking about a past emotional event is a fifth path. Vicarious emotional experience – witnessing another person with whom one is not directly engaged – is the sixth path. Others instructing us about what to be emotional about is the seventh path. Norm violation is the eighth path. Last is voluntarily assuming the appearance of emotion.

Elsewhere (Ekman, 2003) I have built upon these ideas to explain when we will be able to change what we become emotional about, how to accomplish such changes, and also when it will be nearly impossible to make such changes. But that is the subject for another chapter.

References

Bandura, A. (1977). *Social learning theory.* Englewood Cliffs, NJ: Prentice-Hall.

Bointen, F. (1996). Autonomic response patterns during voluntary facial action. *Psychophysiology, 33*, 123–131.

Boucher, J. D., & Brant, M. E. (1981). Judgment of emotion: American and Malay antecedents. *Journal of Cross-Cultural Psychology, 12*, 272–283.

Ekman, P. (2003). *Emotions Revealed*. New York: Time Books; London: Weidenfeld & Nicolson.

Ekman, P., & Davidson, R. J. (1993). Voluntary smiling changes regional brain activity. *Psychological Science, 4*, 342–345.

Ekman, P., & Friesen, W. V. (1975). *Unmasking the face*. Englewood Cliffs, NJ: Prentice-Hall.

Ekman, P.; Levenson, R. W.; & Friesen, W. V. (1983). Autonomic nervous system activity distinguishes between emotions. *Science, 221*, 1208–1210.

Fodor, J. (1983). *The modularity of mind: An essay on faculty psychology*. Cambridge, MA: MIT Press.

Frijda, N. H. (1986). *The emotions*. Cambridge: Cambridge University Press.

Frijda, N. H.; Manstead, A. S. R.; & Bem, S. (Eds.). (2000). *Emotions and beliefs: How feelings influence thoughts*. Cambridge: Cambridge University Press.

Goldie, P. (2000). *The emotions: A philosophical exploration*. New York: Oxford University Press.

Goleman, D. (2003). *Destructive emotions*. New York: Bantam Books.

Hebb, D. O. (1949). *The organization of behavior*. New York: Wiley.

Lazarus, R. S. (1991). *Emotion and adaptation*. New York: Oxford University Press.

LeDoux, J. (1996). *The emotional brain*. New York: Simon & Schuster.

Levenson, R. W.; Carstensen, L. L.; Friesen, W. V.; & Ekman, P. (1991). Emotion, physiology, and expression in old age. *Psychology and Aging, 6*, 28–35.

Levenson, R. W., & Ekman, P. (2002). Difficulty does not account for emotion-specific heart rate changes in the directed facial action task. *Psychophysiology, 39*, 397–405.

Levenson, R. W.; Ekman, P.; & Friesen, W. V. (1990). Voluntary facial action generates emotion-specific autonomic nervous system activity. *Psychophysiology, 27*, 363–384.

Levenson, R. W.; Ekman, P.; Heider, K.; & Friesen, W. V. (1992). Emotion and autonomic nervous system activity in the Minangkabau of West Sumatra. *Journal of Personality and Social Psychology, 62*, 972–988.

Myer, E. (1974). Behavior programs and evolutionary strategies. *American Scientist, 62*, 650–659.

Öhman, A. (2000). Fear and anxiety: Evolutionary, cognitive and clinical perspectives. In M. Lewis and J. M. Haviland-Jones (Eds.), *Handbook of emotions* (2d ed.; pp. 573–593). New York: Guilford Press.

Parkinson, B., & Manstead, A. S. R. (1992). Appraisal as a cause of emotion. In M. S. Clark (Ed.), *Emotion (Review of Personality and Social Psychology*, Vol. 13) (pp. 122–149). Newbury Park, CA: Sage.

Parkinson, B., & Manstead, A. S. R. (1993). Making sense of emotion in stories and social life. *Cognition and Emotion, 7*, 295–323.

Roseman, I. J., & Smith, C. A. (2001). Appraisal theory: Overview, assumptions, varieties, controversies. In K. R. Scherer, A. Schorr, and T. Johnstone (Eds.), *Appraisal processes in emotion: Theory, methods, research* (pp. 3–19). New York: Oxford University Press.

Scheff, T. J. (1979). *Catharsis in healing, ritual and drama*. Berkeley: University of California Press.

Scherer, K. R.; Schorr, A.; & Johnstone, T. (Eds.). (2001). *Appraisal processes in emotion: Theory, methods, research.* New York: Oxford University Press.

Tooby J., & Cosmides, L. (1990). The past explains the present: Emotional adaptations and the structure of ancestral environments. *Ethology and Sociobiology, 11,* 375–424.

9

Feelings Integrate the Central Representation of Appraisal-driven Response Organization in Emotion

Klaus R. Scherer

ABSTRACT

From antiquity, most philosophers and psychologists have implicitly assumed that the nature of an individual's emotional experience is determined by his/her subjective interpretation of the eliciting event. Appraisal theories of emotion, pioneered by Arnold and Lazarus, have made this assumption explicit and have generated empirically testable hypotheses on emotion-specific appraisal profiles and their effects on physiological responses, motor expression, and feeling states. Current appraisal theories will be critically reviewed and compared to competing theories. A number of central issues of debate will be highlighted. The research evidence in this domain will be summarized, illustrated by a number of representative experiments from the Geneva Emotion Research Group. Special emphasis will be given to models of the appraisal process that attempt to tie into current developments in cognitive science and dynamic systems modeling.

The very title of the Amsterdam Symposium, "Feelings and Emotions," implies that these two terms should not be used as synonyms: The copula suggests that they are different and distinguishable. Unfortunately, the need to define these two concepts differentially has not always been heeded by scholars in this area and much confusion has been the result. One can argue, for example, that the famous James–Cannon debate is due to James's using the term "emotion" when he probably meant "feeling" (see Scherer, 2000a, pp. 155–156). There is an unabated tendency to use these two terms interchangeably, and further misunderstanding, followed by futile debate, can be predicted. Further progress in modeling the process of emotion can be achieved only if the central concepts are clearly defined and differentiated from each other, especially when they represent different but interrelated aspects of the underlying process, as is the case with feeling and emotion.

In this chapter I will address three main topics related to this issue. First, I will briefly review the notion of a component process as the central defining characteristic of emotion and suggest considering feeling (or subjective experience) as one of these components. More precisely, I propose to view the feeling component of emotion as a monitoring system that consists of a central representation of the response organization, including the underlying cognitive processes in an emotion episode. In many ways this monitoring function makes feeling a rather special component, in that it integrates the representation of changes in the other components during the duration of an emotion episode. Second, I will review the central role of cognitive evaluation (at different levels of neural organization; see van Reekum & Scherer, 1997) of events that are pertinent for the individual's well-being in eliciting and differentiating emotional response components, including feeling. In addition to providing an overview of the central assumptions of this approach, shared by all appraisal theorists, I will focus on the component process model of emotion (Scherer, 1984, 2001a), which postulates a process of coordination or synchronization of different components, driven by the evaluation or appraisal of external or internal events. Third, I will raise the much neglected issue of how the information from the various components to be monitored is integrated into the overarching feeling component. In order to form coherent *qualities of feeling*, a variety of highly heterogeneous elements with widely varying characteristics, both with respect to the type and the dynamics of the underlying systems, need to be seamlessly fused. One particularly interesting issue in this context concerns the determinants of the intensity of subjective experience or feeling.

FEELING AS A COMPONENT OF EMOTION

Historically, most scholars of emotion have started from the assumption – explicit or implicit – that the phenomenon of emotion consists of several components, each of which fulfills a specific function in the adaptation to the situation that has triggered the emotion process (Frijda, 1986; Scherer, 1984). Table 9.1 (adapted from Scherer, 2001a) shows an attempt to list the components of emotion together with their respective functions and the organismic subsystems that subserve them.

Virtually all aspects of mental and somatic functioning are involved in this adaptive reaction, since an emergency mechanism like emotion needs to recruit, for a limited period of time, all of the resources of the organism in the service of adaptation to the consequences of an event that is appraised by the individual as highly relevant to its well-being. I have suggested that emotions are distinguished from other mental and behavioral states by a high degree of coordination or synchronization of the components that are normally more or less dissociated in serving separate functions (Scherer, 1984, 2000b). This definition also allows one to discriminate emotion from other affective states such as moods, interpersonal stances, preferences

TABLE 9.1. *Relationships between Organismic Subsystems and the Functions and Components of Emotion*

Emotion function	Organismic subsystem and major substrata	Emotion component
Evaluation of objects and events	Information processing (CNS)	Cognitive component
System regulation	Support (CNS, NES; ANS)	Neurophysiological component
Preparation and direction of action	Executive (CNS)	Motivational component
Communication of reaction and behavioral intention	Action (SNS)	Motor expression component
Monitoring of internal state and organism-environment interaction	Monitor (CNS)	Subjective feeling component

Key: CNS = central nervous system; NES = neuro-endocrine system; ANS = autonomic nervous system; SNS = somatic nervous system

or attitudes, and emotional personality dispositions for which one would expect a much lower level of synchronization (see Scherer, 2000c, for a design feature approach to classifying different types of affective states).

The feeling component has a special status in the emotion process, as it integrates and regulates the component process. If subjective experience is to serve a monitoring function, it needs to integrate *all* information about the continuous patterns of change in all other components, as well as their coherence. Thus, feeling is an extraordinarily complex conglomerate of information from very different systems.

It is generally assumed that feelings are conscious phenomena and that the only access to measuring feelings is via verbal report. Unfortunately, this widespread assumption holds only for the visible tip of a huge iceberg. I have suggested that one should conceptualize the problem as shown in Figure 9.1, using a Venn diagram in which a set of overlapping circles represent the different aspects of feeling (see Kaiser & Scherer, 1997). The first circle (A) represents the sheer reflection or representation of changes in all synchronized components in some kind of monitoring structure in the central nervous system (CNS). This structure is expected to receive massive projections from both cortical and subcortical CNS structures (including proprioceptive feedback from the periphery). The second circle (B), only partially overlapping with the first, represents that part of the integrated central representation that enters awareness and thereby becomes conscious, thus constituting the feeling qualities, the

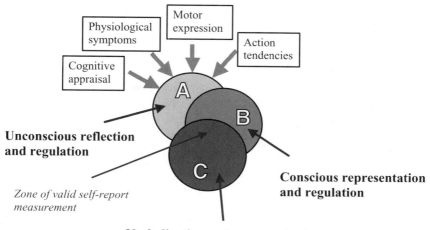

FIGURE 9.1. Venn Diagram of Three Hypothetical Types of Central Representation of Component Processes

qualia with which philosophers and phenomenologically minded psychologists have been most concerned. Thus, this circle corresponds most directly to what is generally called "feelings." The conscious part of the monitoring component feeds the process of controlled regulation, much of which is determined by self-representation and socionormative constraints. My hypothesis is that it is the degree of synchronization of the components (which might in turn be determined by the pertinence of the event as appraised by the organism) that will generate conscious experience.

So far, we have little hope of getting even close to measuring the processes represented by these two circles. All that is currently available to research scrutiny is the tip of the iceberg – the individual's verbal account of a consciously experienced feeling, represented by the third circle (C) in Figure 9.1. Drawing this circle as only partially overlapping with the circle representing conscious experience (B) is meant to suggest that the verbal account of feelings captures only part of what is consciously experienced. This selectivity can be due in part to control intentions – the individual may not want to report certain aspects of his/her innermost feelings. Most important, verbal report relies on language, and thereby on the emotion categories and other pragmatic devices available to express the *qualia* that are consciously experienced. Apart from capacity constraints (the stream of consciousness cannot be completely described by a discrete utterance), it may not be unreasonable to claim that these linguistic devices are incapable of completely capturing the incredibly rich texture of conscious experience.[1]

THE PROCESS OF APPRAISAL

While many theories of emotion focus on particular aspects of these complex processes, for example, motor expression, action tendencies, feeling states, or verbal labels (see Scherer, 2001), only *appraisal theories of emotion* explicitly include all components in the attempt to explain both the elicitation and differentiation of emotion. An appraisal view of the emotion process implies that the nature and intensity of the emotion are predominantly determined by the subjective evaluation of the meaning and consequences of an event for the individual concerned. Explicit appraisal theory started with pioneering suggestions by Arnold and Lazarus, followed by a number of psychologists who have elaborated on this notion (see Schorr, 2001, for a historical account). Most of the theorists in this tradition have postulated sets of dimensions or criteria for event evaluation, attempting to predict the typical appraisal results (in terms of configurations or profiles) that will produce certain types of emotions. Table 9.2 shows a simple example of this type of prediction, consisting of theoretically derived hypotheses on typical appraisal profiles for major emotions. Quite remarkably, the fundamental assumption, the set of criteria, and the detailed predictions show strong convergence for the different appraisal theorists (see Ellsworth & Scherer, 2003; Scherer, 1999a; Roseman & Smith, 2001). In the last two decades there has been an enormous amount of empirical research trying to test these theoretical suggestions, mostly using self-report, which generally tends to confirm many of the theoretical predictions. A comprehensive survey of the major theories, the repertoire of methods currently used to assess appraisal, the major empirical findings, and critical assessments can be found in Scherer, Schorr, and Johnstone (2001).

One of the critiques leveled against appraisal theory is that it cannot explain all instances of emotional arousal or all types of affective processes. However, appraisal theorists have asserted repeatedly, and emphatically, that appraisal theory was never intended to do this (e.g., Ellsworth, 1991). Simple preferences, moods generated by memory recall,

---

[1] There is not sufficient space to discuss the meaning of those portions of circles B and C that do not overlap with circle A and thus do not reflect any underlying component changes due to emotion elicitation. Suffice it to say that the generation of consciousness can be seen as an active, constructive process with a tendency toward the establishment of complex meaning structures, as described by the pars-pro-toto mechanism. The part of the verbal report circle (C) that does not overlap with the circle representing conscious experience (B) can be conceptualized as the surplus meaning carried by the semantic fields of emotion words and expressions that automatically produce connotations which do not necessarily correspond in toto to the nonverbal experience.

TABLE 9.2. *Predictions of Prototypical Appraisal Profiles for Four Modal Emotions*

Stimulus Evaluation Checks	Joy/ Happiness	Anger / Rage	Fear / Panic	Sadness
Novelty	high	high	high	low
Intrinsic pleasantness	high	open	low	open
Goal significance				
Outcome probability/ certainty	high	very high	high	very high
Conduciveness/ consistency	conducive	obstructive	obstructive	obstructive
Urgency	low	high	very high	low
Coping potential				
Agency/responsibility	self/other	other	other/nature	open
Control	high	high	open	very low
Power	high	high	very low	very low
Adjustment	high	high	low	medium
Compatibility with standards/value relevance/legitimacy	high	low	open	open

psychoendocrinological changes (as, for example, during the female menstrual cycle), incitements to aggression, or emotional effects of music, are all instances of affective phenomena that may well be outside of the jurisdiction of appraisal theory (although this depends partly on how appraisal is defined and delimited; see Scherer, 2001b). However, there seems to be increasing acceptance of the idea that what philosophers call the "garden variety of emotion" – that is, anger, fear, joy, sadness, jealousy, shame, guilt – are, in the large majority of cases, determined by the protagonist's subjective appraisal of the meaning of a particular event (see, e.g., Ekman, this volume).[2]

The *transactional* approach (Lazarus, 1966) proposed by appraisal theory (i.e., taking into consideration not only the characteristics of the eliciting

---

[2] Given this increasing convergence of opinion, it was surprising to hear Damasio suggest, at the Amsterdam Symposium, that emotions are elicited by "emotionally competent stimuli." While there may well be stimuli, or features thereof, that have intrinsic, evolutionarily anchored meaning and thus produce similar emotions in all humans (see Öhman, this volume), these are hardly responsible for the wide gamut of extremely differentiated emotional processes in which most people, and most behavioral scientists, are centrally interested. Lazarus's (1966) pioneering suggestion of the central importance of subjective appraisal was precisely directed against the then prevailing medical notion that there were specific stressors (which one could gloss as "stress competent stimuli" in Damasio's parlance) that would reliably produce stress. It is interesting to note how much resistance there is to replacing deterministic models of stress and emotion elicitation by transactional, psychological models.

stimulus but also characteristics of the individual) is absolutely essential in explaining the fact that the very same stimulus or event can produce very different emotions for different individuals, depending on their motivational disposition, their current needs or goals, or their perceived coping potential. For example, students will react to comparable examination results very differently, depending on their appraisal of the causes and consequences of these results (Folkman & Lazarus, 1985; Smith & Ellsworth, 1987). Similarly, missing one's baggage when arriving at an airport will provoke rather different emotional reactions, depending on the appraised consequences of having to wait for it to arrive and the perceived probability of its being lost (Scherer & Ceschi, 1997). The results of the appraisal process will determine not only the type of emotion or blend of emotions but also the intensity. It is important to note that it is *subjective* appraisal, which may differ quite markedly from objective reality, that determines the emotional response. Stable individual differences in cognitive functioning or appraisal styles may consistently affect event appraisal and the consequent emotional reactions (see van Reekum & Scherer, 1997), including appraisal biases that could be involved in the etiology of affective disturbances such as anhedonia or depression (see Kaiser & Scherer, 1997).

It should be noted that these emotion-constituent appraisal processes are strongly determined by social factors (see also the contributions by Manstead and Fischer and by Parkinson in Scherer et al., 2001). While some of the appraisal criteria (like novelty and intrinsic unpleasantness) may have an evolutionary basis and function in a universal fashion (see Öhman, this volume), most are, at least in part, heavily influenced by sociocultural factors such as norms, values, and expectations. Thus, the individuals' notions of what is relevant to their well-being, the satisfaction of their needs, and the attainment of their goals are clearly dependent on cultural models and expectations, quite apart from the effect of norms and moral prescriptions that govern the appraisal of what is fair or morally adequate. In addition to these stable, "dispositional" effects of culture on the appraisal processes of the individual, the immediate social context may play a very powerful role. Thus, the identification with a reference group or the salience of particular social rules in a particular situation may have a very powerful impact on the appraisal process (Garcia-Prieto & Scherer, in press). It can be expected that the social context in question serves like a filter for the perception and interpretation of fundamental appraisal criteria and affects the relative weighting of different criteria.

While the fundamental transactional approach is common to all appraisal theorists, there are major differences with respect to the detailed predictions on emotion differentiation (see Scherer et al., 2001, for a comprehensive overview). A central issue concerns the number and type of emotions to be explained. Whereas most appraisal theorists start from the assumption of a limited number of more or less basic emotions, I have explicitly suggested that there are as many different emotions as there are appraisal outcomes (Scherer, 1984). The basis of this claim is that it is difficult to see what evidence there is for the existence of "basic" or "fundamental" emotions other than the frequency of use (by laymen and scientists alike) of a certain number of natural language labels such as anger, fear, joy, sadness, and the like. To my knowledge, it has not been empirically demonstrated that there are coherent response types consisting of specific patterns of cognitive appraisal, central and peripheral neurophysiological activity, facial, vocal, and bodily expression, motivational action tendencies, *and* subjectively reported feelings. On the contrary, much of the literature reports failures to find "basic-emotion-specific" response patterning (Banse & Scherer, 1996; Cacioppo et al., 2000; Gosselin, Kirouac, & Doré, 1995), or even reports of dissociation between physiological and expressive reactions, on the one hand, and verbal reports of feeling, on the other (Myrtek & Brügner, 1996).

Admittedly, the existence and frequent usage of relatively equivalent emotion labels in most languages, and the coupling of some of these terms to observable behaviors (e.g., anger-attack, fear-flight), does suggest that there are recurrent prototypes of identifiable motivation-emotion-action "packages." I have called these "packages" *modal emotions* (Scherer, 1994), suggesting that they are based on prototypical and frequently occurring organism-environment-reactions such as frustration, loss, achievement, and so on. However, rather than treating these as unitary mechanisms in the form of innate neuromotor programs (Tomkins, 1962, p. 244) or preestablished neural circuits (Panksepp, 1998), I would consider these "modal" in the sense of frequently occurring combinations of appraisal configurations and loosely patterned types of multimodal response organizations that most languages denote with specific words. While the members of such a fuzzy set overlap more or less with respect to a number of appraisal and response characteristics, they can be rather different from each other. This implies, of course, that the respective feelings, as central representations of the component processes, may also vary widely.

The relative success of different theories in concretely predicting the type of response patterning for different types of emotion episodes can be compared empirically. While it is difficult to find concrete predictions of this kind for many theories of emotion, some appraisal theorists have made determined efforts to predict physiological, expressive, and motivational responses on the basis of appraisal results (e.g., Scherer, 1984; Smith, 1989). For example, my *component process model of emotion* (Scherer, 1984, 1986, 2001a) includes predictions of *componential patterning*. In what follows I will briefly describe the model, which is graphically represented in Figure 9.2.

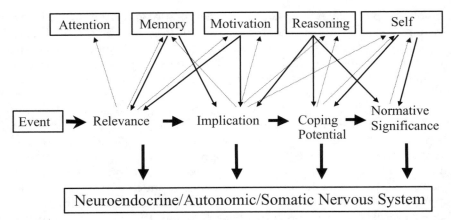

FIGURE 9.2. Central Assumptions of the Component Process Model (reproduced from Scherer, 2001a)

The major structural elements of the model are four appraisal objectives:

1. How relevant is this event for me? Does it directly affect me or my social reference group? (*Relevance*)
2. What are the implications or consequences of this event and how do these affect my well-being and my immediate or long-term goals? (*Implications*)
3. How well can I cope with or adjust to these consequences? (*Coping Potential*)
4. What is the significance of this event with respect to my self-concept and to social norms and values? (*Normative Significance*)

As Figure 9.2 shows, these four classes of assessment are expected to unfold sequentially over time. Each type of assessment draws on (i.e., receives input from) other cognitive and motivational mechanisms (such as attention, memory, motivation, reasoning, and the self-concept), which provide stored information as well as evaluation criteria that are essential for the appraisal process (this input from other systems is represented by the downward-pointing arrows in the model). For each sequential stage of assessment,[3] there are two types of output: (1) a modification of the cognitive and motivational mechanisms that have influenced the appraisal process (represented by upward-pointing dashed arrows); and (2) efferent effects on the periphery, in particular the neuroendocrine system and the autonomous and somatic nervous systems (represented by the downward-pointing boldface arrows).

---

[3] See Scherer, 1999b, 2001a, for a detailed justification of the sequence assumption.

In this component process model, emotion differentiation is predicted as the result of the net effect of all subsystem changes brought about by the outcome profile of the appraisal sequence. It should be noted that each of the major assessment classes consists of a number of constituent appraisal criteria, or, as I call them, stimulus evaluation checks (SECs; see Scherer, 2001a). Based on these assumptions I have proposed a componential patterning theory, which attempts to predict specific changes in the peripheral subsystems that are brought about by concrete patterns of SEC results. The central assumption of the componential patterning theory is that the different organismic subsystems are highly interdependent and that changes in one subsystem will tend to elicit related changes in other subsystems in a recursive fashion. The basic tenet of the theory is that the result of each consecutive check will differentially and cumulatively affect the state of all other subsystems (see Scherer, 2001a).

The predicted patterning of the component states is specific to the unique evaluation "history" of the stimulus concerned. Each SEC result and the changes produced by it "set the scene" for the effects of the following SEC in the sense of "added value" in a complex sequential interaction. The concrete predictions and their justification in the framework of a functional approach that views emotion as adaptation are described in Scherer (1987, 2001a). With my collaborators, I am engaged in a research program, briefly illustrated below, to test these predictions empirically.

With respect to vocal expression, Banse and Scherer (1996) tested the detailed predictions of the theory for the acoustic concomitants of fourteen modal emotions (Scherer, 1986) in a large study using portrayals by professional theater actors. The results showed that a rather large percentage of the hypotheses were confirmed, thus supporting the general approach and many of the specific predictions. Importantly, the empirical results also indicated which predictions might have to be modified and thus serve to focus further theoretical work on specific issues. Currently, our research group is attempting to replicate these results in a study with induced rather than portrayed emotional states (see Johnstone, van Reekum, & Scherer, 2001). The theoretical predictions for facial expressions (Scherer, 1987, 1992, expressed in the form of action unit configurations based on the Facial Action Coding System; Ekman & Friesen, 1978) were recently tested by Wehrle, Kaiser, Schmidt, and Scherer (2001). Synthesized facial expressions based on theoretical predictions derived directly from appraisal profiles were recognized with much better than chance accuracy. Furthermore, the pattern of errors was similar to synthetic expressions modeled after photographs of well-recognized posed expressions. The predictions for facial patterning have also been tested with natural facial expressions filmed in the context of experimental computer games that allow the manipulation of appraisal processes (Schmidt, Wehrle, & Kaiser, submitted; see also Kaiser & Wehrle, 2001). Again, the data generally support the predictions regarding facial patterning based on the sequential check theory of appraisal outlined above, but also indicate cases where the predictions will have to be revised.

With respect to the predictions concerning physiological patterning in the componential process model (Scherer, 1987), our research group has studied peripheral physiological responses to manipulated appraisal responses (in a computer game) for the dimensions of intrinsic pleasantness, goal/need conduciveness, and coping potential. While there are no significant effects for the intrinsic pleasantness manipulation, some of the results for the goal/need conduciveness and coping potential check manipulation are consistent with the predictions of the componential patterning model (van Reekum, Banse, Johnstone, Etter, Wehrle, & Scherer, in press). The predictions of the component process model are continuously adapted on the basis of theoretical evolution and accumulating research evidence, both from our own and other laboratories (see Johnstone, van Reekum, & Scherer, 2001; Kaiser & Wehrle, 2001; Wehrle, Kaiser, Schmidt, & Scherer, 2000; for preliminary restatements).

How well does this model fare in comparison to other theories of emotion? Since there is no agreement on the number or nature of the emotions to be studied, we face a serious dilemma: It is virtually impossible to comparatively test different theories of emotion, due to the absence of a consensually agreed-upon set of criteria as to what constitutes successful prediction. This problem is exacerbated by the confusion as to whether particular theories focus on emotions (in the component process sense described above), on feelings (in the sense of multimodal integration and central representation), or on the conditions for using certain emotion labels in communicating about emotion episodes. Given the absence of a widely accepted analytical distinction among these three alternatives, the problem is rarely acknowledged. In some cases the state of analytical distinction has even fallen behind the achievements made over a hundred years ago. For example, Wundt (1874) proposed his pioneering three-dimensional structure (pleasantness-unpleasantness, excitement-inhibition, and tension-relaxation) that we should describe "simple feelings" as compared to "complex feelings" and "emotions," and discussed the relationships among these three constructs at length.[4] Modern dimensional theorists (see review by Scherer, 2000c) have generally postulated a simple two-dimensional structure for what they indiscriminately call "emotion" or "affect."

Most appraisal theories also fail to draw such fine distinctions. They specify the antecedents for certain emotions in terms of the (generally English) emotion words that stand for what are considered basic emotions

---

[4] A translation of Wundt's discussion of the dimensions of feelings in "Outlines of Psychology" can be found on the web: http://psychclassics.yorku.ca/Wundt/Outlines/.

(see contributions in Scherer et al., 2001). In general (including in my own writing), it is not clear whether these predictions concern what is considered to be the specific multicomponent patterning for these emotions, the feeling states involved, or both. This is of little import in research paradigms that measure or manipulate appraisal results and examine the effect on peripheral response systems (e.g., physiological responses and motor expression). However, as soon as verbal report is used as a dependent variable, in which participants are asked to indicate their emotional experience (using ratings of relative intensity for different emotion labels), one measures feelings rather than emotions – in other words, only one of the components of emotion. Trying to predict such feelings exclusively on the basis of the cognitive appraisal results does not do justice to the componential model advanced above. This model suggests that feeling is a reflection or representation of *all* the component changes produced by the appraisal, not only of cognitive appraisal. As of this writing, I do not know of any study in the appraisal domain that attempts to predict feelings on the basis of both appraisal results and other peripheral responses.

I believe that if we want to progress in theoretical rigor and in our ability to interpret research results, we need to change this situation radically. To this end, I suggest that theorizing and research on appraisal-driven component patterning (*exclusive* of the feeling component), on the one hand, and subjective experience or feeling, on the other, should be decoupled. I submit that this analytical separation will allow us to study either phenomenon more conveniently and then to recombine the two and examine their interrelationships (as well as the recursive processes between them). Specifically, I see two viable approaches: (1) using appraisal theory to predict the response patterning in the physiological, expressive, and motivational components independent of preconceived emotion categories and to examine the types of clusters that can be observed; (2) explicitly studying the feeling component by trying to determine which factors predict the use of a certain label or expression to describe the subjective experience during an emotion episode.

The first research strategy is exemplified by the component process model as described. Using a bottom-up approach, it attempts to predict component process patterning (in the form of a multitude of different configurations) on the basis of manipulated or measured appraisal results. The second research strategy uses a top-down approach. It starts with the assumption that the existence (and frequent usage) of certain emotion labels in natural languages implies that there are feeling states (or, perhaps better, feeling *complexes*) that are integrated across emotion components and over the duration of an emotion episode. Concretely, the utterance "I was really angry" refers to an integrated complex of central representations of cognitive evaluations of a particular event or situation, together with self-perceived changes in physiological, expressive, and motivational response patterns. The aim would be to model, in a top-down fashion, the ingredients of this representation and the process of integration across components and time. The final section of this chapter will provide some preliminary suggestions for the development of such a research strategy.

STUDYING FEELING AS MULTIMODAL INTEGRATION OF SYNCHRONIZED CHANGES IN COMPONENT PROCESSES

Information Integration in the Cognitive Component

So far, appraisal theorists have shown little concern with the issue of how the evaluations made on different appraisal criteria are integrated. Generally, theoretical and statistical predictions are made on the basis of profile matching or regression analysis (see review in Scherer, 1999a) without much explicit discussion of the rules underlying the integration of the appraisal results. An important impetus to remedy that situation comes from a rarely cited contribution to the emotion literature by Anderson (1989), which suggests an *integration function*, strongly affected by the current goals of the organism, that transforms the subjective appraisal results into an implicit response.

I believe that the direction indicated by Anderson's work is of major importance for the further development of appraisal theory. It would be a major breakthrough to be able to predict specific integration rules for the combinations of specific appraisal criteria. For example, we found empirically (van Reekum et al., in press) that levels of coping potential have a very different effect upon psychophysiological responses as a function of goal conduciveness. This is plausible in the sense that coping ability is of less relevance when things are going according to plan. In Anderson's approach, this would be modeled by a configuration rule, predicting that the importance of one of the criteria depends on the level of another. As mentioned above, both stable sociocultural factors and the immediate social context may have a very powerful effect on the weighting of specific criteria and may, in and of themselves, bias the integration of the appraisal criteria toward configuration rules.

The attempt to model information integration in such a fashion as to allow mathematical simulation and empirical investigation will require a high degree of theoretical specification and research sophistication. Apart from precise definition and adequate scaling of the relevant variables, a specification of the transfer functions involved will be needed (see Kappas, 2001). It may also turn out that linear functions, as specified in the rules proposed by Anderson (1989), do not provide an appropriate model of the functions in all cases. I have argued (Scherer, 2000b) that we may need to adopt nonlinear dynamic system analysis as a more appropriate framework for emotion modeling than the classic assumption of linear functions dominating our statistical instrumentarium (e.g., regression analysis).

Information Integration in Other Components

How is the proprioceptive feedback information from other response components (such as vocal and facial expression or psychophysiological symptoms) integrated? While interoception – the conscious proprioceptive representation of internal physiological changes – has been studied systematically (Vaitl, 1996), this is not the case for motor expression. Much of the work on interoception has been concerned with the accuracy of the self-report of physiological parameters, such as heart-rate change, as compared to objective measurement. The question of how the changes in different physiological parameters are integrated has, to my knowledge, not been extensively studied. In facial expression, although there is little formal work, the implicit assumption seems to be that individuals are proprioceptively aware of the prototypical expression of a particular basic emotion. If that were the case, the prototype in question would effectively serve to integrate the proprioceptive feedback originating from different facial muscles. Alternatively, one could assume that the efferent motor command pattern that organizes the innervation of the different muscles involved is centrally represented in an integrated form. In order to be plausible, these assumptions would need to be backed up by the empirical observation of very consistent productions of full-blown prototypical expressions. Such evidence is currently not available from large-scale naturalistic observation. However, posing studies with actors or laypersons generally fail to find that full-blown patterns occur in a consistent fashion for the majority of the encoders. Very often only partial patterns are produced (Galati, Scherer, & Ricci-Bitti, 1997; Gosselin et al., 1995). Other evidence suggesting that the activity of specific facial muscles is available for proprioception comes from work on affect regulation. Ceschi and Scherer (2003) found that children seem to focus on specific strategic muscle groups in the suppression of laughter. Vocal expression is a special case since, in addition to proprioceptive feedback from the muscles involved in the production of vocalization, there is direct perception through bone conduction and via auditory perception. To my knowledge, there is no systematic work on the integration of these different types of information.

Given the rudimentary state of our knowledge about the integration of proprioceptive cues in the different response components of the emotion process, much basic research will be required to obtain a better understanding of the underlying feedback and integration mechanisms. As this very cursory overview suggests, the specificity of each domain may need to be taken into account. Needless to say, neuropsychological findings about the projection and organization of proprioceptive feedback in different domains could provide extremely useful additional information.

Multicomponent Integration

As suggested at the outset, the *qualia* of specific emotional experiences constituting the feeling component seem to be unitary, indivisible phenomena. Given the claim I have made that these feelings represent all of the components of the emotion process, there must be a process of integration of the representations of changes in specific components. One might assume that it is the very process of synchronization that I have proposed as the hallmark of the emotion phenomenon which elicits and organizes this process of integration. It seems safe to assume that this integration occurs outside of awareness. As Anderson suggested, "What does attain consciousness is often, perhaps always, a result integrated across different sense modalities at preconscious stages" (Anderson, 1989, p. 147).

What is the result of the integration of central representations of changes in different components? Are the widely varying types of representations exchanged into a common currency? Or does even the final product of integration still consist of a heterogeneous amalgam of representations reflecting the specific nature of the various components? Proponents of the notion of *qualia* have insisted on the uniqueness of these subjective experiences but have rarely bothered to examine the specific nature of these feelings. In this context, we encounter the same problem that was discussed for the issue of response patterning already mentioned – is there a large, potentially infinite variety of such *qualia*, or rather a limited number of well-defined categories?

As in the case of patterning, I would take a fairly extreme position. Just as I claim that there are as many varieties of response patterning as there are different profiles and histories of appraisal results, I would argue that the *qualia* reflect this variety. My justification for this claim is of a functional nature: If indeed, as I suggest, feelings represent a monitoring system that serves the functions of regulation, it seems appropriate to keep as much detailed information as possible in a central representation to fine-tune any regulation attempts. Specifically, I would expect the integration of proprioceptive information arriving from the different components to be such as to maintain maximal information in unconscious central representation in short-term memory (as symbolized by circle A in Figure 9.1). As mentioned, much of the routine regulation processes is likely to operate at this level and thus benefit from a fairly comprehensive representation of the state of the organism.

As soon as capacity limitation is imposed, further integration will be required. This is the case when part of the unconscious representation becomes conscious or is to be stored in long-term memory (e.g., passing from circle A to circle B in Figure 9.1). One could argue that it is at this point that integration along the lines of dimensions or basic emotion categories occurs. If so, many of the fundamental issues in the field – such as the universality of the affective dimensions or of the discrete emotion categories – take on renewed significance in this context, raising the question of whether these can serve as general organizing systems for the integration of information. However, I believe that even at this level more detailed information is still available in less integrated form. If that were not the case, it would be completely impossible to obtain self-report of appraisal patterns or of experienced symptoms or expression patterns. While it is true that this type of self-report is biased by social stereotypes, as claimed by critics, it is unlikely that it consists exclusively of fabrication. Unless the opposite can be empirically shown to be true, I believe it to be a more plausible claim that individuals do have conscious access to central representations of their appraisals and response patterns. How else could one, for example, consciously monitor one's facial and gestural behavior in order to suppress or modify specific expressions that may be normatively or strategically inappropriate?

A further need for integration occurs upon the passage from circle B to circle C in Figure 9.1, the verbalization of the conscious experience. Obviously, here the common path for integration must be the semantic structures available in language. However, this does not mean that the integration must occur along the lines of discrete emotion categories as represented by single words or concepts. Verbal report is not limited to simple naming; it can use complex expressions and even analogies or metaphors (Lakoff & Kövecses, 1987). Of course, if respondents are invited to respond with respect to a limited number of categories, as identified by labels or dimensions, they will integrate the information retrieved from memory in such a form as to decide among the alternatives. However, this does not constitute evidence that preformed categories or dimensions determine the integration early on in the process. For the functional reasons alluded to before, I suggest that there is only as much integration as is required to store the proprioceptive information from different components in convenient central representations, keeping a maximum of detail.

It should be noted that so far I have only discussed the issue of the *quality* of the subjective experience or feeling and the integration required. The picture changes for the issue of the perceived intensity of the experience. Here, clearly, there is a common currency, the strength or extremity of the feeling, and one can assume that the proprioceptive information from the different components must be integrated toward that common response path. For the sake of terminological clarity, I suggest that one should restrict the term "intensity" to the realm of subjective experience, that is, the feeling component, and use "amplitude" to refer to the strength, size, or extremity of the change in a particular response component.[5] The question then becomes how the respective amplitudes of the responses in the different components are integrated to yield a single subjective intensity response.

The various integration rules proposed by Anderson (1989) seem directly applicable here: Are the amplitudes averaged or multiplied, or are there specific configurational rules? The intensity of feelings (which must be differentiated from the amplitude of the emotional response, for the reasons given above) has, to date, been rarely studied (but see Ortony, Clore, & Collins, 1988; Sonnemans & Frijda, 1994), and little is known about the process of integration. In a recent study attempting to predict intensity on the basis of appraisal results only, Edwards (1998) made the interesting discovery that the best appraisal criteria predictors for maximal intensity of feeling during the emotions episode differ between modal emotions: importance of goal obstructiveness and degree of unexpectedness for fear; feeling socially superior and low self-evaluation for anger/rage; importance of long-term consequences for elation; difficulty of adjustment to loss for sadness; and extent of goal conduciveness for happiness. Edwards's study was limited to the integration of the cognitive appraisal components and did not examine the effect of the central representations of the response components on intensity judgments. Yet, his results are important in illustrating the complexity of the integration rules and their context-specificity.

In the current context, and given the state of my own theoretical reflection, I can only give some very preliminary suggestions concerning the issues that await to be elucidated. In trying to understand integration at different points in the emotion episode and the rules likely to underlie this process, the key issue concerns the *relative weight* given to the different components – appraisal, physiological responses, motor expression, motivation and action tendencies. I think that the large majority of integration rules that we are likely to find will be configurational in nature. In other words, rather than representing stringent algorithms and simple linear functions, the various response components will be weighted more or less strongly and probably in nonlinear fashion. Let me give a simple example: If I know that my emotional response is under close surveillance in a strategic encounter, my integration of proprioceptive cues is likely to give much greater weight to the expression component than in a solitary situation where I have to decide on a cause of action, in which case

[5] This mirrors an important distinction in acoustics where amplitude corresponds to the objectively measurable size of the excursions of the waveform envelope, and intensity (or loudness) to its subjectively perceived equivalent (which is subject to influence from other variables such as fundamental frequency and spectral composition). I expect that a similar situation can be found for the intensity of perceived feelings – they may only partly correlate with the averaged amplitude of the responses.

the analysis of my event evaluation (the cognitive appraisal component) may be more strongly weighted. Thus, as suggested by Anderson (1989), the integration function, particularly the weighting of different components, may be to a very large extent determined by context and goals. Of particular interest in this respect are issues of control and regulation, particularly feeling rules (Hochschild, 1983). The latter may exert strong, normative effects on the weighting of different proprioceptive cues. In this sense, feeling is not only reactive, in the sense of a passive reflection or monitoring of what is happening in the different components; it can also be proactive in defining states to be achieved, thereby eliciting processes of cognitive reevaluation and of physiological and expressive regulation.[6]

The differential weighting of different emotion components in the integration of central representations producing a subjective feeling state can also help to explain a number of thorny issues in emotion psychology. One is the problem of dissociation between reported feeling state and objectively measured parameters. For example, Myrtek and Brügner (1996) found that the reported intensity of feelings of excitement and enjoyment did not correspond to objective measures of increased heart rate. If one admits that feedback from the ANS is only one of several components that are integrated to constitute feeling, and that in the specific situation this response component was not weighted very strongly in the integration process, these results can be easily explained within a component process framework without endangering the notion of subsystem integration as a central aspect of emotion. Similarly, differential weighting of different response components in feeling integration can help to settle the conflicting claims between the proprioceptive (or facial) feedback hypothesis (claiming a positive interrelation between expression and feeling intensity) and the catharsis hypothesis (suggesting a negative relation; see Scherer, 2000a, pp. 188–190, 192). It could be that in cases in which facial feedback effects are found, greater weight is given to expressive cues in feeling integration, whereas in the case of catharsis effects these are devalued (which could be due to regulation attempts, especially in the case of anger and aggression). In any case, rather than treating the quality and intensity of feeling as a given not amenable to componential analysis, it may be useful to examine the integration processes, and particularly the weighting of different types of proprioceptive feedback that produced them.

Temporal Integration

While most emotion theorists endorse the idea of emotion as a process that changes over time, they do have a strong tendency to talk of "emotional

---

[6] A parallel can be drawn here to the distinction between push effects and pull effects in expression (Scherer, 1986).

states," a term which suggests a static, unitary phenomenon rather than a flow of continuously changing component states. However, it is the latter we need to focus on, since the nature of the coordination and interaction between the components, and the reflection of these changes in the feeling component, will change in the course of the emotion episode. Most likely, the unconscious central representations in the monitoring system (circle A in Figure 9.1) faithfully mirror the component processes in real time. If there is the beginning of a temporal integration process at this level, we have little to go on with respect to its nature. Our personal intuition shows that while we can focus on micromomentary changes of feeling, we tend to become aware of our feelings in *experiential chunks*. In other words, there is some phenomenal unity to the feeling in a particular emotion episode, possibly linked to a cause-effect chain as well as to some type of closure.

One could surmise that consciousness fades out as synchronization is reduced. Temporal integration, in the sense of experimental chunking, might thus be determined by the period during which a certain level of synchronization persists. Presumably, the same experiential chunks are available as the basis for verbalization. However, it is possible that there are additional steps of temporal integration due to the packaging by narrative or other pragmatic units in speech. Given that there is little literature on temporal integration, these ideas can provide little more than first, rough hunches about possible directions for further theorizing. It is interesting to note that similar issues of temporal integration have recently been raised in another domain – the subjective experience of pleasure and pain (see Kahneman, 2000, for similar concerns).

CONCLUSION

The crux of the problem for any analytical science is to resynthesize the elements or components of a phenomenon once they have been analytically separated in the attempt to specify the nature and importance of the determinants and their interactions. This chapter has described a potential approach to find a convincing explanation of how the analytically separable parts of the component process in emotion combine to form a phenomenologically indivisible whole – feeling. I have claimed that students of emotion have so far been deficient in accepting this challenge, mostly due to the lack of a clear analytical distinction between emotions and feelings. I submit that a component process approach to emotion can, on the one hand, help to sensitize us to the analytical distinctions to be made, providing tools for studying the elicitation and differentiation of emotional response patterning, and, on the other hand, force us to model the integration of the central representations of these responses into coherent, holistic feeling complexes.

References

Anderson, N. H. (1989). Information integration approach to emotions and their measurement. In R. Plutchik and H. Kellerman (Eds.), *Emotion: Theory, research, and experience. Vol. 4. The measurement of emotion* (pp. 133–186). New York: Academic Press.

Banse, R., & Scherer, K. R. (1996). Acoustic profiles in vocal emotion expression. *Journal of Personality and Social Psychology, 70(3)*, 614–636.

Cacioppo, J. T.; Berntson, G. G.; Larsen, J. T.; Poehlmann, K. M.; & Ito, T. A. (2000). The psychophysiology of emotion. In M. Lewis and J. M. Haviland (Eds.), *Handbook of emotions* (pp. 119–142). New York: Guilford Press.

Ceschi, G., & Scherer, K. R. (2003). Children's ability to control the facial expression of laughter and smiling: Knowledge and behavior. *Cognition and Emotion, 17*, 385–411.

Edwards, P. (1998) Étude empirique de déterminants de la différenciation des émotions et de leur intensité [An empirical study of the determinants of the differentiation and the intensity of the emotions]. Ph.D. thesis, University of Geneva. (Download available from *http://www.unige.ch/fapse/emotion/theses.html*)

Ekman, P., & Friesen, W. V. (1978). *The Facial Action Coding System: A technique for the measurement of facial movement*. Palo Alto, CA: Consulting Psychologists Press.

Ellsworth, P. C. (1991). Some implications of cognitive appraisal theories of emotion. In K. Strongman (Ed.), *International review of studies on emotion* (pp. 143–161). New York: Wiley.

Ellsworth, P. C., & Scherer, K. R. (2003). Appraisal processes in emotion. In R. J. Davidson, H. Goldsmith, and K. R. Scherer (Eds.), *Handbook of the affective sciences* (pp. 572–595). New York: Oxford University Press.

Folkman, S., & Lazarus, R. S. (1985). If it changes it must be a process: Study of emotion and coping during three stages of a college examination. *Journal of Personality and Social Psychology, 48*, 150–170.

Frijda, N. H. (1986). *The emotions*. Cambridge and New York: Cambridge University Press.

Galati, D.; Scherer, K. R.; & Ricci-Bitti, P. (1997). Voluntary facial expression of emotion: Comparing congenitally blind to normal sighted encoders. *Journal of Personality and Social Psychology, 73*, 1363–1380.

Garcia-Prieto, P., & Scherer, K. R. (in press). Connecting social identity theory and cognitive appraisal theory of emotion. In R. Brown & D. Capozza (Eds.), *Social identities: Motivational, emotional, cultural influences*. Hove, England: Psychology Press.

Gosselin, P.; Kirouac, G.; & Doré, F. Y. (1995). Components and recognition of facial expression in the communication of emotion by actors. *Journal of Personality and Social Psychology, 68(1)*, 83–96.

Hochschild, A. R. (1983). *The managed heart: The commercialization of human feeling*. Berkeley: University of California Press.

Johnstone, T.; van Reekum, C. M.; & Scherer, K. R. (2001).Vocal correlates of appraisal processes. In K. R. Scherer, A. Schorr, and T. Johnstone (Eds.), *Appraisal processes in emotion: Theory, methods, research* (pp. 271–284). New York: Oxford University Press.

Kaiser, S., & Scherer, K. R. (1997). Models of 'normal' emotions applied to facial and vocal expressions in clinical disorders. In W. F. Flack, Jr., and J. D. Laird (Eds.), *Emotions in psychopathology* (pp. 81–98). New York: Oxford University Press.

Kaiser, S., & Wehrle, T. (2001). Facial expressions as indicators of appraisal processes. In K. R. Scherer, A. Schorr, and T. Johnstone (Eds.), *Appraisal processes in emotion: Theory, methods, research* (pp. 285–300). New York: Oxford University Press.

Kahneman, D. (1999). Objective happiness. In D. Kahneman and E. Diener (Eds.), *Well being: The foundations of hedonic psychology* (pp. 3–25). New York: Russell Sage Foundation.

Kappas, A. (2001). A metaphor is a metaphor is a metaphor: Exorcising the homunculus from appraisal theory. In K. R. Scherer, A. Schorr, and T. Johnstone (Eds.), *Appraisal processes in emotion: Theory, methods, research* (pp. 157–172). New York: Oxford University Press.

Lakoff, G., & Kövecses, Z. (1987). *Women, fire, and dangerous things: What categories reveal about the mind.* Chicago: University of Chicago Press.

Lazarus, R. S. (1966). *Psychological stress and the coping process.* New York: McGraw Hill.

Myrtek, M., & Brügner, G. (1996). Perception of emotions in everyday life: Studies with patients and normals. *Biological Psychology, 42*, 147–164.

Ortony, A.; Clore, G. L.; and Collins, A. (1988). *The cognitive structure of emotions.* New York: Cambridge University Press.

Panksepp, J. (1998). *Affective neuroscience: The foundations of human and animal emotions.* New York: Oxford University Press.

Roseman, I., & Smith, C. (2001). Appraisal theory: Overview, assumptions, varieties, controversies. In K. R. Scherer, A. Schorr, and T. Johnstone (Eds.), *Appraisal processes in emotion: Theory, methods, research* (pp. 3–19). New York: Oxford University Press.

Scherer, K. R. (1984). On the nature and function of emotion: A component process approach. In K. R. Scherer and P. Ekman (Eds.), *Approaches to emotion* (pp. 293–317). Hillsdale, NJ: Erlbaum.

Scherer, K. R. (1986). Vocal affect expression: A review and a model for future research. *Psychological Bulletin, 99*, 143–165.

Scherer, K. R. (1987). Toward a dynamic theory of emotion: The component process model of affective states. *Geneva Studies in Emotion and Communication, 1(1)*, 1–65. (Download available from *http://www.unige.ch/fapse/emotion/genstudies/genstudies.html*)

Scherer, K. R. (1992). What does facial expression express? In K. Strongman (Ed.), *International Review of Studies on Emotion* (Vol. 2, pp. 139–165). Chichester: Wiley.

Scherer, K. R. (1994). Toward a concept of "modal emotions." In P. Ekman and R. J. Davidson (Eds.), *The nature of emotion: Fundamental questions* (pp. 25–31). New York/Oxford: Oxford University Press.

Scherer, K. R. (1999a). Appraisal theories. In T. Dalgleish and M. Power (Eds.), *Handbook of cognition and emotion* (pp. 637–663). Chichester: Wiley.

Scherer, K. R. (1999b). On the sequential nature of appraisal processes: Indirect evidence from a recognition task. *Cognition and Emotion, 13(6)*, 763–793.

Scherer, K. R. (2000a) Emotion. In M. Hewstone and W. Stroebe (Eds.), *Introduction to social psychology: A European perspective* (3d ed., pp. 151–191). Oxford: Blackwell.

Scherer, K. R. (2000b). Emotions as episodes of subsystem synchronization driven by nonlinear appraisal processes. In M. D. Lewis and I. Granic (Eds.), *Emotion, development, and self-organization: Dynamic systems approaches to emotional development* (pp. 70–99). New York/Cambridge: Cambridge University Press.

Scherer, K. R. (2000c). Psychological models of emotion. In J. Borod (Ed.), *The neuropsychology of emotion* (pp. 137–162). Oxford/New York: Oxford University Press.

Scherer, K. R. (2001a). Appraisal considered as a process of multi-level sequential checking. In K. R. Scherer, A. Schorr, and T. Johnstone (Eds.), *Appraisal processes in emotion: Theory, methods, research* (pp. 92–120). New York: Oxford University Press.

Scherer, K. R. (2001b). The nature and study of appraisal: A review of the issues. In K. R. Scherer, A. Schorr, and T. Johnstone (Eds.), *Appraisal processes in emotion: Theory, methods, research* (pp. 369–391). New York and Oxford: Oxford University Press.

Scherer, K. R. (2001). Emotion, the psychological structure of. In N. J. Smelser & P. B. Baltes (Eds.), *International encyclopedia of the social and behavioral sciences.* Oxford: Pergamon.

Scherer, K. R., & Ceschi, G. (1997). Lost luggage emotion: A field study of emotion-antecedent appraisal. *Motivation and Emotion, 21,* 211–235.

Scherer, K. R.; Schorr, A.; & Johnstone, T. (Eds.). *Appraisal processes in emotion: Theory, methods, research.* New York: Oxford University Press.

Schorr, A. (2001). Appraisal – the evolution of an idea. In K. R. Scherer, A. Schorr, and T. Johnstone (Eds.), *Appraisal processes in emotion: Theory, methods, research* (pp. 20–34). New York: Oxford University Press.

Schmidt, S.; Wehrle, T.; & Kaiser, S. (Submitted). Appraisal profiles of positive and negative emotions in an interactive computer game. Manuscript.

Smith, C. A. (1989). Dimensions of appraisal and physiological response in emotion. *Journal of Personality and Social Psychology, 56,* 339–353.

Smith, C. A., & Ellsworth, P. C. (1987). Patterns of appraisal and emotion related to taking an exam. *Journal of Personality and Social Psychology, 52,* 475–488.

Sonnemans, J., & Frijda, N. H. (1994). The structure of subjective emotional intensity. *Cognition and Emotion, 8(4),* 329–350.

Tomkins, S. S. (1962). *Affect, imagery, consciousness: Vol. 1. The positive affects.* New York: Springer.

Vaitl, D. (1996). Interoception. *Biological Psychology, 42(1–2),* 1–27.

van Reekum, C.; Banse, R.; Johnstone, T.; Etter, A.; Wehrle, T.; & Scherer, K. R. (in press). Psychophysiological responses to emotion-antecedent appraisal in a computer game. *Cognition and Emotion.*

van Reekum, C. M., & Scherer, K. R. (1997). Levels of processing for emotion-antecedent appraisal. In G. Matthews (Ed.), *Cognitive science perspectives on personality and emotion* (pp. 259–300). Amsterdam: Elsevier Science.

Wehrle, T.; Kaiser, S.; Schmidt, S.; & Scherer, K. R. (2000). Studying dynamic models of facial expression of emotion using synthetic animated faces. *Journal of Personality and Social Psychology, 78(1),* 105–119.

Wundt, W. (1874). *Grundzüge der physiologischen Psychologie* [Fundamentals of physiological psychology]. Leipzig: Engelmann.

10

Emotions and Action

Nico H. Frijda

ABSTRACT

This chapter discusses the relationships between emotion and action. Emotion, by its very nature, is change in action readiness to maintain or change one's relationship to an object or event. Motivation, or motivational change, is one of the key aspects of emotions.

Even so, action follows only under certain conditions, including the presence and availability of an action repertoire, an equilibrium of the costs and benefits of action, and the presence of resources and motivation to consider the costs and benefits.

There are trade-offs between selection from the repertoire and the cost-benefit aspects. The repertoire usually includes low-effort actions that considerably expand the influence of emotions on action.

Obviously, emotions have very much to do with action. One would say that emotions exist for the sake of action, for dealing with the environment. Yet, the relationship between emotion and action is variable. There is much emotion without action; there is also much action without obvious emotion. How to understand the relationships?

In this chapter, I shall do two things. First, I argue that motivation for action – changes in motivation, and motivational processes – is part and parcel of what we mean by emotions. Little theory exists, however, to account for it. Second, I explore the conditions under which those motivations do and do not actually lead to action.

EMOTIONS CLOSELY LINKED TO ACTION

The answer to the question of how emotions relate to action depends on what one takes emotions to be, on how one views the central processes involved. Different phenomena can be singled out as pointing to those. Inner feeling has, at a certain time, been considered the central aspect of emotions; and silent inner feeling, loving and suffering and ineffable experience, to be paradigmatic. Emotions have also been seen as first and foremost some sort of judgments. They have been seen primarily as states of autonomic arousal – high heart rate or stomach cramp. However, I want to focus on the role and place of motivation in emotion that readies the individual for action. This would bring emotion and action closely together.

There is good reason to do so. Motivation for action is central among the emotional phenomena. The phenomena of passion are more paradigmatic for emotions than are silent feelings, judgments, or states of arousal. I mean "passion" here in the romantic sense, when a tempest of feeling bursts out in action and breaks through barriers of propriety and self-regard. Emotions in which this is the case may not be frequent, but they are paradigmatic, in that they show that which is in emotions to the full.

Motivation in this sense was the dominant aspect of emotions for MacDougall, or Tomkins, as it is for Izard. Yet it has faded from view in modern psychology, neuropsychology included. Why this should be so I am at a loss to explain. Perhaps it was because the frightened white rat had become paradigmatic for emotion, or the greed for honey of other animals with very little brain. Or perhaps it was because these phenomena are not properly cognitive. Or perhaps it was because of that other twentieth-century obsession with behavior, defined in terms of sequences of movements leading to that mystery element called reinforcement.

Passions are paradigmatic for emotions, not because they exemplify behavior in that latter dried-up sense, but because they exemplify *action*: behavior that not only goes, but goes *somewhere*. Passions blatantly exemplify motivation. A passion *wants* something, it is driven toward something or away from it or would want something if it could. Emotions are closely and intimately related to action by way of their nature as motivational states.

MOTIVATION

Why give motivation such a central place? It is to account for two distinct and major sets of phenomena in emotion that are the two traditional hallmarks of motivation: the phenomena of intent and of energizing of behavior. "Intent" refers to the phenomena of functional equivalence of behaviors, their sharing of a common end state. Biting, hitting, shouting, and insulting in an agonistic encounter all serve to hurt or intimidate an opponent. "Energizing" refers to the feature that behavior does occur, even if it demands effort and other costs, that it seeks to continue in spite of interruptions and obstacles, and that resources are marshaled to accomplish all this. This in turn implies that the subject cares about the end state, and that the action has priority over other goals, the feature that I have called the control precedence of emotions (Frijda, 1986).

The play of motivation is manifest in the fine fiber of emotional behavior; it is what sets emotional action apart from deliberate or habitual action. That play appears in particular in the prosody of behavior, as Lambie and Marcel (2002) call the temporal aspects of behavior and thought. It is what makes movements expressive and what gives dancing, of whatever kind, its emotional charge. Prosody includes differences in speed, in changes in speed, in the forms of change such as the steepness or gradual growth and decay, and in the precision of actions. It also includes differences in the fullness of behavior: one can grasp with one's hand and arm, or also with one's shoulder and upper body, or also with locomotion – all of which differentiate between taking, grasping, and grabbing. Prosody is an almost uncharted domain of phenomena. However, it is examined in and clearly illustrated by respiration. Respiratory patterns vary in many regards: not merely in amplitude and frequency, but also in the amplitude/frequency relationship, in the smoothness or angularity of inspiration/expiration transitions, in the straightness or curvedness of the individual inspirations and expirations, all of which to a large extent are independent dimensions of variation (Boiten, 1993a, 1993b).

Prosody is an aspect not only of movement but also of speech and the flow of thoughts over time; thoughts may come deliberately, or chase one another, none of them coming to completion. Prosody of movements and thought manifests, it would seem, the structure of motivational states. It suggests continuous underlying changes in activation, but also of the degree of focus of that activation as opposed to its more diffuse or global nature, and it suggests the balance between activation and restraint or of tension and countertension (Kreitler & Kreitler, 1972), of letting go and holding back, of the strength of impulsions, inhibitions, and control.

The other aspect of motivation, intent, is manifest in behavioral flexibility and variability. The variations share an outcome, namely particular relational changes such as approach to enhance contact, or approach to process information, or approach to harm, or increasing distance from a source of danger. Flexibility and variation of this sort occur even at low and primitive levels of emotional action. Few emotional actions, at least in mammals, are truly fixed action patterns. Startle may be the only one. Flight is away from a source of danger, whatever the forms of the movements, and with the variation in muscular coordinations that varying circumstances require. Even the reflex-like defensive actions of a newborn kitten, its hissing and extending of claws, are directed toward the source of disturbance. Like grasping, such motor performances can be explained only by preafference, and thus from some sort of goal (Thelen, 1995). The degree to which emotional actions are flexible over phylogeny, and thus appear guided by intent, remains to be examined, but it should be examined. Evolutionary psychologists talk too easily about emotions as patterns of stimulus-elicited behaviors (e.g., Cosmides & Tooby, 2000), without wondering about the mechanisms these actions might presuppose.

One should not underestimate how much in emotion is motivational and involves action readiness. Motivational states include not only those of the evidently striving emotions like fear and anger. Emotions of desire, of course, also exist. And there are many motivational states that do not strike the eyes with conspicuous movements. Interest and curiosity involve striving for cognitive assimilation and mental possession. Sadness involves the motivational state of loss of motivation, which itself may be a motivation for recuperation from pain, perhaps going back on a neural ventrolateral periaquaductal gray disposition (Tucker, Derryberry, & Luu, 2000). As Tan (1999) has emphasized, there are many tonic emotions that comprise tonic motivational states for establishing and retaining a particular relationship for an indefinite duration. They include emotions such as admiration, fascination, suspense, being moved, love in the less sexual sense. These all strive for something, even if that striving only consists of watching and absorbing, of being in communion with, of being near the object. Many of the aesthetic emotions are such tonic emotions. Their aims may go further than absorbing the object, or striving to lose oneself and to fuse with the object. They may extend toward the action tendency of joy, characterized by Fredrickson (2001) as the action tendency to broaden and build, and which includes that readiness to embrace the world called enthusiasm. I remember when I was eighteen years old, after hearing Stravinsky's *Sacre du Printemps* for the first time, I applauded until my fingers hurt, and I left the Concertgebouw floating on the decision to become a good person; I kept that up for two days.

The motivational aspect is often evident in emotional experience, in feeling. Phenomenologically, emotional feeling is to a very large extent awareness, not of the body, but of the body striving, and not merely of the body striving, but of the body striving in the world (Lambie & Marcel, 2002). Emotional experience is, to a large extent, experienced action tendency or experienced state of action readiness. Feelings of anger are not feelings of fists clenched, but of the embodied desire to silence by force a hateful opponent.

Of course, everybody knows that motivation is a major aspect of emotions. We seek pleasure and avoid pain or other occasions for unpleasant emotions. But what I emphasize is that motivation shapes the fine grain of emotions: how they feel, what states of readiness they harbor, what behavior follows, if any, and what the autonomic changes are.

TASKS FOR THEORY

The motivational phenomena discussed set high demands on psychological and neurophysiological theories of emotion. One has to assume processes that make continuously updated projections in time toward coming states, and in space toward objects outside the organism. One has also to account for motivations implying that organisms not only fill deficits (as with hunger and thirst) but also harbor motivations to find, maintain, and stabilize relationships, and to more or less spontaneously explore their surroundings. What processes could account for that? Theories, moreover, have to incorporate low-level intention-like processes of low cognitive articulation, but intention-like processes oriented toward the future nonetheless. Such processes have to be assumed for understanding elementary motor acts such as object grasping by infants as well for understanding open acts like "running away from." Developing theory for these latter motivations is largely a task for the future; but it is a prime task.

There does exist some motivational theory that might do the trick, however, even if it has not been elaborated very much within the context of emotional action. The necessary basic mechanisms are described by Stellar (1977), Gallistel (1980), and Mook (1996). A number of relevant parameters have been studied by Brehm (Brehm & Self, 1989), and there are onsets of neuropsychological theory by Freeman (2000). These theoretical endeavors describe motivational states generated by organismic states, by stimuli, and by situation-setpoint discrepancies; in emotion theory, the outcome of appraisal processes largely fulfills this role. The motivational states embody elementary forms of foresight, in that they implicitly point to a state-to-be; the mechanisms of such foresight are known from the processes of preafference and in the efferent copy mechanisms that match the state of execution of an action with its prospected end state.

The motivational states potentiate relevant action dispositions, either because a link between the two was wired in, or by previous experience, or perhaps by some "insight" into what a to-be-executed action can achieve. They also potentiate the energetic mechanisms. Actual actions are selected from among the potentiated dispositions by additional potentiation from contextual or other cues; this is the dual potentiation model of Stellar (1977). Different action systems respond to different neurohumoral potentiating mechanisms, and to the neural circuits that "organize" the various action repertoires, as discussed in this symposium by Berridge and Panksepp. For a fuller understanding of emotional motivation, it would be worthwhile to investigate the phylogenetic development of flexibility in emotional behavior programs, how it grew out of fixed action patterns, if ever they existed, and where it came from. What we have now is still rudimentary. It is a science of emotion still in the making.

EMOTION, MOTIVATION, AND ACTION

The close relationship between emotions and action readiness presents a paradox. The link between emotion and action is intimate; yet it is weak.

Anger has intimate links to aggression, but few angers actually go that far (Averill, 1983). Sadness induces apathy and crying, but more often than not remains silent and leads merely to a stare. Passions as I sketched them are rare.

The paradox is not very profound. Emotions involve motivations, and links between motivation and action always are both intimate and loose. Many determinants intervene; this is the core assumption of the dual model of motivation just hinted at. But there is an additional link, inside emotions so to speak. Emotions themselves consist of two separate processes: the changes in motivation and the appraisal processes that trigger them, and that Scherer (this volume) has discussed. Note that I use the word "appraisal," as Scherer does, for all processes, automatic or cognitive, that provide objects and events with emotional value or meaning. The processes causing motivational change are sensitive to the outcomes of the appraisal processes; different appraisals tend to play on different sensitivities, and thus on different modes of action readiness (Frijda & Zeelenberg, 2001). This latter link, too, is intimate, and at the same time not strict. It remains a link, and one that can be broken, as Berridge (1999, this volume) has shown, when one of the two processes is silenced by biochemical means.

The link can be broken by other means, too. The outcomes of the appraisal processes may not be heard by the motivational dispositions. This occurs, for instance, in numbing during or after a traumatic event, or under torture when the victim is writhing and moaning but affective experience is absent, the person seeming to see him- or herself from a distance. More frequent are the situations in which the emotional meaning of an event is fully understood but does not obtain emotional reality because of being in the wrong, nonschematic format, as is the case with much verbal information on health and environmental dangers.

The second link, that between motivation and action, is probably the more vulnerable one. There are many reasons for not acting, even when under the sway of emotional motivation. "Between dream and deed are laws, and practical objections," as the Belgian poet Elsschot said. The law and practical objections exemplify the two major conditions for action, even when there is a motivation to act: that an appropriate action repertoire be available, and that it be acceptable. A third determinant is the strength of the emotion, or the urgency or importance of the issue at hand. A fourth is the social eye: social disapproval or support.

ACCEPTABILITY

I begin with the acceptability of actions. The Theory of Reasoned Action (Ajzen, 1989) has stressed its importance in planned behavior, but it plays a role in emotional action as well. Unacceptable actions are suppressed or toned down, or an alternative is sought.

Whether or not an emotion leads to action is influenced by emotion regulation or control, which itself is called forth by the consequences that action may entail. That emotion control intervenes between emotion and action is obvious; still, several points are worth emphasizing. First, emotion regulation results not only from sociocultural norms. There are more grounds for controlling one's emotions. I will come back to them. Second, emotion regulation is itself an emotional matter. Regulation, too, primarily results from emotional motivations. Norm conformity and fear of social censure are emotional matters, but so are other sources of regulation, such as social regard and empathy. Equally emotional, in the end, is emotion control that serves to improve the effectiveness of one's actions. If one wants really to hit and hurt one's adversary, one had better control one's impulse, aim carefully, and when the moment is precisely right – and be sure that it is worth the trouble.

That regulation comes from so many sources is because emotions do not occur in a void. Emotions arise when events impinge on one or several of a person's concerns; but people have many concerns, and emotional actions may have consequences for some of those other concerns. What you gain by your fearful flight you may lose in self-respect.

Emotions are always the outcome of a balance of multiple appraisals, multiple meanings, and relevance to multiple concerns. That emotion follows which stands out most in the balance of influences in appraisal-concern-action readiness relationships. Action depends on settling at a balance within the current perspective on that network of concerns. Action is the result of the cost-benefit balance over the consequences of the action for the total set of the individual's concerns – or, rather, that part of the set that enters consideration. The total set of concerns includes sensitivity to social censure and other forms of punishment, but also the concerns involved in empathy and sympathy, in the pleasures of social harmony, and in the advantages of cooperation. In angry aggression, one may neutralize a competitor at great cost to social harmony and friendship, and even at the cost of missing the gain that the antagonism was about, as DeWaal (DeWaal & Aureli, 1997) described with respect to anger control in primates. It probably does not need emphasizing that moderation by empathy and sympathy needs no social norms: It is within the purview of some animals, as DeWaal (1996, this volume) has been arguing, and it is within the purview of babies, as Draghi-Lorenz (2001) has shown.

Relevance of consequences for other concerns may also facilitate, rather than inhibit, action. Anger may not achieve the desired effects but still yield gains in social prestige and sense of self-worth. Taking revenge may not result in undoing the suffered harm, but it may restore a felt balance of power, social regard, and self-esteem or sense of identity (Frijda, 1994).

Acceptability probably represents some balance between the harms brought by doing and the harms brought by not doing. It will depend on the urgency or importance of the aims at hand. It will be influenced by the attention to the various consequences, their degree of vivacity in imagination, the biasing of attention and strength in favor of the current interaction, and the like. The dynamics of emotion regulation are worth extensive examination.

In balancing costs and benefits, "virtual emotions," that is, anticipated emotions, play the key role. One not only abstains from hurting someone else because of actual empathic distress or guilt feeling, but because empathic distress and guilt feeling be forthcoming if one did hurt. Elster (1999) has discussed that one of the major ways in which emotions can influence action, besides motivating it directly, is when action results from anticipating future emotions. Many social emotions, such as shame, guilt, and jealousy, function primarily in this way. We behave properly and prudently in order not to feel shame or guilt later. We often abstain from marital infidelity to forestall the confusions of jealous quarrels and the empathic distress from the distress of our spouses. Similarly for regret, anger, and vengefulness, for which Frank (1989) has argued the issue.

AVAILABILITY

The other main factor determining that action follows emotion is whether or not some meaningful action is available. There may or may not be some action in one's repertoire to deal with the emotional contingency at hand, and the action may or may not be available in the wider sense of appearing worth the effort and requiring no more than the available effort resources.

One can only act when, in some sense at least, one knows what to do and is able to do it. There must be some relevant action in the repertoire. What is "relevant" is a large and open issue, but, I assume, the inclination to act in response to emotional motivation at least to some extent follows one's expectations of success and the availability of the necessary resources for acting, in technical and social regards and with respect to resources of energy. Probably, expected efficacy of action entertains some relationship to the amount of effort one is willing to invest. In any case, what makes actions that one knows of, or has the ability to perform, "available" and actually part of what one does, appears to me a complex domain that goes far beyond what I am capable of discussing, here or elsewhere. Here, I just mention that having actions in one's repertoire partakes of determining whether emotions lead to action, and I want to mention a few aspects that appear to be of interest for understanding the emotion–action relationship.

One involves the indications for supposing that the link between motivation and the availability of actions is to some degree bidirectional. If there seems to be nothing one can do in a given emotional contingency, emotion tends to change – from fear or anger to despair, for instance. Not seeing the possibility for meaningful action can deeply affect emotional motivation. Not seeing any way out of danger may lead to panic, or to a despair that grows into apathy (Seligman, 1975; Weiss, Glazer, & Poherecky, 1976). Anger that finds no meaningful outlet may lead to harming oneself; one feels one is suffocating. Revenge almost by definition commands only ineffective actions, which may be one of the sources of the cruelty it often instigates.

By contrast, if actions are readily available, motivation may be enhanced, say, from irritation to outright rage. In the appraisal literature, such foresight of what one can and cannot do goes by the name of appraised controllability or coping potential. Coping potential as appraised influences one's emotion (e.g., Roseman, 2001; Scherer, 1999). Instrumental aggression often grows into anger, and having weapons around lowers the anger threshold (Berkowitz & LePage, 1967). Homicide rates are highest in countries where weapons are easily available and their use is well-regarded, as in the United States and the Balkans, and this probably reflects anger intensity as much as merely the scope of aggression. Desire for revenge appears to be stronger when there are socially approved procedures for effecting it (Elster, 1990; Frijda, 1994). Vehement grief may result in impassivity, since no movement, or even wailing, is adequate to the event, as the famous Psammenitus story from Herodotus suggests.

People's repertoire of actions that are relevant to emotional contingencies includes actions that are more inconspicuous than distinctly instrumental activities, and yet are of considerable social importance. There do exist several kinds of low-risk, low-effort actions that are generally available when more demanding ones are not. They may be easily overlooked as actions. One kind includes the involuntary, primitive "expressive" actions such as crying, kicking, shouting, and shooting, kissing and touching, facial expressions, clamming up, and running away. They are ineffective and inappropriate in many emotional confrontations, but even then hard to restrain. They are often insensitive to considerations of ineffectiveness, perhaps because they are automatically linked to emotional motivations, but in part also because they satisfy such motivations: after all, a loud insult does match the efferent copy of hitting the opponent, and a stolen kiss is still a kiss.

Other low-risk, low-effort actions consist of approving or encouraging the actions of others who appear to command more risky and effortful means. Here, of course, is a further way in which emotions influence action, albeit the actions of other people, but that satisfy one's motivations. One votes for budgets that allow for violent actions and one cheers those who ordered them. I stress these types of actions because they form one of the points of entry of sociopolitical context into the emotion–action relationship.

However, the repertoire of simple actions that directly satisfies the aims of action readiness is still small and usually does not fulfill its purpose. Emotional problems tend to be too complex and persistent for that. Most offenses do not yield to angry shouting, and most dangers cannot be escaped from by running away. Emotional motivations usually require that goals be established to devise, plan, and execute corresponding actions.

Emotional goals involve a transformation of the action tendencies that generate them. Motivation is lifted to another level. The push of desire or discomfort is complemented by the pull of the anticipated desired situation. The aims of action tendency remain in force, but the dynamics come from the goal, that is, from the anticipated final state.

IMPORTANCE

But goal formation takes time, effort, invention, and overcoming practical obstacles. The urgency and importance of the emotion must be worth the effort; otherwise the emotion fades after a growl and a feeling. Whether or not it is worth the effort is not a simple matter; of course, the conditions will be different for goals with different scope.

One of the major conditions for the formation of an emotional goal is, I think, when the emotional situation urgently calls for immediate action – as when one is under physical threat, or faced with an opportunity that will rapidly pass by. More interesting and consequential is the felt importance of the event; felt importance is a major emotional dimension. An event is felt as important when it affects one's concerns to a serious degree (Sonnemans & Frijda, 1995), and this is the case when it affects beliefs upon which one's daily decisions rest, one's expectations of what will happen next in the course of life, and one's interactions with other people.

One of the conditions under which this occurs is when one's sense of self is affected: by humiliation, trauma, or shattering of beliefs. The sense of self represents the conception of what counts in how one views oneself, and what counts in guiding one's decisions. It forms the basis of evaluating events and how one could or should respond to them. Persistent emotional goals, and persistent readiness to do something about them, may indeed result from involvement of the self. Hatreds spring from wounded self-regard. Desire for revenge is typical for motivating complex goals, the execution of which may stretch over years, for harms that are, or are felt as, enduring and, in particular, involve one's self-esteem (Frijda, 1996).

One's sense of self is part of what Rimé calls one's "symbolic universe" (Rimé, Phillipot, Boca, & Mesquita, 1992; Corsini & Rimé, 2001). The symbolic universe refers to the sum total of principles that guide one's expectations of how the world is and should be, such as the belief in a just world and the belief that people respond comprehensibly and coherently to what one does. It shapes one's selection and judgments of one's actions and the judgment of those of others. Events that shatter the symbolic universe tend to produce strong emotions, as Corsini found, and presumably make action more likely.

Events relevant to one's symbolic universe include those which are relevant to one's major values and ideology. Emotions aroused by offense to values and ideologies would seem to lead more readily to forming emotional goals for action. The power of ideology to lead to emotional action is, of course, remarkable. Usually peaceful people may spit from rage when their church or everyday morals are at stake. People come to blows when their ideologies are disagreed with, even if others merely disbelieve in one's god, or disagree with that god's presumed proscriptions. Ideologies have to be defended or maintained to a degree that personal well-being has not. One evidently just cannot afford to have someone walk over one's ideological principles. Racist ideology, or the ideology of ethnic particularity, is of course a notorious example of how intense emotions, evoked by events that do not touch immediately on personal well-being, can be, and how common can be the transition into action of those emotions.

This hypothesis of a relationship between the symbolic universe and emotional goals is supported by the nature of moral emotions. By "moral emotions" I do not primarily understand shame and guilt, but all emotions driven by events deemed relevant to moral values. There is moral joy when one sees the tyrant perish; there is moral indignation when someone offends truth, or friendship, or humanity. People are willing to die for defending such principles. Why? In part, I think, because the harmfulness of the relevant events is a truth, and not due to a personal vulnerability or interest. In part it is because, as I said, one's symbolic universe and one's conception of oneself are involved. One cannot afford not to take the emotional impact of the event seriously. As people who tried to save Jews or Tutsis from destruction expressed it: "I could not not have done it"; "I could not have looked myself in the face any longer if I had not answered that which came my way" (e.g., in Block & Drucker, 1992).

Why is relevance to ideology, morality, and the symbolic universe so emotionally powerful? There are at least two reasons. One is that the guidelines of one's conduct and judgment are threatened when ideology, moral views, and the symbolic universe are upset. Another is the social support implied by these various beliefs. One million Mexicans can't be wrong (I refer to a line in a Hitchcock movie), and one can hardly afford to be wrong in front of them. One tends to want to be sure to be right, and one will be supported and acclaimed when right. The impact of ideology, morality, and the symbolic universe on emotion strength and inclinations for action deserves explicit elaboration in any analyses of emotional appraisal.

THE SOCIAL EYE

One of the striking things about the factors influencing the emotion–action relationship is the considerable degree to which all these factors – availability, acceptability, importance – are susceptible to social influence. Whether or not an action appears acceptable depends in part on social norms, and on the model provided by others who do what they do. Whether or not an action is available also depends on the display of those actions by social models. Both also depend on social support for the actions as, for instance, in the case of the low-risk, low-effort actions of applauding actions by others and voting for them.

Whether or not an issue is appraised as important strongly depends on the beliefs that shape appraisal. The nature and strength of many beliefs depend on information that is socially distributed and approved. Who in the United States could doubt that the Iraqis, after invading Kuwait, had abducted Kuwaiti infants from the nurseries? Of course, political propaganda has precisely the purpose of influencing beliefs as well as arousing emotions to obtain public support for political actions – that low-risk, low-effort kind of action mentioned – and perhaps participation in those actions.

The role of social influences, normative or otherwise, is particularly potent in determining emotional action because so much of that action is public action taking place in a social context, under the direct eye of others, and under the direct sway of norms of the moment. The norms may go with or against the actions that one's emotional action readiness calls for, and the social eye thus may favor or block them. In other words, the social environment is often decisive for the occurrence of action, whether in an emotional or instrumental context. People may consider actions to be acceptable from sheer habit of the group, or under group pressure, or for the emotional reasons of group belongingness and group loyalty, as well as from the emotional contagion that a social environment may produce. The literature on violence perpetrated by "ordinary people" provides ample examples (Browning, 1993). By inference, it is a factor of major importance for transforming emotional readiness into action.

Social influence may enhance the acceptability of actions in still another way: by way of the emotions contingent upon the social relationships at hand. These latter emotions – respect, consideration, distrust – modify norms of what is or is not acceptable with regard to these particular targets. Social relationships may redefine these targets and thereby redefine the norms. An example is evident in the key role played by the emotion of contempt in violence, and notably violence toward members of discriminated against social groups.

Contempt, like any other emotion, can be defined by a specific appraisal and a particular action tendency; I follow William Miller (1993) in its definition. Contempt consists of the appraisal of a person as being of such low value as to be disqualified for entering into social interaction as an equal to oneself, while at the same time perceiving that person's presumption to be an equal. It further consists of the action tendency of putting or keeping that person in his/her place, as one of lower value. There is a variant of contempt, radical contempt, in which the other is denied recognition as a human being while arrogating to be one. Contemptuous appraisal is facilitated by a person's exhibiting actual signs of lower value or nonhumanity, such as carrying a number rather than a name, absence of hair and of other cues of individuality, blind obedience to inhuman commands, poverty, and lack of physical fitness. It is of course also facilitated by prior beliefs concerning the targets of contempt, as explicitly fostered by designating those targets by the names of lower animals such as pigs or cockroaches.

The appraisal of contempt implies that a number of the costs of certain actions do not apply, and the same holds for certain norms restraining certain actions. The action tendency implies actions that reinforce signs of contemptuousness, as well as actions that bring or keep the other person in his or her lower place; and cruelty can appear as both efficacious and acceptable. There are very vicious circles here. Cruelty reduces its targets to a state that appears to justify the cruelty. Emotions thus may lead to actions that, by their very nature, modify acceptability and create circumstances that facilitate such modification.

CONCLUSION

I summarize. Emotions exist for the sake of action. Motivation for action is one of the main and major components of emotions, except when the very impossibility to act induces disorganization or loss of motivation.

Motivations potentiate but do not activate actions. Actual action occurs by the conjunction of motivation with factors of situational, personal, and more cognitive kinds. When motivation is aroused, action does or does not ensue, depending on emotion control or regulation, on the availability of a meaningful action repertoire, on the acceptability of the available actions, and on the importance of the emotional event or its effects. Regulation is itself of an emotional nature, as it stems from the anticipated emotional consequences of action for the individual's many concerns. Those concerns include those about social censure, emphatic distress, sympathy, valuing interpersonal relationships, and social harmony.

The balance between emotional motivation and the effects of action for other concerns – and thus the occurrence of action – is strongly influenced by social forces. These include the social determinants of the acceptability of actions, social examples of action availability, and social formation and strength of beliefs that engender emotions. One of the emotions that is central in influencing action acceptability is contempt.

This analysis of the relationships between emotion and action rests on focusing on motivation in emotion. It has been tentative and groping because a coherent theory of such motivation is not available. It is a task for the future. It illustrates the fact that the basic psychology of emotion is still rudimentary. There is a wide gap between the analysis of emotion at the phenomenal or personal level and at the physical or neurophysiological level – as if the latter could explain the former without passing through the middle level, that of functional, psychological analysis.

References

Ajzen, I. (1989). Attitude structure and behavior. In A. R. Pratkanis, S. J. Breckler, and A. G. Greenwald (Eds.), *Attitude structure and function* (pp. 241–274). Hillsdale, NJ: Erlbaum.

Averill, J. R. (1982). *Anger and aggression: An essay on emotion.* New York: Springer.

Berkowitz, L., & LePage, A. (1967). Weapons as aggression-eliciting stimuli. *Journal of Personality and Social Psychology, 7,* 202–207.

Berridge, K. C. (1999). Pleasure, pain, desire, and dread: Hidden core processes of emotion. In D. Kahneman, E. Diener, and N. Schwarz, (Eds.), *Foundations of hedonic psychology: Scientific perspectives on enjoyment and suffering* (pp. 525–557). New York: Sage.

Block, G., & Drucker, M. (1992). *Rescuers: Portraits of moral courage in the Holocaust.* New York: TV Books.

Boiten, F. A. (1993a). *Emotional breathing patterns.* Ph.D. thesis, University of Amsterdam.

Boiten, F. A. (1993b). Component analysis of task related respiratory patterns. *International Journal of Psychophysiology, 15,* 91–104.

Brehm, J., & Self, E. (1989). The intensity of motivation. In M. R. Rosenzweig and L. W. Porter (Eds.), *Annual Review of Psychology, 40.* Palo Alto: Annual Reviews, Inc.

Browning, C. R. (1993). *Ordinary men: Reserve police battalion 101 and the Final Solution in Poland.* New York: Harper Perennial.

Chesnais, J.-C. (1981), *Histoire de la violence.* Paris: Robert Laffont.

Corsini, S., & Rimé, B. (2001). Emotional events and the symbolic universe. *Proceedings, Feelings and Emotions, The Amsterdam Symposium.*

Cosmides, L., & Tooby, J. (2000). Evolutionary psychology and the emotions. In M. Lewis and J. M. Haviland (Eds.), *Handbook of emotions, Second Edition* (pp. 91–115). New York: Guilford.

Davitz, J. R. (1969). *The language of emotion.* New York: Academic Press.

De Waal, F. B. M. (1996). *Good natured: The origins of right anbd wrong in humans and other animals.* Cambridge, MA.: Harvard University Press.

De Waal, F. B. M. & Aureli, F. (1997). Conflict resolution and distress alleviation in monkeys and apes. *Annals of the New York Academy of Sciences. Vol. 807: The integrative neurobiology of affiliation* (317–328).

Draghi-Lorenz, R. (2001). *Young infants are capable of non-basic emotions.* Ph.D. thesis, University of Portsmouth.

Elster, J. (1990). Norms of revenge. *Ethics, 100,* 862–885.

Elster, J. (1999). *Alchemies of the mind*. Cambridge: Cambridge University Press.

Frank, R. H. (1988). *Passions within reason: The strategic role of the emotions*. New York: Norton.

Fredrickson, B. L. (2001). The role of positive emotions in positive psychology: The broaden-and-build theory of positive emotions. *American Psychologist, 56,* 218–226.

Freeman, W. J. (2000). Emotion is essential to all intentional behavior. In M. D. Lewis and I. Granic (Eds.), *Emotion, development, and self-organisation* (pp. 209–235). New York: Cambridge University Press.

Frijda, N. H. (1986). *The emotions*. Cambridge: Cambridge University Press.

Frijda, N. H. (1994). The Lex Talionis: On vengeance. In S. H. M. Van Goozen, N. E. Van de Poll, and J. A. Sergeant (Eds.), *Emotions: Essays on emotion theory* (pp. 263–290). Hillsdale, NJ: Erlbaum

Frijda, N. H.; Markam, S.; Sato, K.; & Wiers, R. (1995). Emotion and emotion words. In J. A. Russell, J. M. Fernández-Dols, A. S. R. Manstead, and J. Wellenkamp (Eds.), *Everyday conceptions of emotion* (pp. 121–144). Dordrecht: Kluwer.

Frijda, N. H.; Mesquita, B.; Sonnemans, J.; & Van Goozen, S. (1991). The duration of affective phenomena, or emotions, sentiments and passions. In K. Strongman (Ed.), *International Review of Emotion and Motivation* (pp. 187–225). New York: Wiley.

Frijda, N. H., & Zeelenberg, M. (2001). Appraisal: What is the dependent? In A. Schorr, K. R. Scherer, and T. Johnston (Eds.), *Appraisal processes in emotion: Theory, methods, research* (pp. 141–156). Oxford: Oxford University Press.

Gallistel, C. R. (1980). *The organization of action: A new synthesis*. Hillsdale: Erlbaum.

Holst, E. von, & Mittelstaedt, H. (1950). Der Reafferenzprinzip. Wechselwirkung zwischen Zentralnervensystem und Peripherie. *Naturwissenschaften, 37,* 464–475.

Horowitz, M. J. (1992). *Stress response syndromes*. (3d ed.). Northvale, NJ: Jason Aronson.

Kreitler, H., & Kreitler, S. (1972). *Psychology of the arts*. Durham, NC: Duke University Press.

Lambie, J., & Marcel, A. (2002). Consciousness and emotion experience: A theoretical framework. *Psychological Review, 109,* 219–259.

Miller, W. I. (1993). *Humiliation.*Ithaca, NY: Cornell University Press.

Mook, D. G. (1996). *Motivation: The organization of action* (2d ed.). New York: Norton.

Panksepp, J. (1998). *Affective neuroscience*. Oxford: Oxford University Press.

Piaget, J. (1976). *Le comportement moteur de l'évolution*. Paris: Gallimard. (English translation: *Behavior and evolution*. New York, Random House, 1978.)

Rimé, B.; Phillipot, P.; Boca, S.; & Mesquita, B. (1992). Long-lasting cognitive and social consequences of emotion: Social sharing and rumination. *European Review of Social Psychology, 3,* 225–258.

Roseman, I. J. (2001). A model of appraisal in the emotion system: Integrating theory, research, and applications. In K. R. Scherer, A. Schorr, and T. Johnstone (Eds.), *Appraisal processes in emotion: Theory, methods, research*. New York: Oxford University Press.

Scheff, T. (1988). Shame and conformity: The deference emotion system. *American Sociological Review, 53,* 395–406.

Scherer, K. R. (2001). Appraisal considered as a process of multilevel sequential checking. In K. R. Scherer, A. Schorr, and T. Johnstone (Eds.), *Appraisal processes in emotion: Theory, methods, research* (pp. 92–120). New York: Oxford University Press.

Sonnemans, J., & Frijda, N. H. (1995). The determinants of subjective emotional intensity. *Cognition and Emotion, 9,* 483–507.

Stellar, E. (1977). Homeostasis, discrepancy, dissonance: A theory of motives and motivation. *Motivation and Emotion, 1,* 103–138.

Thelen, E. (1995). Motor development: A new synthesis. *American Psychologist, 50,* 79–95.

Tomkins, S. S. (1962). *Affect: Imagery and consciousness.* Vol. 1, *The positive affects.* New York: Springer.

Tucker, D. M.; Deryberry, D.; & Luu, P. (2000). Anatomy and physiology of human emotions: Vertical integration of brain stem, limbic, and cortical systems. In J. C. Borod (Ed.), *The neuropsychology of emotion* (pp. 56–79). New York: Oxford University Press.

Varela, F. J.; Thompson, E.; & Rosch, E. (1991). *The embodied mind.* Cambridge, MA: MIT Press.

Weiss, J. M.; Glazer, H. I.; & Poherecky, L. A. (1976). Coping behavior and neurochemical changes: An alternative explanation for the original "learned helplessness" experiments. In A. Serban and A. Kling (Eds.), *Animal models in human psychobiology* (pp. 141–173). New York: Plenum Press.

Zimbardo, P. G. (1970). The human choice: Individuation reason and order versus deindividuation, impulse and chaos. In W. J. Arnold and D. Levine (Eds.), *Nebraska symposium on motivation 1969,* Vol. 16. Lincoln: University of Nebraska Press.

11

Basic Affects and the Instinctual Emotional Systems of the Brain

The Primordial Sources of Sadness, Joy, and Seeking

Jaak Panksepp

ABSTRACT

Primary-process affective processes emerge largely from subcortical action-perception brain systems that elaborate a variety of emotional-instinctual tendencies. This essay highlights how the nature of affect can be clarified by studying ancient brain operating systems that mediate separation distress, social play, and appetitive seeking in all mammals.

> No knowledge would have been more valuable as a foundation for true psychological science than an approximate grasp of the common characteristics and possible distinctive features of the instincts. But in no region of psychology were we groping more in the dark.
>
> – Freud, *Beyond the Pleasure Principle* (1920/1959)

The question "What is the fundamental nature of affect?" is one of the most important and least studied psychological question in the life sciences. If we could understand the neuro-evolutionary nature of affect, we might better understand all other forms of consciousness. Obviously such issues cannot be addressed cogently without neuroscientific strategies. Here I summarize my approach, which seeks to overlay (to *supervene*) basic affective issues onto the intrinsic instinctual emotional systems that evolution constructed into mammalian brains in "deep time" (Panksepp, 1982, 1998a). My overall aim has been to understand the nature of human affective experiences, and this approach is gaining some recognition by investigators of human emotions (e.g., Buck, 1985, 1999; Damasio et al., 2000; Solms & Nersessian, 1999). This synopsis will be largely focused on our work on the topic during the past three decades.

THE MYSTERY OF AFFECTIVE EXPERIENCE

Since affective experiences seem to lie at the core of many of our decision-making processes, the answer to the above question is of foremost importance for the emergence of a deeply scientific psychology. Although the dynamic intrinsic processes of the brain that we call basic affects interact continuously with bodily processes and environmental events, these affects do not have to be learned, even though they are parsed and permuted further by our sophisticated, more recently evolved cortico-cognitive conceptual-analytical processes.

One of the least discussed topics in both neuroscience and the currently blossoming science of human emotions is the fundamental neuro-evolutionary nature of affective processes. Simple systematization and labeling of such processes as locations in dimensional affective space, as is so common in psychology, will not suffice for a deep scientific understanding. Modern brain imaging has dramatically advanced the field, but few recognize that such correlative approaches are not robust enough to reveal causal details.

My goal is to summarize a neuro-evolutionary approach that can resolve such issues. I frame my remarks pointedly in a psychoanalytic context that lost much of its lingering appeal following the onslaught of the neuroscience, cognitive/computational, and biological psychiatry revolutions a generation ago. I do this because Freud, in the footsteps of Darwin, sought to bring emotions, in their full glory, to the forefront of the twentieth-century intellectual agenda. Although his vision failed, at least in mainstream science, he pointed us in the right direction, as had Darwin. Modern neuroscience can now add the needed depth to our discussion of such issues; but, regrettably, investigators have generally been unwilling to regard "affect," especially as experienced by other animals, as a proper topic of inquiry. Affects are subjective experiences that cannot be directly measured, and some believe they are epiphenomena – causally irrelevant aspects of emotions that may exist only in humans (e.g., LeDoux, 1996).

My guiding premise is that affects are basic neurobiological aspects of brain organization in all mammals and perhaps many other animals. The basic affects are ancient evolved processes that helped solve some basic and universal survival problems – namely, the coding of biological values in a variable world of potential rewards and punishments. An obvious corollary of this assertion is that affects have inherited underpinnings. We do not learn to be afraid, to be angry, to be happy, to desire, and to experience pain and loneliness, even though we humans (as well as other animals) learn to whom and in which situations we should express such feelings. My overall working hypothesis is that affects are fundamental properties of rather ancient emotional/instinctual operating systems in action.

Granted these assumptions, the best way to understand how affects emerge in human minds is to unravel their genetic and neural substrates in related animals where the detailed neurobiological studies can be conducted. As Freud put it: "Biology is truly a land of unlimited possibilities. We may expect it to give us the most surprising information and we cannot guess what answers it will return in a few dozen years to the questions we have put to it. They may be of a kind which will blow away the whole of our artificial structure of hypotheses" (1920/1959, p. 73). With a little faith in the hypothetical-deductive method, and abundant theoretically guided neurobehavioral research, we can finally look to neurobiological and evolutionary principles for a fundamental understanding of brain emotional systems and the affective states they generate (Panksepp, 1998a; Panksepp & Panksepp, 2000).

The Instinctual Action-to-Perception Substrates of Emotional Systems

Although there is no adequate taxonomy of affects, we can be confident that there are distinct varieties. Some are more integrally linked to incoming sensory processes (e.g., taste and smell), some to interoceptive drives (e.g., thirst, hunger, etc.), while yet others are more closely linked to the valenced motor-action processes of the brain (e.g., what are typically called the basic emotions), and some to the autonomic relaxations associated with the satisfaction of various drives (e.g., post-prandial and postcopulatory feelings of comfort).

My reading of the evidence is that core processes for the generation of emotional affects (i.e., fear, anger, sadness, joy, etc) are situated in ancient parts of the brain that generate instinctual-emotional action patterns – brain areas we share, with abundant neuroanatomical and neurochemical homologies, with other animals (Panksepp, 1982, 1991, 1998a). However, in clarifying these primitive sources of affect, I am in no way denying the important roles of cognitive appraisals, fantasies, and intentions in optimizing affective goals. I only wish to suggest that an understanding of the *evolved* nature of the affects will not be advanced much at the present time by focusing on those higher processes.

The most illuminating and defensible cross-species translations are bound to emerge from our detailed empirical understanding of the deep subcortical systems that all mammals share in remarkably homologous ways. My perspective is premised on the simple fact that measures of approach and avoidance affirm that the strongest affects in animals and humans are provoked by stimulating specific subcortical systems, especially those where clear instinctual-emotional behavior patterns can be aroused (Heath, 1996; Panksepp, 1985). Such effects are rare from neocortical brain regions, being largely restricted to limbic regions that are richly interconnected with the subcortical substrates of affect. One could easily argue that affects emerge when these primitive systems interact with neural systems that subserve higher mental activities; however, that remains an enormous and a gratuitous assumption. From the vantage of parsimony, as well as the weight of evidence, we should consider that affect arises largely from subcortical neural activities and may be a foundational process for higher forms of consciousness (Panksepp, 1998a, 1998b, 2000c, 2000d).

Few other concrete and testable ideas have been advanced concerning the neurobiological/neurodynamic nature of affective feelings. This is largely because most investigators in behavioral neuroscience have a remarkably difficult time even discussing such concepts as working hypotheses. If they actually work on emotional behaviors, they tend to wrap themselves in a cloak of terminal agnosticism and deny that such "mentalistic" concepts can be topics of rigorous scientific analysis (e.g., LeDoux, 1996, 2000). But the evidence is overwhelming – affect is a true part of neuroanimate nature, and a vigorous discussion must ensue if we truly want to understand the neurobiological nature of human emotional problems, human consciousness, and the fundamental nature of mind.

My inquiries into the nature of affect started with an attempt to understand self-stimulation reward (Trowill, Panksepp, & Gandelman, 1969; Panksepp, 1981), brain substrates of anger (Panksepp, 1971), and hunger (Panksepp, 1974). With the discovery of brain opioids, my interests turned to the study of separation distress, social bonding, playfulness, and animal laughter/joy (Panksepp, 1998a, 2000). We have also pursued work on the affective properties of a brainstem *fear command system* (Panksepp, 1971, 1990, 1996) – a view increasingly supported by subsequent research (Rosen & Schulkin, 1998). This conceptualization is usually ignored by behavioristic/positivistic investigators, who have invested mightily in straightforward classical conditioning models of information input to the higher amygdaloid reaches of this system (see LeDoux, 1996, 2000). In sum, open discussions about the nature of animal emotions are long overdue (Bekoff, 2000), especially if we wish to understand the details of evolutionarily ingrained brain operating systems that are essential for certain basic human experiences.

In broad strokes, Freud probably had it essentially right: We possess an affectively valenced nature that has profound influence over what we think and do. However, we often repress these energies and shield them from our higher cognitive consciousness. As Freud put it, "we know that the pleasure principle is proper to a primary method of working on the part of the mental apparatus, but that, from the point of view of the self-preservations of the organism among the difficulties of the external world, it is from the very outset inefficient and even highly dangerous. Under the influence of the ego's instincts of self-preservation, the pleasure principle is replaced by the reality principle." (1920/1959, p. 7).

With the developmental maturation of the frontal lobes in humans, we develop an exquisite capacity for behavioral inhibition in the service of foresight – to reflect, imagine, and plan, with affective issues in mind – to achieve well-focused, goal-directed behaviors (Barkley, 2001). When those brain tissues are damaged, individuals begin to behave with an affective immediacy that is usually detrimental for the effective pursuit of life activities (Damasio, 1999). Indeed, various higher brain regions provide interfaces between emotional and cognitive/perceptual processes rather than intrinsically creating affect. However, limbic cortices, such as peri-amygdaloid, orbitofrontal, and cingulate, may well be essential for generating higher social feelings such as jealousy, envy, hate, frustration, embarrassment, shame, guilt, and arrogance. But they may only be able to do that by using more basic emotions such as separation distress and so-ciosexual desire as key ingredients within cognitive deliberations. Other limbic cortices such as the insula and claustrum help elaborate affective sensory feeling states such as those of taste, disgust, and pain (Chapman & Nakamura, 2001). The precise transactions that transpire in these tissues, as pursued intensively by investigators such as Rolls (1999), remains an exciting chapter of emotion research that is emerging from a straightforward behavioristic tradition.

HOW MIGHT AFFECT BE ELABORATED IN THE BRAIN/MIND?

Darwin (1872/1998) recognized three general features of emotional systems, namely, the *principle of action*, the *principle of antithesis*, and the principle of *serviceable associated habits*. He also accepted that distinct internally experienced feelings are key features of all emotions, while recognizing that those important aspects were impossible to analyze systematically with the tools available in his era. Freud was confronted by similar conundrums. The task is much easier today because the neuroscience revolution has revealed remarkable neurochemistries that help encode specific psychobehavioral tendencies (Panksepp, 1986, 1993).

Paul MacLean (1990) sought to develop an "epistemic" viewpoint in neuroscience – the study of "the subjective self and its relation to the internal and external environment" (p. 6). He argued that emotional feelings emerge largely from "limbic" circuits. Recently, his ideas (but not his vast empirical contributions) have attracted severe criticism from modern behavioral neuroscientists who disparage the many ambiguities of limbic and emotional concepts (for an overview of such attacks, see Corey & Gardner, 2002). In this combative intellectual climate, is it any wonder that so few are willing to entertain how affective processes may actually emerge from brain dynamics? Parenthetically, many of these same critics all too easily tolerate the comparable ambiguities of constructs such as the amygdala, which is being "extended" as we come to understand the many connectivities and functional continuities.

Besides MacLean's broad and productive limbic system concept (which pointed us neuroanatomically and conceptually in the right direction), there are three additional major lines of thought on this issue: (1) that affective feelings reflect bodily changes accompanying emotions, with a modern variant of this traditional James-Langian perspective being the "somatic marker" hypothesis by Damasio (1994); (2) that feelings are constituted somehow by "read-outs" in higher, neocortical working memory systems (LeDoux, 1996, 2000) or uniquely human linguistic abilities of the forebrain (Rolls, 1999); and, finally, the most monistic view, which I favor: (3) that affective states reflect the intrinsic neurodynamics of neuropeptidergically coded subcortical emotional-instinctual circuits interacting with the intrinsic, primordial "self-representational" structures of midline regions of the upper brainstem, concentrated in areas such as the reticular fields of the periventricular and periaqueductal gray areas (PVG and PAG), which developmentally may guide the programming of higher limbic cortices (Panksepp, 1998b).

Recently, there have been attempts to interface this last view with theories of affect such as Freud's (see Solms & Nersessian, 1999; and Panksepp, 1999b, with the accompanying commentaries). In addition, Damasio (1999b, 2000) and Buck (1999) have reshaped their views by increasingly highlighting the importance of such subcortical systems, albeit they still insist that "read-outs" into higher cerebral spaces are essential for affects to be felt. Of course, considering that emotions constitute widely broadcast "global states" of the nervous system, there is abundant room for all of these viewpoints to contribute to a comprehensive perspective. However, the critical practical issue is where best to initiate relevant analyses that can yield new findings that can be *causally* evaluated in humans. In my estimation, the neurochemical analysis of the evolved executive components will permit that better than any other approach (Panksepp, 1986, 1993, 1998a), and Buck (1999) agrees. This is not to deny that direct measurement of such processes will require direct recording of the relevant brain activities.

The neurodynamic signatures of the basic affective states are most likely to be eventually recorded directly from subcortical brain areas where distinct emotional states can be evoked (Panksepp, 2000a). I suspect that those subcortical organic processes, which provide a fundamental core representation of the organism (e.g., Damasio, 1999; Panksepp, 1998a), generate a primitive "affective consciousness" (i.e., raw feels) through a variety of emotion-specific neurodynamics (e.g., perhaps similar to those described by Clynes, 1978). It is a straightforward concept, capable of being evaluated empirically, that affect arises from the neurodynamics that represent the instinctual expressive character of the various emotional action systems (Panksepp, 1982). Of course, the proposition becomes highly testable in humans only when enough neuroscience details of the underlying operating systems have been deciphered, and the greatest progress so far has been made at the neurochemical level (see Panksepp, 1993, 1998a).

With the advent of modern PET and fMRI brain imaging, it is attractive to assume that higher regions such as anterior cingulate, peri-amygdaloid, insular, perirhinal, orbito-frontal, and other frontal cortical areas that richly connect with PVG and PAG areas will prove essential for everyday experiences of emotions. I personally believe that such views are partly correct. However, those compelling hypotheses are also partly negated by the fact that patients with extensive higher limbic damage still *experience* most of the basic emotions, except for disgust (Adolphs, Tranel, & Damasio, 2003; Damasio, 1999). The main deficit in such patients is a profound impairment in perceiving emotional stimuli in their environments. However, the above investigators still suspect that read-outs in cortical regions, such as somatosensory areas that represent bodily sensations (i.e., somatic markers), are essential for creating the feeling of emotions. To evaluate that possibility for myself, I have personally had rTMS brain stimulation of most of the implicated cortical areas, and regret to report that I experienced no distinct emotional experiences, although my mood was mildly affected, about as expected from prior data, during frontal stimulation (George & Belmaker, 2000). In sum, considering *all* the data, it is difficult to envision how higher neocortical areas that mediate cognitive processes could ever generate affective feelings through mere local "computation."

The existing evidence points toward the likelihood that the infrastructure of affect is fundamentally dependent on deep centro-median subcortical processes (e.g., Panksepp, 1998a, 1998b; 2000b, 2000c). This view is beginning to garner ever more support from modern brain imaging studies. Striking subcortical arousal is evident with functional brain imaging studies ranging from air-hunger (Liotti et al, 2001) to the pleasure of musical peak experiences (Blood et al., 2001), just to name a few (for more, see Panksepp, 2001a). But many higher limbic areas are also aroused. From my perspective, the functions of those higher limbic regions are largely restricted to interfacing primitive emotional functions with cognitions, memories, and plans that are related to perceptions of the external world and that permit effective regulation of emotional processes. Conversely, the subcortical affective systems imbue perceptions with feelings and thereby values (in Freudian terms, yielding the emotional *projections* and *cathexis* of ideas and perceptions).

Indeed, there is now an enormous amount of evidence that such higher brain areas are essential for the recognition of emotional sounds, stories, and facial and bodily expressions, but they contribute comparatively little to the *generation* of affect (although the *modulation* of affect can obviously be controlled by higher cognitive functions). These higher systems surely help organisms to regulate emotions and to learn about the affective nuances of world events (for reviews, see Lane & Nadel, 2000). However, I suspect that the historical bias against the role of subcortical, "instinctual" motor/action processes in the generation of consciousness and emotional states has been and continues to be a great barrier to progress in mind/brain science (Panksepp, 1998b, 2000b, 2000c).

Of course, definitive evidence for where affective states are elaborated in the human brain must come from the analysis of human neuro-subjectivity. Brain stimulation studies have consistently supported a primary subcortical locus of control (Heath, 1996; Panksepp, 1985). This conclusion has recently been dramatically affirmed by the Damasios. In the most comprehensive PET analysis of internally experienced sadness, happiness, fear, and anger (Damasio et al., 2000), human affective arousal was clearly linked to the activities of subcortical systems long implicated in emotional experience in animal studies, with little evidence for neocortical arousal.

An overall summary of the Damasios' data is provided in Figure 11.1. Of 189 brain sites exhibiting significant changes in blood flow, most arousal effects (i.e., increased blood flow) were found subcortically, whereas the neocortex predominantly exhibited reduced arousal (i.e., diminished blood flow). As predicted from animal work, medially situated brainstem areas were selectively aroused in all four affective states. Surprisingly, the amygdala exhibited no significant arousal except during feelings of happiness.

THE PERIAQUEDUCTAL SOURCES OF AFFECT

It seems clear that understanding the functions of tissues that surround the third and fourth ventricles, and especially the intervening periaqueductal gray matter (PAG), deserve our foremost attention in order to understand affect (Panksepp, 1998a,1998b). This brain area, in association with surrounding tegmental and tectal zones, may elaborate primary-process affective self-representation in all mammalian brains. Without that "core SELF," emotional feelings may never developmentally extend throughout the neuroaxis up to the frontal lobes.

Three compelling lines of reasoning suggest we should entertain such a radical idea: (1) It is within the PAG that we find the most massive convergence of emotional information within the brain. (2) It is within the PAG that investigators can evoke the largest diversity of coherent emotional responses with the mildest levels of brain stimulation. (3) Finally, it is within the PAG where the smallest amount of neural damage has the most severe effects on emotional expressions. Indeed, complete damage to the PAG produces a state of severely compromised consciousness (for overview, see Panksepp, 1998b).

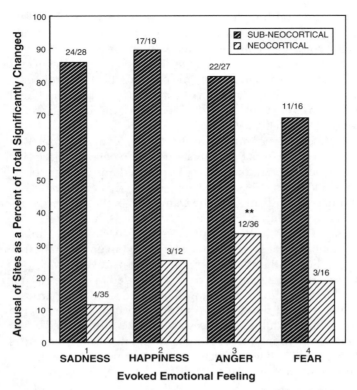

FIGURE 11.1. A summary of 189 brain sites that exhibited significant changes during four self-induced affective experiences (sadness, happiness, anger, and fear) broken down in terms of those that were situated neocortically and those that were found in sub-neocortical areas (data derived from Damasio et al., 2000).

It is noteworthy that PAG has easy access to the ascending reticular activating systems to arouse and regulate activities of many cortico-cognitive parts of the brain. The PAG has massive reciprocal interactions with the diversity of higher brain areas implicated in emotions from anterior cingulate and frontal cortices, down to amygdaloid, basal forebrain, and hypothalamic areas (Holstege, Bandler, & Saper, 1996). During infancy, human children show intense arousal of brainstem areas, but with maturation, the higher systems gain ascendancy as they become more influential in regulating behavior (Chugani, 1998). In short, the elaboration of such SELF-centered affective dynamics, through broad-scale neurochemical broadcasting of the relevant neurodynamics through the rest of the nervous system, may help establish mood-congruent "attractor basins" for perceptions, cognitions, and memories.

Such findings are remarkably consistent with Freud's view that primary-process emotionality guides the development of higher psychic functions.

Thus, even though straightforward pleasure and unpleasure principles may directly regulate behavior during infancy, with the maturation of higher brain areas organisms develop the ability to integrate their behaviors with long-term goals, and so the immediacy of hedonic principles tends to recede into the background while still providing a long-term center of gravity for life decisions. As Freud (1920/1959, pp. 72–73) put it: "The deficiencies in our description would probably vanish if we were already in a position to replace the psychological terms by physiological or chemical ones." Surely "replace" is rather extreme ("supplement" might have been more judicious), but now a study of such supervenience relations can clarify psychological issues enormously. However, in such pursuits, we must avoid the temptations of part–whole confusions. Because psychological processes are woven of many neural components, we will never be able to reduce broad psychological constructs to singular neurological areas, systems, or processes. To minimize part–whole confusions in my own aspiration to identify essential core principles, I have chosen to use capitalizations when I label the core emotional systems.

It is incredibly important to try to identify the epicenters for affect along the neuroaxis. This is the only way we can make major progress on resolving what types of specific neurochemical systems and resulting neurodynamics we need to study in order to understand the fundamental organization of affective processes within the mammalian brain. This could be empirically achieved by contrasting the degree of affective engagement that is induced by "point arousals" at various levels of the neuroaxis – for instance, by placement of the general neuron activator glutamate into distinct areas of the brain such as amygdala, hypothalamus, and PAG, and harvesting place-preference or avoidance measures. I predict that lower areas of the brain will be more essential for affective arousal than similar stimulations of higher areas. This could also be done for any of a variety of neuropeptides: For instance, Gonadotrophin Release Hormone may be essential for certain erotic sexual feelings and urges (Panksepp, 1993), and I would predict that the place-preferences produced with this peptide (de Beun et al., 1991) are probably subcortically mediated. There is already compelling evidence for such a locus of control for endogenous opioids (Olmstead & Franklin, 1997).

The neglect of these lower "animalian" systems in the affect sciences may largely reflect the fact that so few psychologists have had hands-on experience studying them. To highlight their importance, I will now focus on three subcortical emotional systems that we have studied for the past three decades.

THE BRAIN SUBSTRATES OF SADNESS/PANIC

Our work on the nature of separation distress was initiated in 1972 with the discovery of brain opioid receptor systems. This spectacular finding prompted us to consider that such neurochemistries mediate social bonding. Discrete brain systems for social affect were not being actively entertained at that time. The prevailing behaviorist assumption was that such processes arise indirectly via learning experiences associated with primary rewards such as the provisioning of food, water, and warmth. Our hypothesis was based on the similarities between narcotic addiction and social dependence, which share remarkable resemblances: (1) a powerful initial pleasure-attachment phase; (2) a gradual habituation or tolerance phase in which the experienced affective pleasure from interacting with the desired "object" markedly diminishes; and (3) a traumatic withdrawal phase during enforced separation from the attachment "object."

The theory was supported by many pharmacological studies demonstrating the robust capacity of *mu* opioid receptor activity to diminish social aloneness-induced distress (SAD) vocalizations in many species, including dogs, guinea pigs, and domestic chicks (Panksepp et al., 1978a,1978b). Brain stimulation studies highlighted subcortical trajectories of the separation-distress system (Herman & Panksepp, 1981; Panksepp et al., 1988).

Of many other psychoactive agents evaluated, only oxytocin, prolactin, and glutamate receptor antagonists produced similar robust calming effects. Conversely, others such as Corticotrophin Releasing Factor (CRF) and glutamate receptor stimulants, could specifically promote separation vocalizations (Panksepp, 1991, 1998a). A diversity of other social processes were found to be modified comparably in ways compatible with an opioid theory of social affect (Panksepp et al., 1980). These findings were extended to the human clinical realm, with the still controversial opioid-excess theory of autism.

During the subsequent decade, others confirmed and extended these findings (e.g., Kalin, Shelton, & Lynn, 1995; Kehoe & Blass, 1986; Keverne, Nevison, & Martel, 1999), and it is now generally accepted that social-emotional processes are regulated by opioid and oxytocinergic dynamics within mammalian and avian brains (Carter, Lederhendler, & Kirkpatrick 1999; Nelson & Panksepp, 1998). Although a great number of details remain to be worked out, these findings provide a conceptual infrastructure for thinking about many aspects of social affect in humans. When the separation-distress system (or PANIC system, as designated in Panksepp, 1998a) is quiescent, individuals become more emotionally confident and socially dominant (Panksepp, Jalowiec, DeEskinazi, & Bishop,1985), presumably because they have a more "secure emotional base" for their life activities. With the experience of social loss, psychodynamics shift toward a panic, disposing the affective apparatus toward "painful" emotional distress that can cascade into feelings of depression and despair (Panksepp et al., 1991). The lifetime consequences of bonding quality and early attachment difficulties are profound (Meaney, 2001; Panksepp, 2001b).

The implications of these findings for understanding affective consciousness seem straightforward. Those areas of the brain where we can evoke separation calls with electrical stimulation (e.g., Herman & Panksepp, 1981; Panksepp et al., 1988) constitute the core of the emotional "command" circuitry that generates feelings of social loss – from sadness to panic, depending on the intensity of arousal. Opioids, along with oxytocin and prolactin, released along this circuit, are brain neurochemistries that promote feelings of social comfort that accompany friendly companionship. However, such feelings, like air itself, tend to recede into the background of consciousness, only becoming affectively evident with shifts in the underlying psychochemical dynamics. Only when a sense of security is diminished by losing an attachment "object" (or a loved one) does one promptly experience the emotional dependency that arises from the affective potential of the separation distress system.

Thus, rapidly escalating glutamatergic and/or CRF or diminishing opioid activity in these systems precipitate feelings of a psychic pain, a distress that reflects an invigorated motivation to seek social companionship. When such neurochemical imbalances are rectified, social contact can again produce an invigorated pleasurable sense of social satisfaction, even joy. Since we know even less about the positive affective side of such socioemotional systems, we started to investigate the nature of the play-joy systems of the brain.

THE BRAIN SUBSTRATES OF PLAYFUL JOY AND LAUGHTER

Research on rough-and-tumble play in juvenile rats has gradually become a modest growth area in behavioral neuroscience (see Panksepp et al., 1984; Pellis et al., 1997; Vanderschuren et al., 1997). Briefly, there are intrinsic brain systems for rough-and-tumble play that generate positive affect (Normansell & Panksepp, 1990) and may have important consequences for brain development, perhaps through the genetic activation of neuronal growth factors (Panksepp, 2001b). Considering that psychostimulants commonly used to treat human children diagnosed with ADHD can markedly reduce play, I have questioned the wisdom of substituting drug treatment for the natural neurochemically mediated joys of physical play (Panksepp, 1998a,1998b). Indeed, when the PLAY systems of the brain are intensely aroused, we humans tend to exhibit a robust fixed-action pattern – laughter – that may be more prevalent among our fellow animals than has ever been suspected.

Laughter has commonly been deemed unique to humans and perhaps chimpanzees (Provine, 2000), but our work has brought that anthropocentric supposition into question. Rats exhibit robust ~50 kHz ultrasonic chirping response during play as well as during manual tickling by a human experimenter (Knutson et al., 1998; Panksepp, 2000b). We believe this chirping is an evolutionary homologue of primitive human laughter for the following reasons: (1) the vocalization is brought out powerfully by positive social interchange (e.g., play) and even more so by tickling; (2) all fearful and negative affective stimuli we have tested (cat smell, foot shock, new places, being held by the scruff of the neck) reduce this response; (3) individuals that chirp the most in response to tickling also play the most among each other; (4) young animals chirp more than older animals; (5) animals approach hands that have tickled them much more often than those that have petted them, and they are attracted to other stimuli that have been associated with tickling; (6) the response classically conditions rapidly to cues that predict tickling; (7) animals will learn instrumental responses to receive tickling; (8) young animals like to spend more time with older animals that chirp a lot rather than with those that chirp infrequently; (9) just like humans who are more ticklish in certain areas of the body (e.g., the ribs), young rats have "tickle skin" concentrated at the nape of the neck, where they typically direct their own play activities; and (10) the response is a temperamental characteristic of animals, for it can be successfully selected for and against within four generations of selective breeding. For details, see Panksepp (1998a), Panksepp and Burgdorf (1999, 2000, 2003), Burgdorf and Panksepp (2001) and Panksepp, Burgdorf, and Gordon (2000).

Since these results are remarkably robust and clear, we provisionally conclude that rats do, in fact, exhibit and experience a joy-laughter response. Of course, all empirical phenomena remain open to alternative interpretations, and we await major challenges to our views. Until then, we assume that, as we identify brain systems that generate this response in animals, along with the genes responsible, we may reveal the ultimate social joy principles in humans. An understanding of the key neurochemistries may yield new avenues for treating depression. Comparable possibilities exist for the other basic emotional systems.

THE BRAIN SUBSTRATES OF SEEKING

Brain research can reveal emotional systems that traditional psychological analysis has largely overlooked. The trans-hypothalamic SEEKING system, which can support vigorous self-stimulation behaviors, is such an entity. In line with prevailing behaviorist biases, these circuits were initially conceptualized as a "reward" or "reinforcement" system, which led to a large variety of paradoxes that have been extensively discussed elsewhere (Ikemoto and Panksepp, 1999; Panksepp, 1982, 1991, 1992, 1998a). My long-standing theoretical position has been that this system does not mediate consummatory reward, but rather appetitive eagerness. Such distinctions eventually led others to resolve the emerging paradoxes in the reward-pleasure concept along similar lines (Robinson and Berridge, 1993), even though they chose to focus more on the sensory/perceptual aspects of this system rather than on the many other attributes, such as action processes, that deserve equal attention (Panksepp, 1992, 2000c). In any event, practically everyone now agrees that this system is critical for an animal's ability to efficiently seek resources from their variable and often emotionally challenging environments (Schultz, 2001). Here I will focus on only two of the many salient aspects of this system (Panksepp, 1992).

First, to some extent the system is nonspecific, participating in the seeking of all positive resources, including the avoidance of distress (i.e., the seeking of safety). Although the arousal of this system typically has a highly energized positive affective character (i.e., a forward-looking anticipatory exhilaration that led me to originally conceptualize the system in positive "expectancy" terms), the system is also operative in many affectively negative circumstances. At the heart of this system are mesolimbic and mesocortical dopamine systems (for a comprehensive overview, see Ikemoto & Panksepp, 1999). There are many other generalized neurochemical systems of this sort – including prominently the ascending acetylcholine, norepinephrine, and serotonin systems. These systems need to be functionally/psychologically conceptualized in rather broad terms (Panksepp, 1982, 1998a), for they participate in essentially all emotional and cognitive activities ever envisioned. I find it disturbing that, recently, human psychologists are tempted to seek emotional specificity in these general state-control systems. The existence of such generalized systems should encourage us to doubt the prevailing evolutionary psychological assumption that cognitive modules exist that are architecturally "encapsulated" or "impenetrable" to other functions. Every brain faculty interacts with many others in order to operate properly, and distinct psychological functions often share many components.

Second, each emotional system is a learning system, and all learning systems operate by facilitating the salience of many relevant neuroperceptual and behavioral properties. The SEEKING system is a remarkable exemplar of this: It promotes the spontaneous capacity to seek out useful information about the world and to regulate learning. This is exemplified strikingly in the phenomenon of auto-shaping – the tendency of animals to exhibit confirmation biases where external events correlated with satisfying or unsatisfying consequences tend to be perceived as being causally related. This leads animals to behave instrumentally as if their actions could control the world, even in situations where experimenters have formally devised contingencies where no such direct causal control was physically possible (see Panksepp, 1982 and 1991 for details).

DIMENSIONAL VS. EVOLUTIONARY APPROACHES TO EMOTIONS: AFFECTIVE "SELF-REPORT" IN ANIMALS

Our work on social emotions started with the assumption that the separation calls of young animals isolated from companions could be used

as an index of the degree of arousal of an internal emotional process
that reflected their affective experience of social loss (Panksepp, Herman,
Conner, Bishop, & Scott, 1978; Panksepp, 1981). Indeed, a growing number
of psychobiologists now believe that we can use animal vocalizations as
indexes of their affective states (Brudzynksi, 2001; Jürgens, 1998; Newman,
1988), and such measures of affective intensity may eventually be linked
to popular ways of conceptualizing human emotions (Knutson, Burgdorf,
& Panksepp, 2000).

Each emotional system will eventually be found to possess some type
of dimensional structure, but there is not just one single form of "positive
affect," or "negative affect," as is commonly assumed by investigators who
are entranced by factor analytic studies of adjectives. These simplifications
tell us more about how our linguistic systems operate, and how our statistical procedures extract patterns out of self-report data, than how our
emotional systems were formed in the cauldron of evolution. Although
there are some generalized and very primitive neurochemical systems,
such as serotonin and norepinephrine, that may promote certain global
moods, there are also a host of more specific neuropeptide systems that
govern specific motivational and emotional tendencies. These views need
to be integrated coherently, and more direct measures of affect need to be
devised. We have been especially intrigued by the possibility that positive
and negative valence affective measures could be devised for animals.

Recently we have suggested that ultrasonic vocalizations of common
laboratory animals such as rats may be used as "self-reports" of their positive and negative affective states (Knutson, Burgdorf, & Panksepp, 2002).
The 50 kHz chirp appears to reflect appetitive eagerness for many distinct
rewards (Burgdorf, Knutson, & Panksepp, 2000), while the longer 22 kHz
"complaints" occur in many distressing situations (Brudzynski, 2001). This
strategy has turned out to be quite effective in discriminating psychologically attractive drugs from those that are repulsive (Burgdorf et al., 2001),
and we are now entertaining the possibility that these vocalizations may be
used as general indicators of affect, which may be especially useful in analyzing the "switch processes" that characterize drug addictions (Panksepp,
Knutson, & Burgdorf, 2002).

CONCLUSION

It does seem that affective values lie at the heart of our existence as pleasure
and displeasure principles around which our cognitive apparatus revolves.
This in no way denies the "reality principles" that the cortex attempts to
construct with its perceptual and cognitive skills. It simply recognizes that
most of these cognitive skills emerge in the service of various basic needs,
shared by other animals. Freud recognized how the "benevolent illusion"
that rationality exists independently of our animalian tendencies prevents

us from pursuing the deep knowledge about our human condition. As he noted (1920/1959), "The present development of human beings requires, as it seems to me, no different explanation from that of animals" (p. 50). Still, considering our great analytical and delusional skills, it is understandable why so few are tempted to head in that intellectual direction.

In sum, I would submit that it is reasonable to postulate that the basic affective feelings reflect characteristic neurodynamics that generate ancient emotional-instinctual tendencies of the body (i.e., basic "intentions in action"). This is the simplest and least dualistic way to seek an understanding of what basic emotions really are. Clarification of the neurochemistries, especially the function-specific neuropeptides, that underlie the orchestration of many basic organic "states of being" may provide the most *useful* information that we can derive from such studies. Thereby, we should be able to utilize knowledge derived from the brains and behavior of other animals to clarify the human condition and to provide new psychiatrically useful medicines. This can only be achieved by the judicious translation of such animalian neurochemical issues to human studies that seek to probe the phenomenology of affective experiences. To do that well, we will need to deploy new depth-psychological methodologies in humans (Panksepp, 1999) as well as comparable theoretical perspectives in animals. The simplest way to approach such issues is to assume that animal behavior typically does not lie, and that the instinctual emotional actions of animals do reflect the dynamics of their emotional feelings more often than they do not.

References

Adolphs, R.; Tranel, D.; & Damasio, A. R. (2003). Dissociable neural systems for recognizing emotions. *Brain and Cognition, 53,* 61–69.

Barkley, R. A. (2001). The executive functions and self-regulation: An evolutionary neuropsychological perspective. *Neuropsychology Review, 11,* 1–29.

Bekoff, M. (2000a). Animal emotions: Exploring passionate nature. *BioScience, 50,* 861–870.

Blood, A. J., & Zatorre, R. J. (2001). Intensely pleasurable responses to music correlate with activity in brain regions implicated in reward and emotion. *Proceedings of the National Academy of Sciences, 98,* 11818–11823.

Brudzynski, S. M. (2001). Pharmacological and behavioral characteristics of 22 kHz alarm calls in rats. *Neuroscience and Biobehavioral Reviews, 25,* 611–617.

Buck, R. (1985). Prime theory: An integrated view of motivation and emotion. *Psychological Review, 92,* 389–413.

Buck, R. (1999). The biological affects, a typology. *Psychological Review, 106,* 301–336.

Burgdorf, J.; Knutson, B.; & Panksepp, J. (2000). Anticipation of rewarding brain stimulation evokes ultrasonic vocalizations in rats. *Behavioral Neuroscience, 114,* 320–327.

Burgdorf, J.; Knutson, B.; Panksepp, J.; & Shippenberg, T. (2001). Ultrasonic vocalizations index pharmacological aversion in adult rats. *Psychopharmacology, 155,* 35–42.

Carter, C. S.; Lederhendler, I.; & Kirkpatrick, B. (Eds.). (1999). *The integrative neurobiology of affiliation* (pp. 263–273). Cambridge, MA: MIT Press.

Chapman, C. R., & Nakamura, Y. (2001). The affective dimension of pain: Mechanisms and implication. In A. Kazniak (Ed.), *Emotions, qualia and consciousness* (pp. 124–136). Singapore: World Scientific.

Chugani, H. T. (1998). Biological basis of emotions: Brain systems and brain development. *Pediatrics, 102,* 1225–1229.

Clynes, M. (1978). *Sentics: The touch of emotions.* New York: Doubleday.

Cory, G. A., & Gardner, Jr., R. (Eds.). (2002). *The evolutionary neuroethology of Paul Maclean: Convergences and frontiers.* Westport, CT: Praeger.

Damasio, A. R. (1994). *Descartes' error: Emotion, reason, and the human brain.* New York: Avon Books.

Damasio, A. R.; Grabowski, T. J.; Bechara, A.; Damasio, H.; Ponto, L. L. B.; Parvizi, J.; & Hichwa, R. D. (2000). Subcortical and cortical brain activity during the feeling of self-generated emotions. *Nature Neuroscience, 3,* 1049–1056.

Darwin, C. (1872/1998). *The expression of the emotions in man and animals.* 3d ed. New York: Oxford University Press.

De Beun, R.; Geerts, N. E.; Jansen, E.; Slangen, J. L. et al. (1991). Leutenizing hormone releasing hormone-induced conditioned place preferences in male rats. *Pharmacology, Biochemistry, and Behavior, 39,* 143–147.

Fodor, J. (2000) *The mind doesn't work that way: The scope and limits of computational psychology.* Cambridge, MA: MIT Press.

Freud, S. (1920/1959). *Beyond the pleasure principle.* London: The Hogarth Press.

George, M. H., & Belmaker, R. H. (2000). *Transcranial magnetic stimulation in neuropsychiatry.* Washington, DC: American Psychiatric Press.

Heath, R. G. (1996). *Exploring the mind–brain relationship.* Baton Rouge, LA: Moran Printing, Inc.

Herman, B. H., & Panksepp, J. (1981). Ascending endorphinergic inhibition of distress vocalization. *Science, 211,* 1060–1062.

Holstege, G.; Bandler, R.; & Saper, C. B. (Eds.). (1996). *The emotional motor system: Progress in brain research,* Vol. 107. Amsterdam: Elsevier.

Ikemoto, S., & Panksepp, J. (1999). The role of nucleus accumbens dopamine in motivated behavior: A unifying interpretation with special reference to reward-seeking. *Brain Research Reviews, 31,* 6–41.

Jürgens, U. (1998). Neuronal control of mammalian vocalization, with special reference to the squirrel monkey. *Naturwissenschaften, 85,* 376–388.

Kalin, N. H.; Shelton, S. E.; & Lynn, D. E. (1995). Opiate systems in mother and infant primates coordinate intimate contact during reunion. *Psychoneuroendocrinology, 20,* 735–742.

Kehoe, P., & Blass, E. M. (1986). Opioid mediation of separation-distress in 10 day old rats: Reversal of stress with maternal stimuli. *Developmental Psychobiology, 19,* 385–398.

Keverne, E. B.; Nevison, C. M.; & Martel, F. L. (1999). Early learning and the social bond. In C. S. Carter, I. Lederhendler, and B. Kirkpatrick (Eds.), *The integrative neurobiology of affiliation* (pp. 263–273). Cambridge, MA: MIT Press.

Knutson, B.; Burgdorf, J.; & Panksepp, J. (1998). Anticipation of play elicits high-frequency ultrasonic vocalizations in young rats. *Journal of Comparative Psychology, 112,* 65–73.

Knutson, B.; Burgdorf, J.; & Panksepp, J. (2002). Ultrasonic vocalizations as indices of affective states in rats. *Psychological Bulletin, 128,* 961–977.

Lane, R. D., & Nadel. L. (Eds.). (2000). *Cognitive neuroscience of emotion.* New York: Oxford University Press.

LeDoux, J. E. (1996). *The emotional brain.* New York: Simon & Schuster.

LeDoux, J. E. (2000). Emotion circuits in the brain. *Annual Review of Neuroscience, 23,* 155–184.

Liotti, M.; Brannan, S.; Egan, G.; Shade, R.; Madden, L.; Abplanalp, B.; Robillard, R.; Lancaster, J.; Zamarripa, F. E.; Fox, P. T.; & Denton, D. (2001). Brain responses associated with consciousness of breathlessness (air hunger). *Proceedings of the National Academy of Sciences, 98,* 2035–2040.

MacLean, P. D. (1990). *The triune brain in evolution: Role in paleocerebral functions.* New York: Plenum Press.

Meaney, M. J. (2001). Maternal care, gene expression and the transmission of individual differences in stress reactivity across generations. *Annual Review of Neuroscience, 24,* 1161–1192.

Nelson, E., & Panksepp, J. (1998). Brain substrates of infant–mother attachment: Contributions of opioids, oxytocin, and norepinepherine. *Neuroscience & Biobehavioral Reviews, 22,* 437–452.

Newman, J. D. (Ed.). (1988). *The physiological control of mammalian vocalization.* New York: Plenum Press.

Normansell, L. A., and Panksepp, J. (1990). Effects of morphine and naloxone on play-rewarded spatial discrimination in juvenile rats. *Developmental Psychobiology, 23,* 75–83.

Olmstead, M. C., & Franklin, K. B. (1997). The development of a conditioned place preference to morphine: Effects of microinjections into various CNS sites. *Behavioral Neuroscience, 111,* 1324–1334.

Panksepp, J. (1971). Aggression elicited by electrical stimulation of the hypothalamus in albino rats. *Physiology and Behavior, 6,* 311–316.

Panksepp, J. (1974). Hypothalamic regulation on energy balance and feeding behavior. *Federation Proceedings, 33,* 1150–1165.

Panksepp, J. (1981). Hypothalamic integration of behavior: Rewards, punishments, and related psychobiological process. In P. J. Morgane and J. Panksepp (Eds.), *Handbook of the hypothalamus, Vol. 3, Part A: Behavioral studies of the hypothalamus* (pp. 289–487). New York: Marcel Dekker.

Panksepp, J. (1982). Toward a general psychobiological theory of emotions. *The Behavioral and Brain Sciences, 5,* 407–467.

Panksepp, J. (1985). Mood changes. In P. J. Vinken, G. W. Bruyn, and H. L. Klawans (Eds.), *Handbook of clinical neurology. Clinical neuropsychology. Vol. 1.(45),* (pp. 271–285). Amsterdam: Elsevier.

Panksepp, J. (1986). The neurochemistry of behavior. *Annual Review of Psychology, 37,* 77–107.

Panksepp, J. (1990). The psychoneurology of fear: Evolutionary perspectives and the role of animal models in understanding human anxiety. In G. D. Burrows, M. Roth, and R. Noyes, Jr. (Eds.), *Handbook of anxiety, Vol. 3: The neurobiology of anxiety* (pp. 3–58). Amsterdam: Elsevier.

Panksepp, J. (1991). Affective neuroscience: A conceptual framework for the neurobiological study of emotions. In K. Strongman (Ed.), *International reviews of emotion research* (pp. 59–99). Chichester, UK: Wiley.

Panksepp, J. (1992). A critical role for "affective neuroscience" in resolving what is basic about basic emotions. *Psychological Review, 99,* 554–560.

Panksepp, J. (1993). Neurochemical control of moods and emotions: Amino acids to neuropeptides. In M. Lewis and J. Haviland (Eds.), *Handbook of emotions* (pp. 87–107). New York: Guilford Press.

Panksepp, J. (1996). Modern approaches to understanding fear: From laboratory to clinical practice. In J. Panksepp (Ed.), *Advances in biological psychiatry, Vol. 2* (pp. 209–230). Greenwich, CT: JAI Press.

Panksepp, J. (1998a). *Affective neuroscience: The foundations of human and animal emotion.* New York: Oxford University Press.

Panksepp, J. (1998b). The periconscious substrates of consciousness: Affective states and the evolutionary origins of the SELF. *Journal of Consciousness Studies, 5,* 566–582.

Panksepp, J. (1999). Emotions as viewed by psychoanalysis and neuroscience: An exercise in consilience. *Neuro-Psychoanalysis, 1,* 15–38.

Panksepp, J. (2000a). The neurodynamics of emotions: An evolutionary-neurodevelopmental view. In M. D. Lewis and I. Granic (Eds.), *Emotion, Self-Organization, and Development* (pp. 236–264). New York: Cambridge University Press.

Panksepp, J. (2000b). The riddle of laughter: Neural and psychoevolutionary underpinnings of joy. *Current Directions in Psychological Sciences, 9,* 183–186.

Panksepp, J. (2000c). The neuro-evolutionary cusp between emotions and cognitions, implications for understanding consciousness and the emergence of a unified mind science. *Consciousness & Emotion, 1,* 17–56.

Panksepp, J. (2000d). Affective consciousness and the instinctual motor system: The neural sources of sadness and joy. In R. Ellis & N. Newton (Eds.), *The Caldron of Consciousness, Motivation, Affect and Self-organization* (Vol 16, pp. 27–54), Advances in Consciousness Research. Amsterdam: John Benjamins Pub. Co.

Panksepp, J. (2001a). On the subcortical sources of basic human emotions and the primacy of emotional-affective (action-perception) processes in human consciousness. *Evolution and Cognition, 7,* 134–140.

Panksepp, J. (2001b). The long-term psychobiological consequences of infant emotions: Prescriptions for the twenty-first century. *Infant Mental Health Journal, 22,* 132–173.

Panksepp, J. (2003). At the interface of affective, behavioral and cognitive neurosciences. Decoding the emotional feelings of the brain. *Brain and Cognition, 52,* 4–14.

Panksepp, J., & Burgdorf, J. (1999). Laughing rats? Playful tickling arouses high frequency ultrasonic chirping in young rodents. In S. Hameroff, D. Chalmers, and A. Kazniak, *Toward a science of consciousness III* (pp. 231–244). Cambridge, MA: MIT Press.

Panksepp, J., & Burgdorf, J. (2000). 50k-Hz chirping (laughter?) in response to conditioned and unconditioned tickle-induced reward in rats: Effects of social housing and genetic variables. *Behavioural Brain Research, 115,* 25–38.

Panksepp, J., & Burgdorf, J. (2003). "Laughing" rats and the evolutionary antecedents of human joy? *Physiology and Behavior, 79,* 533–547.

Panksepp, J.; Burgdorf, J.; & Gordon, N. (2001). Towards a genetics of joy: Breeding rats for "laughter." In A. Kazniak (Ed.), *Emotions, qualia and consciousness* (pp. 124–136). Singapore: World Scientific.

Panksepp, J.; Herman, B.; Conner, R.; Bishop, P.; and Scott, J. P. (1978). The biology of social attachments: Opiates alleviate separation-distress. *Biological Psychiatry, 9*, 213–220.

Panksepp, J.; Herman, B. H.; Villberg, T.; Bishop, P.; and DeEskinazi, F. G. (1980). Endogenous opioids and social behavior. *Neuroscience and Biobehavioral Reviews, 4*, 473–487.

Panksepp, J.; Jalowiec, J.; DeEskinazi, F. G.; & Bishop, P. (1985). Opiates and play dominance in juvenile rats. *Behavioral Neuroscience, 99*, 441–453.

Panksepp, J.; Knuston, B.; & Burgdorf, J. (2002). The role of emotional brain systems in addictions: A neuro-evolutionary perspective. *Addiction, 97*, 459–469.

Panksepp, J.; Normansell, L. A.; Herman, B.; Bishop, P.; & Crepeau, L. (1988). Neural and neurochemical control of the separation-distress call. In J. D. Newman (Ed.), *The physiological control of mammalian vocalization* (pp. 263–299). New York: Plenum Press.

Panksepp, J., & Panksepp, J. B. (2000). The seven sins of evolutionary psychology. *Evolution and Cognition, 6*, 108–131.

Panksepp, J.; Siviy, S.; & Normansell, L. A. (1984). The psychobiology of play: Theoretical and methodological perspectives. *Neuroscience and Biobehavioral Reviews, 8*, 465–492.

Panksepp, J.; Yates, G.; Ikemoto, S.; & Nelson, E. (1991). Simple ethological models of depression: Social-isolation-induced "despair" in chicks and mice. In B. Olivier and J. Moss (Eds.), *Animal models in psychopharmacology* (pp. 161–181). Basel: Birkhäuser Verlag.

Pellis, S. M.; Field, E.; Smith, L. K.; & Pellis, V. C. (1997). Multiple differences in the play fighting of male and female rats. Implications for the causes and functions of play. *Neuroscience & Biobehavioral Reviews, 21*, 105–120.

Provine, R. R. (2000). *Laughter.* New York: Viking.

Robinson, T. E., & Berridge, K. C. (1993). The neural basis of drug craving: An incentive-sensitization theory of addiction. *Brain Research Reviews, 18*, 247–291.

Rolls, E. T. (1999). *The brain and emotion.* Oxford: Oxford University Press.

Rosen, J. B., & Schulkin, J. (1998). From normal fear to pathological anxiety. *Psychological Review, 105*, 325–350.

Schultz, W. (2000). Multiple reward signals in the brain. *Nature Reviews Neuroscience, 1*, 199–207.

Solms, M., & Nersessian, E. (1999). Freud's theory of affect: Questions for Neuroscience. *Neuro-Psychoanalysis, 1*, 5–14.

Vanderschuren, L.; Niesnik, R.; & Van Ree, J. (1997). The neurobiology of social play behavior in rats. *Neuroscience and Biobehavioral Reviews, 3*, 309–326.

12

Exposure Effects

An Unmediated Phenomenon

R. B. Zajonc

ABSTRACT

The mere repeated exposure paradigm involves repeated exposures of a particular stimulus object and observes the emerging preference for that object. Vast literature on the mere repeated exposure effect shows it to be a robust phenomenon that cannot be explained by an appeal to recognition memory or perceptual fluency. These effects are valid across cultures, species, and diverse stimulus domains. They have been obtained even when the stimuli exposed were not accessible to the participants' awareness, and even prenatally. Empirical research shows that a benign repetition experience can in and of itself enhance positive affect, and that such affect can become attached not only to exposed stimuli but to similar previously not exposed stimuli, and to stimuli totally distinct as well. A new explanation of the phenomenon is offered. Implications for affect as a fundamental and independent process are discussed in the light of neuroanatomical evidence.

The cognitive revolution of the past four decades has exerted an enormous influence not only on *what* we investigate but *how* we do it. In particular, cognitive processes came to be regarded as the major mediators of most significant psychological phenomena. For example, emotional reactions must be mediated by cognitive appraisal (Lazarus, 1982); social phobias are mediated by perceived self-efficacy; and aggression instigated by frustration is mediated by perceived provocation. A related concept is "implicit," a term that connotes an intervening process, but one of which the participant is not aware. There is thus implicit memory, implicit attitude, implicit learning, implicit perception, implicit knowledge, and several others.

An overzealous and indiscriminate commitment to mediators, however, may end up in Zeno's paradox; because if a factor z mediates between x and y, then surely there will be mediators between x and z, between z and y, and so on *ad infinitum*. Some forms of mediation, of course, are useful or necessary, but a knee-jerk appeal to mediators may introduce unwanted complexity, even indeterminacy.

REPEATED EXPOSURE AND ITS EFFECTS

A phenomenon of substantial generality and of fundamental significance – the mere repeated exposure effect – is, I will show, an unmediated process. I begin with an illustrative example. If, on the eleventh day of incubation, the narrow end of a fertile chicken egg is punctured by a syringe and injected with 0.7 ml of 2.5 percent propylane glycol water solution of U.S. certified vegetable coloring, say red, the hatchling will emerge from the shell with bright-red plumage. The same effect can be obtained with all galinatious birds, and perhaps all birds. If we then allow chicks – say, one dyed green and one dyed red – to hatch separately but after twelve hours place them together to remain in each other's company for the next twenty-four hours, these two chicks will prefer each other's companionship to that of all other chicks, even those dyed the same color and those left undyed (Zajonc, Wilson, & Rajecki, 1975). Moreover, when presented with a choice between two potential companions previously not encountered, one red and another green, the red chick will choose a green companion and the green chick will choose a red companion. These preferences can be determined simply by counting the amount of pecking – a good indicator of aggression. Figure 12.1 shows the amount of hostile pecking per minute at an "out-group" target chicken and at an "in-group" target chicken. "Out-group" here means a chicken of coloring other than the coloring that the chick was previously exposed to during its twenty-four-hour first cohabitation. Conversely, "in-group" chicks are those of the coloring to

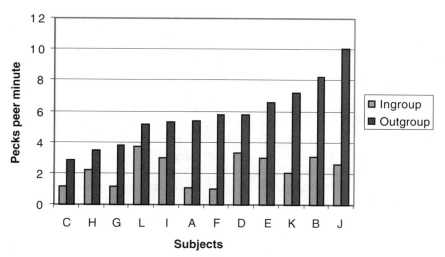

FIGURE 12.1. In-group and out-group aggression following early exposure (Zajonc & Rajecki, 1969)

Experience

Test

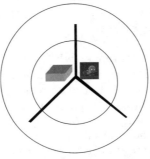

FIGURE 12.2. Exposure conditions (alone, peer, matchbox) and test of affiliative preference (arena) in the Taylor and Sluckin (1964) experiment

which the chick was previously exposed – that is, for red chicks green, and for green chicks red. Chicks of a feather don't. . . .

Many such experiments have been carried out in the days of imprinting, yielding consistent data on the formation of bonds as a function of exposure. For example, Taylor and Sluckin (1964) let newly hatched chicks be raised under three conditions: with a conspecific peer, alone, or with a matchbox (Figure 12.2). After having been so raised, the chick's preferences were recorded. The chicks, one at a time, were placed in an arena that contained three equal pie-shaped segments where the chick could explore or where it could linger: one contained a same-age chick (but not the one they lived with); another segment contained a matchbox; and the third segment was empty. The results – now expressed in measures of attraction – were quite clear. The chicks overwhelmingly preferred the pie-shaped segment that most closely resembled their immediate past experience. Even the matchbox became most attractive following exposure to matchbox, and much more attractive than a live peer (Figure 12.3).

A more dramatic and subtle effect was reported by Pratt and Sackett (1967). These researchers reared young rhesus monkeys under three different conditions. One group was totally deprived of contact (visual and auditory as well) with other monkeys. A second group was reared in separate

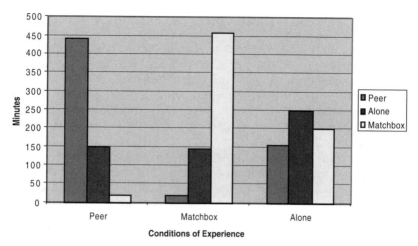

FIGURE 12.3. Time spent by chicks, alone, near peer and near matchbox in the Taylor and Sluckin (1964) experiment

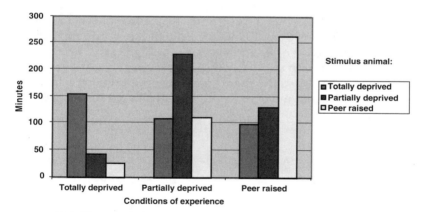

FIGURE 12.4. Time spent by monkeys near totally deprived, partially deprived, and peer-raised stimulus monkeys by subjects that were themselves totally deprived, partially deprived, and peer-raised in the Pratt and Sackett (1967) experiment

cages but in the same room; thus these animals could hear and see each other. The third group was reared in full contact, all in the same cage. As in the Taylor and Sluckin study, the time spent near a stimulus animal constituted the test of affiliation and attachment. The subjects could place themselves near a monkey reared in one of three ways. Of course, none of these monkeys was previously known to the tested subject. The results (Figure 12.4) show, again, that even these subtle behavioral differences that must have emerged in the course of the different forms of contact or its absence were sufficient to produce a level of familiarity sufficient for an affiliative tendency to emerge.

Grier, Counter, and Shearer (1967) exposed chicken eggs during their third week of incubation to sequences of tones. A control group was deprived of this stimulation. A few hours after hatching, the chicks were placed in an area where they could approach a speaker playing the familiar tone sequences or the unfamiliar tone sequences. Predictably, the newly hatched chicks showed strong preferences for the tones that had been played to them *in ovo*.

Exposure effects are readily found with human subjects and with a great variety of stimulus materials. The repeated exposure paradigm used with human participants consists of no more than making a stimulus object accessible to the individual's sensory receptors, without requiring that the individual engage in any sort of behavior, and without offering positive or negative reinforcement. The exposures themselves are sometimes so impoverished that the individual is not aware of their occurrence. Their effects are measured by the resulting changes in preference for the object or approach behavior.

For example, Turkish-like words are presented to subjects with varying frequencies, and following the exposures the participants are asked to judge the stimuli for positivity. They are told that the words are Turkish but are about either good or bad things. We would like, we say, the participants to guess for each word whether it has a positive or a negative meaning. Figure 12.5 shows the results of such an experiment, where the same stimulus when seen more frequently was attributed a more positive meaning.

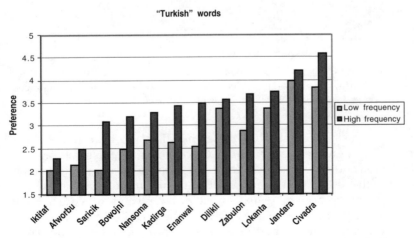

FIGURE 12.5. Preferences for "Turkish" words exposed frequently and infrequently

The study, in fact, has been replicated under field conditions. Zajonc and Rajecki (1969) "advertised" in the University of Michigan and the Michigan State University newspapers the "Turkish" words used previously. For this purpose, a one-inch space in the classified-ads sections was purchased for several repetitions.

In these spaces, over a period of several weeks, the same Turkish-like words used in the experiment just described were printed. Of course, some words were presented frequently, others infrequently. Following the "exposure" campaign, students in various classes and faculty were sent questionnaires asking them to guess the meanings of the Turkish-like words printed in their newspapers. The results clearly indicated that the frequently presented words were attributed more positive meaning.

For almost one century, this type of effect, although not actually demonstrated, was given a mediational explanation. In his textbook, Titchener (1910) offered the explanation that frequently encountered stimuli gain in attractiveness because they are recognized as familiar. He gave an example of the pleasure one experiences in listening to a known piece of music. We enjoy the recognition of a familiar theme, we can anticipate correctly its development, and we "become one with the music."

If Titchener was right, then the stimuli that have gained in attractiveness as a result of exposure should also have gained in ease of recognition. Wilson (1979) investigated this question of whether stimulus recognition is a mediator of enhancement of attractiveness of frequently exposed stimuli. He presented his participants with sequences of tone, some of which were repeated several times. He then played two tone sequences to the subjects, one previously presented and one new, asking them which of the two they liked better and which of the two they had heard previously. Figure 12.6 shows his data, which clearly indicate that recognition of the stimuli does

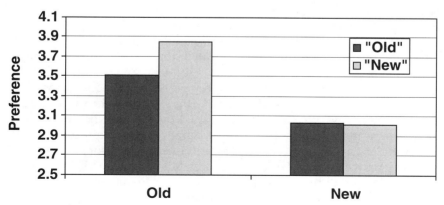

FIGURE 12.6. Preference for frequently presented tone sequences and novel ones that were judged "old" and "new" in the Wilson (1979) experiment

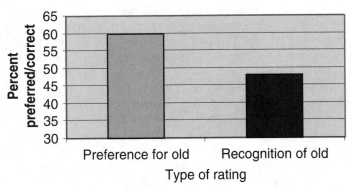

FIGURE 12.7. Preferences for and recognition memory for stimuli presented and novel ones in the Zajonc and Kunst-Wilson (1980) experiment

not mediate the gain in attractiveness. As can be seen from the data, the increased attractiveness of stimuli depends, not on the subjective judgment of familiarity – not on whether a stimulus is judged to be "old" or "new" – but on whether the stimulus was in fact historically old or new.

A more compelling experiment confirms the conclusion that the exposure effect requires no recognition as its mediator. Kunst-Wilson and Zajonc (1980) denied subjects the possibility of recognition by presenting the stimuli repeatedly but at such short intervals that no identification or recognition was possible. In fact, subsequent tests of recognition showed recognition memory to be at chance level. Yet stimuli presented frequently were liked better than stimuli not presented. The results of this experiment are shown in Figure 12.7.

Several replications of this experiment have been carried out since the original Kunst-Wilson and Zajonc study (e.g., Elliott & Dolan, 1998; Seamon, Brody, & Kauff, 1983), all confirming the proposition that recognition is not a necessary mediator of the exposure effect.

But if recognition is not a necessary mediator of the exposure effect, what might be the process whereby repeated stimuli gain in attractiveness? It became apparent from a series of experiments (Zajonc, 2000) that the affective consequence of repeated exposures is actually quite gross and diffuse. It could, therefore, be assumed that the exposures themselves cause a vague and diffuse affective state that "spills over" onto whatever stimuli happen to be in the vicinity. Since the paradigm of mere exposure requires that stimuli be made just accessible to the individual's sensory system, and that no positive or negative consequences follow exposures, the history of repeated stimuli that are neither noxious nor threatening signals that they are safe to be around, that no escape need be contemplated, that no vigilance is required, and that no special attention needs to be paid to these stimuli. In other words, we have here a form of classical conditioning

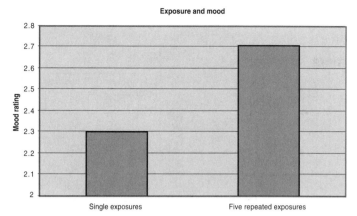

FIGURE 12.8. Mood ratings of subjects following frequent and infrequent stimulus exposures in the Monahan, Murphy, and Zajonc (2000) experiment

where the absence of a harmful event is the unconditioned stimulus for the individual's approach behavior (Zajonc, 2001).

The following experiment revealed that the effects of exposures *in themselves* are capable of inducing a positive affective state in individuals. Monahan, Murphy, and Zajonc (2000) presented, under subliminal viewing conditions, to one group of subjects twenty-five Chinese ideographs, each shown only once. Another group of subjects were presented with five Chinese ideographs, each shown five times. The subjects were instructed to just relax but to pay attention to the screen on which, ostensibly, stimuli would appear, but at such short intervals that they would not be able to see anything. After these exposures, the participants were asked to report their overall mood. Figure 12.8 shows the average mood responses of the participants. It is clear that the repetition of an experience in and of itself is capable of inducing a diffuse mood state.

Can such a diffuse mood state become attached to particular stimuli, thus producing a specific effect? Monahan, Murphy, and Zajonc (2000) repeated the above experiment but after the exposure series asked subjects to judge the likability of three types of stimuli. One group of subjects made these liking ratings after repeated exposures (i.e., five exposures of each of five stimuli). Another group made their liking ratings following one exposure each of twenty-five Chinese ideographs. One type of stimulus to be judged was the stimulus actually shown in the series; the second type of stimulus was of the same category, that is, also a Chinese ideograph. The third type of stimulus was completely distinct. Here the subjects judged random polygons. Figure 12.9 shows that the prior experience of exposures increased the attractiveness of stimuli, whether they were the same ones as previously shown or completely distinct ones. In each of the three

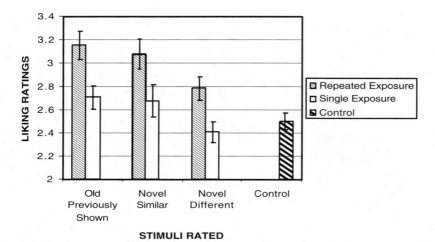

FIGURE 12.9. Preferences for stimuli actually shown, stimuli of the same category but never shown, and novel totally distinct stimuli following frequent and infrequent exposure series in the Monahan, Murphy, and Zajonc (2000) experiment

conditions, the liking for the judged stimuli was greater when they followed repeated exposures than when they followed single exposures.

CONCLUSION

The various experiments reported here and elsewhere in the literature call for a conclusion that the exposure effect does not require an assumption of recognition as a mediator. The history of experience in itself is a sufficient condition for the effect to take place. What is most intriguing about the set of results reported here is that a specific effect of exposures is obtained, not by specific stimuli being distinguished in the person's awareness, but by the diffusion of an undedicated affect. The only process that needs to be assumed is that the conspicuous absence of aversive consequences following the presentation of a conditioned stimulus is a sufficient condition for the development of an approach tendency to that stimulus. One would suppose that the effect documented here must be well known in the advertising industry.

References

Elliott, R., & Dolan, R. J. (1998). Neural response during preference and memory judgments for subliminally presented stimuli: A functional neuroimaging study. *Journal of Neuroscience, 18,* 4697–4704.

Grier, J. B.; Counter, S. A.; & Shearer, W. M. (1967). *Science, 155,* 1692–1693.

Kunst-Wilson, W. R., & Zajonc, R. B. (1980). Affective discrimination of stimuli that cannot be recognized. *Science, 207,* 557–558.

Lazarus, R. S. (1982). Thoughts on the relations between emotion and cognition. *American Psychologist, 37,* 1019–1024.

Monahan, J. L.; Murphy, S. T.; & Zajonc, R. B. (2000). Subliminal mere exposure: Specific, general and diffuser effects. *Psychological Science, 11,* 462–466.

Pratt, C. L., & Sackett, G. P. (1967). Selection of social partners as a function of peer contact during rearing. *Science, 155,* 113–1135.

Seamon, J. G.; Brody, N.; & Kauff, D. M. (1983). Affective discrimination of stimuli that are not recognized: Effects of shadowing, masking, and cerebral laterality. *Journal of Experimental Psychology: Learning, Memory, and Cognition, 9,* 544–555.

Taylor, K. F., & Sluckin, W. (1964). Flocking in domestic chicks. *Nature, 201,* 108–109.

Titchener, E. B. (1910). *A textbook of psychology.* New York: Macmillan.

Wilson, W. R. (1979). Feeling more than we can know: Exposure effects without learning. *Journal of Personality and Social Psychology, 37,* 811–821.

Zajonc, R. B. (2000). Feeling and thinking: Closing the debate over the independence of affect. In J. P. Forgas (Ed.), *Feeling and thinking: The role of affect in social cognition.* (pp. 31–58). Cambridge: Cambridge University Press.

Zajonc, R. B. (2001). Mere exposure: A gateway to the subliminal. *Current Directions in Psychological Science, 10,* 224–228.

Zajonc, R. B., & Rajecki, D. W. (1969). Exposure and affect: A field experiment. *Psychonomic Science, 17,* 216–217.

Zajonc, R. B.; Wilson, W. R.; &. Rajecki, D. W. (1975). Affiliation and social discrimination produced by brief exposure in day-old chicks. *Animal Behavior, 23,* 131–138.

13

Feeling States in Emotion

Functional Imaging Evidence

Joel S. Winston and Raymond J. Dolan

ABSTRACT

An essential feature of emotional states is their association with change in auto-nomic function. The importance of these changes lies in the fact that in many theo-retical accounts of emotion the realization of autonomic states is a primary means through which feeling states are realized. The issue addressed in this chapter is how the brain generates and represents autonomic states of the organism and their im-portance in feeling states. A distinction will be drawn between brain systems that mediate relatively automatic responses to emotional stimuli and systems that are involved in what can be termed conscious feeling states. These distinctions will be illustrated by observations from functional neuroimaging and patients with focal brain lesions and pathology of the autonomic nervous system.

Despite the impact of William James at the end of the nineteenth century, for the best part of several decades in the middle of the twentieth cen-tury, neuroscientists treated "emotion" and "feeling" as interchangeable terms. This approach to the language of emotion, coupled with the behav-iorist movement prevalent in twentieth century psychology, meant that the neuroscientific study of emotion was grossly neglected, often seen as con-ceptually ragged and its practitioners as pursuing "soft science" (Damasio, 1999; Damasio, 1994; Damasio, 1998; LeDoux, 1996; LeDoux, 2000). Recent efforts, however, have put the study of emotion center stage in understand-ing the workings of the brain, proposing roles in cognition (Zajonc, 1980), decision making (Damasio, 1994), perception (Anderson & Phelps, 2001), and even consciousness (Panksepp, 1998; Damasio, 1999). Among the rea-sons that emotion has assumed center stage in neuroscience is a rediscovery of the importance of a dissociation between emotion and feeling (LeDoux, 1996; LeDoux, 2000), which potentially offers a more tractable approach to the neuroscientific study of emotion (Damasio, 2001). Indeed, Antonio Damasio has extended this distinction to formal definitions. Specifically, emotion is defined as "a patterned collection of chemical and neural responses that is produced by the brain when it detects the presence of an emotionally competent stimulus . . . the responses are engendered *automatically*" (emphasis added). This contrasts with feelings that "are the mental representation of the physiological changes that characterise emotions. Unlike emotions . . . feelings are indeed private, although no more subjective than any other aspect of the mind" (Damasio, 2001, this volume).

Though not universally accepted, this distinction between automatically elicited emotional states and experiential (and necessarily subsequent) feeling states is a useful heuristic in reviewing work in the relatively new field of functional neuroimaging of emotion.

AUTOMATICITY AND THE AMYGDALA

A substantial number of neuroimaging studies on emotion have explored the neural responses to emotional faces, often under conditions wherein volunteer subjects are unaware that the emotional aspect of the stimulus constitutes the experimental variable of interest. For example, Morris and colleagues (Morris et al., 1996) and Breiter and colleagues (Breiter et al., 1996) have provided findings implicating the amygdala in automatic processing of fearful faces. In the former study, using PET and involving a block design, subjects were presented with a series of morphed faces from the Ekman and Friesen series (Ekman & Friesen, 1975). The study showed that regional cerebral blood flow (rCBF) in the left amygdala was specifically enhanced to fear and increased monotonically with increasing degree of fear expressed in the face. Debriefing confirmed that subjects were unaware that emotion was the variable of interest in the study. Breiter and colleagues (Breiter et al., 1996), using functional magnetic resonance imaging (fMRI) and a blocked experimental design, showed a response in amygdala to both fearful and happy faces relative to neutral faces. An additional observation was attenuation in amygdala response with repetition of fearful faces. Again, subjects' task in the scanner was designated as gender discrimination, so avoiding any explicit reference to the emotional component of the experimental design. This basic result of an amygdala response to fearful faces has been widely replicated in subsequent studies (Dolan et al., 2001; Hariri et al., 2000; Phillips et al., 1997; Vuilleumier et al., 2001; Whalen et al., 1998).

Neuroimaging of human fear conditioning also implicates the amygdala in fear processing, as might be predicted from the animal literature (for review, see Davis, 1992; LeDoux, 2000) and case reports in humans with discrete brain lesions (Bechara et al., 1995; LaBar et al., 1995). As Buchel and Dolan point out in a recent review of the literature on fear conditioning (2000), the consistent finding in studies of classical aversive conditioning is that the amygdala is a central unit in the processing of CS-US contingency. In other words, the amygdala is the key locus in associating previously

neutral stimuli with acquired aversive value. Commonly in fear conditioning experiments, subjects are unaware of the contingency, or only become
aware of the contingency some time into the experiment. The response in
amygdala, which tends to habituate rapidly (Buchel et al., 1999; Buchel
et al., 1998; LaBar et al., 1998), would consequently seem to take an opposite time – course to subjects' reported awareness of CS+/UCS contingencies. Again, we note an apparent automaticity of amygdala responses,
regardless of the awareness of the contingency. Indeed, in one study, Morris
et al. (1986b) demonstrate that awareness of the conditioned stimulus itself
is unnecessary for an amygdala response.

In a recent study on fearful faces and spatial attention, Vuilleumier and
colleagues (Vuilleumier et al., 2001) addressed the issue of automaticity
in emotional processing in a carefully controlled fashion. These authors
demonstrated that while responses to faces, including fearful faces, in the
fusiform gyrus (an area on the ventral surface of the brain anterior to visual
cortex known to respond to faces) *are* modulated by attention, amygdala
responses to fearful faces are not. In this study, subjects were instructed to
attend to either a horizontal pair or vertical pair of stimuli, which could
be either pairs of houses or faces (Figure 13.1a). Faces were either fearful or neutral. Pairs of faces or houses appeared at either task-relevant or
task-irrelevant locations. The task was a same/different judgment across
the task-relevant location. Regardless of whether fearful faces appeared
at task-relevant or task-irrelevant locations, amygdala responses were of
similar magnitude (Figure 13.1 b, c). In contrast, responses to fearful faces
in the fusiform gyrus were modulated by both attention to the face and the
emotive nature of faces (Figure 13.1 b, d). In a parallel behavioral study, the
authors additionally demonstrate the effectiveness of their experimental
manipulation – subjects were unable to state whether a face was emotional
or neutral immediately after trials in which they had been attending to
houses. In other words the experimental design had induced an inatten-
tional amnesia for nonattended stimuli. Additional evidence that subjects
need not be consciously aware of threatening stimuli in order to generate
amygdala responses to these stimuli has come from a study using masking
of fearful faces (Whalen et al., 1998) and recent studies on a single patient
with blindsight (Morris et al., 2001).

The above leads to the conclusion that the amygdala links pre-perceptual
or pre-attentive sensory processing with emotion. Notably, there is considerable evidence that the amygdala might also be involved in the reverse
process, namely the heightening of perceptual processing in relation to
emotionally salient stimuli. For example, an analysis of functional connectivity, derived from neuroimaging data, between amygdala and extrastriate
cortex in the context of subjects being presented with fearful and happy
faces has revealed increased coupling of activity in these areas when the target face was fearful rather than happy (Morris et al., 1998a). The authors

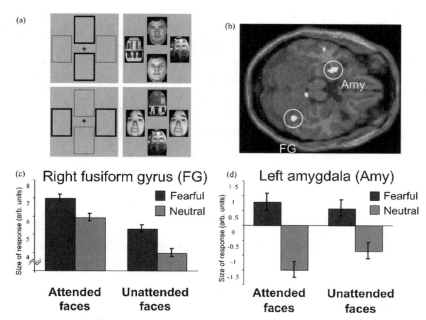

FIGURE 13.1. Differential responses in amygdala and fusiform gyrus dependent on attention and emotion (see Vuilleumier et al., 2001). (*a*) Task design: Faces and houses appeared paired at task-relevant or task-irrelevant locations. The task was to decide whether the pair of stimuli in the task-relevant locations were the same or different. In addition, faces could be fearful or neutral. Subjects were instructed which were the task-relevant locations before they were given a block of trials by bold outlines of the target stimuli locations. (*b*) Main effect of fearful faces relative to neutral faces. Statistical map overlaid onto a horizontal slice from single subject's structural scan demonstrating areas showing greater responses to fearful than to neutral faces. Both left amygdala and right fusiform gyrus exhibit such responses. (*c*) Measures of task- and stimulus-dependent responses in right fusiform gyrus. Note that there is modulation of fusiform responses by both emotion (greater responses to fearful faces) and attention (greater responses when faces were at task-relevant locations). (*d*) Measures of task- and stimulus-dependent responses in left amygdala. Note that there is an effect of emotion (greater responses to fearful faces) but no effect of attention: responses to fearful faces are independent of direction of attention. This suggests that the amygdala is automatically processing the fearful faces.

interpreted this alteration of activity in extrastriate cortex to the presentation of fearful faces as mediated by anatomical back-projections from amygdala (Amaral & Price, 1984). A more recent study, using expressionally transfigured face stimuli (the "Thatcher Illusion"), has replicated this finding of altered coupling between amygdala and lateral occipital cortex in association with emotionally valenced stimuli (Rotshtein et al., 2001). We note also that a recent human lesion study demonstrated that enhanced perception of emotional relative to neutral words during the attentional blink is absent in patients with bilateral amygdala lesions (Anderson & Phelps, 2001). This phenomenon of enhanced perception of emotional items may be the functional consequence of reafferent feedback from amygdala to extrastriate cortical regions.

OTHER AREAS INVOLVED IN GENERATING EMOTIONS

Although the amygdala is clearly important in bridging a gap between perception (or lower-level processes such as object recognition) and emotion (at least for the cases of fear discussed above), there are many other brain areas involved in the generation of the the chemical and neuronal changes that underlie emotional behaviour (Damasio, 1994). Among the key regions are hypothalamic autonomic centers, basal forebrain, and brainstem nuclei. It is of interest that the primate basolateral amygdala has extensive interconnections with all of these areas (Amaral et al., 1992), and it is more than likely that the entire landscape of an emotion includes important components mediated through outputs from these regions. However, relatively few imaging studies on emotion report activations in these structures (for a notable exception, see the recent study by Damasio et al., 2000). The relative absence of activation in these regions may, in part, relate to limitations in current neuroimaging methodologies: these include limited spatial resolutions of a few millimeters; a restricted resolution in the temporal domain of seconds; regional variability in time-courses of neuronal activation; the inability to account for regional variations in neurovascular coupling; and signal dropout in inferior temporal, inferior-medial prefrontal, and brainstem regions (particularly with fMRI).

EMOTIONS OTHER THAN FEAR

It remains unclear whether the human amygdala is a structure devoted more to the processing of fear than to the processing of other so-called basic emotions. Imaging studies of perception of disgust have emphasized activations in the insular cortex and basal ganglia (Gorno-Tempini et al., 2001; Phillips et al., 1998; Phillips et al., 1997; Sprengelmeyer et al., 1998). This distinct pattern of activation in relation to disgust would accord with a more general a priori hypothesis that proposes functional specialization devoted to processing distinct basic emotions. It should also be noted that there is converging evidence from neuropsychology that supports imaging findings in relation to disgust, in that patients with basal ganglia and insula damage have specific impairments in recognition of facial expressions of disgust (Calder et al., 2000; Gray et al., 1997). However, an important caveat with respect to the above neuroimaging data is that, unless critical comparisons are made between fearful- and disgust-evoked activation conditions, one cannot conclude that disgust activates the insula significantly more than fear, nor that fear activates the amygdala significantly more than disgust. To the best of our knowledge, in only one study is such a critical comparison actually reported (Phillips et al., 1998). In this study, using data derived from six subjects, a comparison of evoked responses to fearful minus neutral faces and disgusted minus neutral faces yielded a single point located in amygdala as more significantly activated in response to fearful faces. We note that the coordinate reported for this locus is probably too posterior and lateral for amygdala, and may correspond better to hippocampus. Two separate foci in the left anterior insula were more activated in response to disgusted faces.

This result does suggest a dissociation within regions subserving emotional processing in terms of preferential responses to specific basic emotions. However, we stress that it is a single result in a small number of subjects, and would caution against any strong inference of distinct neural bases for perception of different emotions (Calder et al., 2001) pending confirmatory evidence. Indeed, our considered view is that current findings from functional imaging studies of emotion are unable to resolve the issue of whether there are distinct neural substrates for "basic emotions" (or, indeed, whether there are "basic emotions" at all). At least one study has reported an amygdala response to sad faces (though not to angry ones) (Blair et al., 1999) and, notably, studies have indicated that happy faces activate amygdala relative to neutral faces (Breiter et al., 1996), as well as showing amygdala responses to affectively positive physiological stimuli such as tastes (O'Doherty et al., 2001), suggesting that its role in emotion may not even be limited to negative emotions, as has been suggested by others (Adolphs et al., 1999). The human lesion literature concerning the role of amygdala in recognition of emotion suggests that there is minimally an impairment in recognition of fear subsequent to bilateral amygdala damage, though individual cases with impairments in recognition of anger, sadness, and disgust have also been reported (Adolphs et al., 1994; Adolphs et al., 1995; Adolphs et al., 1999; Broks et al., 1998; Fine and Blair, 2000; Schmolck and Squire, 2001; Young et al., 1996). We anticipate that further neuroimaging and neuropsychological studies may clarify this topic.

THE NEURONAL BASIS OF FEELING STATES

A key component of many classical and modern hypotheses of emotion and feeling has been the crucial role ascribed to the autonomic nervous system in generating feelings. Thus, as James might have elaborated it, we *feel* scared partly because our heart beats faster, and our heart beating faster is itself an index of an emotional response. Though such autonomic activity is only one aspect of the somatic feedback hypothesized to compose emotional responses by James (1884) and Damasio (1994), it has been more extensively studied than other modes of somatic feedback, and we limit our discussion here to studies of the generation and mapping of autonomic states. A series of recent experiments using PET and fMRI have attempted to address the functional neuroanatomy of the autonomic nervous system. Using PET, with simultaneous recording of skin conductance changes elicited by a variety of stimuli, Fredrikson and colleagues (Fredrikson et al., 1998) demonstrated positive correlations between electrodermal activity (EDA) and blood flow in left primary motor, posterior cingulate, and anterior cingulate cortices. One of the strengths of this study was the authors' ability to analyze the association between EDA and blood flow independent of the task effects that generated the conductance changes. Using PET, and different measures of autonomic activity that included heart rate and blood pressure changes, Critchley and colleagues (Critchley et al., 2000a) demonstrated increased activity in cerebellum, pons, right anterior cingulate, and right insula covarying with heart rate and activity in right anterior cingulate and right insula covarying with mean arterial blood pressure. In this study, strenuous exercise and mental stressor tasks were used to generate cardiovascular arousal where an independent baseline for each condition enabled a conjunction analysis allowing identification of regions commonly activated across experimental conditions.

A well-documented problem with PET experiments is the limited temporal resolution. Cerebral blood flow measurements are usually a reflection of integrated activity in the brain typically taken over the time-course of approximately one minute. This makes it impossible to separate cause-and-effect influences on measures of peripheral autonomic arousal. Thus, in the experiments described, the increased blood flow in anterior cingulate reported in both studies might be the cause of the autonomic arousal, or an effect arising out of the central mapping of peripheral autonomic effects. To dissociate these possibilities, Critchley and colleagues used event-related fMRI, with its greatly improved temporal resolution of several seconds (Critchley et al., 2000b). In this study, a variant of a gambling task was undertaken by six subjects while skin conductance measurements and fMRI were simultaneously acquired. Skin conductance responses (SCR – an index of peripheral bodily arousal) were used in the subsequent analysis of the fMRI data by designating peaks in SCR as "events" in the analysis. The authors thus attempted to explain the responses recorded by fMRI by means of events preceding or succeeding peaks in SCR. This allowed the authors to attribute differential brain activity to the generation of SCRs as well as the mapping of neuronal changes consequent upon the occurrence of SCRs. In this study, activity preceding SCR events was evident in cerebellum, lingual gyrus, left medial prefrontal lobe, and fusiform gyrus.

By contrast, activity subsequent to SCR events was demonstrated in right medial prefrontal cortex. Finally, activity both preceding and subsequent to SCR events was evident in regions such as orbitofrontal, bilateral medial prefrontal, and posterior cingulate cortex. The interpretation of these results is that they accorded strongly with a suggested role for ventromedial prefrontal cortex in generating and decoding the significance of "somatic markers" (Bechara et al., 1997; Bechara et al., 1996; Damasio, 1994). Thus, orbitofrontal and medial prefrontal cortices generate and map bodily states, a role that may facilitate guidance of behavior, as suggested by Damasio (1994).

In an experiment addressing the issue of self-modulation of autonomic activity, Critchley and colleagues (Critchley et al., 2001c) trained subjects with biofeedback techniques. Subjects then underwent PET scans in four conditions: instructed to relax using accurate biofeedback information based upon SCR; instructed to relax but provided with inaccurate biofeedback information; and instructed not to relax with both accurate and inaccurate biofeedback. Subjects were informed whether biofeedback information was accurate or inaccurate. Activity in anterior cingulate, left inferior parietal lobule, and globus pallidus was associated with subjects' attempts to relax. Additionally, and importantly, activity in anterior cingulate showed an interaction between between feedback and task, being higher when subjects were instructed to relax and were provided with accurate biofeedback. This suggests that anterior cingulate is involved in the intentional modulation of arousal.

In a study pertaining directly to autonomic arousal and feelings, Critchley and colleagues (Critchley et al., 2001a) used event-related fMRI with simultaneous GSR recording while subjects played a card-gambling game (Figure 13.2a). Eight subjects made decisions about whether the next card in a sequence would be higher or lower than the previous one. There was an objective measure of the risk involved in a given decision, namely the degree of certainty about the value of the next card (certainty was higher when the previous card took an extreme value). Additionally, the recording of SCRs allowed a measure of autonomic arousal association with anticipation of the outcome of each trial. The key finding in this study was the demonstration that a portion of the anterior cingulate cortex responded both to the uncertainty of decisions and to their associated arousal (Figure 13.2b, c). This, in the view of the authors, provided support for the view that "anterior cingulate function reflects integration of cognitive states with adaptive changes in bodily states mediated by the autonomic nervous system."

Some of the hypotheses derived from this work on autonomic regulation have been tested by Critchley and colleagues (Critchley et al., 2001b) in a patient group with pure autonomic failure (PAF). These patients suffer

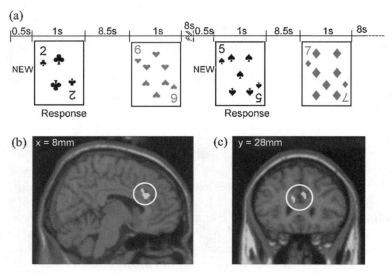

FIGURE 13.2. Anterior cingulate cortex integrates arousal and uncertainty (see (Critchley et al., 2001a). (*a*) Experimental design: The task was a gambling game in which subjects had to predict whether the next card would be higher or lower than the previous one. Card values ranged from 1 to 10. New trials were indicated by the word "new" appearing on screen before the first card. Cards appeared for one second, after which time subjects had to decide whether the next card would be higher or lower. There was then a gap before the next card was revealed. The last four seconds of this gap was the time during which anticipatory arousal was measured. The uncertainty of a given trial was a function of the first card that appeared. In the example in the figure, the first trial is relatively certain, as there is little chance of a card less than 2. The second trial is relatively uncertain, as there is an almost equal chance of a card higher or lower than 6. (*b, c*) Activity in anterior cingulate was modulated by both risk and arousal. Parasagittal (*b*) and coronal (*c*) sections through a template brain with statistical map showing regions where there was significant modulation of the delay period activity by both arousal and uncertainty.

peripheral autonomic denervation in the absence of any other neurological deficit and where there is no known central pathology. Patients thus lack peripheral autonomic change and its associated central representation. Comparing nine PAF patients to eight age-matched healthy controls (using PET) in an experiment where the tasks involved either mental or physical stress (and control tasks), Critchley and colleagues noted that patients showed increased anterior cingulate cortex activity associated with increased exertion. As expected from their medical condition, however, the patients showed no evidence of actual autonomic changes, as indexed by heart rate and blood pressure. This is suggestive of a conceptualization whereby anterior cingulate modulates autonomic function and integrates it with feedback information about ongoing autonomic changes. In the absence of the expected autonomic changes, cingulate activity is increased as it attempts to generate a task-appropriate autonomic tone. Crucially, the authors also documented alterations in emotional experience within the key patient group relative to Parkinsonian patients with similar physical disability, suggesting that an absence of autonomic arousal does impair their ability to experience feeling states.

STUDIES ADDRESSING "FEELINGS"

There have been few attempts since the inception of functional neuroimaging to address the neuronal basis of feelings. The difficulty of this undertaking must be acknowledged, given that the definition of feelings necessarily involves private subjective states. The predominant experimental approach has been to use visual or verbal stimuli as mood inducers and to scan subjects as they report alteration in feeling states. One problem with such study designs is that feelings are necessarily secondary to emotions in most models of feelings and emotions. This renders it difficult to separate the functional neuroanatomy of the feeling from that of the emotion. A fully factorial design, in which feelings occurred in the absence of emotions, might address this issue, but this would seem impossible within the definitions of emotions and feelings provided above. The best alternative would be experiments in which emotions are elicited in both the absence and presence of feelings (even here, one would be incurring the assumption of "pure insertion" [Friston et al., 1996]) but too little research seems to be carried out even along such lines.

Thus, in our view, the bulk of experiments to date confound emotions and feelings. Additionally, experiments on feelings are difficult to quantify because of the subjective nature of the experimental variable. We are reliant on subjects understanding what experimenters mean when they ask them to re-create a feeling of sadness, and to accurately report the intensity and quality of the feeling. Furthermore, the use of a "neutral feeling" baseline is less appropriate than in other types of experiments, as, for instance, in the case of experiments utilizing emotional faces. Re-creating a "neutral" feeling might rely upon the suspension of mnemonic activity, which will confound contrasts of emotional (induced by memory strategies) versus neutral conditions. An approach that can circumvent this problem might involve direct comparison of different emotional conditions, perhaps using post-scanning subjective ratings of experienced emotional valence as covariates of no interest.

In one of the earliest reported studies on emotional feelings, George and colleagues (George et al., 1995) used happy, sad, and neutral faces as well as recall of life events to induce feelings in eleven female subjects. These authors reported widespread increases and decreases in regional CBF in relation to transient sadness and happiness. In particular, they emphasized frontal, temporal, and cingulate as areas in which significant changes in blood flow were seen, depending upon the emotion elicited. A strong point of this study is that a direct comparison of blood flow in the happiness and sadness conditions was made. In this contrast, rCBF increase during sadness in putamen and anterior cingulate, which contrasted with increased during happiness in largely visual areas such as cuneus and occipital cortex. In a similar study by Lane et al. (1997b) subjects underwent ^{15}O PET scans while recalling happy, sad, or disgusting personal events or watching film clips designed to elicit happy, sad, or disgusting feelings. Neutral recall and film conditions were additionally included in the experimental design. In a subtraction analysis, whereby each emotion constituted one activation condition against its own neutral baseline, the authors reported common and distinct patterns of activation for different emotions. However, in failing to contrast the emotional conditions themselves, the authors could make no strong inferences regarding differences between the distinct feeling states.

More recently, Damasio and colleagues (Damasio et al., 2000) have undertaken a large PET study addressing the functional neuroanatomy of feelings involving thirty-nine subjects. A limitation of this study wherein distinct groups of subjects were required to experience sadness and happiness, fear and anger, sadness and anger, and fear and happiness, was a failure to fully counterbalance the pairings of emotions. Consequently, no subject was required to experience both sadness and fear, for example. As with the study of Lane and colleagues (Lane et al., 1997b), the authors describe distinct patterns of activation in relation to different feeling states when contrasted with independent baseline conditions. Note that there are no direct comparisons of activation conditions. An interesting finding was the increase in CBF in midbrain, pontine, and hypothalamic areas regardless of which emotion was experienced, which is supportive of the idea that emotions leading to feelings are associated with changes in autoregulatory (autonomic) functions controlled by such areas (Damasio, 1999; Damasio, 1994). In cortical regions, orbitofrontal, anterior and posterior cingulate, and secondary somatosensory cortices all displayed rCBF increases in relation to the experience of feeling states. This pattern of activity is compatible with the authors' interpretation as reflecting mapping of first-order changes in bodily states. However, in a PET study with limited temporal resolution, and in particular where feelings are self-generated rather than stimulus-driven, it is very difficult to separate cause and effect. Thus, it is possible that a component of activity reported is actually associated with subjects' deliberate modulation of their own bodily states to produce the emotion required. Supportive of this interpretation are data from Critchley and colleagues (Critchley et al., 2001b; Critchley et al., 2001c) indicating that anterior cingulate (for example) is involved in intentional modulation of

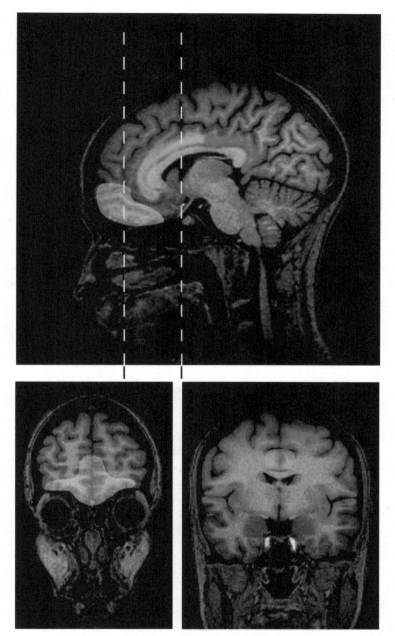

FIGURE 13.3. Brain regions demonstrated to be important in representing emotions and feelings. (*See color insert*)

body states. However, in a study that addressed the attentional modulation of emotional responses, Lane et al. (1997a) demonstrated that anterior
cingulate cortex is activated when subjects are required to pay attention to
their own emotional responses rather that to external features of emotion-
provoking stimuli. Either of these two effects might account for the observations of several authors that anterior cingulate cortex is invoked in
feeling states.

CONCLUSION

In this chapter we have briefly surveyed some of the burgeoning functional
imaging literature on the topic of feelings and emotions. We have noted
that a defining characteristic of emotional responses is their automaticity,
and that a number of studies report obligatory amygdala responses to emotive stimuli independent of subjects' awareness of the stimuli (Morris et al.,
1998b; Whalen et al., 1998), of the emotional nature of the stimuli (Morris
et al., 1996), or of the contingency between the stimulus and its emotive
properties (e.g., early in conditioning studies, before subjects are aware of
CS-US contingencies). These data are highly suggestive that the human
amygdala is a crucial locus in associating stimuli with their appropriate
emotive value. Additional evidence that the amygdala influences neural
responses in perceptual areas (Morris et al., 1998a; Rotshtein et al., 2001)
supports this view. The currently available evidence suggests that the anterior cingulate cortex in particular is involved in generating and mapping
autonomic changes that are central components to feeling states. However,
the empirical data also indicate that widespread cortical areas may provide
the neural basis of feeling states (see Figure 13.3 for summary). What is also
evident is that a distinction between what is termed "emotion" and "feelings" may provide an important conceptual framework for unraveling the
neurobiology of what is generically referred to as emotion.

References

Adolphs, R.; Russell, J. A. & Tranel, D. (1999). A role for the human amygdala in
    recognizing emotional arousal from unpleasant stimuli. *Psychological Science 10*,
    167–171.
Adolphs, R.; Tranel, D.; Damasio, H.; & Damasio, A. (1994). Impaired recognition of
    emotion in facial expressions following bilateral damage to the human amygdala.
    Nature 372, 669–672.
Adolphs, R.; Tranel, D.; Damasio, H.; & Damasio, A. R. (1995). Fear and the human
    amygdala. *Journal of Neuroscience 15*, 5879–5891.
Adolphs, R.; Tranel, D.; Hamann, S.; Young, A. W.; Calder, A. J.; Phelps, E. A.;
    Anderson, A.; Lee, G. P.; & Damasio, A. R. (1999). Recognition of facial emotion
    in nine individuals with bilateral amygdala damage. *Neuropsychologia 37*, 1111–
    1117.

Amaral, D. G., & Price, J. L. (1984). Amygdalo-cortical projections in the monkey (Macaca fascicularis). *Journal of Comparative Neurology 230*, 465–496.

Amaral, D. G.; Price, J. L.; Pitkänen, A.; & Carmichael, S. T. (1992). Anatomical organization of the primate amygdaloid complex. In J. P. Aggleton, (Ed.), *The amygdala: Neurobiological aspects of emotion, memory, and mental dysfunction* (pp. 1–66). New York: Wiley-Liss.

Anderson, A. K., & Phelps, E. A. (2001). Lesions of the human amygdala impair enhanced perception of emotionally salient events. *Nature 411*, 305–309.

Bechara, A.; Damasio, H.; Tranel, D.; & Damasio, A. R. (1997). Deciding advantageously before knowing the advantageous strategy. *Science 275*, 1293–1295.

Bechara, A.; Tranel, D.; Damasio, H.; Adolphs, R.; Rockland, C.; & Damasio, A. R. (1995). Double dissociation of conditioning and declarative knowledge relative to the amygdala and hippocampus in humans. *Science 269*, 1115–1118.

Bechara, A.; Tranel, D.; Damasio, H.; & Damasio, A. R. (1996). Failure to respond autonomically to anticipated future outcomes following damage to prefrontal cortex. *Cerebral Cortex 6*, 215–225.

Blair, R. J.; Morris, J. S.; Frith, C. D.; Perrett, D. I.; & Dolan, R. J. (1999). Dissociable neural responses to facial expressions of sadness and anger. *Brain 122*, 883–893.

Breiter, H. C.; Etcoff, N. L.; Whalen, P. J.; Kennedy, W. A.; Rauch, S. L.; Buckner, R. L.; Strauss, M. M.; Hyman, S. E.; & Rosen, B. R. (1996). Response and habituation of the human amygdala during visual processing of facial expression. *Neuron 17*, 875–887.

Broks, P.; Young, A. W.; Maratos, E. J.; Coffey, P. J.; Calder, A. J.; Isaac, C. L.; Mayes, A. R.; Hodges, J. R.; Montaldi, D.; Cezayirli, E., et al. (1998). Face processing impairments after encephalitis: Amygdala damage and recognition of fear. *Neuropsychologia 36*, 59–70.

Buchel, C., & Dolan, R. J. (2000). Classical fear conditioning in functional neuroimaging. *Current Opinion Neurobiology 10*, 219–223.

Buchel, C.; Dolan, R. J.; Armony, J. L.; & Friston, K. J. (1999). Amygdala–hippocampal involvement in human aversive trace conditioning revealed through event–related functional magnetic resonance imaging. *Journal of Neuroscience 19*, 10869–10876.

Buchel, C.; Morris, J.; Dolan, R. J.; & Friston, K. J. (1998). Brain systems mediating aversive conditioning: An event-related fMRI study. *Neuron 20*, 947–957.

Calder, A. J.; Keane, J.; Manes, F.; Antoun, N.; & Young, A. W. (2000). Impaired recognition and experience of disgust following brain injury. *Nature Neuroscience 3*, 1077–1078.

Calder, A. J.; Lawrence, A. D.; & Young, A. W. (2001). Neuropsychology of fear and loathing. *Nature Reviews Neuroscience 2*, 352–363.

Critchley, H. D.; Corfield, D. R.; Chandler, M. P.; Mathias, C. J.; & Dolan, R. J. (2000a). Cerebral correlates of autonomic cardiovascular arousal: A functional neuroimaging investigation in humans. *Journal of Physiology 523*, 259–270.

Critchley, H. D.; Elliott, R.; Mathias, C. J.; & Dolan, R. J. (2000b). Neural activity relating to generation and representation of galvanic skin conductance responses: A functional magnetic resonance imaging study. *Journal of Neuroscience 20*, 3033–3040.

Critchley, H. D.; Mathias, C. J.; & Dolan, R. J. (2001a). Neural activity in the human brain relating to uncertainty and arousal during anticipation. *Neuron 29*, 537–545.

Critchley, H. D.; Mathias, C. J.; & Dolan, R. J. (2001b). Neuroanatomical basis for first- and second-order representations of bodily states. *Nature Neuroscience 4*, 207–212.

Critchley, H. D.; Melmed, R. N.; Featherstone, E.; Mathias, C. J.; & Dolan, R. J. (2001c). Brain activity during biofeedback relaxation: A functional neuroimaging investigation. *Brain 124*, 1003–1012.

Damasio, A. (1999). *The feeling of what happens: Body and emotion in the making of consciousness*. New York: Harcourt Brace.

Damasio, A. R. (1994). *Descartes' error: Emotion, reason and the human brain*. New York: G. P. Putnam's Sons.

Damasio, A. R. (1998). Emotion in the perspective of an integrated nervous system. *Brain Research Reviews 26*, 83–86.

Damasio, A. R. (2001). Fundamental feelings. *Nature 413*, 781.

Damasio, A. R.; Grabowski, T. J.; Bechara, A.; Damasio, H.; Ponto, L. L.; Parvizi, J.; & Hichwa, R. D. (2000). Subcortical and cortical brain activity during the feeling of self-generated emotions. *Nature Neuroscience 3*, 1049–1056.

Davis, M. (1992). The amygdala and conditioned fear. In J. P. Aggleton (Ed.), *The amygdala: Neurobiological Aspects of Emotion, Memory and Mental Dysfunction*, (pp. 225–306). New York: Wiley-Liss.

Dolan, R. J.; Morris, J. S.; & de Gelder, B. (2001). Crossmodal binding of fear in voice and face. *Proceedings of the National Academy of Sciences U S A 98*, 10006–10010.

Ekman, P., & Friesen, W. V. (1975). *Pictures of facial affect*. Palo Alto, CA: Consulting Psychologists Press.

Fine, C., & Blair, R. J. (2000). The cognitive and emotional effects of amygdala damage. *Neurocase 6*, 435–450.

Fredrikson, M.; Furmark, T.; Olsson, M. T.; Fischer, H.; Andersson, J.; & Langstrom, B. (1998). Functional neuroanatomical correlates of electrodermal activity: A positron emission tomographic study. *Psychophysiology 35*, 179–185.

Friston, K. J.; Price, C. J.; Fletcher, P.; Moore, C.; Frackowiak, R. S.; & Dolan, R. J. (1996). The trouble with cognitive subtraction. *Neuroimage 4*, 97–104.

George, M. S.; Ketter, T. A.; Parekh, P. I.; Horwitz, B.; Herscovitch, P.; & Post, R. M. (1995). Brain activity during transient sadness and happiness in healthy women. *American Journal of Psychiatry 152*, 341–351.

Gorno-Tempini, M. L.; Pradelli, S.; Serafini, M.; Pagnoni, G.; Baraldi, P.; Porro, C.; Nicoletti, R.; Umita, C.; & Nichelli, P. (2001). Explicit and incidental facial expression processing: An fMRI study. *Neuroimage 14*, 465–473.

Gray, J. M.; Young, A. W.; Barker, W. A.; Curtis, A.; & Gibson, D. (1997). Impaired recognition of disgust in Huntington's disease gene carriers. *Brain 120*, 2029–2038.

Hariri, A. R.; Bookheimer, S. Y.; & Mazziotta, J. C. (2000). Modulating emotional responses: Effects of a neocortical network on the limbic system. *Neuroreport 11*, 43–48.

James, W. (1884). What is an emotion? *Mind, 9*, 188–205.

LaBar, K. S.; Gatenby, J. C.; Gore, J. C.; LeDoux, J. E.; & Phelps, E. A. (1998). Human amygdala activation during conditioned fear acquisition and extinction: A mixed-trial fMRI study. *Neuron 20,* 937–945.

LaBar, K. S.; LeDoux, J. E.; Spencer, D. D.; & Phelps, E. A. (1995). Impaired fear conditioning following unilateral temporal lobectomy in humans. *Journal of Neuroscience 15,* 6846–6855.

Lane, R. D.; Fink, G. R.; Chau, P. M.; & Dolan, R. J. (1997a). Neural activation during selective attention to subjective emotional responses. *Neuroreport 8,* 3969–3972.

Lane, R. D.; Reiman, E. M.; Ahern, G. L.; Schwartz, G. E.; & Davidson, R. J. (1997b). Neuroanatomical correlates of happiness, sadness, and disgust. *American Journal of Psychiatry 154,* 926–933.

LeDoux, J. E. (1996). *The emotional brain.* New York.: Simon and Schuster.

LeDoux, J. E. (2000). Emotion circuits in the brain. *Annual Reviews in Neuroscience 23,* 155–184.

Morris, J. S.; DeGelder, B.; Weiskrantz, L.; & Dolan, R. J. (2001). Differential extrageniculostriate and amygdala responses to presentation of emotional faces in a cortically blind field. *Brain 124,* 1241–1252.

Morris, J. S.; Friston, K. J.; Buchel, C.; Frith, C. D.; Young, A. W.; Calder, A. J.; & Dolan, R. J. (1998a). A neuromodulatory role for the human amygdala in processing emotional facial expressions. *Brain 121,* 47–57.

Morris, J. S.; Frith, C. D.; Perrett, D. I.; Rowland, D.; Young, A. W.; Calder, A. J.; & Dolan, R. J. (1996). A differential neural response in the human amygdala to fearful and happy facial expressions. *Nature 383,* 812–815.

Morris, J. S.; Ohman, A.; & Dolan, R. J. (1998b). Conscious and unconscious emotional learning in the human amygdala. *Nature 393,* 467–470.

O'Doherty, J.; Rolls, E. T.; Francis, S.; Bowtell, R.; & McGlone, F. (2001). Representation of pleasant and aversive taste in the human brain. *Journal of Neurophysiology 85,* 1315–1321.

Panksepp, J. (1998). The periconscious substrates of consciousness: Affective states and the evolutionary origins of the SELF. *Journal of Consciousness Studies 5,* 566–582.

Phillips, M. L.; Young, A. W.; Scott, S. K.; Calder, A. J.; Andrew, C.; Giampietro, V.; Williams, S. C.; Bullmore, E. T.; Brammer, M.; & Gray, J. A. (1998). Neural responses to facial and vocal expressions of fear and disgust. *Proceedings of the Royal Society of London Series B: Biological Sciences 265,* 1809–1817.

Phillips, M. L.; Young, A. W.; Senior, C.; Brammer, M.; Andrew, C.; Calder, A. J.; Bullmore, E. T.; Perrett, D. I.; Rowland, D.; Williams, S. C., et al. (1997). A specific neural substrate for perceiving facial expressions of disgust. *Nature 389,* 495–498.

Rotshtein, P.; Malach, R.; Hadar, U.; Graif, M.; & Hendler, T. (2001). Feeling or features: Different sensitivity to emotion in high-order visual cortex and amygdala. *Neuron 32,* 747–757.

Schmolck, H., & Squire, L. R. (2001). Impaired perception of facial emotions following bilateral damage to the anterior temporal lobe. *Neuropsychology 15,* 30–38.

Sprengelmeyer, R.; Rausch, M.; Eysel, U. T.; & Przuntek, H. (1998). Neural structures associated with recognition of facial expressions of basic emotions. *Proceedings of the Royal Society of London Series B: Biological Sciences 265,* 1927–1931.

Vuilleumier, P.; Armony, J. L.; Driver, J.; & Dolan, R. J. (2001). Effects of attention and emotion on face processing in the human brain. An event-related fMRI study. *Neuron 30*, 829–841.

Whalen, P. J.; Rauch, S. L.; Etcoff, N. L.; McInerney, S. C.; Lee, M. B.; & Jenike, M. A. (1998). Masked presentations of emotional facial expressions modulate amygdala activity without explicit knowledge. *Journal of Neuroscience 18*, 411–418.

Young, A. W.; Hellawell, D. J.; Van De Wal, C.; & Johnson, M. (1996). Facial expression processing after amygdalotomy. *Neuropsychologia 34*, 31–39.

Zajonc, R. B. (1980). Feeling and thinking: Preferences need no inferences. *American Psychologist 35*, 151–175.

PART III

FEELINGS AND EMOTIONS: THE PLACE OF PLEASURE

14

The Affect System

What Lurks below the Surface of Feelings?

John T. Cacioppo, Jeff T. Larsen, N. Kyle Smith,
and Gary G. Berntson

ABSTRACT

The structure of affective space has been debated for more than fifty years. According to the model of evaluative space (Cacioppo & Berntson, 1994; Cacioppo, Gardner, & Berntson, 1997), the common metric governing approach/withdrawal is generally a single bipolar dimension at response stages that itself is the consequence of multiple operations, such as the activation function for positivity (appetition) and the activation function for negativity (aversion), at earlier affective processing stages. Accordingly, affective space can be bipolar or bivariate depending on specific circumstances. We further extend the model by reviewing evidence for coactivated emotional states and component processes underlying affect, emotion, and feeling. Two different event-related brain components that reflect implicit affective processing provide specific information on the general location and timing of component affective processing.

Not long ago, the camera was a metaphor for memory, the computer for the brain. Memory, however, does not activate a stored depiction of the event but rather reconstructs the event (Loftus, 1979; Roediger & McDermott, 2000). Contrary to the doctrine of rationality, the inferences drawn from facts (e.g., syllogisms) are not coldly calculated conditional probabilities but a calculus shaped in part by wishful thinking (McGuire, 1981). People do not weigh evidence objectively but generally exercise a confirmatory bias. For example, disagreeing parties who receive mixed messages containing evidence for and against each party's position tend to polarize rather than moderate their attitudes (Lord, Ross, & Lepper, 1979). The metaphors of the camera and the computer failed because they are based on the notion that the brain is a passive, dispassionate recorder and processor of information rather than a builder of meaning in ways sculpted by experience, personal and ancestral.

Research reported in this paper was supported by National Science Foundation Grant No. BCS-0086314.

One way in which this operates is well known. Sense organs filter most of the information available in a given environment, with the brains of different species receiving quite different types and bandwidths of the available information. Visual light is only a small part of the electromagnetic spectrum (400–700 nanometers/millimicrons), with changes across this spectrum perceived as changes in color. The visual perception of the bumblebee, in contrast, does not include the relatively long wavelengths that we see as red, but extends into the region of ultraviolet light below 400 nm into aspects of the environment that are invisible to humans. Moreover, the fusion flicker rate is much faster for bees than humans, so that a movie depiction of a moving object that appears in motion to humans may appear as a series of still images to bees.

Our evolutionary heritage sculpts ongoing perceptions, thoughts, feelings, and actions in a deeper sense as well. Close or occlude your left eye, fixate on the X, and note the presence of the target O. Now move your eye closer or further away from the screen while maintaining fixation on the X. Although the O should disappear at some distance (about 12 inches), the horizontal line is perceptually continuous. The continuity of the horizontal line is a visual construction.

Nowhere should the brain's construction of mental contents based on personal and ancestral experiences be more evident than in feelings and emotion. Traditionally, however, the scientific study of affect and emotion has centered on discrete feeling states. Among the important contributions of the cognitive revolution was the realization that conscious experiences provide a glimpse of only a small subset of the cognitive structures and operations that needed to be explored and understood. Many cognitive (and affective) processes occur unconsciously, with only selected outcomes reaching awareness (Bargh, 2001; Cacioppo, Priester, & Berntson, 1993; Kihlstrom, 1987) yet, as LeDoux (2000) noted, emotion researchers have generally regarded the end products that have reached awareness or behavioral displays as the most appropriate evidence for the study of emotion. In this chapter, we regard feelings and emotions as a subset of the operations of an affect system, whose structure and operating characteristics have been shaped by evolutionary forces to produce generally adaptive behaviors across a very wide range of circumstances.[1]

---

[1] We are not suggesting that evolutionary forces are the *only* influences that produce adaptive behaviors.

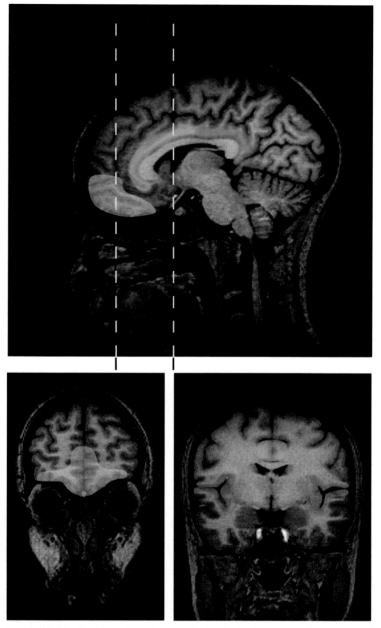

FIGURE 13.3. Brain regions demonstrated to be important in representing emotions and feelings. Color-coded as follows:

Blue: insula (Critchley et al., 2000a; Damasio et al., 2000)
Green: anterior cingulate (Critchley et al., 2000a; Critchley et al., 2001a,b,c; Fredrikson et al., 1998; George et al., 1995; Lane et al., 1997a)
Purple: posterior cingulate (Critchley et al., 2000b; Damasio et al., 2000)
Red: amygdala (Breiter et al., 1996; Morris et al., 1996; Blair et al., 1999; Buchel & Dolan, 2000)
Yellow: ventromedial/orbitofrontal cortex (Critchley et al., 2000b; Damasio et al., 2000)

A   Affective facial expressions of taste 'liking'

Positive 'liking' expressions

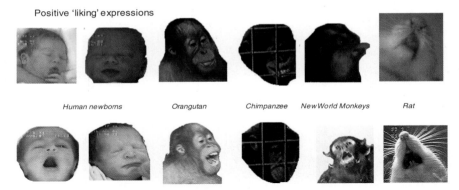

Human newborns   Orangutan   Chimpanzee   New World Monkeys   Rat

Negative 'disliking' expressions

FIGURE 15.2. A. Affective reactions are elicited by sweet tastes from human infants, great apes, monkeys, and rats.

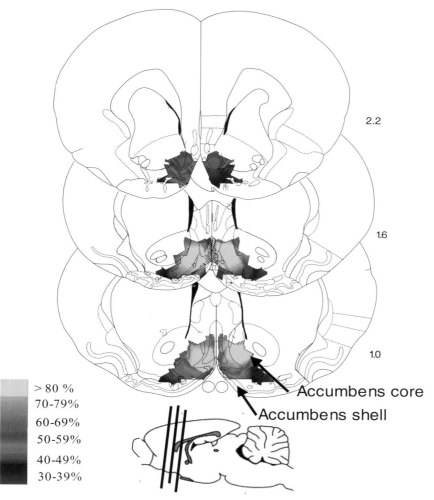

2.2

1.6

1.0

> 80 %
70-79%
60-69%
50-59%
40-49%
30-39%

Accumbens core
Accumbens shell

FIGURE 15.3. A. "Liking" and "wanting" site in nucleus accumbens shell where opioid activation causes increased niceness gloss for sweetness (Peciña & Berridge, 2000). Percentages refer to percent increase in appetitive behavior caused by morphine microinjection (100% = twice baseline amount). Coronal brain slices (face on view) are numbered conventionally; their position is shown in profile view below.

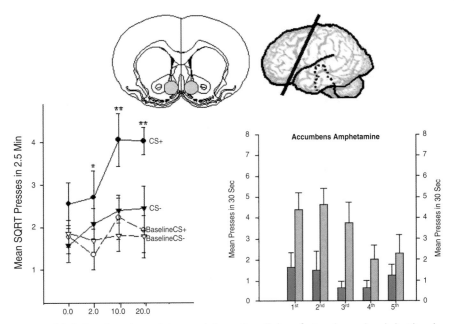

FIGURE 15.4. Irrational cue-triggered "wanting." Amphetamine microinjection in nucleus accumbens magnifies "wanting" for sugar reward – but only in presence of reward cue (CS+). Cognitive expectations and ordinary wanting are not altered (reflected in baseline lever pressing in absence of cue and during irrelevant cue, CS–) (*left*). Transient irrational "wanting" comes and goes with the cue (*right*). Blue bars denote work in the absence of the reward cue; yellow bars show elevation when cue was present. Modified from Wyvell and Berridge, 2000.

NATURAL SELECTION ACTS ON OUTCOMES

In *Expression of Emotions in Man and Animals*, Charles Darwin (1872) articulated three principles in which behavioral expressions reflected a combination of adaptive movements, communicative signals, and general activation. Darwin's principles of serviceable associated habits, antithesis, and actions due to the constitution of the nervous system reflect a more general tenet: that for an animal to survive it must be able to discriminate hostile from hospitable events, to adjust behavior (its own and that of others) accordingly, and to marshal the requisite energy to support the necessary behavioral adjustments. The ability to differentiate between hostile and hospitable stimuli and to respond accordingly is so critical that all animals have rudimentary reflexes for categorizing and approaching or withdrawing from certain classes of stimuli and for communicating to others. Evaluative discriminations are performed in simple organisms by hard-wired stimulus-response connections or fixed action patterns. Human infants are also endowed with a finite set of hard-wired evaluative discriminations (e.g., retreat from nociceptive stimuli, startle response to sudden intense noise). A remarkable feature of humans is the extent to which the evaluative discrimination of stimuli is shaped by learning, cognition, and appraisal processes (Berntson, Boysen, & Cacioppo, 1993; Scherer, this volume). Although only a subset of these evaluative discriminations have been called emotions, and an even smaller subset feelings, the full set of mechanisms involved in evaluative information processing can be thought of as constituent parts of an integrated, heterarchically organized affect system.

Physical constraints generally restrict behavioral manifestations to bipolar (approach/withdrawal) actions. Although one can stay motionless or circle a stimulus at a constant distance, evolution favors the organism that can learn, represent, and access rapidly whether approach or withdrawal is adaptive when confronted by a stimulus. If the affect system evolved to guide behavior toward hospitable and away from hostile stimuli, a valuable consequence of affective processing would be a component of the mental representation that specifies whether stimuli from a given category are harmful or beneficial, likable or dislikable, safe or dangerous, good or bad. Consistent with this reasoning, there is a behavioral efficiency, a conservation of limited cognitive resources, and a reduction in physiological stress that is served by mental representations of general and enduring net action predispositions toward classes of stimuli (Blascovich et al., 1993). Moreover, mental guides for one's actions in future encounters with the target stimuli such as attitudes and preferences are more expected and stable when organized in terms of a bipolar evaluative dimension (e.g., Cacioppo & Berntson, 1994; Fishbein & Ajzen, 1975; Heider, 1946). Almost half a century ago, Brehm (1956) found that individuals, following a selection between two alternatives, spread the appeal of these alternatives by some combination of amplifying the positive features of the chosen alternative, diminishing the negative features of the chosen alternative, magnifying the negative features of the unchosen alternative, and minimizing the positive features of an unchosen alternative. This motivational push toward affective bipolarity was especially strong when subjects initially regarded the alternatives to be similarly appealing. The bipolar (positive/negative) structure that comes from the spreading of alternatives represents a stable endpoint, however, not the states or processes that preceded this endpoint.

With the scientific study of affect and emotion centered on discrete feeling states and behavior, and with the steady state of these feelings in terms of a single evaluative (hostile-hospitable) dimension, measures and theories were developed built around the valence dimension (e.g., Osgood, Suci, & Tannenbaum, 1956; Russell & Carroll, 1999). Studies of the conceptual organization of affect and emotion, for instance, indicate that people conceptually organize feelings and emotions in terms of a circular order around the perimeter of the space defined by a bipolar valence dimension and an orthogonal dimension labeled activation (i.e., a circumplex; Russell, 1980). Using multidimensional scaling of similarity ratings, Russell and other researchers have recovered the circumplex from similarity judgments of emotion-related words in several cultures around the world and from children's similarity judgments of facial expressions (cf. Russell & Carroll, 1999). Thus, the circumplex is viewed not only as a description of the end products of the affect system, but also of people's moment-by-moment affective experiences (cf. Watson & Tellegen, 1985).

There is an understandable appeal to settling for steady-state feelings and behaviors as the appropriate data to model in the area of emotions. After all, these phenomena beckon to be explained. A lesson learned from the cognitive sciences, however, is that the structure and activation of the processes underlying mental contents are not revealed by study of the mental contents alone, that most cognitive and affective processes occur unconsciously, with only selected outcomes reaching awareness (LeDoux, 2000).

Neal Miller (1959, 1961) recognized early that approach and withdrawal are behavioral manifestations that can come from distinguishable motivational substrates. His conflict theory was enriched by conceptualizing approach and withdrawal separately, investigating their unique antecedents and consequences, and examining the psychological constraints that led typically to the reciprocal activation of approach and withdrawal tendencies. Building on this early work and the work of Lang and colleagues (Lang, Bradley, & Cuthbert, 1990), we have proposed a model of the affect system in which the underlying motivational substrates for the processing of appetitive and aversive information are partially separable, characterized by distinct activation functions for positivity and negativity (which refer to the general underlying motivational systems), and coupled through multiple modes of evaluative activation (Cacioppo & Berntson, 1994, 1999; Cacioppo, Gardner, & Berntson, 1997, 1999; Ito & Cacioppo, 1998; Larsen, McGraw, & Cacioppo, 2001). Briefly, a stimulus may vary in terms of the strength of positive evaluative activation (i.e., positivity) and the strength of negative evaluative activation (i.e., negativity) it evokes (see Figure 14.1). The model further posits that positive and negative evaluative processes are distinguishable (stochastically and functionally independent); are characterized by distinct activation functions (e.g., positivity offset and negativity bias principles); are related differentially to ambivalence (corollary of ambivalence asymmetries); have distinguishable antecedents (heteroscedacity principle); and tend to gravitate from a bivariate toward a bipolar structure when the underlying beliefs are the target of deliberation or a guide for behavior (principle of motivational certainty) (Cacioppo et al., 1997).

Positivity and negativity, represented as a bivariate plane in Figure 14.1, represent two broad systems underlying emotion, feelings, and behavior. Although specific emotions and behaviors may differ depending on the stimulus, context, and organismic state, there is an underlying commonality among appetitive affects and behaviors and among aversive affects and behaviors (Diener, 1999). Thus, in the evaluative space model, discrete emotions are conceptualized as constituent elements within two general categories of affective processes.[2] The activation of positivity and negativity, which generally have antagonistic effects on behavior, are combined to produce a response predisposition (see z-axis in Figure 14.1). In a bipolar model, the effects of appetitive and aversive motivation are assumed not only to have antagonistic effects but also to be reciprocally activated (Lang et al., 1990). The evaluative space model does not reject reciprocal activation, but rather subsumes it as one of the three possible modes of activation and explores the antecedents for each mode of evaluative activation. One of the unique predictions made by the evaluative space model, therefore, is that positivity and negativity can be coactivated. In the savanna, for example, animals must come to the water to drink even though their predators come there to hunt. The organism that can process such appetitive and aversive cues in parallel is better able to approach or withdraw from environmental stimuli swiftly than one that can only sample such conflicting cues in serial. Thus, coactivation of positivity and negativity fosters vigilance and directional flexibility in responding.

---

[2] Discrete and dimensional approaches to affect and emotion have been pitted against one another as if they were necessarily competing formulations. In the present formulation, negative discrete emotions are viewed as elements (e.g., analogous to stars) that constitute a broader organization (i.e., negativity dimension, analogous to a galaxy), and positive discrete emotions are viewed as a different set of elements that constitute a second broad organization (i.e., positivity dimension).

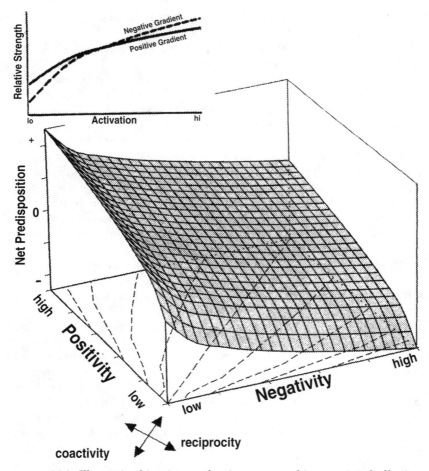

FIGURE 14.1. Illustrative bivariate evaluative space and its associated affective response surface. This surface represents the net predisposition of an individual toward (+) or away from (−) the target stimulus. This net predisposition is expressed in relative units and the axis dimensions are in relative units of activation. The point on the surface overlying the left axis intersection represents a maximally positive predisposition, and the point on the surface overlying the right axis intersection represents a maximally negative predisposition. Each of the points overlying the dashed diagonal extending from the back to the front axis intersections represents the same middling predisposition. Thus, the nonreciprocal diagonal on the evaluative plane – which represents different evaluative processes (e.g., neutral to ambivalence) – yields the same middling expression on the affective response surface. Dashed lines (including the coactivity diagonal) represent isocontours on the evaluative plane, which depict many-to-one mappings between the affective response surface and the underlying evaluative space. These isocontours are illustrative rather than exhaustive. *Figure Inset:* the activation functions depicted separately for positivity and negativity. Adapted from J. T. Cacippo and G. G. Berntson (1994), "Relationship between Attitudes and Evaluative Space," a critical review, with emphasis on the separability of positive and negative substrates. *Psychological Bulletin, 115,* 401–423.

The affect system, according to the evaluative space model, evolved to guide an organism toward hospitable and away from hostile events. The evaluative space model, therefore, also predicts that coactivation is a tense, unexpected, disharmonious state. Coactivation can be advantageous in specific circumstances because, given the antagonistic effects of positivity and negativity, the dynamic range and lability of responses is minimized and directional flexibility is maximized (see Cacioppo & Berntson, 1994, Table 1). Moreover, coactivation may foster faster responses to unexpected movements. Finally, because it is unpleasant, coactivation motivates either a retreat from the eliciting stimulus or circumstance, or a resolution of the evaluative ambiguity. Consistent with this reasoning, ambivalence has been associated with evaluative instability (e.g., Bargh, Chaiken, Govender, & Pratto, 1992; Hass, Katz, Rizzo, Bailey, & Eisenstadt, 1991).

Larsen et al. (2001) conducted three field studies to examine whether coactivation of positivity and negativity is reflected in the self-reports of feelings (e.g., happiness and sadness, bittersweet). Larsen et al. found that individuals were more likely to report feeling both happy and sad immediately after watching the film *Life Is Beautiful* (Study 1), moving out of their college dormitories (Study 2), and graduating from college (Study 3) than in more typical situations (e.g., a typical day on campus). In addition to including standard emotion items such as *happy* and *sad*, in Study 3 Larsen et al. included a more intriguing emotion: *bittersweet*. The term "bittersweet" implies a commingling of positive and negative feelings and is therefore difficult to place in the circumplex and other bipolar frameworks. Yet its inclusion in the lexicon suggests that it can sometimes characterize individuals' feelings. Consistent with this possibility, graduates were not only more likely to report feeling both happy and sad than nongraduates, they also reported feeling more bittersweet than nongraduates. In sum, Larsen et al. replicated the typical finding that happiness and sadness are largely mutually exclusive in routine, steady-state conditions, but demonstrated that these two seemingly opposite emotions can co-occur under certain circumstances.

Additional research has shown that mixed feelings can occur not only in situations as rich as those studied by Larsen et al. (2001), but in situations as simple as a game of chance. In a laboratory experiment with a gambling task, Larsen, McGraw, Mellers, & Cacioppo (in press) presented participants with fifty-fifty chances to win one of two amounts (e.g., seven or eleven dollars) or lose one of two amounts. On winning trials, participants were more likely to feel both good *and* bad about winning the smaller outcome (i.e., a *disappointing win*) than the larger. Even though winning felt good, missing an opportunity to win an even larger amount felt bad. Similarly, participants were more likely to report mixed feelings after they lost the smaller of two amounts (i.e., *relieving losses*) rather than the larger. Thus, losing felt bad even as avoiding a larger loss felt good.

One possibility is that the spotlight of attention focuses on the pleasant and unpleasant aspects of ambivalent situations in turn rather than in parallel. Though attention is limited (e.g., Kahneman, 1973), it can be directed to at least two channels of information (Spelke, Hirst, & Neisser, 1976). De Gelder and Vroomen (2000), for example, found that people can integrate congruent and incongruent emotional cues from the face and tone of voice in judging a target's emotion. Such data notwithstanding, self-report data may ultimately be unable to rule out the possibility that people attend to and experience positive and negative inputs in serial. It is worth noting that the evaluative space model is concerned with coactivation of underlying mechanisms more so than the resulting experience of mixed feelings. Toward that end, priming effects demonstrate that concepts can be coactivated even when one or the other falls outside the spotlight of attention (e.g., Macrae, Milne, & Bodenhausen, 1994).

Although a great deal more work needs to be done, the brain appears to have the capacities posited by the evaluative space model. One of the core predictions of the evaluative space model is that appetitive and aversive information are processed separately at the earliest stages of hedonic information processing and are combined to produce a more integrated guidance in the form of a predisposition to respond positively or negatively. Regions have been identified in animal studies that appear to be preferentially involved in appetitive information processing (e.g., nucleus accumbens, ventral pallidum, paraventricular nucleus); others in aversive information processing (e.g., central amygdala, bed nucleus stria terminalis); and others in both (hypothalamus, anterior cingulate) (see Berridge, this volume; Panksepp, this volume; Damasio, this volume). In a recent functional magnetic resonance imaging (fMRI) study by O'Doherty, Kringelbach, Rolls, Hornak, and Andrews (2001), participants performed a gambling task while in a scanner. An increase in the activity of the lateral orbitofrontal (OFC) was related to the participants' receipt of punishment, and the opposite pattern was recorded in the medial OFC. (Damage to the OFC is associated with impairments in social and emotional behavior.) O'Doherty et al. (2001) concluded that the conceptual representation of reward and punishment may be processed in distinct subregions of the OFC, with the magnitude of activation varying as a function of the magnitude of the reward or punishment. Kawasaki et al. (2001) recorded from single cells in the ventromedial prefrontal region of epileptic patients. They reported cellular firing within 120 ms of stimulus presentation, with different cells firing when pleasant and unpleasant stimuli were presented. These results add to the increasing evidence that the processing of appetitive and aversive information is separable at early stages of information processing.

AFFECTIVE ASYMMETRIES

Affective asymmetries, like cognitive heuristics, constitute an important domain in which the brain creates representations biased by personal and ancestral experiences rather than fastidious depictions of external events. Consider the following empirical results: (1) when people rate someone they do not know, they rate the person on the positive side of the scale's neutral point (Anderson, 1981); (2) when triadic structures are used to depict relationships among oneself (p), another person (o), and a topic (x), people prefer a positive to a negative link (attraction) between oneself and the other (Heider, 1958) whether or not there is balance or agreement – and attraction information is processed more quickly than is agreement or balance information (Cacioppo & Petty, 1981); (3) retrospective voting studies suggest that incumbents are retained if the economy (i.e., the personal resources of the voters) is prospering but are discarded if it is not, with the incumbents being hurt more by deteriorating economic conditions than they are helped by improving economic conditions (Kieweit & Rivers, 1984); and (4) people may be risk-aversive on gains and risk-seeking on losses, although the effects of losses tend to be greater than the effects of gains (Kahneman & Tversky, 1979). These affective asymmetries, which have been puzzling because they are inconsistent in terms of whether positive or negative information is weighted more, are readily explained within the evaluative space model.

Specifically, the separation of appetitive from aversive information processing at early stages before formulating a plan or predisposition to respond made it possible for natural selection to shape distinct activation functions for positivity and negativity (Cacioppo et al., 1997, 1999). We have hypothesized that the activation functions for appetitive (approach) and aversive (withdrawal) affects are both negatively accelerating but differ in activation threshold (higher for positivity than negativity) and gain (higher for negativity than positivity) (see inset, Figure 14.1). These differences in activation functions prescribe two affective asymmetries: (1) a *positivity offset* – the positive system responds more strongly than the negative system at low levels of activation; and (2) a *negativity bias* – as activation increases, the negative system responds more strongly than the positive system. Further, though these features are posited to reflect the default mode of the affect system, the effects of appetitive and aversion stimuli on hedonic activation also depend in part on the affective context in which a stimulus appears. The function of this feature of the affect system is similar to the adaptation seen in various receptor mechanisms: to maximize sensitivity to small variations in stimulation within an ecological niche while accommodating wide variations in levels and ranges of stimulation across ecological niches. This feature is reminiscent of Weber's law: the just-perceptible increment of a stimulus is a constant fraction of the stimulus.

The affective asymmetries described above are consistent with these posited activation functions. The positive asymmetries described by Anderson (1981) and Heider (1958), for instance, emerge in conditions of low affective activation. The rating of unknown people as positive may be based in part on the diagnosticity of neutral information or morality/competence of the behaviors ("Don engages in normal behavior so he is probably OK"; cf. Skorwonski & Carlston, 1989), but it is more difficult to explain the attraction effect in research on cognitive balance in those terms. Moreover, using a procedure developed by Gardner (1995), we examined whether diagnosticity was the critical feature by having participants rate either a hypothetical person (toward whom participants generally felt positive even without any information), an (imaginary) "aguaphore" fish (toward which participants generally felt neutral without any information), and an (imaginary) "entophore" insect (toward which participants generally felt negative without any information) (Cacioppo, Gardner, & Berntson, 1997). Participants rated each after either receiving no additional information or neutral and nondiagnostic information (e.g., the person is susceptible to the laws of gravity; the entophore has six legs). Results indicated that the person, the aguaphore fish, and the entophore insect were each rated slightly more positively after deliberation about neutral and nondiagnostic information.

In contrast, the negative asymmetries such as the effects of economic progress versus economic decline on electoral support for incumbents (Ansolabeher, Iyengar, & Simon, 1990; see also Holbrook, Krosnick, Cacioppo, Visser, & Gardner, 2001) and the relative effects of gains versus losses (Kahneman & Tversky, 1979) are found in conditions of high affective activation. These are just the circumstances in which the affect system should modulate information processing differently, ceteris paribus producing a greater weighting of negative than positive information (see Figure 14.1). Evidence supporting a negativity bias has been found in domains as varied as impression formation (e.g., Skowronski & Carlston, 1989), person memory (e.g., Ybarra & Stephan, 1996), blood and organ donation (e.g., Cacioppo & Gardner, 1993), hiring decisions (e.g., Rowe, 1989), personnel evaluations (e.g., Ganzach, 1995), and voting behavior (e.g., Klein, 1991, 1996); and has been found to characterize the judgments of children as well as adults (e.g., Aloise, 1993; Robinson-Whelen et al., 1997). Taylor (1991) summarizes a wide range of evidence showing that negative events in a context evoke stronger and more rapid physiological, cognitive, emotional, and social responses than neutral or positive events.

Ito, Cacioppo, and Lang (1998a) measured the positive and negative feelings evoked by 472 slides selected to represent the full affective space captured by the International Affective Picture System (IAPS; Lang et al.,

1995). Arousal ratings were used to index the intensity of the affective stimulus (which were plotted on the abscissa), and the unipolar positivity and unipolar negativity ratings were used to index the magnitude of the affective response (which were plotted on the ordinate). Analyses revealed that the intercept was significantly higher for ratings of positive than negative stimuli (i.e., a positivity offset). Results also revealed the slope of the regression line for the ratings of the negative stimuli was significantly steeper than the regression line for the ratings of the positive stimuli (i.e., the negativity bias). Stated more simply, positive stimuli have a greater impact than negative stimuli at comparably low levels of activation, but the opposite is the case at equally high levels of activation.

To assess the generalizability of this effect across stimulus items, Ito, Larsen, Smith, and Cacioppo (1998b) replicated the regression analyses using 620 verbs (e.g., act), nouns (e.g., lion), adverbs (e.g., leisurely), and adjectives (e.g., quiet) from the Affective Norms for English Words (ANEW; CSEA, 1998), and we have subsequently conducted a similar analysis on the 555 trait adjectives from Anderson (1965). As predicted by the evaluative space model, evidence for a positivity offset was found, in that the most neutral positive words were judged slightly but significantly more extreme than the most neutral negative words, and evidence for a negativity bias was found such that the slope of the evaluatively negative words was steeper than the slope of the evaluatively positive words. The human mind treats hedonic information differently when constructing a representation of the world; doing so, at least in the long run, has adaptive advantage over depicting reality objectively and weighting affective information symmetrically.

EARLY AFFECTIVE PROCESSING: EVIDENCE FROM EVENT-RELATED BRAIN POTENTIALS

The extant evidence for affective asymmetries has relied on verbal or behavioral responses. Even the evidence of greater interference in the Stroop task when negative than positive words are presented relies on latency differences in overt response (Pratto & John, 1991). Walter Cannon (1929) long ago suggested that the sympathetic nervous system responds in a fight-or-flight fashion to negative events in order to promote survival. The evidence for the negativity bias based on affective ratings could reflect operations fairly late in information processing. Ito, Larsen, Smith, and Cacioppo (1998b) therefore used event-related brain potentials (ERPs) to test the prediction that affective asymmetries such as the negativity bias emerge early in the processing of appetitive and aversive information, prior to response selection or execution. We used a paradigm developed by Cacioppo, Crites, Berntson, and Coles (1994) to study evaluative categorizations. The experimental task requires the classification of stimuli in terms of their evaluative significance, such as counting the number of positive (or negative) pictures in a short series. A late positive potential that peaks around 550 msec has been identified that is more sensitive to evaluative categorization than response stages (Cacioppo, Crites, Gardner, & Berntson, 1994; Crites, Cacioppo, Gardner, & Berntson, 1995). Ito et al. (1998b) recorded ERPs to positive, negative, and neutral pictures embedded within sequences of other neutral pictures. Results showed: (1) as in prior research, positive or negative stimuli in sequences of neutral stimuli were associated with larger amplitude late positive brain potentials over centroparietal regions that peaked at approximately 550 msec; and (2) the negative stimuli were associated with a larger amplitude late positive potential than was the evaluative categorization of equally probable, equally evaluatively extreme, and equally arousing positive stimuli. These results provide support for the hypothesis that the negativity bias in affective processing occurs early.

In a follow-up, Ito and Cacioppo (2000) used the online measurement of categorization processes provided by ERPs to assess the implicit and explicit categorization of stimuli along evaluative (positive, negative) and nonevaluative (people, no-people) dimensions. Participants were exposed to stimuli that simultaneously varied along both dimensions but were explicitly instructed to categorize along only one of them. As in our prior research, the late positive potential was sensitive to participants' explicit categorization task. However, the late positive potential also revealed implicit categorization along the non-task relevant dimension – for instance, it was larger to a positive/negative picture in a series of negative/positive pictures even when the participants were engaged in a nonevaluative task (counting the number of pictures that depicted humans). More interestingly, clear evidence of an implicit negativity bias was also found, suggesting that, ceteris paribus, negative stimuli spontaneously receive greater processing than positive stimuli. Moreover, the explicit task of categorizing stimuli along a nonevaluative dimension neither diminished nor delayed the late positive potential to variations in the evaluative dimension.[3] We interpreted these results as evidence for the operation of adaptively beneficial implicit categorization processes, triggered by significant proximal stimuli, serving broad, cross-situational goals (Ito & Cacioppo, 2000; see also Collani, Jacobsen, & Schroger, 2001).

The ERP waveform can be represented as a small number of orthogonal underlying components – components that could be measured by examining the covariance between time points in the ERP waveform: those

---

[3] There are limitations to this finding, viz., as hypothesized for low levels of hedonic activation (see Figure 14.1, inset), the negativity bias and implicit categorization effects are not found when using mildly evocative experimental stimuli such as words ("pleasant," "unpleasant") (Cacioppo, Crites, & Gardner, 1996; Crites & Cacioppo, 1996).

which exhibit large intercorrelations are defined as a component (cf. Coles, Donchin, & Porges, 1986). Component loadings index the relationship between amplitude and time (thereby revealing temporal information about the operation of separable implicit processes), and the scalp region over which the component is maximal may help constrain the nature of each implicit process (e.g., occipital region would suggest altered attention or visual processing, centroparietal region would suggest associative processing) (Fabiani, Gratton, & Coles, 2000).

Smith et al. (2001) manipulated the valence of the target stimuli (positive, negative, or neutral) and the probability of the stimuli (frequent vs. rare) in two studies. In each study, principal components analysis confirmed that the P1 amplitude to all frequent stimuli and to rare negative stimuli were larger than P1 amplitude to rare positive stimuli. This component was maximal over the occipital region and peaked at about 140 msec – in the same range of time in which the earliest endogenous attentional components appear. Moreover, this component was only modestly correlated with the LPP, which again was maximal at about 550 msec over the centroparietal areas. Given that the P1 component of the ERP is a proximal index of attention allocation to valenced stimuli, these results suggest an extremely rapid (< 120 ms) differentiation of positive and negative stimuli manifesting as a negativity bias in attention allocation.

Two sources of evidence suggest that the superior colliculus, posterior pulvinar nucleus, and amygdala pathway may underlie the P1 negativity bias. First, patients with striate cortex lesions show preserved abilities to localize and discriminate visual stimuli that are not consciously perceived (blindsight), suggesting that a neural tract involving the superior colliculus and posterior pulvinar nucleus can subserve gross visual discrimination in the absence of visual awareness. Second, neuroimaging studies have revealed correlations between increased blood flow to amygdala, superior colliculus, and pulvinar in response to masked ("unseen") emotional stimuli (e.g., Morris, Öhman, & Dolan, 1999). Thus, while the striate cortex visual pathway affords high resolution visual processing, the superior colliculus and pulvinar pathway afford relatively fast low resolution visual processing that can guide (motivate) attention without intention or awareness (see Winston & Dolan, this volume; Öhman & Wiens, this volume). Such an affective asymmetry serves to guide attentional and cognitive resources to potential threats in the environment even before they can be consciously registered.

COMPONENTS ACROSS LEVELS OF THE NEURAXIS

Although we have depicted positivity, negativity, and the derived affective response predisposition as general processes in Figure 14.1, these results point to another organizing principle of the affect system: these components of the affect system are represented at multiple levels of the brain and nervous system within a heterarchical structure, with distinguishable levels and components that are highly interactive (Berntson et al., 1993; Berntson & Cacioppo, in press). This structure is consistent with Ekman's (this volume) distinction between automatic scanning devices and more deliberative emotional processing; Öhman's (Öhman & Wiens, this volume) distinction between prepared and learned affective responses; and Damasio's (this volume) observation that emotion involves neural components at multiple levels of the neuraxis organized heterarchically beginning in the brainstem and ending in the cortex (Berntson, Cacioppo, & Sarter, in press).

The nineteenth-century neurologist John Hughlings Jackson emphasized the hierarchical structure of the brain, and the re-representation of functions at multiple levels within this neural hierarchy (Jackson, 1884). The notion was that information is processed at multiple levels of organization within the nervous system. Primitive protective responses to aversive stimuli are organized at the level of the spinal cord, as is apparent in flexor (pain) withdrawal reflexes that can be seen even after spinal transection. These primitive protective reactions are expanded and embellished at higher levels of the nervous system (see Berntson et al., 1993). The evolutionary development of higher neural systems, such as the limbic system, endowed organisms with an expanded behavioral repertoire, including escape reactions, aggressive responses, and even the ability to anticipate and avoid aversive encounters. Evolution not only endowed us with primitive, lower-level adaptive reactions, but it sculpted the awesome information-processing capacities of the highest levels of the brain. Thus, neurobehavioral mechanisms are not localized to a single level of organization within the brain, but are represented at multiple levels of the nervous system. At progressively higher levels of organization, there is a general expansion in the range and relational complexity of contextual controls and in the breadth and flexibility of discriminative and adaptive responses (Berntson et al., 1993). But, although higher-level systems confer greater behavioral variability and adaptive flexibility, they do not replace lower neurobehavioral mechanisms.

Adaptive flexibility of higher-level systems has costs, given the finite information-processing capacity of neural circuits. Greater flexibility implies a less rigid relationship between inputs and outputs, a greater range of information that must be processed, and a slower serial-like mode of processing. Consequently, the evolutionary layering of higher-processing levels onto lower substrates has adaptive advantage, in that lower and more efficient processing levels may continue to be utilized, and may be sufficient in some circumstances. For example, pain withdrawal reflexes, mediated by inherent spinal circuits, can manifest in rapid protective responses to pain stimuli. However, ascending pain pathways also convey information to higher levels of the neuraxis that subserve integrative aspects of affective, cognitive, and behavioral reactions such as fear, anxiety, avoidance, and/or aggression. Reflex responses provide a rapid, low-level response, but they are not immutable, as higher neurobehavioral processes can come to suppress or bypass pain withdrawal reflexes (e.g., self-injecting insulin or recovering a billfold from a fire). These organizational features are not limited to somatic systems, but apply to the autonomic nervous system as well (Berntson et al., 1998).

Although we have emphasized the features at the extremes, there is a continuum of neuraxial organization relevant to evaluative processing. We have discussed, for instance, how negative pictures could capture visual attention quickly, an effect we found to manifest in the P140 component of the ERP. Öhman and Mineka (2001) review evidence that people automatically devote more attention to negative (fearful) information than to positive information. Although fast and automatic, this component process can nevertheless be modulated by context. Smith, Larsen, Chartrand, and Cacioppo (2001), for instance, primed participants with positive and negative information, and measured the amount of attention they allocated to each, using both event-related brain potentials (Experiment 1) and a Stroop color-naming task (Experiment 2). Results showed that the attention bias to negative information was attenuated when positive constructs were made accessible.

CONCLUSION

Negative emotion has previously been depicted as playing a fundamental role in calibrating psychological systems; it serves as a call for mental or behavioral adjustment and problem solving, to perform convergent thinking. Positive emotion, in contrast, serves as a cue to stay the course or to explore the environment, to perform divergent thinking (see review by Cacioppo & Gardner, 1999). The separable activation functions provide a complementary, adaptive motivational organization. Species with a positivity offset and a negativity bias enjoy the benefits of exploratory behavior and the self-preservative benefits of a predisposition to avoid, scrutinize, and withdraw from threatening events. These features represent only the rudimentary operations of an affect system, however. A heterarchical organization of the neural components constituting the affect system provides a rich repertoire of processing operations that vary in their speed, contextual control, and behavioral flexibility. Work on the relativity of emotion shows that cognitive factors and physiological states affect the extent to which appetitive or defensive motivations are aroused, and recent work suggests that self-regulatory focus also influences approach and withdrawal gradients (Carver & Scheier, 1990; Higgins, 1997; Shah et al., 1998). The organization of the affect system, its operating characteristics, and its outputs (e.g., affective asymmetries) warrant further study as a reflection of our evolutionary heritage and as a continued force in shaping the mind's construction of the world.

References

Aloise, P. A. (1993). Trait confirmation and disconfirmation: The development of attribution biases. Special Issue: Social context, social behavior, and socialization. *Journal of Experimental Child Psychology, 55,* 177–193.

Anderson, N. H. (1965). Averaging versus adding as a stimulus-combination rule in impression formation. *Journal of Personality and Social Psychology, 2,* 1–9.

Anderson, N. H. (1968). Likableness ratings of 555 personality trait words. *Journal of Personality and Social Psychology, 9,* 272–279.

Anderson, N. H. (1981). Integration theory applied to cognitive responses and attitudes. In R. E. Petty, T. M. Ostrom, and T. C. Brock (Eds.), *Cognitive responses in persuasion* (pp. 361–397). Hillsdale, NJ: Erlbaum.

Ansolabehere, S. D.; Iyengar, S.; & Simon, A. (1999). Replicating experiments using surveys and aggregate data: The case of negative advertising. *American Political Science Review, 93,* 901–909.

Bargh, J. A. (2001). The psychology of the mere. In J. A. Bargh and D. K. Apsley (Eds.), *Unraveling the complexities of social life: A festschrift in honor of Robert B. Zajonc* (pp. 25–37). Washington, DC: American Psychological Association.

Bargh, J. A.; Chaiken, S.; Govender, R.; & Pratto, F. (1992). The generality of the automatic attitude activation effect. *Journal of Personality and Social Psychology, 62,* 893–912.

Berntson, G. G.; Boysen, S. T.; & Cacioppo, J. T. (1993). Neurobehavioral organization and the cardinal principle of evaluative bivalence. *Annals of the New York Academy of Sciences, 702,* 75–102.

Berntson, G. G.; Cacioppo, J. T.; & Sarter, M. (2003). Bottom-up: Implications for neurobehavioral models of anxiety and autonomic regulation. In R. J. Davidson, K. R. Sherer, and H. H. Goldsmith (Eds.), *Handbook of affective sciences* (pp. 1105–1116). New York: Oxford University Press.

Blascovich, J.; Ernst, J. M.; Tomaka, J.; & Kelsey, R. M. (1993). Attitude accessibility as a moderator of autonomic reactivity during decision making. *Journal of Personality and Social Psychology, 64,* 165–176.

Boysen, S. T.; Berntson, G. G.; Hannan, M. B.; & Cacioppo, J. T. (1996). Quantity-based choices: Interference and symbolic representations in chimpanzees (*Pan troglodytes*). *Journal of Experimental Psychology: Animal Behavior Processes, 22,* 76–86.

Bradley, M. M.; Lang, P. J.; & Cuthbert, B. N. (1997). *Affective norms for English words.* Center for the Study of Emotion and Attention – National Institute of Mental Health (CSEA-NIMH), University of Florida, Gainesville.

Brehm, J. W. (1956). Post-decision changes in desirability of alternatives. *Journal of Abnormal and Social Psychology, 52,* 384–389.

Cacioppo, J. T., & Berntson, G. G. (1994). Relationship between attitudes and evaluative space: A critical review, with emphasis on the separability of positive and negative substrates. *Psychological Bulletin, 115,* 401–423.

Cacioppo, J. T., & Berntson, G. G. (1999). The affect system: Architecture and operating characteristics. *Current Directions in Psychological Science, 8,* 133–137.

Cacioppo, J. T., & Gardner W. L. (1993). What underlies medical donor attitudes and behavior? *Health Psychology, 12,* 269–271.

Cacioppo, J. T., & Gardner, W. L. (1999). Emotion. *Annual Review of Psychology, 50,* 191–214.

Cacioppo, J. T., & Petty, R. E. (1981). Effects of extent of thought on the pleasantness ratings of p-o-x triads: Evidence for three judgmental tendencies in evaluating social situations. *Journal of Personality and Social Psychology, 40,* 1000–1009.

Cacioppo, J. T.; Crites, S. L., Jr.; Berntson, G. G.; & Coles, M. G. H. (1993). If attitudes affect how stimuli are processed, should they not affect the event-related brain potential? *Psychological Science, 4,* 108–112.

Cacioppo, J. T.; Crites, S. L., Jr.; Gardner, W. L.; & Berntson, G. G. (1994). Bioelectrical echoes from evaluative categorizations: I. A late positive brain potential that varies as a function of trait negativity and extremity. *Journal of Personality and Social Psychology, 67,* 115–125.

Cacioppo, J. T.; Crites, S. L., Jr.; & Gardner, W. L. (1996). Attitudes to the right: Evaluative processing is associated with lateralized late positive event-related brain potentials. *Personality and Social Psychology Bulletin, 22,* 1205–1219.

Cacioppo, J. T.; Gardner, W. L.; & Berntson, G. G. (1997). Beyond bipolar conceptualizations and measures: The case of attitudes and evaluative space. *Personality and Social Psychology Review, 1,* 3–25.

Cacioppo, J. T.; Gardner, W. L.; & Berntson, G. G. (1999). The affect system has parallel and integrative processing components: Form follows function. *Journal of Personality and Social Psychology, 76,* 839–855.

Cacioppo, J. T.; Priester, J. R.; & Berntson, G. G. (1993). Rudimentary determinants of attitude: II. Arm flexion and extension have differential effects on attitudes. *Journal of Personality and Social Psychology, 65,* 5–17.

Cannon, W. B. (1929). *Bodily changes in pain, hunger, fear, and rage.* New York: Appleton.

Carver, C. S., & Scheier, M. F. (1990). Origins and functions of positive and negative affect: A control-process view. *Psychological Review, 97,* 19–35.

Center for the Study of Emotion and Attention – National Institute of Mental Health (CSEA-NIMH). (1995). *The international affective picture system: Digitized photographs.* Gainesville: The Center for Research in Psychophysiology, University of Florida.

Coles, M. G. H.; Donchin, E.; & Porges, S. (1986). *Psychophysiology: Systems, processes, and applications.* New York: Guilford Press.

Collani, G. von; Jacobsen , T.; & Schröger, E. (2000). Evaluatives Priming von Einstellungen und EKP-Messung. In *Deutsche Gesellschaft für Psychologie (Hrsg.) Abstract CD-ROM zum 42. Kongress der Deutschen Gesellschaft für Psychologie.* Lengerich: Pabst Science Publishers.

Crites, S. L., Jr.; Cacioppo, J. T.; Gardner, W. L.; & Berntson, G. G. (1995). Bioelectrical echoes from evaluative categorization: II. A late positive brain potential that varies as a function of attitude registration rather than attitude report. *Journal of Personality and Social Psychology, 68,* 997–1013.

Crites, S. L., Jr., & Cacioppo, J. T. (1996). Electrocortical differentiation of evaluative and nonevaluative categorizations. *Psychological Science, 7,* 318–321.

Darwin, C. (1998). *Expression of the emotions in man and animals* (3d ed.). New York: Oxford University Press. (Original work published 1872.)

de Gelder, B., & Vroomen, J. (2000). The perception of emotion by ear and by eye. *Cognition & Emotion, 14,* 289–311.

Diener, E. (1999). Introduction to the special section on the structure of emotion. *Journal of Personality and Social Psychology, 76,* 803–804.

Fabiani, M.; Gratton, G.; & Coles, M. G. H. (2000). Event-related brain potentials: Methods, theory, and application. In J. T. Cacioppo, L. G. Tassinary, and G. G Berntson (Eds.), *Handbook of psychophysiology* (2d ed.). Cambridge: Cambridge University Press.

Fishbein, M., & Ajzen, I. (1975). *Belief, attitude, intention, and behavior: An introduction to theory and research.* Reading, MA: Addison-Wesley.

Ganzach, Y. (1995). Negativity (and positivity) in performance evaluation: Three field studies. *Journal of Applied Psychology, 80,* 491–499.

Gardner, W. L. (1996). *Biases in impression formation: A demonstration of a bivariate model of evaluation.* Ph.D. dissertation, The Ohio State University.

Gardner, W. L., & Cacioppo, J. T. (1995). Multi-gallon blood donors: Why do they give? *Transfusion, 35,* 795–798.

Hass, R. G.; Katz, I.; Rizzo, N.; Bailey, J.; & Eisenstadt, D. (1991). Cross-racial appraisal as related to attitude ambivalence and cognitive complexity. *Personality and Social Psychology Bulletin, 17,* 83–92.

Heider, F. (1946). Attitudes and cognitive organization. *Journal of Psychology, 21,* 107–112.

Heider, F. (1958). *The psychology of interpersonal relations.* New York: Wiley.

Higgins, E. T. (1997). Beyond pleasure and pain. *American Psychologist, 52,* 1280–1300.

Holbrook, A. L.; Krosnick, J. A.; Visser, P. S.; Gardner, W. L.; & Cacioppo, J. T. (2001). Attitudes toward presidential candidates and political parties: Initial optimism, inertial first impressions, and a focus on flaws. *American Journal of Political Science, 45,* 930–950.

Ito, T. A., & Cacioppo, J. T. (2000). Electrophysiological evidence of implicit and explicit categorization processes. *Journal of Experimental Social Psychology, 36,* 660–676.

Ito, T. A.; Larsen, J. T.; Smith, N. K.; & Cacioppo, J. T. (1998). Negative information weighs more heavily on the brain: The negativity bias in evaluative categorizations. *Journal of Personality and Social Psychology, 75,* 887–900.

Ito, T. A.; Cacioppo, J. T.; & Lang, P. J. (1998). Eliciting affect using the International Affective Picture System: Trajectories through evaluative space. *Personality and Social Psychology Bulletin, 24,* 855–879.

Jackson, J. H. (1958). Evolution and dissolution of the nervous system (Croonian Lectures). In J. Taylor (Ed.), *Selected writings of John Hughlings Jackson* (Vol. 2). New York: Basic Books. (Original work published 1884.)

Kahneman, D. (1973). *Attention and effort.* Englewood Cliffs, NJ: Prentice-Hall.

Kahneman, D., & Tversky, A. (1979). Prospect theory. *Econometrica, 47,* 263–292.

Kawasaki, H.; Adolphs, R.; Kaufman, O.; Damasio, H.; Damasio, A. R.; Granner, M.; Bakken, H.; Hori, T.; Howard, M. A. (2001). Single-neuron responses to emotional visual stimuli recorded in human ventral prefrontal cortex. *Nature Neuroscience, 4,* 15–16.

Kiewiet, D., & Rivers, D. (1984). A retrospective on retrospective voting. *Political Behavior, 6,* 369–393.

Kihlstrom, J. F. (1987). The cognitive unconscious. *Science, 237(4821),* 1445–1452.

Klein, J. G. (1991). Negativity effects in impression formation: A test in the political arena. *Personality and Social Psychology Bulletin, 17,* 412–418.

Klein, J. G. (1996). Negativity in impressions of presidential candidates revisited: The 1992 election. *Personality and Social Psychology Bulletin, 22,* 288–295.

Lang, P. J.; Bradley, M. M.; & Cuthbert, B. N. (1990). Emotion, attention, and the startle reflex. *Psychological Review, 97,* 377–395.

Lang, P. J.; Bradley, M. M.; & Cuthbert, B. N. (1995). *International affective picture system (IAPS): Technical manual and affective ratings.* The NIMH Center for the Study of Emotion and Attention, University of Florida, Gainesville.

Larsen, J. T.; McGraw, P.; & Cacioppo, J. T. (2001). Can people feel happy and sad at the same time? *Journal of Personality and Social Psychology, 81,* 684–696.

Larsen, J. T.; McGraw, A. P.; Mellers, B. A.; & Cacioppo, J. T. (in press). "The agony of victory and the thrill of defeat: Mixed emotional reactions to disappointing wins and relieving losses." Manuscript under review, Princeton University, Princeton, NJ.

LeDoux, J. E. (1995). Emotion: Clues from the brain. *Annual Review of Psychology, 46,* 209–235.

LeDoux, J. E. (2000). Cognitive-emotional interactions: Listen to the brain. In R. D. Lane, L. Nadel et al., (Eds.), *Cognitive neuroscience of emotion. Series in affective science* (pp. 129–155). New York: Oxford University Press.

Loftus, E. F. (1979). *Eyewitness testimony.* Cambridge, MA: Harvard University Press.

Lord, C. G.; Ross, L.; & Lepper, M. R. (1979). Biased assimilation and attitude polarization: The effects of prior theories on subsequently considered evidence. *Journal of Personality and Social Psychology, 36,* 2098–2109.

Macrae, C. N.; Milne, A. B.; & Bodenhausen, G. V. (1994). Stereotypes as energy-saving devices: A peek inside the cognitive toolbox. *Journal of Personality and Social Psychology, 66,* 37–47.

McGuire, W. J. (1981). The probabilogical model of cognitive structure and attitude change. In R. E. Petty, T. M. Ostrom, and T. C. Brock (Eds.), *Cognitive responses in persuasion* (pp. 291–307). Hillsdale, NJ: Erlbaum.

McGuire, W. J., & McGuire, C. V. (1991). The content, structure, and operation of thought systems. In R. S. Wyer and T. K. Srull (Eds.), *Advances in social cognition* (Vol. 4, pp. 1–78).

McGuire, W. J., & McGuire, C. V. (1992). Cognitive-versus-affective asymmetries in thought systems. *European Journal of Social Psychology, 22,* 571–591.

Miller, N. E. (1959). Liberalization of basic S-R concepts: Extensions to conflict behavior, motivation and social learning. In S. Koch (Ed.), *Psychology: A study of a science, Study 1* (pp. 198–292). New York: McGraw-Hill.

Miller, N. E. (1961). Some recent studies on conflict behavior and drugs. *American Psychologist, 16,* 12–24.

Morris, J. S.; Öhman, A.; & Dolan, R. J. (1999). A subcortical pathway to the right amygdala mediating "unseen" fear. *Proceedings of the National Academy of Sciences, 96,* 1680–1685.

Nisbett, R. E., & Wilson, T. D. (1977). Telling more than we can know: Verbal reports on mental processes. *Psychological Review, 84,* 231–259.

Öhman, A., & Mineka, S. (2001). Fears, phobias, and preparedness: Toward an evolved module of fear and fear learning. *Psychological Review, 108,* 483–522.

O'Doherty, J. O.; Kringelbach, M. L.; Rolls, E. T.; Hornak, J.; & Andrews, C. (2001). Abstract reward and punishment representations in the human orbitofrontal cortex. *Nature Neuroscience, 4,* 95–102.

Osgood, C. E.; Suci, G. J.; & Tannenbaum, P. H. (1957). *The measurement of meaning.* Urbana: University of Illinois Press.

Pratto, F., & John, O. P. (1991). Automatic vigilance: The attention-grabbing power of negative social information. *Journal of Personality and Social Psychology, 63,* 380–391.

Robinson-Whelen, S.; Kim, C.; MacCallum, R. C.; & Kiecolt-Glaser, J. K. (1997). Distinguishing optimism from pessimism in older adults: Is it more important to be optimistic or not to be pessimistic? *Journal of Personality and Social Psychology, 73,* 1345–1353.

Roediger, H. L., & McDermott, K. B. (2000). Tricks of memory. *Current Directions in Psychological Science, 7,* 347–353.

Rowe, P. M. (1989). Unfavorable information and interview decisions. In R. W. Eder and G. R. Ferris (Eds.), *The employment interview: theory, research, and practice* (pp. 77–89). Newbury Park, CA: Sage.

Russell, J. A. (1980). A circumplex model of affect. *Journal of Personality and Social Psychology, 39,* 1161–1178.

Russell, J. A., & Carroll, J. M. (1999). On the bipolarity of positive and negative affect. *Psychological Bulletin, 125,* 3–30.

Shah, J.; Higgins, E. T.; & Friedman, R. S. (1998). Performance incentives and means: How regulatory focus influences goal attainment. *Journal of Personality and Social Psychology, 74,* 285–293.

Skowronski, J. J., & Carlston, D. E. (1989). Negativity and extremity biases in impression formation: A review of explanations. *Psychological Bulletin, 105,* 131–142.

Smith, C. A., & Kirby, L. D. (2001). Affect and cognitive appraisal processes. In J. P. Forgas (Ed.), *Handbook of affect and social cognition* (pp. 75–92). Mahwah, NJ: Erlbaum.

Smith, N. K.; Larsen, J. T.; Chartrand, T. L.; & Cacioppo, J. T. (under review). Being bad isn't always good: Evaluative context moderates the attention bias toward negative information.

Spelke, E.; Hirst, W.; & Neisser, U. (1976). Skills of divided attention. *Cognition, 4,* 215–230.

Taylor, S. E. (1991). Asymmetrical effects of positive and negative events: The mobilization-minimization hypothesis. *Psychological Bulletin, 110,* 67–85.

Watson, D., & Tellegen, A. (1985). Toward a consensual structure of mood. *Psychological Bulletin, 98,* 219–235.

Westermann, R.; Spies, K.; Stahl, G.; & Hesse, F. W. (1996). Relative effectiveness and validity of mood induction procedures: A meta-analysis. *European Journal of Social Psychology, 26,* 557–580.

Ybarra, O., & Stephan, W. G. (1996). Misanthropic person memory. *Journal of Personality and Social Psychology, 70,* 691–700.

15

Pleasure, Unfelt Affect, and Irrational Desire

Kent C. Berridge

ABSTRACT

An example of unfelt affect is described in which subliminal facial expressions cause unfelt "liking," which influences people's reactions and beverage consumption without causing conscious emotion. Subcortical brain modules for core processes of nonconscious "liking" and "wanting" have been revealed by affective neuroscience studies, based on behavioral affective reactions that occur even in creatures that cannot speak, such as infants or animals. Core "liking" and "wanting" may normally contribute to conscious pleasure and desire. But these core psychological processes are themselves intrinsically inaccessible and provide a basis for unconscious affective reactions. The process of "wanting" also provides insight into cases of truly irrational desire, where one wants what is neither liked nor expected to be liked.

Sweetness tastes nice. The pleasantness of a sweet taste is a gloss on the mere sensation, added by our brains to the sensory quality of sweetness (Frijda, 2001).[1] Sweets need not be nice – there are nasty sweet tastes in this world too (as when aversions are acquired for particular sweet flavors). But humans are evolutionarily and neurobiologically predisposed to find sweet sensation pleasant. This chapter is devoted to the gloss of niceness, especially the niceness of sensory pleasures (for discussion of nonsensory pleasures, see Frijda, 2001). What is the niceness gloss? How is it added to

---

[1] The idea of pleasure as a "niceness gloss," added to sweetness above and beyond mere sensation, was introduced at the Amsterdam conference by Nico Frijda (in a public discussion with Antonio Damasio). Without fully addressing the interesting point of their contention (the degree to which the affect of sensations is intrinsic to sensory representations or separate from them), I have adopted it as a useful device to link the ideas in this chapter.

I thank Piotr Winkielman and Julie Wilbarger for allowing me to include our unpublished data. I also thank Nico Frijda, Sheila Reynolds, and Piotr Winkielman for helpful discussion of earlier versions of the manuscript.

a sweet sensation by brain systems? And how does it motivate real action – in rational and even irrational ways?

First, I want to examine the possibility that the essence of niceness may be surprisingly nonconscious. Evidence suggests a form of nonconscious "liking" can occur in ordinary human beings without their subjective awareness of it. Nonconscious "liking" may be the core of the niceness gloss that we ordinarily experience as conscious pleasure. But even nonconscious "liking" alone, without subjective feeling, is sufficient to influence behavioral reactions to affect-laden events.

Second, I will briefly address how core "liking" might be organized in the brain. Specifically, opioid synapses in the subcortical forebrain's nucleus accumbens can cause a niceness gloss for sweet tastes, activating a brain circuit for "liking" sweet pleasures.

Third, I will examine a further core incentive process, namely "wanting," which can rather directly translate the pleasure gloss into action. This psychological process and its dopamine brain substrate is only one of several routes to goal-directed action and is not the most complex or interesting psychologically. But under some circumstances "wanting" might cause irrational desires, in a strong sense of irrationality. I define irrational desire here as desire for something that we neither like nor expect to like. In such cases, this "wanting" process becomes interesting indeed.

UNCONSCIOUS EMOTIONAL REACTIONS?

People often may have emotional reactions without knowing why they have them, but they have generally been supposed to know that they have an emotional reaction (Ellsworth & Scherer, 2003; Frijda, 1999). After all, emotions are feelings, and feelings must be felt. Still, let us ask, can there be unfelt affective reactions? And if affect means feeling, this poses a paradox: can there be an unfelt "feeling"?

Two decades of studies have shown convincingly that people can be caused to have emotional reactions by subliminal events they do not consciously perceive (Öhman, Flykt, & Lundqvist, 2000; Zajonc, 1980; Zajonc, 2000). Yet even in such instances of unconscious emotion, it is only the cause and assignment of emotion that proceeds unconsciously. The emotion itself is generally interpreted as being a conscious feeling, detected by asking subjects how they feel.

But a stronger sense of unconscious emotion can be envisioned too. Truly unconscious emotion would mean the emotion itself remains unfelt yet is still evidenced as a valenced reaction in behavior or physiology. This sense of emotion as an unfelt feeling or nonconscious affect seems to turn the ordinary definition of emotion upside down, dropping its most obvious feature, namely, that emotions feel a certain way. But counterintuitive as it is, there are principled reasons from both psychology and affective neuroscience why a nonconscious emotion might be possible (Berridge & Winkielman, 2003; Frijda, 2001; Kihlstrom, Mulvaney, Tobias, & Tobis, 2000; LeDoux, 2000; Winkielman, Zajonc, & Schwarz, 1997; Zajonc, 2000).

The question can be put as an empirical one. Do subliminal causes of affective reactions always produce a conscious emotion (at least when they succeed in influencing reactions)? Or can people actually remain unconscious of their own emotional reaction that is objectively evident in their later behavior (in addition to being unaware of its subliminal cause)? Piotr Winkielman, together with his student Julie Wilbarger, and I recently conducted a collaborative project that demonstrated unfelt affect (Winkielman, Berridge, & Wilbarger, 2000). That study found nonconscious "liking" – a nonconscious pleasure gloss not sensed by the person at the moment it was caused, but which influenced the response toward an affectively laden stimulus moments later.

Winkielman et al. assessed conscious emotional reactions by asking subjects to rate online their subjective mood immediately after subliminal exposure to emotional facial expression. Subliminal stimuli were happy, neutral, or angry facial expressions (only one-sixtieth of a second duration), followed immediately by a second "masking" photograph of a face with a neutral expression shown long enough to be consciously seen (nearly 1/2 sec, and embedded in a distraction task). Participants were aware only of the second neutral face, and not of the preceding emotional expression. All participants denied later having seen any emotional expressions and were unable to recognize them. Participants also rated their own emotional feelings immediately after subliminal exposure, either on a simple hedonic mood scale, or on a more complex twenty-item mood scale (contentment, irritability, etc.). Finally, their evaluation of subjective emotion was counterbalanced with an opportunity to evaluate a "new fruit beverage" (actually lime Kool-Aid).

For example, participants were given a pitcher of beverage and were asked to pour and drink as much as they wished (the amounts were covertly measured) (Winkielman et al., 2000). In another experiment, participants were given a single sip of the beverage after being shown subliminal faces and asked to rate how much they liked the drink, how much they wanted to consume, and how much they would be willing to pay if it were sold in stores.

Unconscious "liking" was produced best in participants who were thirsty (Winkielman et al., 2000). No change in their subjective emotion was produced by subliminal exposure to happy/angry faces. Yet subliminal exposure to happy facial expressions caused thirsty participants to pour themselves about 50 percent more of the fruit-flavored drink than if they had seen only neutral facial expressions (Winkielman et al., 2000). Conversely, they poured 50 percent less than neutral after seeing angry faces. These participants also consumed or swallowed about 50 percent

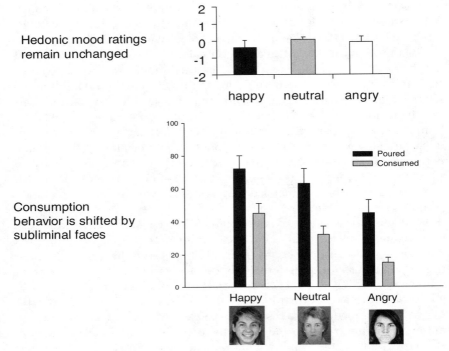

FIGURE 15.1. Unfelt affect controls consumption behavior. *Top:* Ratings of subjective mood were not changed after same subliminal stimuli ("How do you feel right now at this moment?" 10-point hedonic scale). *Bottom:* Pouring and drinking behavior by thirsty men and women was changed after subliminal exposure to happy facial expressions, neutral facial expressions, or angry facial expressions (amount poured of a fruit-flavored drink and amount actually consumed). From Winkielman et al., submitted.

more of what they poured after seeing happy expressions than after neutral expressions (and drank even less after subliminal angry expressions). Their consumption behavior was increased by happy expressions (and decreased by angry expressions) even though they had no conscious awareness of any change in their own mood at the moment subliminal faces are presented (Figure 15.1).

Similarly, the subliminal stimuli altered ratings of liking and wanting given to a sip of the drink and of its monetary value (Winkielman et al., 2000). For example, thirsty participants who were exposed to subliminal happy expressions later gave higher pleasantness ratings and higher answers to the question "How much would you pay for this drink in a store?" They were willing to pay more than twice as much (over 40 cents per can, U.S. currency) after seeing subliminal happy expressions compared to after seeing subliminal angry expressions (less than 20 cents per can). Again, no conscious emotions or mood changes were reported by these participants after subliminal presentations (Winkielman et al., 2000).

Clearly, happy subliminal faces did not make drinkers feel better in general, since they reported no elevation in subjective emotion at all. Nor did subliminal angry faces make them feel worse. Instead the subliminal stimuli produced no conscious emotion at all when presented. Only later, when an affectively laden drink was encountered, did the implicit affective reaction surface into explicit behavior and ratings.

Thus in normal adults under some conditions, unfelt "liking" reactions can influence a person's consumption behavior later, without reportable subjective awareness of the affective reaction at the moment it was caused. Core "liking" in this sense is consistent with Frijda's notion of the pleasure gloss as "a mental process, itself as unconscious as any other mental process, that changes the tuning for inputs and behavioral inclinations" (Frijda, 2001, p. 77) and a process that requires further processing to become conscious. Although it is possible to try to explain subliminal "liking" effects in terms of unconscious cognition rather than unconscious emotion, Winkielman, Wilbarger, and I believe that such cognitive reinterpretations will not succeed in this case (because cognitive manipulations of attention did not alter the effects, whereas biological thirst state played a determining role; for discussion see Berridge & Winkielman, 2003; Winkielman et al., 2000). If my colleagues and I are correct, this may be an example of truly unconscious emotion.

AFFECTIVE NEUROSCIENCE OF CORE "LIKING" FOR PLEASANT TASTES

What could happen in the brain to generate unfelt "liking"? What brain systems might mediate subliminally caused changes in affective reactions to a drink? We can only speculate, but there are some clues to guide us from the affective neuroscience of taste pleasure.

First it is helpful to note a useful behavioral measure of positive affect that has been employed in some affective neuroscience studies – namely, affective facial expressions to the sensory pleasure of taste, which our laboratory has used to examine brain mechanisms that underlie basic "liking" reactions.

A newborn human infant has two distinct patterns of affective facial reactions to tastes, positive versus negative (Steiner, 1973; Steiner, Glaser, Hawilo, & Berridge, 2001). Sweet elicits positive "liking" facial reactions from newborns (e.g., lip sucking, smiles), whereas bitter elicits negative "disliking" reactions (e.g., gapes, nose wrinkling; Figure 15.2).

Positive facial reactions to sweetness might plausibly be accompanied by conscious feelings of pleasure for normal human infants. But there are

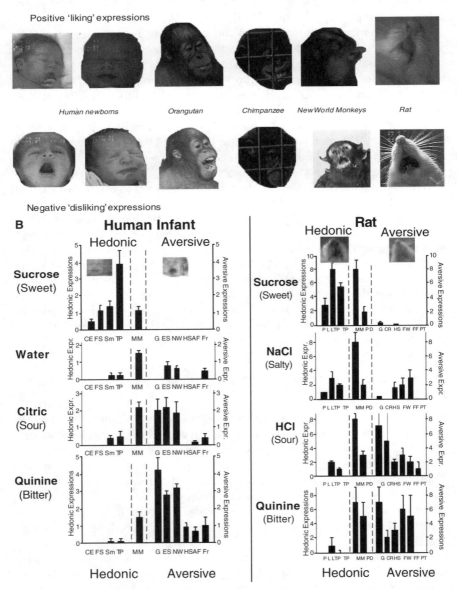

FIGURE 15.2. A. Affective reactions are elicited by sweet tastes from human infants, great apes, monkeys, and rats. B. Human infant affective reactions switch from positive to negative across sweet to bitter tastes (*left*). Affective reactions by rats show a similar gradual switch from positive to negative across tastes (*right*). Modified from Steiner et al., 2001, and Berridge 2000. (*See color insert*)

reasons to think that the facial reaction to pleasure reflects a core process of "liking" rather than the consciousness of the niceness gloss. One reason is that positive affective facial reactions also occur in infants whose consciousness status is more suspect, such as "anencephalic" infants (Steiner, 1973). Anencephalic infants have a brainstem but no cortex, amygdala, or classic limbic system, due to a birth defect that prevents prenatal development of their forebrain. Yet basic tastes elicit normal positive/negative affective reactions from them.

Animals, especially those that prefer sweets, also emit affective facial reactions to sweet versus bitter tastes that can be highly similar to those of human babies (Figure 15.3). Positive facial expressions to sweetness are emitted by chimpanzees, orangutans, and gorillas, various monkeys, and even rats (Berridge, 2000; Steiner et al., 2001). The pattern of positive facial expression becomes increasingly less similar to humans as the taxonomic distance increases between a species and us. But all of these species share some reaction components that are homologous to ours. Those affective reactions share a common evolutionary ancestry and are likely to have similar neural mechanisms (Steiner et al., 2001). This means in practice that one can use mere rats in affective neuroscience studies to examine the brain mechanisms of positive affective reaction to sweetness (Berridge, 2000).

SUBCORTICAL FOREBRAIN SITE CAUSES POSITIVE AFFECTIVE CORE PROCESS: NUCLEUS ACCUMBENS SHELL

The nucleus accumbens is perhaps the most notable brain system of "liking" identified so far (especially its portion named shell; Figure 15.3), because it is a forebrain structure capable of applying a pleasure gloss. It lies at the front base of the brain, just below the prefrontal cortex. Activation of certain neural circuits in the nucleus accumbens causes heightened "liking" for a pleasant taste, as revealed by a recent affective neuroscience experiment conducted by Susana Peciña in our laboratory (Peciña & Berridge, 2000). Nucleus accumbens circuits are one of the few brain systems able to cause an increase in the niceness gloss.

Specifically, selective activation of opioid neurotransmitter receptors on neurons inside the nucleus accumbens of rats causes sweet tastes to elicit extra "liking" reactions. The selective activation was caused by microinjections of morphine (a drug that activates opioid receptors) directly into the nucleus accumbens, made painlessly because the brain cannula had been implanted a week earlier (under anesthesia). Then a few minutes after the morphine microinjection, a bittersweet taste was infused into the rat's mouth while its behavioral affective reactions were videorecorded (Peciña & Berridge, 2000). The rats responded with a distinct shift toward positive affective reactions after the morphine microinjection, indicating they "liked" the taste more (Figure 15.3). Interestingly, morphine

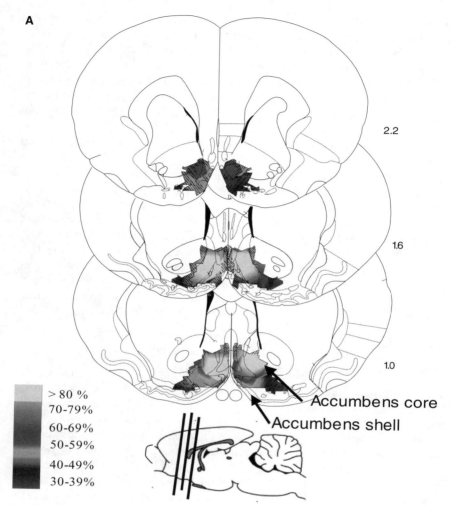

FIGURE 15.3. A. "Liking" and "wanting" site in nucleus accumbens shell where opioid activation causes increased niceness gloss for sweetness (Peciña & Berridge, 2000). Percentages refer to percent increase in appetitive behavior caused by morphine microinjection (100% = twice baseline amount). Coronal brain slices (face on view) are numbered conventionally; their position is shown in profile view below. B. Brain structures of "liking" discussed here (gray), and the dopamine "wanting" system (black). (*See color insert*)

microinjections also caused the rats to eat more of a tasty food than they ordinarily would. This suggests that the accumbens shell activation may increase "wanting" for food, as a consequence of enhancing "liking" for it (Peciña & Berridge, 2000).

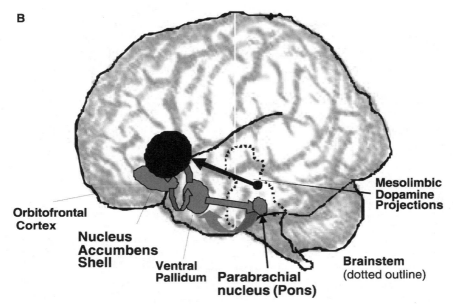

FIGURE 15.3. *(continued).*

The nucleus accumbens is embedded in a larger brain circuit for "liking," which connects to other forebrain structures such as the ventral pallidum, and even to brainstem structures, such as the parabrachial nucleus (Figure 15.3, Berridge, 2003). The ventral pallidum and parabrachial nucleus have been posited by several affective neuroscientists to play important roles in emotion and even in generating a sense of self (Damasio, 1999; Panksepp, 1998). Affective neuroscience studies in our laboratory have found these brain structures share the special ability to cause changes in the niceness gloss, as reflected by "liking" facial reactions to sweet tastes (Berridge, in press).

How do subcortical mechanisms of "liking" reactions to sweet pleasure bear on the subliminal affective reactions to drinks in adult humans found by Winkielman and colleagues? One possibility is that opioid activation patterns in the human nucleus accumbens might be altered by subliminal facial expressions, which activate related brain structures (Morris, Öhman, & Dolan, 1999; Whalen et al., 1998). Altered neuronal activity in the nucleus accumbens (perhaps causing nonconscious "liking") could then change the human affective reaction to a drink, just as morphine microinjection into a rat's accumbens enhances its affective reaction to sweetness and leads to behavioral reaction of greater "liking."

Further, to the degree that conscious feelings of pleasure might be influenced in turn by opioid activation in accumbens, the subjective niceness gloss could be caused by accumbens-to-cortex signals that are relayed to cortical regions in just a couple of synapses, via the ventral pallidum and thalamus (Zahm, 2000). Opioid activation in the nucleus accumbens is widely thought to partly mediate the intense pleasure of stimuli such as heroin for human drug users (Koob & Le Moal, 2001; Wise, 1998), and similar opioid activation mediates normal human subjective feelings of pleasure caused by tasty food (Yeomans & Gray, 1997). Finally, descending projections from frontal cortex to subcortical "liking" structures might permit cognitive appraisals or voluntary intentions to modulate basic emotional reactions (Davidson, Jackson, & Kalin, 2000).

SURPRISING FALSE CANDIDATE FOR "LIKING": MESOLIMBIC DOPAMINE SYSTEM

As our laboratory has examined various brain mechanisms for the sweet pleasure gloss, one of the findings that surprised us most was failure to modulate "liking" whenever we manipulated the mesolimbic dopamine system. The system of dopamine neurons that stretch from the midbrain to the nucleus accumbens is probably the brain's most famous reward system and is often called the pleasure system. But that may be a case of mistaken identity.

There are several reasons why dopamine neurons have been thought to mediate pleasure. Dopamine neurons in rats are turned on by naturally pleasurable events, such as eating a delicious new food or encountering a sex partner (Ahn & Phillips, 1999; Fiorino, Coury, & Phillips, 1997; Schultz, 1998). Dopamine is also turned on by drugs that many people enjoy, such as cocaine, amphetamine, heroin, or ecstasy (Wise, 1998). Further, if dopamine is blocked by other drugs, all these rewards seem to lose certain rewarding properties. At least, animals no longer seem to "want" rewards when their dopamine systems are suppressed, and it has seemed reasonable to many to infer that it is because they no longer "like" rewards (Gardner, 1997; Hoebel, Rada, Mark, & Pothos, 1999; Shizgal, 1999; Wise, 1985).

We therefore expected dopamine manipulations to powerfully alter affective facial expressions to sweet tastes when we began to manipulate the system and were at first surprised to find that they did not. But to make a long story short, dopamine systems do not seem to mediate the pleasure gloss, at least if "liking" is assessed by behavioral affective reactions to the hedonic impact of sweet tastes. We have turned dopamine systems on with amphetamine that causes dopamine release or with electrical stimulation of intervening brain pathways (e.g., Wyvell & Berridge, 2000) and turned them off with drugs that block dopamine receptors (e.g., Peciña, Berridge, & Parker, 1997). We have even selectively destroyed the dopamine system entirely with chemical neurotoxins that damage only dopamine-containing neurons (e.g., Berridge & Robinson, 1998). All these manipulations powerfully altered the degree to which rats "want" tasty food, in the sense of their willingness to work for it or consume it. But they never shifted "liking" facial reactions to a sweet taste. The niceness gloss simply persisted unchanged (as does the ability to learn a new "liking"/"disliking" gloss; for review, see Berridge & Robinson, 1998).

Once over our initial surprise, we tried to suggest a psychological function that could masquerade as sensory pleasure in many studies yet still not be a true niceness gloss. Usually "liking" and "wanting" for pleasant incentives do go together, virtually as two sides of the same coin. But our dopamine studies indicate "wanting" may be separable in the brain from "liking." In particular, mesolimbic dopamine systems seem to mediate only "wanting." My colleagues and I have coined the phrase incentive salience for the form of "wanting" we think is mediated by brain dopamine systems. I should acknowledge our suggestion was strongly guided by earlier views of mesolimbic function (Fibiger & Phillips, 1986; Panksepp, 1986; Valenstein, 1976) and of the psychology of incentive motivation (Bindra, 1978; Toates, 1986).

"Wanting" is not "liking." It is not a sensory pleasure in any sense, conscious or nonconscious. It cannot increase positive facial reactions to sweet taste, or the hedonic impact of any sensory pleasure. Instead, incentive salience is essentially nonhedonic in nature, even though we believe it to serve as one component of the larger composite psychological mechanism of reward learning and incentive motivation (Berridge, 2001; Berridge & Robinson, 1998). Originally "wanting" might have evolved as an elementary form of goal directedness to pursue particular innate incentives even in advance of experience, later becoming harnessed to serve learned "likes." In any case, "wanting" remains a distinct process, and we believe that brain dopamine systems especially attribute incentive salience to reward representation whenever a cue for the reward is encountered. Incentive salience causes the cue and its reward to become momentarily more intensely attractive and sought.

The quotation marks around the term "wanting" serve as caveat to acknowledge that incentive salience means something different from the ordinary sense of the word *wanting*. For one thing, "wanting" in the incentive salience sense need not have a conscious goal or declarative target. Wanting in the ordinary sense, on the other hand, nearly always means a conscious desire for an explicitly expected outcome. In the ordinary sense, we consciously and rationally want those things we expect to like. Conscious wanting and core "wanting" differ psychologically and probably also in their brain substrates (Berridge, 2001; Dickinson, Smith, & Mirenowicz, 2000). Incentive salience or "wanting" depends on mesolimbic dopamine systems. Ordinary wanting for consciously explicit targets, by contrast, may depend more strongly on cortical structures, such as prefrontal cortex and insular cortex (Balleine & Dickinson, 1998; Bechara, Damasio, & Damasio, 2000; Dickinson et al., 2000).

IRRATIONAL DESIRES?

If an outcome is liked, then by rational criteria it should also be wanted. The outcome should be wanted exactly to the degree that it is expected to be liked. "Expected to be liked" is the crucial phrase here. Human expectations of what will be liked can often be wrong – because of ignorance about the outcome, false predictions, or false memory of past outcomes (Elster, 1999; Gilbert & Wilson, 2000; Kahneman, 1999). Expectations are often wrong, but being wrong has nothing to do with what I mean by rational desire. Desires based on wrong expectations are misguided but not irrational. Desire remains rational as long as people still choose what they expect to like. A truly irrational choice would be to choose what you expect not to like.

Does truly irrational choice actually occur? Individuals often choose what they turn out not to like, sometimes based on irrational beliefs (see Elster, 1999). But do individuals ever irrationally choose what they expect not to like? My answer is yes: truly irrational choice can be produced by overactivation of the brain's "wanting" system of mesolimbic dopamine.

ANIMALS AND RATIONAL CHOICE?

It may seem incongruous to turn to animals to distinguish rational versus irrational choice, but the results of animal studies are useful in order to link to our consideration of brain dopamine and mesolimbic function. Let us first lay out what would be needed to make an animal model valid here. A demonstration of irrational pursuit would require: (1) that animals be capable of cognitive expectations of an outcome's hedonic value (wanting in the ordinary rational sense of expected liking); (2) that one be able to assess their rational cognitive wanting; and (3) that one be able to detect when their pursuit deviates from cognitive wanting.

These preconditions may have been met through the work of a leading psychologist of animal learning, Anthony Dickinson of Cambridge University in England, together principally with his former student Bernard Balleine. Dickinson and colleagues developed clever ways to ask a mere rat about its cognitive expectations of reward value, and to detect changes in those expectations (Balleine & Dickinson, 1998; Dickinson & Balleine, in press). They ask rats about their expectations of the value of a food or drink reward in part by testing their willingness to work for the rewards when they must be guided principally by those expectations alone. The rats are first trained to work for the real rewards, which come only every so often, so they learn to persist in working to earn reward.

Then the rats are tested for their willingness to work for these rewards later under so-called extinction conditions, when the rewards no longer come at all. Since there are no longer real rewards, the rats have only their expectations of reward to guide them. Naturally, without real rewards to sustain efforts, performance in the extinction test gradually falls. But since the rats originally learned that perseverance pays off, they persist for quite some time in working based largely on their ordinary wanting for reward.

The issues involved in using a Dickinson-style approach to tease apart ordinary cognitive wanting from cue-triggered "wanting" are rather complex (for more discussion, see Berridge, 2001; Dickinson & Balleine, in press). For our purpose here it is enough to say that these techniques of assessing animals' cognitive expectations of hedonic value can detect when cue-triggered "wanting" suddenly diverges from ordinary cognitive wanting. Combined with appropriate tweaks of the brain, they allow an affective neuroscience of irrational pursuit.

IRRATIONAL PURSUIT: VISCERAL MESOLIMBIC ACTIVATION OF "WANTING" FOR A CUED HYPERINCENTIVE

Truly irrational choice has been produced in our laboratory by the doctoral studies of Cindy Wyvell. She combined brain tweaks, in the form of amphetamine microinjections that activated mesolimbic dopamine systems, with Dickinson's techniques for assessing ordinary cognitive wanting versus cue-triggered "wanting" for a sugar pellet (Wyvell & Berridge, 2000). Dopamine activation caused a transient but intense form of irrational pursuit linked to incentive salience.

In this experiment, Wyvell trained rats first on several days to work for occasional sugar pellet rewards by pressing a lever. On different days, the rats learned a reward cue (CS+) for the sugar pellets, by being exposed to Pavlovian pairings in which sugar was preceded by a light or sound cue. In these cue-learning sessions, rats did not have to work for sugar rewards – instead rewards came freely after each cue. All rats were implanted with microinjection cannulae so that a droplet of amphetamine or of drug-free vehicle solution could be infused into their nucleus accumbens. Finally the rats were tested for work using the Dickinson extinction procedure after they had either received amphetamine microinjections or not. During this test, their performance could be guided only by their expectation of the cognitively wanted sugar, because they received no real sugar rewards. And while they pursued their expected reward, their reward cue (light or sound for 30 seconds) was occasionally presented to them over the course of the half-hour session.

In a related experiment, Wyvell tested the effect of amphetamine microinjections on the niceness gloss of real sugar, by measuring positive hedonic patterns of affective reactions of rats as they received an infusion

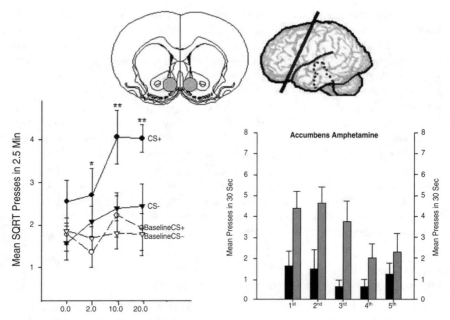

FIGURE 15.4. Irrational cue-triggered "wanting." Amphetamine microinjection in nucleus accumbens magnifies "wanting" for sugar reward – but only in presence of reward cue (CS+). Cognitive expectations and ordinary wanting are not altered (reflected in baseline lever pressing in absence of cue and during irrelevant cue, CS−) (*left*). Transient irrational "wanting" comes and goes with the cue (*right*). Black bars denote work in the absence of the reward cue; gray bars show elevation when cue was present. Modified from Wyvell and Berridge, 2000. (*See color insert*)

of sugar solution into their mouths (Wyvell & Berridge, 2000). In this experiment, amphetamine did not increase positive facial reactions elicited by the taste of real sugar, indicating once again that dopamine did not increase "liking" for the sugar reward.

However, amphetamine microinjection still enhanced "wanting" for sugar in the sense of cue-triggered pursuit of the reward in the first experiment (Figure 15.4). Remember that there are two types of wanting to be assessed here: (1) ordinary wanting, when the rat works guided primarily by its cognitive expectation that it will like the worked-for sugar reward, and (2) cue-triggered "wanting," or incentive salience attributed by mesolimbic systems to the representation of sugar reward that is activated by the cue. What Wyvell found was that activation of dopamine neurotransmission in the accumbens did not change ordinary wanting based on cognitive expectation of liking (measured by baseline performance on the lever). However, amphetamine microinjection dramatically increased cue-triggered "wanting" to more than 400 percent its baseline level.

Cue-triggered "hyper-wanting" is irrational and transient. It is repeatedly reversible, even over the short span of a 30-minute test session (Wyvell & Berridge, 2000). It is triggered by encounter with reward cues, and at that moment it exerts its irrational effect, disproportionate to the cognitively expected hedonic value of the reward. One moment the dopamine-activated brain of the rat simply "wants" sugar in the ordinary sense. The next moment, when the cue comes, the dopamine-activated brain both wants sugar and "wants" sugar to an exaggerated degree, according to the incentive salience hypothesis. A few moments later it has returned to its rational level of wanting appropriate to its expectation of reward. Moments later still, the cue is reencountered, and excessive and irrational "wanting" again takes control.

The irrational level of pursuit thus has two sources that restrict its occurrence and duration: a brain factor (mesolimbic activation) and a psychological factor (presence of reward cue). It seems unlikely that mesolimbic activation stably altered rats' cognitive expectation of how much they would like sugar (which might have rationally increased desire, even though their expectation would be mistaken). That is because amphetamine was present in the nucleus accumbens throughout the entire session but the intense enhancement of pursuit lasted only while the cue stimulus was actually present.

For the brain in a state of mesolimbic activation, the conditioned reward cue becomes a hyperincentive cue, able to trigger an irrational degree of pursuit for the sugar reward, at least for a while. The reward cue causes a momentary irrational desire. Individuals may then "want" what they do not cognitively want – and what they know they will not like (or at least, will not "like" proportionally to their excessive "want").

HUMAN IRRATIONAL CHOICE AND ADDICTION

People have brain dopamine systems too, which may spontaneously activate in many situations. And our brain dopamine systems can be hyper-activated by drugs such as amphetamine or cocaine. If a person's brain dopamine system were highly activated, and the person encountered a reward cue, it seems possible that the person might irrationally "want" the cued reward just like the rat – even if the person cognitively expected not to like it very much.

Human drug addiction may be a special illustration of dopamine irrational "wanting" (Robinson & Berridge, 1993, 2003). Addictive drugs not only activate brain dopamine systems when the drug is taken but may also sensitize them afterward (Robinson, Browman, Crombag, & Badiani, 1998). Neural sensitization means that the brain system becomes hyper-reactive for a long time. The system is not constantly hyper active, but it reacts more strongly than normal if the drug is taken again – in a fashion that is gated by associative context and cues that predict the drug. Neural sensitization occurs to different degrees in different individuals, depending on many factors ranging from genes to prior experiences, as well as on the drug itself, dose, and so on (Robinson & Berridge, 1993; Robinson et al., 1998).

My colleague Terry Robinson and I have suggested that if an addict's mesolimbic system becomes sensitized after taking drugs, that person may irrationally "want" to take drugs again even if they decide they don't "like" them, or like them less than they like the lifestyle they will lose by taking them. This incentive-sensitization theory of addiction thus accounts for why addictive relapse is so often precipitated by encounters with drug cues, which trigger excessive "wanting" for drugs (Robinson & Berridge, 1993, 2003). Cues could trigger irrational "wanting" in an addict whose brain was sensitized even long after withdrawal was over (because sensitization lasts longer), and regardless of expectations of "liking."

Actual evidence that sensitization does indeed cause irrational cue-triggered "wanting" was recently found by Cindy Wyvell in an affective neuroscience animal study similar to the one described above (Wyvell & Berridge, 2001). Rats that had been previously sensitized by amphetamine responded to a sugar cue with excessive "wanting" despite not having had any drug for ten days. Even though they were drug-free at the time of testing, sensitization caused excessively high cue-triggered "wanting" for their reward. For sensitized rats, irrational "wanting" for sugar came and went transiently with the cue, just as if they had received a brain microinjection of drug – but they hadn't. Their persisting pattern of cue-triggered irrationality seems consistent with the incentive-sensitization theory of human drug addiction (Robinson & Berridge, 2000).

IRRATIONALITY IN EVERYDAY LIFE?

Do ordinary people also show irrational cued "wanting" in less extreme situations? Does excessive activation of cue-triggered "wanting" promote irrationally intense pursuit of chocolate, sex, gambling, or other incentives? And can vivid cognitive fantasy ever substitute for cues, triggering in people spontaneous mesolimbic activation and irrational choice? These are intriguing questions about irrational "wanting" in ordinary human lives, but as yet there are no clear answers.

CONCLUSION

Ordinary people seem capable of unconscious emotions in a strong sense of unfelt affective reactions. In normal adults, core "liking" reactions caused by subliminal emotional stimuli may influence a person's "wanting" and consumption of a beverage later, without the person being able to report his or her own affective reaction at the moment it was caused. To generate the core niceness gloss, there appears to be a subcortical network, including the nucleus accumbens, whose output is reflected in objective core "liking" reactions to sweet pleasures. To directly translate "liking" into action, there appears to be a "wanting" dopamine system, which can influence pursuit of rewards independent of cognitive expectations about them. In extreme cases, excessive "wanting" may produce strongly irrational choice, causing individuals to "want" what they do not cognitively want, and to choose what they do not expect to like.

References

Ahn, S., & Phillips, A. G. (1999). Dopaminergic correlates of sensory-specific satiety in the medial prefrontal cortex and nucleus accumbens of the rat. *Journal of Neuroscience, 19(19),* B1–B6.

Balleine, B., & Dickinson, A. (1998). Consciousness – The interface between affect and cognition. In J. Cornwell (Ed.), *Consciousness and human identity* (pp. 57–85). New York: Oxford University Press.

Balleine, B. W., & Dickinson, A. (1998). Goal-directed instrumental action: Contingency and incentive learning and their cortical substrates. *Neuropharmacology, 37(4–5),* 407–419.

Bechara, A.; Damasio, H.; & Damasio, A. R. (2000). Emotion, decision making and the orbitofrontal cortex. *Cerebral Cortex, 10(3),* 295–307.

Berridge, K. C. (2000). Measuring hedonic impact in animals and infants: Microstructure of affective taste reactivity patterns. *Neuroscience and Biobehavioral Reviews, 24(2),* 173–198.

Berridge, K. C. (2001). Reward learning: Reinforcement, incentives, and expectations. In D. L. Medin (Ed.), *The Psychology of Learning and Motivation* (Vol. 40, pp. 223–278). New York: Academic Press.

Berridge, K. C. (2003). Pleasures of the brain. *Brain and Cognition, 52(10),* 106–128.

Berridge, K. C., & Robinson, T. E. (1998). What is the role of dopamine in reward: Hedonic impact, reward learning, or incentive salience? *Brain Research Reviews, 28(3),* 309–369.

Berridge, K. C., & Winkielman, P. (2003). What is an unconscious emotion? (The case for unconscious "liking"). *Cognition and Emotion, 17(2),* 181–211.

Bindra, D. (1978). How adaptive behavior is produced: A perceptual-motivation alternative to response reinforcement. *Behavioral and Brain Sciences, 1,* 41–91.

Damasio, A. R. (1999). *The feeling of what happens: Body and emotion in the making of consciousness* (1st ed.). New York: Harcourt Brace.

Davidson, R. J.; Jackson, D. C.; & Kalin, N. H. (2000). Emotion, plasticity, context, and regulation: Perspectives from affective neuroscience. *Psychological Bulletin, 126(6),* 890–909.

Dickinson, A.; Smith, J.; & Mirenowicz, J. (2000). Dissociation of Pavlovian and instrumental incentive learning under dopamine antagonists. *Behavioral Neuroscience, 114,* 468–483.

Dickinson, A. J., & Balleine, B. (2003). The role of learning in motivation. In C. R. Gallistel (Ed.), *Steven's Handbook of Experimental Psychology* (3d ed., Vol. 3, pp. 497–534), New York: Wiley and Sons.

Ellsworth, P. C., & Scherer, K. R. (2003). Appraisal processes in emotion. In R. J. Davidson, H. H. Goldsmith, and K. R. Scherer (Eds.), *Handbook of Affective Sciences* (pp. 572–595). New York and Oxford: Oxford University Press.

Elster, J. (1999). *Strong feelings : Emotion, addiction, and human behavior*. Cambridge, MA: MIT Press.

Fibiger, H. C., & Phillips, A. G. (1986). Reward, motivation, cognition: Psychobiology of mesotelencephalic systems. *Handbook of Physiology – The Nervous System* (Vol. 4, pp. 647–675).

Fiorino, D. F.; Coury, A.; & Phillips, A. G. (1997). Dynamic changes in nucleus accumbens dopamine efflux during the Coolidge effect in male rats. *Journal of Neuroscience, 17(12)*, 4849–4855.

Frijda, N. H. (1999). Emotions and hedonic experience. In D. Kahneman, E. Diener, and N. Schwarz (Eds.), *Well-being: The foundations of hedonic psychology* (pp. 190–210). New York: Russell Sage Foundation.

Frijda, N. H. (2001). The nature of pleasure. In J. A. Bargh and D. K. Apsley (Eds.), *Unraveling the complexities of social life: A festschrift in honor of Robert B. Zajonc* (pp. 71–94). Washington, DC: American Psychological Association.

Gardner, E. L. (1997). Brain reward mechanisms. In J. H. Lowinson, P. Ruiz, R. B. Millman, and J. G. Langrod (Eds.), *Substance abuse: A comprehensive textbook* (3d ed., pp. 51–85). Baltimore: Williams and Wilkin.

Gilbert, D. G., & Wilson, T. D. (2000). Miswanting: Some problems in forecasting future affective states. In J. P. Forgas (Ed.), *Feeling and thinking: The role of affect in social cognition*. Cambridge: Cambridge University Press.

Hoebel, B. G.; Rada, P. V.; Mark, G. P.; & Pothos, E. N. (1999). Neural systems for reinforcement and inhibition of behavior: Relevance to eating, addiction, and depression. In D. Kahneman, E. Diener, and N. Schwarz (Eds.), *Well-being: The foundations of hedonic psychology* (pp. 558–572). New York: Russell Sage Foundation.

Kahneman, D. (1999). Assessments of individual well-being: A bottom-up approach. In D. Kahneman; E. Diener, and N. Schwartz (Eds.), *Well-being: The foundations of hedonic psychology*. New York: Russell Sage Foundation.

Kihlstrom, J. F.; Mulvaney, S.; Tobias, B. A.; & Tobis, I. P. (2000). The emotional unconscious. In E. Eich (Ed.), *Cognition and Emotion*. New York: Oxford University Press.

Koob, G. F., & Le Moal, M. (2001). Drug addiction, dysregulation of reward, and allostasis. *Neuropsychopharmacology, 24(2)*, 97–129.

LeDoux, J. (2000). Cognitive-emotional interactions: Listen to the brain. In R. D. Lane, L. Nadel, and G. Ahern (Eds.), *Cognitive neuroscience of emotion* (pp. 129–155; Series in affective science). New York: Oxford University Press.

Morris, J. S.; Öhman, A.; & Dolan, R. J. (1999). A subcortical pathway to the right amygdala mediating "unseen" fear. *Proceedings of the National Academy of Sciences of the United States of America, 96(4)*, 1680–1685.

Oehman, A.; Flykt, A.; & Lundqvist, D. (2000). Unconscious emotion: Evolutionary perspectives, psychophysiological data and neuropsychological mechanisms. In R. D. Lane, L. Nadel, and G. Ahern (Eds.), *Cognitive neuroscience of emotion* (pp. 296–327; Series in affective science). New York: Oxford University Press.

Panksepp, J. (1986). The neurochemistry of behavior. *Annual Review of Psychology, 37*, 77–107.

Panksepp, J. (1998). *Affective neuroscience: The foundations of human and animal emotions.* Oxford: Oxford University Press.

Peciña, S., & Berridge, K. C. (2000). Opioid eating site in accumbens shell mediates food intake and hedonic 'liking': map based on microinjection Fos plumes. *Brain Research, 863,* 71–86.

Peciña, S.; Berridge, K. C.; & Parker, L. A. (1997). Pimozide does not shift palatability: Separation of anhedonia from sensorimotor suppression by taste reactivity. *Pharmacology Biochemistry and Behavior, 58(3),* 801–811.

Robinson, T. E., & Berridge, K. C. (1993). The neural basis of drug craving: an incentive-sensitization theory of addiction. *Brain Research Reviews, 18(3),* 247–291.

Robinson, T. E., & Berridge, K. C. (2003). Addiction. *Annual Review of Psychology, 54(1),* 25–53.

Robinson, T. E.; Browman, K. E.; Crombag, H. S.; & Badiani, A. (1998). Modulation of the induction or expression of psychostimulant sensitization by the circumstances surrounding drug administration. *Neuroscience and Biobehavioral Reviews, 22(2),* 347–354.

Schultz, W. (1998). Predictive reward signal of dopamine neurons. *Journal of Neurophysiology, 80(1),* 1–27.

Shizgal, P. (1999). On the neural computation of utility: Implications from studies of brain stimulation reward. In D. Kahneman, E. Diener, and N. Schwarz (Eds.), *Well-being: The foundations of hedonic psychology* (pp. 500–524). New York: Russell Sage Foundation.

Steiner, J. E. (1973). The gustofacial response: Observation on normal and anencephalic newborn infants. *Symposium on Oral Sensation and Perception, 4,* 254–278.

Steiner, J. E.; Glaser, D.; Hawilo, M. E.; & Berridge, K. C. (2001). Comparative expression of hedonic impact: Affective reactions to taste by human infants and other primates. *Neuroscience and Biobehavioral Reviews, 25(1),* 53–74.

Toates, F. (1986). *Motivational systems.* Cambridge: Cambridge University Press.

Valenstein, E. S. (1976). The interpretation of behavior evoked by brain stimulation. In A. Wauquier and E. T. Rolls (Eds.), *Brain-stimulation reward* (pp. 557–575). New York: Elsevier.

Whalen, P. J.; Rauch, S. L.; Etcoff, N. L.; McInerney, S. C.; Lee, M. B.; & Jenike, M. A. (1998). Masked presentations of emotional facial expressions modulate amygdala activity without explicit knowledge. *Journal of Neuroscience, 18(1),* 411–418.

Winkielman, P.; Berridge, K. C.; & Wilbarger, J. (2000). Unconscious affect for doing without feeling: Subliminal facial expressions alter human consumption. Unpublished manuscript.

Winkielman, P.; Zajonc, R. B.; & Schwarz, N. (1997). Subliminal affective priming resists attributional interventions. *Cognition and Emotion, 11,* 433-465.

Wise, R. A. (1998). Drug-activation of brain reward pathways. *Drug and Alcohol Dependence, 51(1–2),* 13–22.

Wise, R. A. (1985). The anhedonia hypothesis: Mark III. *Behavioral and Brain Sciences, 8,* 178–186.

Wyvell, C. L., & Berridge, K. C. (2000). Intra-accumbens amphetamine increases the conditioned incentive salience of sucrose reward: Enhancement of reward "wanting" without enhanced "liking" or response reinforcement. *Journal of Neuroscience, 20(21)*, 8122–8130.

Wyvell, C. L., & Berridge, K. C. (2001). Incentive-sensitization by previous amphetamine exposure: Increased cue-triggered 'wanting' for sucrose reward. *Journal of Neuroscience, 21(19)*, 7831–7840.

Yeomans, M. R., & Gray, R. W. (1997). Effects of naltrexone on food intake and changes in subjective appetite during eating: Evidence for opioid involvement in the appetizer effect. *Physiology and Behavior, 62(1)*, 15–21.

Zahm, D. S. (2000). An integrative neuroanatomical perspective on some subcortical substrates of adaptive responding with emphasis on the nucleus accumbens. *Neuroscience and Biobehavioral Reviews, 24(1)*, 85–105.

Zajonc, R. B. (1980). Feeling and thinking: Preferences need no inferences. *American Psychologist, 35*, 151–175.

Zajonc, R. B. (2000). Feeling and thinking: Closing the debate over the independence of affect. In J. P. Forgas (Ed.), *Feeling and thinking: The role of affect in social cognition* (pp. 31–58). New York: Cambridge University Press.

16

Some Perspectives on Positive Feelings and Emotions

Positive Affect Facilitates Thinking and Problem Solving

Alice M. Isen

ABSTRACT

The work reviewed in this chapter indicates that positive affect facilitates careful, thorough thinking and problem solving, and promotes a flexible, responsive approach to situations that fosters new learning as well as utilization of existing knowledge. Evidence indicates that these processes also facilitate pro-social behavior and flexibility in social perception. In addition, research has shown that positive affect increases some kinds of motivation by influencing some of its components as well. Thus, the chapter argues for a conceptualization that integrates affect, cognition, and behavior/motivation (the traditional trichotomy of mind) and recognizes the fact that they mutually influence one another. The chapter argues against the common assumption that affect and cognition are separate, competing systems or approaches, and shows, instead, that they have mutual influence and are subject to similar processes. Likewise, it is shown that motives arising out of affect need not be more compelling than motives arising from other sources. The data suggest, further, that positive and negative affect, rather than being opposites, have distinct effects. A neuropsychological theory of the influence of positive affect on cognitive functioning is discussed, and the chapter calls attention to the potential benefits to be had from integrating the neuropsychological, behavioral, and cognitive levels of analysis in studying affect.

The focus of this chapter is on positive affect and, in particular, on the growing body of empirical literature investigating positive affect's influence on thought processes and behavior. This literature shows that positive affect generally facilitates thinking and problem solving, and has a number of other beneficial effects as well. Thus, a major goal of the chapter is to dispel the popular misconception that positive affect interferes with systematic cognitive processing and causes superficial, careless thinking.

Secondarily, the chapter also focuses on the need to integrate recent understandings from cognitive neuroscience into our thinking about positive

The author thanks Nico Frijda for helpful comments on an earlier draft of this chapter.

263

affect and its influence on cognition and behavior. To illustrate this possibility, a recent neuropsychological hypothesis, the dopamine hypothesis (Ashby, Isen, & Turken, 1999), which has been proposed as a possible way of integrating some understandings from cognitive neuroscience with this social psychology/affect work, is described.

AFFECT, COGNITION, AND MOTIVATION

"Affect" is used here as the most general term for the emotion domain, and in much of the empirical work and thinking regarding affect these states are defined operationally, in terms of the things that induce them. The inductions represent things that can happen to people as they go about their daily lives, and the feeling states that those events induce. Other terms, such as "emotions" or "mood," are avoided here only because they have connotations that may confuse the issue; "affect" is simply the most general term, encompassing all of the others.

Importantly, the term "affect" (or even "feeling") is used in this work to refer not just to the feeling component of which the person is aware, but to the entire affective cascade, with its cognitive, neurological, physiological, motivational, and behavioral components, as well as the feeling component. Thus, in this work, these various components – feelings, cognitions, motivation, behavior, neurological processes – are not considered separate entities or domains, but are integrated and seen as part of one single whole (see Isen, in press, for discussion).

This is in contrast to the common assumption that affect and cognition are competing processes. That is, one often sees this distinction made in contrasts such as "rational versus emotional" decisions, as if thinking rationally did not allow taking emotional factors or feelings into account, as if responding to the emotional aspects of situations could not be rational, or as if feeling an emotion interfered with thinking. Quite to the contrary, the question of how a given alternative in a choice will make one feel, for example, can be a very reasonable aspect of the choice situation to consider; and one recent approach has even proposed it as a formal component in the decision-making model (Mellers, 2000, this volume).

In fact, it could be argued that *not* paying attention to feeling-related aspects of the decision alternatives (e.g., how one will feel about it later) is the less rational course of action. Although it is possible to think of examples in which feeling an emotion may lead to overweighting of the feeling-related attributes of a decision, it is just as possible to think of examples of insufficient consideration being paid to feeling-related aspects of decision alternatives. Further, many studies have shown that affect (especially positive affect) at the time of making a decision can actually improve the decision-making process, enabling people to take more factors into account and to integrate them in their consideration (e.g., Estrada, Isen, & Young, 1997; Isen, 2000; Isen, Rosenzweig, & Young, 1991).

Motivation, too, has been found to be influenced by mild positive affect, and again the influence appears to be primarily a facilitative one. For example, mild positive affect has been found to promote intrinsic motivation and to lead people to enjoy what they are doing more (Isen & Reeve, 2002), and a recent set of studies has shown that positive affect increases the components of expectancy motivation (e.g., Ilgen, Nebeker, & Pritchard, 1981) that are relevant to the task under consideration (Erez & Isen, in press).

Thus, the dichotomy between affect and cognition breaks down when one tries to understand it more precisely, and similarly, motivation has been shown to be influenced by affect and cognition as well. Thus, it is important to recognize that affect, cognition, and motivation occur together and have mutual influence on one another.

One reason for abandoning the older, dichotomous, way of thinking is that the idea of a dichotomy between thinking and feeling gives rise to several misconceptions about affect itself and what its impact will be on thinking and behavior. These include, that positive affect (or all affect) disrupts thinking; that affect always takes precedence over other motives or thoughts, or is irresistible; that positive affect and negative affect are symmetrical or have parallel influences; and that separate areas of the brain are involved in affective versus cognitive functioning so that affect and cognition compete for brain resources. However, much evidence contrasts with such a view.

For example, as we shall see in this chapter, positive affect influences the content and process of cognition and appears to involve activation of the same brain regions (frontal areas) as underlie thinking and planning (Ashby et al., 1999). Research has shown that positive affect can serve as a retrieval cue for positive material in memory (e.g., Isen, Shalker, Clark, & Karp, 1978; Teasdale & Fogarty, 1979; Teasdale & Russell, 1980), cues social material in memory (see Isen, 1990), cues cognitions related to fairness (Labroo & Isen, 2002), and facilitates memory, in part by enabling effective organization (e.g., Isen, Daubman, & Gorgoglione, 1987; Lee & Sternthal, 1999). In addition, positive affect has been found to facilitate problem solving, including creative problem solving (e.g., see Isen, 1999, 2000).

The conclusion that is supported by much of the empirical work is that positive affect generally facilitates flexibility, the ability to respond appropriately to the situation or task at hand, in thinking and problem solving. Sometimes people assume that if thinking is flexible or creative, it must not be systematic or careful (e.g., Forgas, 2002; Schwarz & Bless, 1991). But much of the empirical work actually shows that the thinking fostered by positive affect is not only flexible and creative, but *also* careful and thorough, and involves purposive deployment of attention (Derryberry,

1993; Isen et al., 1991). Later we will look at some of this evidence in more detail.

VARIETIES OF AFFECT

Before examining the evidence, it should be noted that the research described here involved mild positive affect, induced in randomly assigned groups, by everyday means. The interventions used included events such as finding a coin in the return-slot of a public telephone, receiving an inexpensive free sample, receiving a cookie, winning a computer game, hearing positive feedback regarding one's performance on an unimportant task, seeing five minutes of a nonsexual, nonaggressive comedy film, or receiving (not consuming) a small bag of wrapped hard candies. Thus, people experienced some small success, happiness, gain, or pleasure, and then their performance or reactions were compared with those of a neutral control group in which no affect was induced. Because of the random assignment to conditions, it is possible to draw conclusions about cause; and because of the mildness and naturalness of the affect inductions, it seems likely that such affective states occur frequently in life.

However, this work may not speak to the effects of very intense affect, which may or may not produce the same kinds of effects as does more common affect. It is usually assumed that intense, and especially negative, affect serves an alerting function and dominates behavior. But actually we do not have a lot of empirical evidence about what the effects of intense or disruptive affect would be in humans, other than introspective self-reports (possibly on account of ethical concerns about strong, negative affect inductions). There is work on drug-induced euphoria and sexual arousal, but these more complex, focal feeling states, as well as other intense affects, are beyond the scope of the present chapter.

An interesting finding that is emerging is that the mild affect inductions discussed in this chapter have often been found to have similar effects to those of affective traits or dispositions. For example, work by Staw and Barsade (1993) reports improved problem-solving performance for people high in "positive affectivity" (e.g., Watson & Tellegen, 1985), the measured quality or disposition to be happy and cheerful, just as has been found for induced positive affect. Likewise, Aspinwall and her colleagues have found similar results for the measured quality of optimism (e.g., Aspinwall, 1998), and have even found similar effects for induced positive affect and optimism on processes related to coping. Thus, there is growing evidence that induced mild positive affect and a positive disposition may have similar effects, and there has been speculation that repeated instances of positive affect during development may contribute to the development of a positive or optimistic disposition (e.g., Isen, 1990).

THE RELATIONSHIP BETWEEN POSITIVE AND NEGATIVE AFFECT

A word is in order about the relationship between positive and negative affect. As noted, the focus of this chapter is on *positive* affect. On the basis of the empirical literature, it is reasonable to treat positive and negative affect separately – not as opposites, but as different kinds of phenomena. There is renewed debate in the literature about the nature of positive and negative affect (e.g., Russell, 1999; Tellegen & Watson, 1999), but in terms of their impact, the evidence indicates that they are different, not mirror images of one another. Thus, it is not appropriate to assume that what has been found regarding positive affect will apply somehow to negative affect as well, possibly in the inverse. For example, although the literature shows that positive affect generally promotes helping behavior, studies investigating the influence of negative affect have not usually found reduced helping (see Isen, 1987, for discussion). Similarly, in the literature on affect and cognition, positive affect has been shown to serve as an effective retrieval cue for positive material, and one that is spontaneously used by people to organize their thoughts. However, negative affect, especially sadness, typically has not been as effective at cueing negative material (e.g., see Isen, 1987, 1990, for discussions).

SOME EFFECTS OF POSITIVE AFFECT

Social Behavior

Empirical research over the past thirty years indicates that positive affect increases pro-social behavior, such as helpfulness and sociability (see Isen, 1987, e.g., for review). All else being equal, people in whom mild positive affect has been induced are more helpful and generous to others (e.g., Cunningham, Steinberg, & Grev, 1980) and more socially responsible (e.g., Berkowitz, 1972). For example, in one series of studies, people who were offered a cookie, or who found change in the coin-return of a public telephone, or who had been told they had succeeded on a task, donated more to a charity collection can and were more helpful to a stranger passing by who needed help (Isen, 1970; Isen & Levin, 1972). Research has also shown that positive affect can reduce interpersonal conflict (e.g., Baron, 1984) and can facilitate face-to-face negotiations (Carnvale & Isen, 1986).

In the negotiation study by Carnevale and Isen (1986), when people bargained face-to-face, those in whom positive affect had been induced achieved better negotiation outcomes (in fact, the best outcome possible for both parties in the situation), and enjoyed the process significantly more, compared to those in a control condition. In contrast, negotiators in the control condition most often broke off negotiation without reaching any agreement.

There is reason to believe that the improved outcomes for those in the positive-affect condition were attributable not just to social factors but to cognitive changes, as well, that facilitated the process and outcome. This is because success on the bargaining task required reasoning integratively about possibilities and making trade-offs among alternatives. People in the positive-affect condition also showed more understanding of the other party's payoff matrix when asked about it after the session. This suggests that they had been better able than controls to take the other party's perspective during the session. Thus, there is evidence that the difference in the positive-affect group's outcome was due to improved cognitive processes, not just greater sociability.

Another series of studies has investigated what positive affect does to negotiation in a situation in which there is less chance of using a "problem-solving" approach and people are faced with a zero-sum, win-lose, situation (Labroo, Isen, & Shanteau, 2000). These studies found that, after three rounds, when told that a co-player (in actuality there was no co-player) had chosen the "cooperate" response (which represented a switch from "compete" to "cooperate"), people in positive affect cooperated (which also represented a switch) immediately, to a greater extent than did controls. On average, they responded to their co-player's cooperativeness with a cooperative response of their own on the very next round. (The controls eventually cooperated as well, but one round later.) These results, thus, also show that positive affect fosters flexibility in thinking and responding, even in a competitive situation.

Cognitive Processes

Flexible Thinking. A large and diverse body of research indicates that positive affect enables flexible thinking. This includes, for instance, flexible categorization of neutral material, involving semantic categories, product categories, brand extensions, person types, and social groups; more diverse and less typical word associations to neutral stimuli; and openness to ideas (e.g., Barone, Miniard, & Romeo, 2000; Estrada et al., 1997; Isen & Daubman, 1984; Isen, Johnson, Mertz, & Robinson, 1985; Isen, Niedenthal, & Cantor, 1992; Kahn & Isen, 1993; Urada & Miller, 2000). In addition, many studies, conducted in diverse settings, among participants ranging from young adolescents to practicing physicians and managers in organizations, show that positive affect increases creativity and results in more successful problem solving (see Isen, 1999, for review and discussion).

Problem Solving. Other studies indicate that positive affect influences decision-making and problem-solving processes, leading them to be both more efficient and more thorough (e.g., Isen et al., 1991). For example, in one study that examined the search patterns and choices of advanced medical-student subjects performing a disease-identification task, results showed that people in the positive-affect condition solved the assigned problem (identifying the patient who had the target disease) earlier than controls, and then went beyond the assigned task to do more with the materials, such as diagnosing the other patients or suggesting treatments. Their decision protocols also showed that they integrated the material more, and were less confused (Isen et al., 1991). Flexibility is also likely to have been playing a role in these findings, but the results emphasize that the thinking that was fostered by positive affect was thorough and careful (as well as efficient).

Another recent study looking at the influence of positive affect on physicians' diagnostic processes showed more details of these effects. Doctors in the positive-affect condition correctly identified the domain of the illness they were attempting to diagnose, significantly earlier than controls, showed significantly less tendency than controls to distort or ignore new information that did not fit with their initial diagnostic hypothesis, and gave no sign of any tendency to engage in superficial or faulty processing or to jump to a conclusion without sufficient evidence (Estrada et al., 1997). This demonstration of increased flexibility in considering the evidence is particularly important because it shows that the physicians in the positive-affect group were more open to information – even information that disconfirmed what they were thinking. Thus, the "openness" fostered by positive affect is not limited to increased access to people's own preexisting cognitive structures or preconceptions, an idea currently promoted by some authors (e.g., Bless et al., 1996; Forgas, 2002).

Positive Affect and Improved Coping. A growing body of work in the coping literature indicates that positive affect may help people when they are dealing with problems (see Aspinwall, 1998; Aspinwall & Taylor, 1997, for review). For example, people in positive affect have been found to be less defensive (Reed & Aspinwall, 1998; Trope & Pomerantz, 1998) and to show superior coping skills and styles, including task persistence (Aspinwall & Taylor, 1997). Interestingly, however, a recent study found that people in positive affect disengaged more rapidly from unsolvable tasks if there were solvable tasks to be done, and performed better on the solvable tasks (e.g., Aspinwall & Richter, 1999). This, too, may reflect cognitive flexibility.

Cognitive Flexibility and Social Interaction

As we have seen, and compatibly with the call for integration of affect, cognition, and behavior raised in the first section, the cognitive and social effects of positive affect seem to be related. In fact, it seems that we have had difficulty talking about affect's influence on social behavior without also referring to its impact on flexible thinking and problem-solving ability more generally. That is, an important reason that positive affect contributes to improved social interaction and negotiation outcomes may be that the positive affect leads to integrative thinking about both parties' needs, in the context of the interaction or task and the opportunities provided by the situation.

For another clear example, flexibility in perspective taking may contribute to the increased helpfulness that results from positive affect. There is evidence that broadening of focus occurs as a result of positive affect. In one study that reported that positive affect increased helping, Isen (1970) also found evidence for a broader range of attention among participants who had succeeded, relative to those who had failed. Such broadened focus may play a role in deciding to help another person, because one is more likely to be aware of the other's need. Current work is increasing our understanding of this broadening effect in several contexts (e.g., Dovidio, Gaertner, Isen, Rust, & Guerrera, 1998; Fredrickson, 1998; Isen, 1990; Isen, Daubman, & Gorgoglione, 1987; Kahn & Isen, 1993; Urada & Miller, 2000).

Increased flexibility in thinking also helps to explain another aspect of the helping literature, namely, that people who are experiencing positive affect do not stop attending to their own welfare when they help others (e.g., Isen & Simmonds, 1978), but rather seem to attend to the needs of both. Compatibly, very recent evidence indicates that people in positive affect are sensitive to mistreatment or unfairness toward either themselves or others, and think more of fairness and unfairness than people in neutral affect (Labroo & Isen, 2002).

Findings in the groups literature may also reflect the influence of positive affect on flexibility in thinking. For example, in a study by Dovidio, Gaertner, Isen, and Lowrance (1995), people in a positive-affect condition were more likely than controls to form an inclusive group representation of their own group and a different group. The positive affect and the change in group representation that resulted from the affect gave rise to better evaluations of the out-group members and lower levels of intergroup bias.

Further, in four studies investigating the influence of positive affect on crossed categorization, Urada and Miller (2000) found that positive affect changed the representation and improved the evaluation of out-group members when they shared an important quality with the in-group, but not when they shared only an unimportant quality. This finding illustrates, as do several others in the literature, that positive affect does not act as a simple biasing factor, but rather promotes consideration of the important aspects of the situation.

Flexible Consideration of Situations and Possible Outcomes, or Response Bias?

The research literature indicates that positive affect does not lead to simple biasing or distortion of perception or decision making, but rather to detailed and responsive consideration of materials and situations. Many studies show significant interactions with aspects of the materials, such as valence, importance, interestingness, other tasks that need to be done in the situation, and various other aspects of the context.

For example, studies have shown that positive affect leads to improved evaluation of neutral or ambiguous material but not of clearly positive or negative material (e.g., Schiffenbauer, 1974). Similarly, positive affect has been found to influence people's first associates to neutral words, resulting in those associates' being more unusual, but not people's associates to negative or positive words (Isen et al., 1985). A study looking at categorization of people into person types found that positive affect influenced classification of marginal category representatives into positive person categories but not of marginal category representatives into negative person categories (Isen et al., 1992). As mentioned above, Urada and Miller (2000) found that positive affect changed the group representation, and increased the acceptance, of out-group members if they shared an important characteristic with the in-group, but not if they shared only an unimportant characteristic. For another example, a study in organizational psychology showed that positive affect influenced task perceptions and satisfaction for an "enriched task," one that allows autonomy and sense of control, but not for an unenriched, routine task (Kraiger, Billings, & Isen, 1989). All of these results indicate that positive affect does not just bias thinking and response globally or simplistically, like a filter, but rather, promotes careful thought about the relevant materials in the situation, and flexible responding based on that consideration.

Positive Affect Reduces Dangerous Risk Taking. Another area in which interactions between affect and aspects of the situation have been found is risk taking. Positive affect appears to increase risk taking in low-risk or hypothetical situations, but it actually leads to risk avoidance in situations of high, real risk, or possible meaningful loss (e.g., Isen & Geva, 1987; Isen & Patrick, 1983).

Additional work on this topic suggests, further, that these effects result from separate influences of positive affect on the subjective probability of losing and the perceived negative utility of the loss (e.g., Isen, Nygren, & Ashby, 1988; Nygren, Isen, Taylor, & Dulin, 1996). That is, positive affect influences both of these components of the decision process, but in opposite directions, reducing the subjective probability of losing but at the same time increasing the expected negative utility of the potential loss. These significant interactions and complex results illustrate again that positive affect does not simply bias thinking in a positive direction or cause people to distort situations by ignoring potential negative elements. In fact, results of one study that included a thought-listing task, following the risk measure, showed that people in the positive-affect condition had significantly more thoughts about the potential loss than did controls

(Isen & Geva, 1987). It should also be noted that these results are incompatible with the idea that positive affect has simplifying effects or only leads to affect-congruent judgment whenever it "infuses" thought (Forgas, 2002), because they show that positive affect has different effects simultaneously on different components of the same task. Thus they indicate that positive affect leads to consideration of the details and possible outcomes of situations.

Variety Seeking. Another area in which significant interactions were found between affect and the details of the situation is variety seeking. A series of studies has shown that people in positive-affect conditions, more than controls, want variety, for example, in snack-food choices – but only if the options involved are safe and enjoyable (Kahn & Isen, 1993). When the description of the items (e.g., low-salt) suggested that they might taste bad, people in positive affect no longer showed this greater preference for variety. These significant interactions, again, indicate that positive affect influences thinking in a manner that involves elaboration and evaluation of outcomes, rather than just by biasing responding in a positive direction or rendering it simple or impulsive.

Are Affective Motives Special?

These findings of interaction between induced affect and aspects of the context also illustrate that behavior is multidetermined and that motives induced by affect do not necessarily take precedence over other motives. They can *sometimes* take precedence because they may involve some urgent need – and these are the ones we typically think of when we think of affect – but the motives prompted by positive affect, or even mild negative affect, are not always of that nature and do not necessarily take precedence over other motives in the situation. For example, a motive of affect maintenance, which is thought to arise out of mild positive affect (e.g., Isen et al., 1988; Isen & Simmonds, 1978), does not always govern the resultant behavior (e.g., Aspinwall, 1998; Isen & Geva, 1979). Neither does desire to help another person, another goal that in general is promoted by positive affect (e.g., Isen & Simmonds, 1978).

This is a point worth considering in more detail, for two reasons. First, sometimes it is assumed that a motive such as affect maintenance, because it has been identified, is the *only* motive that arises when a person feels happy, or that it takes precedence over all other considerations (e.g., Erber & Erber, 2000). But, as we have seen, positive affect leads to flexible responsiveness to the requirements and opportunities afforded by situations, and this involves consideration of multiple motives in most circumstances.

Second, the significant interactions that have been observed also indicate that affect, at least mild, positive affect and the motives it induces, are not irresistible, automatic, or possessing of special, privileged status in determining behavior. The interactions depend on the meaning of the situations or the stimuli to the people. Thus, they indicate that people in the affect condition are considering options, priorities, and possible outcomes before deciding what to do.

To summarize, then, a large body of research examining the kind of positive affect that can occur frequently in everyday life indicates that mild positive affect, besides increasing helpfulness and social responsibility, also increases cognitive flexibility, creativity, and innovation. For example, people in whom positive affect has been induced show more unusual (but still reasonable) word associations to neutral words, more liking for nontypical products, and more flexible categorization of neutral words into topic categories, of products into product classes, of people into positive categories (but not negative), and of other-group members into in-groups. They show greater preference for variety among safe, enjoyable alternatives, but not among dubious alternatives.

This increased flexibility is reflected in task performance, with the result that people in positive affect usually show improved problem solving of many kinds, improved social interaction, more openness to information, and careful attention to the details and implications of situations. In an integrative-bargaining task, people in positive affect have better negotiation outcomes than controls, enjoy the task more, and are better at taking the other person's perspective. They also perform more flexibly in zero-sum negotiations and have the opportunity for better outcomes there as well.

People in positive affect distinguish between safe and dangerous situations, avoid taking dangerous risks, but consider the potential loss in the situation carefully en route to that decision. Thus, there is no evidence that they distort or ignore negative information or information that does not fit with their current hypotheses. Neither is there evidence that they do not take in new data or learn new things. Quite to the contrary, the evidence suggests that they are more open to new information and more flexible in considering it. The evidence also supports the idea that people in positive affect do not become superficial or mindless in their thinking, but that they remain purposive and deliberate.

INTEGRATING THE NEUROPSYCHOLOGICAL LEVEL OF ANALYSIS

As noted at the beginning of this chapter, it is useful to integrate the neuropsychological level of analysis with the cognitive and behavioral in studying psychological processes. In order to begin that task, one can start by observing effects of, in this case positive affect, and asking whether there are any neurological processes known to produce similar effects. Recently, it has been suggested that the neurotransmitter dopamine may play an important role in the influence of positive affect on cognition and be-havior, because the dopamine system has been found to underlie several processes that also characterize positive affect (e.g., Ashby et al., 1999).

First, a large literature suggests that dopamine plays an important role in processes related to reward and learning from reward (see Ashby et al., 1999, for review). At the same time, reward may well involve a state similar to the kinds of positive affect conditions studied in the affect literature described here.

Second, dopamine in the anterior cingulate region of the brain has been shown to be important in cognitive perspective taking or set switching (e.g., Owen et al., 1993; see Ashby et al., 1999), and conditions that are known to involve reduced dopamine, such as Parkinson's Disease, are characterized by impaired performance on such tasks. As we have seen, the evidence seems very clear that positive affect promotes cognitive flexibility and the ability to switch perspectives. Therefore, it is plausible that positive affect involves a release of dopamine to frontal brain regions involved in set switching.

Further, as described earlier in the chapter, this flexibility or set-switching ability may be a crucial component in many of the behavioral, as well as cognitive, effects of positive affect that have been observed. For ex-ample, flexibility may play a role in the relationship between positive affect and helpfulness that was discussed earlier. As people can shift attention and perspective, they are better able to see things from other people's per-spectives, and may therefore be more generous and "understanding," in both senses (the emotional and the cognitive) of that word. Thus, enhanced social functioning is also compatible with the dopamine hypothesis of the mediation of positive affect.

Because frontal brain regions, responsible for processes such as thinking, working memory, and so forth, contain dopamine receptors, this hypothe-sis also predicts that positive affect should activate those frontal brain areas and thus facilitate processes related to thinking. This would be compatible with the data presented earlier showing that positive affect usually facili-tates cognitive performance, and it would predict additional effects of this type for positive affect.

Interestingly, Depue and colleagues, adopting an individual-differences approach, have also suggested that the dopamine system is implicated in something possibly related to positive affect, extraversion (e.g., Depue & Collins, 1999). Their work has reported increased levels of brain dopamine activity among people who score relatively high in that characteristic. Other work has also found that people scoring relatively high in disposi-tional "positivity" or "optimism" show increases in problem-solving per-formance (e.g., Staw & Barsade, 1993).

Relating "extraversion" to positive incentive motivation, Depue and colleagues suggest that "extraverts" have a ventral tegmental area (VTA) dopamine system that increases their positive incentive motivation or approach behavior. They indicate that the characteristic VTA dopamine system of extraverts may develop through either genetic or experiential processes, but that by adulthood it is a stable characteristic.

Given Depue's view, it might seem difficult to argue that mild positive affect inductions, randomly assigned, could be having their effects through activation of the dopamine system. However, it is likely that whatever dopamine system exists in a person, that system is activated by events that cause release of dopamine. Further, it is especially interesting that recent findings suggest that cognitive and behavioral events can influence neurobiological structures themselves, including the VTA dopamine system (e.g., Cabib & Puglisi-Allegra, 1999; Isom & Heller, 1999; Miller, 1996). This means that the dopamine system might be changed by affective experiences, after all.

In sum, then, the evidence suggests that induced positive affect may have its effects through the brain dopamine system, even if there are individual differences in this system. Most likely, the full picture will be more complex and will involve more than one neurotransmitter. But the work linking positive affect and brain function seems to point in an exciting new direction, worthy of further development.

CONCLUSION

The work reviewed in this chapter indicates that positive affect promotes social interaction, helpfulness, generosity, and social responsibility, while not undermining attention to a person's own long-term welfare. Furthermore, positive affect facilitates flexible thinking and problem solving, and at the same time gives rise to careful, thorough thinking. The research indicates that, contrary to some earlier misconceptions, under most circumstances positive affect does not impair the ability or motivation to think carefully, thoroughly, and systematically. In fact, it enhances these. And a neuropsychological mechanism that would enable such enhancement has been proposed.

These points contradict some of people's stereotypes about affect – notably, that it leads to superficial, flawed thought processes. Possibly because of this stereotype, too, some preliminary early research had more influence than it otherwise might have had. Nonetheless, many authors did not find results compatible with the suggestion that positive affect impairs systematic processing, and recent studies have undermined it further (e.g., Bless et al., 1996; Estrada et al., 1997; Isen, 2000, for discussion; Isen et al., 2002; Isen et al., 1991; Smith & Shaffer, 1991; Staw & Barsade, 1993).

Furthermore, the recent suggestion by Bless, Schwarz, and their colleagues (e.g., Bless et al., 1996) that positive affect leads to reliance on existing cognitive structures, or so-called top-down processing, seems incomplete. Rather, the evidence suggests that positive affect fosters *both* the ability to take in new data and knowledge *and* the ability to activate and use existing knowledge structures (e.g., Estrada et al., 1997).

Beyond dispelling the myth that positive affect interferes with systematic processing and learning, two other goals of this chapter were to encourage integration in thinking about affect, cognition, and motivation, and to encourage integration of information from multiple levels of analysis (cognitive, behavioral, and neuroscience) in our understanding of affect. The data indicate that affect, cognition, and motivation influence one another. Second, the processes underlying each may be similar, if not identical. This means, for example, that motives that stem from affect are not necessarily more urgent, pressing, or determining of behavior than other motives. They can be, depending on the circumstances, but that is because of the circumstance, not because of the affective nature or origin of the goal. For example, there is evidence that positive affect leads to a motive to maintain that positive state. Yet this does not mean that such a motive will be the only one, or even the most influential one at any given time. The evidence suggests, to the contrary, that people in positive affect, *more* than controls, pay attention to negative information, if it is useful.

As regards the integration of levels of analysis (cognitive, behavioral, and neuroscience), it has been proposed that many of the cognitive effects of positive affect may be mediated by the brain dopamine system (e.g., Ashby et al., 1999; Depue & Collins, 1999). This implies that positive affect may especially facilitate tasks that are controlled by brain regions containing dopamine receptors, which include frontal regions associated with thinking, problem solving, and cognitive and behavioral flexibility. This way of thinking about the situation may provide a more specific basis for defining the kinds of tasks that may, or may not, be facilitated by positive affect, and thus may offer an alternative to the use of vaguely defined concepts such as "heuristic" versus "systematic" processing (see Isen, 1993, 2000, for discussion).

This is not an argument in favor of simple reductionism, however. Rather, it is a call for integration of the cognitive, behavioral, and neuropsychological levels of analysis. As is clear from the data reviewed in this chapter, people's thinking and behavior is purposive – they have plans, goals, and strategies, and these influence their interpretations of situations, their feelings, and their behavior. The neuropsychological level of analysis is a tool that can aid in our understanding of the nature and effects of affect, but it cannot substitute for understandings based on the cognitive and behavioral levels of analysis. These levels of analysis can inform one another, a fact illustrated in part by the realization that the dopamine hypothesis of the mediation of the effects of positive affect on cognition arose from observations at the behavioral and cognitive levels that positive affect improves performance and increases cognitive flexibility.

It is important to note that discussion of the neurological processes in the relationship between affect and cognition and behavior does not in any way imply that the relationships are genetically determined, unchangeable, occur automatically, or are irresistible. Neurological processes are initiated in response to environmental events, and it even seems that neurological structures themselves may be affected by experiences. Further, and most important, the data reviewed in this chapter show that very small positive interventions can produce marked effects on processes that are now understood to be mediated by neurological events.

Likewise, just because neurological processes mediating the effects have been identified, one should not assume that these effects and processes are automatic. In fact, the evidence underscores the role played by people's plans, goals, understandings, and expectations in determining their reactions to the situations in which they find themselves. Evidence from many laboratories indicates that events may not generate positive affect unless they are interpreted and integrated by the person. Moreover, even once dopamine is released, the specific reactions may still depend on aspects of context and people's plans and goals (possibly governing uptake and release of more than one neurotransmitter). The many studies showing significant statistical interactions between affect and situational aspects of the task indicate that the implementation of any added potential for flexibility depends on people's resolution of the possibilities, constraints, contingencies, and so forth that they understand.

In closing, the work reviewed in this chapter illustrates the importance and power of positive affect. In contrast, it seems that psychology, and perhaps other fields as well, have been overly focused on negative phenomena, and that includes negative affect. The accumulating data indicate that it is well worth studying positive phenomena, such as helping, fairness, and positive affect, in their own right, not just as counterpoints to negative phenomena. In the affect domain, it is becoming more and more clear that the different emotions may not be just opposite ends of a continuum, but rather may have quite different determinants, effects, and processes associated with them. If that is the case, then it may be very misleading to take negative affect – especially intense negative affect or emotion that prompts immediate and narrow response and dominates the motivational possibilities in a situation – as the model for all affect.

References

Ashby, F. G.; Isen, A. M.; & Turken, A. (1999). A neuropsychological theory of positive affect and its influence on cognition. *Psychological Review, 106,* 529–550.

Aspinwall, L. G. (1998). Rethinking the role of positive affect and self-regulation. *Motivation and Emotion, 22,* 1–32.

Aspinwall, L. G., & Richter, L. (1999). Optimism and self-mastery predict more rapid disengagement from unsolvable tasks in the presence of alternatives. *Motivation and Emotion, 23 (3)*, 221–245.

Aspinwall, L. G., & Taylor, S. E. (1997). A stitch in time: Self-regulation and proactive coping. *Psychological Bulletin, 121*, 417–436.

Baron, R. A. (1984). Reducing organizational conflict: An incompatible response approach. *Journal of Applied Psychology, 69*, 272–279.

Barone, M. J.; Miniard, P. W.; & Romeo, J. B. (2000). The influence of positive mood on brand extension evaluations. *Journal of Consumer Research, 26*, 386–400.

Berkowitz, L. (1972). Social norms, feelings, and other factors affecting helping and altruism. In L. Berkowitz (Ed.), *Advances in experimental social psychology* (Vol. 6, pp. 63–108). New York: Academic Press.

Bless, H.; Clore, G. L.; Schwarz, N.; Golisano, V.; Rabe, C.; & Wolk, M. (1996). Mood and the use of scripts: Does a happy mood really lead to mindlessness? *Journal of Personality and Social Psychology, 71*, 665–679.

Cabib, S., & Puglisi-Allegra, S. (1999). Of genes, environment, and destiny. *Behavioral and Brain Sciences, 22*, 519.

Carnevale, P. J. D., & Isen, A. M. (1986). The influence of positive-affect and visual access on the discovery of integrative solutions in bilateral negotiation. *Organizational Behavior and Human Decision Processes, 37*, 1–13.

Cunningham, M. R.; Steinberg, J.; & Grev, R. (1980). Wanting to and having to help: Separate motivations for positive mood and guilt induced helping. *Journal of Personality and Social Psychology, 38*, 181–192.

Depue, R. A., & Collins, P. F. (1999). Neurobiology of the structure of personality: Dopamine, facilitation of incentive motivation, and extraversion. *Behavioral and Brain Sciences, 22*, 491–569.

Derryberry, D. (1993). Attentional consequences of outcome-related motivational states: Congruent, incongruent, and focusing effects. *Motivation and Emotion, 17*, 65–90.

Dovidio, J. F.; Gaertner, S. L.; Isen, A. M.; & Lowrance, R. (1995). Group representations and intergroup bias: Positive affect, similarity, and group size. *Personality and Social Psychology Bulletin, 21*, 856–865.

Dovidio, J. F.; Gaertner, S. L.; Isen, A. M.; Rust, M.; & Guerra, P. (1998). Positive affect, cognition, and the reduction of intergroup bias. In C. Sedikides, J. Schopler, and C. A. Insko (Eds.), *Intergroup cognition and intergroup behavior* (pp. 337–366). Mahway, NJ: Erlbaum.

Erez, A., & Isen, A. M. (In press). The influence of positive affect on the components of expectancy motivation. *Journal of Applied Psychology*.

Estrada, C. A.; Isen, A. M.; & Young, M. J. (1997). Positive affect facilitates integration of information and decreases anchoring in reasoning among physicians. *Organizational Behavior and Human Decision Processes, 72*, 117–135.

Forgas, J. P. (2002). Feeling and doing: Affective influences on interpersonal behavior. *Psychological Inquiry, 13*, 1–28.

Fredrickson, B. L. (1998). What good are positive emotions? *Review of General Psychology, 2*, 300–319.

Heller, W. (1997). Emotion. In M. Banich (Ed.), *Neuropsychology: The neural bases of mental function*. New York: Houghton Mifflin.

Ilgen, D. R.; Nebeker, D. M.; & Pritchard, R. D. (1981). Expectancy theory measures: An empirical comparison in an experimental situation. *Organizational Behavior and Human Performance, 28,* 189–223.

Isen, A. M. (1970). Success, failure attention and reactions to others: The warm glow of success. *Journal of Personality and Social Psychology, 17,* 107–112.

Isen, A. M. (1987). Positive affect, cognitive processes and social behavior. In L. Berkowitz (Ed.), *Advances in experimental social psychology* (pp. 203–253). New York: Academic Press.

Isen, A. M. (1990). The influence of positive and negative affect on cognitive organization: Implications for development. In N. Stein, B. Leventhal, and T. Trabasso (Eds.), *Psychological and biological processes in the development of emotion* (pp. 75–94). Hillsdale, NJ: Erlbaum.

Isen, A. M. (1993). Positive affect and decision making. In M. Lewis and J. Haviland (Eds.), *Handbook of emotions* (pp. 261–277). New York: Guilford.

Isen, A. M. (1999). On the relationship between affect and creative problem solving. In S. Russ (Ed.), *Affect, creative experience, and psychological adjustment* (pp. 3–17). Philadelphia: Taylor & Francis.

Isen, A. M. (2000). Positive affect and decision making. In M. Lewis and J. Haviland-Jones (Eds.), *Handbook of emotions,* (2d ed. pp. 417–435). New York: Guilford.

Isen, A. M. (2002a). A role for neuropsychology in understanding the facilitating influence of positive affect on social behavior and cognitive processes. In C. R. Snyder and S. J. Lopez, (Eds.), *Handbook of positive psychology.* Oxford: Oxford University Press.

Isen, A. M. (2002b). Missing in action in the AIM: Positive affect's facilitation of cognitive flexibility, innovation, and problem solving. *Psychological Inquiry, 13,* 57–65.

Isen, A. M. (In press). Positive affect as a source of human strength. In L. Aspinwall and U. Staudinger (Eds.), *The psychology of human strengths.*

Isen, A. M.; Christianson, M.; & Labroo, A. A. (2002). The nature of the task influences whether positive affect facilitates task performance. Manuscript. Cornell University.

Isen, A. M., & Daubman, K. A. (1984). The influence of affect on categorization. *Journal of Personality and Social Psychology, 47,* 1206–1217.

Isen, A. M.; Daubman, K. A.; & Gorgoglione, J. M. (1987). The influence of positive affect on cognitive organization: Implications for education. In R. E. Snow and M. J. Farr (Eds.), *Aptitude, learning, and instruction* (pp. 143–164). Hillsdale, NJ: Erlbaum.

Isen, A. M.; Daubman, K. A.; & Nowicki, G. P. (1987). Positive affect facilitates creative problem solving. *Journal of Personality and Social Psychology, 52,* 1122–1131.

Isen, A. M., & Geva, N. (1987). The influence of positive affect on acceptable level of risk: The person with a large canoe has a large worry. *Organizational Behavior and Human Decision Processes, 39,* 145–154.

Isen, A. M.; Johnson, M. M. S.; Mertz, E.; & Robinson, F. G. (1985). The influence of positive affect on the unusualness of word association. *Journal of Personality and Social Psychology, 48,* 1413–1426.

Isen, A. M., & Levin, P. F. (1972). The effect of feeling good on helping: Cookies and kindness. *Journal of Personality and Social Psychology, 21,* 384–388.

Isen, A. M.; Niedenthal, P.; & Cantor, N. (1992). The influence of positive affect on social categorization. *Motivation and Emotion, 16*, 65–78.

Isen, A. M.; Nygren, T. E.; & Ashby, F. G. (1988). The influence of positive affect on the perceived utility of gains and losses. *Journal of Personality and Social Psychology, 55*, 710–717.

Isen, A. M., & Patrick, R. (1983). The influence of positive feelings on risk taking: When the chips are down. *Organizational Behavior and Human Performance, 31*, 194–202.

Isen, A. M., & Reeve, J. M. (2002). Positive affect promotes intrinsic motivation. Manuscript. Cornell University.

Isen, A. M; Rosenzweig, A. S.; & Young, M. J. (1991). The influence of positive affect on clinical problem solving. *Medical Decision Making, 11*, 221–227.

Isen, A. M.; Shalker, T. E.; Clark, M.; & Karp, L. (1978). Affect, accessibility of material in memory and behavior: A cognitive loop? *Journal of Personality and Social Psychology, 36*, 1–12.

Isen, A. M.; & Simmonds, S. F. (1978). The effect of feeling good on a helping task that is incompatible with good mood. *Social Psychology, 41*, 346–349.

Isom, J., & Heller, W. (1999). Neurobiology of extraversion: Pieces of the puzzle still missing. *Behavioral and Brain Sciences, 22*, 524.

Kahn, B., & Isen, A. M. (1993). The influence of positive affect on variety-seeking among safe, enjoyable products. *Journal of Consumer Research, 20*, 257–270.

Kraiger, K.; Billings, R. S.; & Isen, A. M. (1989). The influence of positive-affective states on task perceptions and satisfaction. *Organizational Behavior and Human Decision Processes, 44*, 12–25.

Labroo, A. A., & Isen, A. M. (2002). Positive affect cues fairness in consumer judgment. Manuscript, Cornell University.

Labroo, A. A.; Isen, A. M.; & Shanteau, J. (2000). The influence of positive affect on strategic decision making in "Prisoner's dilemma" situations. Paper presented at the annual meeting of the Society for Judgment/Decision Making, New Orleans.

Lee, A., & Sternthal, B. (1999). The effects of positive mood on memory. *Journal of Consumer Research, 26*, 115.

Mellers, B. A. (2000). Choice and the relative pleasure of consequences. *Psychological Bulletin, 126 (6)*, 910–924.

Miller, G. A. (1996). How we think about cognition, emotion, and biology in psychopathology. *Psychophysiology, 33*, 615–628.

Nygren, T. E.; Isen, A. M.; Taylor, P. J.; & Dulin, J. (1996). The influence of positive affect on the decision rule in risk situations: Focus on outcome (avoidance of loss) rather than probability. *Organizational Behavior and Human Decision Processes, 66*, 59–72.

Owen, A. M.; Roberts, A. C.; Hodges, J. R.; Summers, B. A.; Polkey, C. E.; & Robbins, T. W. (1993). Contrasting mechanisms of impaired attentional set-shifting in patients with frontal lobe damage or Parkinson's disease. *Brain, 116*, 1159–1175.

Reed, M. B., & Aspinwall, L. G. (1998). Self-affirmation reduces biased processing of health-risk information. *Motivation and Emotion, 22*, 99–132.

Schiffenbauer, A. (1974). Effects of observer's emotional state on judgments of the emotional state of others. *Journal of Personality and Social Psychology, 30*, 31–36.

Schwarz, N., & Bless, H. (1991). Happy and mindless, but sad and smart? The impact of affective states on analytic reasoning. In J. P. Forgas (Ed.), *Emotion and social judgment* (pp. 55–71). Oxford: Pergamon.

Smith, S. M., & Shaffer, D. R. (1991). The effects of good moods on systematic processing: "Willing but not able, or able but not willing?" *Motivation and Emotion, 15*, 243–279.

Staw, B. M., & Barsade, S. G. (1993). Affect and managerial performance: A test of the sadder-but-wiser vs. happier-and-smarter hypotheses. *Administrative Science Quarterly, 38*, 304–331.

Teasdale, J. D., & Fogarty, S. J. (1979). Differential effects of induced mood on retrieval of pleasant and unpleasant events from episodic memory. *Journal of Abnormal Psychology, 88*, 248–257.

Teasdale, J. D., & Russell, M. L. (1983). Differential aspects of induced mood on the recall of positive, negative and neutral words. *British Journal of Clinical Psychology, 22*, 163–171.

Trope, Y., & Pomerantz, E. M. (1998). Resolving conflicts among self-evaluative motives: Positive experiences as a resource for overcoming defensiveness. *Motivation and Emotion, 22*, 53–72.

Urada, M., & Miller, N. (2000). The impact of positive mood and category importance on crossed categorization effects. *Journal of Personality and Social Psychology, 78*, 417–433.

Watson, D. A., & Tellegen, A. (1985). Toward a consensual structure of mood. *Psychological Bulletin, 98*, 219–235.

17

Pleasure, Utility, and Choice

Barbara A. Mellers

ABSTRACT

When making choices, people usually imagine how they will feel about the consequences. This chapter provides an account of the anticipation process and uses it to
predict choice. Decisions from several experiments are consistent with a theory in
which people are assumed to evaluate alternatives by making trade-offs between
predicted pleasure and pain. Then they choose the alternative with greater expected
pleasure.

The field of decision making has long benefited from the interdisciplinary
contributions of philosophers, economists, statisticians, and many others.
These interdisciplinary contibutions can be categorized into two camps.
One camp specifies how people *should* make choices if they wish to obey
fundamental rules of logic and probability. The other camp focuses on what
people actually *do* when making choices. While rational theories rely on
beliefs and utilities, descriptive theories look to psychological processes
including cognitive limitations, social norms, and cultural constraints to
explain actual choices and the reasons behind alleged deviations from
rationality.

Both camps are well aware that emotions influence choice. Rational theorists have addressed the question of whether emotions should influence
choice, and descriptive theorists have explored how emotions influence
choice. This chapter presents a descriptive account of decision making that
focuses on anticipated pleasure. We propose that, when making a choice,
people imagine how they will feel about future consequences. Comparisons of qualitatively different feelings are made in terms of pleasure and
pain. That is, people evaluate each alternative by balancing imagined pleasure against imagined pain and select the alternative with greater average
pleasure.

BACKGROUND AND FOREGROUND EMOTIONS

Emotions have direct and indirect effects on choice. Indirect emotions, such as moods, temperaments, and dispositions, occur regardless of whether or not people make a decision. These emotions shape choices in a variety of ways. Happiness produces faster and more efficient decisions (Isen & Means, 1983), more creative problem solving (Isen, 1987), greater associations among ideas, and greater enjoyment in pleasurable tasks (Isen, 1993). Sadness leads to longer response times, greater discrimination between strong and weak arguments, and greater analytical thinking. Anger produces faster responses and less discriminate use of information, and fear leads to greater pessimism and risk aversion (Bless, Bohner, Schwarz, & Strack, 1990; Fiedler, 1988; Forgas, 1992; Luce, 1998; Luce, Bettman, & Payne, 1997; Lerner & Keltner, 2001).

Direct emotions occur when people make decisions. These emotions can take two forms: process emotions and anticipated emotions. Process emotions reflect feelings about the act of deciding. People might feel annoyed when they have no good options or conflicted when they have too many good options (Dhar, 1997; Tversky & Shafir, 1992). People might feel anxious when the stakes are high, the time is short, or the information is ambiguous (Janis & Mann, 1977).

Anticipated emotions are imagined feelings about future outcomes of a choice. These emotions may involve fear, guilt, anger, sadness, or joy. In some cases, these emotions might be qualitatively different and hard to compare. In these cases, pleasure and pain provide the common currency for comparison.

We have studied the process by which people anticipate the pleasure and pain of outcomes and have tried to relate those emotions to choice. We now summarize some of our results.

INVESTIGATING PLEASURE

Several of our studies use what decision theorists call "the gambling paradigm." Participants are asked to make choices between gambles with monetary outcomes of wins or losses. Such choices have clear-cut probabilities and outcomes and, most important, they are easy to manipulate (Mellers et al., 1997, 1999). On any given trial, respondents are presented with two gambles shown as pie charts on a computer screen. Different regions of the pie charts represent wins or losses. In many studies, amounts range from +US$32 to −US$32 and are large enough to produce strong emotional reactions. Participants select the gamble they prefer to play. The gamble is resolved, and the outcome is displayed. Finally, participants rate their emotional reaction to the outcome.

In some tasks, gambles are only "partially" resolved. A spinner appears in the center of the chosen gamble, while the unchosen gamble vanishes.

The spinner begins to rotate, eventually stops, and participants learn the outcome. This situation matches many real-world choices. People do not know what would have happened if they had made the other choice. In other tasks, gambles are "completely" resolved. Spinners appear in the center of both gambles and rotate independently. When the spinners stop, participants learn the outcomes of chosen and unchosen gambles. This information – either expected or imagined – can have powerful effects on choice (Parker, Stradling, & Manstead, 1996; Ritov & Baron, 1990; Simonson, 1992).

We have investigated the pleasure of monetary wins and losses. To examine *anticipated* pleasure, we ask participants to make a choice between gambles with hypothetical outcomes. When the gamble is resolved, people imagine how they would feel. To investigate *actual* pleasure, we ask participants to make choices between gambles with real outcomes. When gambles are resolved, they rate their feelings about what actually happened to them. Anticipated pleasure and actual pleasure are expressed on a category rating scale from 50 (very happy) to −50 (very unhappy).

Emotions are inherently relative, and anticipated pleasure is no exception. Anticipated pleasure depends on changes, not final states. In the gambling paradigm, at least three reference points are salient. The status quo is by far the most important. People are well aware of the difference between adding $5 to their pocketbooks and taking $5 out. A second reference point is the other outcome of the "chosen" gamble. When people imagine an outcome, they are sensitive to whether it is better or worse than the gamble's other outcome. Such comparisons across states of the world (or places the spinner could stop) are called "elation" and "disappointment," respectively (Bell, 1985; Loomes & Sugden, 1986). A third reference point is the outcome of the "unchosen" gamble. Decision makers are also sensitive to whether their outcome is better or worse than the outcome of the gamble they did not choose. Such comparisons across choices are called "rejoicing" and "regret," respectively (Bell, 1982; Loomes & Sugden, 1982).

Figure 17.1 shows the effects of disappointment and regret in our gambling studies. Emotional reactions to $8 wins and $8 losses are presented on the on the left and right, respectively. Slopes of the lines represent disappointment effects; both gains and losses of $8 are more pleasurable when the reference point (i.e., the other outcome of the *chosen* gamble) is worse (−$32) than when the reference point is better ($32). Spaces between the lines represent regret effects. Again, outcomes are more pleasurable when the reference point is worse than when the reference point is better.

Reference points have enormous effects on the pleasure of gains and losses. Feelings about an $8 win range from "very pleasurable" when both reference points are $32 losses to "just above neutral" when both reference

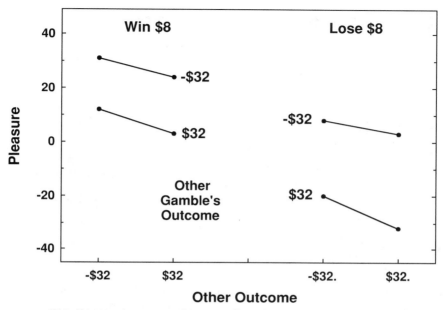

FIGURE 17.1. Disappointment and regret effects for wins and losses of $8, respectively. Each point is the average of three means that differ in the probability of the obtained outcome (.5 or .8), and all else is held constant.

points are $32 wins. Feelings about an $8 loss range from "very painful" when both reference points are $32 wins to "slightly pleasurable" when both reference points are $32 losses. In fact, disappointment and regret effects can make losses more pleasurable than gains. Feelings about losing $8 when both reference points are −$32 are more positive than feelings about winning $8 when both reference points are +$32 (10 vs. 3, respectively).

Comparisons of disappointment and regret effects have revealed that regret is often greater in magnitude than disappointment. Regret, unlike disappointment, involves the element of control. Accountability and/or responsibility often go with regret, but not with disappointment, and these feelings may influence the weight of the comparisons (Kahneman & Miller, 1986; Markman, Gavanski, Sherman, & McMullen, 1995; Zeelenberg, van Dijk, van der Pligt, Manstead, van Empelen, & Reinderman, 1998).

THE ASYMMETRY OF COMPARISONS

In their classic theory of risky choice, Kahneman and Tversky (1979) and Tversky and Kahneman (1992) proposed that people evaluate outcomes relative to the status quo, and that value is asymmetric around the zero point. The pain of a loss is greater in magnitude than the pleasure of

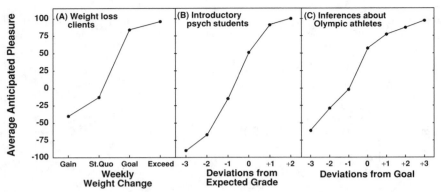

FIGURE 17.2. The asymmetry of comparisons. Slopes are steeper below the reference point than above the reference point. Panels show imagined weight loss relative to the weekly goal, imagined grades relative to the expected grade, and imagined feelings of Olympic athletes with their performance relative to their expected performance.

an equivalent gain. This asymmetry holds around personal comparisons, social comparisons, and even counterfactual comparisons. Negative contrasts have greater impact than positive contrasts. As seen in Figure 17.1, even a gain can *feel* like a loss when compared to an even larger gain.

Figure 17.2 shows the asymmetry in nongambling contexts when the reference point depends on personal expectations and desires (Mellers & McGraw, 2001). Panel A shows results from a dieting study. Clients in a commercial weight-loss program were asked to predict their weekly weight loss and anticipate how they would feel about various outcomes. The next week when clients returned, they learned their actual weight and reported their feelings about the outcome. Clients felt slightly pleased about exceeding their weekly goal by one pound, but quite unhappy about falling short of their goal by the same amount.

Panel B of Figure 17.2 shows results from a grading study. At the beginning of the quarter, undergraduates who had decided to take a course in introductory psychology were asked to predict their course grade and anticipate their feelings about all possible grades. The following quarter, the same undergraduates told us their actual grades and their emotional reactions. Getting one grade higher than expected felt mildly good, but getting one grade lower than expected was quite a blow.

Panel C presents findings from a study in which students were asked to imagine the feelings of Olympic athletes who were given information about the medal received and the medal expected. The students reported that Olympic athletes who exceeded their expectations by one place would be slightly happier, but those who fell short of their expectations by the same amount would be much more disappointed.

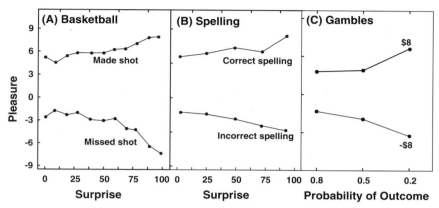

FIGURE 17.3. Surprise effects in tasks of chance and skill. Anticipated pleasure is plotted against surprisingness. Unlikely outcomes are emotionally amplified relative to likely outcomes.

THE WEIGHT OF COMPARISONS

Not all reference points are equally important. Those which are more believable, more salient, more controllable, and more mutable have greater psychological impact. We have found that comparisons between an outcome and a reference point are weighted by the surprisingness of the outcome. Surprise is based on luck or skill, but it can also depend on other factors, such as the vividness of that outcome, the availability of the outcome, and the ease with which it comes to mind. Unexpected or surprising outcomes – either good or bad – have greater emotional impact than expected outcomes (Shepperd & McNulty, 2002). We call this result the surprise effect.

Figure 17.3 presents three examples of surprise effects. Panel A shows results from a task of physical skill. In this case, surprise depends on one's assessment of one's own ability. Recreational basketball players took shots from predesignated locations on the court. Before each shot, they judged their confidence in success. After each shot, they judged their emotional reaction. With tasks of skill, surprise is inferred from confidence. When a player *misses* a shot, we assume that surprise is directly related to confidence. When a player *makes* a shot, we assume that surprise is inversely related to confidence. Surprise is either confidence (with a failure) or confidence subtracted from 100 percent (with a success). Panel A shows that more surprising successes are more pleasurable, and more surprising failures are more painful.

Panel B shows surprise effects from a task of mental skill. In this study, undergraduates participated in a spelling bee. They heard a word, tried to spell it, and judged their confidence that they were correct. Students were then shown the spelling of the word and rated their feelings about their performance. Pleasure is plotted against surprisingness, as derived from judged confidence. Once again, unexpected successes are more pleasurable, and unexpected failures are more painful.

Panel C shows surprise effects from a gambling study. With tasks of chance, surprise depends on objective probabilities. The anticipated pleasure of an $8 win is greater when the chances are smaller (20%) than when they are larger (80%). Similar effects occur with losses. In sum, surprising wins are more pleasurable than expected wins, and surprising losses are more painful than expected losses for tasks of both skill and chance.

DESCRIBING ANTICIPATED PLEASURE

The effects of comparisons and beliefs shown in Figures 17.1 through 17.3 can be explained by an account we call decision affect theory (Mellers et al., 1997, 1999). Imagine a decision maker faced with a choice between Gambles 1 and 2. Gamble 1 has two outcomes, A and B. When the decision maker anticipates the pleasure of outcome A, the process can be represented as:

$$R_A = J\,[u_A + d(u_A - u_B)^*(1 - s_A)], \tag{1}$$

where R_A is the anticipated pleasure of A, J is a linear function that converts an imagined feeling to a numerical response, u_A and u_B are the utilities of outcomes A and B relative to the status quo, and $d(u_A - u_B)$ is a disappointment function that represents the pleasure of A relative to B, the other outcome of the gamble. Finally, s_A is the belief that outcome A will occur, and $1 - s_A$ is the surprisingness of A (i.e., the belief that A will *not* occur). The disappointment function is weighted by the surprisingness of A relative to B.

Now consider the anticipated pleasure of outcome A when the decision maker imagines that outcome C will occur if Gamble 2 is chosen. The anticipated pleasure of outcome A in the context of outcome C is:

$$R_{A(C)} = J\,[u_A + d(u_A - u_B)^*(1 - s_A) + r(u_A - u_C)^*(1 - s_A s_C)] \tag{2}$$

where the first two terms on the right-hand side of the equation are identical to those in Equation 1, and the third term, $r(u_A - u_C)$, is the comparison of A with C. This function is the regret function and is weighted by $(1 - s_A s_C)$, the surprisingness of the joint event of A and C.

Decision affect theory predicts that anticipated pleasure reflects weighted changes relative to salient reference points. The utility of A, u_A, is the pleasure of A relative to the status quo. The disappointment function, $d(u_A - u_B)$, is the pleasure of A relative to B, and the regret function,

$r(u_A - u_C)$, is the pleasure of A relative to the C. The impact of the disappointment and regret functions varies with the surprisingness of the imagined outcome. This theory has done an excellent job describing judged pleasure of outcomes in both experimental and observational studies (Mellers, 2000; Mellers et al., 1997, 1999).

RELATING ANTICIPATED PLEASURE TO CHOICE

Recent interest in the relationship between emotions and choice has led to numerous theoretical developments that differ in their assumptions about which reference points are important and the functional form of the comparisons (Bell, 1982, 1985; Gul, 1991; Inman, Dyer, & Jia, 1997; Loomes & Sugden, 1982, 1986; Zeelenberg, van Dijk, Manstead, & van der Pligt, 2001). All of the theories assert that people anticipate their feelings relative to anchors, sum those feelings over outcomes, and select the option with greater anticipated pleasure. Our theory, called subjective expected pleasure theory, falls into this general framework (Mellers et al., 1999). We further propose that the anticipated pleasure of outcomes can be described by decision affect theory. Then we assume that, when evaluating an option such as a gamble, people weigh their anticipated feeling about each outcome by the likelihood that they will experience that emotion and aggregate over anticipated emotions. Finally, they select the gamble with greater average pleasure.[1]

Let us return to the decision maker facing the choice between Gambles 1 and 2. When that decision maker anticipates the pleasure of outcomes independent of outcomes of other gambles, subjective expected pleasure theory predicts that the average pleasure of Gamble 1 will be:

$$s_A R_A + s_B R_B \tag{3}$$

where s_A and s_B are the beliefs that outcomes A and B will occur, and R_A is the prediction of anticipated pleasure from decision affect theory (Equation 1). The expected pleasure of Gamble 2, with outcomes C and D is:

$$s_C R_C + s_D R_D, \tag{4}$$

and our decision maker selects the gamble with greater average pleasure.

Now consider a more complex case in which the anticipated pleasure of an outcome depends on imagined outcomes of the *other* gamble. The

---

[1] Pleasure does not necessarily imply hedonism. It comes from many sources, including acts of virtue or relief from pain. Likewise, pain arises from an aggressive impulse, a sense of injustice, or frustration from falling short of a goal.

average pleasure of Gamble 1 depends on the anticipated pleasure of A in the context of C and D and B in the context of C and D, as follows:

$$s_A[s_C R_{A(C)} + s_D R_{A(D)}] + s_B[s_C R_{B(C)} + s_D R_{B(D)}]. \tag{5}$$

where $R_{A(C)}$ is the anticipated pleasure of outcome A in the context of outcome C from decision affect theory (Equation 2). The expected pleasure of Gamble 2 follows a similar pattern:

$$s_C[s_A R_{C(A)} + s_B R_{C(B)}] + s_D[s_A R_{D(A)} + s_B R_{D(B)}], \tag{6}$$

and the gamble with greater average pleasure is selected.

Subjective expected pleasure theory is similar to the leading rational account of choice known as subjective expected utility theory (Savage, 1954). In subjective expected utility theory, choices are based on a comparison of the average utilities of options. The choice between Gambles 1 and 2 would be a comparison of the expected utility of Gamble 1:

$$s_A u_A + s_B u_B, \tag{7}$$

where s_A and s_B are the beliefs that A and B will occur and u_A and u_B are the utilities of the outcomes with the expected utility of Gamble 2:

$$s_C u_C + s_D u_D. \tag{8}$$

Decision makers select the gamble with greater expected utility.

The key difference between our descriptive theory and the rational one is the distinction between anticipated pleasure and utility. Pleasure often differs from utility. The *utility* of a smaller win can never be greater than the *utility* of a larger win. But the pleasure of a smaller, surprising win can exceed the pleasure of a larger, expected win. Furthermore, the utility of a loss can never be greater than the utility of a win. But the pain of a loss that could have been much larger can be less than the pain of a win that could have been much larger. These differences between utilities and emotions are predicted by decision affect theory.

SUBJECTIVE EXPECTED PLEASURE THEORY

We have examined the extent to which subjective expected pleasure theory predicts choice proportions in five gambling studies. Predictions for the theory were obtained for group data in the following way. First, decision affect theory was fit to mean judgments of anticipated pleasure separately in each condition (as in Equations 1 or 2). Second, estimated parameters of the theory were used to compute the average anticipated pleasure of each gamble (as in Equations 3 and 4). Third, predicted choices were based on the assumption that people preferred the gamble with greater average pleasure.

The correlation between aggregated choice proportions and binary pre-dictions of subjective expected pleasure theory ranged from 0.66 to 0.86 across the five studies, with an average correlation of 0.74. These correla-tions may seem low, but it is important to keep in mind that predictions for choice were obtained from fit of another theory (decision affect theory) to another set of data (anticipated pleasure). Decision affect theory provides a theoretical framework for both pleasure and choice.

How well does the theory predict individual choices? To answer this question, we examined the correlation between individual choices and predictions using data from Mellers et al. (1999).[2] First, we fit each indi-vidual's judgments of anticipated pleasure to decision affect theory. Using parameters from decision affect theory, we calculated the average plea-sure of each gamble. Then, to compute predicted choices, we assumed that individuals would select the gamble with greater average pleasure. The median correlation between predicted and actual choices was 0.34 and 0.38 in conditions with partial and complete feedback, respectively. These correlations, though much lower than those based on group data, differed significantly from zero for virtually all of the seventy-four subjects.

Tests of subjective expected pleasure theory with observational stud-ies are more difficult for two reasons. First, we used participants who had already made a choice, so we did not know the other options under consid-eration. Second, all participants in each study made the same choice (taking a course, having a pregnancy test, or joining a weight-loss program). De-spite these difficulties, there is a weak, though testable, implication of the theory. For each individual, we can ask whether the expected pleasure of the chosen option was greater than zero. That is, does the average pleasure of the chosen option exceed that of the status quo?

Figure 17.4 shows the average anticipated pleasure of the chosen option for individuals in three observational studies. Panel A presents data from a pregnancy study. Women who were waiting for a pregnancy test at Planned Parenthood imagined how they would feel about negative or positive test results. They also told us the probabilities that each result would occur. A small percentage of women felt very unhappy, but for the majority, the expected pleasure of the chosen option of unprotected sex was positive. Similar patterns appeared with the grading and dieting experiments in Panels B and C. On average, most of the students expected to feel good about their performance in the course. Similarly, clients at the weight-loss program expected to be pleased, on average, with their dieting attempts. Thus, the majority of participants in the three studies chose options that

---

[2] When we fit decision affect theory to individual judgments of anticipated pleasure, we assumed that subjective beliefs were equivalent to objective beliefs and utilities were power functions with exponents that could differ for gains and losses.

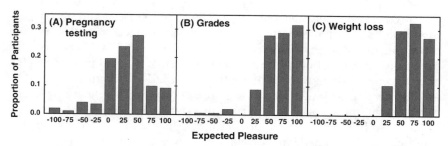

FIGURE 17.4. Tests of subjective expected pleasure theory in three observational studies. The theory predicts that the average pleasure of the selected option will be greater than zero. For most subjects the prediction holds.

were associated with positive expected feelings, as predicted by subjective expected pleasure theory.

HOW ACCURATELY DO PEOPLE ANTICIPATE PLEASURE?

If decision makers compare options by attending to expected pleasure, the accuracy of their affective forecasts becomes essential. Inaccurate predictions could easily lead to suboptimal choice (Kahneman, 1994). Several experiments have identified errors in affective forecasting (Loewenstein & Schkade, 1999). Some of these errors are different forms of myopia. One such error arises when we allow our immediate feelings to have undue influence on our predictions of future feelings. When feeling happy, people overestimate the probability of a favorable outcome, underestimate the chances of an unfavorable outcome, and retrieve more happy memories (Johnson & Tversky, 1983; Nygren, Isen, Taylor, & Dulin, 1996; Wright & Bower, 1990).

Another error occurs when people focus on the immediate but irrelevant features of future outcomes. Gilbert, Pinel, Wilson, Blumberg, and Wheatley (1998) asked assistant professors to predict their feelings about getting and not getting tenure. Not surprisingly, the same professors expected to be happy if they received tenure, and extremely unhappy otherwise. Some time later, Gilbert et al. interviewed the same professors, found out what had happened, and asked them how they actually felt. Those who had been denied tenure were much happier than they had expected to be.

Schkade and Kahneman (1998) also demonstrated that, when predicting affect, people tend to focus on features of an outcome that are salient at the moment. They asked students in the Midwest and California to judge how happy they were and how happy they thought other students like them living in the other region were. Schkade and Kahneman's survey was designed to highlight the advantages of California – better climate, more

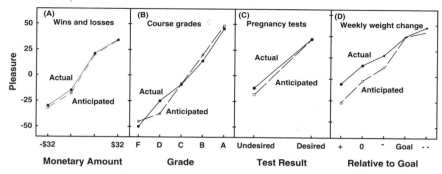

FIGURE 17.5. Accuracy tests of anticipated pleasure. Anticipated and actual pleasure, shown as dashed and solid lines, respectively, from the gambling, grading, pregnancy, and dieting studies. For the most part, average forecasts are accurate, although dieters tend to expect to feel worse about gaining weight than they actually feel.

cultural opportunities, and greater natural beauty over the Midwest. Both Californians and Midwesterners thought students in California would be happier, but in fact, the groups were equally happy on average.

Some of our experiments allow us to check the accuracy of affective forecasts. Figure 17.5 shows average anticipated pleasure (dashed lines) and average actual pleasure (solid lines) as a function of outcomes in the gambling, grading, pregnancy, and dieting experiments. Participants were reasonably good, on average, at forecasting their feelings. In the gambling study, the dashed and solid lines were quite close. Even at the level of the individual decision maker, average errors between anticipated and actual feelings about monetary outcomes rarely deviated significantly from zero. Students in the grading study were also reasonably accurate at forecasting their feelings about course grades. Moreover, women at Planned Parenthood could also predict their feelings about test results.

The only experiment that showed systematic deviations between actual and anticipated feelings was the dieting study. Clients expected to feel worse about gaining (or not losing) weight than they actually felt. They overestimated the pain of an undesirable outcome. However, this prediction error might have been strategic; clients may have tried to convince themselves that they would feel worse about gaining weight in an effort to control their behavior. We now turn to the topic of strategic emotions.

STRATEGIC EMOTIONS

In a classic paper, Taylor and Brown (1988) argued that people are often overly optimistic about themselves and their assessment of the future.

Moreover, such inflated self-perceptions could be strategic if they led to more creative and productive work (Taylor, 1989; Taylor and Brown, 1994). Despite the potential virtues, excessive optimism can have the undesirable effect of setting people up for disappointment.[3] People appear to be aware of this problem and often take actions to avoid disappointment by adjusting their beliefs downward to more realistic or even pessimistic levels (Sanna, 1999; Shepperd, Ouellette, & Fernandez, 1996; Taylor & Shepperd, 1998; Taylor & Gollwitzer, 1995; van Dijk, Zeelenberg, & van der Pligt, 2001). In one example, Shepperd et al. (1996) asked college sophomores, juniors, and seniors to estimate a starting salary for their first postgraduate job. Salaries were predicted at the beginning and end of the spring term. Only seniors looking for jobs immediately after graduation lowered their estimates at the end of the term, right before they would face the world. People are aware that bad news feels worse when unexpected, and they strategically change their expectations to avoid disappointment.

Strategic shifts of emotions can also occur *after* a decision was resolved if the outcome was bad. Tykocinski, Pick, and Kedmi (2001) identified a process they call retroactive pessimism. In an attempt to regulate disappointment, people change their beliefs about the likelihood of an unfavorable outcome and take the position that the event was inevitable. Decision affect theory predicts that such shifts in belief, both before and after the decision is resolved, can diminish the pain of unfavorable outcomes.

CONCLUSION

Anticipated pleasure is inherently relative and governed by change with respect to reference points. Kahneman and Tversky have suggested that the pain of a loss has greater impact than the pleasure of comparable gain, an effect they called loss aversion. Furthermore, they asserted that change around the status quo has differential impact, with negative comparisons having greater impact than positive comparisons. We have found similar asymmetries around other reference points. Not only is the pain of a loss greater than the pleasure of an equivalent gain, but the pain of a *relative* loss is greater in magnitude than the pleasure of a comparable *relative* gain.

Effects of reference points have been investigated with functional imaging studies. Breiter, Aharon, Kahneman, Dale, and Shizgal (2001) presented participants with monetary gambles. A spinner appeared in the center

---

[3] Harrison and March (1994) have also argued, albeit on entirely different grounds, that when people make decisions, they often expect too much and set themselves up for disappointment.

of each gamble, rotated, and eventually stopped. Breiter et al. examined neurological responses to constant outcomes that were either the best or the worst possible consequences of the gamble. Dopamine neurons in several regions of the brain were sensitive to reference point effects. Holding all else constant, greater activation of dopamine neurons occurred when the *same* outcome was the best possible consequence of the gamble than when it was the worst.

The anticipated pleasure of outcomes also varies with beliefs about what will occur. Unexpected outcomes are more intense than expected ones; surprising good outcomes are more pleasurable, and surprising bad outcomes are more painful. Once again, there are parallels between judgments of anticipated pleasure and electrophysiological studies of dopamine neurons (Schultz et al., 1992, 1993, 1997). When monkeys expect a reward, dopamine neurons start to fire. When monkeys receive that reward, neuronal firing depends on prior expectations. Unexpected rewards lead to greater firing than expected rewards.

We have summarized the effects of outcomes, comparisons, and surprise in an account of anticipated pleasure called decision affect theory. The theory predicts that anticipated pleasure is relative and governed by changes and beliefs. This account of pleasure has also been applied to choice. We offer a theory of choice called subjective expected pleasure theory in which people anticipate the pleasure of outcomes, weigh their feelings by the chances they will occur, sum over outcomes, and select options that, on average, provide them with greater pleasure. Anticipated pleasure can be described by decision affect theory.

Are people aware of the expected pleasure associated with risky options? Schwartz (1997) investigated this question by asking people to judge the average pleasure they imagined feeling each time they played a gamble, if they could play it an infinite number of times. People were quite good at judging their average feelings, and overall evaluations of gambles were closely related to the subjective expected pleasure of the gambles.

Another way to investigate the awareness of expected pleasure is to look into whether participants are capable of using different hedonic choice rules. In a two-part study, Schwartz, Mellers, and Metzger (1999) asked people to make choices between gambles and judge the pleasure of monetary outcomes. Later, they asked the same people to make choices between the same gambles, but this time, they were instructed to either maximize the pleasure of their experiences or minimize the displeasure of their experiences. Predictions for these hedonic choice rules could be constructed by examining the judged pleasure of outcomes from the first part of the study and determining, for each individual, what choice would maximize pleasure or minimize displeasure. Participants did not follow instructions perfectly, but they did adjust their choices in the right directions. The results provide further evidence that people are, at least to some extent, aware of the influence of emotions on choice and at least partially capable of controlling their choices to achieve hedonic goals.

How *Should* Emotions Influence Choice?

Emotions have traditionally been regarded as impediments to rational choice. They wreak havoc on orderly thought and interrupt logical reasoning. However, some theorists have recognized the beneficial effects of emotions. Darwin (1872) noted that many emotional expressions are adaptive. Surprise often leads people to open their eyes as wide as possible and obtain as much new information as they can. Anger often leads to aggressive expressions. Chimpanzees who are threatened show their teeth and in the process signal their ability, and perhaps intention, to attack. Such expressions have evolved for long-term survival.

Scherer (1984) argues that emotions may have evolved to replace reflexes, instincts, and simple stimulus-response chains. The decoupling of a single response from an eliciting stimulus allows opportunities for a wide array of reactions. Fridja (1986) has noted that emotions help to mobilize behavior by serving as relevance detectors. Others point out that emotions provide useful information about our internal states (Clore & Parrott, 1991; Clore, Schwarz, & Conway, 1994; Schwarz, Bless, & Bohner, 1991).

Frank (1988) has stressed the advantages of emotions as solutions to commitment problems. Some choices require difficult-to-reverse commitments that may run counter to short-term interests. Couples considering marriage and children may feel reluctant to enter into an agreement for fear of the other leaving when a more attractive mate becomes available. The bonds of romantic love can provide solutions that work far better than detailed contracts. Emotions solve social problems as well by providing constraints for proper behavior. Most people can imagine feeling guilty about lying or cheating, and those imagined feelings encourage socially acceptable behavior. Positive feelings also provide constraints. Widely known and shared positive feelings about fairness deter people from behaving selfishly.

The topic of how people *should* use their emotions is a controversial one. Some argue that regret and disappointment are often momentary feelings that distract us from long-range plans. On the other hand, the emotional consequences of decisions may be just as important as the material consequences. In this view, emotions are an essential part of what it means to be rational (Damasio, 1994). These philosophical debates are not easily resolved. However, it is abundantly clear that cognition and emotion are closely intertwined, and connections between these processes are highly relevant to decision making. We believe rationality and emotion-based decision making are not as far apart as was once thought. Our results suggest that the rational theory may be a special case of certain emotion-based choices.

References

Bell, D. E. (1982). Regret in decision making under uncertainty. *Operations Research, 30*, 961–981.

Bell, D. E. (1985). Disappointment in decision making under uncertainty. *Operations Research, 33*, 1–27.

Bless, H.; Bohner, G.; Schwarz, N.; & Strack, F. (1990). Mood and persuasion: A cognitive response analysis. *Personality and Social Psychology Bulletin, 16*, 331–335.

Breiter, H. C.; Aharon, I.; Kahneman, D.; Dale, A.; & Shizgal, P. Functional imaging of neural responses to expectancy and experience of monetary gains and losses. *Neuron, 30*, 619–639.

Clore, G. L., & Parrott, W. G. (1991). Moods and their vicissitudes: Thoughts and feelings as information. In J. Forgas (Ed.), *Emotion and social judgment* (pp. 107–123). Oxford: Pergamon Press.

Clore, G. L.; Schwarz, N.; & Conway, M. (1994). Emotion and information processing. In R. S. Wyer and T. K. Srull (Eds.), *Handbook of social cognition* (2d ed., pp. 323–417). Hillsdale, NJ: Erlbaum.

Damasio, A. (1994). *Descartes' error: Emotion, reason, and the human brain.* New York: Grosset/Putnam.

Darwin, C. (1872). *The expression of the emotions in man and animals.* New York: New York Philosophical Library.

Dhar, R. (1997). Consumer preferences for a non-choice option. *Journal of Consumer Research, 24*, 215–231.

Fiedler, K. (1988). Emotional mood, cognitive style, and behavioral regulation. In K. Fiedler and J. Forgas (Eds.), *Affect, cognition, and social behavior* (pp. 100–119). Toronto: Hoegrefe International.

Forgas, J. P. (1992). Affect in social judgments and decisions: A multi-process model. *Advances in experimental social psychology* (Vol. 25, pp. 53–60). New York: Academic Press.

Frank, R. (1988). *Passions within reason.* New York: Norton.

Frijda, N. H. (1986). *The emotions.* Cambridge: Cambridge University Press.

Gilbert, D. T.; Pinel, E. C.; Wilson, T. C.; Blumberg, S. J.; & Wheatley, T. P. (1998). Immune neglect: A source of durability bias in affective forecasting. *Journal of Personality and Social Psychology, 75*, 617–638.

Gul, F. (1991). A theory of disappointment aversion. *Econometrica, 59*, 667–686.

Harrison, J. R., & March, J. G. (1984). Decision making and postdecision surprises. *Administrative Science Quarterly, 29*, 26–42.

Inman, J. J.; Dyer, J. S.; & Jia, J. (1997). A generalized utility model of disappointment and regret effects on post-choice valuation. *Marketing Science, 6*, 97–111.

Isen, A. M. (1987). Positive affect, cognitive processes, and social behavior. In L. Berkowitz (Ed.), *Advances in experimental social psychology* (Vol. 20, pp. 203–253). New York: Academic Press.

Isen, A. M. (1993). Positive affect and decision making. In M. Lewis and J. M. Haviland (Eds.), *Handbook of emotions* (pp. 261–277). New York: Guilford Press.

Isen, A. M., & Means, B. (1983). The influence of positive affect on decision-making strategy. *Social Cognition, 2*, 18–31.

Janis, I. L., & Mann, L. (1977). *Decision making*. New York: Free Press.

Johnson, E., & Tversky, A. (1983). Affect, generalization, and the perception of risk. *Journal of Personality and Social Psychology, 45*, 20–31.

Kahneman, D. (1994). New challenges to the rationality assumption. *Journal of Institutional and Theoretical Economics, 150*, 18–36.

Kahneman, D., & Miller, D. (1986). Norm theory: Comparing reality to its alternatives. *Psychological Review, 93*, 136–153.

Kahneman, D., & Tversky, A. (1979). Prospect theory. *Econometrica, 47*, 263–292.

Lerner, J., & Keltner, D. (2001). Fear, anger, and risk. *Journal of Personality and Social Psychology, 81*, 146–159.

Loewenstein, G. (1996). Out of control: Visceral influences on behavior. *Organizational Behavior and Human Decision Processes, 65*, 272–292.

Loewenstein, G., & Schkade, D. (1999). Wouldn't it be nice? Predicting future feelings. In D. Kahneman, E. Diener, and N. Schwarz (Eds.), *Well-being: The foundations of hedonic psychology* (pp. 85–108). New York: Russell Sage Foundation.

Loomes, G., & Sugden, R. (1982). Regret theory: An alternative of rational choice under uncertainty. *Economic Journal, 92*, 805–824.

Loomes, G., & Sugden, R. (1986). Disappointment and dynamic consistency in choice under uncertainty. *Review of Economic Studies, 53*, 271–282.

Luce, M. F. (1998). Choosing to avoid: Coping with negatively emotion-laden consumer decisions. *Journal of Consumer Research, 24*, 409–431.

Luce, M. F.; Bettman, J.; & Payne, J. (1997). Choice processing in emotionally difficult decisions. *Journal of Experimental Psychology: Learning, Memory, and Cognition, 23*, 384–405.

Markman, K.; Gavanski, I.; Sherman, S. J.; & McMullen, M. (1995). The impact of perceived control on the imagination of better and worse possible worlds. *Personality and Social Psychology Bulletin, 6*, 588–595.

Mellers, B. A. (2000). Choice and the relative pleasure of consequences. *Psychological Bulletin, 126*, 910–924.

Mellers, B. A., & McGraw, A. P. (2001). Anticipated emotions as guides to choice. *Current Directions, 10*, 210–214.

Mellers, B. A.; Schwartz, A.; Ho, K.; & Ritov, I. (1997). Decision affect theory: Emotional reactions to the outcomes of risky options. *Psychological Science, 8*, 423–429.

Mellers, B. A.; Schwartz, A.; & Ritov, I. (1999). Emotion-based choice. *Journal of Experimental Psychology: General, 128*, 332–345.

Nygren, T.; Isen, A.; Taylor, P. J.; & Dulin, J. (1996). The influence of positive affect on the decision rule in risk situations. *Organizational Behavior and Human Decision Processes, 66*, 59–72.

Parker, D.; Stradling, S. G.; & Manstead, A. S. R. (1996). Modifying beliefs and attitudes toward exceeding the speed limit: An intervention study based on the theory of planned behavior. *Journal of Applied Social Psychology, 26*, 1427–1453.

Ritov, I., & Baron, J. (1990). Reluctance to vaccinate: Omission bias and ambiguity. *Journal of Behavioral Decision Making, 3,* 263–277.

Sanna, L. J. Mental simulations, affective, and subjective confidence: Timing is everything. *Psychological Science, 10,* 339–345.

Savage, L. J. (1954). *The foundations of statistics.* New York: Wiley.

Scherer, K. R. (1984). On the nature and function of emotion: A component process approach. In K. R. Scherer and P. Ekman (Eds.), *Approaches to emotion* (pp. 293–318). Hillsdale, NJ: Erlbaum.

Schkade, D. A., & Kahneman, D. (1998). Does living in California make people happy? *Psychological Science, 9,* 340–346.

Schultz, W.; Apicella, P.; & Ljungberg, T. (1993). Responses of monkey dopamine neurons to reward and conditioned stimuli during successive steps of learning a delayed response task. *Journal of Neuroscience, 13,* 900–913.

Schultz, W.; Apicella, P.; Scarnati, E.; & Ljungberg, T. (1992). Neuronal activity in monkey ventral striatum related to the expectation of reward. *Journal of Neuroscience, 12,* 4594–4610.

Schultz, W.; Dayan, P.; & Montague, P. R. (1997). A neural substrate of prediction and reward. *Science, 275,* 1593–1599.

Schwartz, A. (1997). *Expected feelings about risky options.* Unpublished Ph.D. dissertation. University of California, Berkeley.

Schwartz, A.; Mellers, B. A.; & Metzger, T. (1998). Manipulating hedonic strategies of choice. In J. Shanteau, B. A. Mellers, and D. Schum (Eds.), *Decision research from Bayesian approaches to normative perspectives: Reflections on the contributions of Ward Edwards.* New York: Kluwer.

Schwarz, N.; Bless, B.; & Bohner, G. (1991). Mood and persuasion: Affective states influence the processing of persuasive communications. In M. Zanna (Ed.), *Advances in experimental social psychology* (Vol. 24, pp. 161–199). San Diego, CA: Academic Press.

Shepperd, J. A., & McNulty, J. K. (2002). The affective consequences of expected and unexpected outcomes. *Psychological Science, 13,* 85–88.

Shepperd, J. A.; Ouellette, J. A.; & Fernandez, J. K. (1996). Abandoning unrealistic optimism: Performance estimates and the temporal proximity of self-relevant feedback. *Journal of Personality and Social Psychology, 70,* 844–855.

Simonson, I. (1992). The influence of anticipating regret and responsibility on purchasing decisions. *Journal of Consumer Research, 19,* 1–14.

Taylor, S. E. (1989). *Positive illusions: Creative self-deception and the healthy mind.* New York: Basic Books.

Taylor, S. E., & Brown, J. (1988). Illusion and well-being: A social psychological perspective on mental health. *Psychological Bulletin, 103,* 193–210.

Taylor, S. E., & Brown, J. (1994). Positive illusions and well-being revisited: Separating fact from fiction. *Psychological Bulletin, 116,* 21–27.

Taylor, S. E., & Gollwitzer, P. M. (1995). Effects of *mindset* on positive illusions. *Journal of Personality and Social Psychology, 69,* 213–226.

Taylor, S. E., & Shepperd, J. A. (1998). Bracing for the worst: Severity, testing, and feedback as moderators of the optimistic bias. *Personality and Social Psychology Bulletin, 24,* 915–924.

Tversky, A., & Kahneman, D. (1992). Advances in prospect theory: Cumulative representation of uncertainty. *Journal of Risk and Uncertainty, 5,* 297–323.

Tversky, A., & Shafir, E. (1992). Choice under conflict: The dynamics of deferred decisions. *Psychological Science, 6*, 358–361.

Tykocinski, O.; Pick, D.; & Kedmi, D. (2001). Retroactive pessimism: A different kind of hindsight bias. Manuscript under review.

Van Dijk, W. W.; Zeelenberg, M.; & van der Pligt, J. (2001). Blessed are they who expect nothing: Lowering expectations as a way of avoiding disappointment. Manuscript under review.

Wright, W., & Bower, G. (1992). Mood effects on subjective probability assessment. *Organizational Behavior and Human Decision Processes, 52*, 276–291.

Zeelenberg, M.; van Dijk, W. W.; Manstead, A. S. R.; & van der Pligt, J. (2000). On bad decisions and disconfirmed expectancies: The psychology of regret and disappointment. *Cognition and Emotion, 14*, 521–541.

Zeelenberg, M.; van Dijk, W. W.; van der Pligt, J.; Manstead, A. S. R.; van Empelen, P.; & Reinderman, D. (1998). Emotional reactions to outcomes of decisions: The role of counterfactual thought in the experience of regret and disappointment. *Organizational Behavior and Human Decision Processes, 75*, 117–141.

PART IV

FEELINGS AND EMOTIONS IN THEIR SOCIOCULTURAL CONTEXT

18

The Development of Individual Differences in Understanding Emotion and Mind

Antecedents and Sequelae

Judy Dunn

ABSTRACT

The chapter examines the relations between children's understanding of others' inner states and their socioemotional experiences and relationships, both concurrently and over time, and the place of talk in these developments. It is framed within a relationship perspective, draws on evidence from longitudinal studies of children, and discusses what we need to know now.

INTRODUCTION

No one who has been around young children can fail to have noticed the emotional drama of their lives – the intensity and frequency of their displays of anger, delight, distress, and humor. If you listen to what they are saying – their questions, jokes, stories, and arguments – their interest in and curiosity about emotions are also strikingly evident. There has of course been a long tradition, since Darwin, of research that charts the developmental changes in children's emotional behavior, and the organization of emotions, a tradition that continues today. There is also flourishing research on the regulation of emotional behavior and its relation to developmental psychopathology, and to close relationships more generally (Eisenberg, 2000; Eisenberg et al., 1995). This chapter however focuses not on these active areas of study, but on another theme that is increasingly prominent in developmental work on emotions. This is the significance, antecedents, and sequelae of individual differences in children's early understanding of emotions. As adults, our understanding of other people's feelings plays a crucial role in our relationships, in our interpretation of people's actions and intentions. What do we know, and what do we need to know,

The research reported in this chapter was supported by grants from the NICHD and the ESRC.

about individual differences in the development of this understanding in children?

The hottest topic in cognitive developmental research for the last decade has been the development of children's understanding of mind – the striking growth of children's grasp of the connections between what people think, believe, and remember, and their actions that takes place during the preschool years. The normative changes in children's discovery of the mind have been mapped in a burst of experimental research, elegantly summarized in Astington (1993). Surprisingly, until relatively recently, much of this research focusing on the developments in children's understanding of mental states has not included a specific examination of their understanding of feelings. Yet there is a powerful case for seeing this understanding of feelings as key to the later development of understanding mental states. Very young children explain people's actions at first in terms of emotions and desires; and then, through their social experiences, Bartsch and Wellman (1995) argue, they come to incorporate the notion of belief into their understanding of why people behave the way they do. An important implication of this argument is that an understanding of cognitive states arises through an earlier understanding of emotional states – that the framework for children's reflection on the links between inner states and human action is initially constructed through children's interest in feelings (Bartsch & Estes, 1996). Bartsch and Estes point out that this has wide implications for our understanding of development – that accounts of metacognition will have to be anchored in a much broader understanding of development.

This chapter will consider some of the ways in which the recent work on emotional understanding is beginning to bridge gaps between ideas on cognitive and emotional development, between interest in language and in understanding, and between social relationships and cognitive development. The primary focus is upon individual differences rather than normative change.

For the background to what I want to discuss I shall go back to some of the first naturalistic observations I did of young children. As I trailed, in good ethological fashion, after toddlers and preschoolers in people's kitchens and living rooms, I was impressed by the apparent sophistication of some of the children I was watching, during their second year and third year, in terms of the emotional understanding their actions reflected (Dunn, 1988). They engaged, for instance, in *teasing* their siblings – behavior in which they managed to tune their actions to just what would annoy or upset their sibling. Such attempts occurred with increasing frequency during the second year of life. They were very responsive to distress or upset shown by other family members, and during the second year made increasingly successful attempts to *comfort* the distressed person. From early in the second year they were able to join in the pretend play of their siblings and other children, *sharing an imaginative world* in which their own contributions were increasingly sophisticated. The children were adept at drawing their parents' attention away from their siblings and toward themselves, and they were particularly attentive to exchanges between other family members that involved the expression of anger, distress, or humor. Perhaps most striking of all, they engaged in acts that were apparently deliberate attempts to *deceive* their parents, to shift blame away from self to sibling.

Many of these actions involved some grasp of what others were feeling, were intending or likely to do, and some – the deceitful acts for instance – suggested some deliberate manipulation of others' beliefs. These acts were shown by very young children, and the maturity of these children's social understanding in their second and third year was in many ways discrepant with the picture of children's developing understanding that more formal assessments gave (e.g., Perner, 1991). Other studies focusing on naturalistic observations have since replicated the general points highlighted in this research. Thus Newton and Reddy have established the pattern of early deceptive acts shown by children in their third and fourth year, and have shown that such deceptive acts are most evident in situations when children are in conflict with parents over issues of control, when the children had "their backs to the wall" (Newton, 1994; Newton & Reddy, submitted).

Why should children show this cleverness in the midst of family dramas – was it simply a question of the familiarity of family members, or did the emotional dynamics of family interactions play a part? And what explains the marked individual differences in children's sophistication that have been found in studies of early emotion understanding and mind reading? The broad issue addressed in this chapter is the question of how the extraordinary developments in cognition about the mind, mapped by those studying children's "theory of mind," and in children's understanding of emotions are related to the social emotional contexts, the pragmatics of children's lives and relationships. In particular, the focus is on why some children should be relatively sophisticated in their understanding of emotion and mind, and others much less so, and what this means for their future development. My own research approach for trying to understand these connections between understanding and the social lives of children has been to pursue three strategies:

The Study of Understanding in Action. The first strategy is to study children's understanding in action – their grasp of what other people feel, think, and believe, and its relation to action *as it is revealed in their everyday interactions*. Here we have paid special attention to how children handle conflict (how far, for instance they take account of their antagonists' feelings), their talk about why people behave or feel the way they do, their questions about feelings, their stories, their sharing of imaginative worlds with others, and the understanding of feelings and actions revealed in that play, and finally their moral sensibility.

The Relation of Understanding-in-Action to Task Performance. The second strategy is to look at how these aspects of understanding-in-action relate to children's task performance in standard cognitive assessments of emotion understanding and mind reading.

The Use of Longitudinal Studies. The third strategy is to look longitudinally as well as concurrently at how children's emotional experiences and social relationships may be linked to their understanding. The data on which much of the discussion here is based come from a series of longitudinal studies based on both naturalistic observations and standardized assessments of emotion understanding (Cutting & Dunn, 1999; Dunn, Brown, Slomkowski, Tesla, & Youngblade, 1991b; Dunn & Hughes, 1998; Hughes, White, Sharpen, & Dunn, 2000).

Drawing on the findings of these studies, the focus of this chapter is on four questions:

1. What do we know about the links between individual differences in children's understanding of others' feelings and thoughts as reflected in cognitive assessments and their socioemotional experiences/relationships (both earlier in their lives, and currently)? What is the place of talk, and of close emotional relationships, in the early development of these differences?
2. What is the relation between early individual differences in understanding of emotions and mind and children's later relationships and emotion understanding?
3. What can we learn about these associations from the study of children with troubled close relationships and difficulties in early emotion understanding?
4. Finally, what do we need to know now?

1. WHAT ARE THE LINKS BETWEEN INDIVIDUAL DIFFERENCES IN EMOTION UNDERSTANDING, MIND READING, AND CHILDREN'S SOCIAL EXPERIENCES?

The main points of what is currently known about antecedent and concurrent links between emotion understanding, mind reading, and social relationships will be briefly summarized. A key issue here concerns the focus on *talk* in many of the central studies in this area.

Talk, Emotion, and the Development of Understanding

Children's ability and propensity to talk about and reflect on emotions as soon as they begin to use language is notable (Bartsch & Wellman, 1995; Bretherton, Fritz, Zahn-Waxler, & Ridgeway, 1986; Brown & Dunn, 1992; Dunn, Brown, & Beardsall, 1991a; Wellman, Harris, Banerjee, & Sinclair, 1995). They increasingly comment on the feelings of others (Smiley & Huttenlocher, 1989). The acquisition of language makes it possible for children to focus and reflect on (and possibly distance themselves from) emotional experiences, through discussion with others. It enables them, as Stern has pointed out, "to share their personal experience of the world with others, including 'being with' others in intimacy, loneliness, fear, awe, and love" (Stern, 1985, p. 182). They can begin to appreciate others' feelings in a new way, and to differentiate between their own and others' emotions. Being able to talk about feelings also leads children to participate in the shared cultural concepts of emotion in their particular cultural worlds, which can of course differ widely, and to talk about past emotions (Fivush, 1991; Fivush, Gray, & Fromhoff, 1987).

The role of language is central in the development of individual differences in emotion understanding. It is evident that many of the standard assessments of children's emotion understanding are language-based. In focusing on individual differences in emotion understanding, are we then simply picking up on differences in children's language abilities? The conventional approach of examining correlations between aspects of social cognition and other developmental domains *partialing out the correlations of each with language* may well be misleading. It is clear from a number of longitudinal studies now, in the United States, the U.K., and Canada, that children who frequently participate in discourse about feelings in their early years are later better able to understand feelings than those who have not had such conversational experiences (Dunn et al., 1991b; Dunn & Brown, 1993; Howe, Petrakos, & Rinaldi, 1998; Hughes & Dunn, 1998). We are language users, and talk about feelings is a major channel through which we come to understand our own emotions and those of others.

A first hint of the significance of talk in emotional development came from an early study of siblings conducted in Cambridge, England (Dunn & Kendrick, 1982). In families in which mothers talked to their firstborn children about the new baby as a person with feelings, needs, and wishes, in the early weeks after the baby sibling had been born, over time both the firstborn and (particularly striking) the younger sibling behaved with more friendliness toward each other than the siblings in families in which the mothers had not discussed the baby's feelings in this way. While direct causal inferences from these correlations were of course not appropriate, the results alerted us to the potential significance of family talk about emotional matters for children's developing relationships. In a further study in Cambridge, we focused more specifically on assessments of emotion understanding, and found that children who grew up in families in which they participated in talk about feelings later did better on formal assessments of emotion understanding (Dunn et al., 1991a). These findings have been replicated in studies in Pennsylvania and in Canada.

What Precipitates Talk about Feelings?

If talk about feelings is of such significance, the question of what precipitates such talk becomes of real importance. What is the emotional context in which these conversations about feelings take place? Are children's emotional experiences implicated in the *development* of understanding, through the discourse that takes place when children are upset, for example? The issue of how emotional experiences may play a role in the development of individual differences in understanding has been relatively neglected in cognitive developmental research. Yet here too there are important lines of evidence that show us the central importance of emotional experience (and of *remembered* emotional experience) in the development of emotional understanding.

Observational studies showed that the children's own emotional state was crucial in the initiation of such discourse: Mothers were more than twice as likely to talk about feelings with their children when their children were upset or angry than when the children were happy or emotionally neutral, and the children were more likely to engage in causal talk about feelings when they were angry or upset (Dunn & Brown, 1994; Dunn & Brown, 1993). What is learned in particular interactions may be importantly linked to the pragmatics and emotional context of the exchange (see also Stein & Miller, 1993). It is not simply the exposure of the child to information about emotions in such talk that matters. Rather a key role in what is learned is the quality of the relationship between child and interlocutor, and the child's relationship goals.

Evidence from Talk about Past Emotional Experiences

A second example of the importance of the affective context for cognitive change comes from work on children's early narratives, showing that it was experiences involving anger, fear, and distress that prompted children to tell coherent stories about the past; the children showed their most sophisticated language skills in the narratives about such negative experiences (Brown, 1995; see also Fivush et al., 1987; Hudson, Gebelt, Haviland, & Bentivegna, 1992). The study of individual differences in conversations, causal talk, and narratives as well as naturally occurring deception establishes the point that the emotional context of children's interactions, and their relationship goals, are central to children's developing understanding of emotions (Dunn, Cutting, & Fisher, 2002).

The Significance of a Relationship Framework

The importance of investigating emotional development within a relationship framework is illustrated by considering the variety of social processes that are implicated in the growth of individual differences among children in their social understanding. For example, in the Pennsylvania study (Dunn et al., 1991b) the findings showed that independent contributions to the variance in emotion understanding and mind reading were made by three groups of very different variables: by *discourse* between child and mother on emotion and mental states; by the children's experience of *cooperative pretend play* with their siblings; and by family differences in the interactions between mothers and older siblings focused on control, which children watched vigilantly. The social processes implicated in the developments in understanding are, these results suggest, very varied in nature.

That study also gave us the first evidence that highlighted the significance of what happened *between children* in the development of emotion understanding. In the Pennsylvania study, observations of the children with their friends at forty-seven months showed that talk about inner states was twice as frequent with friends and sibs as with parents (Brown, Donelan-McCall, & Dunn, 1996; Dunn & Brown, 1994). Much of this talk about inner states and feelings took place in the context of joint pretend play, and indeed the links between frequency of joint pretend with other children and mature sociocognitive understanding were particularly pronounced. These early experiences with other children, moreover, show substantial connections with later friendship quality (Dunn et al., 2002). This pattern of links between children's engagement in talk about inner states, their experience of pretend play with other children, and performance on social cognition tasks, including emotion understanding, has now been shown in a number of studies (Astington, 1993; Howe et al., 1998).

In summary, individual differences in understanding of emotions are, we now know, systematically related to the quality of relationships with friends and siblings as well as with other family members, and to children's experiences of discourse about inner states and of imaginative play. The social processes implicated in these associations include both talk and pretend, and watching other family members, in settings of emotional significance to the children. Other aspects of relationships cited as important in the development of emotion understanding include the security of children's attachment to their mothers, parental socialization techniques, and the emotional expressiveness of parents with their children (Cassidy, Parke, Butkovsky, & Braungart, 1992). New directions in research linking attachment, discourse about emotions, and emotional understanding are considered later. There is now also evidence for other contributing sources of influence, such as genetics, that will not be considered here (see Goldsmith, Lemery, Buss, & Campos, 1999; Hughes & Cutting, 1999).

New Directions: Discourse and Attachment

Two particularly interesting new directions in developmental research have begun to link the part played by conversational experiences in emotion understanding with the quality of family and friend relationships that fosters such talk. One is work within an attachment paradigm. Thus for example, Ross Thompson and his colleagues have shown that mother-child pairs with secure attachment relationships engage in discourse that includes more frequent references to emotion and more moral evaluatives, suggesting that a secure attachment fosters the understanding of negative emotions (Laible & Thompson, 2000). In one study, mothers were asked to discuss with their children incidents in the past in which the children had behaved well and in which they had behaved badly. The emotion-laden discourse about the child's past in which the securely attached pairs engaged, Thompson argues, may make emotions more accessible and less threatening for a child when reflecting on past personal experiences (particularly negatively charged emotional experiences). Interestingly, in Thompson's study maternal references to material consequences of the children's actions, or to moral rules, were unrelated to early conscience development, in contrast to the findings on maternal reference to feelings. The findings link up with our own research on moral development in showing that early conscience development was linked to the children's participation in this discourse about emotions (Dunn, Cutting, & Demetriou, 2000).

Other research that highlights the links between the security of early mother-child attachment, discourse about inner states, and children's social understanding is that of Meins and her colleagues (Meins, Fernyhough, Russell, & Clarke-Carter, 1998), which revealed that children who were securely attached were more successful on mind-reading tasks at four years, and showed greater "mentalizing" abilities at five. The mothers of the securely attached children, according to the researchers, showed particular sensitivity to their children's current level of understanding and used more mental-state terms in their interactions with them – a propensity Meins refers to as "mind-mindedness" (Meins, 1997).

In such research the complex links between the quality of children's relationships, the nature of the conversational world in which they grow up, and the development of their understanding of feelings are beginning to be clarified. The complexity of these links are highlighted by research into the development of children with problems in close relationships, for instance, the studies of young "hard-to-manage" children with problems in attention and inhibitory control.

New Directions: Research on Early Memory

A second exciting new direction in research on early emotional understanding is the work on understanding of the past, which brings together research on developments in memory and emotion, in children's explanations for people's emotions and behavior. As adults we understand that people's actions, emotions, and thoughts are shaped by events and experiences in the past, and as Lagattuta and Wellman (2001) put it: "Achieving a naïve psychological understanding of people requires more than just an awareness of a variety of states and occurrences (e.g., emotions, thoughts, actions) – children must learn to assemble these notions together to provide coherent, holistic explanations of their own and others' lives."

When do children begin to connect such past experiences and emotions to their explanations of why people behave the way they do? Laguttata and Wellman have conducted an intriguing set of experiments focusing on children's explanations for people's emotions in different sets of circumstances; the results indicate growing insight between three and five years of age in the ways that people's reactions to current experiences can be shaped by their emotional experiences from the past. Many three-year-olds, the majority of four-year-olds, and nearly all five- and six-year-olds in their studies could sometimes explain that a person's emotions were caused by being reminded about the past, a *"cognitive cuing" explanation* (Lagattuta, Wellman, & Flavell, 1997). These data are new in the sense that previous work has emphasized the limitations of children's ability to understand appraisal and thinking as a means for alleviating negative emotion. Laguttata and Wellman argue that preschoolers' explanations for negative emotions, particularly those that mismatch or are discordant with current situations, provide an early breeding ground for developing a coherent mental and historical understanding of people. They again emphasize the point that it is emotion understanding that provides the context for later key developments in understanding others. Young children, their data show, recognize that mental recollections are sometimes so powerful that they can induce emotions that do not match current reality – such as feeling angry in a conventionally happy situation because of angry thoughts or memories.

Parallel findings come from longitudinal research on children between four to seven years old, in which we asked the children about causes of sadness/anger/fear in themselves, mothers, siblings, and friends (Hughes & Dunn, 2002). There was an increase between four and seven years in reference to psychological causes of emotions, especially sadness, and explanations in terms of past memories were also given by the children at seven, as in the following comment made by a seven-year-old explaining why someone felt sad, in terms of thoughts about past emotions: "Because he thought of something in his past, something really worrying. . . ."

2. WHAT IS THE LONG-TERM SIGNIFICANCE OF THESE EARLY INDIVIDUAL DIFFERENCES?

From this research linking memory, talk, and emotion understanding we have learned both about normative developmental change and about individual differences. It is notable that such individual differences are marked in children's consideration of the psychological causes of emotions, as in other aspects of emotion understanding. Our second general question is what are the implications of these differences in early emotion understanding for children's later development? One of the striking findings of research over the last decade is the breadth of later differences in children's development that are linked to early differences in emotion understanding. While there is a well-worked area of developmental psychology that has focused on links between (variously termed) social competence, peer popularity, and aspects of "social cognition," three novel themes that have not received much attention will be the focus here: These are the significance of emotion understanding for later friendships, for later moral sensibility, and the costs of social understanding.

Significance for Later Friendships

The first topic concerns the significance of early emotion understanding and experiences with friends for later friendship. It relates to ideas on the representation of relationships; this is a notion familiar to attachment theorists. Here, however, we are concerned with representation of close friendships rather than attachment relationships with caregivers.

In our London research, we studied preschool children's emotion understanding and other sociocognitive skills, and the nature of their social experiences with friends. We included in the investigation the *friend's* sociocognitive abilities as potential contributors to a child's later abilities and friendships (Dunn et al., 2002). Of particular interest, the study examined not only children whose friendships were maintained over the transition to school, but also those whose friendships were "interrupted" or broken through circumstances and who therefore had to form new friendships after their transition to school. In this deprived area of London, many families moved between neighborhoods, were rehoused, and their children changed schools. The middle-class families in the sample were also quite mobile, and school changes interrupted several of their friendships.

What the analyses showed was that the quality of children's early friendships explained variance in the later friendships – specifically in the *insight* and *liking* of the friend at school age. In this pattern of association with the quality of friendship at school, it was not simply the child's own early emotional understanding but that of his/her preschool friend, and their shared pretend experiences, which independently contributed to the quality of their "new" school friendships three years later. The evidence indicates that representation of that earlier relationship was linked to the quality of the new relationships formed at school, and that the emotion understanding of *both* preschoolers in the original relationship were linked to the quality of the later friendship. The data illustrate the more general point that we need to view the development of emotion understanding within a relationship framework (Dunn, 2003).

Significance for Later Moral Sensibility

Early individual differences in emotion understanding are also related to later differences in the response of children to the moral issues that face them daily in their family and school lives – transgressions involving harm to others (accidental or intentional), cheating, breach of rules, lying, and deceiving. In two studies, one in the United States and one in London, we have found that children showing more emotion understanding at the preschool stage showed greater moral sensibility in their justifications about moral judgments years later (Dunn, Brown, & Maguire, 1995; Dunn et al., 2000).

Thus, moral judgments and justifications at school age were, in the London study, correlated with earlier emotion understanding, mind-reading skills, and language abilities. Regression analyses showed that emotion understanding contributed significant independent variance to the later differences in moral sensibility, beyond the variance explained by the other variables (Dunn et al., 2000). In a similar set of analyses we found not only that children's early emotion understanding, and their friends' early socioemotional understanding, but also their shared pretend experiences related to children's moral sensibility in their later school years. Again, the findings from the earlier study in Pennsylvania were replicated and extended in the London studies. And the key importance of viewing the development in social understanding within a relationship framework was again illustrated.

Are There Later Costs of Sophistication in Understanding Feelings?

The third point concerning the sequelae of early emotion understanding is rather different, and perhaps a surprise. It concerns the possible costs of early sophistication in reading minds and feelings. Early maturity in understanding the feelings and judgments of others does not guarantee a happy life. In both our U.S. and our London studies, we have found that the children who were especially sophisticated in early reading of others' feelings and inner states were, when they started school, particularly sensitive to other people's critical views of them, and were likely to judge their own failures in schoolwork more harshly than children who had not been so sensitive to other people during the preschool years. Early success on the assessments of emotion understanding predicted unique variance in the measure of sensitivity to criticism over and above the variance explained by concurrent sociocognitive abilities.

A similar picture emerged from interviews with children about their experiences in the first year of school. Children who had performed well on the preschool emotion understanding measure were, during their first year at school, more likely to describe difficulties with some of their peers – they were more likely to comment that some of the other children did not like them (Cutting & Dunn, 2002). In both the Pennsylvania study and the larger London study, the findings suggested that children who were particularly sensitive to the views, feelings, and judgments of other people in fact found some aspects of their social lives at school more painful.

3. WHAT CAN WE LEARN FROM THE STUDY OF CHILDREN WITH TROUBLED RELATIONSHIPS?

The longitudinal follow-up studies in the United States and U.K. described above give a consistent picture of the sequelae of early individual differences in emotion understanding and mind reading. These sequelae are not trivial, but are evident in the children's moral sensibility and the quality of their intimate relationships with friends – so central to the lives of children at school. The research highlights the potential significance of early social and emotional experiences with friends and siblings; it implicates talk and joint imaginative play as key social processes, as well as the usefulness of a relationship framework for understanding the development of understanding feelings. What, then, are the implications for children who have early problems in relating to other children, who do not experience the shared imaginative games that are a core feature of preschool friendships? What is the role of early emotion understanding and emotion regulation in the pattern of problems for these children?

Research on children who have problems of emotional and behavioral control and attention, termed by Campbell as "hard to manage" preschool children (Campbell, 1994, 1995), can help us to pursue the question of how emotion understanding and social relationships may be linked. The early onset of the combination of conduct disorder and attention problems that characterize these children carries long-term significance for a range of later problems and antisocial behavior. Epidemiological studies of hyperactive children indicate that it is dyadic relationships rather than popularity with a peer group that are particularly likely to trouble these children. Investigations of the processes underlying their difficulties have focused in particular on possible cognitive problems, problems of inhibitory control, and patterns of family relationships. In our longitudinal study of a community sample of children who as preschoolers were rated as hyperactive and conduct-disordered, and therefore at particular risk for later problems (Hughes et al., 2000), the children as four-year-olds indeed had a distinctive cognitive profile. They scored poorly on assessments of emotion understanding and affective perspective-taking, and on standard mind-reading tasks, and showed better understanding of belief dependency on emotions in the context of a *trick* rather than a *treat* (cf. the suggestion by Happe & Frith [1996] that such children have a theory of nasty minds).

The children also showed markedly antisocial behavior when playing with a friend (e.g., bullying, teasing, failing to respond empathetically when the friend was hurt, reacting with anger to unintentional actions by the friend). Other aspects of their friendships differed, too, from those of the control-group children, who were selected to be of the same gender, social background, and neighborhood. It was in the area of emotion regulation, emotion understanding, and inhibitory control that the children were most notably different from the control-group children.

Of particular interest were differences that became apparent when the children's pretend play was studied (Dunn & Hughes, 2001). Shared imaginative play is a core feature of friendship between four-year-olds. Not only did the "hard-to-manage" children engage less successfully in shared play with their friends, but the themes of their own pretend were much more likely to involve violence than the play of the other children. Thus, fighting, hurting, death, killing were common themes for these children (Dunn & Hughes, 2001). Most strikingly, the frequency with which children engaged in this violent pretend predicted both later antisocial behavior in a competitive situation (Hughes, Cutting & Dunn, 2001) and relative lack of moral sensibility (Hughes & Dunn, 2000).

Through their angry aggressive behavior, their failure to respond appropriately to the emotions of their friends, and their preoccupation with violence, these "hard-to-manage" children were missing those experiences with close friends that appear to foster understanding in others. Their communicative experiences at home were also different from those of the control children, containing less frequent connected conversations with their mothers (Brophy & Dunn, 2002). Thus the children's problems were far broader than a focus on cognitive difficulties might suggest; the pattern of results reminds us that we must pay attention to the emotional aspects of their interaction, their responses to their friends' emotions, and the quality of their relationships both with their friends and their mothers.

Parallel arguments have been put forward that individual differences in children's emotion processes and regulation may underlie some of the

individual differences that have been found in social information processing and empathy of bullies and aggressive children (Arsenio & Lemerise,
2001).

4. WHAT DO WE NEED TO KNOW NOW?

Research on emotional development within the framework of children's
close relationships has taught us some key lessons but has also raised a
series of challenging developmental questions. We have learned that if we
are to clarify how children use their emotional understanding, we have to
pay attention to the emotional quality of particular interactions and children's relationship goals; that we need to include both children's earlier
emotional experiences within particular relationships and their cognitive
abilities; that in studying the social processes implicated, attention has to be
paid to both affective and communicative dimensions of children's experiences in their relationships. To make any progress toward understanding
causal mechanisms, we need both experimental and naturalistic strategies.

Among the challenging questions raised, the following stand out:

*What developmental changes are there in the links between emotional experiences
and children's understanding of others?*

In early childhood, the significance of the affective context for the use
children make of their developing understanding of others' emotions is
clear. How does this change as children grow up? As children's powers
of metacognition increase, are they less at the mercy of their emotions, as
some of the research on children's handling of conflict indicates (Dunn &
Herrera, 1997)? Does the significance of emotion for what children learn in
particular interactions decrease?

*How is understanding of emotion related to other aspects of children's social
understanding?*

To what extent should understanding of emotion be differentiated from
other aspects of understanding inner states – for example, from their understanding of mind? Does the relation between these change as children
grow up? In the developmental account given by Bartsch and Estes (1996),
emotion understanding is seen as playing a foundational role: Understanding of cognitive states is thought to develop from the early understanding of emotion. Does this relation change as children grow through
middle childhood? More generally, should emotion understanding be seen
as one aspect of more general cognitive ability? One way of answering
the issue of how far emotion understanding and other aspects of cognitive abilities should be differentiated is through studying the sequelae of
early emotion understanding and mind-reading abilities. Here the story
so far is rather inconsistent, and needs further attention; the finding that

differences in attachment security are related to some aspects of understanding inner states *but not others* (Meins et al., 1998) also deserves further investigation.

Children with adjustment and relationship problems: How does their emotional understanding differ as they grow up?

With the exception of studies of autism, most research on the early beginnings of emotional understanding and relationships has focused on children within the normal range. The research on hard-to-manage preschool children has suggested that there is a range of intriguing differences in the children's early affective understanding, emotion regulation, executive function, and antisocial behavior, their communication with their parents and relationships with their friends. Studying these links in children who have language and communication problems would be of obvious value, both social and theoretical. Parallel arguments about the significance of emotional regulation and processing in social information processing of bullies and aggressive children highlight the importance of further research into these links (Arsenio & Lemerise, 2001).

More broadly, what is the relation of language and verbal communication to affective understanding as children grow up?

What is the significance of cultural and class differences for developmental pathways?

The focus of most research into affective development and understanding has been on middle-class children growing up in the United States and in Europe. Yet we know that educational differences are implicated in individual differences in socialization practices, in affective understanding, and in children's theory of mind abilities. We know, too, that cultural groups differ strikingly in emotional expression and regulation, in shared cultural concepts of their social world (Lutz & White, 1986; Shweder & LeVine, 1984). These cultural influences on the perception and classification of experiences are importantly mediated through relationships (Hinde, 1987). The challenge of investigating the links between children's emotional understanding, their interactions in which this understanding is fostered, and their varied cultural worlds is one that needs to be addressed in a far wider range of cultural groups, and within a developmental framework.

References

Arsenio, W. F., & Lemerise, E. A. (2001). Varieties of childhood bullying: Values, emotion processes, and social competence. *Social Development, 10(1),* 59–73.

Astington, J. W. (1993). *The child's discovery of the mind.* Cambridge, MA: Harvard University Press.

Bartsch, K., & Estes, D. (1996). Individual differences in children's developing theory of mind and implications for metacognition. *Learning and Individual Differences, 8(4)*, 281–304.

Bartsch, K., & Wellman, H. M. (1995). *Children talk about the mind.* Oxford: Oxford University Press.

Bretherton, I.; Fritz, J.; Zahn-Waxler, C.; & Ridgeway, D. (1986). Learning to talk about emotions: A functionalist perspective. *Child Development, 57*, 529–548.

Brophy, M., & Dunn, J. (2002). What did mummy say? Dyadic interactions between young 'hard-to-manage' children and their mothers. *Journal of Abnormal Child Psychology, 30*, 103–112.

Brown, J. R. (1995). What happened?: Emotional experience and children's talk about the past. Unpublished manuscript.

Brown, J. R.; Donelan-McCall, N.; & Dunn, J. (1996). Why talk about mental states? The significance of children's conversations with friends, siblings, and mothers. *Child Development, 67(3)*, 836–849.

Brown, J. R., & Dunn, J. (1992). Talk with your mother or your sibling? Developmental changes in early family conversations about feelings. *Child Development, 63(2)*, 336–349.

Campbell, S. B. (1994). Hard-to-manage preschool boys: Externalizing behavior, social competence, and family context at two-year follow-up. *Journal of Abnormal Child Psychology, 22(2)*, 147–166.

Campbell, S. B. (1995). Behavioural problems in preschool children: A review of recent research. *Journal of Child Psychology and Psychiatry and Allied Disciplines, 36*, 113–149.

Cassidy, J. C.; Parke, R. D.; Butkovsky, L.; & Braungart, J. M. (1992). Family-peer connections: The roles of emotional expressiveness within the family and children's understanding of emotions. *Child Development, 63*, 603–618.

Cutting, A., & Dunn, J. (2002). The cost of understanding other people: Social cognition predicts young children's sensitivity to criticism. *Journal of Child Psychology and Psychiatry, 43*, 849–860.

Cutting, A. L., & Dunn, J. (1999). Theory of mind, emotion understanding, language and family background: Individual differences and inter-relations. *Child Development, 70(4)*, 853–865.

Dunn, J. (1988). *The beginnings of social understanding* (1st ed.). Cambridge, MA: Harvard University Press.

Dunn, J. (2003). Emotional development in early childhood: A social relationship perspective. In R. J. Davidson, K. R. Scherer, and H. H. Goldsmith (Eds.), *Handbook of affective Sciences*. Oxford: Oxford University Press.

Dunn, J., & Brown, J. R. (1993). Early conversations about causality: Content, pragmatics and developmental change. *British Journal of Developmental Psychology, 11(2)*, 107–123.

Dunn, J., & Brown, J. R. (1994). Affect expression in the family, children's understanding of emotions, and their interactions with others. Special Issue: Children's emotions and social competence. *Merrill Palmer Quarterly, 40(1)*, 120–137.

Dunn, J.; Brown, J. R.; & Beardsall, L. (1991a). Family talk about feeling states and children's later understanding of others' emotions. *Developmental Psychology, 27(3)*, 448–455.

Dunn, J.; Brown, J. R.; Slomkowski, C.; Tesla, C.; & Youngblade, L. (1991b). Young children's understanding of other people's feelings and beliefs: Individual differences and their antecedents. *Child Development, 62(6),* 1352–1366.

Dunn, J.; Brown, J. R.; & Maguire, M. (1995). The development of children's moral sensibility: Individual differences and emotion understanding. *Developmental Psychology, 31(4),* 649–659.

Dunn, J.; Cutting, A.; & Demetriou, H. (2000). Moral sensibility, understanding others, and children's friendship interactions in the preschool period. *British Journal of Developmental Psychology, 18(2),* 159–178.

Dunn, J.; Cutting, A.; & Fisher, N. (2002). Old friends, new friends: Predictors of children's perspectives on their friends at school. *Child Development, 73,* 621–635.

Dunn, J., & Herrera, C. (1997). Conflict resolution with friends, siblings, and mothers: A developmental perspective. *Aggressive Behavior, 23,* 343–357.

Dunn, J., & Hughes, C. (1998). Young children's understanding of emotions within close relationships. *Cognition and Emotion, 12(2),* 171–190.

Dunn, J., & Hughes, C. (2001). "I got some swords and you're dead!": Fantasy and friendship in young "hard to manage" children. *Child Development, 72,* 491–505.

Dunn, J., & Kendrick, C. (1982). *Siblings: Love, envy and understanding.* London: Grant McIntyre, Ltd.

Eisenberg, N. (2000). Emotion, regulation, and moral development. *Annual Review of Psychology, 51,* 665–697.

Eisenberg, N.; Fabes, R. A.; Murphy, M.; Maszk, P.; Smith, M.; & Karbon, M. (1995). The role of emotionality and regulation in children's social functioning: A longitudinal study. *Child Development, 66,* 1239–1261.

Fivush, R. (1991). Gender and emotion in mother-child conversations about the past. *Journal of Narrative and Life History, 1,* 325–341.

Fivush, R.; Gray, J. T.; & Fromhoff, F. A. (1987). Two-year-olds talk about the past. *Cognitive Development, 2,* 393–409.

Goldsmith, H. H.; Lemery, K. S.; Buss, K. A.; & Campos, J. (1999). Genetic analyses of focal aspects of infant temperament. *Developmental Psychology, 35,* 972–985.

Happe, F., & Frith, U. (1996). Theory of mind and social impairment in children with conduct disorder. *British Journal of Developmental Psychology, 14,* 385–398.

Hinde, R. A. (1987). *Individuals, relationships, cultures.* Cambridge: Cambridge University Press.

Howe, N.; Petrakos, H.; & Rinaldi, C. (1998). "All the sheeps are dead. He murdered them": Sibling pretense, negotiation, internal state language and relationship quality. *Child Development, 69(1),* 182–191.

Hudson, J. A.; Gebelt, J.; Haviland, J.; & Bentivegna, C. (1992). Emotion and narrative structure in young children's personal accounts. *Journal of Narrative and Life History, 2,* 129–150.

Hughes, C., & Cutting, A. (1999). Nature, nurture and individual differences in early understanding of mind. *Psychological Science, 10(5),* 429–432.

Hughes, C., & Dunn, J. (1998). Understanding mind and emotion: Longitudinal associations with mental-state talk between young friends. *Developmental Psychology, 34(5),* 1026–1037.

Hughes, C., & Dunn, J. (2000). Hedonism or empathy?: Hard-to-manage children's moral awareness, and links with cognitive and maternal characteristics. *British Journal of Developmental Psychology, 18(2),* 227–245.

Hughes, C., & Dunn, J. (2002). "When I say a naughty word." Children's accounts of anger and sadness in self, mother, and friend: Longitudinal findings from ages four to seven. *British Journal of Developmental Psychology, 20,* 515–535.

Hughes, C.; Cutting, A. L.; & Dunn, J. (2001). Acting nasty in the face of failure: Longitudinal observations of "hard to manage" children playing a rigged competitive game with a friend. *Journal of Abnormal Child Psychology, 29,* 403–416.

Hughes, C.; White, A.; Sharpen, J.; & Dunn, J. (2000). Antisocial, angry and unsympathetic: 'Hard to manage' preschoolers' peer problems, and possible social and cognitive influences. *Journal of Child Psychology and Psychiatry, 41(2),* 169–179.

Lagattuta, K. H., & Wellman, H. M. (2001). Thinking about the past: Early knowledge about links between prior experience, thinking, and emotion. *Child Development, 72,* 82–102.

Lagattuta, K. H.; Wellman, H. M.; & Flavell, J. H. (1997). Preschoolers' understanding of the link between thinking and feeling: Cognitive cuing and emotional change. *Child Development, 68(6),* 1081–1104.

Laible, D. J., & Thompson, R. A. (2000). Mother-child discourse, attachment security, shared positive affect, and early conscience development. *Child Development, 71,* 1424–1440.

Lutz, C., & White, G. M. (1986). The anthropology of emotions. *Annual Review of Anthropology, 15,* 405–436.

Meins, A.; Fernyhough, C.; Russell, J. T.; & Clarke-Carter, D. (1998). Security of attachment as a predictor of symbolic and mentalising abilities: A longitudinal study. *Social Development, 7,* 1–24.

Meins, E. (1997). *Security of attachment and the social development of cognition.* Hove: Psychology Press.

Newton, P. (1994). Preschool prevarication: An investigation of the cognitive prerequisites for deception. Ph.D., diss., Portsmouth University.

Newton, P. E., & Reddy, V. (Submitted). Pseudo-constructs in developmental theorising: The case of pseudo-deception.

Perner, J. (1991). *Understanding the representational mind.* Cambridge: MIT Press.

Shweder, R. A., & LeVine, R. A. (1984). *Culture Theory.* Cambridge: Cambridge University Press.

Smiley, P., & Huttenlocher, J. (1989). Young children's acquisition of emotion concepts. In C. Saarni and P. Harris (Eds.), *Children's understanding of emotion: Cambridge studies in social and emotional development* (Vol. 9, pp. 27–49). New York: Cambridge University Press.

Stein, N., & Miller, C. (1993). A theory of argumentative understanding: Relationships among position preference, judgements of goodness, memory and reasoning. *Argumentation, 7,* 183–204. Amsterdam: Kluwer Academic Publishers.

Stern, D. (1985). *The interpersonal world of the infant.* New York: Basic Books.

Wellman, H.; Harris, P.; Banerjee, M.; & Sinclair, A. (1995). Early understanding of emotion: Evidence from natural language. *Cognition and Emotion, 9,* 117–149.

19

Emotional Intelligence

What Do We Know?

Peter Salovey, Marja Kokkonen, Paulo N. Lopes, and
John D. Mayer

ABSTRACT

This chapter describes recent advances in the scientific study of emotional intelligence. Setting the idea of an emotional intelligence in a historical context, the authors' four-branch model of these competencies is then described. Research on the measurement of emotional intelligence, especially as a set of abilities rather than as self-reported personality traits, is described. The psychometric properties of a new measure of emotional intelligence, the Mayer-Salovey-Caruso Emotional Intelligence Test (MSCEIT), are presented, as are preliminary findings concerning the predictive validity of this construct in the domains of family, school, and workplace.

The starting point for the idea that there could be an emotional intelligence is that, rather than "hijacking" one's thoughts and behaviors (Goleman, 1995, p. 13), emotions often serve adaptive, purposeful, and helpful functions (Leeper, 1948). It is the emotional system, in this view, that focuses attention, organizes memory, helps us to interpret social situations, and motivates relevant behavior. Accordingly, it makes little sense to place emotions in opposition to reason and rationality (de Sousa, 1987). The concept of emotional intelligence, which elsewhere (e.g., Mayer & Salovey, 1997) we have defined as the ability to perceive, understand, manage, and use emotional information, simply takes this functionalist perspective one step further by calling attention to the need for research on individual differences in the ability to reason about emotions and to use emotions in reasoning.

Although the idea of an emotional intelligence strikes some investigators as nearly an impossibility (e.g., Roberts, Zeidner, & Matthews, 2001),

Preparation of this chapter was facilitated by grants from the National Cancer Institute (R01-CA68427), the National Institute of Mental Health (P01-MH/DA56826), and the Donaghue Women's Health Investigator Program at Yale to Peter Salovey and a fellowship from the Portuguese Science and Technology Foundation to Paulo N. Lopes. For more information about obtaining the MSCEIT for research, see *www.emotionaliq.org*.

321

neuroscientists such as Damasio (1984) have provided colorful examples of the kinds of cognitive and behavioral deficits that result when individuals suffer damage to centers of the brain integral to the perception and experience of emotion. We share his view that "higher cognition requires the guidance provided by emotion" (Adolphs & Damasio, 2001, p. 45). Not that emotions cannot, on occasion, leave us terribly misguided, but we believe greater emphasis should be placed on the fact that we have evolved an intelligent emotional system rather than a set of vestigial processes no longer relevant to thinking and acting in the modern world (Darwin, 1872).

The idea that individuals might differ in the skills with which they identify and understand their emotions, manage these feelings, and use them to think rationally and behave adaptively is not actually new. The history of psychological research on emotion has witnessed attempts to measure, for example, accuracy in recognizing emotions (e.g., Buck, 1976, 1984; Gross & Bailif, 1991; Campbell, Kagan, & Krathwohl, 1971; Kagan, 1978; Rosenthal, Hall, Archer, DiMatteo, & Rogers, 1979); communicating emotional expressions in the face (e.g., Hall, 1984), using words to describe feelings (e.g., Bagby, Parker, & Taylor, 1993a, 1993b; Bretherton, Fritz, Zahn-Waxler, & Ridgeway, 1986; Lane, Quinlan, Schwartz, Walker, & Zeitlin, 1990); appreciating display rules (e.g., Saarni, 1979); responding with empathy (e.g., Flury & Ickes, 2001; Ickes, 1993; Mehrabian & Epstein, 1970); and managing emotions with self-regulatory strategies (e.g., Thayer, Newman, & McClain, 1994). Indeed, other investigators have developed frameworks organizing emotional competencies from developmental (e.g., Saarni, 1990, 1999) and other perspectives (e.g., Garner, 1983). For some reason, however, labeling these individual differences as an "intelligence," as we did more than a decade ago, somehow catapulted this field of study into the public imagination (Salovey & Mayer, 1990; see also Payne, 1986, for another use of the term "emotional intelligence"). A best-selling, popular book titled *Emotional Intelligence* certainly helped things along (Goleman, 1995).

It is the purpose of this chapter to argue that the idea of an emotional intelligence is a scientifically reasonable one, that such skills can be measured, and that they predict relevant outcomes. Although the term "emotional intelligence" is now used in many domains – from school-based programs to organizational development (Caruso & Wolfe, 2001; Elias, Hunter, & Kress, 2001), we argue that dismissive attitudes toward the idea are not warranted (Barrett, Miguel, Tan, & Hurd, 2001; Davies, Stankov, & Roberts, 1998; Stankov, 2000). Moreover, we believe that the identification of individual differences in the recognition, understanding, management, and use of emotions may give rise to an increased focus on ideographic aspects of emotional experiences in theorizing about emotion. Whether in philosophy, the neurosciences, or psychology, emotion theory in the past two decades has largely taken a nomothetic approach, identifying, for example, the triggers in the environment or in shared cognitive representations that give rise to emotion. Because individuals vary in the competency with which they process information relevant to emotion or use emotion in reasoning processes, these normative models may not capture variability in actual experiences. As an example, consider the classic romantic jealousy triad: Person O threatens to take X away from Person P. Person P experiences jealousy as he or she becomes aware of the possible loss of the relationship with X. In some individuals, this awareness manifests itself in feelings of anxiety, in others deep sorrow, and in still others, anger and, perhaps, homicidal rage (Salovey & Rodin, 1986, 1989). We believe that the construct of emotional intelligence allows investigators to focus on some of the potential roots of these individual differences.

A FOUR-BRANCH MODEL OF EMOTIONAL INTELLIGENCE

We began work on a model of emotional intelligence in the late 1980s by reviewing the research literature and asking what emotion-related skills and abilities had modern investigators of emotion tried – successfully or not – to operationalize over the years (reviewed in Salovey, Woolery, & Mayer, 2001). Could we pull these skills together into a coherent whole? It seemed that these skills could be grouped into four clusters or "branches" (Mayer & Salovey, 1997; Salovey & Mayer, 1990): (1) perceiving emotions; (2) using emotions to facilitate thought; (3) understanding emotions; and (4) managing emotions in a way that enhances personal growth and social relations. We view a distinction between the second branch (using emotions) and the other three. Whereas the first, third, and fourth branch all involve reasoning about emotions, the second branch uniquely involves using emotions to enhance reasoning. The four branches form a hierarchy, with perceiving emotion as the most fundamental or basic-level skill and managing emotions as the most superordinate skill; the ability to regulate emotions in oneself and others is built up from the competencies represented by the other three branches. We have reviewed the literature concerning individual differences in these four sets of skills elsewhere (e.g., Mayer, Salovey, & Caruso, 2000a, 2000b; Salovey, Bedell, Detweiler, & Mayer, 2000; Salovey, Mayer, & Caruso, 2002; Salovey, Woolery, & Mayer, 2001), although we provide a brief summary here and in Table 19.1.

Perceiving Emotions

Emotional perception involves registering, attending to, and deciphering emotional messages as they are expressed in facial expressions, voice tone, or cultural artifacts. Individuals differ in their abilities to discern the emotional content of such stimuli. These competencies are basic information-processing skills in which the relevant information consists of feelings and mood states. For example, some individuals, called *alexithymic*, have

TABLE 19.1. *The Four-Branch Model of Emotional Intelligence*

Branch Names and Exemplary Skills

Branch 1: Perceiving Emotion
- Ability to identify emotion in one's physical and psychological states
- Ability to identify emotion in other people
- Ability to express emotions accurately and to express needs related to them
- Ability to discriminate between accurate/honest and inaccurate/dishonest feelings

Branch 2: Using Emotions to Facilitate Thought
- Ability to redirect and prioritize thinking on the basis of associated feelings
- Ability to generate emotions to facilitate judgment and memory
- Ability to capitalize on mood changes to appreciate multiple points of view
- Ability to use emotional states to facilitate problem solving and creativity

Branch 3: Understanding Emotions
- Ability to understand relationships among various emotions
- Ability to perceive the causes and consequences of emotions
- Ability to understand complex feelings, emotional blends, and contradictory states
- Ability to understand transitions among emotions

Branch 4: Managing Emotions
- Ability to be open to feelings, both pleasant and unpleasant
- Ability to monitor and reflect on emotions
- Ability to engage in, prolong, or detach from an emotional state
- Ability to manage emotions in oneself
- Ability to manage emotions in others

difficulty expressing their emotions verbally, presumably because they have difficulty identifying those feelings (Apfel & Sifneos, 1979).

Using Emotions to Facilitate Thought

This second branch of emotional intelligence focuses on how emotion affects the cognitive system and, as such, can be harnessed for more effective problem-solving, reasoning, decision-making, and creative endeavors. Of course, cognition can be disrupted by emotions, such as anxiety and fear, but emotions also can prioritize the cognitive system to attend to what is important (Easterbrook, 1959; Mandler, 1975; Simon, 1982), and even to focus on what it does best in a given mood (e.g., Palfai & Salovey, 1993; Schwarz, 1990).

Understanding Emotions

The most fundamental competency at this level concerns the ability to label emotions with words and to recognize the relationships among exemplars of the affective lexicon. The emotionally intelligent individual is able to recognize that the terms used to describe emotions are arranged into families and that groups of emotion terms form fuzzy sets (Ortony, Clore, & Collins, 1988). Perhaps more important, the relations among these terms are deduced – that annoyance and irritation can lead to rage if the provocative stimulus is not eliminated, or that envy often is experienced in contexts that also evoke jealousy (Salovey & Rodin, 1986, 1989). This is the branch of emotional intelligence that we would expect to be most related to verbal intelligence, as typically assessed.

Managing Emotions

The emotionally intelligent individual can repair her negative moods and emotions and maintain positive moods and emotions when doing so is appropriate (it is also sometimes desirable to maintain negative emotional states, such as when one anticipates having to discipline an employee, negotiate with a car salesman, or compete against an enemy). This regulatory process comprises several steps. Individuals must (*a*) believe that they can modify their emotions; (*b*) monitor their moods and emotional states accurately; (*c*) identify and discriminate those moods and emotions in need of regulation; (*d*) employ strategies to change these moods and emotions, most commonly, to alleviate negative feelings or maintain positive feelings; and (*e*) assess the effectiveness of those strategies.

Individuals differ in the expectancy that they can alleviate negative moods. Some people believe that when they are upset they can do something that will make them feel better; others insist that nothing will improve their negative moods. Individuals who believe they can successfully repair their moods engage in active responses to stress, whereas people low in self-efficacy of regulation display avoidance responses, as well as depressive and mild somatic symptoms (Cantanzaro & Greenwood, 1994; Goldman, Kraemer, & Salovey, 1996). The ability to help others enhance their moods is also an aspect of emotional intelligence, as individuals often rely on their social networks to provide not just a practical but an emotional buffer against negative life events (Stroebe & Stroebe, 1996). Moreover, individuals appear to derive a sense of efficacy and social worth from helping others feel better and by contributing to the joy of loved ones.

Integration and Definition

Our definition of emotional intelligence relies heavily on the four-branch model presented above. We consider emotional intelligence an actual intelligence, in the psychological sense of that term, and define it more generally as: "the ability to recognize the meanings of emotions and their relationships, and to reason and problem-solve on the basis of them. Emotional intelligence is involved in the capacity to perceive emotion, assimilate emotion-related feelings [to facilitate cognitive activities], understand the information of those of emotions, and manage them" (Mayer, Caruso, & Salovey, 1999, p. 267).

It is important to distinguish this kind of ability- or competence-based definition of emotional intelligence from those which have been generated by writers focused more on the general public. Goleman (1995, p. 22) based his definition of emotional intelligence on our original one (Salovey & Mayer, 1990), but broadened it to include "knowing one's emotions . . . managing emotions . . . motivating oneself . . . recognizing emotions in others . . . and handling relationships." By 1998, however, Goleman's (1998) definition had so strayed from this conceptualization that it is nearly unrecognizable as related to emotional abilities, including such attributes as self-confidence, trustworthiness, innovation, initiative, optimism, political awareness, and team capabilities. As another example, the developer of a self-report measure of emotional intelligence called the EQi defines emotional intelligence as "an array of noncognitive capabilities, competencies, and skills that influence one's ability to succeed in coping with environmental demands and pressures" (Bar-On, 1997, p. 14) and includes self-actualization, social responsibility, reality testing, impulse control, and optimism. We believe that research progress will be facilitated by definitions that are more narrowly focused on emotional skills and competencies rather than a broad array of valued traits that have in common only the fact that they are not measured by conventional intelligence tests.

MEASURING EMOTIONAL INTELLIGENCE AS A SET OF ABILITIES

We have been working with two task-based tests of emotional intelligence, the Multifactor Emotional Intelligence Scale (MEIS) and the Mayer-Salovey-Caruso Emotional Intelligence Test (MSCEIT). The first represented an attempt merely to show that measuring emotional intelligence reliably as an ability was feasible. The second is a more professional and user-friendly assessment battery, and the one that we recommend for research and applied use. It is considerably shorter and better normed than the MEIS. Elsewhere, we have tried to make the case that ability-based measures may be a more appropriate way to operationalize our model of emotional intelligence as compared to self-report inventories (Mayer, Caruso, & Salovey, 2000).

The Multifactor Emotional Intelligence Scale (MEIS)

The first comprehensive, theory-based battery for assessing emotional intelligence as a set of abilities was the Multifactor Emotional Intelligence

Scale (MEIS), which can be administered through interaction with a computer program or via pencil and paper (Mayer, Caruso, & Salovey, 1998, 1999). The MEIS comprises twelve ability measures divided into four branches, reflecting the model of emotional intelligence presented earlier: (1) perceiving and expressing emotions; (2) using emotions to facilitate thought and other cognitive activities; (3) understanding emotion; and (4) managing emotion in self and others (Mayer & Salovey, 1997). Branch 1 tasks measure emotional perception in Faces, Music, Designs, and Stories. The second branch measures Synesthesia Judgments (e.g., "How hot is anger?") and Feeling Biases (translating felt emotions into judgments about people). Branch 3's four tasks examine the understanding of emotion. Sample questions include, "Optimism most closely combines which two emotions?" A participant should choose "pleasure and anticipation" over less specific alternatives such as "pleasure and joy." Branch 4's two tests measure Emotion Management in the Self and in Others. These tasks ask participants to read scenarios and then rate four reactions to them according to how effective they are as emotion management strategies focused on the self or on others.

The Mayer-Salovey-Caruso Emotional Intelligence Test (MSCEIT)

More recently, we have developed a test of emotional intelligence in an attempt to improve upon the psychometric qualities of the MEIS while shortening the battery to about thirty minutes (Mayer, Salovey, & Caruso, 2001). The Mayer-Salovey-Caruso Emotional Intelligence Test (MSCEIT) contains 141 items, with two subtasks for each of the four branches of emotional intelligence, as illustrated in Table 19.2. Like the MEIS, the MSCEIT can be scored according to a general consensus criterion. That is, if .56 of the sample says that there is a moderate amount of happiness in a face, and a participant agrees, his or her score is incremented by .56. As reported by Mayer, Salovey, Caruso, and Sitarenios (2001), when over two thousand participants' scores on the MSCEIT were calculated, the full-scale, split-half reliability was over .90, and reliabilities for each of the four branches ranged from $r = .79$ to .91 using consensus scoring and $r = .77$ to .90 using expert scoring (these two types of scoring are described below). The progression of tests from the MEIS to various versions of the MSCEIT showed a gradual rise in reliability at the level of the individual tasks. Whereas using consensus scoring on the twelve tasks of the MEIS yielded individual task reliabilities ranging from Cronbach's alphas of .49 to .94 (Mayer et al., 1999), similar scoring for the eight tasks of the MSCEIT V2.0 outlined in Table 19.2 yielded individual task split-half correlations from $r = .65$ to .88 and reliabilities for the four branches from $r = .79$ to .91. (Mayer, Salovey, Caruso & Sitarenios, 2003). Nonetheless, we recommend scoring the MSCEIT at the branch level but not at the task level.

TABLE 19.2. *The Four-Branch Model of Emotional Intelligence as Operationalized by the Mayer-Salovey-Caruso Emotional Intelligence Test (MSCEIT V2.0)*

Branch Names and Exemplary Tasks

Branch 1: Perceiving Emotion
- *Faces*: Identifying emotions expressed in faces
- *Pictures*: Identifying emotions suggested by photographs of landscapes and abstract artistic designs

Branch 2: Using Emotions to Facilitate Thought
- *Sensations*: Matching tactile, taste, and color terms to specific emotions
- *Facilitation*: Indicating how moods and emotions affect cognitive processes such as thinking, reasoning, problem solving, and creativity

Branch 3: Understanding Emotions
- *Blends*: Identifying the emotions that may encompass a complex feeling state
- *Changes*: Noticing how feelings and emotions progress or traverse from one state to another

Branch 4: Managing Emotions
- *Management*: Estimating the effectiveness of various strategies that could modify one's feelings in various situations
- *Relationships*: Estimating the consequences of various strategies for emotional reactions involving other people

Scoring Systems

An issue that comes up in task-based tests of emotional intelligence concerns what constitutes the correct answer. We have experimented with three different criteria for determining the "correct" answer to questions such as identifying the emotions in facial expressions or making suggestions about the most adaptive way to handle emotions in difficult situations. The first involves *target* criteria. Here, we would ask the person whose facial expression is depicted on our test item what he or she was feeling. To the extent that the respondent's answer matched the target's, the answer would be scored as correct. A second approach is to use *expert* criteria. In this strategy, experts on emotion such as psychotherapists or emotion researchers would read test items and provide answers. To the extent that the respondent's answers matched those of the experts, they would be scored as correct. Lastly, the *consensus* criterion involves norming the test on a large, heterogeneous sample. The test taker now receives credit for endorsing answers that match those of the larger group.

One might think that a consensus or a target criterion would not be an appropriate approach to scoring tasks measuring emotional competence. After all, aren't most people misguided about their true feelings? We were able to look at how the target, expert, and consensus criteria are interrelated across some of the MEIS ability tasks. The correlations were actually rather high; half were above r = .52 (Mayer, Caruso, & Salovey, 1999).

As with the MEIS, we used expert and consensus scoring for the MSCEIT, but not target scoring. Rather than using two authors as experts, which is what we had done for the MEIS, however, we asked twenty-one members of the International Society for Research on Emotion (ISRE) to answer the MSCEIT questions. We then scored the MSCEIT according to an expert-consensus criterion, based on the proportion of experts from ISRE who answered each item in a particular way. When over two thousand participants' scores on the MSCEIT were calculated by general- and by expert-consensus scoring, the intercorrelation between the two sets of scores was greater than .90 (Mayer, Salovey, Caruso, & Sitarenios, 2001, 2003).

The Validity of EI Scores

The MSCEIT appears to show appropriate discriminant validity from measures of analytic intelligence and many personality constructs. In a data set collected from 103 college undergraduates (Lopes, Salovey, & Straus, 2003), the MSCEIT was administered along with various personality measures. MSCEIT scores did not appear to be associated with social desirability (Crowne & Marlowe, 1960) or mood. They were not related to scores on measures of public and private self-consciousness (Fenigstein, Scheier, & Buss, 1975), and self-esteem (Rosenberg, 1965). Verbal intelligence, as assessed by the WAIS-III vocabulary subscale and Verbal SAT scores (ranges on both were somewhat restricted in this sample), correlated modestly with the Understanding Emotions branch of the MSCEIT (which relies on knowledge of emotional vocabulary), but verbal intelligence did not correlate significantly with any of the other branches or with the total score.

The correlations between the MSCEIT and the Big Five personality traits (Costa & McCrae, 1992) were generally low. The highest correlation was between the managing emotions branch of he MSCEIT and agreeableness (r = .33). There is clearly discriminant validity with respect to traditional personality constructs when emotional intelligence is measured with the MSCEIT. Other studies using the MSCEIT have also yielded relatively low correlations with personality traits, although these correlations vary to some extent with differences in samples and the personality measures used (Salovey, Mayer, Caruso, & Lopes, 2003).

Two self-report measures tapping the quality of one's social interactions provided some evidence for the convergent validity of the MSCEIT in the Lopes et al. data set. The Managing Emotions branch of the MSCEIT was associated with the Positive Relations with Others subscale of Ryff's (1989) Scales of Psychological Well-Being. This scale assesses satisfaction with the quality of one's engagement in, and support obtained from, the social domain of life. All four branches of the MSCEIT were inversely associated with the negative interaction (with close friend) factor of the Network of Relationship Inventory (NRI; Furman & Buhrmester, 1985). This scale assesses conflict and antagonism in the relationship. The Managing Emotions branch of the MSCEIT also was related to the Social Support factor of the NRI in relation to a parent. This scale measures the degree of companionship, intimacy, and affection in the relationship. The relationships between the MSCEIT and these measures of self-perceived quality of social interaction remained significant even when we controlled statistically for personality traits and verbal intelligence.

There were relatively weak associations between the MSCEIT and self-report measures of the meta-mood experience (the way individuals reflect on their moods). We found correlations in the .2 to .3 range between the MSCEIT branches of Managing and Understanding Emotions and the Mood Repair factor of the Trait Meta-Mood Scale (TMMS; Salovey et al., 1995), which taps into the use of optimistic thinking to regulate negative moods. However, only an abbreviated (although reliable) version of the TMMS was used in this study.

Because the MSCEIT was published in 2001, there are few completed studies in which it has been used to predict actual outcomes in the workplace, home, or school. However, the precursor to the MSCEIT, the MEIS, was used in many studies in several different laboratories, and these findings suggest that the four-branch theory of emotional intelligence has predictive validity. Trinidad and Johnson (2002), for example, explored the relation between emotional intelligence and substance abuse among southern California teenagers. Youths with higher emotional intelligence scores were less likely to have ever smoked cigarettes or to have smoked recently, and were less likely to have used alcohol in the recent past. Schoolchildren scoring higher on the MEIS were rated as being less aggressive by their peers and as more prosocial by teachers than those students with low emotional intelligence (Rubin, 1999). Insurance company customer claim team leaders with higher as compared to lower MEIS scores were rated by their managers as being more effective, and overall team performance for customer service was also correlated with the teams' average MEIS scores (Rice, 1999). Emotional intelligence, as measured by the MEIS, also is associated with scores on measures of empathy (Ciarrochi, Chan, & Caputi, 2000; Mayer, Caruso, & Salovey, 1999; Rubin, 1999) and life satisfaction (Ciarrochi et al., 2000). In a study using a preliminary version of the MSCEIT among other measures, Barchard (2000) found that emotional intelligence predicted year-end grades among college students even after cognitive abilities (e.g., verbal ability, verbal closure, inductive reasoning, visualization) and personality variables (e.g., Big Five) were taken into account. Similarly, scores on the managing emotions branch of the MSCEIT predicted the quality of interactions with opposite-sex individuals (Lopes, Brackett, Nezlek, Schütz, Sellin, & Salovey, in press). Although these findings must be viewed as preliminary, they represent promising suggestions that emotional intelligence can predict relevant behaviors in various life domains, such as school, work, and family. Whether the interesting relationships involving the MEIS are replicated with the MSCEIT awaits further research.

Neuroscience

The validity of emotional intelligence can be established in ways other than merely showing that scores on tests like the MSCEIT predict relevant outcomes in the school, workplace, and social situations. One of these ways is to look at the brain. As the pathways involving the processing of emotional-relevant information are elucidated (for recent reviews, see Dolan & Morris, 2000; Lane, 2000; LeDoux, 1996, 2000), one can attempt to establish that the component skills involved in emotional intelligence have more than just a psychometric reality but also a neurological one.

Such work is beginning to appear in the neuroscience literature. For example, Jaušovec, Jaušovec, and Gerlič (2001) used the MSCEIT to create two groups of participants, those with low-to-average emotional intelligence (Mean = 89, range from 60 to 114) and those with above average emotional intelligence (Mean = 120, range from 116 to 128). These individuals were asked to judge the emotions in pictures of people's faces displayed on a computer. At the same time, EEG activity was monitored over nineteen scalp locations. Overall, there was a significant correlation between MSCEIT scores and EEG frequency, $r (45) = .45$. More important, the groups differed in event-related and induced brain activity in the theta, lower-2 alpha, and upper alpha bands. Individuals scoring higher on the MSCEIT showed less desynchronization in the upper alpha band generally and at the C4 and T6 electrode locations in the lower-2 alpha band. Because desynchronization in the lower alpha band is thought to be related to attentional processes, whereas decreased activity in the upper alpha band is related to semantic memory processes (Klimesch, 1999), Jaušovec and colleagues interpret their findings as meaning that highly emotionally intelligent individuals require less cortical activity needed for tasks like this one, but that those individuals lower in emotional intelligence are less efficient at decoding the semantic meaning of pictures of emotional faces. Their findings suggest that individuals with greater emotional intelligence had fewer problems identifying displayed emotions and used a strategy that was less verbal and semantic and more attentional. Because these findings parallel those for individuals higher or lower in verbal and performance intelligence (Neubauer, Sange, & Pfurtscheller, 1999), Jaušovec et al. believe that emotional intelligence is a distinct component of general intelligence (2001). Obviously, these findings are quite preliminary, and a more fine-grained analysis would examine emotional intelligence at the level of the four branches of our model. Studies using fMRI would seem especially valuable.

CRITICISM

The very idea of an emotional intelligence strikes some as inherently contradictory. The field of psychology, and the broader culture, have often viewed emotions as erratic, immature, and irrational – poor guides to action. Emotions are seen as the very antithesis of a reliable, consistent human intelligence, often depicted as cool, cognitive processes based on so-called rational knowledge. Such a viewpoint may well be a carryover from the Stoics of ancient Greece. Whatever its origins, however, it is a pervasive philosophy. An opposing idea is that emotions contain information that one might use in reasoning, which departs dramatically from this cultural belief (see Mayer, Salovey, & Caruso, 2000a, for a review of EI as a historical and cultural phenomenon). The claim that emotional intelligence not only exists but is, in fact, a standard intelligence is, perhaps, even more radical and controversial. Over the past decade, we have been developing just that idea (Mayer & Salovey, 1997; Mayer, Caruso, & Salovey, 1999; Mayer, Salovey, Caruso, & Sitarenios, 2001, 2003; Salovey & Mayer, 1990).

The most systematic challenges to the idea of an emotional intelligence have come from Roberts and his colleagues (e.g., Roberts, Zeidner, & Matthews, 2001). They are most concerned that questions on tests like the MEIS and MSCEIT do not have an objectively "correct" answer (as would, say, a block-design task on a traditional intelligence test). They are concerned that matching test takers' responses to consensual norms may be a valid way of measuring social conformity but not emotional skills. They also worry about deviations between scores based on general consensus versus expert algorithms, although, as discussed earlier, we report substantial overlap between the two types of scoring (Mayer, Salovey, Caruso, & Sitarenios, 2001, 2003).

It is not ridiculous to argue that there could be "right" answers with respect to questions about emotions. Emotions do convey set meanings, which philosophers have been elucidating for centuries. For example, the experience of anger often designates the presence of a real or perceived injustice or blockage of a desired goal. The experience of sadness indicates a real or perceived loss. In addition, there are evolutionary bases for the meanings of many emotions (e.g., Darwin, 1872). Moreover, emotions develop in predictable patterns that are interrelated with developments in complex social situations. For example, if a person is happy and sad at the same time, only some types or patterns of events could bring about such a reaction, and intelligence is necessary to track down the sort of event that brings such feelings about (e.g., a close-by friend finding a much-wanted job in a faraway city). Emotions, in other words, satisfy a complex, coherent, and consistent symbol system that can be puzzled over, understood, and planned for, in abstract thought.

Moreover, even the developers of so-called objective intelligence tests such as the WAIS relied on consensual and/or expert judgment to establish the correctness of responses for some of the subtasks. For example, the manual for the WAIS-III describes the following procedure that was used to arrive at correct answers for some of the items:

> To refine the scoring criteria of those subtests for which many acceptable responses are possible (Vocabulary, Similarities, Information, and Comprehension . . .), the development team conducted several scoring studies. . . . Two team members independently coded each response, identified discrepancies between the code assignments, and resolved the differences so that each response had only one code. At this point, team members had to agree on the groupings of responses and the assignment of codes but not on what score value to assign a code. . . . After the codes were assigned, the team evaluated the quality of the responses and assigned a score value (0, 1, or 2) to each code on the basis of the accuracy of the response. (The Psychological Corporation, 1997, p. 37)

Although there is a subjectivity to deciding upon ideal answers with respect to tests measuring emotional intelligence, it would be wrong to claim that this is in contrast to the assessment of standard, analytic intelligence. In matters related to social interaction, it is difficult to draw a clear-cut distinction between objective knowledge or skill, on the one hand, and social conformity, on the other. Accurate and skillful management of emotional information necessarily has to reflect social norms and expectations. For example, emotional intelligence entails understanding how other people interpret emotional cues, and how they expect us to handle our emotions. It also entails conforming to those expectations, unless there is good reason to behave differently. As a result, any ability measure of emotional (or social) skills must also reflect, to some degree, social conformity.

Complex, real-life problems often lack a single, clear-cut solution. Sternberg and his colleagues (2000) have argued that this is an important difference between analytical and practical intelligence. Unlike the problems that children are usually given to solve in school, which allow only one right answer, the problems we face in real life are often ill-defined and allow for multiple solutions. Testing analytical skills is clearly easier, and that is one of the reasons why Western education has overemphasized them to the detriment of practical intelligence, creativity, and social and emotional competencies. To move beyond this state of affairs, expand our knowledge base, and evaluate the real importance of nonanalytic skills, it is essential to develop ability tests that take into account the fact that there may be no single correct solution to complex, real-life problems.

Reflection on these issues also brings up a concern about cultural differences in emotional intelligence, especially if there are differences due to culture in the "right" way to behave emotionally in particular situations. There is no doubt that such differences exist. In the United States, one needs only to attend funerals among families of different ethnic origins to experience the inconsistencies in the way grief is expressed. New Englanders of old Yankee stock (with origins among the Puritans of England) tend to appear stoical at funerals, maintaining a "stiff upper lip." Those of us with eastern or southern European roots are likely to grieve more openly. And some African Americans, such as those living in New Orleans, for example, may celebrate a loved one's passing on to a better world with joyful singing, jazz music, and a public parade. As can be seen in this illustration, it is not the case that emotional intelligence necessarily means blunting, controlling, or inhibiting emotional expression, but rather behaving in ways that are considered adaptive in a particular cultural or situational context.

There are at least two ways in which these cultural differences can be addressed in the measurement of emotional intelligence. One is to develop consensual norms (or expert norms, for that matter) separately for various cultures. Of course, this approach presents the challenge of deciding how narrowly to "slice" cultures. So, for instance, are different norms needed for Parisians versus French-speaking residents of Geneva or Brussels? Another approach is to attempt to identify situations to include on measures such as the MSCEIT that produce relatively universal consistencies in responses. So, for example, the MSCEIT task having to do with identifying facial expressions of emotion was based on classic work by Ekman and his colleagues concerned with more or less universally recognized emotions.

A FINAL COMMENT

In the midst of the debate about whether emotional intelligence is a useful construct and the swirl of psychometric data concerning its measurement, it is easy to forget that the goal here is to describe people – people with particular strengths in appreciating and using emotions as guides to thinking and action. In that spirit, we would like to end this chapter by providing a sense of such individuals. The young woman quoted below participated in a qualitative study of emotional intelligence among gifted teenagers (Mayer, Perkins, Caruso, & Salovey, 2001). This sixteen-year-old was the highest scoring in EI in the sample using the Multifactor Emotional Intelligence Scale (MEIS; Mayer, Caruso, & Salovey, 1999). She described a conflict she had had with some friends:

Once my friends wanted to sneak in someone's room and paint him while he slept. It began as joking around ("Wouldn't this be funny; could you believe it if?"). Then it slowly evolved into dares ("I bet you wouldn't," or "I dare you to."). I felt like it was betraying the trust I had with the other person, I didn't feel right with sneaking up on a sleeping person with no way to defend himself, and I thought doing this would make the person have his feelings hurt. I know how little pranks like this could really hurt someone's feelings, make them feel like everyone is making fun of them, taking away their dignity and disrespecting them. I won't do that to someone because I understand how badly that can hurt. [How did you handle it?] Told them straight out that it was a degrading thing to do and they shouldn't be so cruel. Asked them how they would like it? [Relation to long-term goals?] I'm not sure. One of my everyday goals is to try my hardest not to judge or make fun of someone. [Parents' reaction?] They would have been proud, but it's just one of those things that sort of never gets talked about because they would have also said I ruined a perfectly harmless joke. [Parents' goals?] My parents want me to be respectful. (Mayer et al., 2001, p. 136)

There is little doubt that this young woman can identify emotions, understand them, manage them, and use this information as the basis for subsequent thought and action. In this sense, she is emotionally intelligent. More important, the concept of emotional intelligence provides a way of describing her assets that, we suspect, is not captured in most theories of intelligence or personality.

References

Adolphs, R., & Damasio, A. R. (2001). The interaction of affect and cognition: A neurobiological perspective. In J. P. Forgas (Ed.), *The handbook of affect and social cognition* (pp. 27–49). Mahwah, NJ: Lawrence Erlbaum Associates.

Apfel, R. J., & Sifneos, P. E. (1979). Alexithymia: Concept and measurement. *Psychotherapy and Psychosomatics, 32,* 180–190.

Bagby, R. M.; Parker, J. D. A.; & Taylor, G. J. (1993a). The twenty-item Toronto Alexithymia Scale: I. Item selection and cross-validation of the factor structure. *Journal of Psychosomatic Research, 38,* 23–32.

Bagby, R. M.; Parker, J. D. A.; & Taylor, G. J. (1993b). The twenty-item Toronto Alexithymia Scale: II. Convergent, discriminant, and concurrent validity. *Journal of Psychosomatic Research, 38,* 33–40.

Barchard, K. A. (2000). Does emotional intelligence assist in the prediction of academic success? Unpublished manuscript, University of British Columbia, Vancouver.

Bar-On, R. (1997). *Emotional Intelligence Quotient Inventory: A measure of emotional intelligence.* Toronto: Multi-Health Systems, Inc.

Barrett, G. V.; Miguel, R. F.; Tan, J. A.; & Hurd, J. M. (2001). *Emotional intelligence: The Madison Avenue approach to science and professional practice.* Akron, OH: Barrett & Associates.

Bretherton, I.; Fritz, J.; Zahn-Waxler, C.; & Ridgeway, D. (1986). Learning to talk about emotions: A functionalist perspective. *Child Development, 57,* 529–548.

Buck, R. (1976). A test of nonverbal receiving ability: Preliminary studies. *Human Communication and Research, 2,* 162–171.

Buck, R. (1984). *The communication of emotion.* New York: Guilford Press.

Campbell, R. J.; Kagan, N. I.; & Krathwohl, D. R. (1971). The development and validation of a scale to measure affective sensitivity (empathy). *Journal of Counseling Psychology, 18,* 407–412.

Caruso, D. R., & Wolfe, C. J. (2001). Emotional intelligence in the workplace. In J. Ciarrochi, J. P. Forgas, and J. D. Mayer (Eds.), *Emotional intelligence in everyday life: A scientific inquiry* (pp. 150–167). Philadelphia: Psychology Press.

Catanzaro, S. J., & Greenwood, G. (1994). Expectancies for negative mood regulation, coping, and dysphoria among college students. *Journal of Consulting Psychology, 41,* 34–44.

Ciarrochi, J. V.; Chan, A. Y. C.; & Caputi, P. (2000). A critical evaluation of the emotional intelligence construct. *Personality and Individual Differences, 28,* 539–561.

Costa, P. T., Jr., & McCrae, R. R. (1992). *NEO-PI-R Professional Manual – Revised NEO Personality Inventory (NEO-PIR) and NEO Five-Factor Inventory (NEO-FFI).* Odessa, FL: Psychological Assessment Resources.

Crowne, D. P., & Marlowe, D. (1960). A new scale of social desirability independent of psychopathology. *Journal of Consulting Psychology, 24,* 349–354.

Darwin, C. (1872). *The expression of emotions in man and animals.* Chicago: University of Chicago Press.

Damasio, A. R. (1994). *Descartes' error: Emotion, reason, and the human brain.* New York: Putnam.

Davies, M.; Stankov, L.; & Roberts, R. D. (1998). Emotional intelligence: In search of an elusive construct. *Journal of Personality and Social Psychology, 75,* 989–1015.

de Sousa, R. (1987). *The rationality of emotion.* Cambridge, MA: The MIT Press.

Dolan, R. J., & Morris, J. S. (2000). The functional anatomy of innate and acquired fear: Perspectives from neuroimaging. In R. D. Lane and L. Nadel (Eds.), *Cognitive neuroscience of emotion* (pp. 225–241). New York: Oxford University Press.

Easterbrook, J. A. (1959). The effects of emotion on cue utilization and the organization of behavior. *Psychological Review, 66,* 183–200.

Elias, M. J.; Hunter, L.; & Kress, J. S. (2001). Emotional intelligence and education. In J. Ciarrochi, J. P. Forgas, and J. D. Mayer (Eds.), *Emotional intelligence in everyday life: A scientific inquiry* (pp. 133–149). Philadelphia: Psychology Press.

Fenigstein, A.; Scheier, M. F.; & Buss, A. H. (1975). Public and private self-consciousness: Assessment and theory. *Journal of Consulting and Clinical Psychology, 43,* 522–527.

Flury, J., & Ickes, W. (2001). Emotional intelligence and empathic accuracy. In J. Ciarrochi, J. P. Forgas, and J. D. Mayer (Eds.), *Emotional intelligence in everyday life: A scientific inquiry* (pp. 113–132). Philadelphia: Psychology Press.

Furman, W. (1996). The measurement of children and adolescents' perceptions of friendships: Conceptual and methodological issues. In W. M. Bukowski, A. F. Newcomb, and W. W. Hartup (Eds.), *The company they keep: Friendships in childhood and adolescence* (pp. 41–65). New York: Cambridge University Press.

Furman, W., & Buhrmester, D. (1985). Children's perceptions of the personal relationships in their social networks. *Developmental Psychology, 21,* 1016–1024.

Gardner, H. (1983). *Frames of mind*. New York: Basic Books.

Goldman, S. L.; Kraemer, D. T.; & Salovey, P. (1996). Beliefs about mood moderate the relationship of stress to illness and symptom reporting. *Journal of Psychosomatic Research, 41*, 115–128.

Goleman, D. (1995). *Emotional intelligence*. New York: Bantam Books.

Goleman, D. (1998). *Working with emotional intelligence*. New York: Bantam Books.

Gross, A. L., & Bailif, B. (1991). Children's understanding of emotion from facial expressions and situations: A review. *Developmental Review, 11*, 368–398.

Hall, J. A. (1984). *Nonverbal sex differences: Communication accuracy and expressive style*. Baltimore: Johns Hopkins University Press.

Ickes, W. (1993). Empathic accuracy. *Journal of Personality, 61*, 587–609.

Jaušovec, N.; Jaušovec, K.; & Gerlič, I. (2001). Differences in event-related and induced electroencephalography patterns in the theta and alpha frequency bands related to human emotional intelligence. *Neuroscience Letters, 311*, 93–96.

Kagan, N. (1978). *Affective sensitivity test: Validity and reliability*. Paper presented at the annual meeting of the American Psychological Association, San Francisco, CA.

Klimesch, W. (1999). EEG alpha and theta oscillations reflect cognitive and memory performance: A review and analysis. *Brain Research Review, 29*, 169–195.

Lane, R. D. (2000). Neural correlates of conscious emotional experience. In R. D. Lane and L. Nadel (Eds.), *Cognitive neuroscience of emotion* (pp. 345–370). New York: Oxford University Press.

Lane, R. D.; Quinlan, D. M.; Schwartz, G. E.; Walker, P.; & Zeitlin, S. B. (1990). The levels of emotional awareness scale: A cognitive-developmental measure of emotion. *Journal of Personality Assessment, 55*, 124–134.

LeDoux, J. (1996). *The emotional brain: The mysterious underpinnings of emotional life*. New York: Simon and Schuster.

LeDoux, J. (2000). Cognitive-emotional interactions: Listening to the brain. In R. D. Lane and L. Nadel (Eds.), *Cognitive neuroscience of emotion* (pp. 129–155). New York: Oxford University Press.

Leeper, R. W. (1948). A motivational theory of emotions to replace "emotions as disorganized response." *Psychological Review, 55*, 5–21.

Lopes, P. N.; Brackett, M. A.; Nezlek, J. B.; Schütz, A.; Sellin, I.; & Salovey, P. (in press). Emotional intelligence and social interaction. *Personality and Social Psychology Bulletin*.

Lopes, P. N.; Salovey, P.; & Straus, R. (2003). Emotional intelligence, personality, and the perceived quality of social relationships. *Personality and Individual Differences, 35*, 641–658.

Mandler, G. (1975). *Mind and emotion*. New York: Wiley.

Mayer, J. D.; Caruso, D. R.; & Salovey, P. (1998). *Multifactor Emotional Intelligence Scale (MEIS)*. (Available from John D. Mayer, Department of Psychology, University of New Hampshire, Conant Hall, Durham, NH 03824)

Mayer, J. D.; Caruso, D.; & Salovey, P. (1999). Emotional intelligence meets traditional standards for an intelligence. *Intelligence, 27*, 267–298.

Mayer, J. D.; Caruso, D.; & Salovey, P. (2000). Selecting a measure of emotional intelligence: The case for ability scales. In R. Bar-On and J. D. A. Parker (Eds.), *The handbook of emotional intelligence* (pp. 320–342). San Francisco: Jossey-Bass.

Mayer, J. D.; Perkins, D. M.; Caruso, D. R.; & Salovey, P. (2001). Emotional intelligence and giftedness. *Roeper Review, 23,* 131–137.

Mayer, J. D., & Salovey, P. (1997). What is emotional intelligence? In P. Salovey and D. Sluyter (Eds.), *Emotional development and emotional intelligence: Implications for educators* (pp. 3–31). New York: Basic Books.

Mayer, J. D.; Salovey, P.; & Caruso, D. (2000a). Emotional intelligence as zeitgeist, as personality, and as a mental ability. In R. Bar-On and J. D. A. Parker (Eds.), *The handbook of emotional intelligence* (pp. 92–117). San Francisco: Jossey-Bass.

Mayer, J. D.; Salovey, P.; & Caruso, D. (2000b). Models of emotional intelligence. In R. J. Sternberg (Ed.), *The handbook of intelligence* (pp. 396–420). New York: Cambridge University Press.

Mayer, J. D.; Salovey, P.; & Caruso, D. (2001). *The Mayer-Salovey-Caruso Emotional Intelligence Test (MSCEIT).* Toronto: Multi-Health Systems, Inc.

Mayer, J. D.; Salovey, P.; Caruso, D.; & Sitarenios, G. (2001). Emotional intelligence as a standard intelligence. *Emotion, 1,* 232–242.

Mayer, J. D.; Salovey, P.; Caruso, D.; & Sitarenios, G. (2003). Measuring emotional intelligence with the MSCEIT V2.0. *Emotion, 3,* 97–105.

Mehrabian, A., & Epstein, N. (1972). A measure of emotional empathy. *Journal of Personality, 40,* 525–543.

Neubauer, A. C.; Sange, G.; & Pfurtscheller, G. (1999). Psychometric intelligence and event-related desyncrhonization during performance of a letter matching task. In G. Pfurtscheller, G. Lopes, and F. H. Lopes da Silva (Eds.), *Handbook of electroencephalography and clinical neuropsychology, event-related desynchronization* (Vol. 6, pp. 219–232). Amsterdam: Elsevier.

Ortony, A.; Clore, G. L.; & Collins, A. (1988). *The cognitive structure of emotions.* Cambridge: Cambridge University Press.

Palfai, T. P., & Salovey, P. (1993). The influence of depressed and elated mood on deductive and inductive reasoning. *Imagination, Cognition, and Personality, 13,* 57–71.

Payne, W. L. (1986). A study of emotion: Developing emotional intelligence; Self-integration; relating to fear, pain and desire. *Dissertation Abstracts International,* 47(01), p. 203A. (University Microfilms No. AAC 8605928). (Ph.D. dissertation, Union Graduate School, Cincinnati, OH. Original dissertation work submitted and accepted, May 1983)

Rice, C. L. (1999). A quantitative study of emotional intelligence and its impact on team performance. M.A. thesis, Pepperdine University, Malibu, CA.

Roberts, R. D.; Zeidner, M.; & Matthews, G. (2001). Does emotional intelligence meet traditional standards for an intelligence? Some new data and conclusions. *Emotion, 1,* 196–231.

Rosenberg, M. (1965). *Society and the adolescent self-image.* Princeton, NJ: Princeton University Press.

Rosenthal, R.; Hall, J. A.; Archer, D.; DiMatteo, M. R.; & Rogers, P. L. (1979). *The PONS test manual: Profile of Nonverbal Sensitivity.* New York: Irvington Publishers.

Rubin, M. M. (1999). Emotional intelligence and its role in mitigating aggression: A correlational study of the relationship between emotional intelligence and aggression in urban adolescents. Unpublished manuscript, Immaculata College, Immaculata, PA.

Ryff, C. D. (1989). Happiness is everything, or is it? Explorations on the meaning of psychological well-being. *Journal of Personality and Social Psychology, 57,* 1069–1081.

Saarni, C. (1979). Children's understanding of display rules for expressive behavior. *Developmental Psychology, 15,* 424–429.

Saarni, C. (1990). Emotional competence: How emotions and relationships become integrated. In R. A. Thompson (Ed.), *Nebraska symposium on motivation* (Vol. 36, pp. 115–182). Lincoln: University of Nebraska Press.

Saarni, C. (1999). *Developing emotional competence.* New York: Guilford Press.

Salovey, P.; Bedell, B. T.; Detweiler, J. B.; & Mayer, J. D. (2000). Current directions in emotional intelligence research. In M. Lewis and J. M. Haviland-Jones (Eds.), *Handbook of emotions* (2d ed., pp. 504–520). New York: Guilford Press.

Salovey, P., & Mayer, J. D. (1990). Emotional intelligence. *Imagination, Cognition, and Personality, 9,* 185–211.

Salovey, P.; Mayer, J. D.; & Caruso, D. (2002). The positive psychology of emotional intelligence. In C. R. Snyder and S. J. Lopez (Eds.), *The handbook of positive psychology* (pp. 159–171). New York: Oxford University Press.

Salovey, P.; Mayer, J. D.; Caruso, P.; & Lopes, P. N. (2003). Measuring emotional intelligence as a set of abilities with the Mayer-Salovey-Caruso emotional intelligence test. In S. J. Lopez and C. R. Snyder (Eds.), *Positive psychology assessment: A handbook of models and measures* (pp. 251–265). Washington, DC: American Psychological Association.

Salovey, P.; Mayer, J. D.; Goldman, S. L.; Turvey, C.; & Palfai, T. P. (1995). Emotional attention, clarity, and repair: Exploring emotional intelligence using the Trait Meta-Mood Scale. In J. W. Pennebaker (Ed.), *Emotion, disclosure, and health* (pp. 125–154). Washington, DC: American Psychological Association.

Salovey, P., & Rodin, J. (1986). Differentiation of social-comparison jealousy and romantic jealousy. *Journal of Personality and Social Psychology, 50,* 1100–1112.

Salovey, P., & Rodin, J. (1989). Envy and jealousy in close relationships. *Review of Personality and Social Psychology, 10,* 221–246.

Salovey, P.; Woolery, A.; & Mayer, J. D. (2001). Emotional intelligence: Conceptualization and measurement. In G. Fletcher and M. Clark (Eds.), *The Blackwell handbook of social psychology: Interpersonal processes* (pp. 279–307). London: Blackwell.

Schwarz, N. (1990). Feelings as information: Informational and motivational functions of affective states. In E. T. Higgins and E. M. Sorrentino (Eds.), *Handbook of motivation and cognition* (Vol. 2, pp. 527–561). New York: Guilford Press.

Simon, H. A. (1982). Comments. In M. S. Clark and S. T. Fiske (Eds.), *Affect and cognition* (pp. 333–342). Hillsdale, NJ: Erlbaum.

Stankov, L. (2000). Structural extensions of a hierarchical view on human cognitive abilities. *Learning and Individual Differences, 12,* 35–51.

Sternberg, R. J.; Forsythe, G. B.; Hedlund, J.; Horvath, J. A.; Wagner, R. K.; Williams, W. M.; Snook, S. A.; & Grigorenko, E. L. (2000). *Practical intelligence in everyday life.* New York: Cambridge University Press.

Stroebe, W., & Stroebe, M. (1996). The social psychology of social support. In E. T. Higgins and A. W. Kruglansky (Eds.), *Social psychology: Handbook of basic principles* (pp. 597–621). New York: Guilford Press.

Thayer, R. E.; Newman, J. R.; & McClain, T. M. (1994). Self-regulation of mood: Strategies for changing a bad mood, raising energy, and reducing tension. *Journal of Personality and Social Psychology, 67*, 910–925.

The Psychological Corporation (1997). *WAIS-III, WMS-III technical manual*. San Antonio, TX: Author.

Trinidad, D. R., & Johnson, C. A. (2002). The association between emotional intelligence and early adolescent tobacco and alcohol use. *Personality and Individual Differences, 32*, 95–105.

20

Culture and Emotion

Models of Agency as Sources of Cultural Variation in Emotion

Batja Mesquita and Hazel Rose Markus

ABSTRACT

This chapter discusses in what ways culture influences emotional processes. The authors propose that different cultural models of agency may influence various aspects of emotions, thus accounting for cultural variance. A distinction is made between a conjoint model of agency, more common in collectivist cultures, and a disjoint model of agency, more often found in individualist cultures. Studies are reviewed that compare members from individualist and collectivist cultures in their selection of emotional events, their appraisal of events, and the way they cope with events.

CULTURE AND EMOTION: MODELS OF AGENCY AS SOURCES OF
CULTURAL VARIATION IN EMOTION

We must admit that we have always thought of our own emotions as *natural*, not cultural. The reason, we suspect, is that our emotions were socialized to fit the cultural realities within which we lived for many years: Dutch and North American middle-class environments, respectively. As long as our emotions were in concordance with the cultural environment that afforded and supported them, the cultural constitution of these emotions remained invisible to us.

We both gained some perspective on the culture-specificity of our emotions when we came to engage in cultural environments with which our emotions were at odds. For the first author, this happened upon moving to the United States. American people initially seemed unnaturally happy, smiling a lot and asserting several times a day that they felt "great." Consequently, her own emotions, which had been previously in harmony with a Dutch context, suddenly felt culturally particular and inadequate in the new American environment. Often, those Dutch emotions seemed slightly depressed (i.e., not happy enough) or even ungrateful (i.e., not happy enough for the occasion).

341

This contrast between Dutch and American emotions is compatible with the literature. In the middle-class American context it is important to attain success through individual hard work (Wierzbicka, 1994), and this will boost one's self-esteem. Self-esteem, a central concern in America, is associated with the desirable emotion of happiness (e.g., D'Andrade, 1984; Heine, Lehman, Markus, & Kitayama, 1999). Americans tend to create and maintain happiness in many different ways – by praising, complimenting, and encouraging each other, and by avoiding being critical or inattentive.

Happiness does occur in the Dutch context, but it is not particularly promoted. Compliments, for example, are not as common, and the desire to please not as pronounced as in America. Not to "give a damn what others may think" is "to live your life to the full" (Van Der Horst, 1996, p. 231). It is Dutch practice to be articulate, which means *not* to be afraid to speak up for oneself even if this may hurt or dismay another person (Stephenson, 1989; Van Der Horst, 1996). In this context, it is important to be aware of, as well as to vent, anger, frustration, and disappointment.

The Dutch yielding to anger or disappointment is in fact *one* way of achieving an independent self, a self that sets clear limits, and that does not let others get in its way. It is an independent self that asserts itself in the way emotions are felt and expressed. Americans also strive to express their thoughts and to achieve an independent self, but this is typically accomplished by placing an emphasis on achievement and self-esteem, and thus by the promotion of happiness. The differences between these two cultures, however similar they are in many other ways – Western, individualist, wealthy – illustrate the case to be made in this chapter. Models of "how to be," including how to feel, think, and act, are differentially distributed in various cultural contexts, and thus the modal and moral emotional experiences that are organized by these models will be different as well.

Our personal example also raises the question of what happens to one's emotions when one relocates to a new cultural environment. Because emotions are constituted and afforded by the particular sociocultural contexts in which they occur, we believe that they will change once their constituting contexts change. Living in the United States for several years, and engaging in practices of praise and the avoidance of criticism, has helped the first author to become attuned to the American context, and thus to experience happiness American-style. Increasingly, she *feels*, rather than just displays, the right emotion in the right context. Thus, it seems that emotional experience is not just shaped by the native culture but also sustained – or, in this case, changed – by the concurrent cultural conditions. Along with changing cultural contexts, emotions themselves will change.

In this chapter we will provide further evidence that different cultural contexts promote different *feelings*, not just different ways of expressing those feelings. The evidence to be discussed contrasts the emotions constructed in Anglo-American contexts with those constructed in East Asian cultural contexts. As should be clear from our introduction, however, cultural contexts much less different from one another, such as those of the Netherlands and the United States, will also shape emotions in particular and importantly different ways.

THE CONCEPTUALIZATION OF CULTURAL DIFFERENCES IN EMOTIONS

Cross-cultural research has suggested the universality of a number of facial, vocal, and bodily expressions, antecedent events, appraisals, action-readiness modes, and physiological changes associated with certain emotions (for reviews of this evidence, see Mesquita & Frijda, 1992; Mesquita, Frijda, & Scherer, 1997). Currently, there is more evidence available for similarities than for differences in emotions. However, we believe that the failure to establish cultural differences in emotional phenomena is due to a lack of theory about those differences (Mesquita, in press). In previous research, differences in emotions were yielded as by-products in the search for similarities in emotions. This meant that no systematic hypotheses were developed with respect to possible differences. An understanding of cultural variations in emotions requires a theory of the ways in which cultures may differentially shape and afford emotions. Our discussion of differences in emotional lives across cultures will be guided, then, by a conceptualization of emotions that allows for the finding of cross-cultural differences in the phenomena.

Consistent with many current theories of emotion, we conceive of emotions as configurations of multiple aspects, such as appraisal, action readiness, and behaviors (e.g., Ellsworth, 1994; Frijda, 1986; Shweder, 1991, this volume). Different aspects of emotions do not automatically follow from each other; each aspect of emotion has its own determinants in addition to the eliciting event. This conceptualization allows for finding differences with respect to each aspect of emotions individually, and thus to establish many degrees of difference in emotion. The view of emotions as multi-aspect phenomena that *emerge* is in stark contrast with the idea that emotions are basic, invariant states of the body that can be turned on and off.

It is important to draw a distinction between emotional practice and emotional potential. Emotional *practices* refer to the actual emotions that people experience and express, the combinations of activated outputs. The *potential for emotions* refers to the emotional responses that people are capable of having in principle, and from which they select outputs (Mesquita & Ellsworth, 2001; Mesquita et al., 1997). As emotions unfold, certain outputs from the potential for each aspect of emotions are activated. The combined outputs from each emotional aspect form the emotional practice, or the actual experience (Mesquita, 2002). Whereas many cross-cultural studies traditionally have focused on the potential for emotions (e.g., the potential to recognize facial expressions in similar ways [Ekman et al., 1987; Izard, 1994]), work on emotional practices in other disciplines, such as anthropology, suggests that cultural differences in emotions are primarily to be expected at the level of emotional practices (e.g., Abu-Lughod, 1986; Briggs, 1970). The cultural differences in emotions discussed in this chapter are best represented as differences in emotional practices.

Cultural differences in emotion practices may be a result of differences in the likelihood that certain outputs will be activated (Mesquita, 2002). For example, in comparison to members of some other cultures, Americans tend to appraise relatively many events, particularly positive ones, in terms of personal agency (Mesquita & Ellsworth, 2001). Such appraisals are not exclusive to American culture, and therefore the frequency differences in agency appraisal should not be conceived of in terms of emotion potential. Rather, the relatively high tendency for Americans to appraise positive events as their own doing is to be represented as a cultural difference in emotional practice. A differential output activation seems to lie at the base of it. In the current example, Americans' claim of agency is consistent with their emphasis on people's own contributions to positive outcomes. Thus, the cultural likelihood of selecting particular emotional outputs – agency appraisals in this case – may depend on the centrality of the emotional output to the pertinent cultural practices. It can be plausibly assumed that, whereas outputs consistent with the cultural practices are more likely to be activated, outputs that are at odds with the cultural practices are less likely to be activated (Mesquita, 2002). Thus, we propose that emotional experience fits in with what cultures are about, with the cultural realities. Emotions are constituted by these cultural realities.

CULTURE: MODELS OF AGENCY

The "right" way to feel in a given cultural context is closely linked to the normative and habitual social behavior in this context. This joint shaping of ways of being and ways of feeling occurs because the "I" who feels an affective state or an emotion has as its referent a particular self and way of being. For example, in many European American contexts, normatively good actions are understood to originate in an independent and autonomous self, and the actions of this self are disjoint, that is, in some ways separate or distinct from the actions of others. In many East Asian contexts, normatively good actions are understood to originate in an interdependent self, and the actions of this self are conjoint, that is, in some ways impelled by others, in relationship and in interaction with others. In both cases "good" actions foster the "right" feelings, and the "right" feelings instigate "good" actions. Specifically, given this link, one way to organize cultural variation in emotional experience is to examine sociocultural variability in agency or in being-in-action.

Cultural realities differ with respect to their prevalent cultural models of agency (Markus & Kitayama, in press). Models of agency are defined as implicit frameworks of ideas and practices about how to be that construct the actions of the self, others, and the relationships among those actions. These models are not so much verbal propositions as ways in which reality, including the psychological reality, is constituted. They are reflected and fostered, for example, in the types of relationships that are sanctioned and condoned, the language, and the public messages as conveyed by the media, books, and educational policies (Markus, Mullally, & Kitayama, 1997). In each of these reality-constituting practices, certain types of self-in-action are afforded, expected, or shaped. Although models of agency are typically invisible to those who engage in or enact them, they are defining of the nature of intentional individuals and their relationships. They are the means by which people make sense of and coordinate their actions alone and in concert with one another.

We shall compare and contrast models of agency that we label as "disjoint" with models of agency we label as "conjoint." These models are differentially distributed in different social contexts and foster different emotional experiences in these contexts. Disjoint models of agency are very common in European American contexts, especially in some parts of middle-class America, while conjoint models of agency are relatively common in East Asian cultural contexts. It is likely that most Americans, depending on the situation, can and do enact both types of models, hybrids of these models, and still other models, and the same is true for Asians, yet their relevant sociocultural contexts are likely to differ in the prevalence of these models.

The distinction between disjoint and conjoint agency rests primarily with whether or not others are actively referenced and centrally implicated in an individual's action. Models of agency always refer to and prescribe patterns of social relations. Yet models of agency that construct action as social and as residing in the relationship between self and others, where agency is explicitly constructed as conjoint, are systematically different in a number of important respects from models of action where agency is explicitly constructed as disjoint – separated from others, residing in and emanating from motives or self-generated intentions or goals. Agency is not separate from context, or opposed to it, but instead is patterned by the ideas and practices of various contexts.

According to a disjoint model of agency, in particular the American model, one is focused on the self. The self should be unique, free from others, and, as noted, happy and positive. The perception of the world should be organized according to the meanings that events carry for the individual: How do I feel about this? What does this mean for me? Models of disjoint agency involve the notion that one should actively control and influence the environment, thus ensuring that the individual is and remains independent, free, and happy. Action should be freely chosen, self-motivated, and primarily the result of one's own goals and intentions. This understanding of agency has direct implications for the definition and expression of the self as *independent*, as well as for the definition of relationships as modifiable to fit the self's needs and desires. Relationships are self-chosen, and an individual tends to dissociate him- or herself from the relationship when the latter is perceived to be harmful to personal concerns or goals.

According to a conjoint model of agency, the prevalent model in East Asian cultural contexts, individuals experience themselves as interdependent selves – as in-relation-to-others, as belonging to social groups, or as significantly and reciprocally enmeshed in families, communities, or work groups. Perception of the environment should be structured according to the meanings events have for others, or to the situation in general. Actions require the consideration and anticipation of the perspective of *others* and are a consequence of the fulfillment of reciprocal obligations or expectations. Agents do not experience themselves as free from others, but rather reference each other, thus trying to improve the fit between what one is doing and what is expected. In fact, a no-self, or a self that does not direct action but rather accommodates itself to the requirements of others and of the context in general, constitutes the Confucian ideal. A primary consequence of conjoint agency is the definition, expression, and affirmation of the self as *interdependent*. This work builds on and extends the distinction between independent and interdependent self-construals (Markus & Kitayama, 1991). In this chapter we emphasize differences in "the self in action" in order to connect the earlier work with research on emotions, and that is why we have chosen to use the term "agency."

People universally experience themselves, at least some of the time, as intentionally acting within the world or as being agentic (Markus & Kitayama, in press). Yet conceptions and implications of "agency" can vary quite dramatically across cultures. Being a person in the world, acting, and relating are not simply automatic reactions to stimuli. One cannot just "be" in a general, unspecified way. In fact, a defining feature of our species is that we enter into worlds that are already constructed according to particular ideas and ways of doing things (Bruner, 1990; Holland, Lachicotte, Skinner, & Cain, 1998). Being, acting, and relating are culturally saturated processes that entail engagement with culture-specific sets of meanings and practices, the cultural models of agency. We discuss evidence to suggest that these models of agency constitute the emotional practice.

EMOTION ANTECEDENTS

Worlds as Sought Out

Emotion practices, the kinds of emotions that people actually have in a given cultural context, are largely dependent on the world as encountered, or on the types of events that people meet in their daily lives. There is a growing volume of evidence to suggest that cultural realities – the worlds that people encounter – are shaped in ways that reflect and perpetuate particular cultural models of agency (Befu, 1986; Benedict, 1946; Karasawa, 2001; Lewis, 1995; Miller, Fung, & Mintz, 1996). These different realities would seem to give rise to different emotions. Thus, the first way in which cultural models of agency affect emotions is through their embodiment in the worlds as encountered.

Models of agency also importantly affect the situations that we prefer and seek out, beyond explicit rules of what one should do or not do. Disjoint models of agency afford preferences for being different and unique, whereas conjoint models of agency are more likely to create a preference for being like others, connected, and in harmony. A study by Kim and Markus (1999) nicely illustrates this. It examines how these preferences are manifest in individual action – a choice among alternatives. The researchers argue that whereas uniqueness in a disjoint model of agency feels good because it is associated with freedom and independence, it feels bad in a conjoint model, where it is associated with being vulnerable and uncomfortable because one is not fitting in. The prediction was, therefore, that East Asians would try to avoid uniqueness because it makes them feel vulnerable and uncomfortable, whereas Americans would seek uniqueness out, as it makes them feel good and strong and independent.

In this study, East Asians and European Americans – passengers waiting at the San Francisco airport – were asked to complete a questionnaire. As a gift for completing the survey, participants were asked to choose one pen from a group of five pens, one or two of which were different from the others. Americans chose the unique or less common pen more frequently than the East Asians, 74 percent compared to 24 percent. Cultural models thus helped to determine the emotional value of the unique versus the common pen, and this valence influenced choice behavior. The alternative explanation that the East Asians were more modest, not wanting to deplete the pen with the highest commodity, is unlikely. The experimenter ostensibly took the pens from a big storage bag containing more of each kind. This experiment thus provides some support for the idea that cultural models of agency help to determine the emotional value of certain situations, and in that manner, influence the choice of behavior.

Cultural models should not be seen as static, internal representations. Rather, they are achieved in constant dynamic interaction with the cultural environment. When that environment changes, emotional experience – what is pleasant and preferable – changes as well. This was demonstrated by a replication of the pen study, this time including participants who moved across cultural contexts, from an environment where a disjoint model of agency prevails to an environment with a predominantly conjoint model of agency (Kim, 2001). The participants were Korean American college students who were visiting Korea as part of a summer international exchange program. The exchange program lasted for approximately two months. In one condition of the experiment, the pen-choice study was done one week after the classes began, and in the other condition, with an independent sample of students, it was done five weeks after the classes began. This study revealed that the length of time spent in Korea had very dramatic consequences for the pattern of preference. After one week, 45 percent of the participants preferred the unique pen. In contrast, after five weeks, the preference had changed quite a bit, and the percentage of participants who chose the unique pen dropped to only 17 percent. Thus, even within this short time span, the cultural connotations of the unique pen seemed to have changed from positive (as in "freedom" and "independence") to negative and uncomfortable (as in "deviant"). As individuals engage in particular models, so do their preferences, because they behave in meaningful and appropriate ways, that is, ways congruent with the particular models of agency.

There is some evidence that different cultural models also affect the relative focus on either avoiding negative or achieving positive outcomes (e.g., Elliott, Chirkov, Kim, & Sheldon, 2001; Lee, Aaker, & Gardner, 2000). This is implicit in some of our previous examples. Whereas Americans focus on the *accomplishment* of positive outcomes, thus to gain self-esteem and happiness, East Asians seem to be more concerned with not falling short of social expectations, and thus with *avoiding* negative outcomes and the shame associated with them. A disjoint model of agency thus has been associated with a promotion focus, whereas a conjoint model of agency has been related to a prevention focus.

There is some support for the idea that whether positive events are sought out or negative events avoided may have implications for the particular emotional practices. In a North American context, Higgins, Shah, and Friedman (1997) found evidence that a prevention focus fosters relaxation or relief when the goals are achieved, and anxiety when the goals are not reached. On the other hand, these authors found that a promotion focus affords feelings of happiness when the goals are achieved, and feelings of sadness when the goals are not met. In a cross-cultural vignette study on success and failure, Lee and colleagues (2000) found that the American group, consistent with what should be hypothesized on the basis of their cultural focus on promotion, reported a higher intensity of happiness/depressed emotions than relief/anxiety emotions. Conversely, a Chinese group, consistent with their focus on prevention, reported a higher intensity of relief/anxiety than happiness/depressed emotions. This is some first evidence that the differences in the worlds sought out are responsible for differences in emotional practices, that is, in the prevalent types of emotions.

In sum, cultural models of agency motivate the selection of situations. They render certain situations more right, more pleasant, and more desirable, whereas others are not right, unpleasant, and undesirable. They also assign relative value to the promotion of situations that are right versus the avoidance of situations that are not right. These preferences need not be, and often are not, conscious, but they guide respondents' behavior, and they affect the situations that are created and sought out. Engaging in the cultural models thus means to selectively participate in and construct the world that serves as the context for emotional practices.

The Relevance of Cultural Differences in Antecedents

Differences in the world as encountered and sought out are important to the understanding of emotions across cultures, because the occurrence of these differences means that the *basic* or *modal* emotional experiences vary across cultures. Understanding the cultural models of agency that constitute the context for emotional experience will thus significantly add to insights into the experiences that people in the relevant cultures actually have. Cultural models of agency influence emotional practices beyond their influence on the worlds as encountered and sought out. The very structure and nature of emotions as they occur also appear to be shaped by the cultural models.

APPRAISAL

Valence

Whereas the American model of agency appears to foster a positive outlook on life and on the self, East Asian cultural models do not seem to favor the positive. Consistent with these cultural models, several of our studies have suggested that Americans tend to appraise emotional situations as more pleasant than do East Asians (Kitayama, Markus, & Kurokawa, 2000; Mesquita & Karasawa, 2002; Mesquita, Karasawa, & Chu, in preparation). Mesquita, Karasawa, and Chu (in preparation) found in a large experience-sampling study among American, Japanese, and Taiwanese students that, on average, American students appraised the emotional situations in their lives as positively different from neutral, whereas Japanese and Taiwanese students evaluated their lives on average as neither positive nor negative. The difference between American appraisals of pleasantness, on the one hand, and Japanese and Taiwanese, on the other, was significant. The sample size of each of the groups was around fifty, and per respondent we measured about twenty-eight emotional events throughout a week. The finding that Americans evaluate their experiences as more positive on average than East Asians, whose evaluations are balanced, has been replicated in many studies (e.g., Kitayama, Markus, & Kurokawa, 2000; Kitayama, Mesquita, & Karasawa, 2002), adopting a variety of methodologies that rule out that the results can be explained from a mere response bias.

Self-focused versus Other-focused Pleasantness

Interestingly, pleasantness itself also appears to be different across different cultures, in ways that are closely tied with the models (Markus & Kitayama, 1994). Whereas disjoint models of agency define active control over one's environment and independent achievement as pleasant experiences, conjoint models will emphasize the connection with other people as conditional to pleasantness.

Several studies have found support for a relatively strong association between pleasantness and connection or engagement in Japan and, conversely, between pleasantness and personal competence or disengagement from others in the United States (Kitayama et al., 2000; Kitayama et al., 2002; Mesquita & Karasawa, 2002). For example, Kitayama and his colleagues (2000) distinguished between positively engaged emotions, such as *amae*, or in the American translation "feel like being babied," and positively disengaged emotions, such as "on top of the world." They also distinguished a category of general positive feelings (e.g., calm, happy). Participants were asked to rate the frequency of emotions within each of those three categories of positive emotions. The study yielded that Japanese felt good when they were positively engaged, whereas Americans felt good when they were in control of how they were doing. That is, in the Japanese group general positive feelings were most closely associated with *engaged positive* emotions (*amae* or feeling like being babied). Positive feelings in the U.S. group were most closely associated with *interpersonally disengaged* emotions (proud, superior, top of the world). This and other studies support the notion that cultural models of agency shape the nature of pleasantness (and unpleasantness). Together, these studies make a case that pleasantness can be a different experience in different cultures.

Appraisal or Antecedents?

To some extent the differences in appraisal practices may reflect differences in the ecology of antecedent events. It is very plausible that there *are* more pleasant situations in the United States, and that there *are* more situations in Japan than in the U.S.A. that are relevant to interpersonal connection. It is thus very likely that at least some of the differences in appraisal can be reduced to the different worlds that are encountered and created in different cultures.

However, some evidence is emerging that the cultural differences are also inherent in the appraisal process itself, and therefore that cultural models of agency are reflected in the very way individuals appraise their environment. The evidence comes from a study by Kitayama, Matsumoto, Markus, and Norasakkunkit (1997) on differences in self-esteem appraisals in the U.S.A. and Japan. Consistent with the cultural models of agency, Americans were found to interpret situations more readily as self-esteem-enhancing, whereas Japanese appraised them more readily as self-esteem-decreasing.

In a first study, American and Japanese students described situations of failure and success. These situations were presented to new groups of respondents. In the actual study, American and Japanese respondents appraised the same stimulus situations, which were either of American or of Japanese origin, and which described either success or failure. Despite the similarity in emotional stimuli, different appraisal tendencies were established in these two cultural groups (Figure 20.1). Americans judged that their self-esteem would increase more in success situations than it would decrease in the failure situations. By contrast, the Japanese students judged that their self-esteem would decrease more in the failure situations than it would increase in the success situations (Kitayama et al., 1997). Interestingly, situations provided by the culture itself proved particularly powerful in eliciting the desired psychological tendencies. The tendency of Americans to appraise situations as self-enhancing was particularly

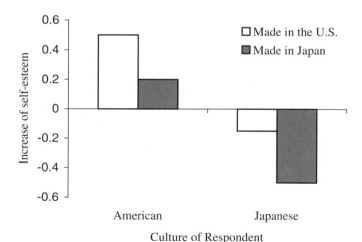

FIGURE 20.1. Self-Esteem Change: Increase of self-esteem on success situations (scale 1–4) *minus* the decrease of self-esteem on failure situations (scale 1–4).

strong for success situations that were generated by Americans. On the other hand, the tendency of Japanese toward self-criticism was particularly strong for failure situations that were generated by Japanese. Thus, interpretations consistent with the cultural model were most strongly suggested by events that were generated by that culture.

The Bigger Picture

The picture emerges that emotional practices vary along with the particular models of agency. Those models produce different contexts, different choices within a given context, and different constructions or appraisals of the context. Culture shapes emotions in any way it can: There is "redundancy" in the working of culture (Levy, 1978). A disjoint model of agency generates more situations in which the individual can feel free and unique, promotes individuals to make choices that affirm their uniqueness and separation from others, and affords appraisals of situations as pleasant and self-esteem-enhancing that, again, add to the idea that the person is unique and autonomous. The cultural model of agency is thus inescapably part of the construction of emotional practices.

COPING

Models of agency can be seen to affect emotional coping as well. By emotional coping, we mean all ways in which an individual attempts to arrange a new fit between the individual and his/her world after some emotional event. "Coping," in our definition, refers to the course of emotions rather than to some post-emotion process; it includes *appraisals* in the context of coping, *action readiness, plans and goals* set within the emotional context, and *behaviors*.

Successful coping should be grounded in the cultural models of agency, because these models dictate what can be considered a fit between an individual and her world, and they also offer, or even prescribe, what are acceptable ways of achieving it. Thus the ways in which emotions develop through coping are presumably constrained and afforded by the cultural models of agency.

Mesquita, Karasawa, Haire, and Izumi (2002) collected some evidence that coping with emotions varies according to cultural models of agency. They conducted a large interview study in which American and Japanese respondents, men and women, community and student samples, were asked to report situations in which they had encountered an offense. The researchers hypothesized that American and Japanese coping with offense would differ greatly in ways that were predictable and understandable from the two different models of agency, disjoint and conjoint respectively.

The most frequently reported ways of coping in the American group were in fact consistent with a disjoint model of agency. The vast majority of Americans reported blaming the offender, aggression, and distancing oneself of the relationship, whereas only a small minority of Japanese did. All three of these coping responses can be considered consistent with a disjoint model of agency. Blaming is a way of reaffirming the positive value of the self by attributing responsibility to another. Blaming, aggression, and distancing all create a clear distinction between the individual and the offender, a coping choice that seems much more readily available to those who are independent, in principle, of the relationship. Aggression, furthermore, is a clear attempt to actively influence the environment and involves pressure to change the relationship in order to fit the individual's goals. Finally, distancing oneself from a relationship that had a negative impact on the self illustrates the priority given to individual well-being over the importance of the relationship. Thus, Americans tend to cope with offense in ways that (*a*) salvage positive self-esteem, (*b*) actively influence the offender, and (*c*) prioritize the concerns of the individual over those of the relationship. These coping outcomes are consistent with disjoint models of agency.

In contrast, Japanese cultural models of agency suggest different coping goals, such as maintaining or improving relationships (Heine et al., 1999; Markus & Kitayama, 1991) and adjusting to relationships in ways that do not disturb them (Morling, Kitayama, & Miyamoto, 2002). Consistent with these goals, many Japanese respondents reported doing nothing, taking responsibility for the offense, and seeking closeness to the offender, while very few American respondents endorsed these ways of coping. Doing nothing is a way of adjusting to the environment without disrupting the normal course of events. Taking responsibility and seeking closeness are coping responses that seek the opposite effect of blaming: keeping the other close and repairing the relationship. These coping responses also exemplify how the other person's perspective is taken. The respondent wonders: "Why did the offender behave as he or she did" rather than "What do I feel?" Japanese coping with offense is thus geared toward (*a*) adjustment to the situation, (*b*) reestablishing or maintaining relationships, and (*c*) taking an outside-in perspective. This is well illustrated by an example of a Japanese self-report:

Offense: My mother takes care of me too much. She treats me as a child. So I said to her: "I am twenty years old. Please, let me free." But she said, "I should watch you, because you are not mature enough."
Coping: I really wanted to make her understand [closer], but there is no way. I know that because of my twenty years of experience with my mom. There is nothing I can actually do [nothing], but I am going to try and show her I am okay [relationship goal]. I wonder if this will continue forever [not codable]. (Japanese female student)

In sum, as the models of agency vary across these cultural contexts, so do ways of coping, and thus the emotions.

Coping or Antecedents?

Cultural differences in the course of emotions may be due to differences in eliciting events or, alternatively, to differences in the coping process itself. Again, differences in coping would not be any less "real" if they were due primarily to the cross-culturally different contexts in which they arose. Whatever the source, differences in coping represent significant differences in the modal emotional practices, and thus in the emotional experiences that people in different cultures have. Moreover, the creation and construction of the emotional context are based on real psychological processes, processes of emotion and motivation.

However, in order to assess whether cultural models of agency were reflected in coping directly, Idzelis, Mesquita, Karasawa, and Hayashi (2002) also examined if the cultural differences in coping with offense would hold when keeping the stimulus situations constant. The researchers asked American and Japanese students to imagine they were the protagonists in a number of the situations that had been reported in the interview study on coping. For each situation, the participants indicated the extent to which they would have certain appraisals, behaviors, and emotions. Some responses (e.g., aggression) were consistent with disjoint models of agency and derived from frequent responses in the American groups of the interview study (Mesquita, Karasawa, Haire et al., in preparation), whereas other responses (e.g., doing nothing) were consistent with conjoint models of agency and derived from frequent responses in the Japanese groups of respondents in the interview study. By and large, the cultural differences in coping that were found in the interview study were replicated in the vignette study. Furthermore, the origin of the situations did not interact with the type of coping, which means that the tendencies to cope in culture-specific ways were seen as much for vignettes generated in the United States as for vignettes generated in Japan. As an illustration of the results, Figure 20.2 shows the interaction with respect to behaviors. Americans reported more "American" behaviors, which were consistent with disjoint models of agency. On the other hand, Japanese reported more "Japanese" behaviors, that is, behaviors that are consistent with conjoint models of agency. Emotional practices of coping thus seem to be different along with the models of agency, even when the contexts of elicitation are artificially kept constant.

Coping as a Constituent of Emotional Practices

It is clear that cultural models of agency shape emotional practices in many different ways. One way would be through coping. Individuals'

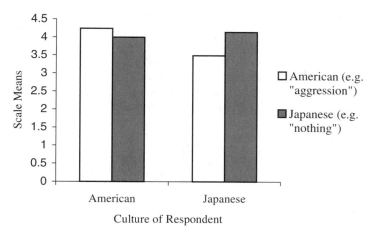

FIGURE 20.2. Cultural Differences in Coping with Offense: Behavior [$F(1,90) = 7.75$ ($p < .01$)].

coping behaviors will contribute to the development of new situations that in turn will elicit new emotions. Americans who cope with offense by reemphasizing the independence of the individual and by demonstrating proactive agency may in fact meet with interpersonal distance and self-affirmation. On the other hand, because Japanese cope with offense by repressing disruptive responses, and by maintaining and emphasizing the relational status quo, they are more likely to create situations of harmony and connectedness that will be the new emotion-eliciting contexts for emotional responses. Thus, coping itself will contribute to the cultural practices which then shape the emotional practices.

CONCLUSION

There are thus important cultural differences in emotions that can be predicted and understood, but more importantly connected to each other, in the light of cultural models of agency. The influence of cultural models goes beyond providing content to an otherwise static and universal emotion process; cultural models affect the very processes of emotions themselves. The selection of contexts, the response selection within components of appraisal, the coping that is entailed by the emotions, are all guided and afforded by cultural models.

The quest for cultural differences has thus led us to take seriously what many psychologists have maintained for a long time: Emotions are processes rather than static entities. The cultural shaping of emotions becomes most apparent when we focus on process characteristics of emotions, that is, processes of response activation. Within a culture, situations tend to be selected and appraisals and ways of coping activated in ways that are consistent with the particular model of agency in that culture. Cultural differences are thus largely a matter of process. Of course, the research discussed only addresses differences in process characteristics in a very indirect way. Differential processes of response activation have been inferred from culturally different rates of certain responses. One way to further the research on cultural differences in emotional practices would thus be to study the mechanism of response activation more directly. This would be a new venue in emotion psychology.

Importantly, the approach that we have taken is a functional one. The very course of emotions – the ways in which the potential of emotions is realized – appears to differ as a function of cultural models of agency. This is not to say that people in a culture are willingly adjusting their emotions to the prescriptions of the culture. As we have discussed, cultural models of agency are typically invisible to those who engage in the model. Yet, cultural models serve as motivating forces by the values they attach to different situations and emotion outputs. Obviously, those values can be either negative, thus motivating one to avoid certain situations or outputs, or positive, inducing approach or promotion. Very importantly, culture is reflected not just in regulation post hoc, but is reflected in all aspects of emotion.

References

Abu-Lughod, L. (1986). *Veiled sentiments*. Berkeley: University of California Press.

Befu, H. (1986). An ethnography of dinner entertainment in Japan. In T. S. Lebra and W. P. Lebra (Eds.), *Japanese culture and behavior. Selected readings* (pp. 108–120). Honolulu: University of Hawai'i Press.

Benedict, R. (1946). *The chrysanthemum and the sword: Patterns of Japanese culture*. Boston: Houghton Mifflin.

Briggs, J. L. (1970). *Never in anger: Portrait of an Eskimo family*. Cambridge, MA: Harvard University Press.

Bruner, J. (1990). *Acts of meaning*. Cambridge, MA: Harvard University Press.

D'Andrade, R. G. (1984). Culture meaning systems. In R. A. Shweder and R. A. Levine (Eds.), *Culture theory: Essays on mind, self, and emotion* (pp. 88–119). Cambridge: Cambridge University Press.

Doi, L. T. (1973). *The autonomy of dependence*. Tokyo: Kodansha.

Ekman, P.; Friesen, W. V.; O'Sullivan, M.; Chan, A.; Diacoyanni-Tarlatzis, I.; Heider, K.; Krause, R.; LeCompte, W. A.; Pitcairn, T.; Ricci-Bitti, P. E.; Scherer, K. R.; Tomita, M.; & Tzavaras, A. (1987). Universals and cultural differences in the judgements of facial expressions of emotion. *Journal of Personality and Social Psychology, 53(4)*, 712–717.

Elliott, A.; Chirkov, V.; Kim, Y.; & Sheldon, K. (2001). A cross-cultural analysis of avoidance (relative to approach) personal goals. *Psychological Science, 12*, 505–510.

Ellsworth, P. C. (1994). Sense, culture, and sensibility. In S. Kitayama and H. R. Markus (Eds.), *Emotion and culture: Empirical studies of mutual influence*. Washington, DC: American Psychological Association.

Frijda, N. H. (1986). *The emotions*. Cambridge: Cambridge University Press.

Heine, S. J.; Lehman, D. R.; Markus, H. R.; & Kitayama, S. (1999). Is there a universal need for positive self-regard? *Psychological Review, 106(4)*, 766–794.

Higgins, E.; Shah, J.; & Friedman, R. J. (1997). Emotional responses to goal attainment: Strength of regulatory focus as a moderator. *Journal of Personality and Social Psychology, 72*, 515–525.

Holland, D.; Lachicotte, W., Jr.; Skinner, D., & Cain, C. (1998). *Identity and agency in cultural worlds*. Cambridge, MA: Harvard University Press.

Idzelis, M.; Mesquita, B.; Karasawa, M.; & Hayashi, A. (2002). *Cultural differences in emotional coping: American and Japanese responses to offense*. Paper presented at the Third Annual Meeting of the Society for Personality and Social Psychology, February, Savannah, GA.

Izard, C. E. (1994). Innate and universal facial expressions: Evidence from developmental and cross-cultural research. *Psychological Bulletin, 115*, 288–299.

Karasawa, M. (2001). Nihonnjinnni okeru jitano ninnshiki: Jikohihan baiasuto tasyakouyou baiasu [A Japanese mode of self-making: Self-criticism and other enhancement]. *Japanese Journal of Psychology, 72(4)*, 198–209.

Kim, H. (2001). *Deviance: Uniqueness and time in context*. Paper presented at the Society for Personality and Social Psychology, San Antonio, TX.

Kim, H. H. W., & Markus, H. R. (1999). Deviance or uniqueness, harmony or conformity? A cultural analysis. *Journal of Personality and Social Psychology, 77(4)*, 785–800.

Kitayama, S.; Markus, H. R.; & Kurokawa, M. (2000). Culture, emotion, and well-being: Good feelings in Japan and the United States. *Cognition and Emotion, 14(1)*, 93–124.

Kitayama, S.; Matsumoto, D.; Markus, H. R.; & Norasakkunkit, V. (1997). Individual and collective processes in the construction of the self: Self-enhancement in the US and self-criticism in Japan. *Journal of Personality and Social Psychology, 72(6)*, 1245–1267.

Kitayama, S.; Mesquita, B.; & Karasawa, M. (2002). The emotional basis of independent and interdependent selves: The intensity of experiencing engaging and disengaging emotions in the US and Japan. Manuscript under review.

Lee, A. Y.; Aaker, J. L.; & Gardner, W. L. (2000). The pleasures and pains of distinct self-construals: The role of interdependence in regulatory focus. *Journal of Personality and Social Psychology, 78(6)*, 1122–1134.

Levy, R. I. (1978). Tahitian gentleness and redundant controls. In A. Montagu (Ed.), *Learning non-aggression: The experience of non-literate societies* (pp. 222–235). New York: Oxford University Press.

Lewis, C. C. (1995). *Educating hearts and minds*. New York: Cambridge University Press.

Lutz, C. (1988). Ethnographic perspectives on the emotion lexicon. In V. E. A. Hamilton (Ed.), *Cognitive perspectives on emotion and motivation* (pp. 399–419). New York: Kluwer Academic.

Markus, H. R., & Kitayama, S. (1991). Culture and self: Implications for cognition, emotion, and motivation. *Psychological Review, 98(2)*, 224–253.

Markus, H. R., & Kitayama, S. (1994). The cultural construction of self and emotion: Implications for social behavior. In S. Kitayama and H. R. Markus (Eds.), *Emotion and culture: Empirical studies of mutual influence* (pp. 89–130). Washington, DC: American Psychological Association.

Markus, H. R., & Kitayama, S. (In press). Models of agency: Sociocultural diversity in the construction of action. *Nebraska symposium on motivation.*

Markus, H. R.; Mullally, P. R.; & Kitayama, S. (1997). Selfways: Diversity in modes of cultural participation. In U. Neisser and D. A. Jopling (Eds.), *The conceptual self in context: Culture, experience, self-understanding* (pp. 13–61). Cambridge: Cambridge University Press.

Mesquita, B. (2001a). Culture and emotion. Different approaches to the question. In T. J. Mayne and G. A. Bonanno (Eds.), *Emotions. Current issues and future directions* (pp. 214–250). New York: Guilford Press.

Mesquita, B. (2001b). Emotions in collectivist and individualist contexts. *Journal of Personality and Social Psychology, 80(1),* 68–74.

Mesquita, B. (2002). Emotions as dynamic cultural phenomena. In R. Davidson, H. Goldsmith, and K. R. Scherer (Eds.), *The handbook of the affective sciences* (pp. 871–890). New York: Oxford University Press.

Mesquita, B., & Ellsworth, P. C. (2001). The role of culture in appraisal. In K. R. Scherer and A. Schorr (Eds.), *Appraisal processes in emotion: Theory, methods, research* (pp. 233–248). New York: Oxford University Press.

Mesquita, B., & Frijda, N. H. (1992). Cultural variations in emotions: A review. *Psychological Bulletin, 112(2),* 179–204.

Mesquita, B.; Frijda, N. H.; & Scherer, K. R. (1997). Culture and emotion. In P. Dasen and T. S. Saraswathi (Eds.), *Handbook of cross-cultural psychology* (Vol. 2, pp. 255–297). Boston: Allyn & Bacon.

Mesquita, B., & Karasawa, M. (2002). Different emotional lives. *Cognition and Emotion, 16(1),* 127–141.

Mesquita, B.; Karasawa, M.; & Chu, R. L. (In preparation). *Predictors of pleasantness in three cultures: A comparison between the United States, Japan, and Taiwan.* Winston-Salem: Wake Forest University.

Mesquita, B.; Karasawa, M.; Haire, A.; & Izumi, S. (In preparation). The emotion process as a function of cultural models: A comparison between American, Mexican, and Japanese cultures.

Miller, J. G.; Fung, H.; & Mintz, J. (1996). Self-construction through narrative practices: A Chinese and American comparison of early socialization. *Ethos, 24,* 237–280.

Morling, B.; Kitayama, S.; & Miyamoto, Y. (2002). Cultural practices emphasize influence in the United States and adjustment in Japan. *Personality and Social Psychology Bulletin, 28(3),* 311–323.

Shweder, R. A. (1991). *Thinking through cultures.* Cambridge, MA: Harvard University Press.

Stephenson, P. H. (1989). Going to McDonalds in Leiden: Reflections on the concept of self and society in the Netherlands. *Ethos, 17,* 226–247.

Van Der Horst, H. (1996). *The low sky: Understanding the Dutch.* Den Haag, The Netherlands: Scriptum Books.

Wierzbicka, A. (1994). Emotion, language, and cultural scripts. In S. Kitayama and H. R. Markus (Eds.), *Emotion and culture: Emperical studies of mutual influence.* Washington, DC: American Psychological Association.

21

Emotion Norms, Emotion Work, and Social Order

Peggy A. Thoits

ABSTRACT

The social origins and functions of emotion norms are examined. Emotion norms both reflect and sustain the social structures in which they develop. Individuals undergo emotional socialization and are subject to pressures to conform, especially adults in service and professional jobs, who actively manage reactions that violate social expectations. Efforts at emotional conformity help to sustain the social order, maintain hierarchy, and build solidarity. Emotional deviants are usually stigmatized and subjected to social control, but under some conditions they can become agents of social change.

An experiment by Dutton and Aron (1974) is often used in psychology textbooks to illustrate the role of cognition in emotional experience. The study was intended to demonstrate that physiological arousal can be misattributed to the wrong cause. Men who were approached by an attractive experimenter after crossing a suspension bridge over a deep gorge were more likely to indicate romantic or sexual interest in the experimenter, in contrast to men who had crossed a low wooden bridge over a stream. Dutton and Aron concluded, consistent with Schachter's two-factor theory of emotion (Schachter & Singer, 1962), that emotions are in part determined by available cognitive cues, not by physiological reactions alone.

The idea that our perceptions affect our experiences has a long and honorable tradition in sociology, too. But the results of the Dutton and Aron study are sociologically interesting for other reasons. If one conducts a quick thought experiment, substituting an attractive *male* experimenter approaching *women* who have just traversed a swaying or a stable bridge, one arrives at a different set of probable results: Women would be less likely to misattribute their state of arousal to romantic or sexual interest in the male experimenter. It is more socially acceptable for women to admit fear than for men; it is more socially acceptable for men to show open interest in the opposite sex than for women. In short, the original

359

experiment "worked" because it was grounded in shared social norms about gender-appropriate emotional behaviors – norms taken for granted by the experimenters. Bringing these implicit norms to the forefront and elaborating their implications for interpersonal behavior, societal organization, and group survival is sociology's ongoing contribution to the interdisciplinary dialogue about the nature and functions of emotion and affect. The purpose of this chapter is to highlight the personal and social origins and consequences of emotion norms in group life.

Hochschild (1979) introduced the concept of "emotion norms," an umbrella term covering two important subsets of social rules, "feeling norms" and "expression rules." Feeling norms indicate the range, duration, intensity, and/or targets of emotions that are appropriate to *feel* in specific situations ("You're supposed to be happy at a wedding," "You shouldn't feel so guilty about that," "It's time for you to let go of your anger"). Expression rules guide appropriate *displays* of emotion in given situations (e.g., passionate kissing in public is improper, big boys shouldn't cry, one should show gratitude for a gift).[1] Hochschild argued that both types of emotion – private, subjective experiences and public, observable expressions – are subject to social rules and social control.[2]

If affects are governed by social expectations (as a wealth of evidence reviewed here will show), then several theoretical implications follow. First, because emotion norms (like all norms) are social constructions, they will vary in content over time, cultures, and contexts, both reflecting and sustaining the social structures in which they develop. Second, because emotion rules (like all rules) are learned, children and adults undergo emotional socialization and are subject to pressures to conform. Third, because individuals are motivated to seek approval and avoid sanctions, they will hide, transform, or otherwise manage emotions that occasionally violate emotional expectations (as they hide occasional rule-breaking behaviors). Fourth, such efforts at emotional conformity (like efforts at behavioral conformity) have functional social consequences. Finally, because some individuals refuse or fail to obey emotion norms (as they do other norms), "emotional deviants" (Thoits, 1985) will be labeled, stigmatized, and subjected to social control, or, under some conditions, they may become agents of social change. How emotion norms are produced by and themselves help to produce social order and social change in these ways will be elaborated further in this chapter.

---

[1] Expression norms correspond to what Ekman (Ekman, Friesen, & Ellsworth, 1982) termed "display rules."

[2] In contrast, Ekman (e.g., Ekman et al., 1982) and others consider basic emotions to be innate reactions to environmental stimuli, free from cultural or social regulation; only emotional displays are socially controlled. The evidence reviewed here will indicate otherwise.

Most sociological research on emotion examines one or more of the implications listed above, which generally center on the causes or consequences of adherence to and deviations from societal feeling and expression norms. Those who investigate the determinants of emotional conventions usually take a social construction of reality approach (e.g., Cancian, 1987; Denzin, 1990; Illouz, 1997); those who study consequences typically emphasize the adaptive functions of emotional regulation and conformity (e.g., Cahill, 1999; Clark, 1997). Because symbolic interactionist theory merges constructionist and functionalist thinking, this approach tends to dominate sociological research on affect in sociology.

Briefly, symbolic interactionism views self and society as reciprocally related; individuals are both products and producers of social order (McCall & Simmons, 1978; Stryker & Statham, 1985). Through social interaction, people learn to categorize themselves and others, learn the behavioral expectations attached to their own and others' role-identities, and are motivated to meet others' expectations in order to gain approval and rewards. When actors conform to others' expectations in their identity performances, they are in effect maintaining the social order. This is the structural-functionalist aspect of the theory: Society shapes (i.e., socializes) the self, and the well-socialized self in turn sustains society.

But the self is not simply a social product. The possibility of social construction or social change also resides in human nature. Symbolic interactionists assume that humans are creative, spontaneous creatures, capable of exerting choice and self-determination when circumstances allow. Improvisation is a routine feature of daily life, making possible the renegotiation of identity meanings and behavioral expectations. New norms, values, beliefs, and behaviors are among the many potential innovations that, if widely adopted by other people, can be constructed or changed.

Where do emotions and emotion norms fit in such thought? To role-identities are attached not only behavioral expectations but expectations for feelings and expression. These norms are part of the broader emotion culture acquired in social interaction. Well-socialized actors are motivated to abide by these emotion norms but are not always able to do so. The structural origins of dissident feelings, how those feelings are reworked to meet social expectations, and the consequences of conforming and deviant emotions for self and society are thus fodder for sociological inquiry.

THE SOCIAL CONSTRUCTION OF EMOTIONS, EMOTION CULTURE, AND EMOTION NORMS

Because emotion norms both reflect and shape people's affective experiences, it may be useful to clarify the sociological view of emotions in general. Within anthropology, psychology, and sociology, disagreements persist regarding whether emotions are cultural constructions or cultural universals. Despite such debates, a majority of sociologists have adopted a middle-of-the-road approach to the issue of emotional hard-wiring (e.g., Kemper, 1987; Thoits, 1985). Drawing from evolutionary psychologists, they acknowledge the innate, biological basis of the primary or basic emotions (e.g., fear, anger, sadness, happiness, disgust) and the adaptive functions of these emotions for the survival of the species (Ekman et al., 1982). Drawing from anthropology and social history, sociologists recognize that the meanings of emotions, even basic ones such as anger and sadness, have varied across places, peoples, and time (e.g., Levy, 1984; Kleinman & Kleinman, 1985; Shweder, 1994; Stearns & Stearns, 1986). For example, Levy (1984) and Kleinman and Kleinman (1985) observed that bereaved Tahitians and Chinese adults who were uprooted during the Cultural Revolution, respectively, "hyper-cognized" (overemphasized) the somatic aspects of grief and depression and "hypo-cognized" (ignored) the affective components of these states, complaining that they were sick, overcome with fatigue, drained of energy, and so forth, rather than sad. Stearns and Stearns's (1986) historical research showed that, as the Industrial Revolution transformed the nature of work (creating more service, managerial, and professional jobs) and altered the meaning of family life (from the locus of farm livelihood to an emotional haven from an impersonal, highly competitive world), middle-class Americans came to view angry feelings as disruptive and insisted on anger control at work and at home. Research showing differences in subjective experience across cultures and time convinced sociologists that not only emotion norms but the meaning of emotional experiences themselves were cultural constructs, at least in part (few would claim that emotions are *solely* social constructions).

Focusing on the socioculturally malleable aspects of emotion, then, sociologists have contributed to this interdisciplinary body of research by more closely examining both the content of "emotion culture" (Gordon, 1989) and its structural origins. Emotion culture consists of beliefs about the nature, causes, distributions, value, and dynamics of emotions in general as well as of specific feelings, such as love, anger, and jealousy. In Western emotion culture, for example, emotions are thought to be bodily reactions to external stimuli, women are viewed as more emotional than men, negative emotions are regarded as undesirable, intense affective states are thought to dissipate with time, and some feelings (infatuations, lust) and emotional displays (tantrums) are believed to be characteristic of the young but not the very old. These tenets and many others, including norms regarding situationally appropriate feelings and emotional displays, constitute a large body of folk knowledge, passed down from one generation to the next.

Sociologists have traced changes in emotion culture, including changes in emotion norms, to changes in social structure. Structure can be broadly described as the ways in which human relationships are organized. It is a truism to observe that culture reflects social structure, but structural patterns are also products of culture. It is almost impossible to disentangle cultural and structural influences at a single point in time. However, longitudinal studies allow an examination of the interplay between the two forces. Typically, structural arrangements alter more quickly than cultural ideologies or norms, so that beliefs about what "ought" to be thought, felt, or done by societal members lag behind what they actually think, feel, or do. These differential rates of change in patterned behaviors and in beliefs help to unravel the reciprocal relations between structure and culture.

As an example, Lofland (1985) has argued that the intensity and duration of grief experiences have increased over the twentieth century in Western countries as social arrangements have changed. Specifically, as infant mortality has plunged and life expectancy has lengthened, bereavement has become less frequent in people's lives, so each death carries greater emotional impact. Family size has shrunk and nuclear families increasingly live separately from kin, making emotional attachments among coresident family members more intense, again augmenting the impact of loss. Leisure time has increased and bigger homes allow greater privacy, giving individuals more opportunities to withdraw and brood upon loss, lengthening the duration of grief. In short, demographic shifts and alterations in the structure of family life have intensified and prolonged the bereavement experience.

Note that Lofland describes changes in subjective *experiences* over time, rather than changes in emotion norms or emotion culture per se. However, recurrent individual experiences tend to become emotional conventions, or norms. People develop expectations about the intensity and duration of grief based on their own and the often observed experiences of others, and these expectations (norms) are passed on to others. The demographic and structural trends described by Lofland should not only be associated with self-reported grief experiences but with changes in norms regarding how much grief is "normal" and how long it should persist, stated in self-help books and texts for bereavement counselors, for example.

Changes in romantic love norms have also been analyzed structurally. Cancian (1987) has shown that historical changes in American women's roles have "feminized" the meaning and manifestations of love and have generated competing cultural models of commitment to love relationships. Briefly, in shifting the location of work from farm to factory, the Industrial Revolution polarized gender roles. Men became the primary breadwinners, while women became the socioemotional specialists, responsible for the home and family members' emotional well-being. Love and loving thus became culturally linked with females and femininity. However, structural trends over the last fifty years have increased women's economic and political independence, shifting the balance of power in relationships and forcing men to take more responsibility for maintaining love and affection. This more equalized sharing of the "work" of maintaining relationships has resulted in more androgynous cultural models of committed love. In the "independence model," individuals make long-term commitments only after developing strong, independent selves ("I have to find myself first"). In the "interdependence model," individuals achieve self-development through the process of sustaining a commitment. Evidence supports the existence of these two ideological models in contemporary American emotion culture (Cancian, 1987; Cancian & Gordon, 1989).

These and other studies (e.g., Stearns & Stearns, 1986) suggest that structural changes indeed alter cultural ideologies about emotion. Although emotion culture typically reflects and reinforces social structures, cultural content may also be deliberately shaped by "culture-producing institutions" (Denzin, 1990), especially the mass media. Illouz (1997) has demonstrated that Western images of romantic love (associated with youth, beauty, freedom, pleasure, and intimacy) and romantic practices (candlelight dining, going dancing, traveling to isolated, exotic settings) are products of advanced capitalism. In ads, films, TV shows, and novels, the ritual consumption of luxuries and sexual intimacy in isolated settings are repeatedly associated with romance. So deeply ingrained in the American psyche are these images that couples automatically use them to characterize their most intimate and authentic romantic experiences. Although Illouz's interviewees are clearly aware that their concepts are a product of consumer culture, they still internalize and actualize these cultural fabrications in their subjective experiences of and normative expectations for romantic love.

Hochschild (1983) has offered perhaps the most influential observations of the effects of capitalist structure on emotion culture and affective experience in her pioneering study of Delta flight attendants. Hochschild argued that the postindustrial shift in Western nations toward service economies (i.e., based more on the provision of services and less on the production of food and goods) has generated demands for workers skilled in self-presentation and emotional control. In service work, profit generally depends on pleasing the customer or client, so employers exert economic control over employees' emotional self-presentations with warnings, firings, promotions, and pay raises. In Hochschild's terms, such jobs involve "emotional labor." For "service with a smile" to be profitable, however, smiles must be genuine – one must smile and "really mean it." Thus, not only workers' expressive displays but their private feelings become commodities to be exchanged for a salary or wage. To meet companies' demands for "genuine" feelings, employees routinely engage in "emotion work" or "emotion management" to produce those feelings, risking, Hochschild suggests, eventual self-alienation or a persistent sense of inauthenticity.

In sum, emotional ideologies and norms not only spring from existing social arrangements that repeatedly evoke particular emotional experiences in societal members, but these may be deliberately created to justify and/or serve the goals of small groups, specific companies, whole industries, or entire social systems. It is important to note that because industrial and postindustrial societies are highly complex, emotion cultures are also likely to be complex. Any one society may contain multiple, overlapping, and potentially conflicting emotional ideologies, and, within them, a great diversity of emotion norms that individuals can use to interpret, evaluate, and justify their own and others' feelings and expressions.

EMOTIONAL SOCIALIZATION

Emotion culture is transmuted into behavior, and hence into social structure, through the process of socialization. Emotional socialization is the acquisition of the emotional knowledge, values, and skills that are appropriate to a person's age, gender, race/ethnicity, social class, and so on. In contrast to psychologists, who largely have focused on *how* children learn the meaning of feelings and expressive displays (e.g., operant conditioning, modeling), or *when* in the developmental process various aspects of this knowledge are acquired, sociologists have focused on *what* children and adults learn in the process of emotional socialization. The transmission of normative content is important because emotion norms not only define situationally appropriate feelings and displays but are intended to impel experience and action ("you *should* feel this," "you *must not* show that"). Understanding normative content, then, should better predict individuals' affects and behaviors.

Only a few studies have examined the emotion norms that are taught to children or adolescents (Leavitt & Power, 1989; Pollak & Thoits, 1989; Simon, Eder, & Evans, 1992). Most sociological research on emotional socialization has focused instead on adults who are entering new social roles (spouse, parent, employee) and acquiring the values, skills, and knowledge needed to perform them. An avalanche of these studies analyzed emotional socialization on the job, following in Hochschild's (1983) ground-breaking footsteps.

Studies of supermarket clerks (Tolich, 1993), fast food and sales workers (Leidner, 1993), and the like confirmed and elaborated Hochschild's observations that sales and service employees are explicitly admonished to smile and are trained in techniques of suppressing and transforming unacceptable emotions. However, many other occupations, particularly professional ones (e.g., psychiatrists, physicians, mortuary directors, paralegals, attorneys, wedding consultants), also require their practitioners to adhere to specific emotion norms, and they transmit techniques for handling improper feelings (although emotional socialization is often informal and implicit). For example, medical students learn that it is important to maintain a stance of affective neutrality toward patients through watching and imitating the comportment and practices of their instructors and advanced peers (Hafferty, 1988; Smith & Kleinman, 1989). Even skilled laborers, such as high-steel ironworkers, receive informal socialization in the dominant emotion norms of their occupation (never show fear, never lose emotional control) and implicit training in emotion management (Haas, 1977). In short, a multitude of studies show emotional socialization to be an important aspect of occupational training for workers in a wide variety of jobs, not just sales and service.

Taken together, studies of adult emotional socialization on the job raise a set of more general issues. First, virtually all studies showed that despite extensive training in the emotion norms of their occupations, workers often had difficulties in experiencing or expressing the emotional states that were expected of them.[3] Why do well-socialized individuals sometimes feel or display what they should not, or *not* feel or display what they should? Second, studies showed that people employed a broad array of strategies to bring their actual feelings back in line with normative expectations. Do emotion management strategies relate systematically to individuals' structural circumstances? Third, some investigations suggested that frequent or prolonged emotion management efforts could damage individuals' psychological well-being. Are attempts at emotional conformity truly damaging? Research on "emotion work" has suggested answers to these questions.[4]

EMOTION WORK: CAUSES, PATTERNS, AND CONSEQUENCES

Causes of Discrepant Emotions

Hochschild (1983) implied a structural answer to the question of the origins of non-normative feelings, observing that the organization of air travel changed dramatically over the decades, creating a "speedup" and intensification of job demands for flight attendants. Cabins are crowded, flights are delayed, passengers must receive meals in shorter amounts of time, and attendants take the brunt of passengers' tempers, sexism, and occasional drunken unruliness. These highly stressful conditions of work differ considerably from the relaxed conditions in which the company emotion norms for flight attendants were originally developed.

---

[3] Several investigators point out that problematic relationships with supervisors and coworkers are also key sources of inappropriate emotions and emotion management efforts on the job (Lively, 2000; Morris & Feldman, 1996; Pugliesi, 1999). So clients or customers are not the only causes of emotional norm violations in the occupational realm.

[4] The term "emotion work" or "emotion management" is more inclusive than "emotional labor." Emotion work occurs not only on the job but also in other domains of life, as people try to align their feelings with normative expectations attached to a particular situation. "Emotional labor" refers to emotion work performed on the job in order to meet company standards.

A more general principle is suggested here. When structural conditions are complex, multifaceted, and/or highly demanding, but the norms that apply to those situations are simple and clear, individuals are more likely to experience inappropriate emotions (Thoits, 1985). People react emotionally to cues in an immediate situation, but these reactions conflict with norms that apply to the modal or idealized situation. Although such structural strains are commonly found in occupational settings, they have been well documented in other adult role domains, particularly parenting (e.g., Frude & Goss, 1981).

Other structural causes can be cited. People who perform multiple roles may experience inappropriate feelings due to conflicting emotional expectations attached to those roles (Thoits, 1985). Working parents with a sick child at home are an example: Anxiety or upset about the child is perfectly acceptable, even required, for parents, but these feelings are improper and distracting at work. Similar conflicts may be experienced by individuals who were raised in two cultural traditions with competing emotion norms. Periods of structural change can also make non-normative feelings more common. When social arrangements are varied or in flux, individuals experience new, unexpected, or unusual life transitions (e.g., acquiring or becoming a stepparent, "coming out of the closet"). Because these transitions are not ritualized (unlike graduations, weddings, and retirements), they lack well-defined norms for behavior *or* emotion. Lacking standards against which to evaluate their emotional reactions, people worry that their feelings are somehow wrong (Thoits, 1985). Alternatively, emotional reactions that were appropriate in one time period may become unacceptable in another – for example, possessive jealousy became a forbidden emotion among hippies during the sixties' countercultural revolution.

Finally, regardless of structural causes, people's innate or spontaneous emotional reactions to environmental stimuli can conflict with existing emotion norms. Individuals may react to certain foods with disgust, to heights with paralyzing fear, or to the sight of an amputee with horror, but be expected not to have these reactions at all or to mask them. Such emotional conflicts are especially common in occupations that require workers to perform acts that most people have been taught to regard as forbidden or taboo: killing, butchering, handling dead or naked bodies, touching genitals, cleaning up blood and feces, and so forth. In these jobs, innate *and* well-socialized reactions to forbidden and/or disgusting tasks must be suppressed or transformed through emotion work.

Strategies of Emotion Management

Studies clearly show that inappropriate emotions are distressing to those who experience them. Interestingly, research along this line has focused almost exclusively on parents (Graham, 1981; Power & Krause-Eheart, 1995;

Taylor, 2000). For example, mothers excoriate themselves when they lose their tempers at their babies and conclude, sometimes from a single episode of anger, that they are bad parents (Graham, 1981). That one must love and never be angry at one's child are strongly held parental norms.

Such norm violations motivate well-socialized actors to attempt to alter their feelings or displays, not just to hide them. Studies of emotion management have focused on parents' emotion-management strategies (e.g., Frude & Goss, 1981; Graham, 1981) or, following Hochschild's lead again, on strategies used by workers in a dizzying array of occupations, from beauty salon operators (Gimlin, 1996) and sheltered workshop supervisors (Copp, 1998) to trial attorneys (Pierce, 1995), among many others. Several patterns are evident in this literature.

In occupations that require emotional detachment (e.g., physician, funeral director, police officer), individuals engage in "cognitive work" (Hochschild, 1979) – reframing a situation so that it elicits the proper emotional state. For example, medical and mortuary personnel distance themselves by reconceptualizing patients' bodies as objects, viewing patients' problems as scientific or mechanical problems to be solved, discussing their work in neutral technical language, and joking about harrowing or disgusting situations (Cahill, 1999; Hafferty, 1988; Pogrebin & Poole, 1995; Smith & Kleinman, 1989).

In occupations requiring the feeling and display of positive or pleasant emotions (e.g., mothers, table servers), individuals often resort to "bodily work"(Hochschild, 1979) – altering their physiological states with deep breathing, alcohol or drugs, exercise, and the like. Mothers and waiters temporarily leave the situation, vent their true feelings in private to other personnel, and manipulate their physiological reactions to change their states (e.g., Frude & Goss, 1981; Lively, 2000). However, flight attendants are an exception; they rely more on cognitive strategies and expression management, perhaps because airplanes have no "backstage" areas to which attendants can retreat and vent (Lively, 2000).

Finally, in occupations in which workers must show and/or inspire negative emotions in other people (e.g., bill collectors, trial attorneys), "expression work" predominates – persistently performing a desired state in order to generate and feel it (Sutton, 1991; Pierce, 1995; Hochschild, 1983). For example, bill collectors behave as though they were irritated or angry, the process of playacting generates arousal, and they become more convincingly intimidating in the process (see Thoits, 1996).

Jobs involving emotional labor require workers not only to regulate their own feelings (self-management) but also to influence the emotions of their clients or customers (interpersonal emotion management). Researchers have dwelt on self-management processes because they are ways of indirectly evoking desired states in others. Attention has only recently turned to direct forms of interpersonal emotion management – techniques that actively manipulate other people's emotions (Cahill & Eggleston, 1994; Francis, Monahan, & Berger, 1999; Leidner, 1993; Lively, 2000; Thoits, 1996).

Perhaps not surprisingly, actors often apply to others strategies that work for themselves (Thoits, 1986). For example, Lively (2000) studied the process of "reciprocal emotion management" among paralegals. For a distressed coworker, paralegals cognitively reframed the stressful situation, encouraged her to vent, took her out for a drink or a walk, and so on. Francis (1997) showed that support groups for the divorced and the bereaved manipulated members' cognitions about themselves and their circumstances in order to change their feelings. Francis also investigated the use of humor as an interpersonal emotion management tool in medical settings (Francis et al., 1999), finding that jokes usually reduced tension in audiences when offered by status equals, but often failed or offended when exchanged between patients and physicians. Goading and inducing physical exertion were other ways to elicit emotions in other people deliberately (Thoits, 1996), while demands for expression control dampened intense emotions in others (Whalen & Zimmerman, 1998).

Although studies of interpersonal emotion management strategies are still few in number, future research will likely show that the strategies that emotion "managers" most frequently employ vary systematically with structural circumstances and intended emotional states, just as they do for techniques that individuals use on themselves. Understanding how other people's emotions can be directly manipulated should help to explain how such crucial group phenomena as cohesion, cooperation, and loyalty happen, as well as causes of conflict, discrimination, injustice, and cruelty.

The Consequences of Emotional Labor

A number of authors have warned that workers who engage in frequent self- or other-focused emotion management efforts may suffer from self-alienation, a sense of inauthenticity, or emotional "burnout" (Maslach, 1982). The evidence at present is mixed. Emotional labor has been linked to several negative outcomes, including sexual problems, emotional and physical exhaustion, lowered self-esteem, insensitivity to the distress of others, self-alienation, job dissatisfaction, and increased psychological distress (Hochschild, 1983; MacRae, 1998; Pierce, 1995; Pogrebin & Poole, 1995; Power & Krause-Eheart, 1995; Pugliesi, 1999; Wharton, 1996). On the other hand, Tolich (1993) observed that checkout clerks experienced their emotional performances as both self-alienating (due to a loss of autonomy) *and* liberating (as an assertion of competence). Lively (2001) found that paralegals took great pride in their ability to maintain self-control in the face of stressful demands. Workers who frequently manage others' emotions report a sense of empowerment or self-enhancement (Leidner, 1993; Stenross & Kleinman, 1989).

Firm conclusions cannot be drawn from studies that differ so greatly in research methods, outcome indicators, and types of emotional labor examined, but it is clear that emotion work on the job does not inevitably damage workers' sense of authenticity or well-being. A key condition may be the degree to which employees view their self-focused and other-focused emotion management efforts as effective. Emotion-management failure is painful and undermines individuals' identities and self-esteem (Graham, 1981; MacRae, 1998; Power & Krause-Eheart, 1995; Taylor, 2000). Success likely has positive effects.

Virtually all of the research on emotion work reviewed here suggests that most people are strongly motivated to conform to the emotion rules of their industry or culture – they put real effort into transforming their actual feelings or expressions into those that are expected. People conform because they are socialized to seek social approval and other rewards, and/or they do so because they want to avoid sanctions that are attached to persistent or egregious rule violations (gossip, reprimands, firing, etc.). Regardless of people's motivations, emotional conformity has important social consequences, beyond those for individuals themselves. Three broad classes of outcomes have been discussed: the maintenance of the social order, the reproduction of social inequality, and the generation of social solidarity.

SOCIAL FUNCTIONS OF EMOTIONAL CONFORMITY AND THE "ROLE-TAKING EMOTIONS"

Obviously, when people alter their spontaneous feelings or expressions to meet normative requirements, they are sustaining, rather than challenging or changing, the existing social order. Less obvious, however, is the fact that when people conform to emotional expectations, they are also reproducing status inequalities that are embedded in that social order. This is because emotional expectations and the emotional skills necessary to meet those expectations are distributed differentially by social status.

Cahill (1999) introduced the concept of "emotional capital" to refer to the sum total of an individual's emotional knowledge and skills. (Emotional capital thus includes the acquisition of emotion culture as well as abilities to understand, display, regulate, and transform one's own and others' emotions. Thus, it is highly similar to what psychologists have termed "emotional intelligence" [Salovey & Mayer, 1989].) People accumulate different amounts and kinds of emotional capital, depending on their status characteristics, such as age, gender, race/ethnicity, and social class. Because different social positions (e.g., entertainers, athletes, day-care workers) require specific types of emotional knowledge and skills, persons with appropriate forms of emotional capital tend to select and be selected for those positions differentially, which in turn maintains the inequalities tied to those positions. This process is most evident in the occupational realm. "People occupations" attract and hire female and middle-class workers who have been trained to attend closely to emotions and to manage feelings (Hochschild, 1983). Working-class boys who have been encouraged to master and mask their fears select and are selected for high-steel ironwork as a career (Haas, 1977). Sons and daughters of funeral directors have sufficient prior experience in coping with death and dead bodies to follow in their parents' footsteps (Cahill, 1999). Differential selection sustains the gender and social class composition of these occupations, and this stratification in turn perpetuates cultural expectations about the emotionality and emotional skills of specific social groups (again, culture and social structure are mutually reinforcing).

The reproduction of social inequality that occurs at the social system level can also be observed within organizations. Lively (2000, 2001) and Pierce (1995) reported that mostly female paralegals are expected to show deference and support to predominantly male attorneys and clients, while frequently being demeaned, insulted, or ignored in return. Paralegals transform their frustrations by using a variety of emotion work strategies (e.g., they view attorneys and clients as spoiled children) and interpret their ability to maintain a pleasant demeanor as an indicator of their professionalism and competence. Ironically, however, by reworking the negative feelings caused by their devalued status in the law firm and by seeing this as a marker of their own moral superiority and professionalism, paralegals help to perpetuate rather than challenge their place in the firm's hierarchy.

Clark (1990) describes these hierarchy-maintaining processes as "micropolitics" – the losing, gaining, or keeping of power, rank, standing, or "place." Emotions are indicators of relative social standing; high-status individuals receive respect and liking, low-status persons are offered contempt or disdain. Individuals deliberately manipulate other people's emotions in order to sustain, usurp, upset, or withhold social placement from some and to convey it to others (or themselves). In short, micropolitical emotional exchanges and manipulations are crucial aspects of the creation and perpetuation of social inequality, and the success of these acts depends upon individuals' relative possession of the requisite emotional capital.

Emotional capital not only includes knowledge of emotion culture and skill at managing one's own and others' emotions, but the ability to experience what have been called the "self-conscious emotions" (Tangney, 1999) or the "reflexive role-taking emotions" (Shott, 1979), such as shame, guilt, embarrassment, pride, and vanity. These "social emotions" result from evaluating the self from the perspective of other people and finding oneself either at fault or favored. Guilt and embarrassment cause individuals to engage in reparative behaviors to restore a positive self-image in their own and others' eyes (Shott, 1979; Tangney, 1999). Pride (self-approval derived from others' approval) encourages behaviors that conform to social norms and values (Barrett, 1995; Tangney, 1999).[5] In general, then, the re-flexive role-taking emotions motivate efforts to conform to social rules, helping, again, to maintain the social order.

Role-taking skills allow the acquisition of other social emotions, the pro-social affects of empathy, sympathy, and pity (Clark, 1997; Shott, 1979). Empathic role-taking emotions are evoked by "mentally placing oneself in another's position and feeling what the other feels [empathy] or what one would feel in such a position [sympathy]" (Shott, 1979, p. 1324). The capacity for these feelings is another key form of emotional capital. Sensitivity to the emotions of others makes one better able to anticipate and meet people's normative expectations and better able to manipulate others' emotions for their benefit or one's own gain. Obviously, such skills are marketable in a service-based economy.

More fundamentally, empathic emotions help to produce social solidarity. Research consistently shows that empathy prompts helping behavior (Eisenberg & Fabes, 1990; Shott, 1979). (By acting to relieve the distress of another, one's own vicarious distress is alleviated.) Helping behavior in turn generates positive emotions in the recipient (gratitude, liking), forges or reinforces social bonds, creates obligations to reciprocate in kind, and improves the overall welfare of the group (Clark, 1997). Perhaps because empathy and sympathy are so crucial for the production and maintenance of social solidarity, they are governed by a set of norms that closely regulate their exchange (e.g., one should not make false claims or too many claims to sympathy, one should reciprocate others' sympathy; Clark, 1997).

In sum, social order, social inequality, *and* social cohesion are by-products of individuals' emotional capital.

EMOTIONAL DEVIANCE AND SOCIAL CHANGE

Although analysts tend to focus on the positive adaptive functions of individuals' role-taking emotions and their efforts at emotional conformity, these outcomes are by no means determined. Emotion management efforts sometimes fail (Hochschild, 1983; Thoits, 1986, 1996; Copp, 1998). Emotion work failure is probable when the structural strains that generate inappropriate emotions are recurrent or persistent, or when emotion-management assistance from others is lacking (Lively, 2000; Thoits, 1986). When one or both of these conditions occur, emotion work attempts may be unsuccessful, and individuals will suffer from prolonged or repeated undesirable feelings and expressive displays, that is, from *emotional deviance* (Thoits, 1985).

---

[5] Shame has less desirable social consequences, prompting social withdrawal and angry and aggressive reactions toward people who are thought to share one's negative view of the self (Tangney, 1999; Scheff, 1988).

There have been few empirical examinations of the consequences of emotional deviance. However, three theoretical possibilities have been raised: Individuals who display persistent inappropriate affect may be labeled by observers as emotionally disturbed (Pugliesi, 1987; Thoits, 1985); they may label themselves as disturbed (Thoits, 1985); or they may seek out similar others to validate their deviant feelings as understandable and justifiable, and pursue social change (Wasielewski, 1985).

With respect to attributions of disorder, emotional deviance plays an important role in clinicians' and laypersons' recognition of psychological problems (Thoits, 2000). As the various editions of the *Diagnostic and Statistical Manual of Mental Disorders* (*DSM*) have become more specific over time in their criteria for diagnoses, multiple references have appeared to "inappropriate affect," emotions "far out of proportion to reality," emotional displays that are "intense," "excessive," or "flat," and the like (American Psychiatric Association, 1994). In fact, violations of emotion norms are essential defining criteria for roughly 30 percent of the disorders listed in *DSM-IV* (Thoits, 2000). Ordinary adults, too, associate odd or inappropriate emotional behaviors with mental illness (Link, Phelan, Bresnahan, Stueve, & Pescosolido, 1999; Pugliesi, 1987). When presented with descriptions of individuals reacting typically to common life troubles and individuals displaying classic *DSM-IV* symptoms of major depression and other disorders, a nationally representative sample of adults made sharp distinctions between conventional and deviant emotional states (Link et al., 1999). Thus, both clinicians and laypersons connect deviant emotional reactions to psychiatric disturbance.

Given such associations, persons who persistently or repeatedly exhibit deviant feelings and/or expressive displays are likely to be labeled as mentally ill by other people and forced into treatment, or, alternatively, well-socialized actors may label themselves as in need of treatment and seek it out (Thoits, 1985). Labeling results in the social control of deviant members of society and/or their emotional resocialization in treatment, thus preserving current social understandings and avoiding social disruption.

However, in special circumstances, deviant emotional states may be validated by others and become motivations for pursuing social change. People often seek out similar others who are experiencing the same problematic situations and feelings – self-help groups help to fill this need (Coates & Winston, 1983). Individuals are usually comforted to know that others have had the same feelings and understand them. Typically, too, self-help groups instruct members in methods of achieving emotional "health" or "recovery" (e.g., Francis, 1997). In these ways, self-help groups act to maintain conventional emotion norms and restore individuals to conventional feelings and behaviors (Thoits, 1985). However, when individuals' deviant emotional reactions are in response to injustice or oppression, these shared feelings may be crucial in the transformation of similar others into counter-normative peer groups, deviant subcultures, or protest movements. A charismatic leader who manipulates and legitimates the feelings and the new emotion norms of the group may facilitate social change (Wasielewski, 1985). In short, because individuals are not totally determined by the structures or cultures in which they live, but can exercise agency, creativity, and autonomy, they may, in unjust or oppressive circumstances, redefine their deviant feelings as valid and proceed to use these new normative understandings to persuade others to pursue social change.

CONCLUSION

Traditionally in sociological thought, self and society have been linked through social roles (Stryker & Statham, 1985). In sociological approaches to affect, however, emotion norms bridge the gap between the individual and the group. Individuals acquire knowledge of emotion culture, including emotion norms, and develop a variety of emotional skills. With such emotional capital, social actors try to meet cultural standards for feelings and expression, and in the process, they re-create and sustain existing social arrangements, inequalities, and solidarities. However, individuals also introduce modifications or new twists in appropriate emotions or displays that may be validated and adopted by others, initiating a process of social change. Social structural arrangements, in turn, generate recurrent emotional experiences that become expectable, conventional, and eventually normative – part of the emotion culture that individuals absorb. In short, emotion norms and the emotion work processes that maintain them are intermediate theoretical mechanisms linking macro- and microlevel phenomena.

This interplay between society and the individual perhaps is best seen in studies of the causes and consequences of emotional labor, a topic that has preoccupied sociologists and may increasingly capture the attention of historians, anthropologists, and social psychologists, given global shifts from preindustrial and industrial societies to service- and information-dominated economies. Observing such trends, one might ask whether pressures to conform to emotion norms for pay will produce widespread self-alienation and social estrangement, or whether such emotional abilities might become sources of efficacy and pride. Is the concept of emotion *work* itself simply a product of Western culture, which celebrates the value of individual freedom from constraint? In cultures that elevate collectivism, might not people locate their authentic selves in their conformity to others' emotional expectations?[6] These are only a few of the kinds of questions that

---

[6] I am grateful to Batja Mesquita for suggesting the latter two interesting questions.

are raised when emotion norms – and the emotion management processes that sustain or change them – become a central focus of analysis.

References

American Psychiatric Association. (1994). *Diagnostic and statistical manual of mental disorders: DSM-IV*. Washington, DC: American Psychiatric Association.

Cahill, S. E. (1999). Emotional capital and professional socialization: The case of mortuary science students (and me). *Social Psychology Quarterly, 62*, 101–116.

Cahill, S. E., & Eggleston, R. A. (1994). Managing emotions in public: The case of wheelchair users. *Social Psychology Quarterly, 57*, 300–312.

Cancian, F. M. (1987). *Love in America: Gender and self-development*. New York: Cambridge University Press.

Cancian, F. M., & Gordon, S. L. (1989). Changing emotion norms in marriage: Love and anger in U.S. women's magazines since 1900. *Gender and Society, 2*, 308–342.

Clark, C. (1990). Emotions and micropolitics in everyday life: Some patterns and paradoxes of "place." In T. D. Kemper (Ed.), *Research agendas in the sociology of emotions* (pp. 305–333). Albany: State University of New York Press.

Clark, C. (1997). *Misery and company: Sympathy in everyday life*. Chicago: University of Chicago Press.

Coates, D., & Winston, T. (1983). Counteracting the deviance of depression: Peer support groups for victims. *Journal of Social Issues, 39*, 169–194.

Copp, M. (1998). When emotion work is doomed to fail: Ideological and structural constraints on emotion management. *Symbolic Interaction, 21*, 299–328.

Denzin, N. K. (1990). On understanding emotion: The interpretive-cultural agenda. In T. D. Kemper (Ed.), *Research agendas in the sociology of emotions* (pp. 85–116). Albany: State University of New York Press.

Dutton, D. G., & Aron, A. P. (1974). Some evidence for heightened sexual attraction under conditions of high anxiety. *Journal of Personality and Social Psychology, 30*, 510–517.

Eisenberg, N., & Fabes, R. A. (1990). Empathy: Conceptualization, measurement, and relation to prosocial behavior. *Motivation and Emotion, 14*, 131–149.

Ekman, P.; Friesen, W. V.; & Ellsworth P. (1982). What are the similarities and differences in facial behavior across cultures? In P. Ekman (Ed.), *Emotion in the human face* (2d ed., pp. 128–143). Cambridge: Cambridge University Press.

Francis, L. E. (1997). Ideology and interpersonal emotion management: Redefining identity in two support groups. *Social Psychology Quarterly, 60*, 153–171.

Francis, L. E.; Monahan, K.; & Berger C. (1999). A laughing matter? The uses of humor in medical interactions. *Motivation and Emotion, 23*, 155–174.

Frude, N., & Goss, A. (1981). Maternal anger and the young child. In N. Frude (Ed.), *Psychological approaches to child abuse* (pp. 52–63). Totawa, NJ: Rowman & Littlefield.

Gimlin, D. (1996). Pamela's place: Power and negotiation in the hair salon. *Gender and Society, 10*, 505–526.

Gordon, S. (1989). The socialization of children's emotions: Emotional culture, exposure, and competence. In C. Saarni and P. Harris (Eds.), *Children's understanding of emotions* (pp. 319–349). New York: Cambridge University Press.

Graham, H. (1981). Mothers' accounts of anger and aggression towards their babies. In N. Frude (Ed.), *Psychological approaches to child abuse* (pp. 39–63). Totowa, NJ: Rowman & Littlefield.

Haas, J. (1977). Learning real feelings: A study of high steel ironworkers' reactions to fear and danger. *Work and Occupations, 4,* 147–170.

Hafferty, F. W. (1988). Cadaver stories and the emotional socialization of medical students. *Journal of Health and Social Behavior, 29,* 344–356.

Hochschild, A. R. (1979). Emotion work, feeling rules, and social structure. *American Journal of Sociology, 85,* 551–575.

Hochschild, A. R. (1983). *The managed heart: Commercialization of human feeling.* Berkeley: University of California Press.

Illouz, E. (1997). *Consuming the romantic utopia: Love and the cultural contradictions of capitalism.* Berkeley: University of California Press.

Kemper, T. D. (1981). Social constructionist and positivist approaches to the sociology of emotions. *American Journal of Sociology, 87,* 2, 336–362.

Kemper, T. D. (1987). How many emotions are there? Wedding the social and the autonomic components. *American Journal of Sociology, 93,* 2, 263–289.

Kleinman, A., & Kleinman, J. (1985). Somatization: The interconnections in Chinese society among culture, depressive experiences, and the meanings of pain. In A. Kleinman and B. Good (Eds.), *Culture and depression: Studies in the anthropology and cross-cultural psychiatry of affect and disorder* (pp. 429–490). Berkeley: University of California Press.

Leavitt, R. L., & Power, M. B. (1989). Emotional socialization in the postmodern era: Children in day care. *Social Psychology Quarterly, 52,* 35–43.

Leidner, R. (1993). *Fast food, fast talk: Service work and the routinization of everyday life.* Berkeley: University of California Press.

Levy, R. I. (1984). Emotion, knowing, and culture. In R. A. Shweder and R. A. Levine (Eds.), *Culture theory: Essays on mind, self, and emotion* (pp. 214–237). Cambridge: Cambridge University Press.

Link, B. G.; Phelan, J. C.; Bresnahan, M.; Stueve, A.; & Pescosolido, B. A. (1999). Public conceptions of mental illness: Labels, causes, dangerousness, and social distance. *American Journal of Public Health, 89,* 1328–1333.

Lively, K. J. (2000). Reciprocal emotion management: Working together to maintain stratification in private law firms. *Work and Occupations, 27,* 32–63.

Lively, K. J. (2001). Occupational claims to professionalism: The case of paralegals. *Symbolic Interaction, 24,* 343–365.

Lofland, L. (1985). The social shaping of emotion: The case of grief. *Symbolic Interaction, 8,* 171–190.

MacRae, H. (1998). Managing feelings: Caregiving as emotion work. *Research on Aging, 20,* 137–160.

Maslach, C. (1982). *Burnout: The cost of caring.* Englewood Cliffs, NJ: Prentice-Hall.

McCall, G. J., & Simmons, J. L. (1978). *Identities and interactions.* New York: Free Press.

Morris, J. A., & Feldman, D. C. (1996). The dimensions, antecedents, and consequences of emotional labor. *Academy of Management Review, 21,* 986–1010.

Pierce, J. L. (1995). *Gender trials: Emotional lives in contemporary law firms.* Berkeley: University of California Press.

Pogrebin, M. R., & Poole, E. D. (1995). Emotion management: A study of police response to tragic events. In M. G. Flaherty and C. Ellis (Eds.), *Social perspectives on emotion* (Vol. 3, pp. 149–168). Stamford, CT: JAI Press.

Pollak, L. H., & Thoits, P. A. (1989). Processes in emotional socialization. *Social Psychology Quarterly, 52,* 22–34.

Power, M. B., & Krause-Eheart, B. (1995). Adoption, myth, and emotion work: Paths to disillusionment. In J. G. Flaherty and C. Ellis (Eds.), *Social perspectives on emotion* (vol. 3, pp. 97–120). Stamford, CT: JAI Press.

Pugliesi, K. (1987). Deviation in emotion and the labeling of mental illness. *Deviant Behavior, 8,* 79–102.

Pugliesi, K. (1999). The consequences of emotional labor: Effects on work stress, job satisfaction, and well-being. *Motivation and Emotion, 23,* 125–154.

Salovey, P., & Mayer, J. D. (1989). Emotional intelligence. *Imagination, Cognition, and Personality, 9,* 185–211.

Schachter, S., & Singer, J. (1962). Cognitive, social and physiological determinants of emotional state. *Psychological Review, 69,* 379–399.

Scheff, T. J. (1988). Shame and conformity: The deference-emotion system. *American Sociological Review, 53,* 395–406.

Shott, S. (1979). Emotion and social life: A symbolic interactionist analysis. *American Journal of Sociology, 84,* 1317–1334.

Shweder, R. A. (1994). "You're not sick, you're just in love": Emotion as an interpretive system. In P. Ekman and R. A. Davidson (Eds.), *The nature of emotion: Fundamental questions* (pp. 32–45). Oxford: Oxford University Press.

Simon, R. W.; Eder, D.; & Evans, C. (1992). The development of feeling norms underlying romantic love among adolescent females. *Social Psychology Quarterly, 55,* 29–46.

Smith, A. C., & Kleinman, S. (1989). Managing emotions in medical school: Students' contacts with the living and the dead. *Social Psychology Quarterly, 52,* 56–69.

Stearns, C. Z., & Stearns, P. N. (1986). *Anger: The struggle for emotional control in America's history.* Chicago: University of Chicago Press.

Stenross, B., & Kleinman, S. (1989). The highs and lows of emotional labor: Detectives' encounters with criminals and victims. *Journal of Contemporary Ethnography, 17,* 435–452.

Stryker, S., & Statham, A. (1985). Symbolic interaction and role theory. In G. Lindzey and E. Aronson (Eds.), *Handbook of Social Psychology* (3d ed., pp. 311–378). New York: Random House.

Sutton, R. I. (1991). Maintaining norms about expressed emotions: The case of bill collectors. *Administrative Science Quarterly, 36,* 245–268.

Tangney, J. P. (1999). The self-conscious emotions: Shame, guilt, embarrassment and pride. In R. Dalgleish and M. Power (Eds.), *Handbook of cognition and emotion* (pp. 541–568). New York: John Wiley and Sons.

Taylor, V. (2000). Emotions and identity in women's self-help movements. In S. Stryker and T. J. Owens (Eds.), *Self, identity, and social movements* (pp. 271–299). Minneapolis: University of Minnesota Press.

Thoits, P. A. (1985). Self-labeling processes in mental illness: The role of emotional deviance. *American Journal of Sociology, 92,* 221–249.

Thoits, P. A. (1986). Social support as coping assistance. *Journal of Consulting and Clinical Psychology, 54,* 416–423.

Thoits, P. A. (1996). Managing the emotions of others. *Symbolic Interaction, 19,* 85–109.

Thoits, Peggy A. (2000). Emotion and psychopathology: A sociological point of view. Paper presented at the International Society for Research on Emotions, August, Quebec City, Canada.

Tolich, M. B. (1993). Alienating and liberating emotions at work: Supermarket clerks' performance of customer service. *Journal of Contemporary Ethnography, 22,* 361–381.

Wasielewski, P. L. (1985). The emotional basis of charisma. *Symbolic Interaction, 8,* 207–222.

Whalen, J., & Zimmerman, D. H. (1998). Observations on the display and management of emotion in naturally occurring activities: The case of "hysteria" in calls to 911. *Social Psychology Quarterly, 61,* 141–159.

Wharton, A. S. (1996). Service with a smile: Understanding the consequences of emotional labor. In C. L. MacDonald and C. Sirianni (Eds.), *Working in the service society* (pp. 91–112). Philadelphia: Temple University Press.

PART V

FEELINGS, EMOTIONS, AND MORALITY

22

On the Possibility of Animal Empathy

Frans B. M. de Waal

ABSTRACT

Animal empathy has received little attention. In monkeys and apes, however, it is not unusual for one individual to respond emotionally to the distress of others. These responses have been measured in observational research and tested experimentally, allowing the conclusion that emotional resonance and targeted helping are within the capacity of other animals.

THE EVOLUTION OF EMOTIONAL LINKAGE

When Carolyn Zahn-Waxler visited homes to find out how children responded to family members who were instructed to feign sadness (sobbing), pain (crying), or distress (choking), she discovered that children a little over one year of age already comfort others. Since expressions of sympathy emerge at an early age in virtually every member of our species, they are as natural as the first step. An unplanned sidebar to this study, however, was that some household pets appeared to be as worried as the children by the "distress" of a family member, hovering over them or putting their heads in their laps (Zahn-Waxler et al., 1984).

The possibility that animals possess empathy and sympathy has received scant systematic attention due to two factors. One is fear of anthropomorphism, which has created unnecessary taboos surrounding animal emotions (de Waal, 1999). The other hampering influence has been Huxley's (1894) dualism between nature and ethics, which still dominates the thinking of some contemporary biologists. This "nature red in tooth and claw" view has little room for kindness, human or animal.

I am grateful to Stephanie Preston for inspiring some of the ideas discussed here, and for critical references to a sometimes obscure literature, as well as to Lisa Parr for sharpening my thinking about empathy. I also thank the editors for comments on a previous version of the manuscript.

As a result, even though emotional linkage seems central to the survival of cooperative animals, it has been ignored except for a few scattered studies. A review is particularly timely now that evolutionists are returning to the original Darwinian position, formulated in *The Descent of Man*, which assigns ethics a central place in human evolution. Moreover, Darwin explicitly postulated continuity with other animals, as when he claimed that "many animals certainly sympathize with each other's distress or danger" (Darwin, 1871, p. 77). Current attention to the evolution of interindividual commitment (Frank, this volume; Nesse, 2001), community-level altruism and cooperation (Sober & Wilson, 1998; Boehm, 1999), and morality as an outgrowth of animal sociality (de Waal, 1996; Flack & de Waal, 2000), confirms that the time is ripe for an exploration of the mechanisms that permit individuals to connect emotionally in adaptive ways. The summary of current knowledge of animal empathy to come draws on two comprehensive theoretical reviews by Preston and de Waal (2002a, 2002b), to which the reader is referred for more details.

Social animals have a great need for the coordination of action and movement, collective response to danger, communication about food and water, and assistance to those in need. Responsiveness to the behavioral states of conspecifics ranges from a flock of birds taking off all at once because one among them is startled by a predator to a mother ape who returns to a whimpering youngster to help it from one tree to the next by draping her body as a bridge between the two. The first is a reflex-like transmission of a fear response that may not involve any understanding of what triggered the initial reaction. The second seems more insightful, involving anxiety in the female who hears her offspring's whimpers, assessment of the possible reason for its distress, and an attempt to ameliorate the situation. There exists ample evidence of one primate coming to another's aid in a fight, putting an arm around a previous victim of attack, or other emotional responses to the distress of others. In fact, almost all communication among nonhuman primates seems emotionally mediated. We are familiar with the prominent role of emotions in human facial expressions (Ekman, 1982), but when it comes to monkeys and apes – which have a similar, homologous array of expressions (van Hooff, 1967) – emotions are probably equally important (de Waal, in press).

When the emotional state of one individual induces a matching or closely related state in another, we often speak of "emotional contagion" (Hatfield et al., 1993). The term "affective resonance" seems preferable, however, since it avoids the disease connotations of the term "contagion" (i.e., the implication of inevitability and undesirability) as well as the assumption of an exact match between the subject's and object's emotions. Even if affective resonance is undoubtedly a basic phenomenon, there is more to it than simply one individual being affected by the emotional state of another: the two individuals often engage in direct interaction. Thus, a rejected youngster may throw a screaming tantrum at its mother's feet, or a preferred associate may approach a possessor of food to beg by means of sympathy-inducing facial expressions, vocalizations, and hand gestures. In other words, emotional and motivational states often manifest themselves in behavior specifically directed at certain partners. The emotional effect on the other is therefore not a by-product, but actively sought.

With increasing differentiation between self and other, and an increasing appreciation of the precise circumstances underlying the emotional states of others, affective resonance develops into empathy. Empathy encompasses – and could not possibly exist without – affective resonance, but it goes beyond it in that it places filters between the other's state and one's own, adding a cognitive layer (Eisenberg & Strayer, 1987).

Two mechanisms related to empathy are sympathy and personal distress, which in their social consequences are each other's opposites. Sympathy is defined as "an affective response that consists of feelings of sorrow or concern for a distressed or needy other (rather than the same emotion as the other person). Sympathy is believed to involve an other-oriented, altruistic motivation" (Eisenberg, 2000, p. 677). Personal distress, on the other hand, makes the affected party selfishly seek to alleviate its *own* distress, which is similar to what has been perceived in the object. Personal distress is not concerned with the situation of the empathy-inducing other (Batson, 1991). A striking monkey example has been offered by de Waal (1996, p. 46): the screams of a severely punished or rejected infant will often cause other infants to approach, embrace, mount, or even pile on top of the victim. Thus, the distress of one infant seems to spread to its peers, which then seek contact to soothe their own arousal. Inasmuch as personal distress lacks cognitive evaluation and behavioral complementarity, it seems to stay at the level of affective resonance.

That most modern textbooks on animal cognition do not index empathy or sympathy does not mean that these capacities are not essential; it only means that they have been overlooked by a science traditionally focused on individual rather than interindividual capacities. Tool use and numerical competence, for instance, are seen as hallmarks of intelligence, whereas dealing appropriately with others is not. However, the survival of many animals depends on how they fare within their social group, both in a cooperative sense (e.g., concerted action, information transfer) and competitive sense (e.g., dominance strategies, deception). It is therefore in the *social* domain that one expects to find some of their highest cognitive achievements. Selection must have favored mechanisms to evaluate the emotional states of others and quickly respond to them in adaptive ways. Empathy is precisely such a mechanism..

In human behavior, there exists a tight relation between empathy and sympathy, and its expression in psychological altruism (e.g., Batson et al., 1987; Eisenberg & Strayer, 1987; Hoffman, 1982; Hornblow, 1980; Wispé, 1986). It is reasonable to assume that the altruistic and caring responses of other animals, especially mammals, rest on similar mechanisms. These mechanisms therefore evolved out of a need for a cooperative group life.

EARLY ANIMAL EXPERIMENTS

As pointed out by Preston and de Waal (2002a), there exists an intriguing older literature by experimental psychologists on empathy, even though most of the time the words "empathy" and "sympathy" were placed between quotation marks. The investigators seemed skeptical that what they were studying had much to do with shared emotions. This literature, produced mainly in the 1960s, has been largely ignored by subsequent generations (but see de Waal, 1989; Parr et al., 1998; Hauser, 2000) even though it remains relevant. These studies involve some experimental protocols that are unlikely to be permitted today.

Rats and Pigeons

In a paper provocatively entitled "Emotional Reactions of Rats to the Pain of Others," Church (1959) established that rats who had learned to press a lever to obtain food would stop doing so if their response was paired with the delivery of an electric shock to a neighboring rat in full view and hearing. This inhibition habituated rapidly, but nonetheless suggested that there is something quite aversive about the reactions of others to pain. Perhaps such reactions arouse negative emotions in those who see and hear them.

Following Allport (1924), Church sought the explanation in conditioning theory: the sight of another individual in pain may have become associated with negative consequences. Pain or trouble tends to afflict multiple individuals at the same time, hence the sight of one rat in pain is generally bad news for others. In other words, there is negative conditioning to the perception of distress in conspecifics. To test this hypothesis, Church shocked the neighboring rat for thirty seconds each time that the subject pressed a lever after which the subject itself was shocked for one second. After this experience, subjects showed such fear of shock that they largely stopped pressing the bar if it shocked another rat, and maintained this suppression far better than rats without the experience. A control group that had been trained with one-second shocks but not paired with shocks to another rat failed to show the same inhibitions. Church's conclusion was that the pain response of a companion rat only has aversive effects if it has been paired in the past with pain to the subject itself. However, this conditioning result, which was successfully replicated with pigeons by Watanabe and Ono (1986), does not address the issue of why *untrained* rats (and pigeons) are aversive to causing pain in others. Before shocks had been given to any of these subjects, they spontaneously stopped using the bar if doing so shocked a companion.

In another experiment, rats were confronted with a companion in a highly uncomfortable situation – strapped in a harness, hoisted up with its feet off the floor, convulsively wriggling and squealing. Subjects could correct the other's situation by pressing a bar, which lowered the hoist, thus reducing the other's distress. Rice and Gainer (1962) found that rats spontaneously, without any special training, helped out distressed companions by lowering them back to the floor. They called this an "altruistic response," using quotation marks because they did not really believe that it was altruistically motivated. In a follow-up experiment, Lavery and Foley (1963) demonstrated that rats would perform the same bar-pressing response to help out a companion if prerecorded vocalizations of distressed rats were played in a loop, and even more so if white noise was played. They concluded that there was no specific quality to rat squealing, and that noise in general – in fact, any unpleasant noise – activates a motivation to turn it off. Thus, Lavery and Foley saw the distress signals of rats as part of a general continuum of noxious stimulation. From another study of the "altruistic response" in rats, however, Rice (1964) concluded that the increase in lever pressing in the original hoisted-rat paradigm may not have been due to vicarious distress, because if rats are truly distressed and fearful they become inactive and withdrawn.

In sum, these experiments demonstrate that rats are willing to deprive themselves of food, however temporarily, in order to prevent the suffering of another rat, or at least to get rid of the sights and sounds of its suffering. Rats will also work to reduce the distress exhibited by other rats. The studies added training procedures to show that one can obtain the same outcome by (*a*) specifically conditioning rats to associate the distress signals of others with pain to themselves, or (*b*) pairing the distress of another rat with an artificial unpleasant stimulus. But neither of these extensions takes anything away from the initial spontaneous effects, and neither excludes the possibility that rats react the way they do because they are sensitive to the emotional states of others. The flaw in the thinking of these psychologists – typical of the time – was a confusion between the effects of training, on the one hand, and naturally evolved means of communication, on the other, as if demonstration of the first in some way detracts from the second.

Monkeys

In the same year that Church's empathy study on rats appeared, Miller and coworkers published the first of a series of pioneering papers on the transmission of affect in rhesus macaques (Miller et al., 1959). They found that monkeys react with avoidance to pictures of conspecifics in a fearful pose, and that this reaction is stronger than that toward a negatively conditioned stimulus. Miller built upon this study in developing an ingenious cooperative avoidance paradigm. At first, a monkey, A, was restricted in a primate chair and trained to respond to a clicker sound paired with a shock. Monkey A learned to press a bar that turned off both the sound and the shock. If the monkey reacted fast enough to the clicker, no shock was received.

The next step was to strap a second monkey, B, in a chair in a different room (Figure 22.1). This monkey was in the same situation as A but lacked a bar to turn off the shock. Monkey B was filmed with a short-circuit video camera, the black-and-white image of which was transmitted to a screen visible to monkey A. Monkey A had retained its bar to turn off shocks – now delivered to both monkeys at the same time – but had lost the clicker warning sound. Only monkey B could hear this sound. In other words, monkey B (the "stimulus" animal) knew when a shock was coming, and this monkey's face was visible on the video screen to monkey A, who had the ability to prevent the shock from being delivered.

In this cooperative setup, monkeys A and B were about as good at avoiding painful stimulation as monkey A had been on its own in the original shock-avoidance paradigm (Miller et al., 1963). Monkeys are thus capable of extracting information from the face of a conspecific using preexisting knowledge about their species' communication. In a review of his work, Miller (1967, p. 131) noted that "It was our conviction that a monkey was a much more skilled interpreter of facial expression in another monkey than was man."

In research resembling that on rats, one of Miller's coworkers found that monkeys will press a bar to prevent painful stimulation to another monkey even if they themselves are not being shocked. The subjects seemed quite upset seeing another monkey leap and run around in response to shock, reacting to this sight with "piloerection, urination, defecation, and excited behavior" (Mirsky et al., 1958, p. 437). This reaction suggested state-matching between subject and object as expected in the case of affective resonance. Physiological support for this mechanism came from heart-rate measures collected in the cooperative avoidance paradigm. Monkeys A and B showed similar heart-rate changes in these tests. When the same paradigm was used to obtain rewards cooperatively, heart-rate patterns were similar as well, even though communication about impending rewards was less efficient, and heart-rate acceleration less pronounced, than during cooperative shock avoidance (Miller, 1967).

Finally, perhaps the most compelling evidence for the strength of empathic reaction in monkeys came from Wechkin et al. (1964) and Masserman et al. (1964). They found that rhesus monkeys refuse to pull a chain that

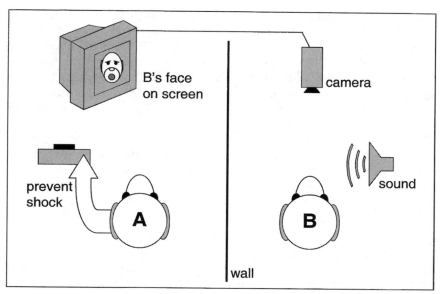

FIGURE 22.1. The cooperative avoidance paradigm of Miller et al., 1963, in which monkey B hears a sound announcing a shock, and monkey A sits in another room, watching a video monitor that shows B's face live. Monkey A uses this behavioral information to press a bar that prevents shock to both A and B.

delivers food to themselves if doing so shocks a companion. One monkey stopped pulling for five days, and another one for twelve days, after witnessing shock delivery to another monkey. These monkeys were literally starving themselves to avoid shocking another monkey, and they maintained this response to a far greater degree than has been reported for rats and pigeons. Such sacrifice relates to the tight social system and emotional linkage among macaques, as supported by the finding that the inhibition to hurt another was more pronounced between familiar than unfamiliar individuals (Masserman et al., 1964).

These findings on monkeys amplify those on rats, in that they show strong, untrained reactions to the emotions of conspecifics, such as a quick reading of another's facial cues and remarkable self-sacrifice to avoid inflicting pain. Furthermore, the monkey work shows evidence of physiological matching between subject and object.

GREAT APES

Anecdotes of "Changing Places in Fancy"

Qualitative accounts are a respectable starting point for research, even though they do not permit a choice between alternative explanations and should therefore never be taken as final proof (de Waal, 1991). Such accounts support the view that our closest relatives show strong emotional reactions to others in pain or need. Thus, Yerkes (1925, p. 246) reports how his bonobo, Prince Chim, was so extraordinarily concerned and protective toward his sickly chimpanzee companion, Panzee, that the scientific establishment might not accept his claims: "If I were to tell of his altruistic and obviously sympathetic behavior towards Panzee I should be suspected of idealizing an ape."

Ladygina-Kohts (1935, p. 121) noticed similar empathic tendencies in her young chimpanzee, Joni, which she raised at the beginning of the previous century, in Moscow. Kohts, who analyzed Joni's behavior in the minutest detail, discovered that the only way to get him off the roof of her house after an escape (much better than any reward or threat of punishment) was by arousing sympathy:

If I pretend to be crying, close my eyes and weep, Joni immediately stops his plays or any other activities, quickly runs over to me, all excited and shagged, from the most remote places in the house, such as the roof or the ceiling of his cage, from where I could not drive him down despite my persistent calls and entreaties. He hastily runs around me, as if looking for the offender; looking at my face, he tenderly takes my chin in his palm, lightly touches my face with his finger, as though trying to understand what is happening, and turns around, clenching his toes into firm fists.

These are just two out of many reports gathered and discussed by de Waal (1996, 1997) which suggest that, apart from emotional connectedness, apes have an appreciation of each other's situation and a degree of perspective taking. One striking report in this regard concerns a bonobo female empathizing with a bird at Twycross Zoo, in England:

One day, Kuni captured a starling. Out of fear that she might molest the stunned bird, which appeared undamaged, the keeper urged the ape to let it go. . . . Kuni picked up the starling with one hand and climbed to the highest point of the highest tree where she wrapped her legs around the trunk so that she had both hands free to hold the bird. She then carefully unfolded its wings and spread them wide open, one wing in each hand, before throwing the bird as hard she could towards the barrier of the enclosure. Unfortunately, it fell short and landed onto the bank of the moat where Kuni guarded it for a long time against a curious juvenile. (de Waal, 1997, p. 156)

Obviously, what Kuni did would have been totally inappropriate with a member of her own species. Having seen birds in flight many times, she seemed to have a notion of what would be good for a bird, thus giving us an anthropoid illustration of the empathic capacity so enduringly described by Smith (1759, p. 10) as "changing places in fancy with the sufferer."

Primate empathy (including the famous story of Binti-Jua, a female gorilla that rescued a three-year-old boy who had fallen into her enclosure at the Brookfield Zoo in Chicago, in 1996) is such a rich area that O'Connell (1995) was able to conduct a content analysis of thousands of qualitative reports. The investigator counted the frequency of reports of three types of empathy, from affective resonance to more cognitive forms, including an appreciation of the other's situation and giving aid that is tailored to the other's needs. Understanding the emotional state of another was particularly common in the chimpanzee, with most outcomes resulting in the subject comforting the object of distress. Monkey displays of empathy were far more restricted, but did include the adoption of orphans and reactions to illness, handicaps, and open wounds. Having myself extensively worked with both monkeys and apes, and having noticed the same striking differences in helping and comforting responses, I agree with O'Connell (1995) that the difference probably says more about the animals than the observers.

It is important to stress the incredible power of the ape's empathic response, which makes these animals take great risks on behalf of others. Whereas, in a recent debate about the origins of morality, Kagan (2000) asserted as self-evident that a chimpanzee would never jump into a cold lake to save another, it may help to quote Goodall (1990, p. 213) on this issue:

In some zoos, chimpanzees are kept on man-made islands, surrounded by water-filled moats. . . . Chimpanzees cannot swim and, unless they are rescued, will drown if they fall into deep water. Despite this, individuals have sometimes made heroic efforts to save companions from drowning – and were sometimes successful. One adult male lost his life as he tried to rescue a small infant whose incompetent mother had allowed it to fall into the water.

The only other groups of animals for which a similar array of strong helping tendencies is known are dolphins and elephants. This material, too, is largely descriptive (dolphins: Caldwell & Caldwell, 1966; Connor & Norris, 1982; elephants: Moss, 1988; Payne, 1998), yet here again it is hard to accept as coincidental the fact that scientists who have watched these animals for any length of time have numerous such stories, whereas scientists who have watched other social animals have few, if any.

Consolation Research

De Waal (1982, p. 67) described how two adult female chimpanzees in the Arnhem Zoo colony used to console each other after fights: "Not only do they often act together against attackers, they also seek comfort and reassurance from each other. When one of them has been involved in a painful conflict, she goes to the other to be embraced. They then literally scream in each other's arms."

First systematically documented by de Waal and van Roosmalen (1979), but also hinted at by Goodall (1968), consolation is defined as reassurance and friendly contact directed by an uninvolved bystander to one of the combatants in a preceding aggressive incident. For example, a third party goes over to the loser of a fight and gently puts an arm around her shoulders. Consolation is not to be confused with so-called reconciliation, defined as a reunion between former opponents (de Waal & van Roosmalen, 1979). One major difference is that reconciliation seems selfishly motivated, such as by the imperative to restore a disturbed relationship (reviewed by de Waal, 2000, and Aureli & de Waal, 2000), whereas the advantages of consolation for the actor remain unclear. The actor could probably have walked away from the scene without negative consequences.

Information on chimpanzee consolation is well-quantified. De Waal and van Roosmalen (1979) based their conclusions on an analysis of hundreds of post-conflict observations, and a replication study by de Waal and Aureli (1996) included an even larger sample in which the authors sought to test two relatively simple predictions. They reasoned that if third-party contacts indeed serve to alleviate the distress of conflict participants, these contacts should be directed more at recipients of aggression than at aggressors, and more at recipients of intense than of mild aggression. Comparing third-party contact rates with baseline levels, the investigators found support for both predictions (Figure 22.2).

Possibly, bystanders become distressed by the sight of an aggressive incident, which makes them seek comfort for their own emotions through the act of consolation. However, this "personal distress" explanation raises intriguing, unanswered questions. First, why would the witnessing of aggression between others induce a state of distress rather than of aggressive arousal? After all, both kinds of emotions are on display. Only if the bystander identifies more with the victim than with the aggressor does it make sense for him/her to be distressed. Second, why would alleviation of one's own distress be sought by approaching another distressed party? If the goal is to seek comfort for oneself, there is no reason why bystanders should approach precisely the individual who caused their vicarious distress, and may well do so again. They could just as easily approach others around them; but they do not. On the other hand, directing comforting behavior at the victim of aggression makes perfect sense if distress alleviation of the *other* is the actor's objective. Finally, why do consolers rarely show external signs of distress themselves (Figure 22.3)? Is their own distress level just low, or is the absence of signs of distress due to their ability to separate their own situation from that of the other? These fundamental questions need to be worked out further before we can tackle the process of consolation through more observation and experimentation.

Curiously, consolation has thus far been demonstrated in great apes only. When de Waal and Aureli (1996) set out to apply exactly the same

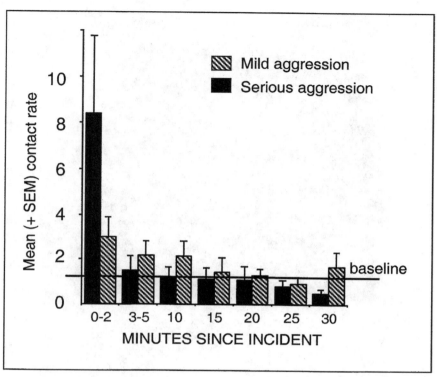

FIGURE 22.2. The rate with which third parties contact victims of aggression in chimpanzees, comparing recipients of serious and mild aggression. Especially in the first few minutes after the incident, recipients of serious aggression receive more contacts than baseline. After de Waal & Aureli, 1996.

observation protocols as used previously on chimpanzees to detect consolation in macaques, they failed to find any. This came as a surprise, because reconciliation studies, which employ essentially the same design, have shown reconciliation in species after species – not only in chimpanzees, but in all kinds of monkeys, and even in some nonprimates (Schino, 2000). Why, then, would consolation be restricted to apes?

The closest that monkey studies have come is when Verbeek and de Waal (1997) and Arnold and Barton (2001) found that individuals actively solicit contact with third parties after a fight. Inasmuch as these contacts are not initiated by the third parties themselves, they do not fit the definition of consolation, however. Instead of hinting at empathy, they only suggest a *need* for reassurance in distressed individuals. Another study, by Call et al. (2002) did find increased contact made by third parties with victims of aggression in stump-tailed macaques. But even if this does fit the definition, the authors note that if these contacts were indeed consolatory one

FIGURE 22.3. A typical instance of consolation in chimpanzees, in which a juvenile puts an arm around a screaming adult male who has just been defeated in a fight with his rival. Consolation has been demonstrated with quantitative methods in chimpanzees (Figure 22.2) but thus far not in monkeys. Photograph by the author.

would expect them to include calming behavior, such as grooming, which demonstrably reduces heart rate in monkeys (Aureli et al., 1999). What they found instead was behavior such as sociosexual mounting, which may help buffer aggression. In other words, stump-tail macaques contact recent victims of aggression perhaps more in order to protect than to reassure them. Post-conflict third-party affiliation, as the topic has become known in the literature, remains a rich area in which to explore possible differences in empathy between monkeys and apes (de Waal & Aureli, 1996; Watts et al., 2000).

Perception of Emotion

Comparative studies of emotional processing in humans and great apes are relatively nonexistent, which constitutes a major gap in our understanding of the extent to which emotional awareness has played a role in shaping social life. To amend this situation, Parr and coworkers applied computerized techniques to face recognition and emotional processing in chimpanzees. First, apes learned to control a cursor on a computer screen via a joystick, after which they were trained on Matching-to-Sample (MTS). Upon selection of a sample image by contacting it with the cursor, two comparison images would appear on the screen, one of which was similar to the sample on a predetermined criterion.

Using this MTS task with digitized black-and-white portraits of conspecifics, chimpanzees were capable of recognizing unfamiliar faces on the first testing session, even if the correct choice was a *different* photograph of the same individual. They also recognized facial similarities between mother and offspring, and were able to match species-typical facial expressions produced by different individuals (Parr et al., 1998, 2000; Parr & de Waal, 1999).

In a study of emotional processing, five-second video clips were shown depicting emotionally charged scenes, such as a detested veterinary procedure or a favorite food item. The apes were then required to match the video to one of two species-typical facial expressions serving as "happy" and "sad" face, that is, a play-face normally seen in tickling matches and a teeth-baring expression normally seen in frustration or after defeat (Figure 22.4). This task differed from the previous MTS task in that, instead of looking for visual similarities between the sample video and the facial photographs, subjects were required to use emotional valence as the basis for matching. The response, which was untrained, was measured upon first presentation of the stimuli. Since the chimpanzees accurately matched stimuli according to their shared meaning, they seemed to have understood the emotional significance of their own facial expressions. Measures of peripheral skin temperature confirmed that the video clips emotionally affected the chimpanzees (Parr, 2001).

LEVELS OF EMPATHY

In reviewing emotional linkage in other animals, we have seen evidence of (*a*) sacrifice, including starvation, to prevent pain to others; (*b*) rewards associated with the elimination of another's distress; (*c*) accurate reading of another's face so as to prevent harm to self and other; (*d*) powerful aiding responses guided by some degree of understanding of another's situation; (*e*) spontaneous consolation of distressed individuals; and (*f*) use of pictures of facial expressions to correctly label emotional scenes. This list is impressive enough to favor the idea of empathy in other animals – an unsurprising possibility in light of what we know about human empathy. It would be bizarre indeed if a human capacity that is so pervasive, emerges so early in life, and has such powerful physiological correlates

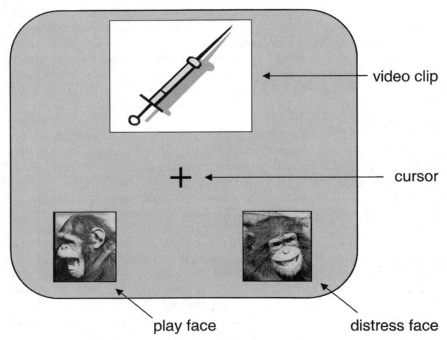

FIGURE 22.4. Chimpanzees have been trained to use a joystick to select images on a computer screen. The ape first watches a 5-sec video clip of either a pleasant or a frightening situation (e.g., a veterinarian holding an injection needle), after which one of two facial images can be selected: a "happy" face (the play face, used in playful situations) and a "sad" face (the bared-teeth face, normally seen in losers of fights). Without specific training on these particular videos, subjects spontaneously selected the emotionally suitable face (Parr, 2001).

had emerged de novo in evolutionary history. It seems logical to assume that empathy is phylogenetically continuous (Preston & de Waal, 2002a, 2002b).

This is a critical point, as the literature includes accounts of empathy as a purely cognitive affair, even to the degree that it is questioned whether apes, let alone other animals, can possess it (Povinelli, 1998; Hauser, 2000). In this "top-down" view, empathy requires mental-state attribution, also known as theory-of-mind (TOM). But even if TOM probably involves empathy, is not it likely that empathic capacities precede TOM both phylogenetically and ontogenetically? Precisely this position has been defended in relation to autistic children. Contra earlier assumptions that autism reflects lack of TOM, autism is noticeable well before the age at which TOM normally emerges. Williams et al. (2001) therefore argue that the main deficit concerns the socioaffective level, which then negatively impacts the more sophisticated forms of interpersonal perception that derive from it later in development.

This is more in line with the "bottom-up" view adopted here, depicted as a Russian doll in Figure 22.5, according to which empathy covers all ways in which one individual's emotional state modifies another's. Preston and de Waal (2002b) propose that at the core of this empathic capacity is the automatic activation of the subject's internal representations of a state or situation whenever it perceives another individual in a similar state or situation. This in turn activates the subject's somatic and autonomic responses appropriate to this state or situation. Since these processes rely on the subject's previous experiences, and since familiar and bonded individuals share more experiences, their representations may be more similar. In addition, these individuals are motivated to pay attention to each other, so that we can expect stronger empathic responses between them.

This Perception-Action Model (PAM) fits well with recent evidence for a link at the cellular "mirror-neuron" level between perception and action (di Pelligrino et al., 1992), as well as with the somatic marker hypothesis of Damasio (1994). The same connection between perception and action is suggested by the impaired emotional recognition in human patients with damaged somatosensory brain areas, which suggests that identification of another's emotions requires internal representations of their emotional state (Adolphs et al., 2000). In other words, to feel what another feels requires that one internally (neurologically, behaviorally, physiologically) mimic their emotional state, something we, and probably a host of other animals, do involuntarily and instantly.

The idea that perception and action share common representations is anything but new: it goes as far back in history as the first treatise on *Einfühlung*, the German concept translated into English as "empathy" (Wispé, 1991). When Lipps (1903) introduced *Einfühlung*, which literally means "feeling into," he speculated about *innere Nachahmung* (inner mimicry) of another's feelings along the same lines as proposed by the PAM. Accordingly, empathy is often an automatic, insuppressible process, as demonstrated by electromyographic studies of invisible muscle contractions in people's faces in response to pictures of human facial expressions (e.g., Dimberg et al., 2000). Accounts of empathy as a higher cognitive process tend to neglect these "gut-level" reactions that are far too rapid to be under cortical control: people automatically and unconsciously mimic what they see, which then feeds back into their own emotions by re-creating the other's emotional state.

This is not to say that higher cognitive levels of empathy are irrelevant; but they are built on top of this firm, hard-wired basis without which we would probably be at a loss about what moves other people (Preston & de Waal, 2002b). Thus, at the center of the Russian doll is affective resonance, around which the higher levels of empathy are constructed. The

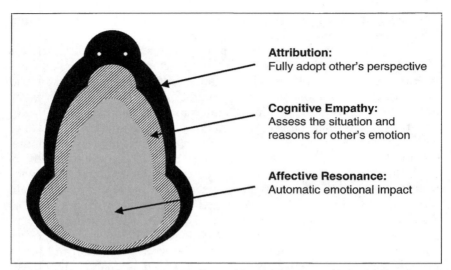

FIGURE 22.5. Russian doll model of empathy. In this model, empathy covers all processes leading to related emotional states in subject and object, with at its core affective resonance: immediate, often unconscious state matching. Higher levels of empathy build on this hard-wired socioaffective basis, such as cognitive empathy (which includes an understanding of the reasons for the other's emotions) and mental-state attribution (which fully adopts the other's perspective). It is assumed here that the outer layers cannot exist without the inner ones.

second layer, cognitive empathy, implies appraisal of another's predicament or situation (cf. de Waal, 1996). The subject not only responds to the signals emitted by the object, but shows some understanding of the reasons based on clues from the other's behavior and circumstances. Cognitive empathy makes it possible to furnish *targeted* help that takes the needs of the other into account, such as when one ape helps another out of a tree (Figure 22.6), or tries to make a bird fly. These responses go well beyond affective resonance yet would be hard to explain without an emotional motivational component.

Targeted help in response to specific, sometimes novel situations probably requires a distinction between self and other that allows the other's situation to be divorced from one's own while maintaining the emotional link that motivates behavior. Assuming that cognitive empathy requires self-awareness, Gallup (1982) was the first to speculate about a possible connection with mirror self-recognition (MSR). This view is supported both developmentally, by a correlation between the emergence of MSR in children and advanced helping tendencies (Bischof-Köhler, 1988), and phylogenetically, by the presence of complex helping and consolation in great apes and humans, which are also the only primates with MSR. The

FIGURE 22.6. Cognitive empathy (i.e., empathy combined with appraisal of the other's situation) allows for aid tailored to the other's needs. In this case, a mother chimpanzee reaches out to help her son down from a tree after he has screamed and begged (see hand gesture). Targeted help may require a distinction between self and other, an ability suggested to underlie mirror self-recognition, such as is found in humans, apes, and dolphins. Photograph by the author.

recent evidence for MSR in dolphins (Reiss & Marino, 2001), a distantly related but highly altruistic mammal, nicely fits this hypothetical connection between increased self-awareness, on the one hand, and cognitive empathy, on the other.

Finally, the third and highest level of empathy is achieved when one individual is capable of fully adopting another's perspective, thus entering the other's "shoes," if not its mind. Whether apes possess this capacity is under debate. Some studies report negative evidence – which is notoriously hard to interpret – whereas other studies report positive evidence. The conclusion thus far is that we are facing a mixed bag of results (Call, 2000). Certainly, the targeted helping and intentional deception reported for apes strongly hints at attributional capacities (O'Connell, 1995;

de Waal, 1996), yet it must be added that this is irrelevant to the question of whether animals have empathy. Empathy is not an all-or-nothing phenomenon: it covers a wide range of emotional linkage patterns, from the very simple and automatic to the very sophisticated. It seems logical to try first to understand the basic forms, which are widespread indeed, before addressing the interesting abilities that cognitive evolution has constructed upon this foundation.

References

Adolphs, R.; Damasio, H.; Tranel, D.; Cooper, G.; & Damasio, A. R. (2000). A role for somatosensory cortices in the visual recognition of emotion as revealed by three-dimensional lesion mapping. *Journal of Neuroscience, 20,* 2683–2690.

Allport, F. H. (1924). *Social psychology.* Cambridge, MA: Riverside Press.

Arnold, K., & Barton, R. A. (2001). Postconflict behavior of spectacled leaf monkeys (Trachypthecus obscurus). II. Contact with third parties. *International Journal of International Primatology, 22,* 267–286.

Aureli, F., & de Waal, F. B. M. (2000). *Natural conflict resolution.* Berkeley: University of California Press.

Aureli, F.; Preston, S. D.; & de Waal, F. B. M. (1999). Heart rate responses to social interactions in free-moving rhesus macaques (Macaca mulatta): A pilot study. *Journal of Comparative Psychology, 113,* 59–65.

Batson, C. D. (1991). *The altruism question: Toward a social-psychological answer.* Hillsdale, NJ: Erlbaum.

Batson, C. D.; Fultz, J.; & Schoenrade, P. A. (1987). Distress and empathy: Two qualitatively distinct vicarious emotions with different motivational consequences. *Journal of Personality, 55,* 19–39.

Bischof-Köhler, D. (1988). Über den Zusammenhang von Empathie und der Fähigkeit sich im Spiegel zu erkennen. *Schweizerische Zeitschrift für Psychologie, 47,* 147–159.

Boehm, C. (1999). *Hierarchies in the forest: The evolution of egalitarian behavior.* Cambridge, MA: Harvard University Press.

Caldwell, M. C., & Caldwell, D. K. (1966). Epimeletic (care-giving) behavior in Cetacea. In K. S. Norris (Ed.), *Whales, dolphins, and porpoises* (pp. 755–789). Berkeley: University of California Press.

Call, J. (2000). Intending and perceiving: Two forgotten components of social norms. *Journal of Consciousness Studies, 7,* 34–38.

Call, J.; Aureli, F.; & de Waal, F. B. M. (2002). Post-conflict third-party affiliation in stumptail macaques. *Animal Behaviour, 63,* 209–216.

Church, R. M. (1959) Emotional reactions of rats to the pain of others. *Journal of Comparative and Physiological Psychology, 52,* 132–134.

Connor, R. C., & Norris, K. S. (1982). Are dolphins reciprocal altruists? *American Naturalist, 119,* 358–372.

Damasio, A. R. (1994). *Descartes' error: Emotion, reason, and the human brain.* New York: Putnam.

Darwin, C. (1982 [1871]). *The descent of man, and selection in relation to sex.* Princeton, NJ: Princeton University Press.

de Waal, F. B. M. (1989). *Peacemaking among primates.* Cambridge, MA: Harvard University Press.

de Waal, F. B. M. (1991). Complementary methods and convergent evidence in the study of primate social cognition. *Behaviour, 118,* 297–320.

de Waal, F. B. M. (1996). *Good natured: The origins of right and wrong in humans and other animals.* Cambridge, MA: Harvard University Press.

de Waal, F. B. M. (1997). *Bonobo: The forgotten ape.* Berkeley: University of California Press.

de Waal, F. B. M. (1998 [1982]). *Chimpanzee politics: Power and sex among apes.* Baltimore, MD: The Johns Hopkins University Press.

de Waal, F. B. M. (1999). Anthropomorphism and anthropodenial: Consistency in our thinking about humans and other animals. *Philosophical Topics, 27,* 255–280.

de Waal, F. B. M. (2000). Primates – A natural heritage of conflict resolution. *Science, 289,* 586–590.

de Waal, F. B. M. (In press). Darwin's legacy and the study of primate visual communication. In P. Ekman, R. Davidson, F. B. M. de Waal, & J. Campos (Eds.), *Emotions inside out: Celebrating 130 years of Darwin's* "Expression of Emotion in Man and Animals." New York: New York Academy of Sciences.

de Waal, F. B. M., & Aureli, F. (1996). Consolation, reconciliation, and a possible cognitive difference between macaque and chimpanzee. In A. E. Russon, K. A. Bard, and S. T. Parker (Eds.), *Reaching into thought: The minds of the great apes* (pp. 80–110). Cambridge: Cambridge University Press.

de Waal, F. B. M., & van Roosmalen, A. (1979). Reconciliation and consolation among chimpanzees. *Behavioral Ecology and Sociobiology, 5,* 55–66.

Dimberg, U.; Thunberg, M.; & Elmehed, K. (2000). Unconscious facial reactions to emotional facial expressions. *Psychological Science, 11,* 86–89.

di Pellegrino, G.; Fadiga, L.; Fogassi, L.; Gallese, V.; & Rizzolatti, G. (1992). Understanding motor events: A neurophysiological study. *Experimental Brain Research, 91,* 176–180.

Eisenberg, N. (2000). Empathy and sympathy. In M. Lewis and J. M. Haviland-Jones (Eds.), *Handbook of emotion* (2d ed.; pp. 677–691). New York: Guilford Press.

Eisenberg, N., & Strayer, J. (1987). *Empathy and its development.* New York: Cambridge University Press.

Ekman, P. (1982). *Emotion in the human face.* 2d ed. Cambridge: Cambridge University Press.

Flack, J. C., & de Waal, F. B. M. (2000). 'Any animal whatever': Darwinian building blocks of morality in monkeys and apes. *Journal of Consciousness Studies, 7,* 1–29.

Gallup, G. G. (1982). Self-awareness and the emergence of mind in primates. *American Journal of Primatology, 2,* 237–248.

Goodall, J. (1968). The behaviour of free-living chimpanzees in the Gombe Stream Reserve. *Animal Behavior Monographs, 1,* 161–311.

Goodall, J. (1990). *Through a window: My thirty years with the chimpanzees of Gombe.* Boston: Houghton Mifflin Company.

Hatfield, E.; Cacioppo, J. T.; & Rapson, R. L. (1993). Emotional contagion. *Current Directions in Psychological Science, 2,* 96–99.

Hauser, M. D. (2000). *Wild minds: What animals really think.* New York: Holt.

Hoffman, M. L. (1982). Affect and moral development. *New Directions for Child Development, 16,* 83–103.

Hornblow, A. R. (1980). The study of empathy. *New Zealand Psychologist, 9,* 19–28.

Huxley, T. H. (1989 [1894]). *Evolution and ethics.* Princeton, NJ: Princeton University Press.

Kagan, J. (2000). Human morality is distinctive. *Journal of Consciousness Studies, 7,* 46–48.

Ladygina-Kohts, N. N. (2001 [1935]). *Infant chimpanzee and human child: A classic 1935 comparative study of ape emotions and intelligence.* Ed. F. B. M. de Waal. New York: Oxford University Press.

Lavery, J. J., & Foley, P. J. (1963). Altruism or arousal in the rat? *Science, 140,* 172–173.

Lipps, T. (1903). Einfühlung, innere Nachahmung und Organempfindung. *Archiv für die gesamte Psychologie, 1,* 465–519.

Masserman, J.; Wechkin, M. S.; & Terris, W. (1964). Altruistic behavior in rhesus monkeys. *American Journal of Psychiatry, 121,* 584–585.

Miller, R. E. (1967). Experimental approaches to the physiological and behavioral concomitants of affective communication in rhesus monkeys. In S. A. Altmann (Ed.), *Social communication among primates* (pp. 125–134). Chicago: University of Chicago Press.

Miller, R. E.; Banks, J. H.; & Ogawa, N. (1963). Role of facial expression in "co-operative avoidance conditioning" in monkeys. *Journal of Abnormal and Social Psychology, 67,* 24–30.

Miller, R. E.; Murphy, J. V.; & Mirsky, I. A. (1959). Relevance of facial expression and posture as cues in communication of affect between monkeys. *Archives of General Psychiatry, 1,* 480–488.

Mirsky, I. A.; Miller, R. E.; & Murphy, J. V. (1958). The communication of affect in rhesus monkeys I. An experimental method. *Journal of the American Psychoanalytic Association, 6,* 433–441.

Moss, C. (1988). *Elephant memories: Thirteen years in the life of an elephant family.* New York: Fawcett Columbine.

Nesse, R. M. (2001). *Evolution and the capacity for commitment.* New York: Russell Sage.

O'Connell, S. M. (1995). Empathy in chimpanzees: Evidence for theory of mind? *Primates, 36,* 397–410.

Parr, L. A. (2001). Cognitive and physiological markers of emotional awareness in chimpanzees. *Animal Cognition, 4,* 223–229.

Parr, L. A., & de Waal, F. B. M. (1999). Visual kin recognition in chimpanzees. *Nature, 399,* 647–648.

Parr, L. A.; Hopkins, W. D.; & de Waal, F. B. M. (1998). The perception of facial expressions by chimpanzees, Pan troglodytes. *Evolution of Communication, 2,* 1–23.

Parr, L. A.; Winslow, J. T.; Hopkins, W. D.; & de Waal, F. B. M. (2000). Recognizing facial cues: Individual recognition by chimpanzees (Pan troglodytes) and rhesus monkeys (Macaca mulatta). *Journal of Comparative Psychology, 114,* 47–60.

Payne, K. (1998). *Silent thunder.* New York: Simon & Schuster.

Povinelli, D. J. (1998). Can animals empathize? Maybe not. *Scientific American.* *www.sciam.com/1998/1198intelligence/1198povinelli.html*

Preston, S. D., & de Waal, F. B. M. (2002a). The communication of emotions and the possibility of empathy and altruism in nonhuman animals. In S. Post,

L. G. Underwood, J. P. Schloss, and W. B. Hurlburt (Eds.), *Altruistic love: Science, philosophy, and religion in dialogue* (pp. 284–308). Oxford: Oxford University Press.

Preston, S. D., & de Waal, F. B. M. (2002b). Empathy: Its ultimate and proximate bases. *Behavioral and Brain Sciences, 25*, 1–72.

Reiss, D., & Marino, L. (2001). Mirror self-recognition in the bottlenose dolphin: A case of cognitive convergence. *Proceedings of the National Academy of Science, 98*, 5937–5942.

Rice, G. E. J. (1964). Aiding behavior vs. fear in the albino rat. *Psychological Record, 14*, 165–170.

Rice, G. E. J., & Gainer, P. (1962). "Altruism" in the albino rat. *Journal of Comparative and Physiological Psychology, 55*, 123–125.

Schino, G. (2000). Beyond the primates: Expanding the reconciliation horizon. In F. Aureli and F. B. M. de Waal (Eds.), *Natural Conflict Resolution* (pp. 225–242). Berkeley: University of California Press.

Smith, A. (1937 [1759]). *A theory of moral sentiments*. New York: Modern Library.

Sober, E., & Wilson, D. S. (1998). *Unto others: The evolution and psychology of unselfish behavior*. Cambridge, MA: Harvard University Press.

van Hooff, J. A. R. A. M. (1967). The facial displays of the Catarrhine monkeys and apes. In D. Morris (Ed.), *Primate ethology* (pp. 7–68). Chicago: Aldine.

Verbeek, P., & de Waal, F. B. M. (1997). Postconflict behavior in captive brown capuchins in the presence and absence of attractive food. *International Journal of Primatology, 18*, 703–725.

Watanabe, S., & Ono, K. (1986). An experimental analysis of "empathic" response: Effects of pain reactions of pigeon upon other pigeon's operant behavior. *Behavioural Processes, 13*, 269–277.

Watts, D. P.; Colmenares, F.; & Arnold, K. (2000). Redirection, consolation, and male policing: How targets of aggression interact with bystanders. In F. Aureli and F. B. M. de Waal (Eds.), *Natural conflict resolution* (pp. 281–301). Berkeley: University of California Press.

Wechkin, S.; Masserman, J. H.; & Terris, W. (1964). Shock to a conspecific as an aversive stimulus. *Psychonomic Science, 1*, 47–48.

Williams, J. H. G.; Whiten, A.; Suddendorf, T.; & Perrett, D. I. (2001). Imitation, mirror neurons and autism. *Neuroscience and Biobehavioral Review, 25*, 287–295.

Wispé, L. (1986). The distinction between sympathy and empathy: To call forth a concept, a word is needed. *Journal of Personality and Social Psychology, 50*, 314–321.

Wispé, L. (1991). *The psychology of sympathy*. New York: Plenum.

Yerkes, R. M. (1925). *Almost human*. New York: Century.

Zahn-Waxler, C.; Hollenbeck, B.; & Radke-Yarrow, M. (1984). The origins of empathy and altruism. In M. W. Fox and L. D. Mickley (Eds.), *Advances in animal welfare science* (pp. 21–39). Washington, DC: Humane Society of the United States.

23

Emotional Gifts and "You First" Micropolitics

Niceness in the Socioemotional Economy

Candace Clark

ABSTRACT

Patterned exchanges of emotions in everyday life help build walls of indifference or enmity and webs of affiliation. Interview and observational data show that the "nice" person and the "micro-hero" give emotional gifts and use a variety of "you first" strategies to safeguard others' emotions and micropolitical places.

INTRODUCTION

Whether people are aware of it or not, human emotionality is an ongoing stream, and what Westerners refer to as emotions – the bits of experience from this stream that a given culture has recognized, labeled, and scripted – pervade every aspect of social life. As more recent evidence bears out (see, e.g., Sally, 2000, p. 579; Scheff, 1990; Wentworth & Ryan, 1992; Wentworth & Yardley, 1994; and Zajonc, 1998), the words that Hume wrote in 1740 were quite apt: "no object is presented to the senses, nor image form'd in the fancy, but what is accompany'd with some emotion or movement of spirits proportion'd to it . . . however custom may make us insensible of this sensation, and cause us to confound it with the object or idea . . ." ([1740] 1978, p. 373). If we think about it, we realize that even seemingly routine cognitive and physical tasks such as reading a term paper, balancing the checkbook, glancing at a stranger walking down the street, or doing laundry are accompanied by emotions, be they strong or weak. If our attention is caught in the action, our emotions concern it; if our attention wanders from the task, our emotions stray elsewhere.

Furthermore, most emotions arise when people are interacting with others, either face-to-face (see, e.g., Kemper, 1978) or in imagination. Mead ([1934] 1962) and Cooley ([1902] 1983) recognized almost a century ago that our self-concepts depend heavily on the reflected appraisals of relevant

402

others, which we carry with us in our minds and which we rarely manage to escape. Who does not know mature adults who are still evaluating themselves according to the remembered judgments of their teachers or parents? As Wentworth and Yardley wrote: "[F]rom the very core of our being we are inwardly linked with others in society. All of our knowing and feeling is influenced by the fact of our mind-self having been formed out of living with others in a persisting pattern of relations. Each person is an actual psychological-experiential blend of significant and anonymous others" (1994, p. 27). Both emotionality and social interaction are virtually omnipresent, and each colors the other. Moreover, although few scholars have taken on the task of explaining it (but see Wentworth & Yardley, 1994), our self-concepts are brimming with emotions that arise in face-to-face interaction, memory of past interaction, and imagined interaction.

Beyond the fact of the mere pervasiveness of emotion in the microworlds of ordinary social actors, it is sociologically important to focus on the fact that emotions flow between and among people. Although it is highly improvisational (Scheff, 1990), the flow is patterned rather than random, and the patterned flow of emotions shapes and creates both social bonds and social barriers.

We can readily understand that, particularly in late-modern Western societies, love, liking, gratitude, and sympathy are key elements in the webs of affiliation that connect people. And because the flow of these emotions tends to be based on some sort of exchange principles (Collins, 1987; Hochschild, 1983; Dressel, 1989; Clark, 1997), the webs are woven tighter through the feelings of obligation a recipient experiences.

With regard to social divisions, emotions such as disgust and disdain may both reflect existing divisions and serve to perpetuate them. Emotions such as anger, exasperation, and fear can create walls of indifference or enmity. And as Scheff and Retzinger (1991) argued, emotions such as shame and humiliation can spiral into anger and rage, and eventually destroy bonds.

Perhaps less obvious, though, some emotions connect people while dividing them on the basis of their relative interpersonal power, or what Goffman (1951) called "place." Place arrangements are distinct from matters of intimacy and social distance, and they are not merely pecking orders. Rather, a person's place in an encounter or relationship is a situated identity that serves to guide interaction. Just as emotions pervade all human encounters and relationships, so too do matters of place. We ask: Who has the edge, the advantage, over whom in this situation? and Where do I stand relative to these other people? Emotions help social actors to answer these questions. For instance, my feelings of respect, embarrassment, or admiration mark for me my inferior "place." Your feelings of disgust, hauteur, or exasperation mark for you your superior "place." Especially when such feelings are displayed to others, who then read and react to them, they play a major role in negotiating place arrangements in everyday microhierarchies.

Thus, understanding how emotions flow in everyday life could go a long way toward explaining an age-old sociological paradox: social life is marked by both connections and divisions. I will approach these issues by focusing on the giving and withholding of emotional gifts. As I have learned through my studies of sympathy and niceness, these seemingly simple emotional gifts can be enormously consequential for individuals' lives and for the social order.

EMOTIONS AS GIFTS

Before we can look sociologically at how emotions work in everyday life, it is important to realize that emotions refer to something, and the object of an emotion can be oneself or others. Thus, only some emotions are indications to the self about the self (e.g., "I feel homesick/ sad/elated/surprised/afraid"). Scheff (1990) would say that even these emotions concern more than the self – most of them reflect perceptions of the state of one's social bonds.

Other common emotions are "extrojected" (Kemper, 1978), or indications to the self about the self's feelings about others. Emotions such as gratitude and jealousy are exclusively about others. And although emotions such as annoyance, admiration, disgust, sympathy, or anger *can* sometimes be about the self, they most often concern family members, coworkers, friends, enemies, and various others. A person may keep these emotions to oneself or may display, or target, them at others.

Some other-targeted emotions can be called emotional gifts. By emotional gifts I mean the emotions that one social actor expresses or displays (verbally or nonverbally) to another that have value because they are scarce – that is, they are not given indiscriminately or limitlessly – and because they create positive emotions in the other. For example, one's expression of liking for a friend, if it has not been too freely or commonly conferred on others, is a gift that may cause the target to feel self-worth or satisfaction. A sister's appropriately timed display of gratitude for a brother's favor is a gift that may produce in the brother a sense of pride or gratification. Or a customer's withholding or "working down" of annoyance at a server's bungling is a gift that can spare the server embarrassment. Of course, as with any gift (see, e.g., Schwartz, 1967), the donor may wittingly or unwittingly cause the target to feel hurt, angry, or belittled because emotional gifts can carry meanings (e.g., "I know what you need and what's good for you," "If I give you a gift first, you can never overcome the fact that you are indebted to me," and "My gift shows that I have more resources than you") that point to the target's inferior place.

Once we begin to consider emotional gifts, we see that it is not only the fact that emotions are given and taken, but also *how* they are given and taken, that shapes social interaction and social bonds. People usually give (and withhold) emotional gifts – what Hochschild, the preeminent sociologist of emotions, called "feeling currency" (1983, p. 78) – in patterned and culturally approved ways. Perhaps unconsciously echoing anthropologist Pitt-Rivers's earlier analysis of honor and shame in traditional cultures, which was based on the concepts of "honor due," "honor claimed," and "honor paid" (1966), Hochschild wrote in *The Managed Heart* (1983, p. 56) of "emotions owed and owing, due and payable." Hochschild developed a theory of "feeling rules" to explain that certain emotions (or at least emotional displays) are due to others in particular settings, for instance sympathy at a funeral and joy at a wedding. Also, certain emotions are due to particular social actors regardless of the setting (for example, love to one's child and gratitude to a benefactor), while other emotions (such as anger) are to be withheld from those with "status shields" (e.g., the boss). Finally, emotions are owed as repayment for others' gifts. Many of us do not want to admit it, but, as Hochschild phrased it, when people find that owed feelings "come hard," they realize "that we keep a mental ledger with 'owed' and 'received' columns for gratitude, love, anger, guilt, and other feelings" (1983, p. 78). Furthermore, the fact that people devise many ways in which to do emotion work in order to work up or work down their feelings implies that they believe they should follow the feeling rules that say they owe feeling currency to others.

In Hochschild's next major work on the way two-earner couples deal with and think about the household division of labor (1989), she took her ideas about feelings owed and received to the level of relationships. Focusing on the "second shift," the extra housework and child-rearing burdens placed on women in many modern marriages, she tackled the question of why some couples, whose marriages appeared to the outside world to be so inequitable as to be heading for the divorce courts, managed to coexist. She argued that an "economy of gratitude" (pp. 110–127, 156–158) between spouses is a key component in creating enough pleasure and satisfaction so that neither leaves the relationship. "When couples struggle," Hochschild wrote, "it is seldom simply over who does what. Far more often, it is over the giving and receiving of gratitude" (1989, p. 18).

First, a spouse must pay some gratitude to the other for his or her contributions to their relationship. Also, a spouse must receive from the other the amount of gratitude that he or she wants or expects. Some of those Hochschild interviewed had to stretch to generate feelings of gratitude for their spouses. For instance, one wife who worked longer hours and received much higher pay than her husband said she was grateful to him for accepting a career woman as his wife. In order to create a balanced economy of gratitude, Hochschild noticed, some spouses created elaborate "family myths" to paper over problems that could threaten feelings of gratitude (Hochschild, 1989, pp. 43–49). Thus, another working wife and mother who had felt that her husband was not contributing much to household chores or child rearing eventually convinced herself of the myth, to which he readily subscribed, that his efforts at walking the dog and keeping the garage clean constituted his "half" of the second shift.

When the economy of gratitude became sufficiently unbalanced among some of Hochschild's interviewees, what she called a "nurturance crunch" ensued, characterized by "emotional absenteeism" (pp. 122–123) and "a dearth of small gestures of caring" (1989, p. 118). In other words, the emotional gifts stopped flowing. Even though gifts – emotional or otherwise – should not be demanded, they are expected (see also Mauss, [1925] 1954; Schwartz, 1967; Kemper, 1978). A social actor who fails to receive expected emotional gifts might feel slighted and in turn withhold his or her own emotional gifts. We could say a spiral of withdrawal has begun. Emotional exchange slows to a standstill. The social bond is threatened or broken.

THE SOCIOEMOTIONAL ECONOMY

Hochschild recognized that, "taken together, emotion work, feeling rules, and interpersonal exchange make up our private emotional system" (1983, p. 76). But I believe her ideas can be greatly expanded. We can envision the private emotional system, with its feeling currency and economy of gratitude, more broadly as a "socioemotional economy" (Clark, 1997) in which, perhaps, gratitude may serve as the pennies, sympathy as the dimes, and love as the quarters. It is in this economy, this more-or-less orderly exchange system, that people give and withhold emotional resources, form social bonds and divisions, negotiate microhierarchical arrangements, and derive identity and self-worth.

As I see it, a society's socioemotional economy, though highly improvisational, is a patterned, organized system for managing the day-to-day flow, or give-and-take, of socioemotional resources among members of a community. It is an intricate and largely unrecognized, taken-for-granted system, one that has marketplace features (Collins, 1987; Dressel, 1989). It parallels and is at many points intertwined with the money-goods-and-services economy. And, it is every bit as consequential. From relationships, membership in communities, and even brief encounters, people may draw nothing and feel themselves at a remove and excluded from the interaction, or they may derive many valuable resources – among them help, attention, sex, company, advice, encouragement, information, and emotions such as sympathy, love, and gratitude. That these resources have no set price tags does not negate the idea that they have worth and utility. They contribute to emotional satisfaction, self-worth, and identity, helping to stave off the late-modern malaise that Giddens (1991) called "existential anxiety" and

Berger and Luckmann (1967) called "anomic terror." In this sense, they are valuable gifts.

The workings of the socioemotional economy became more noticeable to the average U.S. citizen after destructive attacks in September 2001 set off outright horror and panic. These attacks greatly inflamed Americans' existential anxiety and anomic terror, and patterns of everyday interaction changed quickly and dramatically. Almost immediately, many Americans began showing greater respect and concern for each other. News commentators marveled not only at emergency workers' heroism in their rescue efforts and citizens' donations of money and blood; they also noted their astonishment at New York City motorists' newfound courtesy to each other on the roads and pedestrians' new proclivity to make eye contact with and even smile at passersby on the sidewalks. A *New York Times* article reported this conversation as a daughter tells her father about a bomb scare at her school on September 20:

"The kids who have cell phones are calling their parents and then they do something so unusual. They go up to other kids they don't even know and ask if anyone would like to call their parents, you know, offering them their phones; other kids announce that they live only two, three blocks away, and if anybody wants, they can come stay at their houses if they don't want to be out in the street. Everybody became so generous. It was almost worth the scare to see it." (Price, 2001)

U.S. President George W. Bush, in a televised news conference a month after the attacks, also expressed his amazement and delight that one unintended result had been Americans' new appreciation of the importance of spouses, children, friends, and communities. Social psychologists were probably less surprised than Bush to discover that feelings of vulnerability to outside threats would increase people's need for and witting or unwitting efforts to create social cohesion and cement bonds. For my part, I was not surprised at the increased salience of the socioemotional economy during these times. The give-and-take of what might seem to be trivial emotional gifts provided vital and sorely needed social glue, as it also does, though less perceptibly, in tranquil times.

Although actors in the socioemotional economy may not realize it, they create margins or accounts of socioemotional credits for each other, credits that can be held in reserve, cashed in, replenished, or even used up entirely. For instance, in Wiseman's (1979) observational study of homeless men in the U.S.A., she found that social workers, medical personnel, and mission workers held accounts for the men as long as they paid with deference and respectability to keep their accounts open. In fact, she noted, the men had to pay in advance. Maintaining what she called their "social margin" in this way entitled them to help, food, shelter, and money. It seems likely that the more general social margin contributes to specific margins for particular emotional gifts. For example, the respondents and subjects in my research on patterns of sympathy give-and-take (Clark, 1997) created "sympathy margins" for others; those who claimed too many sympathy credits from their accounts often found any new claims to sympathy refused. For instance, people with chronic illness or a string of disasters in a row might have justifiable need for others' sympathy and concern, but others would and could give only so much. The miserable often minimized their claims to protect their significant others and their sympathy margins.

Some critics have complained that looking at socioemotional exchanges in this way is a false economic analogy. On the other hand, in the anthropological view, the two universal bases for social order throughout history have been kinship (exchanges based on reciprocal role performance) and reciprocity (exchanges of roughly equally valuable commodities). And, as Scheff (1990, pp. 64, 79) argued, sequencing, or turn taking – the essence of exchange – is present in human infants, is pancultural, and is possibly hard-wired in our species. Thus, in accord with Simmel (1978) and Lévi-Strauss (1969), I believe the analogy goes the other way: it is the money-goods-and-services economy – what we commonly think of nowadays as "the economy"– that is the simplistic, stylized, institutionalized, concretized analogy (see also Stauth & Turner, 1988). It has evolved in modern times from the very complex, millennia-old systems of give-and-take that have characterized all the cultures on which the anthropologists have reported. As Simmel saw it, sociation and exchange became reified in money.

There is, however, a danger in using the term "economy." Readers may automatically imagine an exchange model based *purely on reciprocity*: one hour's work, or one computer, or one smile equals a fixed number of euros. This simplistic model is not even applicable to the money-goods-and-services economy, where prices and wages are negotiated and change with supply and demand, bartering is common, and the black market is ever present. And it is not the model I propose for the socioemotional economy.

Within this economy, emotional gifts flow between social actors according to feeling rules that are predicated largely on what Davis, Gardner, and Gardner (1941) called "social logics," or learned sets of assumptions and predictions that "make sense" within a given culture (e.g., in Western cultures it "makes sense" that a person betrayed will feel angry or hurt, or a person who receives too much sympathy will become "soft"). Social logics are less obvious and prescriptive than specific rules, and for that reason alone they may influence thinking, feeling, and acting more unexpectedly and more profoundly. The rules and logics of the socioemotional economy differ for intimates and strangers, and they vary from culture to culture and subculture to subculture (see, e.g., Dodd, 1987). The rules and logics are also profoundly gendered, but an adequate discussion of gender differences in expectations and in emotional experience and emotional exchange would fill far too many pages to include here.

Following Gouldner (1973), I believe the explicit exchange rules of the socioemotional economy are based on one or another – or more likely on some combination – of three underlying logics. First is a traditional logic of *complementary role performance*. For example, a spouse might say, "If we perform the complementary roles of husband and wife that we have negotiated, both our needs will be met." This logic helps to shape the particular rules for giving and taking that the spouses create.

A second exchange logic is the utilitarian logic of *reciprocity*: a person who receives something of value from others is obligated to return something of value; a person who gives something of value to others is entitled to expect returns. Examples of rules stemming from this logic might be, "If you do me a favor, I'll do you a favor"; or "I will type your memos if you pay me $50." Yet reciprocity need not involve the same people to be interpersonally effective (Lévi-Strauss, 1974). For example, one of my own respondents, a middle-aged businessman, had expected friends with whom he had sympathized in the past to give expressions of sympathy, not to him, but to his hospitalized son; he was angry with them when they did not (interview, 1986). Another of my respondents, a young woman who was helped by a stranger at a car wash, said: "It was neat that a stranger was kind enough to help out. I felt thankful. It meant a lot. It made *me* want to do something nice for a stranger" (interview, 1999). She felt an urge to return something of value, not merely gratitude to her benefactor, but a commensurate service to another stranger in the larger community.

Third is the exchange logic of *beneficence*, which is spelled out most completely in the New Testament of the Bible. The beneficent person might say, "I will give to you because you are needy – especially if you are unable to repay me; and if I become needy some other beneficent person will give to me."

For my respondents and the subjects in my research on sympathy, the most common social logic for the exchange of socioemotional gifts *among family members and intimates* – at least in American society today – appeared to be the blended logic of *reciprocal complementarity*. That is, spouses and children continue to perform complementary role obligations – be they traditionally defined or some modernized or individually negotiated version – only so long as they believe that the role partner is also doing so. For example, if a husband believes a wife has reneged on her promised contributions to the marriage, or if a wife believes a husband has defected from the team, the partner who feels short-changed can call off the marriage. Parents may disown children who do not repay their investments (although the state gets involved if the children are minors); and one of my recent students successfully divorced her mother in a court of law for "failure to support." Fictive kin and very close friends appear to follow the same blended logic, and it is even easier for them to end a relationship.

With *nonkin and nonintimates*, the social logic underlying exchange also appears to be a blended logic, in this case one of *reciprocal beneficence*. I found, for example, that friends, coworkers, neighbors, and strangers give gifts of sympathy and aid when they think that a sympathy-worthy person needs it – unless they have reason to believe that the other has failed, or would fail, to reciprocate that beneficence in the future. I found very few Good Samaritans out there, perpetually turning their cheeks to those whom they considered ungrateful or calculating.

Microhierarchy and Emotional Gifts

The rules for giving, taking, and reciprocating socioemotional resources in everyday interaction are complicated by place arrangements – who is "superior" and who is "inferior" to whom. For instance, my respondents noted that one should not go overboard in either feeling or displaying deep sympathy or concern toward either an inferior or a superior: a worker should not send an expensive floral display to a boss's father's funeral, and a boss should not break down in sobs over the news that a worker's mother has died. As Schwartz (1967) discovered regarding material gifts between unequals, emotional gifts also should be pegged to place arrangements, lest they threaten or upset those arrangements.

The rules for *reciprocating* emotional gifts are also tied to place. Inferiors are not obligated to return superiors' emotional gifts with similar gifts. For instance, if a veterinarian's office sends a customer a sympathy card when his or her pet dies, the customer is not obligated to send a card if the vet's pet dies. If a professor displays warmth and concern toward students who are having difficulties, the students are expected to offer gratitude or perhaps deference in exchange. But they should not return the favor in kind if they learn that the professor has experienced a setback. If they do so, their actions may be seen as presumptuous, "uppity," or "out of place." And others may quickly "put them in their place."

Even though two people may occupy superior and inferior social statuses (such as boss and worker, professor and student, veterinarian and pet owner, or parent and child), macrohierarchical status discrepancies do not automatically translate into micropolitical place arrangements. That is, the exact social distance between places in a microhierarchy is not determined solely by social status. For example, in some cases, a boss may be one-up relative to a particular worker (and share some emotional interchanges with that worker), and the same boss may be two- or three-up relative to other workers (and share no emotions with them). Or another boss may be three-up relative to all his or her workers (and remain emotionally aloof from them). Cultural capital (Bourdieu, 1986), including one's education, gender, occupation, and social class standing, plays a part in determining place gaps, but interactional skills and micropolitics (which I will discuss in more detail later) play their own parts as well. This is why most of us can think of cases in which an intelligent and efficient secretary with good "people skills" ends up running an office, telling the boss what to do, and helping the boss with his or her personal problems. Or a wily, manipulative teenager can gain a micropolitical advantage by belittling his or her parents, making them quail for fear of losing the child's love. Place gaps, more than social status discrepancies, set the tone for present and future emotional interchanges.

Furthermore, people's places in an encounter or relationship are precarious. Because place arrangements can change in an instant, they are continually negotiated. I call this negotiation "micropolitics" (Clark, 1990). Sometimes micropolitcal actors try to obtain or keep interpersonal power, superior place, and "face" (Goffman, 1967); but sometimes they give up power, place, and face by elevating others or humbly diminishing themselves. That is, social actors sometimes take a "Me First" approach to micropolitics, and at other times a "You First" approach. Either way, micropolitics plays out within the socioemotional economy.

THE "ME FIRST" APPROACH TO MICROPOLITICS

"Me First" micropolitical strategies may be familiar to readers of humorist Stephen Potter's guides to "gamesmanship," "lifemanship," and "one-upsmanship." A person using a Me First approach to an encounter or relationship makes some prior micropolitical assumptions: the situation involves competition, and each party is entitled to compete. The underlying social logic is that other social actors try to make a profit (gain higher place) during encounters, so I am justified in seeking a profit too. This logic is encapsulated in such sayings as "Look out for number one," "Nice guys finish last," and "Do unto others before they do unto you." The Me First micropolitician asks, to turn John F. Kennedy's words on their heads, not "What can I do for my social interaction?" but "What can my interaction do for me?"

Thus, a Me First micropolitician uses methods that aggrandize one's own place and/or reduce others' places. Many of these strategies are implemented by, wittingly or unwittingly, managing the emotions of others. They involve such tactics as:

1. Directing negative emotions such as anger or disgust at another in an effort to make the other feel lowly or inferior
2. Bestowing emotional gifts such as sympathy or patience in a way that underscores one's own virtue and also the recipient's problems or inferior place
3. Flattering or "buttering up" a superior to slip into a more elevated place

4. Causing another to feel guilt over failures to live up to obligations
5. Creating a situation in which one is calm but the other is emotionally flustered or upset (See Clark, 1990, for an extended treatment of these tactics.)

There are undoubtedly many other such strategies. They suggest three important points regarding emotions. First, micropolitical strategies and tactics "work" when the person on the receiving end actually feels belittled or in some way lowered. When this happens, the inferior feels his or her own lower place, and no threat or coercion is necessary to keep him or her there.

Second, people who occupy superior social statuses (e.g., men, bosses, professionals, husbands, and parents) have greater experience, know-how, and leeway to engage in Me First micropolitical strategies than do those in inferior social statuses, who more often must engage in You First strategies (described below). Thus, the superior can often create and reproduce place arrangements in which others feel their inferiority. Of course, the target of any of these strategies may resist with counterstrategies, in which case the micropolitical negotiation goes on – sometimes with surprising results.

Third, people who occupy roughly equal places are not supposed to engage in Me First micropolitical strategies with each other. A person who does so may cause the other to feel embarrassed, disappointed, resentful, or angry. The other may then warily adopt a Me First approach, and the relationship may take on a competitive character.

THE "YOU FIRST" APPROACH TO MICROPOLITICS

As I mentioned above, though, not all micropolitical strategies involve putting others down or elevating oneself. You First micropolitical strategies *elevate others* by improving their place in the microhierarchical arrangement, thereby inspiriting them and enhancing their self-worth and self-esteem. In Harris's (1997) study of friendships, he found that people often act to minimize place inequalities to prevent friends' feelings of belittlement or shame. Even in relationships typically less equal than friendships, superiors may humbly give credit to inferiors, and inferiors may bestow deference and admiration on superiors.

The general outcry over the past few decades against incivility, narcissism, "road rage," airport rage, biting incidents, litigiousness, and the like would make it seem that such You First strategies have become rarer than in the more civil past. They are not (or are no longer), as Goffman (1967) thought, *routine* protective strategies dominating all everyday interaction. You First strategies are gifts, and these gifts have important emotional elements.

A person taking a You First approach begins with several assumptions. First, the situation is not a competition, but rather the parties are interdependent, essentially teammates for the duration of the encounter or relationship. The team may persist over a lifetime; but even if it is a "pickup" team that lasts for only a few moments, the players are mentally and emotionally "on the same side" (Kravanja, 1991). Second, a teammate acts as a fiduciary, a person entrusted to protect and increase another's holdings (including mental and emotional holdings) and power (including place).

The *ideal* social logic of the You First micropolitician is beneficence, as represented in the Golden Rule: "Do unto others as you would have them do unto you." In contrast to one taking a Me First approach, the You First micropolitician asks, "What can I do for my interaction?" The "logical" results will be that the other will gain place, the interaction(s) will be positive, I will be moral, solidarity will increase, and both of us will win in the end. If, as the interaction unfolds, things do not work out this way, the You First micropolitician may revert to the less-than-ideal social logic of reciprocal beneficence: "Do unto others as you would have them do unto you, until they take advantage of you."

The methods of the You First approach also involve managing others' emotions, but in this case the strategies are self-effacement, elevating the other, and producing solidarity. Here, the Me First tactics are essentially reversed:

1. Avoiding aiming negative emotions such as anger or disgust at another in an effort to make the other feel valued
2. Bestowing emotional gifts such as sympathy or patience in a way that downplays one's own virtue and the recipient's problems or inferior place
3. Directing attention and positive emotions such as admiration and appreciation to an inferior to enhance his or her place and lessen the microhierarchical gap
4. Avoiding conduct that causes another to feel guilt over failures to live up to obligations
5. Avoiding conduct that would make the other emotionally flustered or upset

Others may perceive a person who engages in one or more of these strategies in an insincere fashion as a sycophantic Me First micropolitician. They may view one who excessively engages in one or more of these strategies as a "sucker" or a submissive individual who fears others and dares not assert him- or herself. However, they usually consider a sincere, self-assured You First micropolitician to be nice.

In my early research on the role of the sympathizer, it became clear to me that the sympathizer role is often subsumed under the broader social role of the nice person. It also became clear that, although niceness is largely taken for granted, it has become a very important feature of contemporary social life, since the bases for social relations have shifted over the past several centuries away from ascribed status arrangements and toward greater individual choice in interactional partners. Without niceness, everyday life would be a more lonely, humiliating, frightening affair.

In Western societies today, we use the term "nice" to describe people and their behavior quite often. The term is used as an indicator of social worth (as is the term "good" person), and in everyday speech the concept of niceness serves as a capacious umbrella that covers a host of qualities and behaviors. As I will discuss further, this mélange includes being civil, well-mannered, courteous, kind, friendly, sincere, open, empathic, caring, sympathetic, warm, inclusive, humble, altruistic, and generous, and *not* being boorish, ill-mannered, mean, cold, calculating, petty, cruel, snobby, self-centered, hurtful, or greedy. Niceness is not synonymous with the presence of any one of the positive ways of being in the world listed above or the absence of any one of the negative ways of being. Rather, being nice requires a person to exhibit most of the positive and few if any of the negative ways of being. We might call niceness a "meta-role" that subsumes many lesser roles, all of which have to do with the treatment of others in everyday interactions.

We often assume that niceness and non-niceness are personality traits or innate predispositions to treat others in a particular way. However, qualities such as those listed above are ways of acting, thinking, and feeling that have culturally variable expectations and scripts. The scripts can be learned, and indeed parents usually expend a great deal of time and energy to see that their children learn them (see, e.g., Cahill, 1987). Further, a given individual may not enact (or fail to enact) the nice role at every moment or in every encounter or relationship. Rather, one may slip in and out of the nice role many times during a day, in reaction to a wide range of psychological and interactional dynamics. Personality may play a part, but niceness is also a decidedly social phenomenon. The assumptions, logics, and tactics of You First micropolitics are part of the role expectations for the nice person. Yet the expectations and scripts for niceness go beyond micropolitics.

NICENESS IN THE SOCIOEMOTIONAL ECONOMY

One way to gain social worth is to enact the social role of the good person or honorable person, adhering to expectations for major institutional roles in the community, kin system, and workplace. Another way to win approval and social worth is to enact the social role of the nice person. That is, a person can be a good citizen, parent, child, plumber, or sociologist without being nice. And a person can be nice without being a good citizen, parent, or plumber. The nice person manages well in the socioemotional economy by giving to others and inspiriting them, thereby earning "social capital" (Bourdieu, 1986) that can elicit others' socioemotional resources (and financial rewards; see, e.g., Coleman, 1988). The nice person may pay substantial costs for giving to others (some of which I will explain later) but also may elevate him- or herself in the bargain.

Sometimes one person can elevate another via the money-goods-and-services economy, as when a boss gives a worker a free vacation or when an anonymous donor spreads his or her wealth or engages in what Wuthnow (1991) called "acts of compassion." More often, people uplift and inspirit others by offering them socioemotional resources in everyday encounters in the socioemotional economy. Such resources, which include emotional gifts, are the media of niceness.

As I have learned through my interviews and observations over the past five years, at the most general level, being nice is an *emotional* strategy that entails proactively and reactively taking care of others' emotions (to the extent allowed by the intimacy level and place arrangement of the relationship). The social role of the nice person requires giving emotional gifts and giving them appropriately. Sometimes the gift may be a single emotional display – a smile or a hug – that produces a positive feeling in another. And, as we have seen, it may be a You First micropolitical gift.

But often the gift is one of sustained emotion work. Among my respondents, topping their lists of what made both men and women nice were thoughtfulness and consideration for others' feelings and opinions, coupled with the willingness to go out of one's way to pitch in and help others. This kind of conduct requires a vigilant, selfless, and imaginative stance toward others.

In essence, the nice person is an unwitting though respectful believer in what Goffman called the "civil religion of self" (1971, p. 63), in which the self has become sacred and each social actor must cherish and protect others' privacy, "egos," and face. As Elias ([1939] 1978) also noted, the increasing importance of the self in Western cultures over the past several centuries has been accompanied by an increase in the importance placed on individuals' emotions. As a further result, Elias's civilized person – like the one I call the nice person – keeps his or her own concerns and emotions in check and focuses on not offending others' sensibilities or causing them emotional distress.

Perhaps the cardinal rule for being considered nice is to notice and repay other people's positive acts and emotional gifts. At a minimum, the nice person should show appreciation and gratitude for others' kindnesses, but often he or she is expected to go further, reciprocating with actions and emotional gifts of his or her own. Failure to reciprocate for another's gifts, or trying to "make a profit" from a relationship, rules out a person's chances of acquiring nice status. Unless there are mitigating circumstances, the person who fails to reciprocate will cause others to feel "taken advantage of." They may then see him or her as someone lacking in common courtesy or decency, or even see that person as a "user." (But, of course, if the other people are very nice, or if they are intimates, they may search for and sometimes invent the mitigating circumstances that could explain away the ingrate's actions.)

Being considered nice can sometimes be the result of *lucky role performance*, that is, by blindly or self-servingly following the culture's niceness scripts and formulas without having genuine understanding or concern for others. People who attempt to be nice in this way often *act* nicely. They *do* what they think would make most people happy. That is, they follow rules of etiquette, send greeting cards when the calendar and Hallmark demand, write thank-you notes, give compliments, attend funerals, perhaps engage in volunteer work, and give gifts on appropriate occasions. If one's actions, demeanor, and expressions just happen to produce positive feelings in others, they may view the lucky formula follower as a nice person.

However, if others suspect that the person lacks true empathy or is insincere, they tend to discount the person's actions, devalue the gift, and resent the obligation and indebtedness they feel. Worse, if they suspect a hidden desire to get returns on one's investments (sometimes called "getting over"), they view the other as a Me First micropolitician.

To be considered genuinely nice, one must convince others that one's own mind and emotions are engaged on their behalf. As my respondents pointed out, the non-nice have an excessive focus on the self and a deficient focus on others, while the nice can suspend their own concerns. The genuinely nice person must not appear to be following formulas, but rather should determine what could make a specific person happy or sad and enhance that person's sense of place, self-worth, self-esteem, and general well-being.

A first step involves showing an interest in and concern for the other and actively trying to empathize or, to use Mead's ([1934] 1962) words, "take the attitude of the other." Empathizing involves paying careful attention to the other (many of my respondents mentioned listening as a key to niceness). Then, the person being nice should try to head off anything that would produce the other's sadness or loss of place and foster that which would yield the other's happiness and elevated place. At a minimum, the genuinely nice person should monitor his or her own actions and emotional displays to make sure they please rather than offend. For instance, one might mute one's own anger at the other, suppress one's envy (Hochschild, 1983, p. 18), and generally withhold criticisms that one suspects would produce unhappiness in the other.

If another person already is experiencing unpleasant circumstances, the person being nice should react by trying to ameliorate the situation, perhaps by offering assistance, advice, or sympathy. Certainly, a nice person would not impose on the other his or her own claims or demands that might be excessive in the unhappy circumstances.

We can see that the costs of being nice can be relatively high. If the costs are particularly high, we could say that the nice person is engaging in *acts of microheroism*. The microhero or microheroine does not jump into a river to rescue a drowning child. Rather, the microhero or -heroine jumps into the interactional stream to rescue someone from loss of face, loss of place, or negative emotions. One example came from a middle-aged mother of three young boys, a secretary in a busy office, speaking about one of her bosses:

Once when Bernard came in after the Christmas holiday and we were talking about how it had gone, he said Christmas just didn't seem the same to him anymore since his parents had died. He had always loved receiving candy canes, oranges, and cookies, but since they died he hadn't had any. You could tell he was feeling so sad.

So I wrote myself a little note, and the next year I found the note and went out and got all the things that reminded him of the good Christmases. I called him in and told him I had a little surprise for him. You should have seen him! He was so touched he cried. I was so happy I could do it for him. (Field notes, 1999)

This woman could have merely sent her boss a card, but instead she took time and money from her own family to save him from feeling that his life lacked continuity. And she risked being embarrassed if he had not appreciated the gift – or if he himself had felt embarrassed and reacted gruffly.

Another rather extreme example of microheroism came from one of my respondents who described a week-long drying-out session that a group of friends conducted for another friend who was drinking heavily and on the verge of losing his job, his family, and his health. The friends "kidnapped" the drinker and locked him, sans alcohol, in one of their homes. They set up large counseling sessions in which ten to twelve people would talk for hours with the drinker to try to convince him of his merits and talents and get him to change his ways. Between sessions, they took turns staying with him so that he was never alone at any hour of the day or night. And after a week, it worked. The group of microheroes sacrificed a great deal of time they could have spent with their families, doing routine household chores that had piled up, or enjoying themselves. Their selfless concern for their friend certainly qualifies as microheroism.

The most heroic deeds, however, were those that came hard – when people did not want to carry them out but did so anyway. For example, one woman explained:

It was Arlene's 81st birthday, and it was cold and snowy, and none of her children were coming to town to see her. Now, Arlene has started failing lately and she keeps coming over at dinnertime and calling at all hours. She talks all the time anyway, and now she gets mixed up and says bizarre things. Craig just ignores her when she comes over.

Usually I feel sorry for her and take her a plate of food at least once a day because I don't think she cooks anymore. And I was going to take her some food on her birthday, but I decided I couldn't just do that. So I invited her over for dinner, and I invited some of the other neighbors. Craig took his plate into the TV room, but the rest of us had dinner and cake around the table and sang Happy Birthday. The neighbors brought little presents, and I got her something too. She took pictures of us all and was so happy, and it didn't take *that* much trouble. (Field notes, 1999)

This woman spent time and effort that she did not relish spending, and she also risked alienating her husband. Most costly of all was the risk that giving the birthday party would create a greater sense of intimacy and equality of place with her neighbor, who was already interfering in her life.

Although these examples illustrate niceness above and beyond the normal, even those considered the nicest of people have their limits. Those who sacrifice so much as to be viewed as suckers or chumps get demoted from nice status. Because suckers and chumps do not make their niceness scarce and do not dole it out judiciously, they may lose respect in others' eyes. Their gifts are devalued and do not have the intended result. What is worse, these nice guys may finish last if others take advantage of their penchant for niceness. For these reasons, the person being nice has to be an *expert* player in the socioemotional economy, understanding how and when to give and reciprocate for emotional gifts and when to withhold them.

Being nice requires skill, time, effort, and sometimes money, yet there are substantial individual rewards. Among these rewards are the emotions of delight and joy that can accompany caring about and giving to others. Feelings of intersubjective connection to others helps protect against "the ontological precariousness of social arrangements (with its associated terrors)" that are so characteristic of our "deeply social species" (Wentworth & Yardley, 1994, p. 32). Positive self-feelings derive from acting morally or in accord with religious principles (see, e.g., Brennan & London, 2000). "Emotional energy" (Collins, 1990) can result from engaging in ritual behavior such as being nice, and it can carry over into every corner of one's microworld. One may avoid negative reactions and closed margins that would follow if one were considered unpleasant, uncivil, mean, egotistical, or nasty. And others bestow the rewards of esteem, social capital, and social margin when one behaves nicely. Beyond – but of course feeding back to – the individual level, the social importance of niceness and microheroism, especially in times of rapid social change or unrest, cannot be underestimated.

CONCLUSION

In this chapter I have tried to show that emotions have vast significance for the workings of human interaction in Western societies. Focusing on the giving and withholding of emotional gifts permitted me to consider how emotions flow among social actors. Without such a consideration, we will never know how personal relationships, work relationships, groups, and communities cohere or fragment. Nor will we understand how microhierarchy arises, reproduces itself, and sometimes changes. Perhaps some of the concepts I have put forth here – the socioemotional economy, emotional gift margins, micropolitics, and niceness and microheroism – can extend the important early work of Hochschild, Wentworth, Scheff, Collins, and many others. Perhaps these concepts can help to make sense of, or at least draw attention to, the complexity of the issues facing sociological emotions researchers.

At the same time, I have tried to point up the importance of taking a sociological vantage point for understanding emotions. Human emotionality does not – cannot – occur in individuals detached from social history, culture, structural arrangements, microhierarchy, language, self-concepts, and all that makes up collective life. Instead, emotionality occurs among deeply interdependent, deeply social creatures who not only inhabit but in each moment create and re-create their own symbolic and hierarchically arranged microworlds.

References

Berger, P. L., & Luckmann, T. (1967). *The social construction of reality*. New York: Doubleday.

Bourdieu, P. (1986). The forms of capital. In John G. Richardson (Ed.), *Handbook of theory and research for the sociology of education* (pp. 241–58). New York: Greenwood Press.

Brennan, K. M., and London, A. S. (2001). Are religious people nice people? Religiosity, race, interview dynamics, and perceived cooperativeness. *Sociological Inquiry*, 71(2), 129–144.

Cahill, S. E. (1987). Children and civility: Ceremonial deviance and the acquisition of ritual competence. *Social Psychology Quarterly*, 50, 312–321.

Clark, C. (1990). Emotions and micropolitics in everyday life: Some patterns and paradoxes of 'place.' In Theodore D. Kemper (Ed.), *Research agendas in the sociology of emotion* (pp. 305–333). Stony Brook: SUNY Press, 1990.

Clark, C. (1997). *Misery and company: Sympathy in everyday life*. Chicago: University of Chicago Press.

Coleman, J. S. (1988). Social capital in the creation of human capital. *American Journal of Sociology*, 94, S95–S120.

Collins, R. (1987). Interaction ritual chains, power, and property: The micro-macro connection as an empirically-based theoretical problem. In Jeffrey C. Alexander et al. (Eds.), *The micro-macro problem*. Berkeley: University of California Press.

Collins, R. (1990). Stratification, emotional energy, and the transient emotions. In Theodor H. Kemper (Ed.), *Research agendas in the sociology of emotions* (pp. 27–57). Stony Brook: SUNY Press, 1990.

Cooley, C. H. (1983 [1902]). *Human nature and the social order*. New Brunswick, NJ: Transaction.

Davis, A.; Gardner, B. B.; and Gardner, M. R. (1941). *Deep South: A social anthropological analysis of caste and class*. Chicago: University of Chicago Press.

Dodd, D. J. (1987). Feelings as capital: The existential world of black Americans. Paper presented at the annual meetings of the Southern Sociological Society, Atlanta, GA.

Dressel, P. (1989). Exchange rules and the sociology of emotions. Paper presented at the annual meetings of the Southern Sociological Society, Norfolk, VA.

Elias, N. (1978 [1939]). *The Civilizing Process*. Vol. 1: *The history of manners*. Trans. Edmund Jephcott. New York: Pantheon.

Giddens, A. (1991). *Modernity and self-identity: Self and society in the late modern age*. Cambridge: Polity.

Goffman, E. (1951). Symbols of class status. *British Journal of Sociology, 2*, 294–304.

Goffman, E. (1967). *Interaction ritual: Essays on face-to-face behavior*. Garden City, NY: Doubleday.

Gouldner, A. (1973). *For sociology*. New York: Basic Books.

Harris, R. (1997). Status inequality and close relationships: An integrative typology of bond-saving strategies. *Symbolic Interaction, 20*, 1–20.

Hochschild, A. R. (1983). *The managed heart: The commercialization of human feeling*. Berkeley: University of California Press.

Hochschild, A. R. (1989). *The second shift: Working parents and the revolution at home*. New York: Viking Penguin.

Hume, D. (1978 [1740]). *A treatise of human nature*. Oxford: Oxford University Press.

Kemper, T. D. (1978). *A social interactional theory of emotions*. New York: Wiley.

Kravanja, M. E. (1991). Temporary isles: Cognition in pick-up games. Unpublished paper, Rutgers University.

Lévi-Strauss, C. (1969). *The elementary structures of kinship*. Trans. by James Harle Bell, John Richard von Sturmer, and Rodney Needham. Ed. Rodney Needham.

Lévi-Strauss, C. (1974). Reciprocity, the essence of social life. In Rose L. Coser (Ed.), *The family: Its structures and functions* (pp. 3–12). New York: St. Martin's.

Mauss, M. (1954 [1925]). *The gift: Forms and functions of exchange in archaic societies*. Trans. Ian Cunnison. Glencoe, IL: Free Press.

Mead, G. H. (1962 [1934]). *Mind, self, and society: From the standpoint of a social behaviorist*. Ed. by Charles W. Morris. Chicago: University of Chicago Press.

Pitt-Rivers, J. (1966). Honour and social status. In John G. Peristiany (Ed.), *Honour and shame* (pp. 19–78). Chicago: University of Chicago Press.

Price, R. (2001). Conversations from the new New York. *New York Times Magazine*, Internet ed., November 11.

Sally, D. (2000). A general theory of sympathy, mind-reading, and social interactions, with an application to the prisoners' dilemma. *Social Science Information, 39(4)*, 567–634.

Scheff, T. J. (1990). *Microsociology: Discourse, emotions, and social structure*. Chicago: University of Chicago Press.

Scheff, T. J., & Retzinger, S. M. (1991). *Emotions and violence: Shame and rage in destructive conflicts*. Lexington, MA: Lexington Books.

Schwartz, B. (1967). The social psychology of the gift. *American Journal of Sociology, 73*, 1–11.

Simmel, G. (1978). *The philosophy of money*. Boston: Routledge and Kegan Paul.

Stauth, G., and Turner, B. S. (1988). *Nietzsche's dance: Resentment, reciprocity, and resistance in social life*. Oxford and New York: Blackwell.

Wentworth, W. M., & Ryan, J. (1992). Balancing body, mind, and culture: The place of emotion in social life. In David D. Franks and Victor Gecas (Eds.), *Social perspectives on emotions* (Vol. 1, pp. 25–44). Greenwich, CT, and London: JAI Press.

Wentworth, W. M., & Yardley, D. (1994). Deep sociality: A bioevolutionary perspective on the sociology of human emotions. In William M. Wentworth and John Ryan (Eds.), *Social perspectives on emotions* (Vol. 2, pp. 21–55). Greenwich, CT, and London: JAI Press.

Wiseman, J. P. (1979). *Stations of the lost: The treatment of Skid-Row alcoholics*. 2d ed. Chicago: University of Chicago Press.

Wuthnow, R. (1991). *Acts of compassion: Caring for others and helping ourselves*. Princeton, NJ: Princeton University Press.

Zajonc, R. B. (1998). Emotions. In D. T. Gilbert, S. T. Fiske, and Gardner Lindsey (Eds.), *The handbook of social psychology* (4th ed., pp. 591–632). Boston: McGraw-Hill.

24

Introducing Moral Emotions into Models
of Rational Choice

Robert H. Frank

ABSTRACT

Traditional rational choice theorists view the moral emotions as obstacles to the pursuit of narrow self-interest. This paper challenges this view. Drawing on evidence that moral emotions facilitate mutual cooperation in social dilemmas, it suggests they are not only consistent with, but perhaps even necessary for, the pursuit of self-interest.

Traditional rational choice models ignore the emotions. When rational choice theorists do speak of them, usually it is to characterize them as obstacles to the pursuit of self-interest (see, e.g., Hirschman, 1997). Modern neuroscientists offer a different view. Damasio and others, for example, have observed that, although patients with lesions in the emotional centers of the brain are typically able to make complex rational calculations, they often cannot focus on the most pressing tasks at hand (Damasio, 1995). In Damasio's account, the emotions promote self-interest by making people more likely to apply their cognitive capacities where they will do the most good. In this sense, his account is in harmony with functional accounts of human behavior that originate in rational choice theory. Each assumes that behavior is molded by the imperatives of narrow self-interest.

But there are also other ways in which the emotions – in particular, the moral emotions – lead us to abandon narrow self-interest. We leave tips at out-of-town restaurants we will never visit again. We donate bone marrow in an effort to save the lives of perfect strangers. We find wallets and return them with the cash intact. We vote in presidential elections. These observations pose a clear challenge to the narrow self-brand of rational choice theory.

In my 1988 book, *Passions Within Reason*, I suggested that the moral emotions are in fact consistent with, and perhaps even necessary for, the effective pursuit of material self-interest. It is true, just as rational choice theory claims, that defection is a dominant strategy in one-shot prisoner's dilemmas. Yet individuals can escape that logic if those who are predisposed to cooperate can identify similar others and interact selectively with them – since, after all, mutual cooperation yields higher material payoffs than mutual defection. I cited evidence that people driven by moral emotions such as sympathy and guilt are indeed more likely than narrowly selfish rational actors to achieve mutual cooperation in one-shot prisoner's dilemmas.

In that earlier work, I characterized the problem confronting participants in social dilemmas as one of having to identify person-specific signals that mark some individuals as trustworthy trading partners. Recent work in social psychology, however, suggests that this characterization misses something fundamental. In this chapter, I argue that the problem of achieving mutual cooperation is much better viewed as a dynamic process in which potential trading partners forge conditions that make them more likely to elicit cooperative tendencies in one another.

THE EVOLUTION OF BEHAVIORAL TENDENCIES

Social scientists who recognize the limitations of the self-interest assumption often respond by simply assuming a broader range of human objectives. Tips in out-of-town restaurants? We leave them because we care not only about our personal wealth, but also about holding up our end of the implicit understanding with the server. Voting in presidential elections? We do it because we care about fulfilling our civic duty. And so on.

The problem here is that if social scientists are totally unconstrained in terms of the number of goals they can attribute to people, virtually any behavior can be "explained" after the fact simply by positing a taste for it. And as students of the scientific method are quick to emphasize, a theory that can explain everything ends up explaining nothing at all. To be scientifically valuable, a theory must make predictions that are at least in principle capable of being falsified.

And hence the dilemma confronting proponents of rational choice theory: versions that assume narrow self-interest are clearly not descriptive, whereas those to which goals can be added without constraint lack real explanatory power. Yes, people seem to get a warm glow from giving to charity. But why does doing that give them a warm glow? Why do they not get a warm glow from *not* giving to charity, since they will end up with more money for their own purposes that way, and since the absence of any individual's gift will make no perceptible difference?

Evolutionary psychology offers a principled way of resolving this dilemma. Instead of making essentially arbitrary assumptions about people's goals, it views our goals not as ends in themselves but rather as means in our struggle to acquire the resources needed to survive and reproduce. I begin with a simple example that illustrates how a simple evolutionary game-theory model can be adapted to shed light on the emergence of co-operative tendencies supported by moral emotions. Next, I explain why this model is somewhat misleading to the extent that it encourages us to view behavior as the result of individual personal characteristics. I will then summarize the results of studies that support an alternative charac-terization of cooperative behavior – namely, that it results from a history of interaction that helps to create and strengthen bonds of sympathy between potential partners.

AN EVOLUTIONARY MODEL OF SUSTAINABLE COOPERATION

Evolutionary psychologists explain the modern human taste for sweets by noting that because the sugars in ripened fruit were easier for our primate ancestors to digest, individuals with a taste for these sugars would be more likely to have acquired the nutrients required for survival and reproduc-tion. A similar approach can be used to analyze how other tastes might have emerged, in particular, a taste for cooperation. Consider, for exam-ple, a population consisting of two types of individuals, "cooperators" and "defectors." The two types interact in pairs, and there are three types of pairs: those consisting of two cooperaters (C-C), those consisting of two defectors (D-D), and those consisting of one of each (C-D). The correspond-ing payoffs are as follows: C-C, 4 units each; D-D, 2 units each; and C-D, 6 units for D, 0 for C. These payoffs confront the partners with a monetary version of the standard prisoner's dilemma. What will happen when these two types are thrown into a survival struggle against one another? The an-swer depends critically on how easily the two types may be distinguished from one another. I will consider three possibilities in turn.

Cooperators and Defectors Look Alike

Suppose, for argument's sake, that cooperators and defectors look exactly alike, thus making it impossible to distinguish between them. In this hypo-thetical ecology, individuals will then pair at random. Naturally, coopera-tors (and defectors, for that matter) would prefer to pair with cooperators, but because everyone looks the same, they must take their chances. The expected payoffs to both defectors and cooperators therefore depend on the likelihood of pairing with a cooperator, which in turn depends on the proportion of cooperators in the population.

If c denotes that proportion, a cooperator's probability of interacting with another cooperator is c, and his probability of interacting with a de-fector is $1-c$. The expected payoff for cooperators is thus given by

$$P_C = c(4) + (1 - c)(0) = 4c. \tag{1}$$

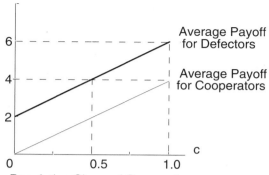

FIGURE 24.1. Average Payoffs When Cooperators and Defectors Look Alike

The corresponding expression for the average payoff for defectors is given by

$$P_D = 6c + (1 - c) = 2 + 4c. \qquad (2)$$

The average payoff relationships for the monetary values assumed in this illustration are shown in Figure 24.1.

When cooperators and defectors look exactly the same, how will the population evolve over time? The rule in Darwinian models is that each individual reproduces in proportion to its average payoff, since those with larger material payoffs have the resources necessary to raise larger numbers of offspring.[1] If the average payoff curves for the two types intersected, the result would be a stable population share for each type. In the current case, however, the average payoff curves do not intersect. Since defectors always receive a higher expected payoff here, their share of the population will grow over time. Cooperators, even if they make up almost the entire population to begin with, are thus destined for extinction. When cooperators and defectors look alike, genuine cooperation cannot emerge.

This case constitutes the crude Darwinian metaphor that underlies the widespread assumption among modern social scientists that human motivation is essentially egoistic. By this I do not mean that modern social

---

[1] In very recent times, of course, there has been a *negative* relationship between income and family size. But if preferences were forged by natural selection, the relationship that matters is the one that existed during most of evolutionary history. And that relationship was undisputedly positive: periods of famine were frequent and individuals with greater material resources saw many more of their children reach adulthood. Moreover, most early societies were polygynous – their most wealthy members usually claimed several wives, leaving many of the poor with none.

scientists think that egoism necessarily leads to good outcomes. Note in Figure 24.1, for example, that in a population consisting only of cooperators ($c = 1.0$), everyone's payoff would be 4 units, or twice as much as everyone gets in the equilibrium consisting only of defectors. But the mere fact that cooperation is socially valuable does not ensure that it will evolve. As Darwin clearly recognized, traits that are harmful to groups can evolve if they promote the survival and reproduction of individual group members.

Cooperators and Defectors Are Easily Distinguished

Now suppose everything is as before except that cooperators and defectors are perfectly distinguishable from each other. For concreteness, suppose that sympathy is the emotion that motivates cooperation, and that there is an observable symptom of it (perhaps a "sympathetic manner"). Defectors lack this observable symptom; or, more generally, they may try to mimic it but fail to get it exactly right.

If this symptom is observable at a glance, the tables are completely turned. Cooperators can now interact selectively with one another and be assured of a payoff of 4 units. No cooperator need ever interact with a defector. Defectors are left to interact with one another, for which they get a payoff of only 2 units. Since all element of chance has been removed from the interaction process, payoffs no longer depend on the proportion of cooperators in the population (see Figure 24.2). Cooperators always get 4, defectors always get 2. This time the cooperators' larger payoffs enable *them* to raise larger families, which means they will make up an ever-growing share of the population. When cooperators can be easily identified, it is the defectors who face extinction.

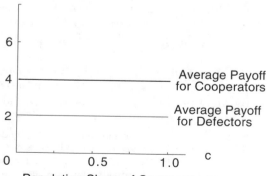

FIGURE 24.2. Average Payoffs When Cooperators and Defectors are Perfectly Distinguishable

Mimicry without Cost or Delay

The defectors need not surrender without a fight, however. Suppose a mutant strain of defectors emerges, one that behaves exactly like other defectors but in which each individual has precisely the same symptoms of trustworthiness as cooperators. Because this particular strain of defectors looks exactly the same as cooperators, it is impossible for cooperators to discriminate against them. Each imposter is therefore just as likely to interact with a cooperator as a genuine cooperator is. This, in turn, means that the mutant defectors will have a higher expected payoff than the cooperators.

The nonmutant defectors – those who continue to look different from cooperators – will have a lower payoff than both of these groups and, as before, are destined for extinction. But unless the cooperators adapt in some way, they too face the same fate. When defectors can perfectly mimic the distinguishing feature of cooperators with neither cost nor delay, the feature loses all power to distinguish. Cooperators and the surviving defectors again look exactly alike, which again spells doom for the cooperators.

Imperfect Mimicry and the Costs of Vigilance

Defectors have no monopoly on the power to adapt. If random mutations alter the cooperators' distinguishing characteristic, the defectors will be faced with a moving target. Imagine that symptoms by which cooperators originally managed to distinguish themselves can be only imperfectly mimicked by defectors. If the two types could be distinguished at a glance, defectors would again be doomed. But suppose it requires effort to differentiate between a cooperator and a defector. For concreteness, suppose inspection costs one unit. Paying this cost is like buying a pair of invisible glasses that enable cooperators and defectors to be distinguished at a glance. For those who do not pay, the two types remain perfectly indistinguishable.

To see what happens this time, suppose the payoffs for the three types of pairings are as before, and consider the decision facing a cooperator who is trying to decide whether to pay the cost of vigilance. If he and other cooperators pay it, he can be assured of interacting with another cooperator, and will thus get a payoff of $4 - 1 = 3$ units. If he does not, his payoff is uncertain. Cooperators and defectors will look exactly alike to him and he must take his chances. If he happens to interact with another cooperator, he will get 4 units. But if he interacts with a defector, he will get zero. Whether it makes sense to pay the 1-unit cost of vigilance thus depends on the likelihood of these two outcomes.

Suppose the population share of cooperators is 90 percent. By not paying the cost of vigilance, a cooperator will interact with another cooperator 90 percent of the time, with a defector only 10 percent. His payoff will thus have an average value of $(0.9)(4) + (0.1)(0) = 3.6$. Since this is higher than the 3-unit net payoff he would get if he paid the cost of vigilance, it is clearly better not to pay it. Now suppose the population share of cooperators is not 90 percent but 50 percent. If our cooperator does not pay the cost of vigilance, he will now have only a fifty-fifty chance of interacting with a defector. His average payoff will thus be only 2 units, or 1 unit less than if he had paid the cost. On these odds, it would clearly be better to pay it.

The numbers in this example imply a "break-even point" obtained by solving the following equation for c:

$$4c = 3, \tag{3}$$

which yields $c = 0.75$. Thus, when the population share of cooperators is 75 percent, a cooperator's expected payoff if he does not pay the cost of vigilance ($4c$) is exactly equal to his certain payoff if he does (3). A cooperator who does not pay the cost has a 75 percent chance at a payoff of 4 units, and a 25 percent chance of getting zero, which means an average payoff of 3 units, the same as if he had paid the cost. When the population share of cooperators is below 75 percent, it will always be better for him to pay the cost of vigilance. When the population share of cooperators is above 75 percent, it will never be better for him to pay the cost of vigilance.

With the break-even rule in mind, we can now say something about how the population will evolve over time. When the population share of cooperators is below 75 percent, cooperators will all pay the cost of vigilance and get a payoff of 3 units by cooperating with one another. It will not be in the interests of defectors to bear this cost, because the vigilant cooperators would not interact with them anyway. The defectors are left to interact with one another, and get a payoff of only 2 units. Thus, if we start with a population share of cooperators less than 75 percent, the cooperators will get a higher average payoff, which means that their share of the population will grow.

In populations that consist of more than 75 percent cooperators, the tables are turned. Now it no longer makes sense to pay the cost of vigilance. Cooperators and defectors will thus interact at random, which means that defectors will have a higher average payoff. This difference in payoffs, in turn, will cause the population share of cooperators to shrink.

For the values assumed in this example, the average payoff schedules for the two groups are plotted in Figure 24.3. As noted, the cooperators' schedule lies above the defectors' for shares smaller than 75 percent, but below it for larger shares. The sharp discontinuity in the defectors' schedule reflects the fact that, to the left of 75 percent, all cooperators are vigilant, while to the right of 75 percent, none of them is. Once the population share of cooperators passes 75 percent, defectors suddenly gain access to their

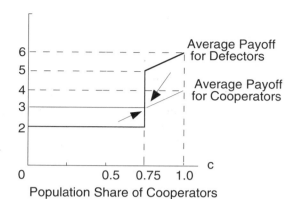

FIGURE 24.3. Average Payoffs with Costs of Scrutiny

victims. The evolutionary rule, once again, is that higher relative payoffs result in a growing population share. This rule makes it clear that the population in this example will stabilize at 75 percent cooperators.

The assumed payoffs and cost of vigilance are merely illustrative. The point of the example is that when there are costs of vigilance, there will be pressures that pull the population toward some stable mix of cooperators and defectors. Once the population settles at this mix, members of both groups have the same average payoff and are therefore equally likely to survive. There is an ecological niche, in other words, for both groups. This result stands in stark contrast to the view that only opportunism can survive in a bitterly competitive material world.

TOWARD A MORE REALISTIC MODEL

Darwinian models like the ones illustrated in these examples are clearly stick-figure caricatures. Although they may capture important features of the reality they attempt to represent, they cannot hope to embody the complex range of human behavior and emotion triggered when individuals have conflicting interests. Yet even such simple models often afford powerful insights.

It is precisely for that reason, however, that we are often prone to interpret them too literally. For though people often do differ in their general tendencies toward aggressive behavior, most of us have the capacity to behave either aggressively or deferentially, according to the specific situational cues that confront us.

A shortcoming of my stick-figure model of the evolution of cooperation is that it encourages us to view people as being either cooperative or not. Under the influence of this model, I once equated the task of solving prisoners' dilemmas to the task of finding a trustworthy trading partner. But social psychologists have long been skeptical about the existence of stable individual differences of this sort. On their view, differences in behavior are often far more likely to be explained by the details of the situation than by stable differences in individual traits (see, e.g., Mischel, 1968). This insight seems clearly applicable to situations that test our willingness to cooperate. Although individual differences in the overall tendency to cooperate surely do exist, most of us are in fact more complex creatures who cannot be easily assigned to a single category from the cooperator/defector pair. All but the most extreme sociopaths have within them the capacity to experience sympathy for others and to weigh others' interests when deciding what to do. And although almost all of us have cooperated in situations in which it would have paid to defect, most of us have also let others down on occasion.

I now believe that the search for a reliable trading partner is not a quest to identify an indiscriminately trustworthy individual, but rather a process of creating conditions that make us more likely to elicit cooperative tendencies in one another. In a remarkably insightful and stimulating paper, David Sally (2000) has summarized a large literature that bears precisely on this process.

The Emergence of Sympathy

Beginning with the writings of David Hume and Adam Smith, Sally traces the intellectual history of the concept of sympathy and reports on some extremely fascinating results on the mechanics of how it develops in human interactions. Many studies, for example, demonstrate how our attitudes are often influenced by seemingly mindless and irrelevant physical motions. Thus, if you are pulling a lever toward you when an experimenter shows you a Chinese ideograph, you are much more likely to give the image a positive evaluation when you are queried about it later. But if you are pushing a lever away from you when you are shown the ideograph, you are much more likely to give it a negative evaluation later (Cacioppo, Priester, & Berntson, 1993). If you put a pen between a person's teeth – forcing him to smile, as it were – and then show him a cartoon, he is much more likely to find it funny than if he does not have a pen between his teeth (Strack, Martin, & Stepper, 1988).

Similar mechanical stimulus-response patterns are also strongly implicated in the processes by which sympathetic bonds form between people. An important factor in these processes is the concept of valence – an evaluation that is either positive or negative. Psychologists have identified a universal human tendency to assign an initial valence in response to virtually every category of stimulus – even words that may seem neutral, or photographs, or visual scenes of any kind (Lewin, 1935; Bargh, 1997).

It is the same, apparently, with persons. When you meet someone, you make an initial up-down categorization very quickly, probably before you are even consciously aware of it (if indeed you ever become consciously aware of it). Likeness seems to play a role in these judgments (Lazarsfeld & Merton, 1954). You are more apt to assign positive valence to someone who is like you in some way – say, in dress, speech patterns, or ethnic background. Reputation matters, as does the character of your initial exchange. Distressingly, attractiveness also seems important. Physically attractive persons are far more likely than others to receive a positive initial evaluation (Eagly et al., 1991; Sally, 1999).

Once the initial valence has been assigned, a biased cognitive filter appears to become activated. You still evaluate further aspects of your experience with a new acquaintance, but with a slant. If the initial evaluation is positive, you are much more likely to treat ambiguous signals in a positive light. But if your initial impression is negative, you are more likely to assign negative interpretations to those same signals. Such positive feedback effects often make first impressions far more important than we might like them to be on ethical grounds.

Given the importance of such cognitive and emotional feedback effects, the development of successful personal relationships hinges powerfully on getting off to a good start. If your first experience in a relationship is positive, you engage further. But if you begin with a negative experience, things are likely to get worse.

Psychologists report that an important component of normal sympathetic responses in relationships is a subconscious impulse to mimic what your conversation partner is doing. If she smiles, you smile. If she yawns, you yawn. If she leans to one side, you lean the same way (Bavelas et al., 1986; Hatfield et al., 1994). Although such mimicry turns out to be critically important, most people are not consciously aware of it. In one study, for example, a group of confederates had separate conversations with two groups of participants – a control group in which the confederates interacted without special inhibition, and a treatment group in which the confederates consciously did not mimic the postures and other movements and expressions of their conversation partners (Chartrand & Bargh, 1999). Participants in the treatment group reported generally negative feelings toward the experimenter's confederates, while those in the control group found the same confederates generally likeable. Apart from the suppression of physical acts of mimicry in the treatment group, no other observable details of the interactions differed between groups. This finding is consistent with the view that people may subconsciously interpret failure to mimic as signifying a deficit of sympathy.

Studies of how the appearance of married couples evolves over time also suggest that physical mimicry is an important aspect of social interaction. In one study, participants were shown individual wedding-year photos of a large sample of men and women, and were then asked to guess which men had married which women. The accuracy of their guesses was no better than chance. But when other participants were given the same matching task on the basis of individual photos taken after twenty-five years of marriage, the accuracy of their guesses was far better than chance (Zajonc et al., 1987). Over the course of a quarter-century of married life, apparently, the furrow of the brow, the cast of the lip, and other subtle details of facial geography seem to converge perceptibly.

The process of bonding with another person influences, and is influenced by, physical proximity and orientation. Being too close invites a negative response, but so does being too far away (where "too close" and "too far" depend partly on cultural norms; Hall, 1982). Gaze is also important (Sally, 2000). Frequency and intensity of eye contact correlates strongly with the duration and intimacy of personal relationships (Patterson, 1973). Among recent acquaintances, both extremely high levels of eye contact and extremely low levels often prove aversive. If experimenters seat participants too close together, they will look at one another less frequently than if they are seated at a more comfortable distance (Argyle & Dean, 1965).

The intensity of the initial interaction – even if purely the result of chance – has important consequences for long-term bonding. For example, combat troops who were under heavy shelling in the same unit corresponded with one another for many more years and much more frequently than combat troops who were not shelled heavily in the same engagement (Elder & Clipp, 1988).

Mere exposure also matters. As Robert Zajonc and his colleagues have shown, the simple fact that we have been repeatedly exposed to an initially neutral stimulus – such as a Chinese ideograph or the shape of a polygon – is enough to make us like it (see Chapter 12 in this volume). Repeated exposure to persons has essentially the same effect. Relative to people we have never seen, we strongly prefer to interact with those whom we have seen repeatedly – in the same elevator or on the same train platform – even though we have never acknowledged one another's presence before (Brockner & Swap, 1976). And, as David Hume wrote, "When we have contracted a habitude and intimacy with any person; tho' in frequenting his company we have not been able to discover any very valuable quality, of which he is possess'd; yet we cannot forbear preferring him to strangers, of whose superior merit we are fully convinc'd" (Hume, 1740, p. 352).

Laughter also seems to be important in the development of relationships. Why do we have such a pronounced capacity to experience mirth in our interactions with one another? While other animal species may have something analogous to this capacity, even our closest relatives among primates do not have it to anything like the same degree. One possibility is that laughter not only promotes the development of social bonds; it may also be an unusually effective test of shared sympathy and understanding. People who find the same things funny often find they have many other attitudes and perceptions in common.

In short, the emergence of sympathetic bonds among people is a very complex physical, cognitive, and emotional dance. People feel each another out, respond to one another, choose to develop closer bonds with some, and abandon further contact with others. This brief account describes only a small sample of the literature surveyed in David Sally's paper. Suffice to say, however, that this literature suggests a far more complex phenomenon than the one I sketched in *Passions Within Reason*. My simple stick-figure model gave the impression that some people feel sympathy toward others and some people do not, suggesting that the challenge is to interact selectively with those in the first group. David Sally's insight is that it would be far more descriptive to say that most people have the capacity to experience sympathy for the interests of others *under the right circumstances*. The challenge is to forge relationships in which mutual sympathy will develop sufficiently to support cooperation.

CAN COOPERATION SUCCEED?

My basic claim is that certain nonegoistic motives or preferences (possibly strongly situationally dependent ones) can help solve prisoner's dilemmas and other commitment problems. For this claim to hold, people must somehow be able to discern the presence of these motives in one another. How can you know whether your potential trading partner feels enough sympathy for your interests to refrain from cheating you?

Since the publication of Charles Darwin's 1872 book, *The Expression of Emotions in Man and Animals*, much has been learned about the observable manifestations of motivational states. Psychologists, for example, have confirmed Darwin's claim that certain facial expressions are characteristic of specific emotions. These expressions, which are the result of complex combinations of facial muscle movements, are extremely difficult to produce on demand, yet appear spontaneously when the corresponding emotion is experienced (see, e.g., Ekman & Rosenberg, 1997, and Ekman, Friesen, & Ancoli, 1980; but, for a dissenting view, see Fernandez-Dols et al., 1997).

Consider, for instance, the schematic expression shown in Figure 24.4. The distinct configuration of the eyebrows – elevated in the center of the brow, sloping downward toward the sides – is produced by a specific combination of the pyramidal muscles (located near the bridge of the nose) and the corrugator muscles (located near the center of the brow), which also produce the mid-brow furrows characteristic of this expression. Only 15 percent of experimental participants are able to produce this expression

FIGURE 24.4. The Expression of Grief, Sadness, or Concern

on demand (Ekmen, 1985, p. 134). In contrast, virtually all participants exhibit it spontaneously when they experience grief, sadness, or concern.

Psychologists have also found that posture and other elements of body language, the pitch and timbre of the voice, the rate of respiration, and even the cadence of speech are systematically linked to underlying motivational states. Because the relevant linkages are beyond conscious control in most people, it is difficult to conceal from others the experience of certain emotions, and equally difficult to feign the characteristic expressions of these emotions on occasions when they are not actually being experienced. For this reason, such clues provide reliable information about the emotions we trigger in others.[2] In addition to facial expressions and other physical symptoms, we rely on reputation and a variety of other clues to predict how potential partners will treat us in specific situations (for a discussion of the role of reputation and other factors, see chapter 4 of my *Passions Within Reason*).

Can we in fact identify people who are emotionally predisposed to co-operate with us? Tom Gilovich, Dennis Regan, and I present evidence from an experimental study that appears to support this possibility (see Frank, Gilovich, & Regan, 1993b). In that study, we found that participants of only brief acquaintance were able to predict defection with better than twice chance accuracy in a one-shot prisoner's dilemma game. In a de-briefing session, participants were asked to fill out a form explaining why

---

[2] The term "preferences" may not fully capture the essence of what we are trying to assess in potential partners. "Character" or "moral sentiments" may come closer.

they predicted cooperation from some partners and defection from others. Their responses were generally consistent with the notion that cooperation may be explained less by individual traits of character (the naïve characterization of my stick-figure model) than by the nature of the interactions between specific partners. For example, participants would offer reasons like "we had a pleasant conversation" when explaining their prediction that a specific partner would cooperate, or like "we really didn't seem to hit it off" when explaining why they thought another partner would defect. And although many participants cooperated with both partners, and still others defected with both, there were also many who cooperated with one partner and defected with the other. Whatever mechanisms may have generated these predictions, the experiment suggests that the accuracy rates needed to support mutually beneficial cooperation can be achieved even on the basis of relatively brief interaction, at least when the stakes are small.

And as the following thought experiment suggests, substantially higher accuracy rates may be possible among people who know one another well:

Imagine yourself just having returned from a crowded sporting event to discover that you have lost an envelope containing $5,000 in cash from your coat pocket. (You had just cashed a check for that amount to pay for a used car you planned to pick up the next morning.) Your name and address were written on the front of the envelope. Can you think of anyone, not related to you by blood or marriage, who you feel certain would return your cash if he or she found it?

Most people answer this question affirmatively. Typically, the persons they name are friends of long duration, choices that seem natural for two reasons. First, the more time one spends with someone else, the more opportunities there are to observe clues to that person's emotional makeup. And second, the more time people spend with a friend, the deeper their emotional bonds are likely to be. Sympathy, affection, and other emotions that motivate trustworthy behavior are likely to be more strongly summoned by interactions with close friends than with perfect strangers.

Notice that although the people named are usually ones with whom we engage in repeated interactions, the particular episode involving the cash is not a repeated game: keeping the cash would not lead to retaliation in the future, because there would be no way of knowing that your friend had found and kept the cash. You are also unlikely to have direct evidence regarding your friend's behavior in similar situations in the past. When pressed, most people respond that they chose the people they did because they felt they knew them well enough to be able to say that they would *want* to return the cash. The prospect of keeping a friend's cash would make them feel so bad that it just wouldn't be worth it. If you chose the people you named for roughly similar reasons, then you accept the central premise of the signaling argument, which is that we can solve prisoner's dilemmas by identifying others who will be sufficiently likely to engage with us in mutual cooperation.

DOES STUDYING ECONOMICS INHIBIT COOPERATION?

The self-interest model of rational choice predicts that people will defect in one-shot prisoner's dilemmas. Does working with that model, as professional economists do over the course of many years, alter one's expectations about what others will do in social dilemmas and, in turn, one's own behavior in these situations? Tom Gilovich, Dennis Regan, and I (1993a) offer evidence that it does.[3] We found, for example, that economics training – both its duration and its content – affects the likelihood that students will defect in prisoner's dilemma games. In one version of our experiments, economics majors were almost twice as likely to defect than noneconomics majors. This difference could stem in part from the fact that people who elect to study economics are different from others in the first place. But we also found at least weak evidence for the existence of a training effect. The differences in cooperation rates between economics majors and non-majors increased with the length of time that students had been enrolled in the major. We also found that relative to a control group of freshmen astronomy students, students in an introductory microeconomics course were more likely in December than in September to expect opportunistic behavior on the part of others.

DYNAMIC EFFECTS AND CYCLES OF COOPERATION

When behavioral predispositions cannot be observed with certainty, we must decide whether to interact with a given partner on the basis of an estimate of the probability that he or she will cooperate. These estimates will depend on information specific to the individual partner, and also on the perceived base rate of cooperation. We are more likely to interact with a given partner when that base rate is high than when it is low.

Now suppose that someone experiences an epiphany and decides to cooperate more frequently. By so doing, he increases the base rate of cooperation as perceived by those with whom he interacts. This, in turn, raises those people's estimates of the likelihood that a given potential partner will cooperate. Some people whose initial pessimistic estimates kept them on the sidelines will now be moved to join the interacting population, raising the base rate of cooperation still further. When and if a new equilibrium is reached, it will be one in which there is a larger – possibly substantially larger – rate of cooperation.

---

[3] Frank, Gilovich, & Regan, 1993a; Marwell & Ames (1981); and Carter & Irons (1991) report similar findings.

If we start with a population with an initially high equilibrium rate of cooperation, an essentially similar dynamic can be set in motion by a spontaneous act of defection. Such an act lowers others' estimates of the likelihood that a given potential partner will cooperate, making them in turn less likely to cooperate, with ripple effects spreading as before.

Such dynamics might thus generate cyclical variation in the rate of observed pro-social behavior. The model I describe here is insufficiently rich to predict such details as the rate of cyclical variation or the amplitude of the differences between end points. But the model does make clear how any spontaneous change – positive or negative – in the rate of cooperation could tend to be self-reinforcing. In any event, there is at least some independent evidence that pro-social behavior is a cyclical phenomenon. For example, in his 1982 book *Shifting Involvements*, Albert Hirschman described oscillations in pro-social behavior in several countries during the twentieth century, with peaks coming at intervals of approximately twenty years.

STRATEGIC ISSUES

Robert Solomon has stressed the importance of viewing emotions not as purely exogenous events but rather as something over which we often have considerable control (see, e.g., Chapter 2 in this volume). The literature that describes how sympathetic bonds develop among people is strongly supportive of this view. In predictable ways, people react to the things we do and say to them, and we react to the things they say and do. Over time these reactions change both them and us. And because the outcomes of our choices are to a large extent predictable, decisions about the details of interpersonal interaction have a potentially strategic dimension.

Consider the decision to associate with someone. In the absence of unexpected negative feedback, and sometimes even in the presence of it, deciding to spend time with someone is tantamount to a decision to like him and to develop sympathy for his interests. If his values were initially different from yours, a decision to spend time together is likely to diminish those initial differences. Our choice of associates, therefore, is at least in part a strategic choice about the kind of values we want to hold.

The knowledge of how sympathetic bonds emerge between people also has strategic implications for the design of organizations and institutions. Most university administrations are keenly aware, for example, of how sympathy (and antipathy) can affect people's decisions in promotion cases. Accordingly, few universities delegate ultimate decision power in such cases to a faculty member's departmental colleagues. Most rely heavily on ad hoc committees composed of faculty outside the department.

Widespread prohibitions on gift-giving in institutional settings can be understood in a similar way. The fear is not, for example, that by giving a gift to a professor the student will bribe the professor to overrule his or her honest judgment about the true grade he or she feels the student deserves. Rather, it is that the gift may foster a strong sympathetic bond between the two, which in turn may distort even the professor's most determinedly objective assessment of the student's performance.

Knowledge of the processes that forge sympathetic bonds among people also sheds light on the common practice of cronyism among corporate executives and political leaders. When such people ascend to positions of power, their first step is often to hire assistants from the ranks of their long-standing friends and subordinates. This practice invariably exposes them to the criticism that they value loyalty above competence. Yet in order for leaders to achieve the goals they were chosen to implement, they require subordinates who are not only competent but also trustworthy. And because the sympathetic bonds that support trust are strongest when nurtured over a period of many years, the preference for long-term associates is, on its face, neither surprising nor blameworthy. What would be cause for alarm would be the observation that an executive's long-term friends and executives were mostly incompetent hacks, and those are choices for which we have every reason to hold a potential executive accountable.

CONCLUSION

Traditional rational choice theories confront a painful dilemma. Without making specific assumptions about people's goals, they cannot generate testable implications for observable behavior. Most rational choice models thus assume that people pursue narrowly selfish goals. Yet people make anonymous gifts to charity, leave tips at restaurants on interstate highways, vote in presidential elections, and take a variety of other costly actions with little prospect of personal gain. Some analysts respond by introducing tastes for such behavior. But if the list of goals is not circumscribed in any way, virtually any behavior can be rationalized just by positing a taste for it. A man drinks the used crankcase oil from his truck and then writhes in agony and dies? No problem, he obviously really must have liked crankcase oil.

Darwinian analysis offers a principled way of resolving this dilemma, one that is not vulnerable to the crankcase-oil objection. Evolutionary models view our goals, not as ends in themselves, but as means to acquire the material resources. In this framework, we are free to offer a "taste for cooperation" to explain why people cooperate in one-shot prisoner's dilemmas, but only if we first can explain how having such a taste might help a person acquire the resources needed to survive and reproduce.

I have argued that cooperation in one-shot prisoner's dilemmas is sustained by bonds of sympathy among trading partners. The models I employed in my earlier work on this subject encouraged the view that some people have genuinely cooperative tendencies while others do not. I now believe it is far more accurate to say that most people have the capacity to develop bonds of sympathy for specific trading partners under the right set of circumstances. The preference for cooperation is not an unconditional one, but rather one that depends strongly on the history of personal interaction between potential trading partners. But this amendment, in the end, is a detail. Even traditional preferences depend on context in essentially similar ways. We do not desire food at every moment, for example, but only after a suitable delay since the ingestion of our last meal.

Narrow versions of the rational choice approach leave the moral emotions completely out of the picture. Naked self-interest is not an unimportant motive, of course, and these models can help us understand much of the observed human behavioral repertoire. But there is also much that is simply beyond the reach of these models. And there is some evidence that the models themselves may do social harm by encouraging us to expect the worst from others. By giving us a principled framework for broadening our assumptions about human motives, the Darwinian approach points the way to long overdue enrichments of the narrow rational choice approach.

References

Argyle, S. T., & Dean, J. (1965). Eye contact, distance, and affiliation. *Sociometry, 28*, 289–304.

Axelrod, R. (1984). *The evolution of cooperation*. New York: Basic Books.

Bavelas, J. B.; Black, A.; Lemery, C. R.; & Mullett, J. (1986). I *show* how you feel: Motor mimicry as a communicative act. *Journal of Personality and Social Psychology, 50*, 322–329.

Bargh, J. A. (1997). The automaticity of everyday life. *Advances in Social Cognition, 10*, 1–61.

Cacioppo, J. T., Priester, J. R.; & Berntson, G. G. (1993). Rudimentary determinants of attitudes, II: Arm flexion and extension have differential effects on attitudes. *Journal of Personality and Social Psychology, 65*, 5–17.

Carter, J., & Irons, M. (1991). Are economists different, and if so, why? *Journal of Economic Perspectives, 5* (Spring), 171–177.

Chartrand, T. L., & Bargh, J. A. (1999). The unbearable automaticity of being. *American Psychologist, 54*, 462–479.

Damasio, A. (1995). *Descartes' error: Emotion, reason, and the human brain*. New York: Avon.

Darwin, C. (1965 [1872]). *The expression of emotions in man and animals*. Chicago: University of Chicago Press.

Elder, G. H., & Clipp, E. C. (1988). Wartime losses and social bonding: Influence across 40 years in men's lives. *Psychiatry, 51*, 177–198.

Eagly, A. H.; Ashmore, R. D.; Makhijani, M. G.; & Longo, L. C. (1991). What is beautiful is good, but . . . : A meta-analytic review of research on the physical attractiveness stereotype. *Psychological Bulletin, 110*, 109–128.

Ekman, P. (1985). *Telling lies*. New York: W. W. Norton.

Ekman, P.; Friesen, W. V.; & Ancoli, S. (1980). Facial signs of emotional experience. *Journal of Personality and Social Psychology, 39,* 1125–1134.

Ekman, P., & Rosenberg, E. (Eds.). (1997). *What the face reveals: Basic and applied studies of spontaneous expression using the facial action coding system (FACS).* New York: Oxford University Press.

Fernandez-Dols, J. M.; Sanchez, F.; Carrera, P.; & Ruiz-Belda, M. A. (1997). Are spontaneous expressions and emotions linked? An experimental test of coherence. *Journal of Nonverbal Behavior, 23,* 163–177.

Frank, R. H. (1988). *Passions within reason.* New York: W. W. Norton.

Frank, R. H.; Gilovich, T.; & Regan, D. (1993a). Does studying economics inhibit cooperation? *Journal of Economic Perspectives, 7* (Spring), 159–171.

Frank, R. H.; Gilovich, T.; & Regan, D. (1993b). The evolution of one-shot cooperation. *Ethology and Sociobiology, 14* (July), 247–256.

Hall, E. T. (1982). *The hidden dimension.* New York: Anchor Books.

Hatfield, E.; Cacioppo, J. T.; & Rapson, R. (1994). *Emotional contagion.* Cambridge University Press.

Heimer, M. (1969). *The long count.* New York: Athenum.

Hirschman, A. O. (1997). *The passions and the interests.* Princeton, NJ: Princeton University Press.

Hirshleifer, J. (1987). On the emotions as guarantors of threats and promises. In John Dupre (Ed.), *The latest on the best: Essays in evolution and optimality* (pp. 307–326). Cambridge, MA: MIT Press.

Hume, D. (1978 [1740]). *A treatise of human nature.* Oxford: Oxford University Press.

Lazarsfeld, P. F., & Merton, R. K. (1954). Friendship as a social process. In M. Berger (Ed.), *Freedom and control in modern society* (pp. 18–66). Princeton, NJ: Van Nostrand.

Lewin, K. (1935). *A dynamic theory of personality.* New York: McGraw-Hill.

Marwell, G., & Ames, R. (1981). Economists free ride, does anyone else? *Journal of Public Economics, 15,* 295–310.

Mischel, W. (1968). *Personality and assessment.* New York: Wiley.

Patterson, M. L. (1973). Compensation in nonverbal immediacy behaviors: A review. *Sociometry, 36,* 237–252.

Sally, D. (1995). Conversation and cooperation in social dilemmas: A meta-analysis of experiments from 1958 to 1972. *Rationality and Society, 7,* 58–92.

Sally, D. (2000). A general theory of sympathy, mind-reading, and social interaction, with an application to the prisoners' dilemma. *Social Science Information, 39(4),* 567–634.

Smith, A. (1966 [1759]). *The theory of moral sentiments.* New York: Kelley.

Strack, F.; Martin, L. L.; & Stepper, S. (1988). Inhibiting and facilitating conditions of the human smile: A nonobtrusive test of the facial feedback hypothesis. *Journal of Personality and Social Psychology, 54,* 768–776.

Zajonc, R. B.; Adelmann, P. K.; Murphy, S. T.; & Niedenthal, P. M. (1987). Convergence in the physical appearance of spouses. *Motivation and Emotion, 11,* 335–346.

25

Virtue and Emotional Demeanor

Nancy Sherman

The gestures which we sometimes call empty are perhaps in fact the fullest things of all.

(Erving Goffman, 1967)

ABSTRACT

I argue in this chapter that emotional demeanor (especially in facial expression) is often a crucial way we show moral regard for others. I explore the extent to which such expression is subject to control and consider the problem of insincerity in posing facial expressions. For a robust discussion of these issues, I turn to Seneca's *De Beneficiis* (On Doing Kindnesses). Seneca's concerns in this work overlap in significant ways with those of Erving Goffman in his classic account of deference rituals.

INTRODUCTION

When we think about moral character we sometimes focus on faces and bodies. In particular, we think about emotional attitude and how it is conveyed in physical and facial comportment. So we talk about "a look of concern," "a compassionate embrace," "a reassuring smile," "an empathetic tone of voice." What is salient is emotional demeanor, or, to adapt a Kantian phrase, the "emotional aesthetic" of virtue (Kant, 1964, 405).

I emphasize "adapt," for Kant is a controversial figure to appeal to in matters of the emotions. On an orthodox reading, his notion of an

An ancestor of this paper was presented at a conference on moral cultivation at Santa Clara University (March 2001), at Trinity College, Dublin (April 2001), and at the Royal Institute of Philosophy (July 2001). I am grateful to these audiences for helpful discussion, as well as to my emotions seminar students (Spring 2001) at Georgetown. I also would like to thank Elisa Hurley for her help with the final draft of this essay, and to Alisa Carse and Maggie Little for ongoing discussion of these issues.

emotional "aesthetic" of virtue is meant to keep emotion at arm's length from morality, construed more narrowly in terms of willed action.[1] The emotional quality of action, its manner and tone, becomes something of optional trim, "a garment that dresses virtue to advantage," as he puts it, not itself substantive to morality (Kant, 1963a, p. 282).

In contrast, I take the "emotional aesthetic" of virtue (or character) to be substantive to character. I argue for a conception in which emotional expression is crucial to the way in which we exhibit and appraise moral character. The view is roughly Aristotelian. Indeed, a familiar theme in Aristotle's *Nicomachean Ethics* (1992) is that virtuous states of character are expressed in terms of both appropriate action and appropriate emotions. To hit the mean is to get it right with respect to both:

> For instance, both fear and confidence and appetite and anger and pity and in general pleasure and pain may be felt both too much and too little, and in both cases not well; but to feel them at the right times, with reference to the right objects, towards the right people, with the right motive, and in the right way, is what is both the mean and best, and this is characteristic of virtue. Similarly with regard to actions also there is excess, defect, and the mean. Now virtue is concerned with emotions and actions, in which . . . the mean is praised and is a form of success; and being praised and being successful are both characteristics of virtue. (Aristotle, 1992, 1106b18–24; cf.1104b13–14, 110618ff., 1108a30ff.)

So, for example, showing anger or indignation on a particular occasion may be morally requisite for expressing a sense of justice. Moreover, to express the sentiment correctly requires both a moral sensitivity to the particular requirements of the occasion and a capacity to modulate one's emotional experience and expression in a way that meets those requirements. One misses the mark if anger is somehow displaced onto the wrong object, or is inappropriately excessive or timid, or is motivated by a hot temper rather than an appreciation of the injustice at hand. So, for example, one's moral response is inappropriate if, in expressing outrage to a friend who has been unjustly victimized, one explodes in a way that exacerbates the friend's fear rather than shows solidarity. To express appropriate emotions, Aristotle holds, is integral to the moral response. It is constitutive of whether or not one acts morally well.

In this broadly Aristotelian spirit, I explore in this chapter the general relation of emotional expression (and in particular, the facial expression of emotion) to character. I proceed as follows. In section 2, I argue against the view that emotions are primarily modes of passivity by appealing to research on affect regulation and emotional development. In section 3, I consider psychological and sociological literature on the facial expression of emotion and the role of such expression in showing due regard toward

---

[1] See my *Making a Necessity of Virtue* (1997) for a less orthodox reading.

others. To illustrate the claim further, I turn in section 4 to an oft-neglected ancient text, Seneca's *De Beneficiis* (On Doing Kindnesses). A key theme in this work is the role of emotional demeanor in small, everyday kindnesses. The text is of special interest, insofar as Seneca, as a Roman Stoic, is not an author whom we would expect, *ex ante*, to be promoting the place of emotional expression in morality. That he does so may suggest something of the indispensability of emotions in moral responsiveness. In section 5, I conclude with an overview of my claims in the chapter.

EMOTION, REGULATION, AND MORAL ASSESSMENT

A broad implication of the Aristotelian view is that we have some control over our emotional lives, both in terms of our emotional experiences and our expression of those experiences. For if to call something "praiseworthy" implies not simply "what is recommended and exemplary" (or "what reflects well on us") but, more strongly, "what we can be held accountable for," then emotions and their expressions are states over which we can exercise some degree of control. Moral responsibility or accountability implies control.

The matter is complex, and a full philosophical treatment would cut across a wide swath of literature on moral responsibility for actions, character, and emotions.[2] Rather than delve into that literature here, I want to offer more empirically based remarks that argue for a degree of agency and control in emotional experience. I begin with research on affect regulation and emotional development in the early stages of infancy. For even then we are not merely passive with regard to affect. So, for example, Alan Sroufe (1995) has argued that the differentiation of emotions, emerging in the second half-year, involves active attention and cognitive efforts as well as deliberate attempts on the part of the infant to manipulate her environment to bring about certain emotional effects. Even before this, the three-month-old will smile most vigorously at mobiles she can put into motion or in response to smiles she can herself elicit from a caregiver. In the reciprocal exchange of smiles, the young child is learning how to enhance and sustain her experience of pleasure. From seven to nine months, the infant continues to modulate the sources of her affects through intentional bids to parents (through vocalization, touching, and cajoling) to share in emotionally positive experiences (Sroufe, 1995, p. 74). By eight months a child can anticipate the joy she will find in a peek-a-boo game and make efforts to bring about that joy by grabbing the diaper that is hiding her mother's eyes (Sroufe, 1995, p. 153). During the next phase (9–12 months),

---

[2] For a good overview of the literature on responsibility, see Fischer, 1986, and Fischer & Ravizza, 1993. The material covered in the next six paragraphs overlaps with work in Sherman, 1999. For a related discussion, see Sherman, 2000.

when strong attachment emotions are in evidence, the infant begins to regulate her separation anxiety and find ways to self-soothe in the absence of more mature structures for internalizing an absent parent. Also, by the first year, the child has the skill to regulate emotion by gaze aversion and other controls involving intensification and deintensification (miniaturization) of expressive behavior. So while a ten-month-old's crying is all or nothing, by twelve months an infant can fight to hold back tears. Pout and crying faces can appear but then evaporate (Malatesta, Culver, Tesman, & Shepard, 1989, pp. 7–8; Sroufe, 1995, pp. 107, 124–130).

The essential point is that, even in the first year, infants do not experience their emotions (or emotional precursors) in a purely passive way. Through their intentional bids with adults, infants seek to elicit, intensify, and share emotional experiences; through gaze aversion and other controls of their expressive behavior, they seek ways to tolerate and manage emotions that are distressing and frustrating. Even before one year of age, the young child is figuring out how to live the emotional life, how to be more, rather than less, an agent of emotional experience.

A conception of emotional agency emerges just as vividly in the psychoanalytic developmental literature. The pioneer in this field is Margaret Mahler (Mahler, Pine, & Bergman, 1975). On Mahler's account, the early path of emotional development moves through the successive phases of autism (marked by its inward rather than outward focus), to symbiosis (a period of discovering others and forming attachments), and separation-individuation (the beginnings of a toddler's independence). The phases chart the "hatching out process," or ultimate "psychological birth" of the human infant at roughly three years after biological birth. For our purposes, what is key is the cracking of the "autistic shell" during the symbiotic and subsequent separation-individuation phase.

Much has been written on the symbiotic phase (roughly 2–9 months), with its focus, as Sroufe notes, on the positive, reciprocal engagements of caregiver and infant. This is the period of intense visual dialoguing between mother and infant, of sustained facial gazing, of "mirroring" sequences in which the mother's gleam in her eyes evokes bright and shiny eyes in the child. It is the period in which attachment and merger experiences are created, often, though not exclusively, through the eyes (Schore, 1999, pp. 71–82). But in addition to the development of empathetic synchronies crucial for the formation of attachment ties, the dialoguing of the symbiotic period marks the beginning of an education of the emotions. Infant observers point to the psychobiologically attuned mother who does not simply mirror back the child's affective rhythms and intensities, but helps modulate them, dispensing stimulation in a way that both keeps the infant from potentially disorganizing states, and amplifies and elaborates capacities for tolerating prolonged positive stimulation (Schore, 1999, pp. 85–91; Stern, 1974, pp. 187–213). These are periods of fine-tuning the synchrony, of regulating from the outside the child's capacity for experiencing the precursors of emotions in ways that are not purely passive. The parent's role, according to these theorists, is to permit the child to endure the early manifestations of the positive emotions of interest, excitement, and joy in a way that at once stretches the boundaries of tolerance without overwhelming the child (Malatesta, Culver et al., 1989, pp. 7–8; Schore, 1999, p. 89). But, significantly, and this is the point I wish to emphasize, the child also plays a role, even in this predominantly externally driven regulation. For it is the child's cues of gaze attention and aversion that typically direct the well-synchronized parent's input:

A mother's most effective technique in maintaining an interaction seems to be a sensitivity to her infant's capacity for attention and need for withdrawal – partial or complete – after a period of attending to her. Although there appears to be continuous attention to the mother on the part of the infant, stop-frame analysis uncovers the cyclical nature of the infant's looking and not looking. By looking away, infants maintain some control over the amount of stimulation they take in during such intense periods of interaction. (Brazelton & Cramer, 1990; as quoted in Schore, 1999, p. 85)

With the onset of physical mobility and a developed musculature, the child at about ten months of age advances, according to the Mahlerian schema, from the symbiotic phase to the separation-individuation phase, with its central practicing and rapprochement subphases. The practicing subphase (10–18 months) is just that – a period of practicing separation and the emotional self-control required as the child becomes psychologically and physically separate from parents. The rapprochement subphase (18–24 months) is marked by the ambivalent return to parents after discovering that independence poses challenges in terms of separations and losses, conflicts and struggles. The world is, as Mahler et al. put it, no longer the child's oyster (Mahler et al., 1975, p. 78). The thrill of independence is marked by the toddler's realization that one's efforts sometimes fail, that there are big people out there who can often do things more skillfully than the small child can. Whatever the disagreements about the precise timing of separation and individuation, we can focus, as before, on the continued emergence of emotional self-regulation and agency during this general period. Put generally, the problem of this period is how to regulate emotion in the face of autonomous forays into the environment. The child partly solves the problem, as before, through deliberate, intentional bids to parents for assistance in emotional regulation. Mahler et al. refer to the phenomenon as "refueling," regular "checking back" to the parent for emotional reassurance and confidence (Mahler et al., 1975, p. 77). Here, by reading distal facial cues from the parent and self-regulating in line with those cues, the child learns to make sense of emotional challenges in her environment and to moderate her own responses to them.

Much more can be said by way of empirical evidence for emerging, developmental structures that regulate affect. But we need to clarify a conceptual issue at this point. Even if the developmental data point to structures that regulate affect, some of these structures will involve unconscious and involuntary mediation through cognitive and psychobiological processes, while others will mark more intentional and explicitly voluntaristic bids. So, for example, does the fact that a child at three or four years can begin to use language to verbalize feelings or imagination to hold an absent parent in mind (Mayes & Cohen, 1992) point to a kind of voluntary control over emotions?

Yes and no. Certainly in the case of the young child who is just learning how to deploy her newly emergent capacities, we have guarded hopes. Education revolves precisely around learning how to use these new skills as a part of impulse control, communication, and self-soothing. But once we reach adulthood, being able to use language and reflection to moderate and shape emotions does seem a reasonable requirement on most of us much of the time. The requirement is routinely imposed upon us in being responsible parents, spouses, and friends. And while we may not always be successful in our attempts at emotional change or growth, especially in the context of intimate relationships, we are typically held responsible for trying.

Still, there is something to the idea introduced at the beginning of this section that emotions can redound to us and be subject to weaker forms of esteem and disesteem than the language of responsibility and "praise" or "blame" suggests. So we might think positively of a woman as "bright" and "sunny," and she, in turn, might identify herself with those emotional attributes, much in the way she thinks of herself as having certain physical attributes or as having a certain ethnicity or religion or ancestral history. It is part of who she is, part of her loose sense of identity, something about which she might herself feel pride. But all the same, it is not something directly or indirectly her doing.

Do emotions and their expression "belong" to us in this sort of way? Are they states with which we identify (and others identify us with), yet which are largely accidental, outside the sphere of moral accountability?

The idea is attractive and certainly captures the vulnerability (and passivity) to which emotions can subject us. They can descend upon us unbidden and overextend their stay; vestiges of early emotional temperaments or encrusted defense structures can unconsciously frame how we process the world; bad luck and tragedy can bring on a welter of emotions that crowds out others that may be morally required. These are all-too-familiar upheavals of emotional life. Still to focus just on these moments is to underrate what we *can* do to cultivate our emotional lives. Indeed, that emotions can be responsive to reason is just as familiar a part of emotional living. So imagine a moment in which we catch ourselves being amused at a sexist joke. Disappointment over our own response might lead to thoughts about why the joke was not so funny, so that next time around we respond quite differently. Or again, we may find ourselves peeved at another's remarks, but then lighten up once we realize that we have wildly overreacted. These are common enough occurrences in emotional life. They are the reflective stuff of psychotherapy, but of ordinary reflection as well. They suggest that any picture of emotions that underplays the degree to which we can effect emotional change is seriously lopsided.

EMOTIONAL DEMEANOR

We have talked about emotions as mental states over which we have some degree of control. But can we control the expression of emotions in terms of the looks we wear on our faces? That faces are crucial modes of emotional communication is not new. Tomkins (1962, 1982), Izard (1971), and Ekman (1982) have done pioneering work on the emotional expressiveness of the face, and numerous developmentalists have shown the crucial role of the smile (Spitz, 1965) and eye gaze (Baron-Cohen, 1999; Butterworth, 1991; Schore, 1994) in both developmentally early and mature forms of emotional responsiveness.

If we hold, loosely with Aristotle, that we are morally appraised for moral action in a way that includes its manner, then the face (and perhaps, too, vocalization and body posture) becomes part of what we assess. They are part of the emotional aesthetic of character, and often part of what we might call a thick conception of moral action. Yet the face is often something over which we have little control. Our eyes can wander and our eyeballs roll, we can grimace or chuckle, blush, crack a smile or furrow our brow – all without too much consciousness. Our eyes can show fear toward our captors in a way we wish they did not.

But while faces sometimes leak inner states, they do not always do so. Indeed, some of us are fairly good at masking or "posing" facial expressions. At such times, we control emotional demeanor. So we may smile as a sign of gratitude even if we do not feel quite so kindly disposed inside, or we may effect involvement through eye gaze even when we feel mildly bored. The sociologist Erving Goffman (1967) details these aspects of demeanor comportment as part of a more complex discussion of the ceremonial rituals involved in deference behavior. Goffman's idea is that through demeanor (including dress and deportment, but also physical and emotional bearing) an individual creates an image of herself which may be part of showing deference or due regard. And dissembling may be part of demeanor display:

It appears that deference behavior on the whole tends to be honorific and politely toned, conveying appreciation of the recipient that is in many ways more complimentary to the recipient than the actor's true sentiments might warrant. The actor typically gives the recipient the benefit of the doubt, and may even conceal low regard by extra punctiliousness. Thus acts of deference often attest to ideal guidelines to which the actual activity between actor and recipient can now and then be referred. (Goffman, 1967, p. 60)

Put differently, "regard is something the individual constantly has for others, and knows enough about to feign on occasion" (Goffman, 1967, p. 58). This is not to deny that candor might, on occasion, render the more appropriate and respectful signal, as when concealment of boredom bars a recipient from important feedback. But even here, the poise and timing of one's emotional display may be crucial to the message and a reasonable part of showing due regard.

That there are occasions when due regard requires dissembling implies that we actually have such capacities for deliberate, facial posing. According to Paul Ekman (1982), there is evidence that we can pose emotional expressions as early as the preschool years. As adults we share, cross-culturally, a repertoire of core facial expressions corresponding to specific, basic emotions (surprise, disgust, sadness, anger, happiness, fear) that we have some facility in posing and reading. Presumably, the better we know others, the more successful we are in reading a wider range of emotional expressions and, too, in discriminating sincere from posed displays.

The expectation of finding interest, regard, joy, sympathy, or indignation in faces has its seeds in infancy. As we have said, our first lessons in social dialogue involve tracking eye gaze and finding joy in the mutual to-and-fro of smiling. Ruptures in attunement can come from the failure of a parent to adequately mirror (in facial behavior as well as other body movements) a child's own engagement or rhythm (Stern, 1985). Facial expressions are a part of establishing mutuality, but are also instrumental to signaling crucial information about the environment. Thus, recall Mahler's toddler who glances back to parents in order to read distal facial cues (what others have called "social referencing"; Klinnert et al., 1983). In such cases, parents may pose an expression, not in order to be honorific, but didactic. In reading and mimicking expressions, the child begins to self-regulate affect (Greenspan, 1989).

In the next section, I leave behind contemporary research on emotional demeanor and turn to an ancient discussion of the topic. The text in question is Seneca's *De Beneficiis*.[3] Here we have a rich though sorely neglected account of how emotional demeanor becomes part of the microeconomy of doing kindnesses.

SENECA ON KINDNESS AND ITS EMOTIONAL EXPRESSION

Seneca's *De Beneficiis* is an essay on just that subject – doing favors, showing gratitude, "sorting out a matter which more than anything else holds society together" (Seneca, *De Beneficiis* [hereafter *Ben.*] 1.4.2). The spirit of the project parallels that of Goffman: in the latter's words, to show in the

---

[3] I quote from J. Cooper and J. Procopé's edition. However, I translate *De Beneficiis* as "On Doing Kindnesses" and not, as they do, "On Favours."

symbolic expressions of regard how a "recipient is told that he is not an island unto himself" (Goffman, 1967, 72).

To read Seneca's *De Beneficiis*, like reading Goffman's work on deference and demeanor, is to be reminded just how social details, including an aesthetic of emotional demeanor, morally matter – that the furrow on a brow, a smile of engagement, a hesitant look, all may be morally significant in specific circumstances. Moreover, for Seneca, they are not mere matters of etiquette, at least in the conventional sense of "add-on's" supplemental to substantive morality. To the contrary, they are part of the casuistry of kindness itself; they fill in, in far more detail than Aristotle at his most descriptive offers, what is involved in morally appropriate emotion as well as action.

One of Seneca's preoccupations in this work is to show that the material details of kindness matter. No one should give "winter clothes at midsummer" or "a present of gladiators or animals for the arena when the show has already been put on" (*Ben.* 1.12.3). One should give presents to others that bring "the greatest pleasure" and "bring us to mind whenever he comes into contact with it" (1.11.5). This last thought gives us a glimpse of a tension that arises between Seneca's views here and his general subscription to Stoic doctrines elsewhere. Most briefly put, Stoic doctrine urges detachment from material goods in so far as such goods are not themselves essential to genuine happiness. They may be "preferred" rather than "dispreferred," but either way they are to be regarded as "indifferents" that lie outside of happiness. Genuine happiness becomes a matter of what we can fully control. On the Stoic view, that points to virtue, and virtue alone, informed by reason. It would take us too far afield to try to resolve this tension here, or the related tension introduced, as we shall see in a moment, by Seneca's unabashed and seemingly un-Stoic embrace of the emotions as part of the full expression of virtue. As I argue elsewhere (Sherman, forthcoming), the latter tension can be mitigated somewhat within a Stoic account of the emotions. But that excursus is beyond the scope of the present discussion.

Just as the material details of kindness matter according to this treatise, so too do the nuances of emotional attitude and expression. In the best sorts of acts of kindness, emotions are expressive of deeper positive attitudes. But even when the appropriate internal attitudes are absent, making an effort to "show" the right emotional signs is still part of the requirement of virtue. Success at that effort is far better, Seneca suggests, than letting one's emotions betray one's reluctance or ambivalence. Thus, appearances and presentations matter, including the emotions we wear on our face and convey through our body language and voice. The garments that dress virtue, or in some cases hide its absence, have moral weight.

The evidence is striking and plentiful. So, Seneca insists, we should not give a gift in a way that is "humiliating (*contumliose*)." For we are so

constituted that insults "go deeper than any services" and are more "tena-
ciously remembered" than kindnesses (*Ben.* 1.1.8). Similarly, "no one can
feel gratitude for a favor haughtily tossed down or angrily thrust on him"
(1.1.7), or given with groaning or flaunting (1.7.3), or "furrowed brows" or
"grudging words" (1.1.5) or with an "insolent expression" or "language
swollen with pride" (2.11.6), or with "a silence that gives an impression of
grim severity" (2.3.1), or in a way that is simply "irritating" (2.6.2). It is like
giving bread with stones in it (2.7.1). Showing arrogance in gift-giving undermines the deed itself: "There are many who make their kindnesses hateful by rough words and superciliousness. Their language and annoyance
are such as to leave you regretting your request was ever granted" (2.4.1).
Again, he exhorts, "don't remonstrate when giving an act of kindness; save
that for another time. No element of unpleasantness should be mixed with
it" (2.6.2). In short, gifts that are true kindnesses are bestowed "with a look
of human kindness" (2.13.2), be it in the language of words and voice or
facial and bodily expression. Proper emotional bearing is also required on
the part of the recipient in conveying gratitude:

When we have decided to accept, we should do so cheerfully. We should express
our delight and make it obvious to our benefactor so that he gets an immediate
reward. To see a friend joyful is due cause for you, still more to have made him
joyful. We must show how grateful we are by pouring out our feelings and bearing
witness to them not only in his presence but everywhere. (*Ben.* 2.22.1)

Thus, even when words fail, a feeling of indebtedness ought to "show on
our faces" (2.25.2). That we may lack genuine feelings of indebtedness does
not necessarily excuse us from giving the impression that we have them. To
appeal to Ekman and Goffman, facial posing becomes a way of conveying
due regard.

To argue that emotional comportment matters is, in a sense, to argue
that appearances matter, that, as Seneca repeats, "impressions" or "looks"
of kindness are part of the moral economy. And they are even if there is
a tad of hypocrisy in the display. So just as certain actions, according to
the standard Stoic conception, are duties or appropriate (*kathêkonta*) even
when they lack proper motivation, so too certain looks and appearances are
duties even when the corresponding inner state is absent. The requirement
to cultivate appearances is captured well in this passage:

No gratitude is felt for a favour which has long stuck to the hands of whoever
granted it, which he seemed unhappy to let go, giving as though he were robbing
himself. Even if some delay should intervene, we should do everything to avoid
the *appearance* of having had to think whether to do it (*ne deliberasse videamur*).
(*Ben.* 2.1.1; italics added)

In a similar spirit, we are to contrive to make favors appear as if they
have been unsolicited: "To give the impression not of having been asked

(*ne rogati videamur*) [to perform some action]. . . . we should make an immediate undertaking and prove by our very haste that we were on the point
of actions, even before we were approached." (*Ben.* 2.2.1)

But in all this there is something morally worrisome about the idea of
cultivating appearances. Is Seneca saying we should be complacent in our
own insincerity or tolerant when others hide problematic feelings behind
an acceptable veneer? Should we all become practiced in the art of cover-
up and plastic smiles, and not worry too much about a conversion of the
heart? Moreover, is the focus on demeanor a way of short-circuiting a
deeper education of character?

This is not the spirit of his moral counsel. Two points can be made.
First, Seneca is suggesting that specific emotional expressions, however
limited or superficial, are nonetheless crucial ways of respecting others and
showing due engagement or concern. While *properly motivated right* actions
(*katorthômata*; i.e., the actions that characterize the Stoic sage) remain the
aim of a complete moral education; performing morally *appropriate* actions
(*kathêkonta*) must suffice for those of us who fall short.

The second (two-pronged) point is that the cultivation of appearances
can itself be educative. It can lead to a conversion of the heart in the prac-
titioner as well as set an instructive example to onlookers who take their
cues from others' appearances. With respect to the first prong, to try on
appearances can be self-exhortative, a way of coaxing along a corresponding inner change. (Recall Pascal's advice to the skeptic: practice as if you
believe and you will find yourself believing.)[4] We nurse a change from
the outside in, as it were. Current research on facial feedback mechanisms lends some support to this process. Experiments have shown that
those who read the "funnies" with upturned lips find the cartoons funnier
than those whose lips are not in the smiling position (Strack, Martin, &
Stepper, 1988, pp. 768–77). Other studies confirm that overt facial expression can affect the intensity of emotional arousal (Ekman, 1982). Anticipating this general line of research, Kant says (with a sexism that plagues the
Anthropology), when a woman practices smiling, the facial gesture helps to
promote an inner spirit of benevolence. The general point is less offensively
expressed in the following passage, also from the *Anthropology*:

Men are, one and all, actors – the more so the more civilized they are. They put on
a show of affection, respect for others, modesty and disinterest without deceiving
anyone, since it is generally understood that they are not sincere about it. And
it is a very good thing that this happens in the world. For if men keep on playing these roles, the real virtues whose semblance they have merely been affecting
for a long time are gradually aroused and pass into their attitude of will. (Kant,
1963a, 151)

---

[4] On this, see De Sousa's (1988) discussion of innocent examples of boot-strapping that do
not shade into deceptions.

Thus, Kant, as dogmatic as he can be about truth telling, is willing here to dismiss the charge of deceit on the grounds that everyone knows the game. It is a wink, wink, nod, nod, with no one being deceived. Moreover, he argues, as we have found in reading Seneca, there are clear pedagogical advantages for stimulating properly grounded virtue through semblance. Kant reiterates the psychological lesson he stated in the *Lectures:* love born from obligation can itself turn into a more genuine love. With time, one acquires "a taste for it" (Kant, 1963b, 197).

CONCLUSION

I have been arguing for the important role of emotional demeanor in the expression of moral character. The claim has been voiced by a variety of philosophers spanning different historical periods: in the ancient world by Aristotle, in the Hellenistic period by Seneca, in the Enlightenment by Kant. As I have argued, the view represents a position made most familiar and plausible by Aristotle. But Seneca, despite his Stoicism, elaborated on the position by concretely showing the role of emotional bearing in the microeconomy of doing kindnesses. Kant, in a similarly unorthodox move given his Stoic leanings, held that emotional demeanor is part of the aesthetic of virtue. And, he claimed, practice on the surface can effect deeper motivational changes.

In focusing my discussion more on emotional demeanor than on emotional experience, I have tried to circumvent some of the usual worries about directly beginning or stopping the occurrence of emotional states or episodes. Granted, I have suggested with Aristotle that we can gradually cultivate emotional dispositions, but this does not guarantee successful exercise of those dispositions on demand. Circumstances may overwhelm us, impulses may elude control, regression may be the order of the day. In the case of emotional expression, in contrast, we seem to have greater control. The research of Ekman and others suggests that facial posing, in particular, is something we can voluntarily affect early on. I have suggested that we should read Goffman's sociological research as adding an important piece to the puzzle and as indicating the crucial role of emotional expression in our displays of care and regard for others. In showing care, respect, and deference to others, we are sometimes called upon to be actors, giving due to others through facial looks and tones that might lack exact counterparts in our heart. At such moments we act from duty, we might say, just as we do when we perform required or recommended actions without necessarily wanting to. Granted, it may seem morally preferable to have outside behavior in synchrony with what is within. Certainly, Aristotle often urges this as an ideal of good character: true virtue lies beyond the stage of needing to bear down on or silence what is wayward.

But such an ideal is a tall order. And to act under the yoke of duty, as Kant would say, is an ineliminable part of morality for us mortals. Even so, we can go a fair way toward appreciating the role Aristotle assigned to emotions without insisting that we must always *feel* the right ones; at times, emotional demeanor may suffice. Moreover, trying on emotions from the outside in may be an indispensable way not only to respect others but to begin to cultivate an inner change.

References

Aristotle. *Nicomachean ethics*. (1992). Trans. D. Ross. Rev. J. L. Ackrill and J. O. Urmson. Oxford: Oxford University Press.

Baron-Cohen, S. (1999). *Mind blindness*. Cambridge, MA: MIT Press.

Brazelton, T. B., & Cramer, B. G. (1990). *The earliest relationship*. Reading, MA: Addison-Wesley.

Butterworth, G. (1991). The ontogeny and phylogeny of joint visual attention. In A. Whiten (Ed.), *Natural theories of mind* (pp. 223–232). Cambridge, MA: Blackwell.

Cooper, J., & J. R. Procopé (Eds.). (1995). *Seneca: Moral and political essays*. Cambridge: Cambridge University Press.

DeSousa, R. (1988). Emotion and self-deception. In B. McLaughlin and A. O. Rorty (Eds.), *Perspectives on self-deception* (pp. 324–341). Berkeley: University of California Press.

Ekman, P. (Ed.). (1982). *Emotion in the human face*. 2d ed. Cambridge: Cambridge University Press.

Fischer, J. M. (Ed.). (1986). *Moral responsibility*. Ithaca, NY: Cornell University Press.

Fisher, J. M., & Ravizza, M. (Eds.). (1993). *Perspectives on moral responsibility*. Ithaca, NY: Cornell University Press.

Goffman, E. (1967). The nature of deference and demeanor. In *Interaction ritual: Essays on face-to-face behavior*. Garden City, NY: Anchor Books.

Greenspan, S. (1989). *The development of the ego: Implication for personality theory, psychopathology, and the psychotherapeutic process*. Madison, CT: International Universities Press.

Izard, C. (1971). *The face of emotion*. New York: Meredith Corporation.

Kant, Immanuel. (1963a). *Anthropology from a pragmatic point of view*. Trans. Mary Gregor. The Hague: Nijoff.

Kant, Immanuel. (1963b). *Lectures on ethics*. Trans. Louis Infield. Indianapolis, IN: Hackett.

Kant, Immanuel. (1964). *Metaphysic of morals*, Part II: *The doctrine of virtue*. Trans. Mary Gregor. Philadelphia: University of Pennsylvania Press.

Klinnert, M. D.; Campos, J. J.; Sorce, F. I.; Emde, R. N.; & Svejda, M. J. (1983). Social referencing: Emotional expressions as behavior regulators. In R. Plutchik and H. Kellerman (Eds.), *Emotion: Theory, research, and experience*, Vol. 2: *Emotions in early development* (pp. 57–86). Orlando, FL: Academic Press.

Mahler, M.; Pine, F.; & Bergman, A. (1975). *The psychological birth of the human infant*. New York: Basic Books.

Malatesta, C.; Culver, C.; Tesman, J. R.; & Shepard, B. (1989). The development of emotion expression during the first two years of life. *Monographs of the Society for Research in Child Development, 54,* 7–8.

Mayes, L., & Cohen, D. (1992). The development of a capacity for imagination in early childhood. *The Psychoanalytic Study of the Child, 47,* 23–47.

Schore, A. (1994). *Affect regulation and the origins of self.* Hillsdale, NJ: Lawrence Erlbaum Associates.

Sherman, N. (1997). *Making a necessity of virtue: Aristotle and Kant on virtue.* Cambridge: Cambridge University Press.

Sherman, N. (1999). Taking responsibility for our emotions. In E. F. Paul, F. D. Miller, & J. Paul (Eds.), *Responsibility* (pp. 294–321). Cambridge: Cambridge University Press.

Sherman, N. (2000). Emotional agents. In M. Levine (Ed.), *The analytic Freud* (pp. 154–176). New York: Routledge.

Sherman, N. (Forthcoming). *Of Manners and Morals,* Christopher Gill (Ed.). Oxford: Oxford University Press.

Spitz, R. (1965). *The first year of life.* Madison, CT: International Universities Press.

Sroufe, A. (1995). *Emotional development.* New York: Cambridge University Press.

Stern, D. (1974). Mother and infant at play: The dyadic interaction involving facial, vocal, and gaze behavior. In M. Lewis and L. Rosenblum (Eds.), *The effect of the infant on its caregiver* (pp. 187–213). New York: Wiley.

Stern, D. (1985). *The interpersonal world of the infant: A view from psychoanalysis and developmental psychology.* New York: Basic Books.

Strack, F.; Martin, L.; & Stepper, S. (1988). Inhibiting and facilitating conditions of the human smile: A nonobtrusive test of the facial feedback hypothesis. *Journal of Personality and Social Psychology, 45,* 768–777.

Tomkins, S. S. (1962). *Affect, imagery, consciousness.* 2 vols. New York: Springer.

Tomkins, S. S. (1982). Affect theory. In P. Ekman (Ed.), *Emotion in the human face* (2d ed., pp. 353–395). Cambridge: Cambridge University Press.

26

Epilogue

Feelings and Emotions: Where Do We Stand?

Nico H. Frijda, Antony S. R. Manstead, and
Agneta H. Fischer

Our main objective in organizing the symposium of which this book is the outcome was to provide an overview of current theory and findings in the study of emotion. As mentioned in the Introduction, the restrictions of our schedule meant that we could not accommodate all relevant viewpoints and findings. This resulted in our selection of twenty-four contributions, here twenty-four chapters.

Although the range and quality of the contributions are impressive, not all of the potentially relevant disciplines are represented. Missing disciplines include computer science, psychiatry, psychoanalysis, and linguistics. Nevertheless, we believe that this volume provides a good reflection of the current state of the art, partly because of the broad range of the topics addressed, but also because many of the chapters refer to important work by others than their authors, both within and outside their own discipline.

For us, the organizers, the symposium was a great pleasure. It contained much that is highly fascinating in terms of new findings and novel insights, providing us with the joys of enhanced understanding and unsuspected implications. We were impressed by the multitude of levels at which emotions can be studied, described, and analyzed. It filled us with respect for the high quality of the presentations and of the reported research.

In this epilogue, we shall try to summarize what we think is the current state of the art, focusing on what seem to us to have been the major contributions over the last three decades. Obviously, however, there is plenty of room for debate as to which have been major contributions rather than revisits to issues that have been addressed by previous thinkers.

The current state of emotion theory can be summarized in terms of several themes, around which our overview will be organized. However, one important feature cuts across them: the sheer explosion of empirical research over the past three decades. Thirty years ago empirical research on emotion had begun to extend beyond the study of autonomic arousal. At the time of Magda Arnold's 1970 Loyola Symposium, research by Lazarus, by Plutchik, by Schachter and Singer, and by Schlosberg was just beginning to be influential. Since then, research on facial expression, on appraisal, on social and cultural factors in emotion and, somewhat later, on the neuropsychology of emotion has blossomed. Reflecting this, no fewer than three journals (*Motivation and Emotion, Cognition and Emotion*, and *Emotion*) have been launched and a large number of monographs and edited volumes devoted specifically to emotion have appeared.

THE NATURE OF EMOTIONS

What is all that research about? What are emotions? The behavioral and experiential phenomena associated with emotion have suggested quite different conceptions of emotion. That still is so, and this variety of conceptions can be recognized in the different tones of the chapters in this volume.

In one of the major current views, emotions are regarded as rapid responses to emergency situations that have evolved in order to cope with the threats and opportunities afforded by the ancestral environment. They can occur automatically in response to rather specific stimuli that demand little in terms of information processing and conscious awareness (see the chapters by Damasio, Ekman, Öhman & Wiens, Panksepp, Zajonc). This view has gained in specificity and prominence over the last three decades. At the same time, it implicitly continues the traditional view of emotions as distinct from "reason" and as "passions," that is, reactions in which the subject is essentially passive.

However, speed does not characterize all emotions; nor do all emotions have to do with emergencies. Moreover, not all emotions are passive. Capacities for regulation and control of emotions form part and parcel of the emotion system, as well as of the phenomenology of emotional experience and behavior. For these reasons, it is argued, as Solomon and Shweder do in their chapters, that emotions cannot be regarded as a natural class. In any case, in other conceptions emotions are viewed primarily as complexes of meanings, meanings-in-action, and desires, which, jointly with the environment and the individual's history, determine a huge variety of behavioral and cognitive phenomena. Emotions are regarded as including judgments with respect to values or concerns, and their contents are seen as matching one's normative and cultural context. People are held responsible, and hold themselves responsible, thus rendering emotions morally relevant (see the chapters by de Waal, Frank, Oatley, Panksepp, Salovey et al., Scherer, Sherman, Solomon, and Thoits).

These differences in the conceptualization of emotions are due in part to different levels in the description of the emotional phenomena, and to different foci of interest: in behavior and neural processes (notably by Berridge, Cacioppo et al., Winston & Dolan, Öhman & Wiens, and

Panksepp), or in feelings, subjective awareness, and how emotions function in the context of self-awareness and social interaction (notably, by Clark, Frank, Mellers, Mesquita & Markus, Oatley, Scherer, Sherman, Shweder, Solomon, and Thoits). In part, however, these differences are substantive ones, and have to do with what sets emotions apart from other psychological functions and the neural machinery responsible for them.

These different conceptions of emotions are related to divergences in views of the differences between individual emotions. In particular, there are the opposing viewpoints of basic emotions theory and multicomponential theory.

Basic emotions theory posits the existence of a restricted set of evolutionarily shaped emotions. In the present volume this point of view is to be found in the chapters by Ekman, Öhman and Wiens, and Panksepp. Each basic emotion is held to consist of a package or brain system of response components that can be traced back to a more or less unitary central disposition, and is triggered by a specific set of stimuli or contingencies. Basic emotions theory contains a hierarchical analysis of the emotion space, involving a top-down system for ordering emotions. All emotions that can be distinguished consist of variants of one or more of the basic emotions. Basic emotions theory forms a powerful force in focusing research toward the biological and possibly universal mechanisms in emotions.

Multicomponential theory (represented here in the chapters by Mesquita & Markus, Scherer, and Shweder) considers emotions as consisting of sets of response components drawn from a components reservoir and more or less freely combined. What may be innate are mechanisms for the components, such as those for appraisal processes, motivational and physiological response dispositions, and certain action programs. There presumably exist as many different emotions as there are patterns of components. Components are individually activated by the appraisal of events. Individual emotions nevertheless are coherent wholes because of interaction or synchronization between the components (see the chapter by Scherer). Componential analysis, as Shweder argues, favors bottom-up comparison of emotions in cross-cultural and developmental research. It thereby frees emotion study from the restrictions of categorical distinctions, whether those distinctions are between what are and what are not emotions, or between what is emotion X or emotion Y.

Between the fully structured conception of emotion found in basic emotions theory and the fully unstructured one of multicomponential theory, there are intermediate conceptions. Organizing principles are sought in various ways, for instance in appraisal (by Scherer), in the dimensions of pleasure and pain in dimensional theories (aspects of which can be seen in the chapter by Cacioppo et al.), or in motivation or action readiness (by Frijda). These various conceptions may not be incompatible. As Cacioppo et al. suggest, different levels of analysis may require different conceptions of the underlying processes. The overall system may possess a heterarchical structure, in which lower-order processes combine in various ways to shape different higher-order processes. This systems viewpoint constitutes one of the integrating perspectives in current theoretical developments. It suggests different conceptualizations when the focus is upon the functioning of emotions in social interaction and within cultural modeling and normative influences. Those influences, as well as neuropsychological findings, have suggested that emotion regulation and control are an integral part of the emotion system, and are not factors external to it merely resulting in inhibitions (see the chapters by Clark, Dunn, Frank, Salovey et al., Solomon, and Thoits; and previous work by Damasio, among others).

Component patterns, however they are interpreted, only imperfectly characterize human emotional reactions and their meaning for the individual. To get a grip on these meanings, analysis has to include the roles played by the individual's history, the narratives in which the emotions are located, their cultural contexts, and their place in social interchange (see the chapters by Clark, de Waal, Mesquita & Markus, Oatley, Sherman, and Thoits).

THE NATURE OF FEELINGS

Researchers are nearly unanimous in distinguishing emotions from feelings. This reflects the common contemporary view that emotional processes exist independently of awareness and may occur without awareness, and that feelings have a special place in emotional reactions. What that place is, and how feeling relates to the various functionally defined processes (such as cognitive and motor ones), and to neural and neurochemical ones, has emerged as a new domain of empirical and theoretical investigation (see the chapters by Cacioppo et al., Damasio, Panksepp, Scherer, and Winston & Dolan).

Feeling itself has regained respectability. Efforts are being devoted to investigating its nature and content. One of the major recent gains concerns recognition of the need to distinguish among different levels of feeling. There are more diffuse or primitive and more articulate or reflexive levels. Most of the work relevant to this issue was not featured in our symposium (see Lambie & Marcel, 2002), but some of the contributions include reflections suggesting that different neural processes may be involved in different forms of feeling (see the chapters by Damasio, Panksepp, and Winston & Dolan).

In line with the classic theorizing by James, feelings are thought by many investigators to reflect feedback from bodily responses and action. However, other processes are being recognized as equally important in feeling, such as pleasure and pain, desires, intentions or goal settings, or actions-as-planned, as discussed by Berridge, Cacioppo et al., Damasio, Frijda, and

Scherer. At more articulate levels of feeling, cognitive processes of varying degrees of complexity and reflectiveness are major constituents. Feelings are being regarded, notably by Damasio and Scherer, as integrating information from all response components, and as serving to monitor and guide emotional response. This view, as Scherer's chapter shows, poses the problem of discovering the rules of integration, including the integration of event information, body information, and person information into experiences of self (as discussed by Damasio, Panksepp, and Solomon).

COGNITIVE PROCESSES AND AUTOMATICITY

Among the major exploits over the last three decades has been the development of the cognitive approach to emotions. On the occasion of the previous Feelings and Emotions Symposium, this was evident in the landmark contributions by Arnold, by Lazarus and his colleagues, and by Schachter. Since then this approach has developed into the appraisal approach to emotion and emotional disturbances. It profoundly influences our understanding of what constitutes different emotions, or variants of the "same" emotions (see the chapters by Mesquita & Markus, Shweder, and Solomon). It also permits varied accounts of the meanings of different emotions, of the roles of emotions in social interaction, and of the content and consequences of understanding emotions in others. Moreover, it offers the promise of understanding the causal mechanisms involved in the emergence of emotions. Emotion arousal appears to depend quite generally on the context in which stimuli or events appear, rather than on the affectively potent stimuli per se. Emotional value and emotion intensity, for instance, depend on the relation of these stimuli to reference points such as expectations and norms. Examples of these dependencies can be found in the chapter by Mellers and her research on the valence effects of surprise. The cognitive approach has made emotion research relevant to understanding decision-making and economic behavior, and to the ways in which such behavior deviates from rational decision models. It also made it relevant to seeking to understand psychopathology (see the chapter by Öhman & Wiens, which criticizes this understanding).

The cognitive approach to emotion has led to a large amount of research that links self-reports on appraisal, or experimental manipulations of appraisals, to self-reports of different emotions. Such research has been, and continues to be, conducted in various cultural-comparative settings. The cognitive approach has also led to the experimental investigation of the possible causal relationships between emotion-eliciting events and aspects of emotional response such as facial and vocal expressions, changes in action readiness, or emotion self-ascriptions (see the chapters by Ekman, Frijda, and Scherer). One of the problems encountered in such research is the failure to apply anything other than simple linear models to analyze the relationships between these variables (see the chapter by Scherer).

Problems also arise in specifying the cognitive processes that play a role in emotions. Emotions have since ancient times been contrasted with rationality and reason. Evidence for the interaction between emotional and cognitive processes has blurred this distinction. There also are arguments to the effect that emotions enhance reason and rational decision making; Damasio and Frank have both developed such arguments. On the other hand, there remain empirical and theoretical grounds for maintaining a basic distinction between emotion and reason. Emotions and cognitive assessments may be in conflict, as Öhman and Wiens describe in connection with fear, and as Berridge shows in connection with desire. In his chapter Elster argues that emotions and reason are each to be characterized by non-overlapping, and partly incompatible, properties, to be defined in terms of system attributes rather than types of processes.

The cognitive approach has encountered powerful opposition on the grounds that aspects of the emotional response can be aroused automatically. The cognitive approach makes strong claims with respect to causality, holding that appraisals trigger emotions (see Scherer's chapter). One of the major developments during the past three decades has been the emergence of extensive and varied evidence that affective responses (liking and dislike, or processes that influence the liking or dislike of subsequent stimuli) can occur rapidly, ubiquitously, and in the absence of conscious awareness as well as of nonconscious cognitive mediation. Elementary stimuli can directly evoke emotional reactions, also without cognitive mediation or awareness. Fragmentary information, presented below the threshold of awareness, may suffice for certain emotional reactions, or prepare the ground for the response to more complex information. All this is described in the chapters by Berridge, Öhman and Wiens, Panksepp, Winston and Dolan, and Zajonc. Such evidence leads to the view that much in emotional awareness, including self-reports, may be irrelevant to what actually elicited the emotion or consist of after-the-fact justifications. Many emotions, moreover, show "cognitive encapsulation," that is, an insensitivity to relevant information or an insensitivity of emotion processes to variations in attention, as illustrated in the chapters by Öhman and Wiens and Winston and Dolan.

At the same time, in many elementary and automatic reactions, information from context and from the individual's history does play a role. The automaticity research leads to questions about the relative roles of the relevant processes and cognitive variables in the general occurrence of animal and human emotions. Some of the contrast between the approach emphasizing cognitive processes and the approach emphasizing automatic processes is softened by the recognition that emotion processes may occur and even co-occur at different levels of complexity, articulation, and neural functioning. Such diversity of levels is generally recognized by contemporary investigators, and with respect to most relevant subdomains such as those of sensitivity to emotionally relevant information, appraisal, response construction, and regulation (see the chapters by Cacioppo et al., Damasio, de Waal, Ekman, Frijda, Öhman & Wiens, Panksepp, Scherer, and Solomon). Interactions between activity at the various levels are also generally recognized, although the details have yet to be worked out.

The automaticity of certain emotional reactions to stimuli of which the subject is unaware underscores the question of what feelings are good for. What is the functional role of feeling? Clark, Damasio, Dunn, Mesquita and Markus, and Panksepp all propose tentative answers to this question, albeit at different levels of analysis.

PLEASURE AND PAIN

Pleasure and pain are among the most distinctive aspects of feeling. For several decades they were almost absent from emotion theory. They have now returned to the forefront of empirical investigation and theoretical analysis. Pleasure and pain are regarded as fundamental. They have appeared as ubiquitous responses to information, even when nonconscious and only partly identified. They are understood not only as feeling states, but more broadly as affective processes that dictate stimulus salience and acceptance or nonacceptance, influence evaluation of subsequent neutral stimuli, and sensitize the organism to approach and avoidance, even when they are nonconscious. As feeling states, they appear to be irreducible to body sensations. They are of central concern in many different contexts: as processes that can be nonconscious, that have particular temporal dynamics, that influence cognitive and social flexibility and performance, that have signal value, and that are central in decision making (see the chapters by Berridge, Cacioppo et al., Isen, Mellers, and Zajonc). There are concentrated research efforts to elucidate the underlying psychological and neural processes (Berridge, Cacioppo et al., and Isen). One line of research seeks to elucidate the relationships between pleasure and other basic processes, finding that pleasure has functional and motivational consequences different but not always opposite from those of pain, and evidence suggestive of separate underlying neural processes. Research on pleasure allows positive emotions to receive functional interpretations that go beyond a return to homeostasis (Cacioppo et al. and Isen), and shows that pleasure processes are distinct from those governing approach or wanting (Berridge).

How pleasures and pains are evoked is still a mostly uncharted domain. Appraisal theory assumes appraisals of ultimate benefits or harms, and thus refers to these. How these elementary pleasures and pains are generated – the processes by which certain tastes or organ sensations obtain a "niceness" gloss and activate the opiate system, while others do not, for instance – remains unclear. There are some promising endeavors, however. An example, and a possible model for other research, is Zajonc's explanation (see his chapter) of the effects of mere exposure – the tendency to like familiar stimuli.

EMOTIONS AND THE BRAIN

Affective neuroscience is one of the domains that has shown impressive progress over the last thirty years. It was neither a very lively nor a coherent field then; it is a highly active and prominent field now. Both emotion and feeling have become respectable topics in neuroscience. A massive amount of novel information has been produced that not only is providing information about the neural and neurochemical processes involved in emotional phenomena but also makes important contributions to the functional understanding of emotions.

We shall limit ourselves here to the contributions from affective neuroscience discussed in the chapters in this volume. One of these concerns the wide array of areas and circuits that have been shown to play a role in emotions. These range from the lower brainstem and midbrain to the prefrontal and cingulate cortices, with the amygdala being prominent in several regards. Another major contribution concerns the central place of neuropeptides in emotional processes, with some of these being linked to functionally definable circuits (such as endogenous opiates to pleasure and separation distress).

The findings on brain circuits involved in emotional phenomena shows the relevance to them of subcortical circuits, as far down as the brainstem periaquaductal gray. One of the major findings that underlined the place of subcortical processes has been the demonstration that emotions (or certain emotional responses) can be evoked by a rapid "low road" that engages only fragmentary information from the eliciting situation or cortical circuits. Another set of findings provides evidence for the vital role played by parts of the prefrontal cortex in responses to emotionally complex stimuli, and in modifying such responses (see the chapters by Damasio, Panksepp, and Winston & Dolan).

Neuroscience research has demonstrated important functional differentiations in emotion-relevant brain processes. Evidence shows distinctions between areas more involved in triggering or organizing emotions and areas more involved in the execution of responses, and still others that are pertinent to feelings. Evidence has also been adduced to conclude that certain brain circuits fulfill a key role in more or less specific emotions, such as fear, anger, separation distress, or joy and play. Other findings suggest that much of emotion is best conceptualized in terms of more broadly defined processes such as "liking," necessitating novel conceptualizations of basic emotional processes, such as "seeking" or "wanting." Moreover, brain processes have been identified that are essential to social feelings, thus corroborating a biological basis for such feelings. How best to conceive of the functional nature of the various brain processes is one of the current concerns that may lead to linking brain processes more closely with behavioral, physiological, and experiential phenomena (see the chapters by Berridge, Damasio, Isen, Panksepp, and Winston & Dolan).

Fascinating research directions explore the interactions between various neural functions. Certain emotional response mechanisms appear to be context-sensitive whereas others are not; some are responsive to attention, whereas others cannot be so influenced. All this holds out the promise of an analysis of emotion mechanisms at an increasingly deep and subtle level.

Neuroscience research is extending toward the study of feeling. It supports the psychological distinction of levels of subjective experience (more immediate or diffuse, and more reflexive or articulate) and provides evidence for the role of body information and information integration in feeling (see the chapters by Damasio, Panksepp, Winston & Dolan).

EMOTIONS AND SOCIAL INTERACTION

Emotions regarded as evolutionarily shaped adaptations form one theoretical orientation; emotion as that which shapes and cements social interaction forms another, and this latter approach has also increased considerably in scope during the past three decades. The social psychology, sociology, and anthropology of emotions have become prominent subdomains of research in their respective disciplines. The same holds for emotion study in cultural psychology, and for the study of emotions in decision making and economics. The past thirty years have witnessed the emergence of systematic empirical research on emotion in each of these fields.

Emotions have come to be regarded as the major social glue, with extensive empirical research supporting that view. For instance, humans generally appear to desire to share their emotions with others and have others share their emotions with them, as the extensive work by Rimé (1995) has made evident. Emotional exchanges belong to the social fabric and regulate interpersonal relationships (see the chapters by Clark, de Waal, Frank, Mesquita & Markus, Sherman, Solomon, and Thoits). This is so by virtue of capacities for empathy, and by sensitivity to sympathy and the detection of suffering in others. The attendant emotions form an important basis of moral behavior and moral rules, and may well explain the human inclination toward cooperation that often balances that for competition (see Frank's chapter). Having emotions in itself has moral impact, which is presumably one of their functions. Forms of awareness of suffering in others, sympathy, empathy, and consolation are found among animals, notably apes (see the chapter by de Waal). These emotional propensities may well shed light on the explanation of morality and altruism.

Equally promising is the development of another perspective that takes the social-interactional origins of emotion processes into account: the dynamic perspective. This approach examines how phenomena may emerge from the interaction between individuals and the environment, and between an individual's different capabilities (Lewis & Granic, 2000). Although the dynamic approach was not directly represented at our symposium, Frank's inventive analysis of risky cooperation could be used to illustrate this perspective.

Careful analysis of the role emotions play in social interaction shows that such interaction is shaped both by one's own emotions and by how others perceive one's emotions. Social interaction depends on the manner in which and the degree to which emotions are regulated and steered by the individuals concerned, which in turn depend on their knowledge of emotions and their awareness of their own emotions. These abilities and knowledge constitute what is termed "emotional intelligence." Individuals differ in emotional intelligence, which can be regarded as a more or less stable personality trait (see the chapter by Salovey et al.). Developmental studies indicate that prior experience of social interaction, especially in the context of close relationships, contributes to the acquisition of emotion regulation and steering and emotion knowledge, which in turn contribute to the formation of close relationships such as friendships (see the chapter by Dunn).

EMOTIONS BETWEEN BIOLOGY AND CULTURE

Ever since Darwin, the functional viewpoint has had a dominant place in emotion theory. In the past three decades, evolutionary hypotheses have been extensively used to explain post hoc why the various emotions and emotion processes are as they are. It is argued that they are presumably the most adaptive solutions to ancestral environmental threats and opportunities that required rapid reactions (for examples, see the chapters by Cacioppo et al., Ekman, and Öhman & Wiens). Such functional viewpoints have generally predominated in biological approaches, but recently such ideas can also be found in social and cultural analyses. A rich and perhaps at least as fertile field of research is opening up in investigations of the functional consequences, rather than the possible functional origin, of emotions. Emotions appear to play a number of roles in addition to contributing to solving adaptive problems. For example, emotions are functional in forming social relationships and smoothing social interactions, and also in cognitive functioning, as is illustrated by research on moods (as discussed by Isen). Emotions also are found to be indispensable for goal setting and adaptive decision making, as is evident from clinical data discussed by Damasio and from experimental studies such as those reported by Frank and by Mellers. Emotion research is beginning to penetrate economic theory precisely because of these functional consequences.

The development of functional viewpoints in biological, cognitive, and sociocultural approaches to emotion is also illustrative of the emergence of views that acknowledge the potential compatibility of biological and sociocultural approaches to emotion, despite differences in the ways that emotions are defined and "measured." In recent theorizing, the old controversy between a biological and a cultural view is being abandoned and replaced by the idea that emotions are both biologically and culturally determined. The debate is shifting from the question of whether emotions are biological or cultural to that of the extent to which, and the ways in which, biological givens and cultural influences determine emotions. With regard to the origin of emotions and emotion component patterns, assessing the contributions made by biological dispositions and the social-cultural environment remains a major research issue. Evidence is growing that should enable more precise assessment of the biological contribution. This evidence comes from the near-universality of certain emotion classes and behavior forms, including facial expressions, from phylogenetic continuities such as those discussed in the chapter by de Waal, and from efforts to characterize more closely the functional nature of the neural emotion dispositions, as discussed in the chapters by Berridge, Damasio, and Panksepp.

The study of cultural variability has also vastly extended in scope and sophistication. There is not only research on cultural variation in emotion concepts; a further focus has emerged on variations in emotion components such as appraisal and the concerns underlying emotions, and on the meanings of emotional reactions in the specific social context. The chapters by Mesquita and Markus and by Shweder illustrate these developments. Theoretical notions are being refined that should lead to enhanced understanding of what in emotions might be acquired and what might be given, and how the acquired and the given interlock. The notion of appraisal, the distinction between emotion potential and emotion practice, and the analysis of regulation by norms appear to be promising in this enterprise (see the chapters by Mesquita & Markus, Scherer, Shweder, and Thoits).

CONTROVERSIES AND UNRESOLVED ISSUES

The preceding chapters provide evidence, as did the symposium on which they are based, of the many controversies and unresolved issues in the study of emotion. Such issues spur on research and inject liveliness into academic debate. They go deeply into how one views emotions. One such issue concerns the structure of emotion space. Is it built around basic, innate, neurally given, and evolutionarily shaped emotion dispositions? Or is it built out of emotion processes and components, some of which may be innate but the assembly of which is created by circumstance and modeling?

Another such issue is the role of information or cognition in generating and structuring emotions; phrased differently, what is the role of automatic processes in emotional responding? The issue is distinct from, but related to, that of assessing the role of feeling. Our symposium had the title "Feelings and Emotions," as does the present volume. Although, as we noted above, the distinction between feelings and emotions is commonly accepted, the way in which the phenomena concerned are related is not. Are feelings mere reflections of essentially nonconscious processes? Are they without a functional role in the processes and responses of emotion, or do they influence or even generate some of these processes? Attributing a causal role to feelings not only clashes with the evidence on automatic emotion processes, but also with philosophical considerations of causal determination. Yet common sense and scientific observation suggest that feelings are essential to the conduct of life.

Perhaps the most general unresolved issue concerns the relationship between elementary processes of emotion and everyday emotional responding. The various levels of description of emotional phenomena – say, those of reflex-like evocation of fear reactions, and of emotions as described in narratives – do not easily match. Nor do the analyses of automatic response evocations fit easily with the understanding of more complex events such as frustrations or personal loss. These different levels of analysis are not easy to translate into each other's terms. This is due in part to the absence of satisfactory models of how information from diverse sources is integrated, and in part to the lack of specification of the processes actually involved, even at the level of elementary processes.

Indeed, when surveying current work in emotion, one can argue that research on basic processes is relatively scarce – research at the level, for example, used by Zajonc to account for the mere exposure effect, or by Berridge to distinguish the phenomena of liking and wanting. These are not the only efforts to understand basic processes. Other examples in the present volume are Cacioppo et al.'s work on affective processes, Frijda's chapter on motivational mechanisms, Mesquita and Markus's analysis of the relations between emotion components and culture, Öhman and Wiens's analysis of emotion modules, Scherer's detailing of appraisal, and Thoits's analysis of the operation of emotion norms. However, most of these examples are as yet some way from the level of specification one would ideally like to see. How, precisely, should one conceive of appraisal processes at their various different levels? How do elementary stimuli like certain smells and innately preferred sights evoke positive or negative affect? What is evoked in elementary fear responses: a pattern of action programs, or a modification in motivational state? What process is involved in a motivational state like that of fear or anger? What precisely connects an emotion of awe to culturally shaped beliefs, on the one hand, and elementary fear mechanisms, on the other? What precisely does the amygdala do?

Between the level of behavioral and experiential analysis and that of neural and neurochemical processes – between Dennett's intentional and physical levels of description – there is the functional or psychological level of explanation. In emotion theory, one often leaps directly from the first level to the third; as if the emergence of a pleasure response were truly explained by noting that a smell or sight triggers opiate response in the nucleus accumbens. It may well be that developing the second level of analysis and explanation is one of the major tasks confronting emotion research in the coming period.

In order to accomplish that task, we believe a greater interaction and exchange than is now current among the various disciplines engaged in emotion research is essential. It was one of our impressions during the Amsterdam Symposium that the investigators from one discipline were not always well informed about the ideas and findings current in other relevant disciplines. It is sometimes the case that the problems posed in one's own discipline have been analyzed in detail in another discipline; or that findings in one's own discipline could illuminate the findings in a neighboring discipline. Facilitating closer interaction and greater exchange is of course one of the primary objectives of such symposia. However, this goal can only be truly achieved if the symposium results in an appreciation that other disciplines have data, views, and experiences to offer from which one can profit, and also present challenges to theory and theory formation in one's own discipline.

References

Lambie, J., & Marcel, A. (2002). Consciousness and emotion experience: A theoretical framework. *Psychological Review, 109*, 219–259.

Lewis, M. D., & Granic, I. (Eds.). (2000). *Emotion, development, and self-organization.* New York: Cambridge University Press.

Rimé, B. (1995). The social sharing of emotional experience as a source for the social knowledge of emotion. In J. A. Russell, J. M. Fernandez-Dols, A. S. R. Manstead, and J. C. Wellenkamp (Eds.), *Everyday concepts of emotions: An introduction to the psychology, anthropology, and linguistics of emotion* (pp. 475–489). Dordrecht: Kluwer.

Subject Index

Author Index